For the People, By the People

A History of the
United States
Beginnings to Present

The Peoples Publishing Group, Inc.
Free to Learn, to Grow, to Change

Photograph and Illustration Credits

ISBN 1-56256-091-3

For the People, By the People

For the People, By the People
The Revolutionary U.S. History Program

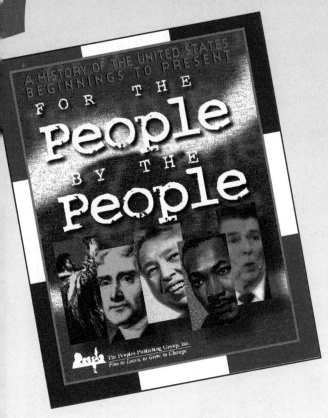

United States history that students really comprehend and succeed with!

Interesting writing tells the full scope of U.S. History as a story, and gives students the *whys* and *hows* they need to connect the facts and comprehend the logical connections!

The Revolution Continues with the Peoples Mainstream Tutor!

Peoples Mainstream Tutor is a student's study guide to U.S. history. It was created by learning specialists to be a student's private tutor, filling the study skills gaps for individual students—freeing teachers to teach!

Over 300 pages: reading comprehension, phonics, map and study skills, and writing activities—for all learning styles. And at a pace every mainstreamed history student needs!

The Tutor is a special study guide for any chronological U.S. History course.

Comprehensive Skills Development and Content at a Pace to Help Students Grow as Quickly as Our Country Has!

Students Are Prepared to Expect Success and Make Logical Connections at the Start of Every Unit

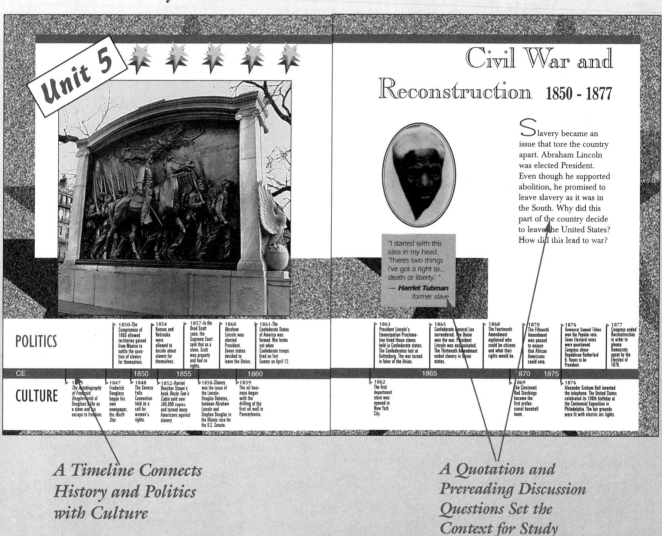

Unit 5

Civil War and Reconstruction 1850 - 1877

Slavery became an issue that tore the country apart. Abraham Lincoln was elected President. Even though he supported abolition, he promised to leave slavery as it was in the South. Why did this part of the country decide to leave the United States? How did this lead to war?

"I started with this idea in my head. There's two things I've got a right to... death or liberty.' "
— **Harriet Tubman**
former slave

POLITICS		1850-The Compromise of 1850 allowed territories gained from Mexico to settle the question of slavery for themselves.	1854 Kansas and Nebraska were allowed to decide about slavery for themselves.	1857-In the Dred Scott case, the Supreme Court said that as a slave, Scott was property and had no rights.	1860 Abraham Lincoln was elected President.	1861-The Confederate States of America was formed. War broke out when Confederate troops fired on Fort Sumter on April 12.	1863 President Lincoln's Emancipation Proclamation freed those slaves held in Confederate states. The Confederates lost at Gettysburg. The war turned in favor of the Union.	1865 Confederate General Lee surrendered. The Union won the war. President Lincoln was assassinated. The Thirteenth Amendment ended slavery in Union states.	1868 The Fourteenth Amendment explained who could be citizens and what their rights would be.	1870 The Fifteenth Amendment was passed to ensure that African Americans could vote.	1876 Democrat Samuel Tilden won the Popular vote. Some Electoral votes were questioned. Congress chose Republican Rutherford B. Hayes to be President.	1877 Congress ended Reconstruction in order to please Democrats upset by the Election of 1876.
CE	1845	1850	1855		1860			1865		1870	1875	
CULTURE	1845 *The Autobiography of Frederick Douglass* told of Douglass's life as a slave and his escape to freedom.	1847 Frederick Douglass began his own newspaper, the *North Star*.	1848 The Seneca Falls Convention held as a call for women's rights.	1852-Harriet Beecher Stowe's book *Uncle Tom's Cabin* sold over 300,000 copies and turned many Americans against slavery.	1858-Slavery was the issue of the Lincoln-Douglas Debates, between Abraham Lincoln and Stephen Douglas in the Illinois race for the U.S. Senate.	1859 The oil business began with the drilling of the first oil well in Pennsylvania.	1862 The first department store was opened in New York City.		1869 The Cincinnati Red Stockings became the first professional baseball team.		1876 Alexander Graham Bell invented the telephone. The United States celebrated its 100th birthday at the Centennial Exposition in Philadelphia. The fair grounds were lit with electric arc lights.	

A Timeline Connects History and Politics with Culture

A Quotation and Prereading Discussion Questions Set the Context for Study

Five units, 100 chapters cover U.S. history completely and with excitement!

Skills development comes first in every chapter, so students are prepared to succeed when they read and study!

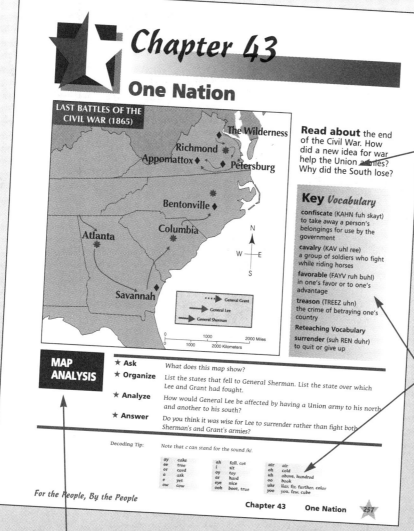

Chapter 43

One Nation

LAST BATTLES OF THE CIVIL WAR (1865)

The Wilderness
Richmond
Appomattox
Petersburg
Bentonville
Atlanta
Columbia
Savannah

N
W — E
S

- ···· General Grant
- → General Lee
- ➡ General Sherman

0   1000   2000 Miles
0   1000   2000 Kilometers

Read about the end of the Civil War. How did a new idea for war help the Union armies? Why did the South lose?

Key *Vocabulary*

confiscate (KAHN fuh skayt) to take away a person's belongings for use by the government

cavalry (KAV uhl ree) a group of soldiers who fight while riding horses

favorable (FAYV ruh buhl) in one's favor or to one's advantage

treason (TREEZ uhn) the crime of betraying one's country

Reteaching Vocabulary

surrender (suh REN duhr) to quit or give up

MAP ANALYSIS

★ **Ask** — What does this map show?

★ **Organize** — List the states that fell to General Sherman. List the state over which Lee and Grant had fought.

★ **Analyze** — How would General Lee be affected by having a Union army to his north and another to his south?

★ **Answer** — Do you think it was wise for Lee to surrender rather than fight both Sherman's and Grant's armies?

Decoding Tip: Note that *c* can stand for the sound /k/.

ay	cake	ah	fall, cot	air	air	
ee	tree	i	sit	oh	cold	
or	cord	oy	toy	uh	above, hundred	
a	ask	ar	hard	oo	book	
e	yet	eye	nice	uhr	liar, fir, further, color	
ow	cow	ooh	boot, true	yoo	you, few, cube	

For the People, By the People

Chapter 43   One Nation   257

Students Won't Miss the Point Because Prereading Questions Focus Them!

Vocabulary and Phonics Decoding Tips Are Keys to Reading Success

Always, Always *Practice Map and Geography Skills!*
The National Geography Standards Version of Map Analysis Skills are Taught in Manageable Steps!

*Y*ou'll Have to Read It to Believe Us!

Each 3-5 paragraph section starts with a question for guided reading and note-taking help. If students can answer the section questions, they understand the content.

Teachers tell us that the writing style is what they've been asking for! Students are interested enough to read and continue.

▲ Major General William Tecumseh Sherman

The top photograph below shows the ruins of Bull Run in Virginia, March 1862.

The bottom photograph below shows the ruins seen from the Circular Church in Charleston, South Carolina in 1865.

43.1 Why did the Confederacy think that the U.S. Election of 1864 might bring independence to the South?

Southerners hoped the Democrats would win the White House in 1864. They knew that Lincoln, the Republicans, and the War Democrats would never give up the war. However, many Northerners were tired of the war. They wanted peace even if the South would be lost to the United States. The Democrats pushed this idea in the Election of 1864. They chose General George B. McClellan to run for President. He promised to stop the war as soon as he took office.

43.2 How did General Sherman affect the war and the Election of 1864?

General William T. Sherman believed in total war. He did not fight against Southern soldiers only. He fought against all Southerners. Crops and animals were **confiscated** or destroyed. Homes, farms, towns, and cities were burned. Railroads were torn up. Sherman made it impossible for the people to care for themselves or their soldiers.

Sherman and other Union troops were very successful. Sherman pushed south into Tennessee. He took Atlanta in September 1864. General Philip Sheridan used Sherman's ideas to take Virginia's Shenandoah Valley. News of these wins thrilled people in the North. It helped President Lincoln, too. He won a second term in 1864.

▲ General John B. Hood

▼ Lt. General Ulysses S. Grant outside a tent in Cold Harbor, Virginia, in June 1864.

18
Hoo
brok
maj
Atl
eve

43.

General Lee S

Sherman and Grant both moved toward Lee's army. Grant pushed south into Virginia. His army had terrible losses. However, Grant kept pushing farther south. Lee had to stretch out his line all the way from Richmond to Petersburg. In the meantime, Sherman moved north from Savannah. He marched his troops into the Carolinas. Sherman left a strip of scorched land behind him. It was 60 miles wide. Sherman kept pushing north. Sherman and Grant planned to pin Lee between their two armies.

43.4 Why did General Lee decide to surrender?

Lee held out against Grant for several months. Then Grant punched through Lee's lines in April, 1865. Lee pulled back. Grant took Richmond. A Union **cavalry** troop made up of African Americans led the army into the city. The Confederate government moved to Danbury, Virginia. General Lee moved the last of his troops to the town of Appomattox Court House on April 8. It was a cloudy evening at Appomattox. Lee's army built camp fires. They shone against the clouds. Lee saw Union fires shining against the clouds, too. He saw that he was blocked on three sides.

Logical Connections among facts help students continue understanding. No laundry lists of seemingly unrelated facts!

*Each chapter ends with a special section
of biography, a multicultural perspective,
or other information to make the time
and culture come alive!*

Biography

▲ Clara Barton

Many women took part in the Civil War. They worked in factories, grew food, and made uniforms and bandages. Before this time, most nurses had been men. Now, there were not enough men to work as nurses. President Lincoln turned to Dorothea Dix. She had worked for years to make hospitals better places. Lincoln put Dix in charge of the government's nursing department. It

trained hundreds of women as nurses. Clara Barton had been the first woman ever hired to work in a U.S. government office. When the war began, she worked as a nurse, too. She helped other women become nurses. Many supplies were not reaching the army. Barton collected money and began shipping supplies herself. Often, she and her wagons were the first to arrive where the army was fighting.

Mary Walker was a doctor who wanted to help wounded soldiers. Many of the men doctors did not believe that she could handle the work. Dr. Walker worked so hard that she finally became an army doctor. She traveled with the army to battle. She was caught by the Confederates in 1864. She was held in prison for four months. Dr. Walker was given the

Congressional Medal of Honor in 1865. She is the only woman to have received the military's highest honor.

Women worked as spies for both sides. Belle Boyd and Rose O'Neal Greenhow worked for the South. They gathered important information. This helped the Confederates win several battles. Elizabeth Van Lew lived in Richmond but worked for the North. She had freed her slaves after her father's death. During the war, she gathered information for the North. She hid Union soldiers who were escaping from Confederate prisons. She hired African Americans to carry her information. Elizabeth Bowser had been one of her slaves. Van Lew got Bowser a job in Jefferson Davis's home. Bowser was then able to spy on the Confederate President.

★★★ CHAPTER REVIEW

Chapter Review *includes two critical-thinking questions that develop one of 12 key skills. Skills are identified. Students know exactly what they are working on!*

Critical Thinking

Write your answers on a sheet of paper, or discuss in class.

Identifying Main Idea ➡️

1. How did Sherman's way of fighting affect the South's limited resources?

Making Inferences

2. Why did General Lee decide to surrender rather than lose the war by being beaten in battle?

Cooperative Learning

LEARNING STYLE
*Verbal
Visual*

3. Work with a partner. Talk to each other about Sherman and total war. Think about what the countryside must have looked like after Sherman's army left. Describe what you might have seen if you had been there. Draw a picture of what you describe. Display your pictures for the class.

*A **Cooperative Learning** activity allows students to use alternative learning styles, and to experience success in a group or with a partner.*

Write About It

*A **Writing** activity for the writing portfolio gives students practice in this important area.*

Writing Portfolio

4. Make up a secret code. Reread the part about Grant and Lee at Richmond and Petersburg. Pretend that you are a Union spy in Richmond. Write a message with news that General Grant could use against General Lee. Put the message in code. Trade messages and codes with someone in the class. Decode each other's messages.

*The student textbook also includes a glossary,
atlas, gazeteer, and primary sources!*

And if your students are using the *Peoples Mainstream Tutor*
alongside this clean-to-read textbook, they're also learning
to take notes that summarize the essential content!

The Closest Thing to a Private Tutor for Every Student!

The Peoples Mainstream Tutor is a consumable study guide for every student. Three pages of guided study for every chapter to accompany any chronological U.S. history course or text—especially For the People, By the People!

Predicting Content Increases Comprehension

Vocabulary Practice in Historical Context

Always, Always *a Timeline Activity to Keep the Sequence of Events Straight—A Must for Comprehension!*

Skills Reminders Focus Students on the Purpose and Steps in Learning

Later, Students Will Return to Check the Predictions They Made at the Beginning of the Section or Chapter, Practicing Their Comprehension Skills.

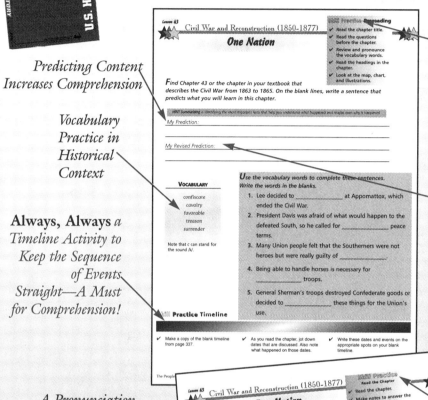

A Pronunciation Key for Important Proper Names

Study Tips Remind Students of Reading and Study Skills to Practice.

Questions About the Content Guide Students to Take Notes That Focus on the Important Facts.

Skills Reminders Focus Students on the Purpose and Steps in Learning.

(Section numbers refer to the *For the People, By the People* textbook, but the content moves chronologically and can easily be used with any U.S. history program that is chronological!)

The Peoples Mainstream Tutor in U.S. History Teaches Content Plus Skills!

For Every On-Level and Mainstreamed Student!

For Every Student Who Needs to Brush Up on Study, Reading, Map, Charts, Tables, Graphs and Diagrams Skills While Learning U.S. History!

Use With any U.S. History Course That Is Chronological

ASK, ACQUIRE, ORGANIZE, ANALYZE, ANSWER is the National Geography Standards Method for Map and Graph Analysis— Distilled for the Reluctant Student!

Students Manipulate the Maps or other graphs, a Manageable Piece at a Time!

Now, Back to Checking Comprehension Predictions!

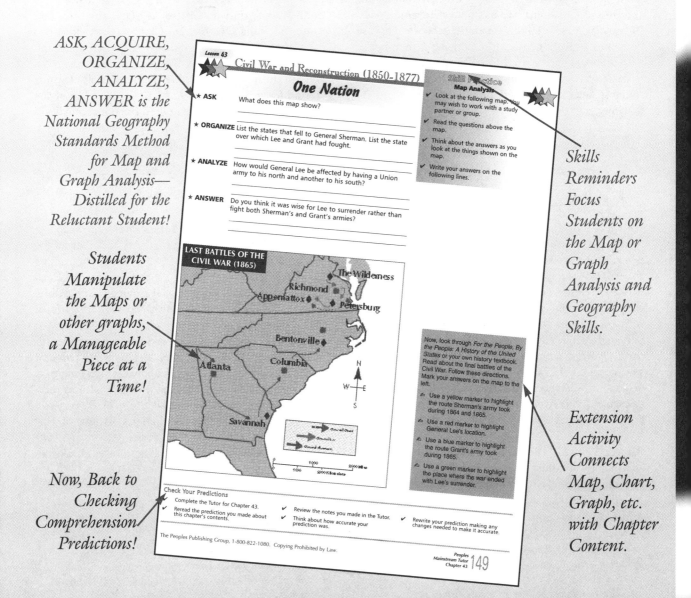

Skills Reminders Focus Students on the Map or Graph Analysis and Geography Skills.

Extension Activity Connects Map, Chart, Graph, etc. with Chapter Content.

For more information on *For the People, By the People,* and *The Peoples Mainstream Tutor,* Call 1-800-822-1080

About the Authors and Creative Team

Jim Eddy, Clanci Brown, and John Allen began their careers as teachers in grades K-12, and shifted their talents for curriculum, writing and editing into educational publishing, where they have worked as a creative team now for more than twelve years. They have helped to create educational materials in social studies and remedial education this entire time, with their roles varying from authors to editors to educational consultants. They have designed books, curriculums, and developed instructional design to further education throughout their careers. They are based in Oklahoma City.

Howard Meredith, Ph.D., reviewed the manuscript extensively. Dr. Meredith is in the Department of American Indian Studies at the University of Science and Arts of Oklahoma. He has published nine books, and managed and edited several textbooks. He also publishes actively in scholarly journals. A member of the Cherokee nation, Dr. Meredith is active in educational and community projects relating to American Indians, and has received five awards for research, teaching, and his books.

Blue Clark, Ph.D., reviewed this manuscript extensively. Dr. Clark is Executive Vice President of Oklahoma City University, with degrees in history, and publications and expertise in U.S. history and American Indian history. Dr. Clark has authored two scholarly history books, one on American Indians and one a regional history, has been editor of five books, and author of more than one-hundred book chapters and professional papers. Dr. Clark is a member of the Creek nation, and is active in both the educational and administrative challenges of managing a university.

The scholarship and vast experience in U.S. history, American Indian history, and education of Dr. Meredith and Dr. Clark were strong forces guiding this book to tell America's story comprehensively, interestingly, and accurately.

Jan First, M.Ed. is currently Acting Administrator of Special Education in the Oklahoma City Public Schools. She is a specialist in learning disabilities, and a certified elementary principal. She has actively worked in public and private schools and provided private tutoring for more than fourteen years, and is active in organizations for exceptional children and bilingual-special education. Ms. First was a member of the Mayor's Committee on Disability Concerns for seven years. Ms. First's guidance in reviewing this book and the *Peoples Mainstream Tutor* ensured that the pedagogy and instructional design of both titles would be solid and elegant.

Barbara Schindler, Ph.D., holds degrees in economics and history, and her Ph.D. is in Adult Education. She has taught in classrooms from elementary school through college and adult education for more than sixteen years, and is currently a faculty member at the University of Oklahoma. Dr. Schindler's teaching expertise includes serving as Supervisor of Social Studies programs for the Oklahoma City Public Schools. Dr. Schindler has authored two educational books as well as professional papers, has presented professional workshops in social studies and multicultural education, and has served as Executive Director of the Democratic Party of Oklahoma. Dr. Schindler is active in national and regional educational and publishing groups, and is on the NCSS/NCATE Portfolio Review Committee. Dr. Schindler's review of this book and the accompanying *Peoples Mainstream Tutor* helped guide both the historical content and instructional design of the program.

Additional key contributors to the project were:

Doreen Smith, Project Manager, Design and Production/ Electronic Page Makeup, *Peoples Publishing*

Kristine Liebman, Photo Research and Electronic Page Makeup, *Peoples Publishing*

Joan Fedus, Electronic Page Makeup, *Peoples Publishing*

Margaret Lepera, Electronic Assistance, *Peoples Publishing*

Edith Bush, Electronic Assistance, *Peoples Publishing*

Janet Kliesch, Electronic Assistance, *Peoples Publishing*

Pencil Point Studio, Interior Design

Northeast Visual Media, Cover Design

Westchester Graphics, Klaus Spitzenberger, Cover Design, *Peoples Mainstream Tutor*

Diane M. Miller, Publisher, *Peoples Publishing*

Table of Contents
For the People, By the People

Photograph and Art Credits ii
A Walk Through
For the People, By the People iii
About the Authors & Creative Team x
Contents xi
Maps in
For the People, By the People xv
Special Features in
For the People, By the People xvi
Scope and Sequence of Skills in
For the People, By the People xvii

UNIT 1: THREE WORLDS MEET BEGINNINGS TO 1620 . . 2

Chapter 1: **East to the Americas** 4
Chapter 2: **The First Americans** 9
Chapter 3: **To Reach Asia** 15
Chapter 4: **Africa** 20
Chapter 5: **Europe Looks to the West.** . 25
Chapter 6: **Exploration and Conquest** . 30
Unit 1 Review 36

UNIT 2: COLONIZATION AND SETTLEMENT 1585-1763 38

Chapter 7: **Europe and North America** 40
Chapter 8: **Successful Colonies** 46
Chapter 9: **Colonies of New England** . 52
Chapter 10: **England Expands** 58
Chapter 11: **The Thirteen Colonies**
             Grow 64
Unit 2 Review 70

UNIT 3: REVOLUTION AND THE NEW NATION 1754-1820S 72

Chapter 12: **The French and**
             the British 74
Chapter 13: **The French and**
             Indian War 80
Chapter 14: **The Cost of the War** 85
Chapter 15: **The Colonies Unify** 91
Chapter 16: **Britain Fights Back** 97
Chapter 17: **Independence** 102
Unit 3 Mid-Unit Review 108
Chapter 18: **War in the North** 110
Chapter 19: **Victory in the South** 116
Chapter 20: **Experiment in**
             Government 121
Chapter 21: **The Constitution** 127
Chapter 22: **The Constitution Works** . . 132
Chapter 23: **A New Crisis** 138
Chapter 24: **The War of 1812** 144
Chapter 25: **New Reputation**
             in the World 149
Unit 3 Review 154

UNIT 4: EXPANSION AND REFORM
1801-1861 156

Chapter 26: **The Nation Grows**. **158**
Chapter 27: **A Changing People** **163**
Chapter 28: **Conflicts with Spain** **169**
Chapter 29: **Factions Form** **174**
Chapter 30: **New Parties—New Ideas**. **179**
Unit 4 Mid-Unit Review. *184*
Chapter 31: **The President and
                  the Economy**. **186**
Chapter 32: **American Life** **191**
Chapter 33: **Western Growth** **196**
Chapter 34: **The Trail of Tears** **202**
Unit 4 Review. *208*

UNIT 5: CIVIL WAR AND
RECONSTRUCTION
1850-1877 210

Chapter 35: **Slavery** **212**
Chapter 36: **Abolition** **217**
Chapter 37: **Political Battles**. **223**
Chapter 38: **Closer to War** **228**
Chapter 39: **The Future of the Nation**. **233**
Chapter 40: **Battle Lines**. **238**
Unit 5 Mid-Unit Review. **244**
Chapter 41: **The Struggle for Control** . **246**
Chapter 42: **The Union Advances** **251**
Chapter 43: **One Nation** **257**
Chapter 44: **Aftermath**. **263**
Chapter 45: **Reconstruction** **269**
Chapter 46: **Deal Making**. **275**
Unit 5 Review. *280*

UNIT 6: INDUSTRIAL
DEVELOPMENT IN
THE U. S. 1870-1900 . . 282

Chapter 47: **Expansion by Railroad**. . . **284**
Chapter 48: **African &
                  Asian Americans** **290**
Chapter 49: **My Native Land** **296**
Chapter 50: **A Recipe for Growth**. . . . **303**
Chapter 51: **Corporate America** **308**
Chapter 52: **A New Way of Life** **313**
Unit 6 Mid-Unit Review. *318*
Chapter 53: **Immigrants
                  and Industry** **320**
Chapter 54: **Cities and Their
                  Problems** **326**
Chapter 55: **Honesty and Change**. . . . **332**
Chapter 56: **Labor** **337**
Chapter 57: **Populism**. **343**
Chapter 58: **Reform** **348**
Unit 6 Review. *354*

UNIT 7: THE EMERGENCE OF MODERN AMERICA 1890-1930 356

Chapter 59: **Out into the World** 358
Chapter 60: **The Progressives** 365
Chapter 61: **Roosevelt's Foreign Policy** 371
Chapter 62: **Problems—Foreign & Domestic** 379
Chapter 63: **The World Goes to War** . . 386
Unit 7 Mid-Unit Review *392*
Chapter 64: **World War I** 394
Chapter 65: **A World at Peace** 402
Chapter 66: **Boom Times** 410
Chapter 67: **The Roaring Twenties** . . . 417
Chapter 68: **Cracks in the Seams** 424
Unit 7 Review *432*

UNIT 8: THE GREAT DEPRESSION AND WORLD WAR II 1929-1945 434

Chapter 69: **The Crash** 436
Chapter 70: **The Great Depression** . . 443
Chapter 71: **The New Deal** 450
Chapter 72: **A Social Experiment** 456
Unit 8 Mid-Unit Review *464*
Chapter 73: **The World of the 1930s** . . 466
Chapter 74: **The March to War** 472
Chapter 75: **Fascist Victories** 478
Chapter 76: **Fighting the War at Home** 487
Chapter 77: **War in Europe** 493
Chapter 78: **Approach to Peace** 499
Chapter 79: **Aftermath** 506
Unit 8 Review *512*

UNIT 9: POSTWAR UNITED STATES 1945 TO EARLY 1970S 514

Chapter 80: **Leading the World** 516
Chapter 81: **The Cold War** 521
Chapter 82: **New Alliances** 526
Chapter 83: **The Korean War** 532
Chapter 84: **The 1950s** 538
Chapter 85: **The Rights of Citizens** . . . 544
Unit 9 Mid-Unit Review *550*
Chapter 86: **Only 90 Miles Away** 552
Chapter 87: **Exploring Space** 558
Chapter 88: **Violence in America** 563
Chapter 89: **Controversial Ideas** 569
Chapter 90: **People Power** 574
Chapter 91: **New Directions** 581
Unit 9 Review *590*

UNIT 10: CONTEMPORARY UNITED STATES 1968 TO PRESENT 592

Chapter 92: **Scandal in the White House** **594**
Chapter 93: **At 200 Years of Age** **600**
Chapter 94: **World Conflicts** **606**
Chapter 95: **The Cold War Heats Up** . **612**
Unit 10 Mid-Unit Review **620**
Chapter 96: **New Federalism** **622**
Chapter 97: **The U. S. and the World** **628**
Chapter 98: **The Changing World Map** **634**
Chapter 99: **Storm Clouds** **640**
Chapter 100: **The Federal Debate** **648**
Unit 10 Review **656**

The Southeastern United States **662**
The Midwestern United States **663**
The Great Plains States of the U.S. . . . **663**
The Mountain States of the U.S. **664**
The Southwestern United States **664**
The West Coast and Pacific States of the U.S. **665**
The Presidents of the United States **666**
The Star-Spangled Banner **668**
The Declaration of Independence **669**
The Constitution and Bill of Rights of the United States **671**
The Constitution Made Easier **678**
The Emancipation Proclamation **685**
The Seneca Falls Declaration of Sentiments and Resolutions **686**
The Civil Rights Act of 1964 . . . . **688**
Glossary **689**
Gazetteer and Index **696**

APPENDICES 674

Atlas **658**
The World **658**
North America **660**
The United States of America **661**
The Northeastern United States **662**

MAPS

North and South America, Ice Ages 4
People of North America, 1400 CE 9
Europe, Africa, and Asia, 1400 CE 15
Portuguese Voyages around Africa,
     1400s CE 20
Columbus's First Voyage to the
     Americas, 1492 25
Spain's Empire in the Americas, 1600 30
European Interests in North America,
     1500s 40
Colonial North America, 1640 46
British Colonies in
     New England, 1650 52
13 Colonies, 1733 58
The Triangle Trade, 1700s 64
French and British Colonies in
     North America, 1754 74
North America before (1754) and
     after (1763) the French
     and Indian War 80
The Beginning of the Revolutionary War,
     1775 91
Early Battles of the Revolutionary War,
     1775-1776 97
George Washington's Surprise Victories,
     1776-1777 110
Last Battles of the Revolutionary War,
     1778-1781 116
The United States of America, 1783 121
States of the U.S.A., 1803 138
Early Battles of the War of 1812,
     1812-1814 144
The End of the War of 1812, 1815 149
United States and the Louisiana
     Purchase, 1803 158
Andrew Jackson's Push into
     Spanish Florida, 1818 169
Slavery in the United States, 1824 174
Electoral College Vote, 1828 179
Growth of the United States,
     1783-1854 196
Native American Removals,
     1820-1840 202
The United States after the Missouri
     Compromise, 1850 212
Kansas-Nebraska Act, 1854 217

Dred Scott's Travels as an
     Enslaved African, 1834-1843 228
Electoral College Vote, 1860 233
Union and Confederate States, 1861 246
Last Battles of the Civil War, 1865 257
Military Districts in the South,
     Reconstruction, 1866-1877 269
Developments in the West, 1870s 284
Indian Territory, 1830-1880s 296
United States Mineral
     Resources, 1870 303
Electoral College Vote, 1892 343
Electoral College Vote, 1896 348
Lands Gained by the United States,
     1867-1899 358
States with Reformed Governments,
     1889-1910 365
The Panama Canal Zone,
     1914-Present 371
Electoral College Vote, 1912 379
World War I, European Allies,
     1914-1917 386
Europe and the Middle East
     after World War I, 1919 402
Voting Rights for Women by State,
     1890-1920 410
European and American Colonies
     in Asia, 1930s 466
Middle Europe, 1938 472
Axis Conquests, 1940 478
World War II in Europe, 1942-1945 493
World War II in the Pacific,
     1941-1945 499
Palestine as Divided by the
     United Nations, 1947 516
The Soviet Union's Satellite Countries,
     1947 521
The Korean War, June-November, 1950 526
The Korean War, September 1950-July 1953 . . 532
The Cuban Missile Crisis, 1962 552
The Vietnam War, 1968 569
The Vietnam War, 1973 581
Wars in the Middle East, 1967-1973 600
Wars in the Middle East, 1979-1980 612
Fighting in Latin America, 1980s 628
The Fall of the Soviet Union, 1989 634
The Gulf War, 1991-1992 640

SPECIAL FEATURES

Chapter 1:   Multicultural Perspective: The Mayans. 8
Chapter 2:   Multicultural Perspective: Native Americans 14
Chapter 3:   Multicultural Perspective: Foods 19
Chapter 4:   Multicultural Perspective: East Africa. 24
Chapter 5:   Yesterday & Today: Hispaniola 29
Chapter 6:   Connections: Chocolate and the Aztecs 35
Chapter 7:   Multicultural Perspective: The Lumbee Indians . . . 45
Chapter 8:   Multicultural Perspective: Pocahontas 51
Chapter 9:   Biography: Anne Hutchinson 57
Chapter 10: Connections: Rhode Island. 63
Chapter 11: Yesterday & Today: Wall Street 69
Chapter 12: Connections: Political Cartoons 79
Chapter 13: Connections: French and British Influence
             in Canada 84
Chapter 14: Connections: Crispus Attucks 90
Chapter 15: Connections: Ralph Waldo Emerson 96
Chapter 16: Biography: Molly Pitcher and Deborah Sampson . . 101
Chapter 17: Connections: Anti-Slavery Leaders
             in the Colonies 107
Chapter 18: A Hero and a Traitor:
             John Paul Jones and Benedict Arnold 115
Chapter 19: Connections: African Americans
             in the Revolution 120
Chapter 20: Biography: Benjamin Franklin. 126
Chapter 21: Yesterday & Today: 17th Amendment 131
Chapter 22: Biography: Benjamin Banneker. 137
Chapter 23: Yesterday & Today: The Democratic Party 143
Chapter 24: Biography: Tecumseh 148
Chapter 25: Yesterday & Today: Communications in
             1812 and Now 153
Chapter 26: Connections: Haiti 162
Chapter 27: Yesterday & Today: The Clothing Industry 168
Chapter 28: Connections: The Monroe Doctrine 173
Chapter 29: Connections: Voting Rights 178
Chapter 30: Connections: Choosing a President. 183
Chapter 31: Connections: The Fur Trade and
             Beckwourth Pass 190
Chapter 32: Connections: The Enslavement Debate 195
Chapter 33: Speaking Out Against the War 201
Chapter 34: Yesterday & Today: The Choctaw and the Irish 207
Chapter 35: Women's Rights 216
Chapter 36: Biography: Frederick Douglass 221
Chapter 37: The Brooks-Sumner Affair. 227
Chapter 38: In Their Own Words:
             The Lincoln-Douglas Debates. 232
Chapter 39: Biography: Jefferson Davis 237
Chapter 40: Connections: Families Take Sides
             in the Civil War. 243
Chapter 41: Connections: Firsts in the Civil War 246
Chapter 42: Biography: Martin R. Delaney and
             Alexander T. Augusta 256
Chapter 43: Biography: Women in the Civil War 262
Chapter 44: Connections: Native Americans
             in the Civil War 268
Chapter 45: Connections: African Americans in Congress 274
Chapter 46: Biography: Lucy Webb Hayes. 279
Chapter 47: Connections: Sandra Day O'Connor 289
Chapter 48: Biography: Booker T. Washington and
             W.E.B. DuBois. 295

Chapter 49: Connections: The Navajo Language and
             World War II 302
Chapter 50: Yesterday & Today: Steam Engines & Computers . . 307
Chapter 51: Biography: Madame C. J. Walker &
             Marjorie Merriwether Post 312
Chapter 52: Connections: Suburbs in the 1800s and Today. . . . 317
Chapter 53: Connections: Statue of Liberty 325
Chapter 54: Biography: Jane Addams and Hull House 331
Chapter 55: Biography: President Ulysses S. Grant. 336
Chapter 56: Biography: Leonora Barry O'Reilly 342
Chapter 57: Biography: Mark Twain. 347
Chapter 58: Biography: Nellie Bly 353
Chapter 59: Biography: Teddy Roosevelt and
             William Howard Taft 364
Chapter 60: Connections: Public Schools 370
Chapter 61: Connections: The Panama Canal. 378
Chapter 62: Biography: Jim Thorpe 385
Chapter 63: Connections: The Balkans. 391
Chapter 64: Connections: WWI Changes the USA 401
Chapter 65: Connections: World War I and Influenza. 409
Chapter 66: Connections: Suffragettes 416
Chapter 67: Connections: Pancho Villa and the Movies 423
Chapter 68: Connections: Carry Nation's War against Alcohol . 431
Chapter 69: The Dust Bowl. 442
Chapter 70: The Bonus Army 449
Chapter 71: Connections: Roosevelt's Banking Laws. 455
Chapter 72: Connections: Presidential Families 463
Chapter 73: Connections: Hitler and American Athletes 471
Chapter 74: Connections: Mein Kampf and Churchill. 477
Chapter 75: Connections: Quiet Heroes 486
Chapter 76: Connections: World War II and
             Japanese Americans 492
Chapter 77: Connections: World War II and
             the Tuskegee Airmen 498
Chapter 78   Connections: The Atomic Bomb 505
Chapter 79: Connections: ODESSA and Simon Wiesenthal. . . . 511
Chapter 80: Biography: Ralph Bunche 520
Chapter 81: Connections: The Iron Curtain 525
Chapter 82: Connections: Blair House. 531
Chapter 83: Connections: North Korea & the U.S. 537
Chapter 84: Connections: Television and the Movies 543
Chapter 85: Connections: Thurgood Marshall and Civil Rights . 549
Chapter 86: Connections: Stolen Votes 557
Chapter 87: Connections: Six Trips to the Moon. 562
Chapter 88: Connections: Arlen Specter and
             the Single Bullet Theory 568
Chapter 89: Connections: Women and
             Environmental Activism 573
Chapter 90: Connections: Rock Music and the 1960s. 580
Chapter 91: Biography: Shirley Chisholm. 589
Chapter 92: Biography: Judge Robert Bork 599
Chapter 93: Connections: Oil Spill in Alaska 605
Chapter 94: Connections: The New South 611
Chapter 95: Connections: Canada and
             the Iranian Hostage Crisis. 619
Chapter 96: Connections: Changing the Constitution 627
Chapter 97: Connections: Oliver North and Iran Contra 633
Chapter 98: Connections: Germany after World War II
             and Today 639
Chapter 99: Biography: General Colin Powell 647
Chapter 100: Terror from Within 655

Scope and Sequence of Skills in the *For the People, By the People* Program

The following chart shows the scope and sequence of skills. Categories: Decoding Skill; Comprehension Skills (Main Idea, Details, Sequence, Summarizing, Cause and Effect, Fact/Opinion, Outlining, Compare/Contrast, Classifying, Drawing Conclusions, Inferences, Predictions); Graphics (Timeline, Map, Chart, Table); Evaluation (Critical Thinking; Cooperative Learning / Learning Styles: Reading, Writing, Visual, Auditory, Verbal, Oral, Listening, Kinesthetic, Tactile; Alt. Assess. Activity; Alt. Assess. Rubric; Writ. Assess. Activity; Writ. Assess. Rubric; Standardized Format).

Program	Decoding Skill	Main Idea	Details	Sequence	Summarizing	Cause and Effect	Fact/Opinion	Outlining	Compare/Contrast	Classifying	Drawing Conclusions	Inferences	Predictions	Timeline	Map	Chart	Table	Critical Thinking	Reading	Writing	Visual	Auditory	Verbal	Oral	Listening	Kinesthetic	Tactile	Alt. Assess. Activity	Alt. Assess. Rubric	Writ. Assess. Activity	Writ. Assess. Rubric	Standardized Format
Unit 1 Opener Text													✓	✓					✓	✓												
Unit 1 Opener Tutor													✓																			
Chapter 1 Text	Sounds of a					✓					✓		✓		✓			✓												✓		
Chapter 1 Tutor	Sounds of a	✓	✓	✓	✓	✓		✓					✓	✓	✓												✓	✓				
Chapter 2 Text	Sounds of e		✓									✓	✓		✓						✓		✓					✓		✓		
Chapter 2 Tutor	Sounds of e	✓	✓	✓	✓	✓	✓	✓			✓		✓	✓	✓			✓										✓		✓		
Chapter 3 Text	Vowel + r		✓			✓							✓		✓						✓							✓		✓		
Chapter 3 Tutor	Vowel + r	✓						✓					✓		✓																	
Chapter 4 Text	Short a	✓				✓	✓					✓	✓		✓			✓			✓							✓		✓		
Chapter 4 Tutor	Short a	✓			✓	✓		✓					✓	✓	✓													✓				
Chapter 5 Text	/uh/ or schwa								✓			✓	✓		✓													✓		✓		
Chapter 5 Tutor	/uh/ or schwa				✓	✓							✓		✓													✓				
Chapter 6 Text	qu = /k/										✓	✓	✓		✓			✓				✓						✓		✓		
Chapter 6 Tutor	qu = /k/					✓		✓					✓		✓																	
Unit 1 Review Text		✓		✓		✓							✓	✓																		
Unit 1 Review Tutor											✓	✓	✓	✓																		
Unit 1 Tests			✓																														
Unit 2 Opener Text					✓			✓					✓		✓			✓	✓	✓			✓					✓				
Unit 2 Opener Tutor													✓		✓																	
Chapter 7 Text	Vowel + r	✓			✓			✓			✓		✓		✓	✓		✓	✓	✓								✓		✓		
Chapter 7 Tutor	Vowel + r												✓		✓																	
Chapter 8 Text	ex		✓		✓								✓		✓									✓				✓		✓		
Chapter 8 Tutor	ex		✓										✓	✓	✓																	
Chapter 9 Text	Short i	✓			✓	✓		✓					✓		✓	✓		✓	✓	✓								✓		✓		
Chapter 9 Tutor	Short i					✓							✓		✓																	
Chapter 10 Text	Sounds of e	✓			✓	✓							✓	✓	✓	✓		✓			✓							✓		✓		
Chapter 10 Tutor	Sounds of e	✓				✓							✓	✓	✓																	

Scope and Sequence of Skills in the *For the People, By the People* Program

Program	Decoding Skill	Main Idea	Details	Sequence	Summarizing	Cause and Effect	Fact/Opinion	Outlining	Compare/Contrast	Classifying	Drawing Conclusions	Inferences	Predictions	Timeline	Map	Chart	Table	Graph	Diagram	Critical Thinking	Reading	Writing	Visual	Auditory	Verbal	Oral	Listening	Kinesthetic	Tactile	Alt. Assess. Activity	Alt. Assess. Rubric	Writ. Assess. Activity	Writ. Assess. Rubric	Standardized Format
Chapter 11 Text	Ph = /f/	✓	✓		✓	✓		✓				✓	✓	✓	✓					✓	✓		✓							✓		✓		
Chapter 11 Tutor	Ph = /f/					✓							✓	✓	✓																			✓
Unit 2 Review Text						✓							✓									✓								✓			✓	
Unit 2 Review Tutor				✓									✓	✓								✓						✓	✓	✓				✓
Unit 2 Test													✓																	✓		✓		✓
Unit 3 Opener Text			✓		✓	✓			✓			✓	✓	✓	✓						✓									✓		✓		
Unit 3 Opener Tutor						✓							✓		✓																	✓		
Chapter 12 Text	Double Consonants		✓			✓							✓	✓	✓						✓											✓		
Chapter 12 Tutor	Double Consonants												✓			✓																✓		
Chapter 13 Text	Sounds of y	✓			✓	✓		✓					✓			✓				✓			✓							✓		✓		
Chapter 13 Tutor	Sounds of y										✓		✓																			✓		
Chapter 14 Text	Sounds of e		✓		✓	✓						✓	✓		✓	✓				✓					✓	✓				✓		✓		
Chapter 14 Tutor	Sounds of e												✓			✓																✓		
Chapter 15 Text	Y=long i	✓	✓		✓	✓						✓	✓	✓		✓							✓		✓					✓		✓		
Chapter 15 Tutor	Y=long i												✓			✓																✓		
Chapter 16 Text	Sounds of e	✓	✓		✓	✓		✓					✓			✓							✓									✓		
Chapter 16 Tutor	Sounds of e					✓							✓			✓																✓		
Chapter 17 Text	Ph = /f/		✓		✓	✓							✓	✓	✓																	✓		
Chapter 17 Tutor	Ph = /f/												✓																			✓		
Mid-Unit 3 Review Text			✓										✓	✓																✓	✓	✓	✓	
Mid-Unit 3 Review Tutor				✓		✓		✓					✓	✓						✓												✓		✓
Mid-Unit 3 Tests			✓			✓							✓																					✓
Chapter 18 Text	Double vowels					✓		✓				✓	✓		✓	✓				✓			✓			✓						✓		
Chapter 18 Tutor	Double vowels					✓							✓		✓	✓																✓		
Chapter 19 Text	Sounds of ue		✓			✓						✓	✓	✓	✓	✓								✓								✓		
Chapter 19 Tutor	Sounds of ue	✓	✓		✓	✓						✓	✓	✓	✓				✓			✓							✓		✓		

Scope and Sequence of Skills in the *For the People, By the People* Program

Program	Decoding Skill	Main Idea	Details	Sequence	Summarizing	Cause and Effect	Fact/Opinion	Outlining	Compare/Contrast	Classifying	Drawing Conclusions	Inferences	Predictions	Timeline	Map	Chart	Table	Graph	Diagram	Critical Thinking	Reading	Writing	Visual	Auditory	Verbal	Oral	Listening	Kinesthetic	Tactile	Alt. Assess. Activity	Alt. Assess. Rubric	Writ. Assess. Activity	Writ. Assess. Rubric	Standardized Format
Chapter 20 Text	Syllables	✓	✓		✓	✓							✓	✓	✓	✓				✓						✓				✓		✓		
Chapter 20 Tutor	Syllables	✓	✓		✓	✓		✓				✓	✓	✓	✓	✓				✓	✓	✓								✓		✓		
Chapter 21 Text	/uh/ or schwa	✓			✓	✓			✓	✓		✓	✓	✓			✓							✓											
Chapter 21 Tutor	/uh/ or schwa								✓	✓	✓			✓	✓		✓																		
Chapter 22 Text	Same sound for a and e	✓			✓	✓					✓		✓	✓	✓		✓																✓		
Chapter 22 Tutor	Same sound for a and e			✓	✓	✓				✓	✓	✓	✓	✓	✓												✓								
Chapter 23 Text	Sounds of a				✓	✓							✓	✓	✓									✓							✓		✓		
Chapter 23 Tutor	Sounds of a	✓				✓							✓	✓	✓																✓				
Chapter 24 Text	Long a followed by silent e			✓	✓	✓							✓	✓	✓																				
Chapter 24 Tutor	Long a followed by silent e					✓							✓	✓	✓																				
Chapter 25 Text	Short e				✓	✓							✓	✓															✓	✓	✓		✓		
Chapter 25 Tutor	Short e	✓		✓		✓							✓																						
Unit 3 Review Text														✓																				
Unit 3 Review Tutor													✓																					
Unit 3 Tests																																		
Unit 4 Opener Text													✓		✓																			
Unit 4 Opener Tutor													✓		✓																			
Chapter 26 Text	Sounds of e		✓		✓	✓		✓				✓	✓	✓	✓					✓	✓	✓						✓				✓	✓	✓
Chapter 26 Tutor	Sounds of e	✓				✓							✓		✓					✓	✓	✓												✓
Chapter 27 Text	Sounds of vowels				✓	✓		✓	✓		✓		✓	✓			✓	✓	✓	✓		✓	✓			✓								
Chapter 27 Tutor	Sounds of vowels	✓	✓										✓							✓											✓			
Chapter 28 Text	Final e	✓	✓		✓								✓	✓	✓																			
Chapter 28 Tutor	Final e												✓		✓																			
Chapter 29 Text	c, q, and k				✓	✓					✓		✓	✓	✓	✓														✓				
Chapter 29 Tutor	c, q, and k	✓											✓	✓	✓					✓				✓	✓									
Chapter 30 Text	Sounds of a	✓	✓		✓	✓					✓		✓	✓	✓	✓				✓					✓					✓				
Chapter 30 Tutor	Sounds of a	✓							✓				✓	✓	✓																			

Categories: Decoding Skill | Comprehension Skills (Main Idea, Details, Sequence, Summarizing, Cause and Effect, Fact/Opinion, Outlining, Compare/Contrast, Classifying, Drawing Conclusions, Inferences, Predictions) | Graphics (Timeline, Map, Chart, Table, Graph, Diagram) | Critical Thinking | Cooperative Learning Learning Styles (Reading, Writing, Visual, Auditory, Verbal, Oral, Listening, Kinesthetic, Tactile) | Evaluation (Alt. Assess. Activity, Alt. Assess. Rubric, Writ. Assess. Activity, Writ. Assess. Rubric, Standardized Format)

Text = Student Text *For the People, By the People*
Tutor = *Peoples Mainstream Tutor*

Scope and Sequence of Skills in the *For the People, By the People* Program

Program	Decoding Skill	Main Idea	Details	Sequence	Summarizing	Cause and Effect	Fact/Opinion	Outlining	Compare/Contrast	Classifying	Drawing Conclusions	Inferences	Predictions	Timeline	Map	Chart	Table	Graph	Diagram	Critical Thinking	Reading	Writing	Visual	Auditory	Verbal	Oral	Listening	Kinesthetic	Tactile	Alt. Assess. Activity	Alt. Assess. Rubric	Writ. Assess. Activity	Writ. Assess. Rubric	Standardized Format
Mid-Unit 4 Review Text				✓		✓				✓			✓	✓														✓	✓	✓	✓	✓	✓	✓
Mid-Unit 4 Review Tutor																																		
Mid-Unit 4 Tests																																		✓
Chapter 31 Text	Sounds of e			✓		✓							✓	✓																✓		✓		
Chapter 31 Tutor	Sounds of e	✓														✓				✓					✓					✓				✓
Chapter 32 Text	Double consonants	✓			✓	✓							✓	✓		✓				✓														
Chapter 32 Tutor	Double consonants					✓										✓																		
Chapter 33 Text	su=/sw/		✓			✓		✓			✓		✓	✓	✓	✓				✓	✓		✓						✓					
Chapter 33 Tutor	su=/sw/											✓	✓		✓																			
Chapter 34 Text	final y = long e	✓				✓							✓	✓	✓					✓						✓						✓		✓
Chapter 34 Tutor	final y = long e			✓		✓																		✓	✓									
Unit 4 Review Text						✓																												
Unit 4 Review Tutor													✓	✓	✓							✓												✓
Unit 4 Tests																																		
Unit 5 Opener Text																																		
Unit 5 Opener Tutor																																		
Chapter 35 Text	c=/k/	✓				✓					✓		✓		✓	✓	✓			✓			✓							✓				
Chapter 35 Tutor	c=/k/												✓			✓																		
Chapter 36 Text	f and ph	✓									✓		✓		✓					✓										✓				
Chapter 36 Tutor	f and ph												✓			✓																		
Chapter 37 Text	ea and ai	✓	✓								✓	✓	✓		✓	✓	✓			✓			✓							✓			✓	
Chapter 37 Tutor	ea and ai												✓			✓								✓					✓					
Chapter 38 Text	sounds of i	✓	✓								✓		✓		✓					✓										✓				
Chapter 38 Tutor	sounds of i												✓			✓																		
Chapter 39 Text	s and c = /k/	✓	✓								✓		✓		✓					✓			✓							✓				
Chapter 39 Tutor	s and c = /k/												✓			✓																		
Chapter 40 Text	sounds of i	✓	✓		✓						✓		✓	✓	✓	✓	✓			✓									✓	✓		✓		

Tutor=Peoples Mainstream Tutor

Scope and Sequence of Skills in the *For the People, By the People* Program

Row	Decoding Skill	Main Idea	Details	Sequence	Summarizing	Cause and Effect	Fact/Opinion	Outlining	Compare/Contrast	Classifying	Drawing Conclusions	Inferences	Predictions	Timeline	Map	Chart	Table	Graph	Diagram	Critical Thinking	Reading	Writing	Visual	Auditory	Verbal	Oral	Listening	Kinesthetic	Tactile	Alt. Assess. Activity	Alt. Assess. Rubric	Writ. Assess. Activity	Writ. Assess. Rubric	Standardized Format
Chapter 40 Tutor	Sounds of i	✓	✓		✓	✓		✓	✓				✓	✓		✓										✓		✓		✓		✓		✓
Mid-Unit 5 Review Text						✓																												
Mid-Unit 5 Review Tutor				✓		✓							✓	✓																✓	✓	✓	✓	✓
Mid-Unit 5 Tests																																✓		✓
Chapter 41 Text	Long e																						✓											
Chapter 41 Tutor	Long e												✓					✓												✓		✓		
Chapter 42 Text	Short vowels	✓			✓	✓		✓			✓	✓	✓	✓	✓					✓										✓		✓		
Chapter 42 Tutor	Short vowels		✓										✓	✓	✓			✓					✓		✓									
Chapter 43 Text	c = /k/	✓			✓	✓		✓			✓	✓	✓	✓	✓					✓												✓		
Chapter 43 Tutor	c = /k/	✓				✓							✓		✓															✓		✓		
Chapter 44 Text	Sounds of a		✓								✓		✓			✓				✓	✓								✓	✓		✓		
Chapter 44 Tutor	Sounds of a					✓		✓					✓		✓																			
Chapter 45 Text	Sounds of air												✓																	✓		✓		
Chapter 45 Tutor	Sounds of air					✓					✓		✓		✓					✓				✓					✓					
Chapter 46 Text	Short a		✓			✓		✓					✓															✓				✓		
Chapter 46 Tutor	Short a			✓						✓			✓			✓										✓								
Unit 5 Review Text																						✓										✓		✓
Unit 5 Review Tutor													✓		✓	✓				✓		✓								✓	✓	✓✓✓		✓
Unit 5 Tests			✓					✓					✓																					
Unit 6 Opener Text													✓							✓										✓				
Unit 6 Opener Tutor													✓																					
Chapter 47 Text	Sounds of e	✓	✓		✓	✓		✓	✓		✓		✓		✓	✓				✓										✓		✓		✓
Chapter 47 Tutor	Sounds of e	✓			✓	✓		✓	✓				✓			✓				✓			✓							✓		✓		
Chapter 48 Text	/uh/ or schwa	✓											✓																					
Chapter 48 Tutor	/uh/ or schwa	✓											✓		✓										✓								
Chapter 49 Text	oo as in troops	✓						✓	✓			✓	✓		✓	✓				✓	✓				✓					✓		✓		

For the People, By the People

Scope and Sequence

xxi

Scope and Sequence of Skills in the *For the People, By the People* Program

Program	Decoding Skill	Main Idea	Details	Sequence	Summarizing	Cause and Effect	Fact/Opinion	Outlining	Compare/Contrast	Classifying	Drawing Conclusions	Inferences	Predictions	Timeline	Map	Chart	Table	Graph	Diagram	Critical Thinking	Reading	Writing	Visual	Auditory	Verbal	Oral	Listening	Kinesthetic	Tactile	Alt. Assess. Activity	Alt. Assess. Rubric	Writ. Assess. Activity	Writ. Assess. Rubric	Standardized Format
Chapter 49 Tutor	oo as in troops	✓	✓		✓	✓							✓	✓	✓					✓						✓				✓				
Chapter 50 Text	Sounds of u	✓			✓	✓							✓	✓	✓																			
Chapter 50 Tutor	Sounds of u	✓											✓	✓	✓					✓														
Chapter 51 Text	Sounds of o				✓	✓		✓	✓				✓	✓		✓					✓								✓	✓				
Chapter 51 Tutor	Sounds of o												✓			✓																		
Chapter 52 Text	Sounds of ur	✓	✓		✓	✓		✓			✓	✓	✓	✓				✓		✓		✓	✓	✓						✓		✓	✓	✓
Chapter 52 Tutor	Sounds of ur												✓					✓																
Mid-Unit 6 Review Text		✓		✓		✓							✓	✓												✓				✓		✓		✓
Mid-Unit 6 Review Tutor													✓																					
Mid-Unit 6 Tests													✓							✓														✓
Chapter 53 Text	tion = /shuhn/	✓	✓		✓	✓							✓	✓						✓									✓	✓		✓		
Chapter 53 Tutor	tion = /shuhn/												✓																					
Chapter 54 Text	Sounds of u	✓	✓		✓	✓							✓	✓			✓			✓								✓	✓	✓		✓		
Chapter 54 Tutor	Sounds of u												✓				✓																	
Chapter 55 Text	Sounds of o	✓	✓		✓	✓							✓	✓				✓		✓									✓	✓		✓		
Chapter 55 Tutor	Sounds of o												✓					✓																
Chapter 56 Text	k and c = /k/	✓	✓		✓	✓							✓	✓	✓	✓				✓					✓					✓	✓	✓	✓	✓
Chapter 56 Tutor	k and c = /k/												✓		✓	✓																		
Chapter 57 Text	final silent e	✓	✓		✓	✓							✓	✓						✓										✓		✓		
Chapter 57 Tutor	final silent e												✓																					
Chapter 58 Text	ti = /sh/	✓	✓		✓	✓				✓			✓	✓						✓					✓	✓	✓			✓	✓	✓	✓	✓
Chapter 58 Tutor	ti = /sh/												✓																					
Unit 6 Review Text		✓	✓	✓	✓	✓							✓							✓										✓	✓	✓	✓	✓
Unit 6 Review Tutor		✓	✓		✓								✓																		✓	✓		✓
Unit 6 Tests		✓	✓			✓							✓							✓										✓		✓		✓
Unit 7 Opener Text														✓																				

Tutor=Peoples Mainstream Tutor

Scope and Sequence of Skills in the *For the People, By the People* Program

Program	Decoding Skill	Comprehension Skills — Main Idea	Details	Sequence	Summarizing	Cause and Effect	Fact/Opinion	Outlining	Compare/Contrast	Classifying	Drawing Conclusions	Inferences	Predictions	Graphics — Timeline	Map	Chart	Table	Graph	Diagram	Evaluation — Critical Thinking	Reading	Writing	Visual	Auditory	Verbal	Oral	Listening	Kinesthetic	Tactile	Alt. Assess. Activity	Alt. Assess. Rubric	Writ. Assess. Activity	Writ. Assess. Rubric	Standardized Format
Unit 7 Opener Tutor													✓		✓					✓		✓							✓					
Chapter 59 Text	Sound of *or*	✓	✓		✓	✓		✓					✓	✓	✓					✓					✓					✓		✓		
Chapter 59 Tutor	Sound of *or*	✓			✓	✓		✓					✓	✓	✓					✓														
Chapter 60 Text	o = /uh/	✓				✓		✓					✓	✓	✓																			
Chapter 60 Tutor	o = /uh/				✓	✓		✓					✓	✓	✓										✓				✓	✓		✓		
Chapter 61 Text	Short a	✓	✓			✓		✓	✓			✓	✓	✓	✓	✓				✓									✓					
Chapter 61 Tutor	Short a				✓	✓		✓					✓	✓	✓										✓									
Chapter 62 Text	/uh/ or schwa	✓									✓		✓	✓	✓					✓					✓					✓		✓		
Chapter 62 Tutor	/uh/ or schwa				✓	✓		✓	✓				✓	✓	✓																			
Chapter 63 Text	Double consonants	✓												✓	✓																			
Chapter 63 Tutor	Double consonants			✓				✓					✓	✓	✓																			
Mid-Unit 7 Review Text		✓	✓			✓							✓	✓									✓											
Mid-Unit 7 Review Tutor		✓			✓			✓					✓	✓	✓										✓					✓	✓	✓	✓	✓
Mid-Unit 7 Tests		✓	✓										✓							✓			✓							✓		✓		
Chapter 64 Text	/uh/ or schwa	✓											✓	✓	✓			✓	✓	✓														
Chapter 64 Tutor	/uh/ or schwa	✓			✓	✓			✓				✓	✓	✓			✓	✓	✓					✓									
Chapter 65 Text	Sounds of c & s	✓											✓	✓	✓																			
Chapter 65 Tutor	Sounds of c & s	✓			✓			✓						✓	✓																			
Chapter 66 Text	c = /k/	✓							✓					✓		✓																		
Chapter 66 Tutor	c = /k/							✓						✓																				
Chapter 67 Text	c = /s/	✓											✓	✓																				
Chapter 67 Tutor	c = /s/				✓	✓		✓						✓	✓		✓				✓					✓				✓	✓	✓	✓	
Chapter 68 Text	/uh/ or schwa	✓											✓	✓	✓		✓																	
Chapter 68 Tutor	/uh/ or schwa	✓			✓	✓		✓					✓	✓	✓						✓					✓				✓		✓		
Unit 7 Review Text		✓	✓										✓	✓		✓							✓							✓		✓	✓	✓
Unit 7 Review Tutor		✓	✓	✓		✓								✓																✓	✓	✓	✓	
Unit 7 Tests														✓						✓					✓					✓		✓		✓

Text = Student Text *For the People, By the People*
Tutor = *Peoples Mainstream Tutor*

Scope and Sequence of Skills in the *For the People, By the People* Program

Program	Decoding Skill	Main idea	Details	Sequence	Summarizing	Cause and Effect	Fact/Opinion	Outlining	Compare/Contrast	Classifying	Drawing Conclusions	Inferences	Predictions	Timeline	Map	Chart	Table	Graph	Diagram	Critical Thinking	Reading	Writing	Visual	Auditory	Verbal	Oral	Listening	Kinesthetic	Tactile	Alt. Assess. Activity	Alt. Assess. Rubric	Writ. Assess. Activity	Writ. Assess. Rubric	Standardized Format
Unit 8 Opener Text													✓	✓								✓												
Unit 8 Opener Tutor													✓					✓					✓											
Chapter 69 Text	ck and ss	✓											✓			✓		✓		✓														
Chapter 69 Tutor	ck and ss												✓																	✓		✓		
Chapter 70 Text	au=/ah	✓	✓		✓	✓							✓	✓						✓					✓									
Chapter 70 Tutor	au=/ah											✓	✓			✓																		
Chapter 71 Text	a consonant e = long a	✓	✓		✓	✓					✓	✓	✓							✓														
Chapter 71 Tutor	a consonant e = long a	✓											✓																	✓				
Chapter 72 Text	c =/k/ and /s/	✓	✓		✓	✓					✓		✓	✓				✓		✓		✓			✓				✓	✓		✓		✓
Chapter 72 Tutor	c =/k/ and /s/												✓							✓														
Mid-Unit 8 Review Text				✓						✓			✓								✓						✓							✓
Mid-Unit 8 Review Tutor													✓					✓												✓	✓	✓	✓	
Mid-Unit 8 Tests																																		
Chapter 73 Text	sc=/sk/	✓	✓		✓	✓							✓	✓	✓			✓		✓	✓													
Chapter 73 Tutor	sc=/sk/		✓			✓					✓	✓	✓		✓					✓														
Chapter 74 Text	Double vowel letters				✓	✓					✓		✓		✓					✓														
Chapter 74 Tutor	Double vowel letters												✓		✓										✓									
Chapter 75 Text	Long a	✓	✓		✓	✓							✓		✓					✓	✓													
Chapter 75 Tutor	Long a												✓		✓					✓														
Chapter 76 Text	tion =/shuhn/	✓	✓			✓							✓	✓	✓			✓		✓	✓													
Chapter 76 Tutor	tion =/shuhn/												✓		✓							✓												
Chapter 77 Text	ck =/k/	✓											✓	✓	✓					✓														
Chapter 77 Tutor	ck =/k/												✓		✓																			
Chapter 78 Text	Final y = long i	✓	✓		✓	✓			✓		✓		✓	✓	✓	✓				✓														
Chapter 78 Tutor	Final y = long i												✓		✓																			
Chapter 79 Text	u =/yooh/	✓				✓					✓		✓	✓		✓		✓		✓					✓							✓		
Chapter 79 Tutor	u =/yooh/	✓									✓		✓	✓	✓					✓										✓				

Scope and Sequence of Skills in the *For the People, By the People* Program

Program	Decoding Skill	Main Idea	Details	Sequence	Summarizing	Cause and Effect	Fact/Opinion	Outlining	Compare/Contrast	Classifying	Drawing Conclusions	Inferences	Predictions	Timeline	Map	Chart	Table	Graph	Diagram	Critical Thinking	Reading	Writing	Visual	Auditory	Verbal	Oral	Listening	Kinesthetic	Tactile	Alt. Assess. Activity	Alt. Assess. Rubric	Writ. Assess. Activity	Writ. Assess. Rubric	Standardized Format
Unit 8 Review Text			✓			✓							✓	✓									✓		✓					✓		✓		✓
Unit 8 Review Tutor													✓	✓																	✓		✓	
Unit 8 Tests														✓																		✓		✓
Unit 9 Opener Text													✓	✓																				
Unit 9 Opener Tutor													✓		✓																			
Chapter 80 Text	ice = /eyes/ and /is/	✓			✓			✓	✓				✓	✓	✓					✓	✓	✓										✓		
Chapter 80 Tutor	ice = /eyes/ and /is/	✓							✓				✓		✓																			
Chapter 81 Text	Sound of x				✓	✓			✓		✓		✓	✓	✓					✓			✓							✓		✓		✓
Chapter 81 Tutor	Sound of x	✓									✓		✓		✓											✓								
Chapter 82 Text	u = /yoo/	✓			✓	✓		✓			✓		✓	✓	✓					✓										✓		✓		
Chapter 82 Tutor	u = /yoo/												✓	✓	✓																			
Chapter 83 Text	Long o and a with Silent e												✓	✓	✓	✓														✓				
Chapter 83 Tutor	Long o and a with Silent e												✓	✓	✓	✓																		
Chapter 84 Text	c = /k/ and /s/	✓	✓			✓							✓	✓	✓	✓				✓					✓	✓			✓	✓		✓		✓
Chapter 84 Tutor	c = /k/ and /s/												✓	✓	✓	✓																		
Chapter 85 Text	Long a				✓	✓		✓					✓	✓		✓														✓		✓		
Chapter 85 Tutor	Long a												✓	✓		✓																		
Mid-Unit 9 Review Text													✓	✓	✓	✓									✓					✓		✓		✓
Mid-Unit 9 Review Tutor													✓	✓		✓																✓		✓
Mid-Unit 9 Tests				✓						✓																								✓
Chapter 86 Text	e = Short i	✓	✓		✓	✓							✓	✓	✓	✓									✓				✓	✓		✓		
Chapter 86 Tutor	e = Short i	✓	✓										✓	✓	✓	✓																		
Chapter 87 Text	Final silent e	✓						✓					✓	✓		✓				✓									✓	✓		✓		
Chapter 87 Tutor	Final silent e												✓	✓		✓				✓														
Chapter 88 Text	c = /s/	✓			✓	✓							✓	✓		✓														✓		✓		
Chapter 88 Tutor	c = /s/				✓	✓							✓	✓		✓																		

Scope and Sequence of Skills in the *For the People, By the People* Program

Program	Decoding Skill	Main Idea	Details	Sequence	Summarizing	Cause and Effect	Fact/Opinion	Outlining	Compare/Contrast	Classifying	Drawing Conclusions	Inferences	Predictions	Timeline	Map	Chart	Table	Graph	Diagram	Critical Thinking	Reading	Writing	Visual	Auditory	Verbal	Oral	Listening	Kinesthetic	Tactile	Alt. Assess. Activity	Alt. Assess. Rubric	Writ. Assess. Activity	Writ. Assess. Rubric	Standardized Format
Chapter 89 Text	Long i	✓				✓							✓		✓					✓						✓				✓		✓		
Chapter 89 Tutor	Long i	✓			✓	✓						✓	✓	✓		✓				✓										✓		✓		
Chapter 90 Text	tion = /shuhn/	✓											✓	✓	✓	✓																✓		
Chapter 90 Tutor	tion = /shuhn/	✓	✓		✓	✓		✓					✓	✓		✓									✓				✓	✓		✓		
Chapter 91 Text	ea = long e		✓										✓		✓		✓			✓					✓							✓		
Chapter 91 Tutor	ea = long e					✓							✓										✓							✓				
Unit 9 Review Text		✓		✓		✓							✓	✓	✓							✓								✓	✓	✓	✓	✓
Unit 9 Review Tutor													✓		✓																			
Unit 9 Tests																																		
Unit 10 Opener													✓	✓							✓													
Unit 10 Opener Tutor															✓																			
Chapter 92 Text	Long i	✓			✓	✓					✓	✓		✓	✓	✓				✓					✓					✓		✓		
Chapter 92 Tutor	Long i		✓		✓	✓		✓				✓	✓			✓				✓										✓				
Chapter 93 Text	Sounds of a					✓							✓	✓		✓																		
Chapter 93 Tutor	Sounds of a	✓			✓	✓							✓		✓					✓									✓	✓		✓		
Chapter 94 Text	Long i													✓		✓					✓													
Chapter 94 Tutor	Long i					✓							✓	✓						✓										✓		✓		
Chapter 95 Text	Sounds of o												✓	✓	✓																			
Chapter 95 Tutor	Sounds of o			✓		✓							✓	✓	✓																	✓		
Mid-Unit 10 Review Text													✓	✓	✓													✓	✓	✓	✓	✓	✓
Mid-Unit 10 Review Tutor																													✓					
Mid-Unit 10 Tests																																		
Chapter 96 Text	Sounds of e	✓	✓			✓							✓	✓		✓				✓	✓									✓		✓		
Chapter 96 Tutor	Sounds of e	✓				✓							✓	✓		✓				✓	✓					✓				✓				
Chapter 97 Text	/uh/ or schwa										✓		✓	✓	✓														✓	✓		✓		
Chapter 97 Tutor	/uh/ or schwa	✓			✓	✓								✓	✓						✓									✓		✓		

Text=Student Text *For the People, By the People*
Tutor=*Peoples Mainstream Tutor*

Scope and Sequence of Skills in the *For the People, By the People* Program

Program	Decoding Skill	Main Idea	Details	Sequence	Summarizing	Cause and Effect	Fact/Opinion	Outlining	Compare/Contrast	Classifying	Drawing Conclusions	Inferences	Predictions	Timeline	Map	Chart	Table	Graph	Diagram	Critical Thinking	Reading	Writing	Visual	Auditory	Verbal	Oral	Listening	Kinesthetic	Tactile	Alt. Assess. Activity	Alt. Assess. Rubric	Writ. Assess. Activity	Writ. Assess. Rubric	Standardized Format
Chapter 98 Text	c = /k/ and /s/	✓							✓				✓		✓	✓				✓					✓					✓		✓		
Chapter 98 Tutor	c = /k/ and /s/				✓	✓		✓					✓	✓	✓																			
Chapter 99 Text	oo = /ooh/	✓									✓	✓	✓		✓								✓						✓			✓		
Chapter 99 Tutor	oo = /ooh/					✓		✓					✓	✓	✓																			
Chapter 100 Text	Vowel + final e	✓			✓	✓					✓		✓			✓													✓					
Chapter 100 Tutor	Vowel + final e					✓		✓								✓				✓	✓													
Unit 10 Review Text										✓			✓	✓									✓						✓	✓		✓	✓	
Unit 10 Review Tutor														✓																✓	✓		✓	✓
Unit 10 Tests																																✓		✓

For the People, By the People

A History of the United States
Beginnings to Present

 The Peoples Publishing Group, Inc.
Free to Learn, to Grow, to Change

Unit 1

POLITICAL

20,000BCE
The Ice Age lowered sea levels, joining Asia to what is now called Alaska. Asians crossed over the Bering Strait and entered Alaska.

CE1000
Leif Ericson reached a land known today as Newfoundland.

CE1419
Portugal's kings sent ships to sail along Africa's shores.

CE1492
Columbus landed at an island he named San Salvador. He claimed all these lands for Spain.

CE1498
Vasco Da Gama sailed around Africa and reached Asia.

20,000 BCE   0 BCE   1400

CULTURE

1200BCE
Olmec civilization began in what is known today as Central America.

600BCE
Mayan people of Mexico and Central America told stories that became a book known as *Popul Vuh.*

300BCE
Native Americans developed farming cultures in the lands that are now part of the Southwest United States.

Three Worlds Meet

BEGINNINGS to 1620

"I write you this, by which you should know that in 33 days I passed over the Indies with the fleet the . . . King and Queen gave me; where I found very many islands . . . and of them all, I have taken possession for their Highnesses . . . ."

— *Christopher Columbus*
Explorer for Spain

$\mathcal{E}$arth is a planet that is almost all water. Only about one-fourth of its surface is land. Scientists believe that all the land was once connected. This great land mass broke apart and formed the continents. Read about two continents that produced a marvelous collection of animals and plants but no humans. How did people arrive? Why?

CE1501
Amerigo Vespucci reached what is now known as Brazil. He said these lands were not Asia but a continent that Europeans had known nothing about.

CE1513
Juan Ponce de Leon claimed for Spain lands that became Florida.

CE1519
Parts of what is now Mexico were conquered for Spain by Cortés.

CE1532
Francisco Pizarro beat the Inca and took their land for Spain. Most of this land became Peru.

CE1539
Hernando de Soto spent three years exploring Florida, Texas, and Oklahoma.

CE1540-1542
Francisco Coronado passed through Arizona, New Mexico, Oklahoma, and Kansas.

CE1588
England defeated the Spanish Armada.

1500

CE1505
People all over Europe read Vespucci's letters about his trip to what is now Brazil. Martin Waldseemüller named all the lands "America" in his new book of world maps.

Chapter 1

East to the Americas

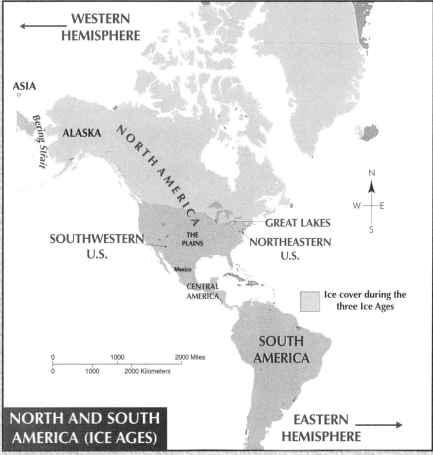

WESTERN HEMISPHERE ←

ASIA

Bering Strait

ALASKA

NORTH AMERICA

SOUTHWESTERN U.S.

THE PLAINS

Mexico

GREAT LAKES

NORTHEASTERN U.S.

N
W — E
S

CENTRAL AMERICA

Ice cover during the three Ice Ages

SOUTH AMERICA

0   1000   2000 Miles
0 1000 2000 Kilometers

NORTH AND SOUTH AMERICA (ICE AGES)

EASTERN HEMISPHERE →

Read about the way in which geography helped bring Asians to the Americas. Where did they decide to live? Why?

Key *Vocabulary*

strait (strayt) a narrow stretch of water flowing between two larger areas of water

extinct (ek STINGKT) none left alive

population (PAHP yuh LAY shuhn) all the people who live in a specific area

civilization (SIV uh luh ZAY shuhn) a group that has reached a stage where people use writing and keep records

MAP ANALYSIS

★ **Ask**   Where is North America closest to Asia?

★ **Acquire**   What body of water is between Asia and Alaska?

★ **Organize**   What places were covered by ice during the Ice Ages?

★ **Analyze**   If sea levels dropped during an Ice Age, the Bering Strait might have become dry. How could people have moved from Asia to Alaska?

★ **Answer**   Where could people have settled in the Americas and still have avoided the ice sheets of an Ice Age?

Decoding Tip: Notice the sound *a* stands for in the vocabulary words.

ay	cake	ah	fall, cot	air	air
ee	tree	i	sit	oh	cold
or	cord	oy	toy	uh	above, hundred
a	ask	ar	hard	oo	book
e	yet	eye	nice	uhr	liar, fir, further, color
ow	cow	ooh	boot, true	yoo	you, few, cube

1.1 What was the Ice Age?

Giant piles of ice cover the oceans at the top of the world. During the winter, the ice cover grows larger. In the spring, some of the ice melts. The ice cover becomes smaller. At different points in the past, the weather was very cold. The ice cover grew very large. It even moved down to cover lands that are now Canada and part of the United States. Each of these times is called an "Ice Age."

The first Ice Age started around 68,000 BCE. It lasted about 40,000 years. A second one started around 23,000 BCE and lasted about 10,000 years. The last Ice Age began around 12,000 BCE and lasted about 4,000 years. During an Ice Age, sea water freezes. It becomes part of the ice cover. So much water is frozen that the seas drop. As the water drops, land can be seen. The Bering **Strait** may have become dry. It may have been a land bridge from Asia to Alaska.

1.2 Why did the first people move to North and South America?

Grass and other plants grew on land that was dry during the Ice Ages. Animals slowly moved from Asia to North America. They ate the grass as they went. The first Americans were Asian hunters. They followed these animals across the land bridge to Alaska.

No one knows which Ice Age was happening when the first Asians reached the Americas. People may even have come to the West during each Ice Age. By 6,000 BCE, people had reached every part of the Americas.

1.3 How did life in the Americas change after the last Ice Age?

The ice cover grew smaller as the last Ice Age ended. The weather turned warmer. Melting water caused new rivers and lakes. Forests and jungles grew on land that had been covered by ice. Many large animals became **extinct**. The early Americans had to hunt smaller animals for food.

Early people found many new kinds of plants in the Americas. They learned which plants were good to eat. Soon, the people began to take care of these plants. Between 6,000 and 5,000 BCE, the people began to grow their own plants. They raised foods that were not known in the rest of the world. Some of these foods were corn, tomatoes, peanuts, potatoes, and pumpkins.

1.4   How did farming affect the people of the Americas?

▼The illustration below shows how the early Native American people worked together to harvest corn.

Farming probably began in lands known as Mexico and Central America today. The most important food was corn.

▲ The photograph above, which was taken in 1889 by F.A. Ames, shows a Navajo hogan and cornfield near Holbrook, Arizona.

People built homes near their fields. They learned how to change this plant. Soon the ears of corn were very large. There was now plenty of food. Families could raise more children. The **population** began to grow. More corn was grown than the people could eat. People began to trade the extra corn. This trade made the people rich. Some small farm villages grew into cities.

Trade in the Americas was between neighbors. The people of Mexico would trade with people in the U.S. Southwest. These people would trade with people who lived on the Plains. The Plains people would then trade with those who lived near the Great Lakes. Goods from one place could reach people all over North and Central America.

Farming and trade caused great changes in the villages and cities. The people became different from each other. Each group came up with new ideas and new ways of living. Talk changed, too. The groups had different ways of speaking. Many great **civilizations** were born in the Western Hemisphere.

☆☆☆

Multicultural
PERSPECTIVE

*P*opol *Vuh* is the name of some special Native American stories. These stories were told by the Mayans. These people built great cities in Mexico and Central America. One story tells about how the first Mayans were born. The gods tried to make people from mud. The mud would not keep its shape. Next, the gods used wood. These people could not think. The gods made them disappear. The third group of people were made of flesh. They became very mean and dangerous. The gods sent a great flood. The people were killed. At last, the gods added water to ground corn. They used this dough to make the first Mayans. The Mayans built about 60 great cities in Central America. There were over ten million Mayans by 650 CE. Mayans still live in Mexico and Central America today.

▲ Cities built in ancient times

★★★ CHAPTER REVIEW

Critical Thinking

Write your answers on a sheet of paper, or discuss in class.

Analyzing Cause and Effect

1. Why did the early Americans always need to move from place to place in search of food?

Drawing Conclusions

2. How did farming help bring about villages and cities?

Cooperative Learning

LEARNING STYLE
Tactile

3. Work with a study partner or group. Use clay to make a map of the lands around the Bering Strait. Build your map in something that can hold water. Shape the clay so that you can see mountains and low spots. Dry out the map. Pour water over the map. Note how the water rises to make coasts and islands.

Write About It

Writing Portfolio

4. Read the following list of sentence starters. Think of an ending for each sentence. Write your sentences on a piece of paper.
   a. When a really large animal is caught, hunters must...
   b. The weather during an Ice Age must be...
   c. The most important development of the Ice Age was...

Chapter 2

The First Americans

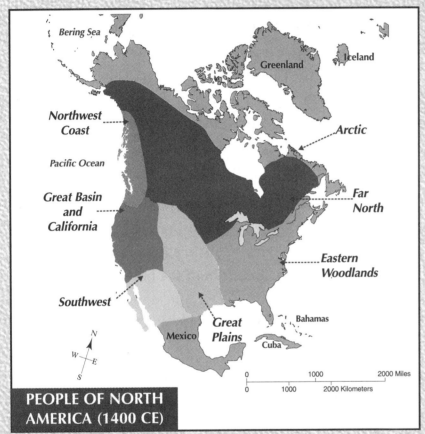

Bering Sea

Greenland

Iceland

Northwest Coast

Arctic

Pacific Ocean

Far North

Great Basin and California

Southwest

Eastern Woodlands

Great Plains

Mexico

Bahamas

Cuba

N
W — E
S

| 0 | 1000 | 2000 Miles |
| 0 | 1000 | 2000 Kilometers |

PEOPLE OF NORTH AMERICA (1400 CE)

Read about the lives of the first Americans. How were they the same? How were their lives different? Why?

Key *Vocabulary*

basin (BAYS uhn) a low area of land

pyramid (PIR uh mid) a building or structure that slopes inward from bottom to top

temple (TEM puhl) a building where people perform religious activities

canal (kuh NAL) a ditch or channel dug to move water from one place to another

MAP ANALYSIS

★ **Ask**   What Native American groups lived in North America?

★ **Acquire**   What Native American groups lived in areas that became the United States?

★ **Organize**   As you go south, the weather gets warmer. How is the weather in the Arctic different from the weather in Mexico and Central America?

★ **Analyze**   Why might the clothing worn by people in the Arctic be different from that worn by people in Mexico?

★ **Answer**   What might have caused Native Americans to develop different lifestyles?

Decoding Tip: Notice the different sounds *e* stands for in the vocabulary words.

ay	cake	ah	fall, cot	air	air
ee	tree	i	sit	oh	cold
or	cord	oy	toy	uh	above, hundred
a	ask	ar	hard	oo	book
e	yet	eye	nice	uhr	liar, fir, further, color
ow	cow	ooh	boot, true	yoo	you, few, cube

2.1 What was life like in the northern parts of North America?

Who would build homes near the North Pole? The Arctic and Far North are cold places. No one knows when the first people appeared there. Two important groups of people decided to live there. One group is called Eskimos. They still live in the Arctic. They were among the last Asians to reach North America. The other group is the people of the Far North. They had left Asia earlier. Both groups lived like the early Asian hunters. They hunted caribou. This animal is a kind of deer. Caribou were very important. The people ate caribou meat. They used its bones to make all their tools. Hides were turned into clothes and tents. Canoes made of hides were used for fishing. The people even caught whales.

Hide tents were used by both the Eskimos and people of the Far North. These homes were used when it was fairly warm. The tents were easy to move. This was important when game was sighted. In winter, Eskimos built ice homes called igloos. The people of the Far North even built log homes. They only lived in these homes during winter.

▲ The photograph above shows an old Eskimo woman sitting in front of a summer skin tent in Point Barrow, Alaska, in 1935. Photograph taken by Stanley Morgan.

2.2 What was life like in areas bordering the Pacific Ocean?

The people of the Northwest Coast, California, or the Great **Basin** did not farm the land. Finding food was never a problem along the Pacific shores. The forests were filled with game. Plenty of fish lived in the rivers and the ocean. People who lived away from the shores had a harder time. The weather and land were dry. Hunting, fishing, and finding plants was not easy.

People of the Northwest built homes of wood boards. They lived in these villages year after year. Totem poles were placed beside their doors. These were tall poles. Each was finely carved. The people carved great boats from giant logs. They

▲ The photograph above shows how early Native Americans dried salmon. This photograph was taken in the Aleut village in Old Harbor, Alaska, in 1889 by N.B. Miller.

took these boats to sea on fishing trips. The people of California and the Great Basin used sticks to build shells of homes. These shells were covered with bark and brush. The people did not build villages and cities. Still, many people lived in California. Only Mexico had more people in all of North America.

2.3   What was life like in Central America?

The first farms were in Central America. The people grew corn, beans, and squash. They had to live near their fields. These farm villages often grew. Some became great cities. The Olmecs built the first great cities in the Americas. They built with stone. They made large **pyramids**, **temples**, and homes for their kings. The Olmecs left their cities. Then, Mayan cities became important. They came up with ways of writing and counting. The Mayans' cities fell, too. No one knows why these cities fell. The children of both people still live in Central America.

The last great civilization of Central America was built by the Aztecs. Tenochtitlan was the most important Aztec city. It was a great city built on an island. A lake circled the city. Many great stone buildings made up the city. The people made fine goods of cotton, feathers, and gold. The Aztec king ruled many other people in Central America. Most of these people hated the Aztecs. The Aztecs had beaten them in war. Many of them were taken to Tenochtitlan. They were killed in the Aztec temples. This was done to please the Aztec gods.

2.4   What was life like in the Southwest?

Farming spread from Central America. Early people of the Southwest farmed the land. They built homes of mud bricks. Villages were sometimes built inside openings found on mountain cliffs. These villages protected the people from

▲ The top photograph shows pumpkins being grown near a single-family Zuni adobe.

▲ The bottom photograph shows part of a Hopi pueblo in Dancers' Rock, Walpi, Arizona. It also shows three Hopi people, ladders, and utensils. Both photographs taken by John K. Hillers, in 1879.

their enemies. The people dug **canals** to bring water to the fields. They grew corn, beans, and squash. Some of them left the cliff villages. They became known as the Pueblos. The Pueblos made fine clothes of cotton. They made beautiful jewelry and fine pots. These goods were traded with people across North America. The Pueblos also built special homes. They were made of brick, too. Some were four and five stories tall. Doors were in the roofs. They could only be reached by ladders. These ladders were pulled up during war. This protected the Pueblos from people like the Apaches and Navajos.

Apaches and Navajos probably moved from Canada to the Southwest. They were like the early Asians. These people moved from place to place. They hunted animals and looked for plants. Sometimes, these people attacked Pueblo villages. They took the Pueblos' food and goods.

2.5   What was life like in the Eastern Woodlands?

Great civilizations were raised in the Eastern Woodlands and Great Plains. One was built around the Great Lakes and in New England. The people built great mounds of earth. Some were used as temples. Others were for the dead. Villages and cities grew up around these mounds. Another civilization took shape along the Mississippi River. It spread out through the Midwest and down into Florida. These people built mounds and cities, too. Some of these cities ruled many places and people. One such city was near what is now St. Louis, Missouri. It was a great city named Cahokia. It was ruled by a king. He lived on top of a mound that was ten

▲ The photograph above shows the Pawnee lodges at Loup, Nebraska, with a family standing in front. Photograph taken in 1873 by William H. Jackson.

stories tall. It was the largest and richest city north of Mexico and Central America.

The mound cities fell. No one knows why. The people of the Eastern Woodlands began living in houses covered with bark. The villages were protected by log fences. Outside the fences were the people's fields. They grew corn, beans, and squash. There was plenty of game in the forests. They rowed bark boats on the rivers and streams. These boats helped the people fish, hunt, and trade.

2.6   What was life like on the Great Plains?

Farming villages on the Great Plains were made up of log homes. Dirt and brush were used to fill any holes. Villages were built near rivers and streams. This land was easy to farm. Women used the water to help grow corn, beans, and squash. Women did all the farming, cooking, and sewing. Times could be hard here. The weather could be very hot or very cold. Few people lived on the Great Plains until the late 1700s and early 1800s.

Men of the Plains people hunted animals. They hunted antelope and buffalo. There were no horses. The men had to follow the animals on foot. Their hunting parties lived in teepees. These tents could be set up and taken down quickly.

▼ The photograph below shows a Wichita camp with teepees in the background and Native American children in the foreground.

Sometimes the men shot the animals with arrows. At other times, they drove the animals over cliffs. No part of an animal was wasted. The people ate the meat. Hides were used as blankets and for clothes. Bones were turned into needles and other tools. The people raised dogs. Dogs carried and pulled goods from one place to another.

☆☆☆

▲ Village of early Native Americans

Native Americans were in touch with each other. The early people of the Southwest mined turquoise stones. They traded these stones for parrots and gold from Central America. Seashells from California and Mexico were sent across North America. The shells were bought by the people who built mounds near the Great Lakes. Copper was mined near the Great Lakes. It was traded, too. There were no horses. People and dogs carried goods from one place to another. They moved by foot and boat. The earliest people of the Southwest are known as the Anasazis. This Navajo word means "ancient ones or ancient enemies." The Anasazis built over 400 miles of roads to help people sell their goods.

CHAPTER REVIEW

Critical Thinking

Write your answers on a sheet of paper, or discuss in class.

1. Why were game, fish, and crops so important to the first Americans?

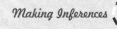

2. How did farming spread through North America?

Cooperative Learning

LEARNING STYLE
Reading Verbal

3. Work with a study partner. Choose a part of the chapter to read aloud. You may wish to record your readings. Check the vocabulary list. See what these words mean. Note how to say these words. Other words might be found in the back of the book. Remember that names can be found there, too.

Write About It

Writing Portfolio

4. Imagine you are a part of an early Native American group. Pretend that you have a friend who lives across the country. Write this friend a letter. Tell your friend about where you live. Also tell how you and your people live.

Chapter 3

To Reach Asia

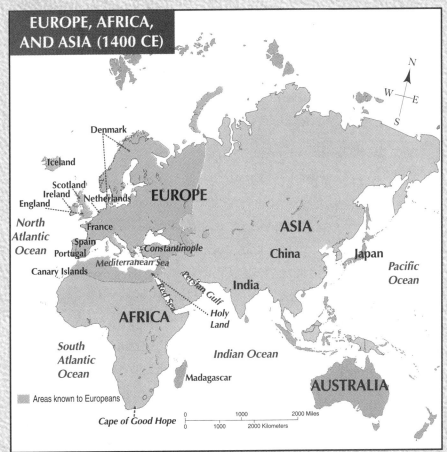

EUROPE, AFRICA, AND ASIA (1400 CE)

N, W—E, S

Denmark
Iceland
Scotland
Ireland   Netherlands
England
EUROPE
North
Atlantic   France
Ocean   Spain
Portugal   Constantinople
Canary Islands   Mediterranean Sea
Persian Gulf
Red Sea
India
Holy
Land
AFRICA
South
Atlantic
Ocean   Madagascar
Areas known to Europeans
Cape of Good Hope

ASIA
China   Japan
Pacific
Ocean

Indian Ocean

AUSTRALIA

0   1000   2000 Miles
0   1000   2000 Kilometers

Read about
Portuguese explorations during the 1400s. Where did they go? Why?

Key *Vocabulary*

empire (EHM peyer) a nation that is made up of many areas and people; ruled by a king or queen known as an emperor or empress

resource (REE sors) something that can be sold and/or used to make an item that can be sold

merchant (MUHR chuhnt) a person who buys goods and sells them for a higher price, or profit, in order to make a living

continent (KAHNT uhn uhnt) one of the globe's great land masses

MAP ANALYSIS

★ **Ask**   What two European nations are at the point where the Atlantic Ocean meets the Mediterranean?

★ **Acquire**   Where is the Western Hemisphere?

★ **Organize** How has the Europeans' knowledge of Earth changed since 1400 CE?

★ **Analyze**   Look at the areas in Africa and the Middle East that were known by the Europeans in 1400. What geographic feature do they share?

★ **Answer**   How did ships affect what the Europeans knew of the world?

Decoding Tip: R following a vowel affects the vowel's sound in some of the vocabulary words.

ay	cake	ah	fall, cot	air	air
ee	tree	i	sit	oh	cold
or	cord	oy	toy	uh	above, hundred
a	ask	ar	hard	oo	book
e	yet	eye	nice	uhr	liar, fir, further, color
ow	cow	ooh	boot, true	yoo	you, few, cube

3.1   What did the people of Europe know of the world in the late 1400s?

Before the late 1400s, Europeans knew little of the world. Of course, they knew Europe very well. They believed there were only three places outside Europe. These places were Africa, Asia, and the Middle East. Few Europeans had ever visited Africa or Asia. They had learned about the Middle East, though. Most Europeans were Christians who believed in Jesus Christ's teachings. The Middle East was ruled mostly by Muslims. These people followed the teachings of Muhammad. Both Jesus and Muhammad had lived in the same place. It was called the Holy Land by Muslims and Christians.

The Holy Land was part of the Middle East. By the 1000s CE, it was ruled by the Muslims. Europe tried many times to take over the Holy Land. These wars were known as the Crusades. The Crusaders would first visit the city of Constantinople. It was the home of Christian kings in the Middle East. This land was known as the Byzantine **Empire**. Much of Europe, Africa, and the Middle East had once been ruled by Rome. The Byzantine Empire was all that was left of the Roman Empire. The Byzantine king sent his people to fight with the Crusaders. Soon, Crusaders took over parts of the Holy Land. The Muslims always returned. Rule passed back and forth for about 400 years.

European learning grew during the Crusades. Europeans discovered many new wonders in the Middle East. They found new ideas in Middle Eastern books. The people of the Middle East knew more about mathematics and medicine than the Europeans. These ideas helped the people of Europe.

3.2   Why were the people of Europe interested in reaching Africa and Asia?

Europeans found more than ideas during the Crusades. Many fine goods could be bought in the Middle East. Trade was very important there. The Middle East handled trade among the people of Africa and Asia. Africa had a great many **resources**. Goods like gold, iron, and salt made some Africans rich. Asians grew spices like pepper and cinnamon. They also made cloth of silk. Europeans were eager to buy these goods. They had goods like wool and leather to trade. No **merchant** had to make the whole trading trip from Europe to Asia. Goods were moved slowly. They were sold from one merchant to another. Money was made in each trade. Prices were very high. People still wanted these goods. Merchants became very rich.

In the late 1400s, Constantinople was in danger. A group of Muslims were moving in from Asia. They were taking over lands ruled by the Byzantine Empire. These Muslims were known as the Ottoman Turks. They were very strong. Constantinople was a very old city. The people knew that they could not beat the Turks. The Byzantine king sent to Europe for help. Only the Turks appeared at the city's walls. These walls were over 1,000 years old. It took the Turks only a few hours to break them down. The Byzantine Empire disappeared. The Turks now ruled the Middle East. They also took charge of trade with Asia. Prices were raised even higher. Europeans knew that they could pay lower prices in Asia. They began looking for a new way to reach these lands.

3.3 How did the Portuguese plan to reach Asia?

Land routes into Asia were blocked by the Ottoman Turks. The Portuguese decided to reach Asia by water. They believed a way could be found around Africa. In 1419, Portugal's kings sent ships to sail along Africa's shores. This route to Asia was very long. It was far longer than the Portuguese believed. Europeans did not know how large the **continent** of Africa is. Many trips were made. Each went a little farther around Africa. Vasco da Gama finally reached Asia in 1498.

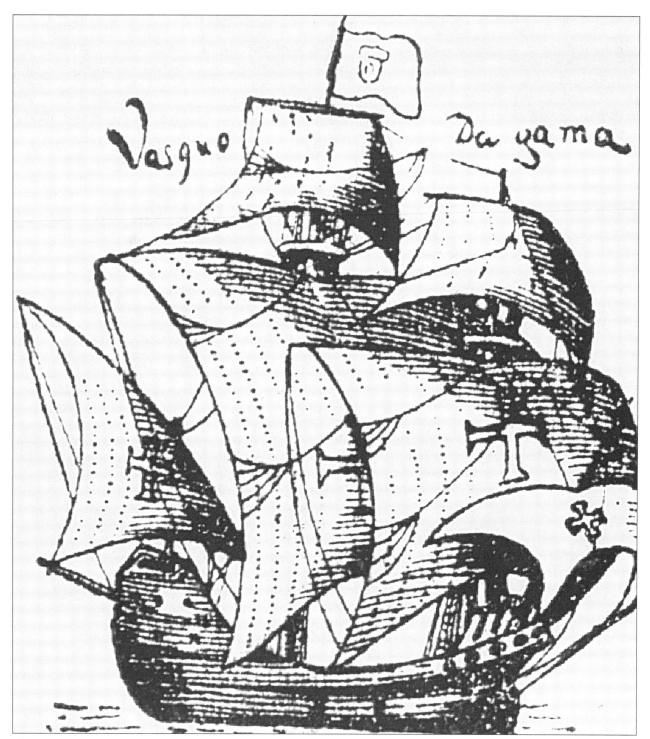

▲ The illustration above shows the ship that Vasco da Gama sailed to reach Asia in 1498.

The Portuguese grew rich by trading with Asia's markets. They also made a lot of money in Africa. Trade had long been important in Africa. It was a land of great riches. Many great kings ruled in Africa.

☆☆☆

Multicultural
PERSPECTIVE

▲ Pepper Seed

Fresh food was a problem for early people. There were few ways to keep it fresh. Meats could be salted. Vegetables could be dried. But these foods had little taste. Adding spices made these foods more pleasant to eat. Crusaders brought a special seed to Europe. It could be ground and added to food. The people loved it. This seed was pepper.

Pepper seed was expensive. It could be worth more than gold. Pepper seeds were often used as money. Homes were even paid for with pepper seeds. The king of England once sold lands and a home for about 300 pepper seeds. These seeds were to be paid every year. A year could never be skipped. The home would go back to the king or queen. Today, the family still pays pepper seeds to Queen Elizabeth II each year.

Pepper helped bring Europeans to Asia. Merchants wanted to buy pepper from the Asians. Then the merchants could resell the pepper in Europe. They would resell it for more money. One ship filled with pepper could make a person very, very rich. Vasco da Gama sailed around Africa to find Asia's Spice Islands. This was where he believed pepper could be found.

★★★ CHAPTER REVIEW

Critical Thinking

Write your answers on a sheet of paper, or discuss in class.

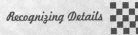 **1.** Why did so many people want to rule the Middle East?

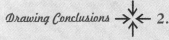 **2.** How did wars in the Middle East change Europe?

Cooperative Learning

3. Work with a study partner. Look at the map that begins this chapter. Read the names on the map. Point out Portugal and Africa. Slide your finger over the ocean. Move from Portugal to the Cape of Good Hope. Then show how to reach Asia. Talk about the distance between Asia and Portugal. Decide if a land route to Asia is shorter.

Write About It

4. Make a chart of trade goods. Take out a piece of paper. Write the names "Europe," "Africa," "Asia," and "Middle East" across the top. Look through the chapter. Note which goods are found in each place. List these goods on your chart.

Chapter 4

Africa

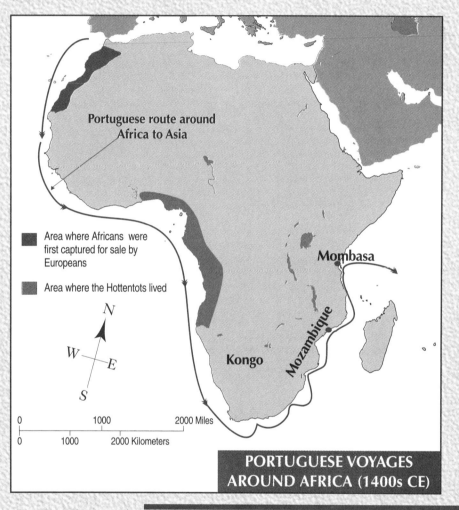

Portuguese route around
Africa to Asia

- Area where Africans were
  first captured for sale by
  Europeans
- Area where the Hottentots lived

Mombasa

Mozambique

Kongo

N
W E
S

| 0 | 1000 | 2000 Miles |
| 0 | 1000 | 2000 Kilometers |

**PORTUGUESE VOYAGES
AROUND AFRICA (1400s CE)**

Read about how the
African people felt
about the Portuguese
explorers. How did the
Portuguese treat the
Africans?

Key *Vocabulary*

thatch (thach)
a mat of plant material that is
used as a roof

advanced (ad VANST)
ahead of in development

embroider (im BROY duhr)
to decorate by sewing with
threads

MAP ANALYSIS

★ **Ask** Which area of Africa do you think the Portuguese explored more fully,
the coast or the inside area?

★ **Analyze** Why were Africans in northeast Africa the first to be captured for sale
by the Portuguese?

★ **Answer** Why was trade with Asia and the Muslims more fully developed in East
Africa than in West Africa?

Decoding Tip: Notice the short *a* sound in two of the vocabulary words.

ay	cake	ah	fall, cot	air	air
ee	tree	i	sit	oh	cold
or	cord	oy	toy	uh	above, hundred
a	ask	ar	hard	oo	book
e	yet	eye	nice	uhr	liar, fir, further, color
ow	cow	ooh	boot, true	yoo	you, few, cube

4.1 How did the Portuguese become rich from the West Africans?

In 1435, two explorers sailed farther south than any other Portuguese had gone. They found no people. But they did see footprints. Some were made by people. Others were made by camels. The explorers returned to Portugal. They told Prince Henry what they had seen. Henry sent them back to Africa. He ordered the Portuguese to bring Africans back to Portugal.

The Portuguese went back to Africa. They caught several African people. The Portuguese were one of the first to bring African people to Europe. The Africans told the Portuguese much about their land. The Portuguese learned a lot. But there was a shameful side. The African people were sold in Portugal as slaves.

By 1448 the Portugal slave trade had become a big business. The Portuguese discovered that they made a lot of money by catching and selling slaves. They made less money by buying and selling spices and gold. So, they moved from village to village catching people to be taken to Portugal and sold.

▼ Enslaved Africans are chained in a coffle and forced to march to the slave forts on the coast.

4.2 What cultures existed in West Africa at this time?

On trips farther south, the Portuguese found villages of people. The Portuguese called them Hottentots. These people raised sheep and cattle. Their jobs were to take care of the animals. The houses in these villages were made of animal hides. The houses had **thatched** roofs.

In 1483 Diogo Cão found where the Congo (Zaire) River runs into the ocean. He and his men followed the river. They found an African kingdom known as Kongo. This kingdom was divided into five states. Each one had its own ruler. The king of the whole kingdom was the Manikongo. People in Kongo were hunters and farmers. They also raised vegetables and cattle. They lived in villages. The houses were mud and had thatched roofs. Some of the workers were smiths. They made things from metal. Some workers made masks and other things from wood. Some sang or played music. Kongo became rich by buying and selling goods.

4.3 How did the Portuguese interact with the cultures of West Africa?

West Africans at first were friendly to the Portuguese. They treated the Portuguese well. Then the Portuguese began to catch and sell the Africans. The Africans turned against them. The Portuguese tried to take over the people of West Africa. The Africans hated the Portuguese and fought against them.

4.4 What cultures existed in East Africa at this time?

In East Africa the Portuguese found big cities. The people were as **advanced** as the people of Portugal. The people of East Africa traded with the Muslims. They had been trading with other countries much longer than West Africans.

▲ The illustration above shows the East African village of Zanzibar.

The East Africans owned sheep, chickens, and cattle. They also grew their own vegetables and fruit on farms. Their clothes were made of fine cloth. Their cloth often was **embroidered** with gold.

4.5   How did the Portuguese interact with the cultures of Africa?

The Portuguese sailed around the Cape of Good Hope to East Africa. They discovered the cities of Mozambique, Mombasa, and Malindi. These cities had been trading with Muslims for many years. Mozambique and Mombasa were Muslim cities. The people did not want the Portuguese in their cities. In Malindi the ruler was glad the Portuguese had come. The Portuguese wanted to take over these three cities. Then they could control trade with India. The Portuguese took over the East African cities of Sofala, Mozambique, and Mombasa. Then they continued taking cities in India. In East Africa the Portuguese became hated as much as they were in West Africa.

☆☆☆

Multicultural
PERSPECTIVE

Mozambique and Mombasa were cities in East Africa in the 1400s. They are still there today. In the 1400s, they were among the most advanced cities in the world. This was because of trade. Arabic and African cultures joined together. Mozambique and Mombasa became cities of great riches.

When Vasco da Gama came to the cities, he was surprised. The buildings were made of stone.

People dressed in clothing made from fine embroidered cloth. They ate many different kinds of foods. The East Africans ate many kinds of fruits and vegetables. These were all grown near the cities. The people ate many kinds of meat. They had chicken, fish, and beef

Today the people in both cities come from many different groups. Many of the buildings were built in the 1500s. In Mombasa, the

older buildings have been made into museums. New buildings have been built to house businesses.

▲ East African port

★★☆ CHAPTER REVIEW

Critical Thinking

Write your answers on a sheet of paper, or discuss in class.

Identifying Fact and Opinion

1. Why did both East and West Africans hate the Portuguese so much?

Comparing and Contrasting

2. What did the Portuguese want to accomplish by exploring Africa? What did the Portuguese actually accomplish?

Cooperative Learning

LEARNING STYLE
Visual Tactile

3. Work with a partner. Draw a diagram of what an East African city such as Mozambique or Mombasa must have looked like. What kinds of buildings were there? What were they used for? You might wish to find information in encyclopedias or other sources. Be sure to label the buildings or areas in your drawing. Tell what each was used for.

Write About It

Writing Portfolio

4. Imagine you are in the crew of a Portuguese exploration ship. Write a diary entry describing what you see as you dock in Mozambique.

Chapter 5

Europe Looks to the West

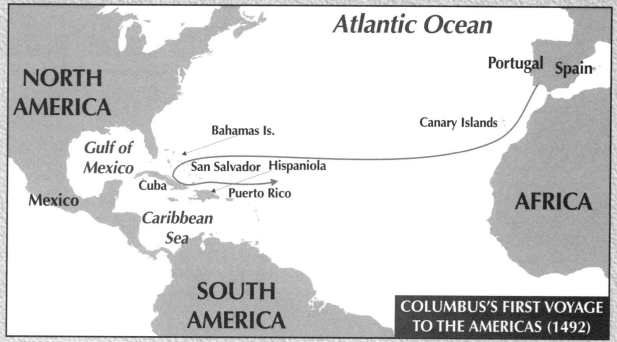

Atlantic Ocean

Portugal Spain

NORTH AMERICA

Canary Islands

Gulf of Mexico

Bahamas Is.

San Salvador   Hispaniola

Cuba

Mexico

Puerto Rico

Caribbean Sea

AFRICA

SOUTH AMERICA

COLUMBUS'S FIRST VOYAGE TO THE AMERICAS (1492)

Read about how Columbus and his crew sailed to the Americas. What was Columbus looking for? Why?

Key *Vocabulary*

distance (DIS tuhnz)
the space between two points or places

voyage (VOI uhj)
a trip made on the ocean

convinced (kuhn VINST)
sure that something is true

MAP ANALYSIS

★ **Ask**   In what direction did Columbus sail from Europe?

★ **Organize**   Name in order the bodies of land Columbus found on his first voyage.

★ **Analyze**   Why did Columbus turn back to the southeast when he reached Cuba?

★ **Answer**   What did Columbus know about the continents of North America and South America after his first voyage? Explain.

Decoding Tip: Notice the different letters that can make the uh sound.

ay	cake	ah	fall, cot	air	air
ee	tree	i	sit	oh	cold
or	cord	oy	toy	uh	above, hundred
a	ask	ar	hard	oo	book
e	yet	eye	nice	uhr	liar, fir, further, color
ow	cow	ooh	boot, true	yoo	you, few, cube

5.1   Who were the first Europeans to reach North America?

Europeans called Vikings reached North America around 1001 CE. This was hundreds of years before Columbus. Vikings lived in Scandinavia. This land is now Denmark, Sweden, and Norway. In the 800s CE, Vikings found and settled a large island. They called it Iceland. In 982 CE, a Viking named Eric the Red sailed west to an even larger island. It was cold and harsh. But Eric wanted it to sound like a good place to live. He named it Greenland. Eric made a second trip to Greenland. With him he brought hundreds of people to live there.

About 1001 CE, Eric's son, Leif, sailed west from Greenland. He wanted to check stories about land seen by Vikings. These Vikings had been blown off course. The stories spoke of many trees. Wood was important to the Vikings. Leif Ericson and his men reached the east coast of what is now Canada. They were the first Europeans to set foot on North America. One place they found was special. It was green and had many vines growing. They called it Vinland. We think that Vinland was on the tip of Newfoundland Island. Settlements were built there but did not last.

5.2   How did Columbus plan to reach Asia?

Christopher Columbus was born in Genoa, Italy, in 1451. As a young man, he went to Portugal. Sailing and mapmaking were very important there. Columbus learned all he could about sailing. Many sailors in Portugal were talking about reaching Asia more quickly. Columbus listened. He thought about the problem. Like other learned people, he knew that the world was round. The seas and land were like a map spread around a ball. He came to believe that Asia lay across the Atlantic Ocean. He thought he could sail west to reach "the Indies." This was the name of the islands of southern Asia.

How long would the trip take? No one knew how much ocean was in between.

Columbus needed money for his plan. He asked Portugal. The Portuguese had their own plan. They hoped to reach India by sailing around Africa. England and France also turned Columbus down. At last, Spain's Queen Isabella and King Ferdinand said they would help. They gave Columbus three ships and the men to sail them. On September 6, 1492 the three ships sailed west from the Canary Islands.

The illustration to the right shows the *Santa Maria*, one of the three ships sailed by Christopher Columbus. ▶

5.3   What did Columbus find?

Columbus was a good sailor. He was also lucky. At the **distance** where he planned to find Asia, he did find land. It was a green island in warm blue waters. It was one of a group now known as the Bahamas. Columbus named it San Salvador. He found what is now Cuba and Hispaniola. In Hispaniola, he started a settlement. He also saw people. Thinking he was in the Indies, he called them Indians. But the great cities of Japan or China were not to be seen. Columbus captured some Indians. He took them back to Spain. They were sold as slaves.

Columbus returned to Spain a hero. A year later, he made another **voyage** across the Atlantic. He took many more ships and people. The Hispaniola colony grew. Columbus thought it would be a trading place with Asia. He claimed the land he found for Spain. Still, some people did not think the land was part of Asia. On his third trip, he reached the continent of South America. A fourth trip reached Central America. Columbus died in 1506. He was still **convinced** he had found a new way to Asia.

5.4   How did Europe learn about the "New World"?

In 1501 an Italian named Amerigo Vespucci sailed west from Portugal. Vespucci found the north coast of Brazil. In letters he told about his trip. Vespucci was the first to see that the land was not a part of Asia. He wrote about the land. He called it a "New World." His letters were read all over Europe. People began to talk about the lands that had been found. One map named the place "America" after Vespucci. Many ships would now set sail for the Americas.

☆☆☆

Yesterday . . .

▲ Christopher Columbus

Near Hispaniola, one of Columbus's ships sank. Columbus had his men save wood from the ship. They built a place for trade on Hispaniola. Columbus left 39 men to live there. It was the first European settlement in the Western Hemisphere since the time of Leif Ericson.

Today . . .

Hispaniola today is made up of two countries. These are Haiti and the Dominican Republic. In 1990 Haiti's people picked Jean Bertrand Aristide to lead them. But then the Haitian army took over. Aristide left for the United States. In the fall of 1994, things changed. The U.S. convinced Haiti's generals to leave. President Aristide returned to lead his people. U.S. soldiers watched for trouble in Haiti until United Nations people came.

▲ The two countries of modern Hispaniola

★★☆ CHAPTER REVIEW

Critical Thinking

Write your answers on a sheet of paper, or discuss in class.

Identifying Main Idea   1. What made Columbus think he could sail west to reach Asia?

Making Inferences   2. Some say Columbus "found" the Americas. But people had already been living there for a long time. Why were the Americas called the "New World"?

Cooperative Learning

LEARNING STYLE
Reading Visual

3. Work with a friend or group. Go to the start of this chapter. Trace the map of Columbus's first trip. In an encyclopedia, find a map of Columbus's other trips. Draw lines showing these trips on your map. Make each line a different color. Number Columbus's trips 1, 2, 3, and 4.

Write About It

Writing Portfolio

4. Write a short news story. Tell about Columbus's first trip to the West. Your story should tell these things:
Who made the voyage. **What** the voyage was. **When** it was made. **Where** it was made. **How** it was made.
Trade papers with a friend. See if you can find the who, what, when, where, and how in your friend's paper.

Chapter 6

Exploration and Conquest

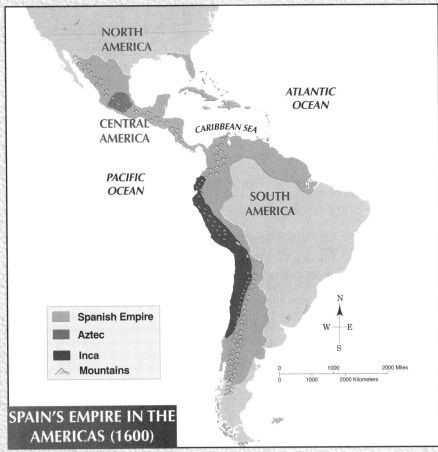

NORTH AMERICA

CENTRAL AMERICA

PACIFIC OCEAN

ATLANTIC OCEAN

CARIBBEAN SEA

SOUTH AMERICA

N
W   E
S

0   1000   2000 Miles
0   1000   2000 Kilometers

Spanish Empire
Aztec
Inca
Mountains

SPAIN'S EMPIRE IN THE AMERICAS (1600)

Read about the Europeans who came to the Americas after Columbus. What were they looking for? Why?

Key *Vocabulary*

circumnavigate
(sur kuhm NAV uh gayt)
to go all the way around

chart (chart)
to record the movements of something

conquistador
(kon KEES tuh dor)
someone who conquers or takes over

disease (diz EEZ)
a sickness, such as smallpox or yellow fever

armada (ar MAHD uh)
a large group of war ships

MAP ANALYSIS

★ **Ask**   Is Spain's land in the New World broken up into parts or is it mostly connected?

★ **Acquire**   Was most of Spain's land in North America or South America?

★ **Organize**   Which empire was larger, the Aztec or the Inca?

★ **Analyze**   Why did Spain control only the outside parts of the American continents?

★ **Answer**   Was Spanish control more likely to spread to the west coast or the east coast of North America? Explain.

Decoding Tip: Notice that the letters *qu* make the sound /k/ in **conquistador**.

ay	cake	ah	fall, cot	air	air
ee	tree	i	sit	oh	cold
or	cord	oy	toy	uh	above, hundred
a	ask	ar	hard	oo	book
e	yet	eye	nice	uhr	liar, fir, further, color
ow	cow	ooh	boot, true	yoo	you, few, cube

6.1 Why did more European explorers come to North America?

After Columbus, more Europeans sailed to the Americas. Some looked for a way to Asia. Some wanted gold. Some wanted to get land for their king or queen. All hoped to become rich and well known. In 1497 England sent John Cabot to the new world. Cabot made two trips. He looked for a northwest passage to Asia. It was not found. But Cabot claimed land for England. In 1524 France sent an Italian named Giovanni da Verrazano. Verrazano sailed down the east side of North America. France called all that land its own. Spain's Juan Ponce de León sailed to Florida in 1513. Ponce de León claimed the land for Spain. Spain now had its eyes on North America.

Ferdinand Magellan wanted to be the first to **circumnavigate** the world. In 1519 he led five ships west from Spain. He sailed around the tip of South America. He then sailed west. Magellan's ships were the first to cross the Pacific Ocean. Magellan himself died on a Pacific island. But one of his ships made it all the way back to Spain.

6.2 What happened to the Aztec and Inca empires?

The Aztec empire was very large. It covered most of what is now Mexico. Aztecs were Native Americans. They built great buildings. They **charted** the sun and stars. They made beautiful things from stone and gold. Aztec gold was important to Spain's Hernando Cortés. He wanted it for Spain. In 1519 Cortés sailed to Mexico. He met with the Aztecs. He also met with their many enemies. His 600 men joined with the Aztecs' enemies. They went to the Aztec city Tenochtitlan. Cortés met with Moctezuma. Moctezuma ruled the Aztecs. He thought Cortés was a god. But Cortés took Moctezuma by surprise. The Spanish conquered the Aztecs.

▲ Reconstruction of the central area of Tenochtitlan shows the developments of the Aztecs before the arrival of the Spanish.

They broke up buildings and took gold. Moctezuma was killed. About 240,000 Aztecs were also killed. The Spanish called the land New Spain. The Aztec way of life was no more.

Another great Native American empire was the Inca. The Incas lived in what is now Peru. They had great stores of gold and silver. They farmed. They made fine houses. But like the Aztecs, they fell to the Spanish. Like Cortés, Francisco Pizarro was a **conquistador**. Pizarro set a trap for the Incas' chief. He was caught. Thousands of Incas were killed. In 1535 Pizarro started the city of Lima. Incas worked for the Spanish. Many Incas died of **diseases** brought by the Spanish.

6.3   What effect did these conquests have on Spain?

Spain grew rich on gold from the New World. Cities were started. Gold and silver were mined. Everything was sent back to Spain. Spain kept building ships. More gold was needed to pay for them. The Spanish looked to North America. It might hold riches like Mexico and Peru. Explorers went north from Mexico into the new land.

One of these was Francisco Coronado. He had heard about gold. He heard of seven cities in Cibola. The cities were said to be filled with gold. Coronado looked for two years. He passed through Arizona, New Mexico, Oklahoma, and Kansas. Coronado's long search came to nothing. Hernando de Soto also looked for the cities. He and his party looked all through the Southeast. They cut through woods and swamps. They saw the Mississippi River. No gold was found. But much was learned about the new land.

6.4 Why did Spanish influence decrease in the New World?

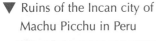
▼ Ruins of the Incan city of Machu Picchu in Peru

Spain was rich and strong. In the 1580s it held land from the Philippines to Peru. Spain's ships were feared. Why did

▲ Illustration of Spaniards landing on a Caribbean island in the 1500s

Spain not take over the New World? Other countries wanted a share. England and the Netherlands were among them.

English ships called "sea dogs" began to attack Spanish ships. Spain's King Philip II grew angry. He put together a group of 130 ships. This group was called the **Armada**. In 1588 they were sent to take over England. England's small ships raced to meet them. Clever English captains had the edge. High winds and rain also worked against the Spanish. They lost the war. Only 76 Spanish ships returned home. No longer did Spain rule the seas. Other countries could now sail to the New World. Spanish ships could not stop them.

Connections

Do you like chocolate? It was first made by the Aztecs. They used seeds from the cacao tree. These seeds were dried into beans. The beans were then ground up. The Aztecs made a rich drink with them. The beans were also important in the Aztec religion. The Aztecs believed the beans were special. Eating them would make a person wise. They also used the beans as money.

Cortés took some of the beans to Spain in 1528. Soon they were used all over Europe. By some mistake, they were called cocoa beans. In the early 1700s cocoa became the drink of the rich in England. Today people all over the world eat chocolate. In Mexico it is still a special food. Molé, a hot Mexican sauce, is made from chocolate.

◀ Early advertisement for Cadbury Cocoa, circa 1890s

★★☆ CHAPTER REVIEW

Critical Thinking

Write your answers on a sheet of paper, or discuss in class.

Making Inferences

Analyzing Cause and Effect

1. Would the Spanish have left the Aztecs alone if not for their gold?

2. Imagine that the Spanish Armada won. How might the United States be different?

Cooperative Learning

LEARNING STYLE
Reading Auditory

3. Work with a friend. Use a tape machine. Read the names of the explorers out loud. Record your reading. Play back your reading and listen. Did you say the names correctly? Check the words in the Pronunciation Gazetteer. Read them again until you make no mistakes. Have your friend do the same reading. Next, read Aztec names. Say Moctezuma and Tenochtitlan. Record them and play them back.

Write About It

Writing Portfolio

4. Look at the picture on page 34. It shows Native Americans meeting the Spanish. Imagine you are one of the Native Americans. What do you think of these men from Spain? Write a paragraph about your thoughts.

REVIEW

Quiz

Number a piece of paper from 1-10. Read the answers that follow each question. Choose the answer for each question. Write the letter of the answer you choose beside the correct number on your piece of paper.

1. **Which group was the first to reach North America?**
   a. Europeans
   b. Africans
   c. Asians
   d. Australians

2. **How did the first Americans live?**
   a. by farming
   b. by hunting animals
   c. by gathering plants
   d. both b and c

3. **Where did farming first take place in the Americas?**
   a. Mexico
   b. U.S. Southwest
   c. on the Great Plains
   d. along the California coast

4. **Which of the following was NOT used by the first Americans for building their homes?**
   a. stone
   b. wood
   c. whale oil
   d. hides

5. **Which area had so much food that farming was not necessary?**
   a. Northwest Coast
   b. California
   c. Great Basin
   d. all of the above

6. **How did the Portuguese finally reach Asia?**
   a. by moving through the Middle East
   b. by sailing around Africa
   c. by sailing west across the Atlantic
   d. by moving east across Europe

7. **Which part of Africa had been trading with Asia before the Portuguese arrived?**
   a. West Africa
   b. East Africa
   c. Southwest Africa
   d. Northeast Africa

8. **Which Europeans reached the Americas before Columbus?**
   a. Vikings
   b. Italians
   c. Spanish
   d. Portuguese

9. **What lands did Columbus always believe that he had visited by sailing west across the Atlantic?**
   a. Russia
   b. the Indies
   c. Vinland
   d. the Americas

10. **Which areas held lands that were taken over by the Spanish?**
    a. Central America
    b. Mexico and California
    c. most of South America
    d. all of the above

RECOGNIZING DETAILS

Add numbers 11–15 to your paper. Read the two lists below. People are listed on the left. What each person did is listed on the right. Match the people with the things that they did. Write your answers on your paper.

11. Asians
12. Vasco da Gama
13. Portuguese
14. Christopher Columbus
15. Ferdinand Magellan

a. the Spanish explorer whose ship was the first to sail around the world
b. the first people to settle in the Americas
c. the first people to sail from Europe to Mombasa and Mozambique
d. the first European to sail around Africa to Asia
e. the explorer for Spain who reached San Salvador in 1492

Look over the things you wrote for these chapters. Choose one that you like the best. Add to your writing. For example, you wrote a diary entry for a Portuguese crew member. You may wish to write an entry for an African who has just met the Portuguese for the first time. You also made a chart of trade goods for Chapter 3. You may wish to add goods listed in other chapters. Trade papers with a study partner. Check each other's work. Make a clean, neat copy. Put it in your portfolio.

Choose something that happened in the first chapter. Write it on a piece of paper. What happened next? Write this beside the first thing that happened. Draw an arrow to connect these two happenings. Add other happenings to your chain. Make a chain of at least three happenings for each chapter.

COOPERATIVE PROJECT: THE EXPLORING GAME

Work with a group. Make a list of the places that you read about in this unit. Now, make a list of the people who reached each place. Work with the class to make one master list of these people. Choose someone to hold the list and keep score. Draw or copy a world map. Make it a very large copy. Place this map on the floor.

Set a time limit for the game. Decide which group will take the first turn. Give a paper clip or eraser to one person from the group. Have the person throw the paper clip onto the map. Have the person tell where the clip landed. Then the group should tell about someone who visited this place. The group earns five points for each correct answer. Total the scores when the time for the game is up.

POLITICS

1587
The third English colony at Roanoke, VA, failed.

1588
England defeated Spain.

1604
The French built Port Royal in what is now Canada.

1607
Jamestown, VA, was the first successful English town built in the Americas.

1614
Dutch colonists built Fort Nassau. It became Albany, New York.

1620
Pilgrims built Plimouth Plantation near Massachusetts Bay.

CE   1585   1600   1625

CULTURE

1500s
Protestants broke from the Catholic Church of Rome and began forming their own churches.

1584
The first English settlers at Roanoke sent potatoes to Europe, where they became a popular food.

1586
The second group of English settlers at Roanoke sent tobacco to Europe, where it also became popular.

1608
John Smith's stories about Jamestown, VA, were printed in England as a way of getting more people to move to the colony.

1619
English women and indentured African servants arrive in Jamestown.

Colonization and Settlement 1585 - 1763

"My family didn't come over on the *Mayflower* but they met the boat."

— **Will Rogers**, actor, comedian, son of the Cherokee Principal Chief

Asians settled all parts of North and South America. They built great cities and developed wonderful cultures. These people and their ways of life all but disappeared. Read about the movement of Europeans into the Americas. How did Europe take over these two continents? Why?

1629
Maine became two colonies— Maine and New Hampshire.

1630
Thousands of Puritans began arriving in Massachusetts Bay Colony.

1660
King Charles II tried to break rule of Puritans in England and North America.

1664
England took over New Netherland and renamed it New York.

1682
Quakers founded Pennsylvania and ruled lands that became New Jersey and Delaware.

1733
James Oglethorpe set up Georgia in lands between Spanish Florida and England's colonies of North and South Carolina.

1650

1700

1640
The first American book, a set of religious poems by different authors, was printed in Cambridge, Massachusetts.

1650
Anne Dudley Bradstreet was the first American poet to become famous in Europe after her first book of poems was printed in London.

1694
Rice seed from Madagascar helped bring about a new cash crop for European colonists in North America.

1729
Benjamin Franklin began publishing the *Pennsylvania Gazette*.

1733
Benjamin Franklin wrote and published the first of his *Poor Richard's Almanack*, which sold well in Europe, too. Franklin became the first American millionaire.

Chapter 7

Europe and North America

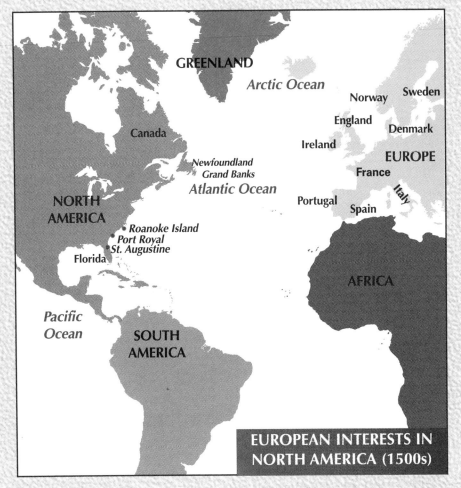

GREENLAND

Arctic Ocean

Norway   Sweden

England

Denmark

Ireland

Canada

Newfoundland
Grand Banks

Atlantic Ocean

EUROPE

France

**NORTH
AMERICA**

Portugal   Italy

Spain

* Roanoke Island
Port Royal
St. Augustine

Florida

AFRICA

*Pacific
Ocean*

SOUTH
AMERICA

EUROPEAN INTERESTS IN
NORTH AMERICA (1500s)

Read about Europe
and its interest in North
America. Where did
Europeans explore and
settle? Why?

Key *Vocabulary*

envy (EN vee)
to want what someone else has

religion (ri LIJ uhn)
the beliefs a person or group
holds about God

protest (PROH test)
to disagree or oppose

charter (CHAR tuhr)
an agreement that is spelled
out in writing

adviser (uhd VEYE zuhr)
a person who shares
knowledge or facts in order to
be of help

MAP ANALYSIS

★ **Ask**   What European nations are closest to Newfoundland?

★ **Analyze**   What part of North America is close to the Arctic?

★ **Answer**   Why would fishing ships leave Newfoundland in the fall and return in late
spring and early summer?

Decoding Tip: Notice *r* following a vowel affects the vowel's sound in some of the vocabulary words.

ay	cake	ah	fall, cot	air	air
ee	tree	i	sit	oh	cold
or	cord	oy	toy	uh	above, hundred
a	ask	ar	hard	oo	book
e	yet	eye	nice	uhr	liar, fir, further, color
ow	cow	ooh	boot, true	yoo	you, few, cube

7.1 What brought Europeans to North America in the 1500s?

Asia and the Americas made Spain and Portugal rich. Other Europeans **envied** this wealth. They wanted some for themselves. Spain and Portugal firmly ruled Mexico and South America. They also guarded the African and South American routes to Asia. Europeans decided to look for an Asian route around the top of North America. They called this route the Northwest Passage. The English and French kings paid Italians to search the northeast shores of North America. Henry VIII of England gave ships to John Cabot. He sailed to North America in 1497. Francis I of France sent Giovanni Verrazano to North America in 1524.

One place in North America was well known to Europeans in the early 1500s. The island of Newfoundland was visited by ships from many European nations. These ships came to fish along Newfoundland's Grand Banks. Millions of fish lived in these waters. Fishing became a very big business. Settlements were built on Newfoundland's shores. No Europeans lived there all year round, however. The people fished the waters during the summer and fall. They returned to Europe when the fishing season was over. France and England both claimed lands in the area. French explorer Jacques Cartier called the northern part of North America "Canada."

7.2 What European country built the first successful settlement in the United States?

Europeans faced problems with **religion** in the 1500s. Some people followed the Catholic church of Rome. Others wanted to break away. These people were known as Protestants because they **protested** against Rome. The rulers of France held with Rome. Some Protestants wanted to leave France. King Charles IV gave them permission to settle in North America. They reached Florida in 1562 and sailed north. They built a town and called it Port Royal. They called the land Carolana for King Charles I. A town in North Carolina is built on this spot today. It is called Port Royal. Times were hard for the settlers. An English ship visited the town. The people took the ship back to Europe.

A second French settlement was built in 1564. This town was built in Florida. It was called Fort Caroline in honor of Charles I. Spain claimed these lands. The Spanish king was angry about the French town. Spanish troops were sent to Florida in 1565. They built a fort and town called St. Augustine. These troops destroyed Fort Caroline. St. Augustine is still part of Florida. It is the oldest European town in the United States.

7.3 How did England affect the settlement of the United States?

England's Queen Elizabeth 1 wanted settlements in North America, too. She gave a **charter** to Sir Humphrey Gilbert. This gave him permission to build settlements. However, she told him to search lands where only Native Americans lived. She did not want trouble with Spain. Gilbert sailed to Newfoundland in 1583. He claimed the island for England. He had plans to build a settlement there. However, he died on the return trip. His half-brother was Sir Walter Raleigh. Raleigh was a powerful man. He was the queen's most trusted **adviser**. Raleigh took over the charter. He sent two ships to North America in 1584. They explored the land and called it Virginia for the queen. Her nickname was "the Virgin queen."

Reports about Virginia were very good. The people brought a new food back with them. The English called it the potato. It became a great favorite all over Europe. Raleigh decided to send settlers to Virginia. They built a town on Roanoke Island, but were not happy. They returned in 1586. They brought another new plant to Europe—the tobacco plant. Many

▶ The illustration shows Sir Walter Raleigh meeting with Native Americans on his expedition at Roanoke Island in what is known today as North Carolina.

Europeans then took up smoking. Raleigh sent a third group to Virginia in 1587. They settled on Roanoke Island, too. They were led by John White. His granddaughter was the first European born in lands that became the United States. She was named Virginia Dare. The settlement needed supplies, so White returned to England. He stayed in England because of a war.

▲ Artist's illustration of the baptism of Virginia Dare

The king of Spain used his money from the Americas to build ships. They formed a huge navy called the Armada. It was sent to England in 1588. This navy was ordered to take over the country for Spain. However, Elizabeth I's ships won the battle. Spain kept its lands in the Americas. Its power in Europe was never the same. After the war, John White returned to Roanoke Island. He reached the settlement in 1591, but all the settlers were gone. The word "Croatoan" was carved into a door post. He felt they might have moved to an island they had called Croatoan. Other people believed the settlers were killed in a battle with Native Americans. A storm forced White to return to England. He never came back to Virginia. The fate of the Roanoke settlers was a puzzle. Raleigh never tried to build another settlement in Virginia.

No one knows exactly what happened to the settlers of Roanoke Island. However, one story is told by people in North Carolina. By the middle 1600s, English people found an unusual group of Indians called the Lumbees. Many settlers arrived in Lumbee lands in the 1730s. The Lumbees surprised the Europeans. Some of the Lumbees had blonde hair and blue eyes. They all spoke English. However, it was English as it had been spoken in the 1500s. Their homes were like those built in Europe. They even farmed in the same way as Europeans.

The Lumbees claim they are descendants of the settlers of Roanoke Island. The early settlers had lost hope when John White did not return. They moved to the mainland and joined with the Lumbee Indians. Finally, they settled in North Carolina. Some of the families said they were descendants of Virginia Dare. They said the name had slowly changed through the years. Now they were the Dial family. The Lumbee Indians still live in North Carolina today. They believe they are the living answer to the Roanoke puzzle.

CHAPTER REVIEW

Critical Thinking

Write your answers on a sheet of paper, or discuss in class.

Analyzing Cause and Effect

1. How did envy and religion bring settlers to North America?

Making Inferences

2. Why did most of the early settlements fail?

Cooperative Learning

LEARNING STYLE
Verbal

3. Work with a study partner. Think about settlers coming to North America. There were no stores or homes waiting for them. They had to bring everything they would need until they could build homes and start farming. Talk about the supplies the settlers had to bring. Compare your ideas with other students'.

Write About It

Writing Portfolio

4. Find the years that are discussed in this chapter. Make a list of these years. Put them in order. Start with the earliest year. Now find out what happened in each year. Write a sentence about each event. Write the sentence beside the correct year.

Chapter 8

Successful Colonies

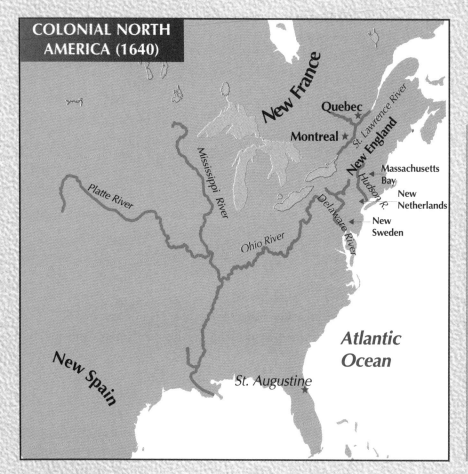

COLONIAL NORTH AMERICA (1640)

New France

Quebec ★

Montreal ★

St. Lawrence River

New England

Massachusetts Bay

New Netherlands

New Sweden

Hudson R.

Delaware River

Mississippi River

Platte River

Ohio River

New Spain

St. Augustine ★

Atlantic Ocean

Read about Europe and its interest in North America. Where did Europeans explore and settle? Why?

Key *Vocabulary*

explore (ek SPLOHR)
to search the unknown in order to find facts

settle (SET uhl)
to found a home or town in a new place

colony (CAHL uh nee)
a community of people living in a new place but keeping close ties to their original government

tobacco (tuh BAK oh)
a plant grown for its leaves which are dried so they can be chewed or smoked

experiment
(ek SPAIR uh muhnt)
to try new methods to see what happens

MAP ANALYSIS

★ **Ask** What European nations formed settlements in areas east of the Mississippi River?

★ **Analyze** What bodies of water are near these settlements?

★ **Answer** Why were oceans and rivers important to these settlements?

Decoding Tip: Notice the sound of ex at the beginning of two vocabulary words.

ay	cake	ah	fall, cot	air	air
ee	tree	i	sit	oh	cold
or	cord	oy	toy	uh	above, hundred
a	ask	ar	hard	oo	book
e	yet	eye	nice	uhr	liar, fir, further, color
ow	cow	ooh	boot, true	yoo	you, few, cube

8.1 What European nations formed successful North American settlements during the early 1600s?

France's Jacques Cartier had **explored** Canada in the 1630s and 1640s. He sailed along the St. Lawrence River. For years afterwards, the French traded with the Indians. They especially traded goods for furs. Beaver furs were used to make French hats. King Henry IV wanted firm rule of these lands. He sent Samuel de Champlain to Canada in 1604. Champlain built a trading fort on the St. Lawrence River. It was called Port Royal. He named the area Acadie, which means "rich." He founded Quebec in 1608 and Montreal in 1611. These lands became known as New France.

England's Queen Elizabeth I died in 1603. Her nephew, James I, became the new king. He gave charters to two companies in 1606. The London Company and the Plymouth Company were closely linked at first. The London Company was to settle lands along the southeast coast of North America. The Plymouth Company was to **settle** along the northeast coast. The London Company sent a ship to Virginia in 1607. The settlers built a town along a river. They named it the James River in honor of the king. The town itself was called Jamestown. Life was difficult and times were hard, but the **colony** did not fail.

The Netherlands and Sweden were interested in North America, too. The Netherlands hired Henry Hudson of England to explore North America. The Hudson River and Hudson Bay were named for him. A company was formed to help settle the area. Dutch settlers from the Netherlands sailed up the Hudson River in 1614. They built Fort Nassau so they could trade with the Indians. A second colony was built on Manhattan Island in 1624. Peter Minuit was sent in 1626 to rule the colony known as New Netherlands. He bought Manhattan Island from the Indians for goods then worth about $24. Minuit led settlers from Sweden to America in

▲ The illustration above shows the artist's vision of colonial Jamestown. Painting, *The Marketplace at Jamestown,* by Sidney King.

1638. They built Fort Christina on the banks of the Delaware River. The colony of New Sweden was never very large. But special homes were built there—log cabins. This kind of home became very popular with early settlers.

8.2   Why did Jamestown succeed when earlier English colonies had failed?

Life was hard for the settlers in Jamestown. The London Company, later known as the Virginia Company, had run ads looking for settlers. The ads made Virginia seem like a land of plenty. The 100 settlers expected more than the land offered. They needed to build homes and grow their own food. Most of the settlers would not work. In six months half of the settlers were dead.

John Smith took charge of the colony. He met with Powhatan, the leader of the Indians in the area. Powhatan ruled 128 villages. Smith traded with Powhatan for food. He kept the colony going. Help arrived in 1608. Food, supplies, and more settlers had been sent from England. They found only 38 settlers still alive in Jamestown. John Smith made the settlers plant corn in the Indian way. However, he was sent back to England in 1609. Supply ships and more colonists were sent to Jamestown. These ships were wrecked in a storm. The people made it to Jamaica. They built two new ships and finally reached Virginia in the fall of 1609. The next winter was very bad. Only 60 colonists were left alive. They started to sail for home. Then they met new supply ships that had been led from England by Lord De La Warr. The settlers turned around and stayed in America. Lord De La Warr explored along the coast. The Delaware River is named for him.

8.3   How did tobacco affect Jamestown?

One settler in Jamestown was a farmer named John Rolfe. The Indians taught him how to grow **tobacco**. He **experimented** with the plants. He came up with a new kind of tobacco in 1612. People liked it better than the old kinds. It sold very well in England. Farmers began growing this tobacco and selling it in England. Their farms spread all along the James River.

▼ The illustration below shows Pocahontas, the daughter of Powhatan, with John Smith.

The colony changed greatly in 1619. Before, all the settlers had been men. In that year, women arrived from England. They married the settlers and began families. The colony was growing, and settlers kept coming. Most did not like the hard work of growing tobacco. A ship from the Netherlands reached Jamestown in 1619. It carried enslaved people from Africa. The settlers bought these people and put them to work in the fields. African slaves were not new to the colonies in North America. Spain had brought enslaved Africans to Florida in 1581. Slavery continued for almost 300 years. Slavery and tobacco helped make Jamestown a success.

A new governor arrived in 1619. He decided to change the colony's government. The colony was divided into 11 parts. Two people were to be elected from each part. These 22 people helped the governor make laws. They were known as "burgesses." This word is an old English name for people who are not slaves but free. The House of Burgesses helped run the colony's government for over 150 years.

Multicultural
PERSPECTIVE

▲ Pocahontas

John Smith told a story about a special Indian woman. Her name was Pocahontas. She was the daughter of Powhatan. She enjoyed Smith's stories about England and Europe. According to Smith, Powhatan ordered his people to kill Smith. But Pocahontas talked her father into letting Smith live. No one is sure if this story is true.

Pocahontas was a real woman. She was the daughter of Powhatan. She married an English settler in 1614. He was John Rolfe. They sailed to England in 1616. She met King James I and was popular in London. She went to fancy balls and parties. The king often invited Pocahontas and her husband to his palace. Her son was born in England. The family began the trip back to Jamestown in 1617. She died of a fever before the ship could reach the open ocean. She is buried in England, but her son returned to America. His descendants still live in Virginia.

★★☆ CHAPTER REVIEW

Critical Thinking

Write your answers on a sheet of paper, or discuss in class.

Making Inferences   1. Why was making money in North America so important to the settlers and rulers of Europe's colonies?

Recognizing Details   2. How did the settlers use the resources they found in North America?

Cooperative Learning

LEARNING STYLE
Reading Visual

3. Work with a study partner or as part of a study group. Think about settlers coming to North America. One important need they had was fresh water. Why was this so important? Look through encyclopedias and other books for facts about water and the way it was used. Make a chart with these facts. Share it with the class.

Write About It

Writing Portfolio

4. Think about the first group of settlers to reach Jamestown in 1607. Their supplies ran low and life became very difficult. Pretend you are a settler. Make a list of supplies you will need until you can grow your own food. Share your list with a study partner or the class.

Chapter 9

Colonies of New England

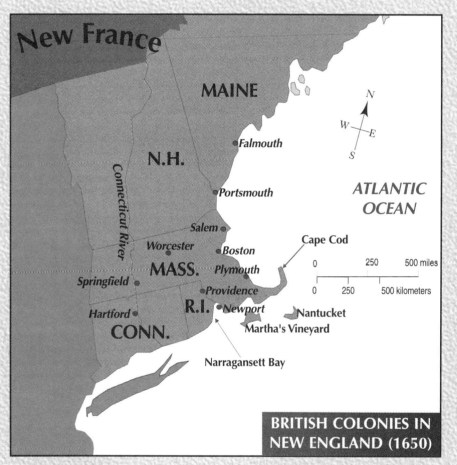

New France

MAINE

N.H.

Connecticut River

Falmouth

Portsmouth

Salem

Worcester   *Boston*

MASS.   *Plymouth*

Springfield

Providence

R.I.   *Newport*

Hartford

CONN.

N
W   E
S

ATLANTIC
OCEAN

Cape Cod

0   250   500 miles

0   250   500 kilometers

Nantucket

Martha's Vineyard

Narragansett Bay

**BRITISH COLONIES IN
NEW ENGLAND (1650)**

Read about the New England colonies. Why did these people leave England?

Key *Vocabulary*

worship (WUHR shuhp)
to pray or take part in a church service

investment (in VEST muhnt)
money paid for some project in hopes of making more money back in profit

govern (GUHV uhrn)
to keep order and make laws for

democracy
(duh MAHK ruh see)
a kind of government in which people rule themselves

MAP ANALYSIS	★ **Ask**	What do the towns of Newport, Plymouth, and Boston have in common?
	★ **Organize**	Which colony was largest in size? Which was the smallest?
	★ **Analyze**	Did the first settlers in New England go far from the coast? Explain.
	★ **Answer**	Would it have been easy for the New England colonies to trade with each other? Explain.

Decoding Tip: Notice the sound of short i in the first two words. The i is short when followed by a consonant and no vowel.

ay	cake	ah	fall, cot	air	air
ee	tree	i	sit	oh	cold
or	cord	oy	toy	uh	above, hundred
a	ask	ar	hard	oo	book
e	yet	eye	nice	uhr	liar, fir, further, color
ow	cow	ooh	boot, true	yoo	you, few, cube

9.1   Who were the Pilgrims?

The Pilgrims were English people who wanted to **worship** their own way. They sailed to America to be free. In the 1600s everyone in England had to belong to the Church of England. It was the law. James I, the king of England, led this church. But some people did not share his ideas. The Pilgrims wanted to be separate from the Church of England. The Pilgrims were also called "Separatists."

James I treated the Pilgrims badly. They had to meet in secret. At last they left England for Holland. There they could worship in their own way. By 1609 they were living in the Dutch city of Leiden. Life in Holland was better. Still, there were problems. The Pilgrims feared losing the English way of life. Their children were becoming more Dutch than English. Also, war with Spain seemed close. Where could they go? Maybe they could go to America. There they could start a new life. A vote was taken. Most decided to sail to America.

9.2   How did the London Company help the Pilgrims reach America?

In England, there were companies that paid for trips to America. They gave their help as an **investment**. They hoped to make back their money and more. To reach America, the Pilgrims needed help. They needed food and supplies. They started a stock company of their own. They put their money together. But more money was still needed. Help came from the London Company. Its members agreed to pay for the Pilgrims' trip. They also made rules for the Pilgrims to follow. The deal was to last seven years. After that time, everything would be split between the company and the Pilgrims.

More than one hundred Pilgrims sailed for America. Of these, 35 were Separatists from Leiden. The Pilgrims sailed on the ship *Mayflower*. They left England on September 16, 1620. It was decided they would sail to Virginia. The crossing was hard. High winds and waves shook the *Mayflower*. The small ship blew north. On November 9, land was sighted in Massachusetts. A month later, a small party found Plymouth Harbor. There the Pilgrims landed. Their new lives had begun.

9.3   What was the Mayflower Compact?

The Mayflower Compact was an agreement to live under new laws. In America the Pilgrims were under no laws. There was talk among some of them. They would not take orders from anyone. Their leaders began to worry. If nothing were done, the whole plan could fall apart.

▼ The illustration below shows Squanto, the Native American who helped the Pilgrims adapt to new land by teaching them the ways of his people.

William Brewster was the head of the group. Brewster had an idea. The Pilgrims would write their own set of laws. Everyone in the group would sign the paper. They would agree to live by these laws. This would hold the group together. The paper was called the Mayflower Compact. It was signed on November 21, 1620. Why was it important? It was a first step in America for Europeans to **govern** themselves. People joined together to make their own laws. **Democracy** took root in a New World colony.

The Pilgrims' first winter was hard. Half died from lack of food. But help came from Native Americans nearby. Few Native Americans had survived the diseases brought by explorers. One of them surprised the Pilgrims by speaking English. His name was Squanto. Years before,

Squanto had been caught by an English sea captain. He had lived in England for nine years. Squanto taught the Pilgrims to grow food the Native American way. Samoset was another. He took the Pilgrims to his chief, Massasoit. A treaty was signed by both sides. They agreed to live in peace. One year after the Pilgrims' landing, there was a special day. Pilgrims joined with Native Americans to feast. It was the first Thanksgiving.

9.4 Why did the Puritans leave England to settle around Massachusetts Bay?

The Puritans were another group who left England to find religious freedom. Like the Pilgrims, the Puritans disliked the Church of England. At first they tried to change it. They wanted to make it "pure." But King Charles I stopped them. (His father, James, had done the same with the Pilgrims.) Sometimes the king used force. The Puritans looked toward North America. There they would be free to worship. In 1630 John Winthrop left with a party of Puritans. The group sailed to New England. Charles I was glad to see the Puritans leave. He let them form their own company. But Charles lost control of the company. The Massachusetts Bay Company was run by the Puritans. They could rule themselves.

From 1630 to 1643 more than 20,000 people sailed to New England. They built many small towns in Massachusetts. The towns were set up by Puritan rules. Each town raised a meeting house. People would gather there to hold church. They would also come together to talk about problems. These town meetings were another step toward democracy.

9.5 Why were other colonies started in New England?

In the 1600s people came to New England for many reasons. Some wanted to worship in their own way. Roger

Comparing Pilgrims and Puritans

Group	Arrival	Colony	Religion	Government
Pilgrims	1620	**Plymouth Colony**	wanted to **separate from** the Church of England	wrote the **Mayflower Compact,** an agreement to live under new laws
Puritans	1630	**Massachusetts Bay Colony**	wanted to **change** the Church of England	started **town meetings** to make laws

Williams was a Puritan with a mind of his own. To him, the Puritans had not been fair to Native Americans. They had bought some land. But other land they had taken. For this and other views, Williams was thrown out of the Massachusetts Bay Colony. He started the Rhode Island colony.

Others wanted a more open government. To them, religion should not decide who takes part. A group in Connecticut acted on this thought. They wrote a plan of government. It was called the Fundamental Orders. Every man who owned land could take part in government.

Of course, some came to New England to get rich. River valleys offered fine land for farming. It took hard work to do well. But new chances were waiting in the colonies.

☆☆☆

Biography
ANNE HUTCHINSON

▲ Anne Marbury Hutchinson

The Puritans came to America to be free. They hated the rules of the Church of England. But the Puritans had rules of their own. People in the Massachusetts Bay Colony had to believe as the Puritans did. Anyone who went against them was wrong.

Anne Marbury Hutchinson (1591-1643) lived in Boston. She was proud to be a Puritan. What she believed was much like everyone else. Anne held meetings in her home. She would explain last Sunday's sermon. Many came to hear her. But Governor John Winthrop and others began to worry. Some of Anne's thoughts seemed different from their own.

Things grew worse. More people followed Anne. They stood up in church. They asked about what had been said. This had been done before, but not often. Winthrop had seen enough. Anne was put on trial. Few spoke up for her. She and her family had to leave the Massachusetts Bay Colony. Saying what you thought could lead to trouble—even in the colonies.

★★☆ CHAPTER REVIEW

Critical Thinking

Write your answers on a sheet of paper, or discuss in class.

Identifying Main Idea

1. Why did the Pilgrims write the Mayflower Compact?

Drawing Conclusions

2. Were the Puritans better off in North America than in England? Why or why not?

Cooperative Learning

LEARNING STYLE
Reading Oral

3. Work with a small group. Sit in a circle. Read over the chapter again. Then take turns telling about parts of the chapter. Make sure to tell the important points. After each person speaks, talk about what was said. Was everything covered? Do some in the group have different thoughts? Continue until all have had a chance to speak.

Write About It

Writing Portfolio

4. Imagine you are a Pilgrim. You have left your home in England. You have sailed to New England. Now you are writing a letter to a friend back home. Tell about what you have seen. Tell about how you feel.

Chapter 10

England Expands

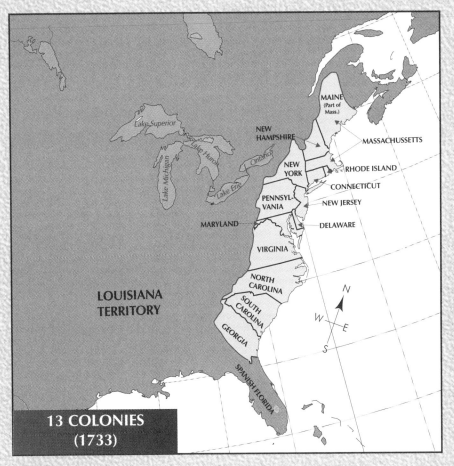

Lake Superior
Lake Michigan
Lake Huron
Ontario
Lake Erie

MAINE (Part of Mass.)
NEW HAMPSHIRE
MASSACHUSSETTS
NEW YORK
RHODE ISLAND
CONNECTICUT
PENNSYL-VANIA
NEW JERSEY
MARYLAND
DELAWARE
VIRGINIA
NORTH CAROLINA
LOUISIANA TERRITORY
SOUTH CAROLINA
GEORGIA
SPANISH FLORIDA

N
W E
S

13 COLONIES (1733)

Read about
England's effect on North America. What lands came under English rule? Why?

Key *Vocabulary*

government (GUHV uhrn muhnt) the person or people who rule a certain place such as a state, colony, or country

limit (LIM uht) to set a point that cannot be passed

debt (det) money owed to another

Reteaching Vocabulary

religion (ri LIJ uhn) the beliefs a person or group holds about God

---

MAP ANALYSIS	★ Ask	What were the names of the 13 English colonies?
	★ Analyze	Why isn't Maine counted as a separate colony?
	★ Answer	What European countries might have been a danger for England's colonies?

Decoding Tip: Note the different sounds e can stand for.

ay	cake	ah	fall, cot	air	air
ee	tree	i	sit	oh	cold
or	cord	oy	toy	uh	above, hundred
a	ask	ar	hard	oo	book
e	yet	eye	nice	uhr	liar, fir, further, color
ow	cow	ooh	boot, true	yoo	you, few, cube

10.1 How did religion affect the colonies of New England?

Puritans came to Massachusetts so they could practice their **religion** freely. Life was hard for colonists who did not share their beliefs. These people were thrown out of Massachusetts. Some of these people built towns south of Massachusetts. These towns became the colony of Rhode Island in 1647. Other people also wanted freedom from Puritan rule. They moved into Connecticut. People from New Netherland were already living there. The two groups did not always get along.

Massachusetts worried about new colonies run by people who were not Puritans. James I gave land to Ferdinando Gorges and John Mason. They began the colonies of Maine and New Hampshire. Massachusetts wanted Puritan ideas to

▼ This painting shows Roger Williams returning from England in 1644 with the first charter for Rhode Island. From a painting by C. R. Grant.

spread to these two colonies. From time to time, it did manage to rule New Hampshire. In 1677, Massachusetts bought Maine from Gorges' family.

Puritans were not the only English people looking for freedom of religion. Like the Puritans, Catholics could be put in jail for their beliefs. Lord Baltimore became a Catholic in 1625. He wanted to build a Catholic colony. Charles I gave him land just north of Virginia. Baltimore died before he could begin the colony. His son founded Maryland. The name honored Charles I's queen, Henrietta Maria. As Catholics, they also wanted to honor the Virgin Mary.

10.2   How did the English Civil War affect the colonies?

Puritans caused a war in England. Parliament had always helped the king make laws. Many Puritans were elected to Parliament in the early 1600s. They wanted more control. Charles I would not give up any power. The king went to war with Parliament. Oliver Cromwell led Parliament's army. The king lost the war in 1649. Parliament had him killed. It then ruled England. Cromwell took over the **government** in 1653. The Puritans in Massachusetts supported Parliament. Virginia had been on the king's side. The two colonies broke off trade. They never went to war against each other, however.

The English took over New Netherland in 1664. Cromwell had died in 1658. Some people wanted to have a king again. Charles I's son became king in 1660. Charles II acted as if he owned New Netherland. He gave it to his brother James. James was the Duke of York and Albany. His troops took over the colony without having to fight. The colony was renamed "New York." New Amsterdam became New York City. Fort Orange, which had earlier been called Fort Nassau, became Albany.

10.3   How did Charles II affect the colonies in North America?

Charles II **limited** the part Puritans could play in English government. He also wanted to break the hold Massachusetts had on its neighbors. Connecticut, Rhode Island, and New Hampshire received new charters in the 1670s. In 1684, Charles II gave a new charter to Massachusetts Bay. These charters gave the king a new right. He could choose each colony's ruling officers. Now the king controlled all these colonies.

Many people helped Charles I's family while Cromwell ruled England. Now Charles II wanted to help these friends. He gave them land in North America. One group began the colony of Carolina. The name honored the king. Two of the king's other friends began East Jersey and West Jersey. William Penn was a Quaker leader. The king owed him money. Penn asked for land instead. Charles II gave him Pennsylvania. The name honored Penn's father, who had helped make Charles II king in 1660. The king said that Penn owned the land. Penn wanted to be friends with the Native Americans who already lived there. He bought some of their land. The two groups lived together in peace for many years.

10.4   Why was Georgia founded?

Fighting broke out between Florida and South Carolina in 1727. South Carolina took over Spanish lands north of St. Augustine. James Oglethorpe received this land from King George II. It was named "Georgia" in his honor. Oglethorpe had a new idea for his colony. English people who could not pay **debts** were put in jail. They could not earn money there. They had to stay in jail for years. Oglethorpe planned to take them to America. There they could earn enough money to pay their debts. Then they could begin new lives.

☆☆☆

The Beginning of the Colonies

Colony	Year	Event
Virginia	1607	London Company built Jamestown.
New York	1614	People from the Netherlands began New Netherland.
	1655	New Netherland took over New Sweden, which had been built along the Delaware river.
	1664	England took over New Netherland. It was renamed "New York."
Plymouth	1620	Plymouth Company began Plymouth colony.
	1691	The king added this colony to Massachusetts Bay.
Maine	1622	Ferdinand Gorges and John Mason were given Maine.
	1629	Colony was divided. Gorges kept name of "Maine." Mason called his colony "New Hampshire."
	1677	Gorges family sold Maine to Massachusetts.
New Hampshire	1622	Colony built as part of Maine.
	1629	Colony was divided from Maine. Mason renamed it "New Hampshire."
Massachusetts	1630	Massachusetts Bay Company founded Massachusetts Bay colony.
Maryland	1634	Lord Baltimore led Catholics to found Maryland.
Connecticut	1635	People who did not follow Puritan beliefs moved into Connecticut.
Rhode Island	1636	Roger Williams founded Providence.
	1647	Providence is joined with nearby towns to form Rhode Island.
Delaware	1638	Swedish people began New Sweden.
	1655	New Sweden was taken over by New Netherland.
	1664	England took over New Netherland.
	1682	English king gave land that had been New Sweden to Pennsylvania.
	1704	Pennsylvania gave up this area. It became the Delaware colony.
North Carolina	1663	Eight English owners began the colony of Carolina.
	1712	Northern part of Carolina became North Carolina.
South Carolina	1663	Eight English owners began the colony of Carolina.
	1712	Southern part of Carolina became South Carolina.
New Jersey	1664	East and West Jersey given to John Berkeley and George Cateret.
	1674	Quakers bought West Jersey.
	1680	William Penn bought East Jersey.
	1702	East and West Jersey became New Jersey.
Pennsylvania	1682	William Penn began Pennsylvania for Quakers.
Georgia	1733	John Oglethorpe began the colony of Georgia.

Connections

▲ Recreation of early settlements

Providence was a village of farms. They were known as plantations. It joined Rhode Island and two other towns in 1647. The new colony was named "Rhode Island and Providence Plantations." This is still the name of the state. Most people simply call it "Rhode Island," however.

★★★ CHAPTER REVIEW

Critical Thinking

Write your answers on a sheet of paper, or discuss in class.

Analyzing Cause and Effect
1. How did religion affect England's government and colonies?

Drawing Conclusions
2. What do you think might have happened to most Native Americans who lived in lands that were settled by the English?

Cooperative Learning

LEARNING STYLE
Reading Visual

3. Work with a study partner or as part of a study group. Look at the chart about the 13 colonies. Put these facts on a timeline. Add other important dates. For example, Rhode Island first received a charter in 1647. Share your timeline with the class.

Write About It

Writing Portfolio

4. Choose one of the 13 colonies. Pretend that you own this colony. You want people to come to your colony from England. Write an ad telling about your colony. Tell why people might want to settle there. Remember to include facts about your colony.

Chapter 11

The Thirteen Colonies Grow

Read about how the colonies grew. What did they do to grow? Did all the people's lives get better?

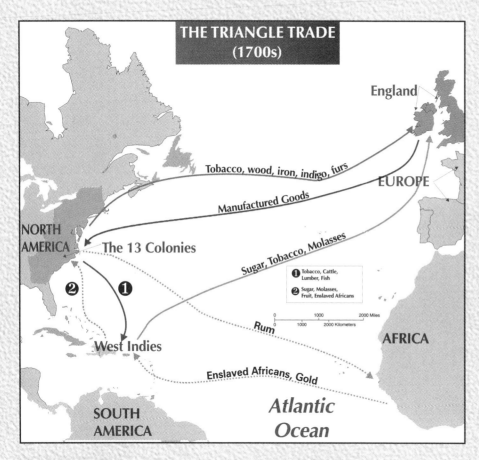

THE TRIANGLE TRADE (1700s)

England

EUROPE

Tobacco, wood, iron, indigo, furs

Manufactured Goods

NORTH AMERICA

The 13 Colonies

Sugar, Tobacco, Molasses

❶ Tobacco, Cattle, Lumber, Fish

❷ Sugar, Molasses, Fruit, Enslaved Africans

❷ ❶

West Indies

Rum

AFRICA

Enslaved Africans, Gold

SOUTH AMERICA

Atlantic Ocean

0   1000   2000 Miles
0   1000   2000 Kilometers

Key *Vocabulary*

geography (jee AHG ruh fee) the features of a place: where it is, what the land is like, what the weather is like, etc.

fertile (FER tuhl) good for growing plants

mercantilism (MUHR kuhn teel iz uhm) trade controlled by one country to help itself

indigo (IN di goh) a plant from the pea family used to make a blue dye

plantation (plan TAY shuhn) a very large farm that grows only one or two cash crops

MAP ANALYSIS	★ **Ask**	*What things were sold to England?*
	★ **Analyze**	*Was trade with England one-way or two-way?*
	★ **Answer**	*Look at the dotted lines. Why was this trade called "triangular trade?"*

Decoding Tip: Notice that the letters *ph* make the sound /f/ in **geography**.

ay	cake	ah	fall, cot	air	air
ee	tree	i	sit	oh	cold
or	cord	oy	toy	uh	above, hundred
a	ask	ar	hard	oo	book
e	yet	eye	nice	uhr	liar, fir, further, color
ow	cow	ooh	boot, true	yoo	you, few, cube

11.1 How did geography affect farming in New England?

Farming in the New England colonies was hard. The **geography** of New England made it so. It was farther north than other colonies. Winter was very long. The time for growing food each year was short. Also, the soil was thin. Most land was full of rocks and trees. First a field had to be cleared. Then it was plowed and planted. The people borrowed Native American ways of farming. With hard work, they could grow enough food to live. They grew beans, peas, corn, and squash. Farms were small and the whole family worked. Besides growing food, each family had to make everything they needed. They baked bread and made soap. They cut down trees to make tables and chairs. Cloth was spun for clothes. Some people even made their own tools and shoes.

▼ Gardening in Jamestown Settlement's recreated fort

Farming was not the only way of life in New England. Some people fished for a living. The ocean was close and full of fish. Large harbors were perfect for fishing boats. Hard workers could catch more fish than they could use. The extra fish were dried and salted. This kept them from going bad. They were then shipped to markets in Great Britain. Some people hunted whales. Oil from whale fat was burned in lamps to light houses.

As fishing grew, more ships and boats were needed. Many worked in the forests cutting down trees for lumber. Wood was sold for many uses. In towns by the sea, barrels were made. Cabinetmakers put together fine tables, chests, and beds. Village blacksmiths pounded pieces of hot iron. They made them into shoes for horses and nails for building. Sometimes they were even called to pull out a bad tooth.

11.2 What did the Middle Colonies do to make money?

In the Middle Colonies farmers had it better than in New England. **Fertile** fields helped. So did warm weather. There were more weeks each year for growing food. Many different things could be grown. Grains, fruits, and vegetables all grew well. More wheat was grown than the Middle Colonies could use. What was left over was sold to other towns. Some was sold to England. Wheat was just one of the cash crops. Cows and pigs were also raised and sold. With more money, farms in the Middle Colonies became larger.

Trapping animals for fur also made money. A large fur trade was started. This was in New York and New Jersey. People in Europe would pay a high price for fur. Bear, fox, and beaver were hunted. The fur was used for hats and coats. Other trade grew in the Middle Colonies. It was run by Great Britain. Ships filled with wood, cloth, and other materials sailed for Britain. There they were made into fine things. Some were then shipped back. They were sold to people in the colonies.

Britain got both raw materials and new markets. Trade run by one country for its own good is called **mercantilism**.

11.3 What were plantations?

Warm weather made the Southern Colonies special. The land was perfect for growing certain things. Among these were rice, tobacco, and **indigo**. Tobacco leaves were dried and used for smoking. Indigo was used to make blue dye for clothes. People in England wanted these things. They were willing to pay a good price. Farms were started to grow one crop. These farms lay along the rivers. Shipping was easy from there. Southern people mostly lived on farms. Few large cities grew in the South.

Growing only one crop in a place caused problems. Tobacco uses up the soil. Every few years the land must rest. It cannot be planted. To do well, a farmer had to own a lot of land. That way he could plant part of it and leave part of it to rest. For this reason, farms in the South were very large. Each one needed lots of workers. These large farms were called **plantations**.

▶ Reenactment of colonists cultivating tobacco outside James Fort, Jamestown Settlement

Where did Southern farmers get workers? At first they used indentured servants. These were European people with little money. They could not pay to sail to America. They promised to work for free for several years. After that time they could do as they pleased. Some started their own farms.

11.4 How did the growth of the colonies affect African Americans and Native Americans?

Southern farms continued to grow. More and more people were needed to work the farms. There were not enough European workers. Ships brought African men and women by the thousands. At first, the African people were treated as servants. Then things got worse. Southern land owners began to buy African people as slaves.

Laws were passed to keep slavery going. No one could teach an African person to read and write. No one could help an African person get away. Those who owned enslaved Africans could do almost anything to them. African families were broken up. Some were killed. Some died from hard work in the hot sun. Southern land owners saw no way except slavery. They thought they would lose everything if slavery were changed. It would not change for a long time.

The colonies also changed the lives of Native Americans. The English took over large fields. They put up fences. Towns and farms grew where Native Americans once hunted and planted. Native Americans were pushed away from the best land. English goods became important to them. They liked English cloth, needles, and pots. They traded for iron knives and arrow points. Sometimes they gave too many furs or skins in return. Sometimes a year's catch would be handed over. Europeans' diseases had already killed many Native Americans. Now their strange new ways were harming those who were left.

Yesterday & TODAY

▲ Slave trading in the colonies

money was used to make new streets. By about 1750, one in every ten people in New York was black. Some were free. Most were enslaved. One large market was on the corner of Wall Street. African men and women were sold there. Even children were sold. Wall Street was a busy place.

Today . . .

Today Wall Street is still a busy place. It holds the largest stock market in the world. People buy and sell shares in companies. Orders come in by phone. They come from all over the world. Money changes hands every second. Millions of dollars are made and lost. Many people buy and sell on Wall Street. African Americans are among them. Some have become

very rich. Wall Street has changed a lot in 250 years.

▲ Wall Street today

Yesterday . . .

Africans were not sold only in the South. The Middle Colonies also had a slave trade. New York put a tax on each African brought in. The

CHAPTER REVIEW

Critical Thinking

Write your answers on a sheet of paper, or discuss in class.

Comparing and Contrasting

1. Why were New England farms smaller than Southern ones?

Making Inferences

2. Why were laws needed to keep slavery going?

Cooperative Learning

LEARNING STYLE
Writing Visual

3. Work with a friend. Write the following on a sheet of paper. Write **New England Colonies**, **Middle Colonies**, and **Southern Colonies**. Leave space between them. Circle each term. Then draw three small circles around each one. In each small circle write a fact. The fact should tell about the term. "Built plantations" is a fact for **Southern Colonies**. Draw lines from the fact circles to their main terms. Can you think of more facts? Write them also. Use your fact circles to learn about this chapter.

Write About It

Writing Portfolio

4. At this time, Native Americans' lives began to change. Imagine how they felt about change. What was most important to them? What were they losing? Write what you think in a poem or in a paragraph.

Quiz

Number a piece of paper from 1-10. Write a, b, c, and d beside these numbers. Read the following sentence beginnings. Four endings follow each one. Choose the ending that best completes the sentence. On your paper, circle the letter that matches the letter of your answer. Be sure you mark your answer beside the correct number.

1. **Explorers reached North America looking for the . . .**
   a. gold of the Incas.
   b. Northwest Passage.
   c. route taken by Magellan.
   d. Arctic Channel.

2. **The first successful European settlement in North America was . . .**
   a. Roanoke.
   b. Fort Caroline.
   c. Carolana.
   d. St. Augustine.

3. **France built successful colonies in an area now known as . . .**
   a. Canada.
   b. Maine.
   c. Carolina.
   d. Manhattan.

4. **In 1607, an English company built the successful settlement of . . .**
   a. Jamestown, Virginia.
   b. Plymouth, Massachusetts.
   c. Boston, Massachusetts.
   d. Quebec, Canada.

5. **The Pilgrims and Puritans came to Massachusetts looking for the freedom to . . .**
   a. live without a king or queen.
   b. set up trade with other countries.
   c. begin a new kingdom of their own.
   d. worship as they pleased.

6. **The first step toward democracy in North America was the . . .**
   a. founding of Jamestown.
   b. granting of a charter to the Massachusetts Bay Company.
   c. signing of the Mayflower Compact.
   d. writing of the Fundamental Orders.

7. **England's colonies were run by . . .**
   a. the king or queen.
   b. the colony's owners.
   c. a company.
   d. all of the above.

8. **England had the most trouble ruling . . .**
   a. Quaker colonies.
   b. Catholic colonies.
   c. Puritan colonies.
   d. all of the above.

9. **Farming and mercantilism were practiced in the . . .**
   a. Southern Colonies.
   b. Middle Colonies.
   c. Northern Colonies.
   d. all of the above.

10. **Slaves grew tobacco, indigo, and rice on plantations in the . . .**
    a. Southern Colonies.
    b. Middle Colonies.
    c. Northern Colonies.
    d. all of the above.

ANALYZING CAUSE AND EFFECT

Add numbers 11–15 to your paper. Read the two lists below. The ideas on the left describe a cause, or something that makes a second event happen. The ideas on the right are effects, the events that are caused. Match these causes and effects. Write your answers beside the correct numbers on your paper.

11. France, England, and the Netherlands explored North America . . .
12. When tobacco became an important crop . . .
13. By coming to New England for freedom of religion . . .
14. Charles II changed charters and began new colonies . . .
15. Since people had trouble making money from farming . . .

a. because they wanted to find a northern route to Asia.
b. Pilgrims and Puritans set up colonies that governed themselves.
c. fishing and ship building became important in the Northern Colonies.
d. more and more farms were built around Jamestown.
e. in order to break the Puritans' power and to pay back loyal friends.

Look over the things you wrote for these chapters. Choose one that you like the best. For example, you wrote a letter to a friend as if you were a Pilgrim settler. Write the friend's answering letter. You may wish to turn your list of dates and happenings into a paragraph that summarizes the chapter. Trade papers with a study partner. Check each other's work. Make a clean, neat copy. Put it in your portfolio.

Write the headings **Cause** and **Effect** on a piece of paper. Think about something that happened in the first chapter. Did it make something else happen? If so, list it under the heading **Cause**. Did an earlier event make it happen? If so, list it under the heading **Effect**. List two causes and effects for each chapter.

COOPERATIVE PROJECT: COLONIAL PUZZLE

Work with a group. Make a list of the 13 English colonies. Trace or draw a large map of these colonies. Do not label the colonies. Glue this map to a sturdy piece of cardboard. Carefully cut out the colonies so that you make them part of a jigsaw puzzle.

Put the pieces in a box. Take turns with the other groups in drawing a puzzle piece from the box. Name the colony that has been drawn. If your group is correct, you earn five points. If not, put the piece back into the box. Now, put the piece into the correct place on the puzzle. If your group places it correctly, you earn another five points. If not, put the piece back into the box. When the puzzle is complete, total the scores to see who wins.

Unit 3

POLITICS

1756 Seven Years' War began in Europe and spread to the colonies in North America. British colonists called it the French and Indian War.

1763 France lost the Seven Years' War and almost all its land in North America.

1765 Britain passed the Stamp Act to raise money from the colonies to pay for the war.

1767 More taxes were put in place with the Townshend Acts.

1774 Parliament passed Intolerable Acts to punish colonists for protesting the new tax laws.

1775 Tax acts caused war between the Americans and Britain.

1776 Colonies declared independence on July 4.

1740   1750   1760   1776

CULTURE

1748 French lawyer Baron de Montesquieu published *The Spirit of the Law.* It included the idea that different people or groups should hold different powers of government. This would keep government fair and honest.

Thomas Paine's pamphlet *Common Sense* sold over 100,000 copies.

Thomas Jefferson wrote the Declaration of Independence.

At Congress's request, Mary Katherine Goddard printed copies of the Declaration of Independence, and sent them to every state.

Revolution and the New Nation 1754 - 1820s

"I am not a Virginian, but an American. "

—*Patrick Henry*,
October 4, 1774,
in a speech at the First
Continental Congress

People from all over Europe came to Britain's colonies in North America. They developed new ideas and ways of life. Read about conflicts that grew between the colonies and Great Britain's government. How did Americans form a new country? Why?

1781
The Revolutionary War ended with the surrender of the British at Yorktown, Virginia.

1783
Peace terms in the Treaty of Paris forced the British to recognize the United States as an independent country.

1789
The states ratified the Constitution and set up the country's federal government.

1803
The United States completed the Louisiana Purchase. The country grew to twice its size.

1812
The War of 1812 stopped British attacks on American shipping. Britain gave up all hope of taking back its former colonies.

1780   1790   1800

1787-Ideas from John Locke's *Two Treatises of Government*, Montesquieu's *The Spirit of the Law*, and American writers like Thomas Paine and Benjamin Franklin helped the Founding Fathers write the United States Constitution.

1787-Alexander Hamilton, James Madison, and John Jay wrote a series of letters called *The Federalist*, in which they urged the states to ratify the Constitution.

1791-Benjamin Banneker joined Andrew Endicott in laying out the country's new capital, Washington, D.C. Endicott later left his job and took the plans for the city. Banneker redrew all the plans from memory.

1812-"The Star-Spangled Banner" was written by Francis Scott Key.

Chapter 12

The French and the British

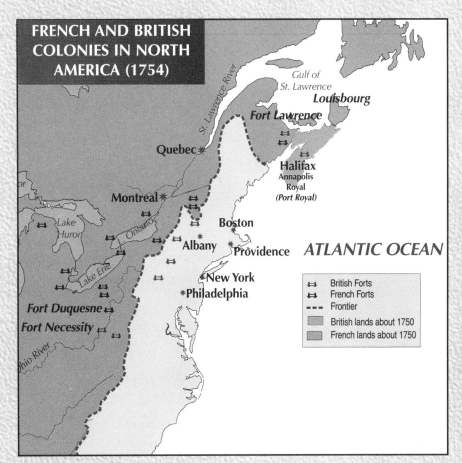

FRENCH AND BRITISH COLONIES IN NORTH AMERICA (1754)

St. Lawrence River
Gulf of St. Lawrence
Louisbourg
Fort Lawrence
Quebec
Halifax
Annapolis Royal (Port Royal)
Montreal
Lake Huron
Ontario
Boston
Albany
Providence
ATLANTIC OCEAN
Lake Erie
New York
Philadelphia
Fort Duquesne
Fort Necessity
Ohio River

British Forts
French Forts
--- Frontier
British lands about 1750
French lands about 1750

Read about how colonists tried to get more land. What trouble was caused? Why?

Key *Vocabulary*

bluff (bluhf) a try at making someone believe something that isn't true

surround (suh ROWND) to place people all around

surrender (suh REN duhr) to quit or give up

alliance (uh LEYE uhns) two or more people or groups working for a common goal

assembly (uh SEM blee) a group of people who meet together to make decisions

MAP ANALYSIS

★ **Ask**   Where do the French forts make a north-south line?

★ **Acquire**   Which country controls the larger area, Britain or France?

★ **Analyze**   What are the French forts placed beside?

★ **Answer**   Which country seems to have a stronger hold on its land in the Northeast? Why?

Decoding Tip: Note the double consonants in all five words (ff,rr,rr,ll,ss). Does doubling a letter change the letter's sound?

ay	cake	ah	fall, cot	air	air	
ee	tree	i	sit	oh	cold	
or	cord	oy	toy	uh	above, hundred	
a	ask	ar	hard	oo	book	
e	yet	eye	nice	uhr	liar, fir, further, color	
ow	cow	ooh	boot, true	yoo	you, few, cube	

12.1 How was New France different from the English colonies?

By the middle 1600s France ruled a large part of North America. It held Canada and the Great Lakes. It held Louisiana and land to the west. New France was larger than England's colonies. But much of New France was too cold for good farming. Thick forests grew there. Many French worked in the fur trade. They would live in the woods all winter. There they would hunt and trap. Much had been learned from Native Americans. In spring the ice would melt. French canoes would appear on the rivers. The little boats would be loaded with furs.

In 1663 Louis XIV took a new interest in America. The French king took over New France. He named a person to rule the colony. He gave rewards to those who would fight for it. He paid them with land. Others were paid to have large families. The number of people doubled. But there were still far more British colonists in America.

New France did not have several religions. The Catholic Church was the only one. The Church owned land. It told the people how to live. Even the king would listen to the Church on important matters.

12.2 What caused the French and the British to fight?

The French fur trade continued to grow. By the 1700s money was pouring into France. Louis XV wanted to protect French land. In the 1750s he sent men to build forts. They raised them in the Ohio Valley. This place was west of the Appalachian Mountains. But England's colonies had their own plans. They wanted the Ohio Valley also. Already some English had moved west. Land companies sold land to settlers. The English and French were not comfortable living side by side. The English were Protestant. The French were Catholic. Their home countries were the world's strongest. They both believed they had a right to the land. Three small wars had already broken out between them. These began in 1689. But nothing had been settled. Some kind of final battle seemed sure to happen. This battle was the French and Indian War.

Native Americans also played an important part. Most of them sided with the French. These were the Huron-Algonquian groups. French trappers lived the same way they did. The French did not fence the land as much as the British. British colonists wanted lots of land. Native Americans saw their own way of life in danger. However, not all Native American groups hated the British. The Iroquois were friends with the British colonists. They would help fight the French.

12.3   How did the French and Indian War begin?

The governor of Virginia was worried. He feared that French colonists were coming too close. The line of French forts reached the Allegheny River. Something had to be done. The governor sent a young Virginia officer to talk to the French. His name was George Washington. Washington told the French to pull out. It was a **bluff**. Virginia's colonists could not force the French to do anything. The French captain knew this. He refused to leave.

In 1754 Washington returned with a war party. He planned to build his own fort. The place where the Allegheny and the Monongahela Rivers meet would be perfect. This place is now called Pittsburgh. Then bad news came. The French had beaten him to the spot. Their new fort was called Fort Duquesne. Fifty miles away Washington and his men built a fort. From there they carried out a surprise attack on the French. At first, it worked. But the French fought back. They **surrounded** Washington's fort. More than 400 Native Americans helped the French. Rain and mud also helped. In three days Washington had to **surrender**.

▲ This illustration shows a typical fort of the 1750s time period, Fort Halifax on the Kennebec River in Maine. It is made up of barracks, a large residential structure, and corner blockhouses.

12.4　Why did the Albany Plan fail?

News quickly reached the colonies. The English were alarmed. Something had to be done to stop the French. A meeting was called in Albany, New York. It was the summer of 1754. Only six British colonies sent people. They were from the north. The Southern Colonies were not worried about the French. Pennsylvania sent Benjamin Franklin. Franklin was smart. He had many interests. He had thought about problems in the colonies. How could the colonies be made stronger? Franklin thought they should work together.

The Albany meeting had one important goal. It would fix the English **alliance** with the Iroquois. They were needed to fight the French. But Franklin wanted something more. He had a plan of his own. He called it the Albany Plan of Union. A union is a group of states or people. The group works together for some reason. Franklin borrowed his plan from the Iroquois nation. He wanted the colonies to join together. They could make one government. It could give orders to the colonies' small armies. Working together, they could beat the French. The government could also tax the colonies. The money would pay for the war.

The people at the meeting liked Franklin's plan. But the colonies had to decide. Their **assemblies** voted against it. They thought it took away too much of their freedom. The British king didn't like the plan either. He feared the colonies joining together. They might become hard to rule. Union would not come for several years.

☆☆☆

Connections

Do you like cartoons? Not all cartoons are just for fun. Some deal with important matters. They present ideas about things in the news. These are called editorial cartoons. Of course, they are supposed to be funny. But they also make a serious point.

Benjamin Franklin drew an editorial cartoon in 1754. It shows a snake. The snake is cut into pieces. Beside each piece are letters. The letters are for colonies. At the bottom are the words "Join, or Die." Franklin wanted the colonies to join together. He wanted them to fight the French. He feared what would happen if they didn't. What did Franklin think would happen?

Today many papers carry such cartoons. They show people in the news. Many times it is the President. The person who draws the cartoon wants to make you laugh. But he or she also wants to make a point. The point can be made very fast. Cartoons take less time to read. Find one in your town's paper. What is it saying?

▲ Benjamin Franklin's editorial cartoon

★★☆ CHAPTER REVIEW

Critical Thinking

Write your answers on a sheet of paper, or discuss in class.

Analyzing Cause and Effect

1. Why did most Native Americans side with the French?

Making Inferences

2. Why couldn't the French and English colonists live together?

Cooperative Learning

LEARNING STYLE
Reading Visual

3. Read this chapter a second time. Think about what the different groups wanted in the war. Then work with a classmate to make a chart. Title it "Reasons for Fighting the French and Indian War." Make three columns. At the top, write **French**, **Native American**, and **British**. Under each group, write all the reasons you can think of.

Write About It

Writing Portfolio

4. Make a list of people and places in this chapter. Read over your list. Have you heard of any of these before? What do you know about them? Write what you know about each person or place. Use facts from this chapter. Save your paper. When you see these names again, you can write more.

Chapter 13

The French and Indian War

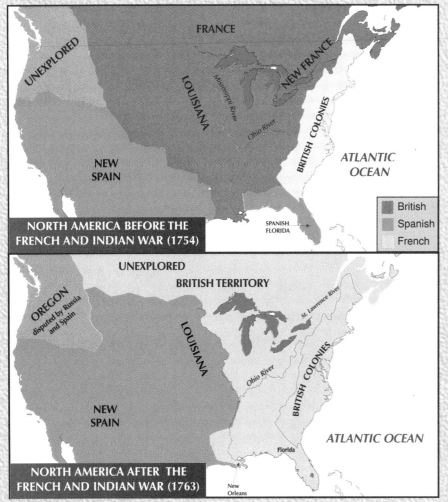

NORTH AMERICA BEFORE THE
FRENCH AND INDIAN WAR (1754)

- British
- Spanish
- French

NORTH AMERICA AFTER THE
FRENCH AND INDIAN WAR (1763)

Read about
England's war with the French and the Indians. Who won the war? Why was the war important?

Key *Vocabulary*

soldier (SOHL juhr) a person who serves in an armed force

ambush (AM bush) to attack by surprise

supply (suh PLEYE) something needed, such as food or water

strategy (STRAT uh jee) careful planning to achieve some goal

treaty (TREE tee) an agreement reached by the parties after a war

MAP ANALYSIS

★ **Ask**   Where did the British gain the most land?

★ **Organize**   In the second map, what body of water is between Spanish land and British territory?

★ **Analyze**   Which country gained the most land overall?

★ **Answer**   What area do you think the British colonists moved into next? Why?

Decoding Tip: Note the different sounds *y* stands for in **supply**, **strategy**, and **treaty**.

ay	cake	ah	fall, cot	air	air
ee	tree	i	sit	oh	cold
or	cord	oy	toy	uh	above, hundred
a	ask	ar	hard	oo	book
e	yet	eye	nice	uhr	liar, fir, further, color
ow	cow	ooh	boot, true	yoo	you, few, cube

13.1 Why did Britain's General Braddock lose the first large battle of the war?

At the start of the war, Britain did poorly. Its generals did not understand how to fight wars in America. They learned a painful lesson. At first they thought things would be easy. British colonies had grown three times larger since 1720. New France had far less people. But the French ruled the inside of the country. They controlled the Mississippi River. They had forts at important points. Most of the Native Americans were their friends. The French could count on their help.

Great Britain's King George II sent **soldiers** to help the colonies. Leading them was General Edward Braddock. Braddock had fought many wars in Europe. There, soldiers lined up and fought in open fields. But in America war was different. There were few open fields. Trees and rocks blocked an army's path. They could be used to hide behind. Both French and Native American fighters were good at using the land. They would hide and attack by surprise. Braddock needed more Native Americans on his side. They could have explained their ways of war.

In 1755 Braddock's 1,200 troops marched toward Fort Duquesne. The French sent a party to **ambush** the British. They hid behind trees. They surrounded the British. Braddock's men had nowhere to go. Their red coats made them easy to see. They were packed in together. Musket balls rained down. Almost 900 British were killed or hurt. Braddock himself was killed.

13.2 How did William Pitt help the British colonies in the war?

The Seven Years' War broke out in Europe. The French and British faced each other there as well. For two years the French won battles in America. The British needed someone new to lead them. In 1757 William Pitt became Minister of

War in Great Britain. He wanted to drive the French out of North America. Pitt did several things to help win the war. He gathered more troops. Most of them he sent to America. He raised taxes to pay for the war. Pitt put better generals in the field. He gave the colonies what they needed to fight. Pitt also had a plan to win the war. He planned to attack the heart of New France. This was Quebec. First the British had to cut off **supply** lines to Quebec. These were at Lake Champlain, the Gulf of St. Lawrence, and the Great Lakes.

13.3   How did the British take Fort Duquesne?

First, the British attacked near Lake Champlain in 1758. They attacked Fort Ticonderoga. Facing them was the French general Louis Joseph de Montcalm. He was good at war **strategy**. Montcalm's 4,000 troops defeated 16,000 British. However, the Battle of Ticonderoga was the last French victory. Now it was Britain's turn.

Second, the British attacked the French fort at Louisbourg. It lay on the Gulf of St. Lawrence. It was the most important line to Quebec. The British won a huge victory. French spirits dropped. British ships now sailed the mouth of the St. Lawrence. They also controlled the seas. The French in North America were isolated. The British marched on. Finally, they came to the forks of the Ohio River. That is where the war had started. They found Fort Duquesne in pieces. The French had blown up the fort. The British put up a new one. They named it after William Pitt. The city of Pittsburgh still stands there.

▼ The illustration below shows French soldiers and Native Americans leading a charge in a battle of the French and Indian War.

13.4 What led to the fall of Quebec?

Quebec fell because of a small path in the cliffs around it. Large numbers of British soldiers crossed the Atlantic. Their goal was to take Quebec. They gathered downriver from the city. General James Wolfe was their young leader. He faced a tough task. Quebec was protected by high cliffs. Some were 350 feet tall. Once past the cliffs, however, things got better. There was a large flat plain. The problem was how to get an army up the cliffs.

Montcalm, the French general, had 15,000 soldiers to defend Quebec. Some were French and some were Native American. He hoped to hold out until winter. By then British ships would be stuck in the frozen river. Wolfe knew this. He attacked in July, 1759. But the French held firm. Two months passed. At last Wolfe found an opening to the west. A small path led up the cliffs. The British climbed up the path at night. They surprised the French. The battle lasted only 15 minutes. Both Wolfe and Montcalm were killed. Quebec, the heart of New France, had to surrender.

13.5 What was Britain's position in the world after the war?

At the war's end Britain was stronger than ever. Britain called 1759 its "wonderful year." It won battles all over the world. In 1763, the Seven Years' War in Europe ended.

All sides signed a **treaty**. It was called the Peace of Paris. The terms favored Britain. Britain took over France's land in Canada. It held all of North America east of the Mississippi. France lost almost everything it had held in North America. Britain was the most powerful country in the world. And it would not give up control of its colonies.

☆☆☆

Connections

At the end of the French and Indian War, Britain held Canada. Canada has kept its ties with Britain. However, they have become weaker. For many years Britain ruled Canada. Beginning in 1867 the British Parliament let Canada rule itself. In 1982 Britain gave up its last power over Canada. This was the power to change Canada's rules of government. But Canada still calls the British crown its own head of state.

France's influence lives on also. Canada has a large group who still speak French. They are mostly in Quebec. Some French Canadians have wanted their own country. In the 1960s some blew up buildings to get their way. But Canada is still one country. Laws have been passed to help those who speak French. Many Canadians take pride in their French past.

 Canada

 British Columbia

 Quebec

 Ontario

 Newfoundland

 # CHAPTER REVIEW

Critical Thinking

Write your answers on a sheet of paper, or discuss in class.

Comparing and Contrasting

1. How did Britain and France fight the war differently?

Recognizing Details

2. In what ways was Britain stronger after the war?

Cooperative Learning

LEARNING STYLE
Writing
Oral

3. Work with a partner or a group. Make cards from six-inch cardboard squares. Write a name on each card. Write the names of people in this chapter. Place the cards face down on a table. Take turns taking one card. Read the name out loud. Then give one fact about that person. Keep on playing until each student has named several facts.

Write About It

Writing
Portfolio

4. Read again the facts about William Pitt. Imagine that you are a news reporter. You are talking to William Pitt. You want to know how he plans to win the war. Write down your questions. Write the answers you think he would give.

Chapter 14

The Cost of the War

Great Britain's Plans for Paying Costs of the War

Act	Year	Law
Proclamation of 1763	1763	stopped colonists from settling west of the Appalachians
Sugar Act	1764	(1) taxed sugar, coffee, and cloth brought into the colonies, (2) also lowered tax on molasses
Currency Act	1764	(1) stopped colonies from printing paper money, (2) made colonists use only gold and silver
Quartering Act	1765	made colonies pay for homes and goods used by British soldiers
Stamp Act	1765	made colonists buy paper with stamps for things like newspapers, letters, birth certificates
Declaratory Act	1766	stated that Parliament had the right to make any laws it wished for the colonies
Townshend Acts	1767	(1) new taxes on more goods brought into the colonies, (2) set up a special group in Boston to make sure these taxes were paid
Tea Act	1773	allowed only the East India Company to sell tea to the colonies
Intolerable Acts	1774	(1) closed Boston Harbor until ruined tea was paid for, (2) took control of Massachusetts government, (3) made Britain place for any trial involving a royal official, (4) made people take British soldiers into their homes and feed them, (5) gave Canada lands claimed by Virginia, Pennsylvania, and New York

Read about
England's plans to pay for the war with the French and the Indians. What made the colonists so angry? Why?

Key *Vocabulary*

tax (taks) money people must pay to their governments

officer (AHF uh suhr) a person who is chosen to carry out special duties

citizen (SIT uh zuhn) a member or a city, state, and/or country

committee (kuh MIT ee) a group of people chosen to carry out special duties

Reteaching Vocabulary
debt (det) money owed to another

CHART ANALYSIS

★ **Ask** — Who made these new laws?

★ **Acquire** — Why were these laws passed?

★ **Organize** — How was the money to be raised?

★ **Analyze** — No colonist could vote for members of Parliament. How might the colonists feel about any laws passed by Parliament?

★ **Answer** — Why might some of these laws have made the colonists angry?

Decoding Tip: Notice the different sounds *e* can stand for.

ay	cake	ah	fall, cot	air	air
ee	tree	i	sit	oh	cold
or	cord	oy	toy	uh	above, hundred
a	ask	ar	hard	oo	book
e	yet	eye	nice	uhr	liar, fir, further, color
ow	cow	ooh	boot, true	yoo	you, few, cube

14.1 Why did the colonists object so strongly to the Proclamation of 1763?

After 1763, Great Britain ruled Canada. This land had been French. The English colonists had fought hard for Britain. Now, they felt it was safe to move into the area. They began moving into lands along the Ohio River. However, the Native Americans began fighting to keep these people out. King George III wanted peace. He did not want colonists to move into the area. He feared they would be too far from British control. The king sent out the Proclamation of 1763. This law said that no colonists could live west of the Appalachian Mountains. Many colonists became very angry. They had fought in the wars for the right to build in this area.

14.2 How did Great Britain plan to pay for the French and Indian Wars?

England's kings ruled with the help of Parliament. Only the British Parliament could set new **taxes** or raise old ones. Parliament was led by a Prime Minister. The Prime Minister reported to the king. In 1762 Britain's Prime Minister was George Grenville. Britain had a huge problem. The war had been costly. The country's **debt** had gone up. It was twice what it had been before these wars. Now, Grenville had to find a way to pay these debts. He turned to Parliament. Grenville and Parliament raised taxes in Great Britain. However, fighting broke out around the country.

Grenville decided that the colonies should help pay some of the war debt. They had gained from the war, too. It also cost money to protect the colonies. Parliament passed Grenville's Sugar Act in 1764. The colonists would have to pay new taxes. The tax would be paid on goods bought from other countries. It covered things like sugar and clothes. The British had had a lot of trouble collecting taxes in North America. Some people sneaked goods into the colonies. This was called smuggling. Britain knew it would have trouble collecting the new taxes. Parliament allowed royal **officers** to search for smuggled goods. They could enter any building at will.

The colonists became very angry. They felt it was fair to pay part of the war costs. However, they felt that they should be able to send members to Parliament, too. That way they could help to make new laws. After all, they were British **citizens**, too. The colonists called Parliament's act "taxation without representation." Parliament held firm. Its members felt that they alone should rule the colonies. They felt that the colonies had only one purpose. That purpose was to make Britain rich and powerful.

14.3 How did acts passed between 1765 and 1766 affect the colonies?

Parliament passed acts between 1765 and 1766. These acts made the colonists very angry. The acts were:

- the Stamp Act,
- the Quartering Act, and
- the Declaratory Act.

The colonists now had to buy special paper for things like newspapers and letters. Each colony had to pay for housing and goods needed by British troops. Nine colonies sent members to a special meeting. It was held in New York City. The members wrote a letter to Parliament and the king. They asked all Americans to stop buying goods from Great Britain. In a few months, British sales were cut almost in half. Parliament ended the Stamp Act in 1766. However, it passed the Declaratory Act on the same day. Now even the law books said that only Parliament could rule the colonies.

14.4 What was the Boston Massacre?

The Townshend Acts of 1767 were hated in all the colonies. New York had never followed the Quartering Act. The Townshend Acts did away with New York's legislature. New taxes were to be paid by all the colonies. Another act set up a new office in Boston. It would make sure that all the new taxes were paid. The colonists made plans to fight these acts.

People made their own clothes. They used raspberry leaves instead of tea. Britain sent more troops to the colonies. In 1770 a group met outside the British army's Boston offices. The people yelled at the British troops. They also threw snowballs. The troops fired on the crowd. Three people were killed. This was called the "Boston Massacre."

▼ The illustration below shows a scene from the Boston Massacre, on March 5, 1770. Painting by John Bufford.

14.5 What caused the Boston Tea Party?

Lord North became Britain's Prime Minister. The Townshend Acts had set up new taxes. However, most of them had never been paid. British sales to the colonies were still very low. Lord North ended the Townshend Acts in 1770. But he still believed in Parliament's right to tax the colonies. He kept the tax on tea. The colonists did not back down. Boston formed a special **committee**. It wrote to the other colonies about Boston's plans to fight the law. The other colonies formed committees, too. They kept the news flowing throughout the colonies.

Parliament passed the Tea Act in 1773. The Tea Act let one British Company sell tea for less than other companies. The colonists felt that Britain might try to take over all business. They decided not to buy the East India Company's tea. The

people of Charleston, South Carolina, locked up the company's tea. New York and Philadelphia made the company's ships turn back to sea. One night the people of Boston went onto a company ship. They threw the tea into the water. This was called the "Boston Tea Party."

▲ The illustration above shows the destruction of tea at Boston Harbor, during the Boston Tea Party in 1773.

14.6   Why did the colonists call Britain's laws of 1774 the "Intolerable Acts"?

Parliament decided that the people of Boston had gone too far. It passed the Coercive Acts to punish Massachusetts. Boston Harbor was to be closed until the tea was paid for. Parliament shut down the Massachusetts legislature. Parliament itself would run the colony. Any trial involving a royal officer was to be held in Britain. Some British troops had no place to stay. Now, they could be put into colonists' homes. The colonists had to feed them, too. Parliament moved Canada's borders. It now owned lands claimed by Virginia, Pennsylvania, and New York. The colonists called these acts the "Intolerable Acts." These acts seemed too bad for the colonists to live with.

All the colonies spoke out against the Intolerable Acts. One governor was quick to act. He shut down the legislature of Virginia. This colonial legislature was known as the House of Burgesses. It had been holding meetings since 1619. Some colonists called for a new way of thinking. All the colonies should join together in the fight for their rights.

☆☆☆

Connections

▲ Crispus Attucks

Crispus Attucks had been a slave. He had run away from his owner. His father had been an African slave. His mother was Native American. She named him "Crispus." It meant "little deer." Attucks led the Boston crowd that threw snowballs at British soldiers. He was one of the three people killed in the Boston Massacre.

 # CHAPTER REVIEW

Critical Thinking

Write your answers on a sheet of paper, or discuss in class.

Comparing and Contrasting 1. How were Parliament's ideas about the colonists different from the way in which the colonists saw themselves?

Making Inferences 2. Why do you think Parliament and the king were so blind to the colonists' wishes?

Cooperative Learning

 3. Work with a study partner or as part of a study group. Pretend to be a colonist or a member of Parliament. Think about each person's beliefs. Discuss these beliefs with your partner.

Write About It

 4. Imagine that you own a newspaper in the colonies. You have to write an editorial for your paper. An editorial tells not only facts but also beliefs. Beliefs are a person's opinions. Write an editorial about an event that happened between 1763 and 1774. Remember to include your opinions.

Chapter 15

The Colonies Unify

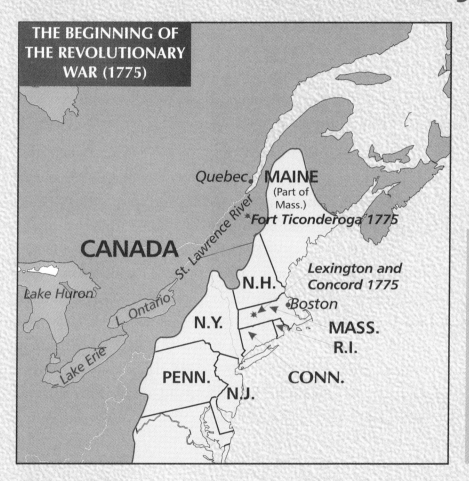

THE BEGINNING OF THE REVOLUTIONARY WAR (1775)

Quebec MAINE (Part of Mass.)
*Fort Ticonderoga 1775
St. Lawrence River
CANADA
Lake Huron
L. Ontario
N.H.
*Boston
Lexington and Concord 1775
N.Y.
MASS.
R.I.
Lake Erie
PENN.
N.J.
CONN.

Read about the colonies' fight against the Intolerable Acts. How did war with Britain begin? Why?

Key *Vocabulary*

unify (YOO nuh feye) to join parts together as one

demand (duh MAND) some decision or action that a person or group insists upon

boycott (BOY kaht) to refuse any dealings with a person or group until certain terms are met

rebellion (ri BEL yuhn) a fight against one's government

MAP ANALYSIS

★ **Ask**   What city controls Boston Harbor?

★ **Analyze** How would closing the harbor to all shipping affect the colony of Massachusetts?

★ **Answer**   Why might surrounding colonies also be affected?

Decoding Tip: Note the long i sound of y in **unify**.

ay	cake	ah	fall, cot	air	air	
ee	tree	i	sit	oh	cold	
or	cord	oy	toy	uh	above, hundred	
a	ask	ar	hard	oo	book	
e	yet	eye	nice	uhr	liar, fir, further, color	
ow	cow	ooh	boot, true	yoo	you, few, cube	

▲ John Adams

▲ Samuel Adams

15.1 What was the purpose of the First Continental Congress?

A special meeting was held in Philadelphia in September, 1774. It was called the First Continental Congress. Only Georgia did not send members to this meeting. The members met to discuss the Intolerable Acts. What could they do? Each colony had protested these laws. Nothing had changed. Now the colonies wanted to work together. They would be much stronger that way. Maybe then they could get Parliament to understand their feelings. The members had different ideas. It was agreed that one plan had to be formed. Nothing could be done if the colonies did not **unify**.

Two main groups affected the First Continental Congress. One group was led by people like John and Samuel Adams of Massachusetts. They wanted to end all trade with Great Britain. Trading would continue only when Parliament ended the Intolerable Acts. Virginians Patrick Henry and Richard Henry Lee supported this idea. The second group was led by another Virginian, George Washington. He and his group did not want to make the king and Parliament too angry. They wanted to move more slowly. Members of this second group did not want to fight with Parliament. They wanted to work with it instead. However, Washington did not have great hopes that these ideas would work. Parliament had not been willing to work with the colonies in the past.

15.2 How did the First Continental Congress plan to resist Britain?

The First Continental Congress unified the colonies. The members passed the List of Resolves on October 14. This was a **demand** for an end of the Intolerable Acts. It stated that Britain had no right to tax the colonies. The Congress also wrote a Declaration of Rights. Thomas Jefferson and James Wilson had formed its main ideas in their own writings. It stated that only the colonies could set taxes and make the laws. It said that the colonists should be loyal to the English king. However, the colonists did not have to be loyal to Parliament. This was especially true when Parliament took rights away from the colonists.

On October 18, the Continental Association was formed. Each colony would form a committee. They would not buy goods from Britain. They would punish people who did buy British goods. Their names would be put in the newspapers. People would be asked to **boycott** shops that sold British goods. The colonies would even take away any goods that had been bought from Britain. The Congress ended on October 26. The members set another meeting for May 10, 1775. It would be held if Britain did not agree to Congress's plans.

Parliament received the news of the First Continental Congress. Its members had different ideas, too. One group was led by William Pitt. They wanted to end the Townshend Acts. They asked that Britain take its troops out of Boston. However, few other members agreed with this small group. King George III was very angry with the Congress's plans. He felt that Massachusetts was staging a **rebellion**. He wanted this stopped. Most of Parliament agreed.

▼ The illustration below shows soldiers in the street during the retreat from Concord, Massachusetts.

15.3 Why did fighting break out in Lexington and Concord in 1775?

Thomas Gage was a British general. He was also the governor of Massachusetts. Parliament ordered him to carry out the Coercive Acts. He was told to use his troops if they were needed. Gage felt that this might cause war to break out. He decided to wait and see what the colonies would do. He learned that the colonists were calling themselves "Patriots." They would fight against Britain. They even formed small armies called "militias." The militia members were called

▼ John Hancock

"minutemen." These people were ready to fight at a minute's notice. The militias were storing arms in the town of Concord, Massachusetts.

General Gage decided to move against Concord. His troops would take away the arms from the militias. On the way they would stop in Lexington. They planned to arrest two militia leaders, Samuel Adams and John Hancock. Gage wanted to surprise the militia. His troops marched out of Boston at night. However, militia members were watching. Paul Revere and William Dawes rode out with the news. On the morning of April 19 the British reached Lexington. Adams and Hancock were gone. The minutemen were ready to fight. However, Captain John Parker knew that there were too many British. He told his militia to back down, but a shot was fired. The British began firing, too. Eight Patriots were killed. The others ran into the woods.

After their win at Lexington, the British moved on to Concord. Minutemen met them at North Bridge outside the town. The fight was too much for the British. They turned back to Boston. William Dawes had been arrested by the British. However, Paul Revere had done his job well. Many militias lined the road back to Lexington. They fired from behind trees, buildings, and fences. 273 British were killed or hurt that day. Only 95 Patriots were killed or hurt.

▼ The illustration below shows the famous ride of Paul Revere.

15.4 How did the colonies react to news about the fighting?

Patriots in Massachusetts had set up their own government. They raised 13,600 people for an army. Other colonies sent troops, too. Connecticut, New Hampshire, and Rhode Island were closest, so their troops were the first to arrive. The Patriots won another battle in May. Ethan Allen led a group called the "Green Mountain Boys." A militia led by Colonel Benedict Arnold joined them. They marched north toward Canada. They surprised British troops at Fort Ticonderoga on

May 10. They took over the fort. They also gained a great store of goods and arms. All the colonies were excited by the news.

Meeting	Year	Colonies	Purpose
First Continental Congress	1774	all but Georgia	plan ways of forcing Parliament to end the Intolerable Acts
Second Continental Congress	1775	all but Georgia	plan ways to fight the British army that was carrying out the Intolerable Acts

15.5 How did the colonists organize their efforts?

The Second Continental Congress first met on the day of the battle at Fort Ticonderoga. Again, only Georgia was missing from the meeting. The colonists knew that a war had to be fought. In order to win, however, they had to organize. The Second Continental Congress became the new government for the colonies. The militias of New England were to be an army. It was called the "Continental Army." The Congress voted to form more militias. Virginia, Maryland, and Pennsylvania would fight with the Continental Army.

▼ George Washington, the Virginia Colonel, painted by C. W. Peale, noted artist who founded the first American art museum in Philadelphia

Now the Continental Army needed a leader. Who would be the best choice? John Adams felt that George Washington was best for the post. He pointed out that Washington had fought in the French and Indian Wars. He had led troops during the war, too. Everyone knew that he was a strong Patriot. They would support him. Washington did not have extreme ideas and views. Most members of Congress would support him for that reason. Also, all of the fighting had happened in New England. These colonies would need help. Washington was from Virginia. The Southern Colonies would be pleased if he became general. Congress agreed. Washington was made Commander-in-Chief of the Continental Army on June 15, 1775.

★★★

Connections

Ralph Waldo Emerson was a great American poet. He wrote about the battles at Lexington and Concord. Here is one verse from that poem.

By the rude bridge that arched the flood,

Their flag to April's breeze unfurled,

Here once the embattled farmers stood,

And fired the shot heard round the world.

◄ The Battle of Lexington

★★☆ CHAPTER REVIEW

Critical Thinking

Write your answers on a sheet of paper, or discuss in class.

Making Inferences 1. What kind of person do you think George III was? Give reasons to support your answer.

Drawing Conclusions 2. How might things have changed for the colonies if Gage had succeeded at Lexington and Concord? Why do you think so?

Cooperative Learning

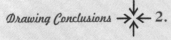

3. Work with a study partner or as part of a study group. Talk about the things that happened before, during, and after the fighting at Lexington and Concord. Name the people who were involved. Choose parts for a skit about these battles. Talk with each other about the kinds of things each person would say and do. Practice your skit. Present it to the class.

Write About It

4. Read the last paragraph of Section 15.5. Notice that John Adams makes a suggestion. He gives reasons to support his ideas. Choose an event from this chapter. Write a sentence telling how you feel about the event. Then list reasons to support your idea. Use these ideas to write a paragraph about the event.

Chapter 16

Britain Fights Back

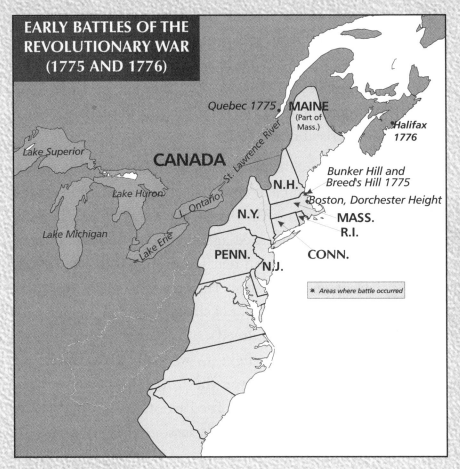

EARLY BATTLES OF THE REVOLUTIONARY WAR (1775 AND 1776)

Quebec 1775

MAINE (Part of Mass.)

Halifax 1776

Lake Superior

CANADA

St. Lawrence River

Lake Huron

N.H.

L. Ontario

Bunker Hill and Breed's Hill 1775

Boston, Dorchester Height

N.Y.

Lake Michigan

Lake Erie

MASS.

R.I.

PENN.

CONN.

N.J.

★ Areas where battle occurred

Read about the war in New England. How did the Continental Army drive the British from New England? Why?

Key *Vocabulary*

represent (rep ri ZENT) to act for someone or something

delegate (DEL i guht) a person who is chosen to act for another person or group of people

petition (puh TISH uhn) a paper written to ask that something be done

professional (pruh FESH uh nuhl) having training in special skills that can be used to earn a living

MAP ANALYSIS

★ **Ask**   What surrounds the city of Boston?

★ **Analyze**   The land near Boston Harbor is hilly. How could American troops on these hills affect the British troops in Boston?

★ **Answer**   Why might Canada be a better spot for the British movement against the Continental Army?

Decoding Tip: Note the different sounds *e* can stand for.

ay	cake	ah	fall, cot	air	air
ee	tree	i	sit	oh	cold
or	cord	oy	toy	uh	*above*, hundred
a	ask	ar	hard	oo	book
e	yet	eye	nice	uhr	liar, fir, further, color
ow	cow	ooh	boot, true	yoo	you, few, cube

16.1   What was the Battle of Bunker Hill?

George Washington was named Commander-in-Chief on June 15, 1775. He was to lead the Continental Army. He made plans to go to Boston. However, the Patriots in Boston heard dangerous news. British Generals William Howe, Henry Clinton, and John Burgoyne had reached Boston. They brought more troops for General Thomas Gage. The British had 6,500 troops in Boston. There were 10,000 Patriots around the city. Now the British wanted guns on the Dorchester Heights. This would help them keep all of Boston. The Patriots moved to Breed's Hill. They set up their guns during the night of June 16. Then the sun came up. General Gage was surprised to see them.

▼ The painting below illustrates a scene from the Battle of Bunker Hill. Painting by John Trumbull.

General Gage decided to take back Breed's Hill. His troops were driven back down. He tried again. The Patriots held their fire. The British came very close. Then the Patriots fired. Once again, the British were pushed back. More British reached Breed's Hill. The British dropped their packs. They charged again. However, the Patriots were out of shells. They had to pull back. The British took Breed's Hill. Then they took Bunker Hill. That day's fighting was called the Battle of Bunker Hill. However, the British lost many troops. Over 1,000 were killed or hurt. The Patriots did not have many losses. The Patriots had learned a lesson. They were able to stand up to Britain's fine army.

16.2   What was the Olive Branch Petition?

The Second Continental Congress **represented** the colonies. All but Georgia sent delegates. Not all the **delegates** wanted the same things. Some wanted to be free of England. John Adams of Massachusetts led this group. Others wanted to remain British. However, they wanted a say in Parliament. John Dickinson of Pennsylvania led these people. The

Congress decided to send a letter to George III. The delegates would stop the war. However, the king had to end the Intolerable Acts. He also had to give Americans seats in Parliament. This letter was called the "Olive Branch **Petition**." An olive branch stands for peace. The letter was sent in July, 1775. The delegates waited for an answer. News came in November. George III would not even read the letter. He would send more troops. He wanted total war. All the delegates made plans to fight. Even Georgia was represented. Its delegates had arrived at Congress in September.

16.3 Why did fighting spread to Canada?

Hopes for peace had been strong. However, war planning had not stopped. News about Britain's plans reached the Continental Congress. A British general wanted to march out of Quebec. He planned to take over western New York. Congress acted quickly. It sent word to Fort Ticonderoga. General Richard Montgomery was to move his troops toward Quebec. He would be met by more troops from Maine. They would be led by Benedict Arnold. Arnold's march was like a terrible dream. It covered 350 miles. The troops had to move through thick forests. There was heavy snow. The food ran out. Finally, Arnold's troops reached Quebec in December. The two leaders moved against the city on December 30. Heavy snow and high winds began. The Patriots could not take the city. Montgomery was killed. Arnold was hurt. However, he would not leave. His men camped around the city. They would not let anyone in or out. More British troops arrived in the spring. Arnold had no choice. He led his troops out of Canada.

16.4 How did other battles with the British rebuild American hopes?

Boston was at the center of the war in 1775 and 1776. Washington took charge two weeks after the Battle of Bunker

Hill. His job was a large one. There were many militias. He made plans to turn them into one army. He also had to see that the troops were trained. General Henry Knox brought needed goods in January, 1776. His troops had dragged arms from Fort Ticonderoga. They had brought 59 pieces of cannon. Washington made a daring plan. On March 4, his army took Dorchester Heights. The cannon were put into place. General Howe was leading the British. He sent troops to push the Patriots off the Heights. However, a storm blew up. Howe's troops pulled back without a fight.

Early Battles of the Revolutionary War

Battle	Date	Result
Lexington	April 19, 1775	British drive Patriots out of Lexington and into the woods.
Concord	April 19, 1775	Patriots stop British at North Bridge. British are pushed all the way back to Boston.
Fort Ticonderoga	May 10, 1775	Patriots take British fort near Canada. They send its guns to Boston.
Bunker Hill	June 16, 1775	Patriots hold Breed's Hill against two British attacks. They pull back after third attack. British move on and take Bunker Hill, too.
Quebec	Dec. 30, 1775	Patriot Generals Montgomery and Arnold fail to take Quebec, Canada. They surround the city. More British troops arrive in the spring, so Patriots move out of Canada.
Dorchester Heights	March 4, 1776	Washington uses guns from Fort Ticonderoga. They are placed on Dorchester Heights. British begin attack, but are driven off by a storm. The Patriots now control Boston. The British leave the city.

Howe decided that he could not hold Boston. He loaded his troops onto ships. About 1,000 people from Boston moved with him. They were called loyalists because they supported Britain and the king. The ships sailed out of Boston Harbor on March 26. They went north to Canada. Howe led his people to Halifax. The British would set up in the north. Now they would run the war from Canada.

New England was free of the British. The Patriots were wild with excitement. The Continental Army had proved itself. It could stand up to a **professional** army. However, the British were not beaten. Now there was a new question. Where and when would the British return?

☆☆☆

  For the People, By the People

Biography

▲ Molly Pitcher

Women fought in this war, too. Mary Ludwig joined her husband on the lines. She carried water to the troops. They gave her the name "Molly Pitcher." She was at the Battle of Monmouth. Her husband was shot. She took his place at the cannon. She became a hero of the war.

Deborah Sampson's family was poor. She became an indentured servant. Her family was given money. She then worked for a set time. The work paid back the money. She worked for a family with 10 sons. They all grew to love her. She was like their daughter and sister. The boys went off to fight for the Patriots. Deborah wanted to fight too. She dressed like a man. Everyone still knew who she was. She went to another town. No one knew her there. They did not see that she was a woman. She became part of the army. She fought with the other troops. Once she was hurt. She kept this a secret. She took care of the wound herself. Then she had to stand guard. Deborah became sick. The doctor learned she was a woman. He took her to her aunt in Sharon, Massachusetts. After the war, her country recognized her efforts. She was given a pension, or a yearly sum for the rest of her life.

★★☆ CHAPTER REVIEW

Critical Thinking

Write your answers on a sheet of paper, or discuss in class.

Analyzing Cause and Effect

1. Why did geography have an important effect on the war?

Drawing Conclusions

2. Why did some Americans disagree about whether or not to remain British?

Cooperative Learning

LEARNING STYLE
Visual

3. Work with a study partner or as part of a study group. Think about the battles in this chapter. Imagine that you have seen one. Tell what you saw. Also, tell how you felt while watching the fight.

Write About It

Writing Portfolio

4. Look over the chapter. Note the important dates. Make a list of these dates. Write a sentence beside each date. Tell what happened. Write one paragraph as a summary of the chapter. Use the sentences from your list.

Chapter 17

Independence

The Road to Independence

Date	Event
January 1776	Thomas Paine produced *Common Sense*. He suggested that the colonies declare their independence and form their own country.
March 1776	British troops left Boston and all of New England. They sailed to Canada and planned to invade western New York.
June 7, 1776	Richard Henry Lee proposed a measure for a vote in Congress. It would establish independence for the colonies.
June 11, 1776	A special committee was set up to write a letter to George III. It would be sent if Congress approved Lee's measure.
June 28, 1776	The committee presented its work to Congress. It was the Declaration of Independence, written by Thomas Jefferson.
July 2, 1776	Congress passed Lee's measure establishing independence for the colonies.
July 4, 1776	Several changes were made in the Declaration of Independence. It was approved by the Congress. Each member had to sign it in order to stay in Congress.

Read about the colonists' changing ideas about Great Britain. How did the Second Continental Congress change the goal of the war? Why?

Key *Vocabulary*

pamphlet (PAM fluht) a small booklet with a paper cover

independence (in duh PEN duhnts) the state of being free from something

representative (rep ri ZENT uh tiv) a person who acts in place of another person or for a group of people

declare (di KLAIR) to tell, state, or announce

revolution (rev uh LOO shuhn) the act of tossing out one kind of government and replacing it with another

CHART ANALYSIS

★ **Ask**   Look at the title. What is the topic of this chart?

★ **Acquire**   What idea did Thomas Paine suggest for the colonies?

★ **Organize**   List the steps followed by Congress in acting on Paine's idea.

★ **Answer**   How did the colonies' relationship with Britain change on July 4, 1776?

Decoding Tip: Note that *ph* can stand for the sound of *f*.

ay	cake	ah	fall, cot	air	air
ee	tree	i	sit	oh	cold
or	cord	oy	toy	uh	above, hundred
a	ask	ar	hard	oo	book
e	yet	eye	nice	uhr	liar, fir, further, color
ow	cow	ooh	boot, true	yoo	you, few, cube

17.1 What idea did Thomas Paine propose?

The colonists had won some important battles, but they still did not have their rights. British troops left New England in March, 1776. They sailed to Canada. They were making new plans. They would move into western New York. Many Loyalists lived in that area. The Loyalists could help the British with their plans. These plans were very clear to most of the colonists. The British would not back down. The Patriots could fight for their rights as British citizens. However, the British would never meet those demands.

Thomas Paine produced a **pamphlet** in January, 1776. He presented a new plan for the Patriots. It was not a new idea. Many people had talked about it for years. Paine wrote simply and plainly. His idea made a great deal of sense. In fact, he called his pamphlet *Common Sense*. What was this idea? Paine felt that the colonies should no longer be British. They should break free of Great Britain. The colonies should fight for **independence**. Over 100,000 copies of *Common Sense* were sold in three months. Washington's troops shared copies with each other. Washington had driven the British from New England. Now more and more colonists wanted the British gone forever.

17.2 Why did the Second Continental Congress agree with Paine's idea?

Independence became important to the Second Continental Congress. **Representatives** of the colonies made up the Second Continental Congress. Each colony was run by a legislature and a governor. The legislatures told their representatives how to vote in Congress. By the middle of 1776, the idea of freedom was spreading. Not everyone agreed. The idea sometimes turned families against each other. Benjamin Franklin was a strong Patriot from Pennsylvania. However, his son William was for the king. He had even been made the royal governor of New Jersey. Other people in New Jersey were Patriots. Even Governor William Franklin's son was a Patriot. The people of New Jersey finally arrested their royal governor. They sent new representatives to Congress. They were told to vote for independence.

Richard Henry Lee was a representative from Virginia. On June 7, 1776, he introduced the idea of independence. He wanted Congress to vote for this idea. He said that ". . . these united colonies are, and of right ought to be, free and independent states." The idea was discussed. One decision was made. The measure could not pass unless all 13 colonies voted for it. Congress did not want to force an unwilling colony to break from Great Britain. Besides, such a colony could be dangerous for the Patriots. British troops could start a base in a loyal colony. A special committee was set up on June 11. It would write a letter to George III. The letter would explain why independence was now necessary. The writing would take time. That time could be spent in raising enough votes for independence.

▼ The illustration below shows the Second Continental Congress voting for independence.

17.3 What ideas were expressed in the Declaration of Independence?

Writing the Declaration of Independence was a great task. Five members were on the committee to write the Declaration. They were from different colonies. They were Benjamin Franklin of Pennsylvania, John Adams of Massachusetts, Robert Livingston of New York, Roger Sherman of Connecticut, and Thomas Jefferson of Virginia.

▼ The illustration below shows Congress signing the Declaration of Independence.

The committee chose Jefferson to do the actual writing. His work took about two weeks.

The Declaration was presented in Congress on June 28. Jefferson wrote it in three main parts. The first part lists the rights held by all people. He even spells out the special rights of British citizens. In the second part, he discusses George III and Parliament. He listed how they had taken away the colonists' rights. The last part **declares** that the colonies will now be independent states. It ends with a promise by all those who sign it. ". . . (W)e mutually pledge to each other our lives, our fortunes, and our sacred honor."

17.4 How did the colonies become the United States of America?

Not everyone in Congress agreed about independence or the ideas in the Declaration. Some members still wanted to be British citizens. However, the idea could not be stopped now.

On July 2, 1776, Congress passed Richard Henry Lee's measure. The colonies were taking their independence. More talk was needed before Jefferson's Declaration was passed. Some members asked for changes that were easily made. However, the idea of slavery almost ended the push for independence.

Jefferson had written that all men are created equal. In truth, some people in the colonies were slaves. Jefferson had written about slavery in the Declaration. He wrote that slavery was a crime. He said that George III had committed a crime by allowing slavery. Representatives from the Southern Colonies did not like this part of the Declaration. They wanted it removed. They would not support independence any other way. John Adams and others felt that this part must stay. They wanted a free and independent country. How could that happen if slavery remained? This would be a good time to end slavery. However, the southern representatives stood firm. Adams and the others decided that independence was too important. They would fight against slavery at a later time. The part about slavery was removed. The Declaration was passed on July 4, 1776.

All the members were to sign the Declaration of Independence. Then it would be sent to George III. Only those members who signed would be allowed to stay in Congress. The members knew the Declaration was dangerous. It turned their fight into a **revolution**. If the Patriots lost the war, the members would be hanged. The members had already faced dangers. British troops had destroyed the New York home of Lewis Morris. He and the others were determined to sign. John Hancock was President of the Congress. He signed first. He wrote in very large letters. He said, "There, I guess King George will be able to read that." Many copies were printed. They were sent to all the colonies. Bells were rung to help spread the news. The people were no longer British. They were no longer colonists. Now they were all Americans.

▼ The illustration below shows the reading of the Declaration of Independence from the east balcony of the State House in Boston in 1776.

Connections

▲ Roger Williams

Many Americans did not like the idea of slavery. Even the early colonists had believed it to be wrong. Roger Williams founded Rhode Island in the 1600s. He would not allow slavery in the colony. James Oglethorpe founded Georgia in 1733. He hated slavery. He set up a law against it. His law did not last very long. The Quakers of Pennsylvania began writing against slavery in the 1680s. Vermont joined Pennsylvania and Rhode Island in the fight against slavery. These states passed laws against slavery by 1780.

Massachusetts has a special nickname. It is known as the "Cradle of Liberty." It had helped the United States become free. However, this state still allowed slavery. Quock Walker was a slave. He lived in Massachusetts. He filed a case in court in 1781. He wanted his freedom. He said slavery was wrong. The court decided that he was right. He was freed. The court also said that slavery must end. All the other slaves living in Massachusetts were freed, too.

 CHAPTER REVIEW

Critical Thinking

Write your answers on a sheet of paper, or discuss in class

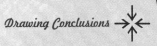 1. Why did most colonists come to support the idea of independence?

 2. Why were the members of the Declaration committee from different colonies?

Cooperative Learning

3. Work with a study partner or as part of a study group. Think about the important dates in this chapter. Make a list of the dates. Use these dates to make a timeline. Be sure to include facts that tell what happened on each date.

Write About It

4. Look over the chapter. Imagine that you own a newspaper in 1776. Write a headline for three stories about the Second Continental Congress. Remember that a headline tells the important facts about what happened. Share your headlines with the class.

Quiz

Number a piece of paper from 1-10. Read each question below. Read the answers that follow each question. Choose the answer for each question. Write the letter of the answer you choose beside the correct number on your piece of paper.

1. **What was the goal of Benjamin Franklin's Albany Plan?**
   a. to drive the French out of North America
   b. to make the British colonies stronger by having them work together
   c. to push Native Americans from lands where the French and British wanted new colonies
   d. both b and c

2. **Who gained lands after the French and Indian War?**
   a. the French
   b. the British
   c. the Spanish
   d. both b and c

3. **Why did the colonists fight against British taxes as a way of paying for the war?**
   a. They had gained nothing from the war.
   b. They were already paying higher taxes than the people of Great Britain.
   c. They had no voice in Parliament, which had set up these taxes.
   d. They felt that the British should help pay the war's costs, too.

4. **Why was the First Continental Congress held?**
   a. to plan ways of forcing Parliament to end the Intolerable Acts
   b. to plan ways of uniting the colonies against French attacks
   c. to plan ways of making the king give up his power over the colonies
   d. both a and b

5. **Why was the Second Continental Congress held?**
   a. to plan a government based on Franklin's Albany Plan
   b. to plan how to raise an army to fight the British
   c. to plan a way in which American members of Parliament would be chosen
   d. to plan a way of pulling Ireland and Scotland into the fight against Great Britain

6. **How did the struggle between the colonies and Britain change after Lexington and Concord?**
   a. The British arrested all the colonies' governors.
   b. Protests against taxes spread into all of the colonies.
   c. War broke out with British troops.
   d. both a and b

7. **Which colony saw most of the early action between the British and the Patriots?**
   a. Virginia
   b. New York
   c. Pennsylvania
   d. Massachusetts

8. **Why did the British leave Boston in March 1775?**
   a. Washington's troops took Dorchester Heights and gained control of the city.
   b. The Patriots kept new British troops from landing at Boston Harbor.
   c. The British knew that taking Philadelphia, Pennsylvania would end the war sooner.
   d. Washington cut the British off from their supplies of food and guns.

9. **What new goal did the colonists set on July 4, 1776?**
   a. a fight to remove George III as king
   b. a fight to push the British out of Canada, too
   c. a fight to gain independence from Great Britain
   d. a fight to take over all the seats in Parliament

10. **How did the Americans present their new goal to the British and the world?**
    a. in the Olive Branch Petition
    b. in the Declaration of Independence
    c. in the Albany Plan of Union
    d. in the book *Common Sense*

RECOGNIZING DETAILS

Add numbers 11–15 to your paper. Read the two lists below. People are listed on the left. What each person did is listed on the right. Match the people with the things that they did. Write your answers on your paper.

11. Thomas Jefferson
12. Iroquois
13. Parliament
14. Patriots
15. Thomas Paine

a. We helped the British in their fighting during the French and Indian War.
b. We fought for our rights to help make the laws that govern the colonies where we live.
c. I wrote the Declaration of Independence.
d. My members are the only people who can make laws for the British colonies.
e. I wrote *Common Sense,* which explains why the colonists should become independent.

Writing Portfolio

Look over the people who are described in these chapters. Choose one person who interests you. Find out more about this person. Write a short report about this person. Trade papers with a study partner. Check each other's work. Make a clean, neat copy. Put it in your portfolio. You may also wish to combine your report with those of your classmates. Put them in a book called "People Who Have Influenced America."

Alternative Assessment

You may wish to work with a study partner. Write the following names across the top of a piece of paper: English Citizen, Colonist, and Patriot. Look through the chapters to find out facts about these people. Make a chart with these facts. List the facts under the headings on your paper. Put facts that are alike in the same row. For example, one row of facts might show these people's ideas about religion. Another row might show their ideas about Parliament. Note that by reading each row you can tell how the people are alike and how they are different. Share your chart with the class.

COOPERATIVE PROJECT: THE WAR IN BOSTON

LEARNING STYLE
Tactile Kinesthetic

Work with a group. Make a list of events and battles that happened in Boston from 1763 to 1776. Look at different maps of the city of Boston. Make a model of Boston. Build small houses out of cardboard. Also make models of important buildings and special spots. For example, you might use clay to form Breed's Hill, Bunker Hill, and Dorchester Heights. Make paper flags that tell what happened at different spots. Put these flags on small sticks. Place the sticks in the correct spots on your diorama. Display your diorama so that other classes can examine it.

Chapter 18

War in the North

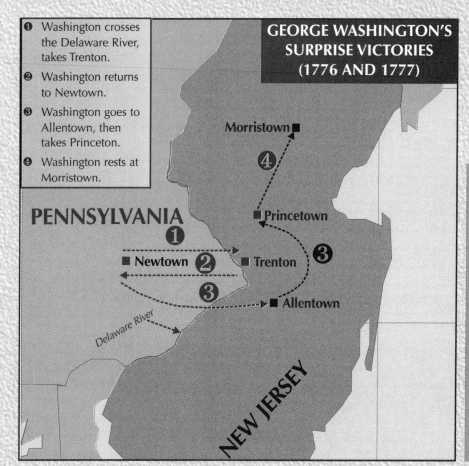

GEORGE WASHINGTON'S SURPRISE VICTORIES (1776 AND 1777)

❶ Washington crosses the Delaware River, takes Trenton.

❷ Washington returns to Newtown.

❸ Washington goes to Allentown, then takes Princeton.

❹ Washington rests at Morristown.

PENNSYLVANIA

Morristown ■

❹

■ Princetown

■ Newtown ❷ ■ Trenton ❸

❸

➤ ■ Allentown

Delaware River

NEW JERSEY

Read about the turning point of the Revolutionary War. What was the most important battle? Why?

Key *Vocabulary*

mercenary (MUHRS uhn air ee) someone who fights in wars for pay

retreat (ri TREET) to back away from danger

reinforcements (ree in FORS muhntz) troops that are sent to help other troops in a war

frontier (fruhn TEER) land that is still wild and has few people living there

traitor (TRAY tuhr) someone who helps the enemy or joins the enemy side

---

MAP ANALYSIS		
★ **Ask**	How many times did Washington cross the Delaware in this period?
★ **Acquire**	To get from Newtown to Trenton, which way did Washington have to go?
★ **Analyze**	Which step was the longest trip for Washington's army?
★ **Answer**	Why might the third step have been a surprise to the British?

Decoding Tip: Note the different sounds that two vowels together can stand for. Look at retreat, frontier, and traitor, in which two vowels together make one sound. Look at reinforcements, in which two vowels together make two sounds.

ay	cake	ah	fall, cot	air	air
ee	tree	i	sit	oh	cold
or	cord	oy	toy	uh	above, hundred
a	ask	ar	hard	oo	book
e	yet	eye	nice	uhr	liar, fir, further, color
ow	cow	ooh	boot, true	yoo	you, few, cube

18.1 What was the British plan to win the war?

▼ Washington at the battle of Trenton. Engraving by Illman Brothers, 1870, from a painting by E.L. Henry.

In 1776 Britain was still certain it could win the war. The British had many more soldiers than the Patriots. They had more ships. They had money for food, clothes, and guns. Also, they could pay **mercenaries** from other countries to help. Most came from Germany. They were called Hessians. Native Americans also helped the British.

As for the Patriots, they had many problems. Few of them could fight all the time. Most had to return home after battles. They had to work in shops and on farms. Their side had far less money for supplies.

The British had a simple plan. They would attack the colonies in the middle. New York would be taken. This would cut off New England from the states in the South. The British could then fight two small separate wars. However, things didn't work out as planned.

18.2 How did George Washington's troops surprise the British?

▼ *Crossing the Delaware,* painting by Emanuel Leutze

At first the British army rolled foward. They were led by Sir William Howe. In New York, Howe's 32,000 men almost destroyed George Washington's army. Washington had to fall back. British forces were camped forty miles outside Philadelphia. Howe set up a line of British posts in New Jersey. Then he settled in for the winter. But Washington came back. It was Christmas night, 1776. Snow filled the air. The Delaware River was choked with ice. Washington and his men crossed the river to Trenton, New Jersey. Hessians held the town.

▲ The picture above shows George Washington at the battle of Princeton on January 3, 1777. Lithograph by D. McLellan, 1853.

They were taken by surprise. They had to surrender.

Howe was shocked and angry. He sent Lord Charles Cornwallis to pin down Washington's army. Again Washington fooled the British. At night his army slipped around Cornwallis's troops. They surprised the British at Princeton. Britain's line of posts was broken. Most of New Jersey again belonged to the Patriots. Their spirits soared. They began to believe they could win.

18.3 Why was the Battle of Saratoga important?

The British tried again to cut America in two. This was early in 1777. General John Burgoyne led troops down from Canada. They took Fort Ticonderoga. The Patriots had to **retreat**. They cut down trees to block the roads. The British slowed down but did not stop. Burgoyne sent a large group to Bennington, Vermont, for supplies. Patriots were waiting for them. Almost the whole British group was killed or caught. Burgoyne now needed **reinforcements**. He kept on going south. General Howe was busy. He was fighting Washington's troops near Philadelphia. Burgoyne made a desperate try to reach Albany. General Horatio Gates led American troops to meet him.

▼ Surrender of General Burgoyne at Saratoga, painting by John Trumbull

▲ Baron von Steuben at Valley Forge, 1777; painting by Augustus G. Heaton

Fighting broke out at Saratoga, New York. The Patriots won two battles at Saratoga. About 5,000 British gave up.

News about Saratoga spread quickly. Great Britain saw things changing. It offered to rule America more lightly. But the states refused to talk. France entered the war. The French sided with the United States. Saratoga was the turning point of the war.

18.4   What happened at Valley Forge?

Not all the news for the Patriots was good. In September 1777, General Howe took over Philadelphia. Washington and his men pulled back. They spent the winter at Valley Forge. It was about 25 miles west of Philadelphia. They built long rows of log cabins. Months of fighting were starting to tell. Washington's troops were hungry and cold. Half had no shoes or socks. Their clothes had been worn to rags. There was no meat to eat. Smoke filled the cabins. The roofs leaked. The floors turned to mud. Many became sick. At least 3,000 died. Those who were strong enough worked. They learned how to march. They learned how to move together in battle. A

German named Frederick von Steuben worked with them. Many Patriots did not leave Valley Forge alive. Those who did were better soldiers.

18.5 How did the Americans win in the West?

Fighting also went on in the West. The war was very different there. Not many people had moved to the Ohio Valley. A few British forts ruled a large area. Native Americans helped the British keep control. The state of Virginia decided to fight for the West.

In 1778 George Rogers Clark was sent to take the area. Clark had only 127 men. But he knew a lot about the **frontier**. He knew how to live off the land. Clark and his men captured two British forts. Then they marched 180 miles to Vincennes. It was winter. The land was flooded. Clark's men had to wade through deep water. At Vincennes, Clark surprised the British. The people of Vincennes were mostly French. They supported the Americans. Clark made the British surrender. Lands west to the Mississippi River came under American rule.

▲ Clark's march against Vincennes, across the Wabash River, through wilderness and flood; painting by Ezra Winter

☆☆☆

A Hero
AND A TRAITOR

▲ John Paul Jones

John Paul Jones was a ship's captain from Scotland. He joined the Patriot cause in 1776. Jones's ship was the first to fly the American flag. Jones led raids on the English coast. In September 1779, he met a group of British ships. He attacked the lead ship. The British ship was much larger than his. The ropes of the two ships became tangled. The British captain called out to Jones. Was he ready to quit? Jones shouted his answer. "I have not yet begun to fight!" The fight lasted three hours. At last the British surrendered. Jones took over the British ship. America had its first hero at sea.

▲ Benedict Arnold

Benedict Arnold was a general in the Revolutionary Army. He had showed himself to be clever and brave. He had fought in the Battle of Saratoga and others. In 1780 he was the head of West Point. This was an important American fort. But Arnold felt he did not get enough attention. He became angry at his fellow Patriots. He decided to turn West Point over to the British. A British spy was caught with papers from Arnold. The papers showed what Arnold planned to do. Arnold escaped to the British side. He fought for the British. He helped burn American cities. Benedict Arnold often is called the worst **traitor** in the war.

★★☆ CHAPTER REVIEW

Critical Thinking

Write your answers on a sheet of paper, or discuss in class.

Making Inferences

1. Why did the Patriots have to use surprise attacks to win?

Analyzing Cause and Effect

2. Why was Saratoga a turning point in the war?

Cooperative Learning

LEARNING STYLE
Verbal Oral

3. Work with a partner or a group. Read over the facts in this chapter. Which ones would belong in a news report? Work together to make up a news report on the war. Make it sound like the news on TV. You might draw or find pictures to go with your report. Present your news report to the class.

Write About It

Writing Portfolio

4. A diary is a book for writing private thoughts. Imagine that you are at Valley Forge. The year is 1778. Describe in your diary what life is like there. What does the camp look like? How do you feel?

Chapter 19

Victory in the South

LAST BATTLES OF THE REVOLUTIONARY WAR (1778-1781)

N.J.

MD.

DEL.

Virginia

Yorktown

Guilford Court House

N. Carolina

King's Mt.

Cowpens

Camden

Wilmington

S. Carolina

Georgia

Charleston

Savannah

★ Major Battles of the Southern Campaign of the Revolutionary War

← American Troops

◄- - English Troops

◄— French Troops

French Navy

English Navy

N W E S

Read about the end of the War for Independence. What things did the Patriots have in their favor? Why?

Key *Vocabulary*

guerrilla (guh RIL uh) a kind of fighting that depends on hiding and surprise attacks

ceremony (SAIR uh moh nee) a formal act or gathering to do something or remember something

negotiate (nuh GOH shee ayt) to talk about or bargain for

sue (soo) to go to court to get something by law

Reteaching Vocabulary

ambush (AM bush) to attack by surprise

MAP ANALYSIS

★ **Acquire** Which southern state saw the most battles in the war's last years?

★ **Analyze** Why were the British in trouble at Yorktown?

★ **Answer** From this map, how would you describe the Americans' plan to end the war?

Decoding Tip: Notice the different sounds that the vowel pair ue can stand for in guerrilla and sue.

ay	cake	ah	fall, cot	air	air
ee	tree	i	sit	oh	cold
or	cord	oy	toy	uh	above, hundred
a	ask	ar	hard	oo	book
e	yet	eye	nice	uhr	liar, fir, further, color
ow	cow	ooh	boot, true	yoo	you, few, cube

                    For the People, By the People

19.1 Why did Britain attack in the Southern states?

In 1778 Britain's army turned to the South. It needed another plan. Three years of fighting had passed. Britain had won most of the battles. However, Britain had not stopped the Revolution. Britain's new plan was to gather its supporters in the South. These people were called Loyalists. Georgia and the Carolinas were full of Loyalists. With their help, Britain planned to capture those states. Then Britain could attack Virginia with all its might. Virginia was the richest state. Its fall would end the Revolution. Or so the British hoped.

At first the plan worked well. British troops took Savannah, Georgia in 1778. A year later, they took Charleston, South Carolina. Charleston was the South's only large city. It almost burnt down. Fighting in the South turned ugly. Both sides showed little mercy. The Patriots again were running low on supplies. They needed food and clothing. Some quit. The low point came at Camden, South Carolina. It was the Patriots' worst loss of the war. Horatio Gates's army was torn apart. Britain's Lord Cornwallis still had a large force. Many worried that the British could not be stopped.

19.2 How did the Americans weaken the British army?

The Patriots found different ways to fight successfully. In the South their army was broken. They couldn't fight large battles. Instead they made **guerrilla** attacks. Some Patriots in the South lived off the land. These were mountain men. They came from what is now Tennessee. They knew the woods and the streams. They hid behind rocks or among trees. They waited for Cornwallis's men to march past. Anyone who strayed would be shot. Sometimes small groups of British went looking for food. Patriots would **ambush** these groups. Small numbers of Patriots caused the British lots of problems.

The mountain men even won a full battle. They beat an army of Loyalists. This was at King's Mountain. After the battle, the mountain men went home. But Cornwallis didn't know this. To be safe, he pulled back. The mountain men bought time for the American cause.

19.3 Why did Cornwallis's army go to Yorktown?

In October 1780 the Americans got a new leader in the South. He was General Nathanael Greene. Like Washington, Greene took care in picking his battles. He would only fight in places he chose himself. He rebuilt the American army in the South. Then he divided it into three parts. Greene thought Cornwallis would divide his own army to stop him.

▼ The illustration below shows American troops planning the siege of Yorktown. Engraving by O.M. Fontaine from a painting by Conder.

Greene was right. It was a dangerous plan. But it gave the Patriots a fighting chance.

The result of Greene's plan was two key battles. The first was at Cowpens, South Carolina. General Daniel Morgan beat a strong British force. The next battle was at Guilford Court House in North Carolina. It was March 15, 1781. Greene's army met Cornwallis's at last. Neither side won. But the British lost twice as many soldiers. Cornwallis's army left for Yorktown, Virginia. Cornwallis hoped to get supplies on the Virginia coast. Instead, he stepped into a trap.

19.4 What caused Britain to surrender?

The Americans saw their chance to win the war. They could surround Cornwallis at Yorktown. The French were able to help. French ships moved into Chesapeake Bay. They cut off a British escape by sea. George Washington moved his army in secret. They marched from New York. A French army came too. Washington cut off the British on the north. Cornwallis couldn't move by land or sea. He had to fight.

▲ The illustration above shows a scene from the battle of Yorktown, which ended with the surrender of Cornwallis in 1781. Lithograph by Turgis.

Washington attacked at Yorktown. Big guns opened fire on the British lines. Foot soldiers then swarmed in. Washington's armies were too much for the British. On October 17, 1781, Cornwallis gave up. Two days later there was a **ceremony** for the surrender. Cornwallis's sword was handed over. A British band played an old song. They played "The World Turned Upside Down." Congress got word of the victory on October 22. Some fighting went on for two more years. But the real war was over.

19.5   What were the terms of the Treaty of Paris?

The United States began to **negotiate** peace in April 1782. France and Britain were still fighting in far places. The Americans and British talked alone in Paris. Benjamin Franklin and John Adams led the Americans. The talks went on for months. In November an agreement was reached. On September 3, 1783, the final Treaty of Paris was signed. In it, the United States' boundaries were set. They reached from Canada to Florida. They went west to the Mississippi. Americans could fish off Newfoundland and Nova Scotia. Britain agreed to America's independence. It had been won with eight years of war. Benjamin Franklin put it in simple words. "We are now friends with England and with all mankind."

☆☆☆

Connections

What did the Revolution do for African Americans? Some fought for the British. They were promised their freedom. Thousands of African Americans left with the British in 1783. Others were in favor of the Revolution. As many as 5,000 African Americans fought for it. They listened to all the talk about freedom. After the war, some acted on it. They went to courts. They **sued** to be set free. Massachusetts and Vermont ended slavery in 1780. Other states in the North began to follow them. But they went slowly. By 1790, there were about 27,000 free blacks in the North. The North would become the center for free blacks in America.

In the South, things were different. Slavery held firm. But some African Americans proved what they could do. The war years brought hard times. Plantation owners left to fight. African Americans were left behind. They had to help run the farms. Sometimes they were the only ones running them. Then the owners came back. They put back the hard rules of slavery. African Americans had to wait for freedom. It would take another huge war to bring change. That would be the Civil War.

▲ African Americans working on the plantations.

CHAPTER REVIEW

Critical Thinking

Write your answers on a sheet of paper, or discuss in class.

 Analyzing Cause and Effect

1. The British won most of the battles with the Patriots. However, they lost the war. Why?

 *Drawing Conclusions*

2. What was the most important part of the Treaty of Paris? Why?

Cooperative Learning

LEARNING STYLE
Visual Auditory

3. Think about the Revolutionary War. How did the battles look and sound? Try to see and hear a battle as if it were on a movie screen or on a video. Describe to a partner what the battle is like.

Write About It

Writing Portfolio

4. A slogan is a catchy phrase or clever use of words. Make up a slogan to urge Americans to joint the fight against the British. Make a poster using your slogan. Decorate your poster with a drawing or design.

Chapter 20

Experiment in Government

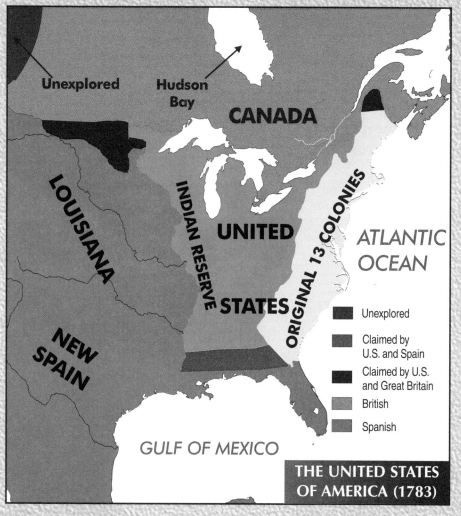

Unexplored

Hudson Bay

CANADA

LOUISIANA

INDIAN RESERVE

UNITED

STATES

ORIGINAL 13 COLONIES

ATLANTIC OCEAN

NEW SPAIN

Unexplored

Claimed by U.S. and Spain

Claimed by U.S. and Great Britain

British

Spanish

GULF OF MEXICO

THE UNITED STATES OF AMERICA (1783)

Read about the problems of setting up our national government. How did ideas about this government change? Why?

Key *Vocabulary*

confederation (kuhn FED uh RAY shuhn) a united group

legislature (LEJ i slay chuhr) a group that makes laws

Executive Branch (ig ZEK yuh tiv • branch) the branch of the government that includes the President

Legislative Branch (LEJ i slay tiv • branch) the branch of the government that includes Congress

Judicial Branch (joo DISH uhl • branch) the branch of the government that includes federal judges and other officers of the court

MAP ANALYSIS	
★ **Ask**	Where were the 13 original states located?
★ **Analyze**	Why would the area held by the British have been such a threat to America?
★ **Answer**	How might Spain cause problems in trade?

Decoding Tip: Notice how the words are divided into syllables.

ay	*cake*	*ah*	*fall, cot*	*air*	*air*
ee	*tree*	*i*	*sit*	*oh*	*cold*
or	*cord*	*oy*	*toy*	*uh*	*above, hundred*
a	*ask*	*ar*	*hard*	*oo*	*book*
e	*yet*	*eye*	*nice*	*uhr*	*liar, fir, further, color*
ow	*cow*	*ooh*	*boot, true*	*yoo*	*you, few, cube*

20.1 What were the powers granted by the Articles of Confederation?

In May of 1776 the men who made up the Second Continental Congress saw that a central government was needed. The 13 states could not have completely independent governments. Congress wrote the Articles of **Confederation**. After all the states agreed to it, it became law in 1781.

The Articles set up a confederation, or group, of states. Each state had its own government. A national **legislature**, called Congress, made all the laws of the central government. The people in this legislature were elected by the voters in each state. Each state, large or small, had only one vote in Congress.

Many colonists did not want a central government that was too strong. Each state made its own laws. However, certain powers were given to the national legislature. Only Congress could begin a war or make peace with other countries. If states could not agree with each other, Congress could settle their differences. Congress could borrow money for national use. It could also print money and make coins. Congress set up national standards for weight and measurement.

Congress had the power to control all the land outside the states. It had power over the Native Americans living outside

The Articles of Confederation

Powers of Congress	Powers of each state
1. make all laws of central government	1. make own laws, except for making war with other countries
2. settle disagreements between states	2. elect seven members to Congress
3. borrow money for national use	3. have only one vote in Congress
4. ask states for money or troops	4. decide whether or not to send troops
5. control territories	5. decide whether or not to do as Congress wants
6. set up national standards for weights and measurements	

the state borders. Congress also could ask the states for troops to fight wars and money to run the government. If changes were needed in the Articles, all 13 states had to agree.

20.2 What were the weaknesses of this form of government?

Under the Articles, the states had a choice. Each state could decide whether to do as Congress voted. If Congress asked the states for money, they could say no.

Great Britain was a problem. The Treaty of Paris asked that British citizens be paid money owed to them by Americans. The states would not agree, so the British stayed in the United States. They refused to trade with America because they were afraid the states would not obey a trade agreement.

Some of Spain's land included the Mississippi River. Western states could not ship their goods to the East. They needed to sail down the Mississippi, around Florida, and up the east coast. Spain would not let them sail on the river. Congress did not have power to make an agreement with Spain so that American ships could sail on the Mississippi.

Britain sold more goods in America than American manufacturers. Too much money went to Britain instead of the American manufacturers. Congress did not have the power to stop trade with Britain. Some states, like Massachusetts, made laws to stop the sale of British goods in America. However, not all states did the same. The states began to disagree with each other. Congress did not have the power to stop the disagreements.

Congress did not have the power to tax people. America did not have enough money to pay soldiers who fought the Revolution. People who had fought for freedom in America were put into prison because they could not pay their debts.

In 1786, Daniel Shays, a Massachusetts farmer, gathered together soldiers who had lost all their money. As a group, they closed courts to stop collection of debts from people who had no money. Shays' Rebellion was finally stopped. But many people decided that the states had too much power and the national government did not have enough.

20.3 Why was a meeting called in Philadelphia in May 1787?

The Virginia legislature saw a need for changes to the Articles of Confederation. The Virginians asked that a meeting of representatives from every state be held at Annapolis, Maryland. They felt that trade between states and with other countries should be controlled.

The meeting was held in September, 1786. Only five states sent representatives. The most important thing that the group did was ask for a meeting to change the Articles. Congress agreed. The meeting would be held in May, 1787, in Philadelphia.

State legislatures picked the men to attend the meeting in 1787. Each man had spent most of his life either fighting for freedom from Britain or helping to make laws for the country or the states. These men are known as the Founding Fathers.

20.4 What happened in the meeting?

The men talked about how to change the Articles of Confederation. Some wanted no changes at all. Some states wanted a strong national government. The men had long discussions about how this country should be governed. The large states usually disagreed with the small states. Each group wanted changes that would help them but not the other. Both groups decided that a new Constitution was the answer.

20.5 What were the Virginia and New Jersey Plans?

The group from Virginia put together a plan now called the Virginia Plan. In this plan, each state would still have its own government. This plan also suggested that the power of a national government should be limited, but stronger than in the past. The national government would be made up of three

parts, or branches. Power would be divided among the three branches: **Executive Branch**, **Legislative Branch**, and **Judicial Branch**. No branch would have more power than any other branch.

The large states liked the Virginia plan. It gave states with more people more seats in the legislature. The small states became very worried. They put together another plan. The New Jersey Plan gave all states the same num-ber of seats in the legislature. The two sides argued about which plan was best.

▲ The engraving above shows the exterior view of Independence Hall in Philadelphia where the Founding Fathers met for the Constitutional Convention of 1787.

20.6 What would the meeting mean for the new country?

Until the meeting in Philadelphia, the 13 states had been separate. During the summer of 1787, this meeting, now called the Constitutional Convention, would change everything. From this convention would come a Constitution on which all our laws would be based. Instead of 13 individual states, there would now be a strong national government. From this point on, the United States became one country.

☆☆☆

Biography

At 81, Benjamin Franklin was the oldest man at the Constitutional Convention. During his long life, Franklin was one of the best-known people in the United States. He was a printer, a publisher, an inventor, and a scientist. Franklin was also the richest man in the United States.

In addition, he helped start the world's first lending library. He also started a fire department and began a program to pave and light the streets of Philadelphia. He set up the first city hospital.

He signed four of the most important documents of our country's history. First he signed the Declaration of Independence. In Europe, he signed the Treaty of Alliance with France. He signed the Treaty of Paris to end the Revolution and the United States Constitution to set up American government.

Even though he was elderly in 1787, Benjamin Franklin presented arguments that brought about decisions on some of the major points of the Constitution. Franklin settled some of the most important arguments with his wisdom.

▲ Benjamin Franklin

★★☆ CHAPTER REVIEW

Critical Thinking

Write your answers on a sheet of paper, or discuss in class.

 Recognizing Details
1. How did states take away power from Congress under the Articles of Confederation?

Identifying Main Idea
2. What weakness showed that the United States needed a strong national government?

Cooperative Learning

 LEARNING STYLE *Oral*
3. Summarize aloud the information in each section of this chapter. Try to answer the section questions with two-sentence answers.

Write About It

 Writing Portfolio
4. Imagine you are at the Constitutional Convention. Write a letter home telling about some of the arguments you are hearing every day.

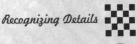

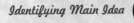

Chapter 21

The Constitution

Powers of Congress

Articles of Confederation

➤ Declare war

➤ Run postal service

➤ Coin money

➤ Set standards of weight and measurement

➤ Make peace treaties

➤ Manage affairs with Native Americans

Constitution

➤ Declare war

➤ Set up the postal service

➤ Coin money

➤ Set standards of weight and measurement

➤ Collect Taxes for public use

➤ Borrow money

➤ Control trade with other countries, among states, and with Native Americans

➤ Establish laws by which people from other countries become citizens

➤ Raise an army and navy

➤ Make the laws that govern this country

Read about a major change in our federal government. What replaced the Articles of Confederation? Why?

Key *Vocabulary*

compromise
(KAHM pruh meyez)
1. an agreement reached when the different sides each give up part of their demands
2. to settle differences by each side giving up something it wants

ratify (RAT uh feye)
to approve

amendment (uh MEND muhnt)
a change

CHART ANALYSIS

★ **Ask** Which powers of Congress are the same for the Articles of Confederation and the Constitution?

★ **Analyze** Which powers did Congress have under the Articles that it does not have today? Which powers does Congress have today that it did not have under the Articles?

★ **Answer** Under which plan is Congress stronger? Explain.

Decoding Tip: Notice how different vowels represent the sound /uh/.

ay	cake	ah	fall, cot	air	air	
ee	tree	i	sit	oh	cold	
or	cord	oy	toy	uh	above, hundred	
a	ask	ar	hard	oo	book	
e	yet	eye	nice	uhr	liar, fir, further, color	
ow	cow	ooh	boot, true	yoo	you, few, cube	

21.1 What was the Great Compromise?

A **compromise** is one way of solving a disagreement. When the Constitution was written in 1787, the writers often disagreed with each other. The biggest disagreement was about how many people each state would have in Congress. This disagreement was solved by the Great Compromise.

The Great Compromise set up Congress in two houses—the House of Representatives and the Senate. The House of Representatives would be elected by the people of each state. The number of representatives from each state would depend on how many people lived in the state. The Senate would be elected by the state legislatures. Each state would send two senators to Congress.

The Great Compromise meant that small states would have fewer representatives in Congress than large states. However, small states would have the same number of senators as large states.

21.2 How did the plan provide for a system of checks and balances?

The men at the Constitutional Convention feared that one branch of the government would have more power than the other branches. They thought that this could become dangerous for the people's freedom. They set up a plan to keep the branches of the government equal in power. This plan is called checks and balances.

The chart on page 129 shows how the system of checks and balances works.

21.3 How did the delegates decide to regulate trade?

Northern states wanted to give the government power to control all trade between the United States and other countries. Southern states were afraid that the national government would stop the slave trade. They were also afraid that the national government would put high taxes on goods imported from other countries. Once again, the states had to compromise.

The national government was given power to control trade between the United States and other countries. It could also control trade between the states themselves. It could place a tax on goods from other countries. Only the national government had these rights.

The national government could not tax goods that were sent from America to other countries. The government also could not stop the slave trade for at least 20 years.

This was a plan for trade that all the states could agree upon.

System of Checks and Balances

Executive Branch (headed by President)

Legislative Branch (Congress)

Judicial Branch (Supreme and Federal Courts)

Executive Branch	Legislative Branch	Judicial Branch
Elected by Electoral College who are chosen by the people	Elected by the people	Chosen by the President
Carries out laws	Makes laws	Must be approved by Senate
Vetoes, or stops, new laws	Amends the Constitution with approval of states	
Makes treaties with other countries	Overturns vetoes with 2/3 vote of Senate	Decides whether or not laws go against the Constitution
Chooses people to head government departments	Must be approved by Senate	
	Must be approved by Senate	

21.4 What were the positions of the Federalists and the Anti-Federalists?

Before the Constitution could become law, it had to be ratified, or approved. One group, called the Federalists, wanted the Constitution to be **ratified**. They felt that a strong national government was good. Some of these people included George Washington, Benjamin Franklin, James Madison, and Alexander Hamilton.

Another group, called the Anti-Federalists, felt that a strong central government would take away the powers of the states. They also thought that people would lose some of their freedoms. They did not want the Constitution to be ratified. Some of these people included Patrick Henry and Samuel Adams.

▲ The illustration above shows a drafted manuscript in James Wilson's handwriting and the only known copy of the first printing of the Constitution of the United States.

21.5 How and when did the Constitution become law?

In late 1787, state legislatures began to vote on the Constitution. Before the end of the year, Delaware, Pennsylvania, and New Jersey had approved it.

In 1788, arguments and elections continued. In that year, Georgia, Connecticut, Massachusetts, Maryland, South Carolina, New Hampshire, Virginia, and New York agreed that the Constitution should be law.

It was not until late 1789 that North Carolina agreed to ratify the Constitution. Rhode Island held out until 1790.

Even though all the states did not approve it until 1790, there were enough states in agreement in 1788 that the Constitution became law then.

☆☆☆

For the People, By the People

Yesterday & TODAY

When the Constitution was first written the Senate was to be elected by state legislatures. This law was in effect until 1919. The Seventeenth **Amendment** changed the way senators were elected.

State legislatures often could not reach a decision and Senate seats were empty. Some states then had only one senator. Also, some senators had bribed state legislators to vote for them. Therefore, the Seventeenth Amendment was ratified. It gave the people the power to elect who they wanted to serve in the Senate. Who are your two senators?

▲ Who are your senators?

★★☆ CHAPTER REVIEW

Critical Thinking

Write your answers on a sheet of paper, or discuss in class.

Making Inferences 1. The government cannot tax goods that the United States sells to other countries. Why is this helpful to the United States' economy?

Making Inferences 2. The government can tax goods from other countries. Why is this also helpful to the United States' economy?

Cooperative Learning

LEARNING STYLE
Reading Writing

3. Write a paragraph that tells the story of each section in this chapter. Try to summarize each section in your paragraph.

Write About It

Writing Portfolio

4. Imagine you are a state legislator from Pennsylvania. Write a letter to your friend who is a state legislator from North Carolina. Tell your friend why you think his state should ratify the Constitution.

For the People, By the People   **The Constitution   Chapter 21** 131

Chapter 22

The Constitution Works

Bill of Rights*

Amendment	Citizens' Rights
FIRST	Freedom of religion, freedom of speech, freedom of the press The right to assemble peacefully The right to petition the government
SECOND	The right to bear arms
THIRD	No troops in people's homes during times of peace
FOURTH	No unreasonable searches and seizures
FIFTH	No taking of life, liberty, or property without due process of law Cannot be retried for the same crime if already found not guilty Cannot be forced to testify against yourself
SIXTH	The right to a speedy and public trial The right to a trial by jury and to call and question witnesses The right to be informed of the nature and cause of the accusation The right to have the assistance of a lawyer
SEVENTH	The right to bring cases between individuals without government involvement The right to trial by jury if more than $20 is involved
EIGHTH	No excessive bails or fines No cruel or unusual punishment
NINTH	Have all other rights not listed in the Constitution
TENTH	The right of states and/or the people to have any powers that are not given to the federal government and not forbidden to the states by the Constitution

* Two other Amendments were sent to the 13 states. They were not ratified. One would require that each member of the House represent 50,000 people. The other would keep Congress from raising its pay.

Read about the way the American government was shaped. Some Americans took sides over government. Why?

Key *Vocabulary*

appeal (uh PEEL) a review by a higher court of a case tried earlier in a lower court

capital (KAP uh tuhl) the city in which government is centered

invest (in VEST) to use money so that profits are earned

political (puh LIT i kuhl) trying to affect or control government decisions

Reteaching Vocabulary
compromise (KAHM pruh meyez) an agreement reached when the different sides each give up part of their demands

CHART ANALYSIS

★ **Ask** What does the title tell you about the contents of the chart?

★ **Acquire** The asterisk tells you that there is a note at the bottom of the chart. What does the note tell you about the Bill of Rights?

★ **Analyze** What is the purpose of the Bill of Rights?

★ **Answer** Why did the people feel it was necessary to list their rights in the Constitution?

Decoding Tip: Note that *a* and *e* can both stand for the same sound.

ay	cake	ah	fall, cot	air	air
ee	tree	i	sit	oh	cold
or	cord	oy	toy	uh	above, hundred
a	ask	ar	hard	oo	book
e	yet	eye	nice	uhr	liar, fir, further, color
ow	cow	ooh	boot, true	yoo	you, few, cube

22.1 What were the results of the first elections in 1788?

George Washington was elected President. John Adams became Vice President. Both were Federalists. Federalists also won most of the seats in Congress. The House of Representatives looked for ways of raising money. The work of the government would have to be paid for. Taxes on goods were proposed. The North wanted taxes that would be good for businesses. The South wanted taxes that would be good for farmers. A **compromise** was reached. Everyone would pay these taxes. However, other countries would pay higher taxes. Rhode Island and North Carolina decided to ratify the Constitution. They were no longer foreign countries. Now they wouldn't have to pay the higher taxes.

The Senate set up the federal court system. Each state has a federal court. These courts can try only cases that involve federal laws. All other cases are tried by state courts. Congress set up district courts. These courts hear **appeals** from federal courts. They also hear cases involving two or more states. Finally, the first Supreme Court was set up. It had six members. The Supreme Court decides if new laws follow the Constitution. Each justice would also be a member of a district court.

The people wanted a list of their rights. The Federalists had promised such a list if the Constitution was ratified. Now it was time to carry out that promise. Many amendments were suggested. The states sent 78 to Congress. Only 12 made the final list. It was sent to the states. The states ratified only 10 amendments in 1791. They are known as "the Bill of Rights."

22.2 What effect did the Cabinet have on government?

The House of Representatives set up different departments. They would carry out the business of the government. The

House put the President in charge of all these offices. However, the Senate had to approve the President's choices. Washington chose Alexander Hamilton as Secretary of the Treasury. Thomas Jefferson was the Secretary of State. Henry Knox became the Secretary of War. Edmund Randolph was Attorney General. Washington made sure these people were from different states. Some were Federalists and some were Anti-Federalists. Washington hoped this would keep the government united. He came to depend on these leaders for advice and help. They became known as "the Cabinet."

Freedom had been won at a large price. Over $50 million had been borrowed to pay for the war. The states had borrowed about $20 million, too. Most of this money was owed to business people. Alexander Hamilton wanted the U.S. government to pay the states' debts. This would make business people strong supporters of the federal government. Thomas Jefferson and other Anti-Federalists thought this plan was unfair. Most of the debts were owed by the northern states. Why should the South help pay debts it didn't owe?

Jefferson worked out a compromise about the national debt. He invited Hamilton and other leaders to dinner. They reached an agreement. Jefferson would help put Hamilton's plan into law. Hamilton would help move the country's **capital**. Philadelphia would be the capital for 10 years. Then it would be moved to a spot in the South. Maryland and Virginia each gave up land. It became the District of Columbia. The capital was built there. It was named Washington City. Now it is known as Washington, D.C.

22.3 What did George Washington's talks with France, Spain, and Great Britain achieve?

The people of France began fighting their king in 1789. Many Americans were happy to see that other people shared their ideas. However, they were shocked when King Louis XVI was killed. After all, Louis XVI had helped the U.S. win its war with Great Britain. Britain and Spain went to war with France. President Washington wrote a special letter in 1793. He said that the United States would not take sides. However, both France and Britain began capturing American ships. They wanted to pull the U.S. into the war.

Washington did not want a new war. He sent delegates to Europe. Some terms were reached in 1795. Britain would stop taking American ships and sailors. It would pull the last of its troops out of the Northwest Territory. Spain and the U.S. set up the exact border between Florida and Georgia. Americans could sail along the Mississippi River. They could trade with Spain's colonies, too. No terms were reached with France.

22.4   Why did two political parties develop?

Alexander Hamilton and Thomas Jefferson had different ideas. Hamilton thought that only rich and wise men should run the government. Jefferson felt that the government should be run by all men who were U.S. citizens. Hamilton wanted to set up a federal bank. It would collect taxes and **invest** the money. Most of the bank would be sold as shares. Jefferson knew that only the rich would be able to buy these shares. A few rich people would then control the government's money. He felt they would become too powerful. Jefferson and his followers formed a second **political** party. They called themselves Democratic-Republicans. They would fight for the rights of the people and of the states.

President Washington wanted to know if the Constitution allowed a federal bank. He asked Hamilton and Jefferson to write about their beliefs. Hamilton said the bank could be set up because it was necessary. The Constitution said the federal government could do anything that was "necessary and proper." Jefferson said the federal government had only those powers listed in the Constitution. It said nothing about banks, so a federal bank could not be set up.

Washington felt that a federal bank was necessary. He helped set up the bank. However, he worried about taking too much power for the federal government. The Democratic-Republicans worked against the bank. Their ideas were printed in some newspapers. Other papers carried the ideas of the Federalists. Washington thought this was a problem, too. He did not like the idea of political parties. Fights between them might hurt the country. This argument about the powers of the government and about political parties still goes on today.

Biography

▲ Benjamin Banneker

Benjamin Banneker was an African American from Maryland. He had been born in 1731. However, he had never been a slave. He had been born free. Banneker had studied hard to become a scientist. He studied math and the stars. A teacher once showed him a watch. He found a picture of a clock. He used them to make his own clock. He made it out of wood. It worked for almost 50 years.

George Washington chose the spot for the District of Columbia. Plans for the city were drawn by Pierre L'Enfant. Andrew Endicott and five others laid out the city. One of these men was Benjamin Banneker. Later, Endicott left his job. He took all the plans for the city. Banneker went to work. He redrew this set of plans. All he had to go on was his memory. The city of Washington was built with Banneker's plans.

 CHAPTER REVIEW

Critical Thinking

Write your answers on a sheet of paper, or discuss in class.

Drawing Conclusions 1. How did George Washington prove that he was a good choice as the first President of the United States?

Comparing and Contrasting 2. Why did differences in ideas help divide the country?

Cooperative Learning

 3. Work with a study partner or as part of a study group. Look at the beginning of this chapter. Read the Bill of Rights. Copy this list on a sheet of paper. Decorate your copy with pictures that illustrate each right. Display your copy in the classroom.

Write About It

 4. Imagine that you are a Federalist or a Democratic-Republican. Think about the beliefs you would hold. Make a list of these beliefs. Write a few sentences that suggest laws that would put these beliefs into effect.

Chapter 23

A New Crisis

British Canada

Vermont
(1791)

Maine
(1788)

New York
(1788)

New Hampshire
(1788)

Mass. (1788)

Rhode Island
(1790)

Pennsylvania
(1787)

Conn.
(1788)

Ohio
(1803)

Northwest Terr.

New Jersey
(1787)

Delaware
(1787)

Maryland
(1788)

Virginia
(1788)

Kentucky
(1792)

Louisiana
(Bought from France in 1803)

Tennessee
(1796)

North Carolina
(1789)

South Carolina
(1788)

Mississippi Territory

Georgia
(1788)

Appalachian Mtns.

Spanish Florida

Mississippi River

STATES OF THE USA
(1803)

Read about the country's earliest political parties. They had a strong effect on the country? Why?

Key *Vocabulary*

immigrant (IM i gruhnt) a person who moves to another country in order to live there

nullify (NUHL uh feye) to strike down or cancel

ballot (BAL uht) the time when a vote is held

expire (ik SPEYER) to end; to run out

MAP ANALYSIS		
★ **Ask**	The 13 colonies could only become states by ratifying the Constitution. Which were the first to become states?	
★ **Analyze**	New York and New Hampshire gave up their claims to the same piece of land. Which state was formed from these lands in 1791?	
★ **Answer**	The Constitution was fully ratified in 1788. How did land west of the Appalachian Mountains become states?	

Decoding Tip: Notice the sound *a* stands for in the vocabulary words.

ay	cake	ah	fall, cot	air	air
ee	tree	i	sit	oh	cold
or	cord	oy	toy	uh	above, hundred
a	ask	ar	hard	oo	book
e	yet	eye	nice	uhr	liar, fir, further, color
ow	cow	ooh	boot, true	yoo	you, few, cube

▲ President John Adams

23.1 What were the results of John Adams's attempts to avoid war with France?

French attacks on American ships led to calls for war. France had been capturing American ships. American sailors were forced to work on French ships. In 1797, France said that it would hang any American found working on a British ship. John Adams had become President after George Washington. President Adams did not want war with France. He sent representatives to France. Three French officials wanted a $250,000 bribe. Then talks could begin. The U.S. representatives became very angry. They left France instead. The three French officials were never named. They were called "X," "Y," and "Z." This crisis was called the "XYZ Affair."

In America, the two political parties could not agree on ways of dealing with France. President Adams and some Federalists wanted peace. Thomas Jefferson and the Democratic-Republicans also wanted a peaceful answer. However, Alexander Hamilton and most Federalists in Congress wanted war. Taxes were raised. The money bought new ships, arms, and ammunition. The Department of the Navy was formed in 1798.

Actual war was never declared against France. However, the two countries' navies met in several battles. They fought between 1798 and 1799. Napoleon Bonaparte took over the French government in 1799. He wanted to end the fighting. Bonaparte agreed to new talks. Peace terms were reached in 1800.

23.2 Why were the Alien and Sedition Acts the result of party politics?

Federalists used the excitement over war for their own ends. They moved to crush the Democratic-Republicans. Federalists in Congress passed the Alien and Sedition Acts in 1798. Three of these laws kept **immigrants** from becoming citizens easily.

▲ Vice President and later, President Thomas Jefferson

Most new citizens had been joining the Democratic-Republican party. The fourth law made it a crime to criticize the President or the government. Anyone who did was put into jail. Many were Democratic-Republican leaders. Others were people who put out newspapers with Democratic-Republican ideas.

Thomas Jefferson and James Madison worked to kill the Alien and Sedition Acts. They fought for the people's rights. They felt these Acts took away rights and freedoms promised in the Bill of Rights. Both men felt that the states could nullify federal acts. They wrote about their beliefs. Virginia and Kentucky passed laws to **nullify** the Alien and Sedition Acts. However, no other states would agree. These ideas led to the strong states' rights movement that continues even today.

23.3 How did the Election of 1800 lead to the 12th Amendment to the Constitution?

No one wanted a repeat of the Election of 1796. John Adams and Thomas Jefferson had been elected President and

Presidential Elections

Year	Name	Position	Party	Electoral Votes	Result
1796	John Adams	President	Federalist	71	President
	Thomas Pinckney	Vice President	Federalist	Unknown	not elected
	Thomas Jefferson	President	Democratic-Republican	68	Vice President
	Aaron Burr	Vice President	Democratic-Republican	unknown	not elected
1800	John Adams	President	Federalist	65	not elected
	Charles Coatsworth Pinckney	Vice President	Federalist	64	not elected
	Thomas Jefferson	President	Democratic-Republican	73	President
	Aaron Burr	Vice President	Democratic-Republican	73	Vice President

NOTE: *Person with most Electoral Votes becomes President. Person with second-highest number of Electoral Votes becomes Vice President. In case of a tie, House of Representatives elects the President and Vice President.*

Vice President. Adams and Jefferson belonged to different parties. People decided the President and Vice President should be from the same party. The members of the Electoral College promised to stand by their parties. The Democratic-Republicans won the most votes. However, they voted for both offices at the same time. This led to a tie between Thomas Jefferson and Aaron Burr.

Breaking the tie led to a new amendment to the Constitution. The Constitution gave the House of Representatives the power to break such a tie. It voted along party lines. The tie held for 35 separate ballots. Alexander Hamilton had never liked Burr. He finally decided to vote for Jefferson. Jefferson was elected President. Burr became Vice President. However, he had worked with the Federalists for a chance to be President. Burr was never trusted again by Jefferson or the Democratic-Republicans.

No one wanted such a thing to happen again. The 12th Amendment to the Constitution was ratified. Now, the Electors would vote for the President and Vice President on separate ballots.

23.4   How did President Jefferson's new ideas about government affect the nation?

President Jefferson did not rush to make a lot of changes. He felt that would harm the country. He kept many Federalist laws. However, he did cut back on the army. Most Americans still feared a large army. They remembered how Britain had used its army to take away their rights.

Jefferson and the Democratic-Republicans would not renew the Alien and Sedition Acts. The Acts were allowed to **expire**. Those people who had been jailed were set free. Any fines they had paid were returned.

The Democratic-Republicans wanted a limited federal government. They accidentally increased the power of the

Supreme Court, though. The Federalists had set up many new offices for federal judges. In his last few days as President, Adams wrote letters appointing these new judges. Secretary of State James Madison was to send the letters. However, the Democratic-Republicans in Congress did away with these offices.

Jefferson told Madison not to send out Adams' letters. One was for William Marbury. Marbury sued Madison in the Supreme Court. He asked the Court to order Madison to send out the letters. The Judiciary Act of 1789 gave the Court this power. However, the Supreme Court said that this power went against the Constitution. Marbury lost his case. But the Supreme Court had put a new idea in place. The Supreme Court has the highest power to decide when laws go against the Constitution.

▲ President Thomas Jefferson

Yesterday...

Thomas Jefferson led the Democratic-Republican party. It changed during the 1800s. However, its strongest belief was in states' rights. Its members wanted a limited form of federal government.

Today...

The Democratic-Republican party became the Democratic party. It changed its ideas in the middle 1900s. Today's Democrats support the idea of a strong federal government. Jefferson would not have approved of this idea.

★★☆ CHAPTER REVIEW

Critical Thinking

Write your answers on a sheet of paper, or discuss in class.

1. How did President Jefferson sometimes act like a Federalist?

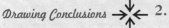

2. Why did George Washington's fears about the dangers of political parties seem to come true?

Cooperative Learning

LEARNING
STYLE
Oral

3. Work with a study partner or as part of a study group. Write these words on separate pieces of paper: Federalist, John Adams, Thomas Jefferson, Democratic-Republican, James Madison, William Marbury. Put the papers in a box. Take turns drawing pieces of paper from the box. Read the name you have drawn. Tell what this person was like. Also tell about the person's ideas.

Write About It

Writing Portfolio

4. Imagine that you are a citizen of the late 1700s. You have just heard about the XYZ Affair. Write a letter to the editor of your local newspaper. Write about your feelings and opinions. Add your letter to those of the rest of the class. Turn them into a booklet for display.

Chapter 24

The War of 1812

EARLY BATTLES OF THE WAR OF 1812 (1812-1814)

British Ship Forming Blockade

Read about the War of 1812. What part did shipping and trade play in the war? Why?

Key *Vocabulary*

impressment (im PRES muhnt) the act of taking sailors from other ships to work on your own ship

blockade (blah KAYD) the act of using ships on a country's coast to keep other ships from bringing in goods

invade (in VAYD) to attack another country by crossing its borders

militia (muh LISH uh) a state or local army made up of regular citizens.

crusade (kroo SAYD) a spirited plan to do something or change something

---

MAP ANALYSIS

This map shows the British blockade of the United States. Read the meaning of the word blockade in the vocabulary. Then answer the questions below.

★ **Ask** Is any part of the United States free from the blockade?

★ **Analyze** Which states would be most affected by the blockade?

★ **Answer** Would lots of ships be needed to carry out this blockade? Explain your answer.

Decoding Tip: Note that the vowel *a* has a long sound when followed by a consonant and a silent *e*.

ay	cake	ah	fall, cot	air	air
ee	tree	i	sit	oh	cold
or	cord	oy	toy	uh	above, hundred
a	ask	ar	hard	oo	book
e	yet	eye	nice	uhr	liar, fir, further, color
ow	cow	ooh	boot, true	yoo	you, few, cube

24.1   Why did the United States become angry with Britain?

In 1807 Britain passed laws that hurt American shipping. The laws were called Orders in Council. They angered many Americans. The laws kept American ships from going straight to France. Ships had to go to a British port first. They had to pay fees. Some were taken over. American trade with Europe had been growing. Now, that trade was in trouble. The United States was already angry with Britain. British ships had been taking British-born sailors off other ships. This was called **impressment**. Sometimes American sailors were taken by mistake. Feelings against the British ran high.

Why did the British pass the new laws? They were fighting France's leader, Napoleon. Napoleon wanted to take over Europe. He already controlled much of it. But Britain's navy held him off. Now British ships began a **blockade** of Europe. They tried to keep supplies from reaching France. This meant keeping out American ships, too.

24.2   Why did the War Hawks want to fight Britain?

The War Hawks were members of Congress who pushed for war with Britain. They were led by Henry Clay of Kentucky and John C. Calhoun of South Carolina. The War Hawks were young and full of fire. They came from the South and the West. They wanted to help Americans move west onto new land. But people were afraid of attacks by Native Americans. The British in Canada backed the Native Americans. Some said the British had brought the tribes together. In truth, Tecumseh and other Native Americans had done that themselves. But the War Hawks blamed Britain.

Not everyone agreed with the War Hawks. New England was against a war. New England shipping was hurt by Britain's new laws. But many in New England favored Britain against

France. The vote for war was close. In the Senate it was 19 to 13. The House voted 79 to 49. Two days before the vote, Britain's Parliament took back the Orders in Council. It was too late. By the time word got through, the war had started.

24.3 Where did most of the War of 1812 take place?

▼ Sailors and officers engaging in combat during a battle at sea.

Most of the war was fought near the Canadian border. The United States tried to **invade** Canada. The Americans thought a quick knockout punch could work. They knew Britain was busy fighting the French in Europe. Britain's power in America was not great. But the United States was also weak. It was not ready for war. Its army was small. Its navy had only 20 ships. Most of the war's early battles were won by the British.

First came the fall of Detroit. That was in August 1812. American troops crossed the Detroit River into Canada. But the British pushed them back into Detroit. There they were surrounded. Detroit was taken by the British. The United States lost two forts in the area. American armies also lost at Queenston Heights and Lake Champlain. The state **militia** groups were to blame. They would not cross into Canada to fight. Trying to invade Canada was a big mistake.

▶ The illustration to the right shows ships engaged in war at sea during the early 1800s.

24.4   Why did the British control the war at sea?

The British navy was the strongest in the world. It controlled the seas through numbers alone. The British had 1,000 fighting ships. The United States had less than 20. British ships set up a blockade of American ports. No ships could get through. American trade almost stopped. The United States couldn't collect money on goods brought in. The country went further into debt.

The United States did win some battles at sea. Small American ships were well armed. Their captains didn't waste a shot. In close fighting they could defeat much larger ships. The *Constitution* won several battles. It seemed impossible to sink. Its nickname was "Old Ironsides." In 1813 Oliver Hazard Perry won the battle of Lake Erie. His ships beat a small British fleet. In 1814 Thomas MacDonough took control of Lake Champlain. He lined up his ships in a narrow channel. Britain's ships had to sail close to the Americans. American guns pounded them. McDonough won in a little over two hours. The British had to pull back into Canada.

Biography

▲ Tecumseh

Tecumseh (1765?-1813) was a Shawnee chief and a great Native American leader. He tried to bring together Native Americans in the east. He urged them to defend their lands from white people. Tecumseh and his brother started a **crusade**. They worked to save Native American lands. They urged Native Americans not to take on the ways of whites. Tecumseh traveled all over. He spoke to Native Americans about the need to work together. He attacked those chiefs who had sold land on their own. He said the land belonged to everyone. It was not their land to sell.

"Sell a country! Why not sell the air, the clouds and the great sea, as well as the earth? Did not the Great Spirit make them all for the use of his children?"

—Tecumseh

Tecumseh was a powerful speaker. He was also a great fighter. In the War of 1812 he fought on the British side. As a general, he led a large force. Tecumseh hoped to win back land for his people. In October 1813, Tecumseh fought in the Battle of the Thames. He would not retreat with the British. He and his men stood and fought. No one saw how Tecumseh died. After his death, Britain lost the help of Native Americans in the war. Tecumseh lived on in the minds of his people.

★★☆ CHAPTER REVIEW

Critical Thinking

Write your answers on a sheet of paper, or discuss in class.

Analyzing Cause and Effect

Making Inferences

1. How did Britain's war with France affect American trade?

2. A large number of Americans were against the War of 1812. Would this have made it harder to fight the war? Why or why not?

Cooperative Learning

LEARNING STYLE
Kinesthetic Tactile

3. Voting in Congress is an important job. Imagine voting on whether to go to war. Work with a group to come up with a "yes or no" question. Make it a question about something in the news. Then make a ballot box from a shoebox or something like it. Have each member write *yes* or *no* on a slip of paper. Tell them to fold their slips. Then let them drop the slips in the box. Count the votes carefully. Then tell the group which side won.

Write About It

Writing Portfolio

4. Think about the reasons for and against the War of 1812. Write three reasons for going to war with Britain. Then write three reasons not to fight the war.

Chapter 25

New Reputation in the World

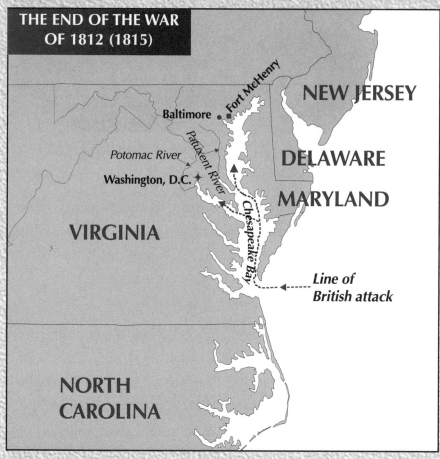

THE END OF THE WAR OF 1812 (1815)

Fort McHenry

Baltimore

NEW JERSEY

Potomac River

Patuxent River

DELAWARE

Washington, D.C.

MARYLAND

Chesapeake Bay

VIRGINIA

← Line of British attack

NORTH CAROLINA

Read about the end of the War of 1812. How did the war change the United States in the eyes of the world? Why?

Key *Vocabulary*

revenge (ri VENJ) taking action against someone in return for something they have done

expert (EKS puhrt) someone who is excellent at some skill

veteran (VET uh ruhn) older and well tested

reservation (rez uhr VAY shuhn) land set aside for a group of people to live on

secession (suh SESH uhn) the act of leaving or breaking away from a group or country

MAP ANALYSIS

★ **Ask** Why did the British sail up the Potomac River to attack Washington, D.C.?

★ **Analyze** What troubles do you see in defending Washington, D.C. and Baltimore?

★ **Answer** Could the United States have defended these cities better with a larger navy? Explain your answer.

Decoding Tip: Note the sound of short *e* in these vocabulary words.

ay	cake	ah	fall, cot	air	air
ee	tree	i	sit	oh	cold
or	cord	oy	toy	uh	above, hundred
a	ask	ar	hard	oo	book
e	yet	eye	nice	uhr	liar, fir, further, color
ow	cow	ooh	boot, true	yoo	you, few, cube

The illustration at right is called the *Capture of the City of Washington,* and it shows the buildings in Washington being destroyed in 1814.

25.1 What did the British do to Washington, D.C., and to Ft. McHenry?

In 1814, the British stormed into Washington, D.C. They set fire to many buildings. Even the Capitol and the White House were burned down. President James Madison had to leave the city. So did others in the government. How could such a thing happen?

By April 1814, the French emperor Napoleon Bonaparte had been defeated in Europe. Britain could now send thousands to fight in America. The British generals wanted to keep American troops from gathering at Canada's line. To do this, the British attacked on the east coast. Their ships moved up the Chesapeake Bay and the Potomac River. American troops couldn't stop the British. At Washington, D.C., the British took **revenge** for an American action. The year before, American troops had burned York (now Toronto) in Canada. Americans were shocked by the British attack. Some were ashamed that their capital had been burned. President Madison named a new Secretary of War, James Monroe.

The British marched on to Baltimore and Fort McHenry. There the Americans did better. They fought hard. Fort McHenry was bombarded by British guns. The firing lasted all night. At dawn, the American flag was still flying. Francis Scott Key saw it from a boat. The sight filled him with pride. Key later wrote "The Star-Spangled Banner."

25.2   Who won the Battle of New Orleans?

▲ A young Andrew Jackson

The Battle of New Orleans was a great victory for the United States. It was fought on January 8, 1815. The battle made Andrew Jackson an American hero. Jackson was in charge of American troops in the Southwest. His job was to keep control of the Mississippi River. A British fleet was sailing from Jamaica to take it. Jackson ordered his men to pile up cotton bales. They set up the piles in long lines. Then the men dropped behind the piles and waited. They were rifle **experts** from Kentucky and Tennessee. The British marched straight into Jackson's trap. On January 8, 1815, Jackson's men opened fire. The cotton bales protected them. In a half hour it was over. More than 2,000 British soldiers were killed or hurt. These were **veteran** soldiers. They had helped stop Napoleon in Europe. But they were no match for Jackson's troops.

News of the American victory went all over the country. Many Americans were proud. But the battle wasn't needed. A peace treaty had been signed 15 days before. The battle took place after the war was over.

25.3   What were the terms of the Treaty of Ghent?

The Treaty of Ghent was an agreement to end the war. It made no real changes. It put things back as they were before the war. Prisoners were set free. Both sides gave up the land they had won. Disputes over boundary lines were put off to a later date. The treaty ended three years of fighting. It didn't do much else.

At first, Britain had wanted more. It wanted the United States to give up land in the north. It wanted to set up a large reservation for Native Americans. Then the United States won some battles. The British changed their minds. They had been through many years of war. Peace was more important than getting land. Both sides wanted the war to end. They met in Ghent, a town in Belgium. The meetings began in August 1814. Nothing was said about the British taking sailors from other ships. Nothing was said about trade or blockades. On December 24, 1814, the treaty was signed.

25.4 What happened at the Hartford Convention?

The Hartford Convention was a meeting of Federalists in New England. They met in Hartford, Connecticut. It was December 1814. Fighting was still going on. The New England Federalists had been against the war from the start. They said the war had hurt shipping in New England. At secret meetings, they talked about leaving the United States. This is called **secession**. New England would become a separate country. They talked about making their own peace with Britain.

In the end, the Federalists took a smaller step. They said the government should not be so free to make war or stop trade. Three days after the Hartford Convention, the Battle of New Orleans was fought. Pride in America's troops turned to anger at the Hartford group. People thought they wanted to quit the United States. They called the Federalists traitors. The Federalist Party fell apart in the next two years.

How was the United States changed by the war? It had not lost or gained any land. But it had held its own against a great power. The United States had grown more important in the eyes of the world.

☆☆☆

Yesterday & TODAY

Yesterday...

Imagine that telephones were around in 1812. If this were true, the War of 1812 might never have happened. The war was fought over trade laws passed by the British. However, Britain offered to change those laws. This was two days before the fighting started. But word traveled slowly. Messages had to come by ship. They sometimes took weeks to arrive. By the time American leaders heard, the war was on. A telephone also could have stopped the Battle of New Orleans.

Peace was signed 15 days before it was fought. Again the message was slow to come.

Today...

Today messages arrive in seconds, not weeks. An attack can be stopped at the last moment. It only takes a telephone call. For years there was a "red phone" in the White House. The President could call the leader of the Soviet Union at once. They could talk·about

urgent trouble spots. Cable TV has also sped up messages. Cable TV was important in the Persian Gulf War. Iraq's leader Saddam Hussein watched cable TV news. So did America's leaders. They listened to what the other side was saying. They sent messages through reporters. The world could see history being made.

★★☆ CHAPTER REVIEW

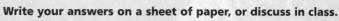

Critical Thinking

Write your answers on a sheet of paper, or discuss in class.

Analyzing Cause and Effect

1. Why did Britain attack Washington, D.C. and Baltimore?

Drawing Conclusions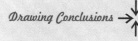

2. Was the War of 1812 necessary? Explain your answer.

Cooperative Learning

LEARNING STYLE
Visual

3. Make a timeline of the War of 1812. Show the important events of the war. These may be battles and other events. Study your timeline to see how one event led to another.

Write About It

Writing Portfolio

4. Choose one of the events from the War of 1812. Write a song about it. Use strong images, as in "The Star-Spangled Banner." If you wish, make up a tune for your song. You might even sing it for the class.

Quiz

Number a piece of paper from 1–10. Write a, b, c, and d beside these numbers. Read the following sentence beginnings. Four endings follow each one. Choose the ending that best completes the sentence. On your paper, circle the letter that matches the letter of your answer. Be sure you mark your answer beside the correct number.

1. **Saratoga was the turning point of the Revolutionary War because the . . .**
   a. British were driven back into Canada.
   b. French decided to help the United States.
   c. British saw that they could lose the war.
   d. both b and c.

2. **The British finally surrendered at . . .**
   a. Cowpens.
   b. Charleston.
   c. Guilford Court House.
   d. Yorktown.

3. **The Articles of Confederation were replaced because they . . .**
   a. gave too much power to the states.
   b. gave too much power to Congress.
   c. were never accepted by all the states.
   d. both a and c.

4. **Our Founding Fathers met to change the Articles of Confederation, but instead they . . .**
   a. brought about a new war with Britain.
   b. decided to keep the Articles.
   c. wrote the Constitution.
   d. both a and c.

5. **To protect Americans' freedoms and rights, the Constitution set up a system that . . .**
   a. balances the powers of government among the branches.
   b. makes each branch's powers the same.
   c. forces the states to keep a check on the balance of power.
   d. all of the above.

6. **The Constitution took over when the states . . .**
   a. elected the members of Congress.
   b. ratified the Constitution.
   c. ratified the Bill of Rights.
   d. signed the Articles of the Constitution.

7. **Federalists set up the offices of government, but Democratic-Republicans . . .**
   a. refused to take any of these offices.
   b. were elected to all of these offices.
   c. set up the U.S. court system.
   d. feared the federal government would be too strong.

8. **Democratic-Republicans took power when . . .**
   a. the people learned that the Alien and Sedition Acts took away their rights.
   b. Federalist judges ruled that voting had been crooked.
   c. Federalist leaders were jailed for breaking the Alien and Sedition Acts.
   d. the war with France was settled by President Jefferson.

9. **The War of 1812 was fought because the British were a danger to American . . .**
   a. towns in the East.
   b. towns in the West.
   c. trade.
   d. farming.

10. **After the War of 1812, the United States' borders . . .**
    a. did not change.
    b. moved farther west.
    c. moved north into Canada.
    d. took in Maine.

ANALYZING CAUSE AND EFFECT

Add numbers 11–15 to your paper. Read the ideas below. The ideas on the left describe a cause, or something that makes a second event happen. The ideas on the right are effects, the events that are caused. Match these causes and effects. Write your answers beside the correct numbers on your paper.

11. To protect the rights they had fought so hard to gain, . . .
12. A promise to add a list of rights to the Constitution caused. . .
13. Because France and Britain were at war, . . .
14. Since Federalists supported a strong federal government, . . .
15. After winning two wars against Britain, . . .

a. most states to ratify the Constitution by 1788.
b. the 13 states to set up a weak government under the Articles of Confederation.
c. most Americans felt a strong sense of pride in their country by the 1820s.
d. Democratic-Republicans fought against their ideas as dangerous to the people's rights.
e. American ships could not trade safely in Europe.

Look over the things you wrote for these chapters. Choose one that you like the best. Add to your writing. For example, you wrote a diary entry about being with General Washington's troops. Imagine that it is now the year 1788. The Constitution has just been ratified. Write a diary entry telling how you feel about the Constitution. Also, tell if the war was worth the effort to achieve the ideas in the Constitution. Trade papers with a study partner. Check each other's work. Make a clean, neat copy. Put it in your portfolio.

You may wish to work with a study partner. Write the names Federalist and Democratic-Republican at the top of a piece of paper. Look through the chapters to find out facts about these people. Make a chart with these facts. List the facts under the headings on your paper. Put facts that are alike in the same row. For example, one row of facts might show how these people feel about the power of the federal government. Another row might show their ideas about the size of the country's army. Note that by reading each row you can tell how the people are alike and how they are different. Share your chart with the class. Combine this chart with the one you prepared in the Mid-Unit 3 Review.

COOPERATIVE PROJECT: LIVING TABLEAUS

Work with a group. Make a list of important events included in these chapters. Discuss what the people did and how they probably acted. Work with your group to draw a picture of what the event looked like. Choose the roles of the people involved. Set up the front of the class with any chairs, tables, etc., that you might need. Stand in the poses shown in your picture. See if the class can guess what event you are presenting. If possible, take photographs of each group's presentation. Write a caption for each photo. Display the photos and captions in the classroom.

Unit 4

POLITICS

► **1803**
The United States bought the Louisiana Territory from France. The size of the country almost doubled.

► **1810**
West Florida joined the United States after becoming independent of Spain.

► **1820**
The Missouri Compromise set the boundaries between slave states and free states.

► **1821**
The Florida peninsula was bought by the United States from Spain.

► **1823**
President James Monroe explain the ideas of the Monroe Doctrin Now, the United States would n allow Europe to interfere with either North or South America.

CE   1800   1820

1789
Samuel Slater built the first spinning factory.

► **1793**
Eli Whitney invented the cotton gin.

◄ **1806**
Lewis and Clark returned from their exploration of Louisiana and the lands that reach to the Pacific Ocean.

► **1807**
Robert Fulton's steamship *Clermont* traveled from Albany to New York City.

► **1825**
Workers completed the 363-r long Erie Canal that joined A to Buffalo, New York.

The first American steam eng built by John Stevens, ran on track in Hoboken, New Jerse

CULTURE

Expansion and Reform 1801 - 1861

Developing the nation became extremely important during the first half of the 1800s. New ideas spread across the growing country. How did the country and its people change during these years? Why?

"One country, one constitution, one destiny. "

— **Daniel Webster**
March 15, 1837

1828
The Tariff of 1828 split the Democratic-Republicans. The Democratic party was formed to fight this tariff.

1830
The Removal Bill was used to move Native Americans out of the Southeast and to lands that are now Arkansas and Oklahoma.

1836
Texas won its war to become a country independent of Mexico.

1845
Congress admitted Texas to the union as a state. Border disputes brought about the Mexican-American War.

1848
Peace talks settled the Mexican-American War. The United States gained lands that became California, Nevada, Utah, New Mexico, and Arizona. Britain and the United States agreed to the boundary between Oregon Territory and Canada.

1830

1840

1850

1830
America's first passenger train began service in South Carolina.

1840
Transcendentalists began a new magazine, *The Dial.* It discussed a new kind of writing based on feelings rather than ideas.

1841
Edgar Allan Poe published "The Murders in the Rue Morgue," one of the first detective stories.

1844
An American artist, Samuel F .B. Morse, invented the telegraph.

1846
Elias Howe built the first sewing machine.

1847
The Post Office put out the first national postage stamps.

1849
Henry David Thoreau wrote against the Mexican-American War in *Civil Disobedience.*

1858
Cyrus Field laid a telegraph cable across the Atlantic Ocean from the U.S. to Europe.

Chapter 26

The Nation Grows

UNITED STATES AND THE LOUISIANA PURCHASE (1803)

BRITISH CANADA

LOUISIANA TERRITORY (Purchased from France in 1803)

MICHIGAN TERRITORY (1800)

INDIANA TERRITORY (1800)

UNITED STATES

MISSISSIPPI TERRITORY (1804-1812)

NEW SPAIN

SPANISH FLORIDA

WEST FLORIDA (1810-1819)

0   250   500 Miles

N W E S

Read about land that was added to the United States. How did France cause the United States to grow? Why?

Key *Vocabulary*

shipping (SHIP eng) the act of moving goods by boat or ship

enslaved (in SLAYVD) in a state of being owned by another person

Reteaching Vocabulary

empire (EHM peyer) a nation that is made up of many areas and people; ruled by a king or queen known as an emperor or empress

treaty (TREE tee) a written agreement reached by two or more countries

MAP ANALYSIS

★ **Ask**   Which territories were created from the Northwest Territory?

★ **Analyze** When did the United States double in size?

★ **Answer**   How would pioneers and immigrants probably feel about this growth of the country?

Decoding Tip: Note the sounds *e* can stand for.

ay	cake	ah	fall, cot	air	air
ee	tree	i	sit	oh	cold
or	cord	oy	toy	uh	above, hundred
a	ask	ar	hard	oo	book
e	yet	eye	nice	uhr	liar, fir, further, color
ow	cow	ooh	boot, true	yoo	you, few, cube

26.1 Why did the transfer of Louisiana from Spain to France cause danger for the United States?

France's wars in Europe seemed likely to spread to both of the Americas. France was led by Napoleon Bonaparte. He wanted to take over Europe. He wanted an **empire** in the Americas, too. Spain was forced to give Louisiana to France. The United States feared this act. France was a stronger country than Spain. Some Americans feared that France might stop American **shipping** on the Mississippi River. President Jefferson sent an offer to Bonaparte. The United States would buy the city of New Orleans. This would keep the river open to Americans.

26.2 What was the Louisiana Purchase?

Bonaparte decided to give up all of Louisiana. His wars were going very well. He needed money, though. He offered to sell all of Louisiana. The United States could have it for $25 million. The United States offered $15 million. Bonaparte accepted. This was a great deal. The United States bought about 800,000 square miles. Each square mile cost a little over $18.

Jefferson worried about this **treaty** with France. He wanted a limited government. Yet, he had led the government in a very powerful act. Was it too powerful? He felt that the act might go against the Constitution. Still, Congress and the country were happy about the treaty. The Senate voted for the treaty. Louisiana became part of the United States on December 20, 1803.

Meriwether Lewis and William Clark were sent to Louisiana. They were to find out what it was like. They received special help. Toussaint Charbonneau joined them. He had bought a Shoshone woman. She was now his wife. She went on the trip, too. Her name was Sacajawea. She led the people to the West.

▲ Meriwether Lewis

▲ William Clark

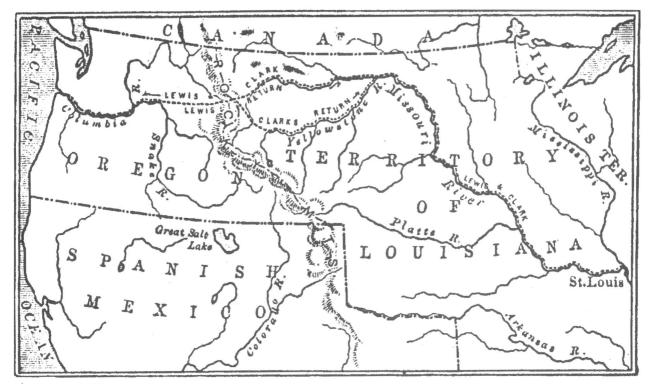

▲ Lewis and Clark's Route

She handled talks with the Native Americans that they met. The trip took three years. It covered more than just Louisiana. The people went all the way to the Pacific Ocean.

26.3 Why did Thomas Jefferson limit trade with France and Great Britain?

New fears of France broke out in 1806. France had taken almost all of Europe. Great Britain had entered the war right after the Louisiana Purchase. The United States had traded with both countries. Britain and France began stopping American ships. The British even took Americans from their ships. They were put to work in British ships. However, American ships could pay both sides. Then they could sail on their way unharmed.

President Jefferson decided to stop France and Britain. He asked Congress for a new law. Americans could not trade with any European country involved in the war. This law did not work well. It hurt the United States more than France or Britain. The law was changed. Now Americans could trade with other countries. They would not trade with France or Britain, though.

The United States saved its ships from Britain and France. It fought the War of 1812 with Britain. A treaty ended this war. Britain agreed to leave American ships alone. Then the British beat the French in 1815. Bonaparte was kept under British guard. Louis XVIII became the king of France. He stopped French attacks on American ships.

26.4 How had the country's shape and its people changed from 1776 to 1816?

The United States gained land from other countries. Britain gave up the Northwest Territory in 1783. France sold Louisiana to the United States in 1803. Over 200,000 French, Spanish, and Native American people lived there. Spanish people also lived in parts of Florida. In 1810, the people of West Florida turned against Spain. They set up their own country. It soon joined the United States.

All these lands made the United States stronger. Americans moved into these lands. They built towns and cities. Many new states were formed. The ideas of the Revolutionary War were working very well for the young country.

☆☆☆

Connections

▲ Illustration shows Columbus's journey

Columbus reached Hispaniola in 1492. A fort was built on the island. It was the first European town in the Americas. **Enslaved** African people were brought to Hispaniola. France took over the east end of the island in 1697. Its farms were very rich. France made more money there than in all of Canada. France turned against its kings in 1789. The enslaved people of Hispaniola wanted to be free, too. They began a war with France in 1791. They won the war. They set up a country called "Haiti." Napoleon Bonaparte wanted Haiti back. He sent an army of 30,000 to Haiti. They took over for a few years. Many of the French died of yellow fever. Then, the war began again in 1803. The people drove out the French in 1804. Bonaparte lost all interest in the Americas. He had even sold Louisiana to the United States just a few weeks before.

 # CHAPTER REVIEW

Critical Thinking

Write your answers on a sheet of paper, or discuss in class.

1. How do you think Native American people felt about the Louisiana Purchase?

2. Why was it important to learn about the lands of the Louisiana Purchase?

Cooperative Learning

3. Work with a study partner or as part of a study group. Make a map of North America. Use clay for the map. Press lines into the clay. These should show the United States in 1776. Also show the Louisiana Purchase, the Northwest Territory, and West Florida. Let the map dry. Paint the United States blue. Paint the Northwest Territory white. Paint the Louisiana Purchase red. Paint West Florida green.

Write About It

4. Find out about lands visited by Lewis and Clark. One place was the Yellowstone area. Another was the Pacific Ocean. Write a paragraph about one of these places. Tell what it was like in 1803. Tell what the place is like today.

Chapter 27

A Changing People

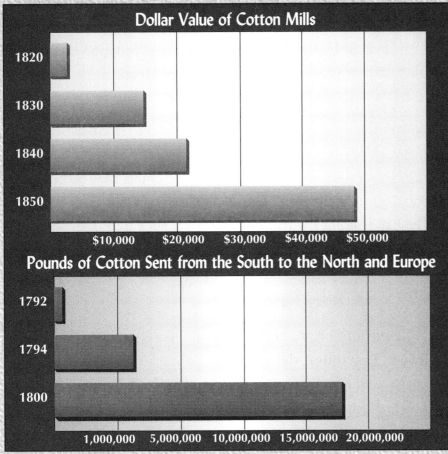

Dollar Value of Cotton Mills

1820	
1830	
1840	
1850	

$10,000 $20,000 $30,000 $40,000 $50,000

Pounds of Cotton Sent from the South to the North and Europe

1792	
1794	
1800	

1,000,000 5,000,000 10,000,000 15,000,000 20,000,000

Read about how people in different parts of the United States lived. What did the different groups expect of the federal government?

Key *Vocabulary*

convenience (kuhn VEEN yuhns) something that makes life easier

territory (TAIR uh tor ee) an area of land

produce (PROH doos) fruits and vegetables

factory (FAK tuh ree) a building where items are manufactured

Reteaching Vocabulary

indigo (IN di goh) a plant from the pea family used to make blue dye

GRAPH ANALYSIS

★ **Ask** The cotton gin was invented in 1793. According to the information on the bar graphs, how did the cotton gin affect the growth of the cotton industry?

★ **Analyze** Why do you think the amount of cotton and the money it produced grew so much over a period of years?

★ **Answer** Before cotton was used widely, most clothes were made from wool and linen. Since the cotton gin made cotton cloth so easy to produce, what do you think happened to the wool and linen industries? Why?

Decoding Tip: Notice the sounds that vowels represent in the vocabulary words.

ay	cake	ah	fall, cot	air	air
ee	tree	i	sit	oh	cold
or	cord	oy	toy	uh	above, hundred
a	ask	ar	hard	oo	book
e	yet	eye	nice	uhr	liar, fir, further, color
ow	cow	ooh	boot, true	yoo	you, few, cube

27.1 How were the lives of people in the West different from those of people in the East?

After the Louisiana Purchase, land west of the Mississippi River became part of the United States. The people who had moved into that land were not part of the rest of the country. There was no cheap way to get to the eastern part of the United States. There were few roads for travel, and they were not good ones. The roads were mainly dirt, and they turned into mud in bad weather. At times travel stopped during the coldest part of winter and during rainy weather.

People who had moved to the West did not have the **conveniences** that people in the East had. Their homes were not comfortable. They had no cities where they could buy and sell goods like the easterners had. People made their own tools, grew their own food, made their own clothing, and built their own homes with what materials they had.

27.2 What problems did people in the western territory have?

People in the western **territory** mainly grew crops for a living. They often did not have enough money to buy their farms. Dishonest people sold them land and charged them too much. Many farmers were cheated out of the money they had worked hard for.

Farmers could not get their **produce** to market before it spoiled. Roads were so bad that they often could not get their produce to market at all. They were then left with rotting fruits and vegetables that could not be sold.

Farmers also needed money to buy seeds and tools. They had no way to get that money, especially if they could not get their produce to market to sell it.

27.3 Why did the North industrialize?

The first big industry in the United States was the clothing industry. It started in the northeastern part of the country. Before the 1790s, clothing was made by women in their homes. Each woman in a family spun thread, wove cloth, and then made the clothes for the whole family.

In 1789 Samuel Slater came to the United States from England. He knew about the machines in England. He had a plan for making cloth in America. He made a spinning jenny, a machine that could spin 12 threads at once. He built the first American **factory**. He hired women to use his machines to spin thread. The thread was then sent to women in their homes to be woven into cloth.

In 1810 Francis Lowell visited England and learned about the power looms used there to weave cloth. When he returned to America, he built a power loom. He also built a factory. He not only had women spinning thread in his factory, he also hired them to weave cloth.

The first factories were built in the North. England had been using machines to produce goods for many years. People who came from England to the United States often stayed in the North. They used their knowledge of machines to build factories like those in England. For that reason, the North became industrialized.

27.4 What crops were the basis of life in the South?

The weather in the South was good for growing crops. Small farmers grew only enough to feed their families and sell a little produce to their neighbors. Other farmers owned hundreds of acres of land and grew huge amounts of cash crops. A cash crop is one that is grown to be sold.

▲ The artwork above illustrates how African Americans worked in the fields picking cotton.

One crop that was grown on a large scale in the South was **indigo**. This was a plant that was (and is still) used to dye cloth a dark blue color. Two other crops that were grown in the South were rice and tobacco. Tobacco was grown mainly in North Carolina and Virginia. South Carolina produced the most rice. Another cash crop was sugar—both sugar cane and sugar beets.

However, another important crop would take over in the South because of the invention of a machine—cotton. Since the late 1700s farmers in the South had grown cotton. Because cotton has big seeds inside the fuzz, the seeds have to be pulled out one at a time before thread can be made. This process took a lot of time, so cotton was not used as much as wool to make cloth.

During the 1790s Eli Whitney invented a machine called the cotton gin. It could comb the seeds out of cotton fuzz in minutes. This invention made cotton a popular thread.

Because there were mills in the North to spin thread and weave cloth, cotton was in great demand in the United States. Then the weaving mills in Europe also began to buy cotton from America. Cotton became the most popular crop to grow in the South.

27.5 How were ideas about federal policies different among the people in the western territories, the North, and the South?

People living in the western territories needed help. They needed roads for travel. They also needed help with money. They wanted to buy land, but they wanted the sale to be controlled by the federal government. This would help keep the sale of land honest. They also wanted to borrow money from banks to buy land and to have enough money for crops. They wanted the government to make sure there would be a market for the fruits and vegetables they grew.

People in the South grew cash crops, but they did not make their own goods. Much of what they needed, like furniture, clothing, tools, and other things, came from Europe. Southerners wanted the government to stop charging high taxes on goods from Europe. They also wanted government to allow slavery to continue. They needed cheap labor. Slavery was even better—it provided free labor to grow cash crops.

People in the North made goods in their factories. They wanted the government to raise taxes on goods from Europe. This would force people to buy goods made in America. They wanted to stop or slow down the sale of goods from other countries.

☆☆☆

▲ The first cotton gin

Before the invention of the cotton gin, the spinning jenny, and the power loom, clothes in America were made by hand. Women in a household usually made all the clothes worn by a family. With the invention of the three machines, everything changed.

Not only was cotton fuzz separated from the seeds at a cotton gin, the thread was spun in a factory. Before long, other machines were invented to do the weaving of cloth and then later to sew the clothes. For almost 100 years, making clothes was a big industry in the United States. Then things turned completely around.

The cost of labor increased so much that designers and manufacturers began to send their clothing to other countries to be made. Clothing made in the United States is very expensive because of the cost of manufacturing. Most clothing produced in the United States is made in small shops. This clothing is very expensive to buy. More and more people again sew their own clothing. The clothing industry has once again become a very small business.

★★☆ CHAPTER REVIEW

Critical Thinking

Write your answers on a sheet of paper, or discuss in class.

Identifying Main Idea

1. Why was travel so important to every part of life in the western territory?

Analyzing Cause and Effect

2. Why did the North and South depend on each other so much in the cotton industry?

Cooperative Learning

LEARNING STYLE
Verbal
Tactile

3. Work with a partner. Draw a diagram or build a model of one of the following machines: a spinning jenny, a power loom, or a cotton gin. Then explain to the group how your particular machine works.

Write About It

Writing Portfolio

4. Imagine you are about to open a cotton mill. Write a newspaper ad asking for workers to work in your mill. Describe the job, what it involves, and the pay and benefits. You will need to do some research to find out more about working conditions during the time described in this chapter.

Chapter 28

Conflicts with Spain

ANDREW JACKSON'S PUSH INTO SPANISH FLORIDA (1818)

Read about the conflicts between Spain and the United States. How did President Monroe deal with the problem? Why?

Key *Vocabulary*

protest (PROH test) to disagree or oppose

criticize (KRIT uh seyez) to find fault with someone or something

circumstance (SUHR kum stants) the way things are at a certain time and place

sympathetic (sim puh THET ik) feeling of support or approval

recognize (REK uhg neyez) to accept a new nation and its right to exist

MAP ANALYSIS

★ **Ask** By gaining Florida, the United States added new port cities. What bodies of water are these on?

★ **Analyze** Which states would feel safer with Florida in American hands?

★ **Answer** Do you think adding Florida helped the United States become a sea power? Explain your answer.

Decoding Tip: Note that the final *e* is silent in **criticize**, **circumstance**, and **recognize**.

ay	cake	ah	fall, cot	air	air
ee	tree	i	sit	oh	cold
or	cord	oy	toy	uh	above, hundred
a	ask	ar	hard	oo	book
e	yet	eye	nice	uhr	liar, fir, further, color
ow	cow	ooh	boot, true	yoo	you, few, cube

28.1　What problems did Spain's control of Florida give the United States?

In 1816, Spain still controlled Florida. This gave the United States three problems. First, the United States did not want another country to hold land so close to it. Spain might become an enemy and start a war. Second, Spain was not doing enough to stop raids by Native Americans. The Seminoles and Creeks were still fighting the United States. The Native Americans resented giving up their land. They often led raids into Georgia. Spain had agreed to stop these Seminole raids. But Spain did not have enough troops in Florida to keep its agreement. Third, Florida had become a home for outlaws. Spain did nothing to make them leave. They ran wild. People in Georgia and Florida lived in fear.

President James Monroe **protested** to Spain. However, the Spanish would not act. Monroe called on General Andrew Jackson to clean up the Georgia-Florida area. He let Jackson follow the Seminoles onto Spanish land. But Jackson was told not to attack any Spanish forts.

▲ President James Monroe

28.2　What was the result of Andrew Jackson's attack on Florida?

Jackson's attack in 1818 led to Florida coming under United States control. His attack was almost too much of a success. Jackson chased the Seminoles from Georgia into Florida. Then he moved on to Pensacola on the coast. He drove out the Spanish governor. He had two British people put to death. Jackson said the British were helping the Seminoles plan their raids. Jackson then claimed Florida for the United States.

President Monroe had mixed feelings. He was glad to have the raids under control. Also, he believed the United States should have Florida. But something had to be done. Spain's

▲ General Andrew Jackson

leaders were very angry. At the same time, it wasn't a good idea to **criticize** Jackson. Jackson was a national hero.

Monroe decided to write a carefule letter to Spain's minister. He admitted that Jackson had gone beyond his orders. But Monroe also took up for his general. Jackson had done the right thing under the **circumstances**, Monroe said. The Spanish saw how easily Jackson had taken Florida. They knew the United States wanted the area. By 1821, a treaty was signed. Florida became part of the United States.

28.3 How did the United States act towards the new Latin American nations?

By 1820, several nations in Latin America had just gained their freedom from Spain. Among them were Colombia, Mexico, Argentina, Chile, and Brazil. The United States was friendly but not too friendly to these new Latin American nations. President Monroe was **sympathetic** to their cause. After all, the United States had been free from Britain for only about 40 years. Monroe wanted to show his country's good

▼ The illustration below shows the flags of some of the new Latin American nations.

will. He wanted the United States to **recognize** these new nations. He wanted the U.S. to say officially that these nations had the right to be nations.

But there were other things to think about. Monroe didn't want the United States caught in the middle of a war. How would the countries of Europe take this? What if Spain tried to get its colonies back? Monroe also wondered if the new nations were strong enough to last. What if they fell apart? Monroe waited and watched. By 1822, he could tell that the new Latin American nations were going to last. The United States Congress voted to **recognize** them.

28.4 What did the Monroe Doctrine do?

The Monroe Doctrine was a warning to Europe. It told Europe's leaders to keep out of the Western hemisphere. It said, "Leave America alone, and it will leave you alone." President Monroe set out this idea in a speech to Congress in 1823. The Monroe Doctrine would remain important for 100 years.

Three reasons caused Monroe to write his speech. First, there were the recent problems with Spain. Second, Russia was making moves in the American Northwest. Monroe wanted them to stop. Third, Greece had won its independence in Europe. Many Americans wanted to show support for Greece. But Monroe had second thoughts. The United States wanted Europe to stay out of its affairs. Should the United States take sides in a European matter?

The Monroe Doctrine

1. Western nations were different from European nations. They were ruled by their own people. Europe still had kings and queens.

2. No more European colonies could be started in the Americas.

3. A European nation could not force its way of government on a nation in the Americas. Doing so would be an act of war.

4. Europe and the Americas must be separate. The United States would take no part in European matters.

Monroe's speech was firm and clear. It left no doubt about the United States' place in the world. The United States was not yet strong enough to back it up. It still counted on Britain for help. But a line was drawn between Europe and America.

☆☆☆

Connections

The Monroe Doctrine has played a large part in American history. Several presidents have acted by its rules. In 1846, James Polk warned European nations to stay out of the Mexican War. In the 1860s, Andrew Johnson stopped Napoleon III from starting a French empire in Mexico. Both Polk and Johnson were following the Monroe Doctrine. Some presidents added to its rules. Ulysses S. Grant told Europe it couldn't trade or sell territories in the West. When the Panama Canal was being dug, Theodore Roosevelt warned Europe. Roosevelt said the canal was the business of the United States and its neighbors only. Roosevelt also wanted the United States to "police" the West. He wanted nations in the Americas to answer to the United States, not to Europe.

In the 20th Century, the Monroe Doctrine became less important. The line between Europe and the Americas grew faint. The United States fought two world wars in Europe. Latin American nations made the United States agree to stay out of their affairs. But even in the 1980s, the Monroe Doctrine seemed alive. Ronald Reagan sent American forces to Granada, an island in the West Indies. Reagan feared that the Soviet Union was building an air base there.

▲ President James Monroe

 CHAPTER REVIEW

Critical Thinking

Write your answers on a sheet of paper, or discuss in class.

 1. Was President Monroe correct to send Andrew Jackson into Florida? What else might he have done?

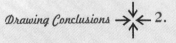 2. Did the Monroe Doctrine make the United States look stronger to the rest of the world? Why or why not?

Cooperative Learning

LEARNING STYLE
Reading
Writing

3. Read sections 28.1 and 28.4 again. Notice that they both contain paragraphs with numbered points. These have the words *first*, *second*, *third*, etc. Make your own list for these sections. Write the numbered points in order. Use your list to help you study.

Write About It

Writing Portfolio

4. A doctrine is a set of rules. Write a doctrine of your own. Write it about how new students should be treated in school. Number the main points. Show your doctrine to another student. See if he or she can suggest other points to include.

Chapter 29

Factions Form

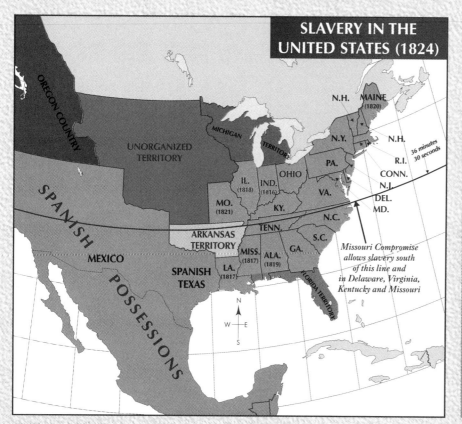

SLAVERY IN THE UNITED STATES (1824)

OREGON COUNTRY

UNORGANIZED TERRITORY

MICHIGAN TERRITORY

N.H.

MAINE (1820)

N.Y.

N.H.

R.I.

CONN.

N.J.

DEL.

MD.

PA.

OHIO

IL. (1818)

IND. (1816)

VA.

MO. (1821)

KY.

N.C.

TENN.

ARKANSAS TERRITORY

SPANISH POSSESSIONS

MEXICO

MISS. (1817)

ALA. (1819)

GA.

S.C.

LA. (1817)

SPANISH TEXAS

FLORIDA TERRITORY

36 minutes 30 seconds

Missouri Compromise allows slavery south of this line and in Delaware, Virginia, Kentucky and Missouri

N W E S

Read about the people of the United States. How did different sections in the country develop different ideas? Why?

Key *Vocabulary*

faction (FAK shuhn) a group that shares ideas that are opposed by another group or groups

equal (EE kwuhl) being treated exactly like others who belong to the same group

balance (BAL uhnts) to keep each side on the same level

candidate (KAN duh dayt) one who runs for an office

elect (i LEKT) to choose by voting; especially when choosing a person to fill an office

MAP ANALYSIS

★ **Ask**   What three sections does this map show?

★ **Acquire**   What line separates slave states from free states?

★ **Organize** Which states can have slaves and which cannot?

★ **Analyze**   Look at the states that were formed between 1812 and 1821. How did Congress alternate forming new states between the sections of the country?

★ **Answer**   Why might it be important to keep a balance between slave states and free states?

Decoding Tip: Note that *c, q,* and *k* can stand for the same sound.

ay	cake	ah	fall, cot	air	air
ee	tree	i	sit	oh	cold
or	cord	oy	toy	uh	above, hundred
a	ask	ar	hard	oo	book
e	yet	eye	nice	uhr	liar, fir, further, color
ow	cow	ooh	boot, true	yoo	you, few, cube

29.1 How did the issue of making Missouri a state cause the nation to divide into factions?

People with different beliefs formed **factions** or groups. People lived different kinds of lives. They formed different ideas. The factions wanted different things from the federal government. The North made goods to sell. They wanted the government to help businesses grow. The people in the South grew crops to sell. They liked laws that helped farmers. The people in the West were farmers, too. They wanted a strong federal government that would help them build up their states.

Arguments over slavery blew up during talks about making Missouri a state. Missouri was part of the Louisiana Purchase. Slavery had been allowed by the Spanish and French. The people of Missouri wanted to keep their enslaved people. Americans in the North wanted these people to be free instead. However, the people in the South wanted slavery to continue in Missouri. Members of Congress even took sides.

The North and South wanted to be **equal** in the Senate. Without Missouri, they were **balanced** in their numbers of Senators. Suppose Missouri kept slavery as a new state. Then, the South would have more members in the Senate. The North would not let such a thing happen. Some people on each side even called for war to settle this problem.

29.2 What was the Missouri Compromise?

Illinois Senator Jesse B. Thomas called for both Missouri and Maine to become states. This kept the Senate balanced between North and South. It was called "The Missouri Compromise." Also, slavery would not be allowed anywhere north of a line between the North and the South. This line roughly followed the northern borders of North Carolina and Tennessee. Missouri was the one exception. However, the Missouri Compromise did not stop all arguments about slavery. The question of slavery would cause problems for many years.

29.3 How did the candidates for President in 1824 reflect the country's factions?

Different factions picked different men to run for President. Congress chose William H. Crawford of Georgia. John Quincy Adams was the choice of New England. He was the son of President John Adams. Kentucky chose Henry Clay. Andrew Jackson was chosen by Tennessee. Each man was a Democratic-Republican.

The three main **candidates** had different ideas. Adams believed in a strong federal government. He also wanted laws to help businesses. Jackson believed that the government should help develop the West. He felt it should protect Westerners from attacks by Native Americans. He believed in states' rights and slavery, too. He owned over 100 enslaved people. Clay shared many of Jackson's beliefs. However, he liked the idea of a strong federal government.

The Election of 1824

Candidate	Party	Popular Vote	Electoral Vote	Result
Andrew Jackson	Democratic-Republican	153,000	99	not enough to win
John Quincy Adams	Democratic-Republican	109,000	84	not enough to win
William H. Crawford	Democratic-Republican	47,000	41	not enough to win
Henry Clay	Democratic-Republican	47,000	37	not enough to win

▲ Secretary of State Henry Clay   ▲ President John Quincy Adams

29.4 Why was the Election of 1824 thrown to the House of Representatives?

The House of Representatives had to **elect** the President. No candidate had won enough votes in the Electoral College. Jackson had more Electoral votes than any other candidate. However, all together they had more votes than Jackson. The House could choose from the top three candidates. However, Crawford was very ill. He was out of the running. That left Jackson, Adams, and Clay in the race.

29.5 Why did the Election of 1824 cause great anger in parts of the country?

Some people felt a secret deal stole the election from Jackson. Clay knew that he could not win. He talked his supporters into voting for Adams. Adams was elected President with this help. Then, Adams chose Clay to be his Secretary of State. Talk about a secret deal made many people very angry. They felt that Jackson had been cheated. The factions pulled even farther apart. They seemed to be pulling the country apart, too.

☆☆☆

Connections

Today, any American citizen can vote beginning at the age of 18. However, this has not always been the case. The first voters in the United States were men. They had to be 21 and own a home or land. Later, some states changed their laws. Men had to be 21 and had to have paid taxes. In the Election of 1824, all men over the age of 21 could vote in the states of Missouri, Indiana, Illinois, New Hampshire, and Vermont.

Some women had voted in the country's early years. New Jersey at first allowed women to vote. This ended in 1806, though. Some women were thought to have voted more than once in the same election. In the same election, some men voted once. Then they dressed up like women and voted a second time. New Jersey wanted to stop this from happening again. It took away women's rights to vote. In later years, some states did allow women to vote. However, not all American women were allowed to vote until 1920.

▲ A suffragette marching for the right to vote

★★★ CHAPTER REVIEW

Critical Thinking

Write your answers on a sheet of paper, or discuss in class.

Making Inferences
1. Suppose there was no Electoral College. How would the Election of 1824 have turned out differently?

Analyzing Cause and Effect
2. Why did the way in which people lived affect their ideas about government?

Cooperative Learning

LEARNING STYLE
Auditory Oral

3. Work with a study partner or as part of a study group. Practice reading a section of the chapter aloud. Then record this section. Play the recording for another group. Talk about the ideas included in this section of the chapter.

Write About It

Writing Portfolio

4. Imagine that you are a voter in the Election of 1824. Think about what happened. Write three sentences about your candidate. Use these sentences to create a campaign poster for your candidate.

Chapter 30

New Parties—New Ideas

ELECTORAL COLLEGE VOTE (1828)

MAINE

UNORGANIZED TERRITORY

MICHIGAN TERRITORY

V.T.

N.H.

NEW YORK MASS.

R.I.
CON.

ILLINOIS INDIANA OHIO PENNSYLVANIA

N.J.
DEL.

MARYLAND

MISSOURI KENTUCKY VIRGINIA

ARKANSAS TERRITORY TENNESSEE NORTH CAROLINA

MISSISSIPPI ALABAMA SOUTH CAROLINA

LOUISIANA GEORGIA

FLORIDA TERRITORY

Andrew Jackson
(Democrat)

John Quincy Adams
(National Republican)

Divided

0   250   500 Miles

Read about changes in the United States. How did two new political parties come about? Why?

Key *Vocabulary*

tariff (TAIR uhf)
a tax that must be paid on goods bought from another country

economy (i KAHN uh mee)
the system through which the people and companies of a certain area make their livings

spoils (spoylz)
the jobs a winning candidate can give to loyal supporters.

protectionism
(pruh TEK shuhn izm)
the idea that the government should take actions to protect businesses

Reteaching Vocabulary

democracy (duh MAHK ruh see)
a kind of government in which people rule themselves

MAP ANALYSIS

★ **Ask**   What vote is shown by this map?

★ **Acquire**   What do the different colors show?

★ **Organize** Which candidates won each state?

★ **Analyze**   How did the West, the South, and the North vote in 1828?

★ **Answer**   Why might these sections have voted differently?

Decoding Tip: Note that a can stand for more than one sound.

ay	cake	ah	fall, cot	air	air
ee	tree	i	sit	oh	cold
or	cord	oy	toy	uh	above, hundred
a	ask	ar	hard	oo	book
e	yet	eye	nice	uhr	liar, fir, further, color
ow	cow	ooh	boot, true	yoo	you, few, cube

30.1 How did the Tariff of 1828 help to form two new political parties?

The **Tariff** of 1828 split the Democratic-Republicans. Two new parties were formed. John Quincy Adams led the National Republicans. They wanted a strong federal government. It could help the **economy** and businesses grow. Andrew Jackson led the Democrats. They wanted a limited federal government. They wanted to protect the people's rights, both rich and poor.

Democratic ideas swept the country. Jackson was elected President in 1828. He was very popular in the South and West. He did not do well in New England. Adams and the National Republicans were too strong there.

30.2 What was the spoils system?

When they enter the White House, most Presidents can hand out jobs to supporters. These jobs are called **spoils**. Putting new people into government offices is called the "spoils system." This fills the Executive Branch with people who support the President and his ideas. President Adams had not followed this plan. He then had to spend much of his time fighting against his own branch of government. Jackson disagreed. He felt it was bad for people to keep their offices too long. That could hurt the ideas of **democracy**. He also wanted the Executive Branch's help with his ideas. He removed many people from office. They were replaced with Democrats.

30.3 How did the role of the Cabinet change under President Jackson?

The Cabinet did not help Jackson in making plans. They simply ran the offices of the Executive Branch. Jackson's real advisers helped him form his ideas. These people held no official posts. Jackson held meetings with them in the White House. Some people said that these people came into the

White House through the kitchen. This group became known as the "Kitchen Cabinet."

30.4 How did the Tariff of 1828 affect the country?

Some people truly liked the Tariff of 1828. People in the South and West fought this law, though. The North wanted **protectionism**. This meant that the government would protect the country's businesses. Northerners liked the Tariff of 1828 because it was based on ideas of protectionism. However, people in the South and West wanted free trade. They did not want any tariffs or other taxes on goods. Why should they pay higher prices just to help out another part of the country?

▼ Vice President John C. Calhoun

30.5 How did the President and Vice President disagree over states' rights?

John C. Calhoun was Vice President. He wanted the states to have strong rights. He led the fight against the Tariff of 1828. Jackson decided that Calhoun went too far with his ideas. Some of Jackson's supporters turned to Calhoun. President Jackson said he still believed in states' rights. However, he said that as President he would not help the states if such an act hurt the country. The Tariff of 1832 lowered taxes on goods. This still did not please the states' rights supporters, though.

Calhoun led South Carolina against the President's ideas. The state voted to nullify both tariff laws. Jackson asked Congress for help. It passed the Force Bill. Jackson could now use the army to collect the tariffs if necessary. South Carolina decided to back down. Its legislature voted to kill the bill to nullify the tariffs. Then, the legislature voted to nullify the Force Bill. Nothing actually came of this. The Force Bill was kept in place. The army was never used to collect any taxes. The fight over states' rights would continue for many years. Giving more power to the states has even become a popular idea in the 1990s.

30.6 How did the Second Bank of the United States affect the country?

Jackson wanted to end the Second Bank of the United States. The charter for the First Bank had ended in 1816. The Second Bank was set up that year. It would end in 1836 unless the President and Congress took action. President Jackson did not like the Second Bank. He felt that its powers did not fit the ideas of the Constitution. It made its rich owners too powerful. Also, the Second Bank was not always able to make sure that state bank notes were good. Bank notes were paper money printed and handed out by individual banks. National Republicans were shocked that Jackson wanted to end the Second Bank. They felt it did a lot of good for the country's economy.

National Republicans thought this issue would help them beat Jackson in 1832. Henry Clay was the party's candidate. He spread the news about Jackson's plans for the bank. This plan did not work. Jackson's win was even bigger than in 1828. He knew he had the people's support. He pulled all the government's money out of the Second Bank of the United States. No bank notes would be allowed. Banks could only hand out gold and silver coins.

☆☆☆

The Election of 1832

Candidate	Party	Popular Vote	Electoral Vote	Result
Andrew Jackson	Democratic	687,000	219	reelected
Henry Clay	National Republican	530,000	49	

For the People, By the People

Connections

Few people actually had much power in choosing the country's early Presidents. The states held meetings of party leaders. The leaders chose the candidates for President and Vice President. Then, the state legislatures chose the members of the Electoral College. Then the members would meet to vote for the President and Vice President. Many people felt this was not a democratic process. By the late 1820s, more and more people had gained the right to vote. Elections changed, too.

One small political party was the Anti-Masonic Party. Each state sent members to its national meeting in 1831. The meeting was called a convention. The convention members chose the party's candidates for President and Vice President. The Democrats and National Republicans liked the idea. They held meetings, too. Jackson became the Democratic candidate. Clay was the National Republican candidate. More people became involved in the election process than ever.

Today, candidates are still chosen at national party conventions. However, the people still do not actually choose the President. They vote for the members of the Electoral College. The people vote for members who have pledged to support a particular candidate. The members of the Electoral College must carry out that pledge and vote for his or her candidate. If the vote is tied or very close, the House of Representatives must then elect the President and Vice President.

▲ In 1992, Democratic candidates Harkin, Clinton, and Kerrey debate in New Hampshire.

★★☆ CHAPTER REVIEW

Critical Thinking

Write your answers on a sheet of paper, or discuss in class.

Classifying

1. Why could President Jackson be called both a supporter of states' rights and of a strong federal government?

Drawing Conclusions →✦←

2. Some people feel that the Electoral College is not needed. Do you think the Electoral College should be kept or done away with? Why?

Cooperative Learning

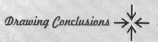

LEARNING STYLE
Reading
Verbal

3. Work with a study partner or as part of a study group. Read the chart that is included in this chapter. Tell facts that are shown in each section of the chart. Compare the two elections. Talk about the ways in which these elections were alike and how they were different.

Write About It

Writing Portfolio

4. Write the following list on a piece of paper: **Tariff of 1828, states' rights, protectionism, free trade, Tariff of 1832, Force Bill, power to nullify**. Put each item on a separate line. Then write a sentence beside each item. Tell about that item.

For the People, By the People   **New Parties—New Ideas**   **Chapter 30**

Quiz

Number a piece of paper from 1-10. Read each question below. Read the answers that follow each question. Choose the answer for each question. Write the letter of the answer you choose beside the correct number on your piece of paper.

1. **Which country took over Louisiana in 1800, causing a danger to the United States?**
    a. Spain
    b. Great Britain
    c. France
    d. the Netherlands

2. **Why did President Jefferson agree to buy Louisiana, even though he felt that the Constitution did not give his office such powers?**
    a. He knew that Britain would buy it if the United States did not.
    b. He wanted to keep European slave traders out of the area.
    c. He wanted to give Native Americans this land in trade for their lands between the Mississippi River and the Appalachians.
    d. He knew that the United States would gain a great deal by meeting the small price Napoleon wanted for all this land.

3. **Which area's economy was based on raising crops to sell?**
    a. the North
    b. the South
    c. the West
    d. both b and c

4. **Which area began to industrialize?**
    a. the North
    b. the South
    c. the West
    d. both b and c

5. **Which area wanted a strong federal government to help it develop and prosper?**
    a. the North
    b. the South
    c. the West
    d. both a and c

6. **How did conflicts with Spain change people's ideas about Europe?**
    a. President Monroe led people to see that Europe should stay out of North and South American affairs.
    b. People learned that Europe must open its markets for American factories to succeed.
    c. Napoleon's wars with Spain led people to see that Spain was the only European country that could be trusted.
    d. all of the above

7. **What issue almost kept Missouri from becoming a state?**
    a. states' rights
    b. slavery
    c. industrialization
    d. Force Bill violations

8. **How did factions cause anger during the Election of 1824?**
    a. Democrats would not allow Democratic-Republicans to vote.
    b. Democratic-Republicans did away with the Electoral College.
    c. Democrats felt that a secret deal among the Democratic-Republicans stole the election from Andrew Jackson.
    d. all of the above

9. **How did the Kitchen Cabinet help President Jackson?**
    a. gave him advice
    b. ran his campaign
    c. worked against the Second Bank of the U. S.
    d. overturned the Tariffs of 1828 and 1832

10. **According to President Jackson, whose interests should come first?**
    a. the states
    b. Congress
    c. the nation
    d. the President

CLASSIFYING

Add numbers 11–15 to your paper. Read the ideas listed below. If Democratic-Republicans would agree with an idea, write A on your paper. If Democrats would agree with an idea, write B on your paper.

11. believed in states' rights
12. wanted protectionism
13. favored the Second Bank of the United States
14. supported the Tariffs of 1828 and 1832
15. encouraged a limited federal government

Look over the writing you did for Chapters 26–30. Work with a study partner or group. Turn your work into stories and ads for a newspaper. Invent a name for your paper. Type up all the stories and ads. Put them together in a newspaper form. Draw pictures for the paper. Display your paper for other classes and for the school.

Work with a partner. Find ideas that would be supported by the Democratic-Republicans and the Democrats. Think up a sentence with one idea. Tell your sentence to your partner. Ask the partner to identify the party that would agree with this sentence. Then, listen to your partner's sentence. Identify the party that would agree with this sentence. Think up one or two sentences each for Chapters 26–30.

COOPERATIVE PROJECT: THE GROWING UNITED STATES

Work with a group. List the areas added to the United States from 1800–1820. Make a clay map of the United States as of 1820. Press lines to show the shapes of the states and territories. Let the map dry. Use red paint for the original 13 states. Use white paint for states that were formed after 1781 and that are east of the Appalachians. Use blue paint for the lands of the Northwest Territory. Use yellow paint for the Louisiana Purchase. Use green paint for lands gained from Spain along the Gulf of Mexico.

Chapter 31

The President and the Economy

The Election of 1836				
Candidate	Party	Popular Vote	Electoral Vote	Result
Martin Van Buren	Democratic	763,000	170	elected
William Henry Harrison	Whig	548,000	73	
Hugh Lawson White	Whig	unknown	26	
Daniel Webster	Whig	unknown	14	

The Election of 1840				
Candidate	Party	Popular Vote	Electoral Vote	Result
Martin Van Buren	Democratic	1,130,000	60	not reelected
William Henry Harrison	Whig	1,300,000	234	elected

Read about the nation's economy. How did it affect the election of the President? Why?

Key *Vocabulary*

panic (PAN ik) a time when people suddenly fear that the economy is failing

deposit (di PAHZ uht) money put into a bank

depression (di PRESH uhn) a time when the economy slows and people are put out of work

issue (ISH ooh) something that needs to be settled or decided

CHART ANALYSIS

★ **Ask**   Which elections are shown by this chart?

★ **Acquire**   How were the candidates alike and different?

★ **Organize**   How did the number of voters change between 1836 and 1840?

★ **Analyze**   Which candidate won each election?

★ **Answer**   Why might the number of voters have changed so much?

Decoding Tip: Note that e can stand for more than one sound.

ay	cake	ah	fall, cot	air	air
ee	tree	i	sit	oh	cold
or	cord	oy	toy	uh	above, hundred
a	ask	ar	hard	oo	book
e	yet	eye	nice	uhr	liar, fir, further, color
ow	cow	ooh	boot, true	yoo	you, few, cube

31.1 Why was the Whig party formed?

Henry Clay's loss to Andrew Jackson in 1832 ended the Democratic-Republican party. There were now two new groups in the United States. Jackson led the Democrats. The other group was made up of those who did not like Jackson. They felt he was too powerful. Some even said that Jackson wanted to be like a king. These people wanted to stop Jackson and his ideas. They formed the Whig party. It was named for an English party of the 1700s. It had fought against England's king and his ideas.

▲ President Martin Van Buren

31.2 What were the results of the Election of 1836?

Jackson and the Democrats had backed Vice President Martin Van Buren in the Election of 1836. He easily beat all the Whig candidates. The members of this party had agreed that they did not like Jackson. They also wanted the government to help the economy. They could not agree on many other ideas, though. They had even chosen three candidates to run against Van Buren. Not one could get enough votes. Van Buren took office. His plan was to continue government along Jackson's ideas.

31.3 How did the Panic of 1837 affect the country?

President Jackson's fight with the Second Bank of the United States had caused some problems. There were not enough coins to help people carry out business. Then Britain called in many of its American loans. Banks had to pay these loans in gold and silver coins. The shortage of coins became even worse.

The country's economy began to fail. This was called the **Panic** of 1837. People in the West did not have enough coins. Land sales dropped. Many people could not pay the loans on the land that they had bought. Banks could not collect on these loans. The banks started to fail. People could not buy as many goods. Factories in the North had to close. The North stopped buying as much cotton from the South. Southern farmers began losing their land, too. States were not collecting as much money in taxes. Some states could not even pay their bills. Things did not get better for six long years.

31.4 What were the results of the Election of 1840?

President Van Buren lost popularity after the Panic of 1837. He would not help banks. He felt this was a power not allowed by the Constitution. He took this idea of Jackson's much further. He got the government out of banking completely. He pulled all the government's money out of state banks. The Treasury Department kept the money. They had vaults in different places around the country. Without government **deposits**, more banks failed.

Whigs used the **depression** to beat the Democrats. They chose General William Henry Harrison to run for President. Neither candidate talked about many of the **issues**. The Whigs described how good they were. They also pointed out the Democrats' flaws. The Democrats began following this plan, too. The Whigs' plan worked. They gained even more favor by promising to help end the depression. Harrison became President.

31.5 Why were the Whigs dissatisfied with their party's President?

Harrison served as President for only one month. At his inauguration, the President spoke on the steps of Congress for three hours. The weather was cold and wet. Harrison became very ill. The President died a month later. Vice President John Tyler became President. Tyler's ideas were

▶ Whig party candidate William Henry Harrison, who was elected president and died in office a month later from natural causes.

more like Jackson's than the Whigs'. He became hated by the Whigs. All the members of his Cabinet quit. They would not help him carry out plans they did not like. The Whigs then began fighting among themselves. They fought with the Democrats, too. The government found it hard to get anything done.

☆☆☆

Connections

Fur trading had helped the country grow. Trappers had moved throughout the Louisiana Purchase and other western lands. Their furs were sold in the East and in Europe. Beaver fur was used to make men's hats. So many beaver were caught, the animal almost died out completely. Many people became rich from the fur trade. However, the fur trade suffered from the Panic of 1837, too.

The fur trappers took on many of the ways of the Native Americans they met. As the trappers worked throughout the West, they also explored the lands. News of their travels reached the East. Americans learned more about these western lands. One special trapper was James Beckwourth. He was a free African American. This trapper moved west over the Rocky Mountains and the Sierra Nevadas. He was the first American to reach the main pass from Nevada into California. It was named "Beckwourth Pass." Today, a highway carries traffic through Beckwourth Pass.

▲ Native Americans hunted animals for fur and other uses.

 # CHAPTER REVIEW

Critical Thinking

Write your answers on a sheet of paper, or discuss in class.

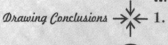 1. Why might someone picked by President Jackson be popular with the people?

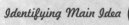 2. How firmly did President Van Buren stand up for what he believed?

Cooperative Learning

LEARNING STYLE
Verbal

3. Work with a study partner or as part of a study group. Talk about money problems people sometimes have. What happens when people spend too much? How can falling behind in paying a loan affect a person? Governments must handle money, too. Talk about government services that could be affected if a government faces money problems.

Write About It

Writing Portfolio

4. Find out about General William Henry Harrison. List facts that would catch the interest of voters in the Election of 1840. Write a few sentences that include these facts. Use the sentences to make a campaign poster for the election.

Chapter 32

American Life

Read about new inventions and new arrivals in the United States. How did they affect the country? Why?

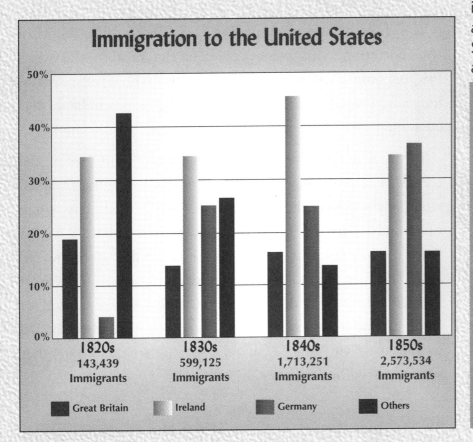

Immigration to the United States

| | 1820s 143,439 Immigrants | 1830s 599,125 Immigrants | 1840s 1,713,251 Immigrants | 1850s 2,573,534 Immigrants |

■ Great Britain ■ Ireland ■ Germany ■ Others

GRAPH ANALYSIS

★ **Ask**   What does this chart show?

★ **Acquire**   How did the population change from the 1820s to the 1850s?

★ **Organize** Which groups made up the largest number of immigrants to arrive in each decade?

★ **Analyze**   Which decade saw the most growth in German immigrants?

★ **Answer**   What problems might cause people to move to a new country?

Decoding Tip: Note that double consonants usually stand for just one sound.

ay	cake	ah	fall, cot	air	air
ee	tree	i	sit	oh	cold
or	cord	oy	toy	uh	above, hundred
a	ask	ar	hard	oo	book
e	yet	eye	nice	uhr	liar, fir, further, color
ow	cow	ooh	boot, true	yoo	you, few, cube

32.1 How did waterways and roads connect the states?

Native Americans and the colonists had used water for **transportation**. Travel along the coasts was easy. People sailed on the Atlantic Ocean and the Gulf of Mexico. Inland, they used rivers. The Mississippi River was a great waterway. However, the Appalachians made water travel impossible from the East to the West.

The federal government built roads to help improve transportation. This helped connect the East to the West. Private companies built roads, too. They charged tolls, or fees, for using these roads. States saw that the roads helped their economies. States began building toll roads to earn money.

Travel was improved when canals were built. Once the canals were dug, they were filled with water. Horses walked along paths beside these waterways. They pulled boats along the canals. This was faster and easier than pulling a wagon down a road. The Erie Canal ran for 363 miles. It connected Lake Erie with New York's Hudson River. Goods from the West flooded into New York. New York City became a center for shipping goods to other states. The goods were also shipped to Europe. New York's economy became so rich that other states started building canals, too.

32.2 How did inventions affect the country?

The invention of the **telegraph** changed **communication**. The mail had carried all messages and news. Days and even weeks could pass before news and letters reached the other side of the country. People voted for the President in November. The results could take months to reach Washington, D.C. That is why the President was not inaugurated until March. The telegraph helped change the country. It could send messages hundreds of miles in just a few seconds. Steam power made great changes in

CANADA

Lake Superior
Lake Huron
Lake Michigan
Lake Erie
Lake Ontario
Mississippi River
Ohio River
Tennessee River

Quebec
Montreal
Ottawa
Toronto
Albany
Buffalo
Detroit
Chicago
Cleveland
Pittsburg
Wheeling
Cumberland
Vandalia
Cincinnati
St. Louis
Nashville
Memphis
Natchez
Mobile
New Orleans
Richmond
Wilmington
Charleston
Savannah
St. Augustine

Boston
New York
Philadelphia
Baltimore
Washington

National Road
Other Roads
Canal

▲ Trade was so important in the early United States that roads and canals were built to connect all the states.

transportation. The first steamboat was built in 1807. These boats could travel rivers, lakes, and oceans very quickly. They could sail easi-ly up streams and against **currents**. Soon, steamboats filled the coun- try's rivers. Goods and people traveled across the country in record times. What about places where boats could not reach? Trains run by steam could reach these places. The train was invented in England. Americans were thrilled by the idea. Trains could go anywhere tracks were laid. Building railroads created many new jobs. Factories began making engines, cars, and tracks. Even more jobs opened up. The 1850s were a boom time for railroads.

32.3   Why did immigration increase?

Problems in Europe caused many people to move to the United States. A blight killed potato crops in Ireland. Many people had lived on potatoes. Now they were starving. Thousands of people left Ireland for the United States. Revolutions broke out across Europe in 1848. However, most of them failed. Many people had to leave Europe or be punished for fighting against their kings and governments. In the United States, they could be free.

Often, **immigrants** were very poor. It was hard to come up with the money to pay for the trip across the ocean. Once they reached the United States, they had no money left. They could not move to the West to buy cheap land. Happily, the United States was growing. It needed more workers. The immigrants took many of these jobs. They worked in factories. They helped build canals and railroads. However, these jobs did not require many skills. Often, the pay was low. Many immigrants remained poor. Since immigrants were in the cities, factories moved to cities, too. Cities grew tremendously. People even began to give up farming for jobs in cities.

32.4 How had enslavement affected the country from 1619 to 1860?

Building and running farms was hard work. Plantations in the South came to depend upon African workers. The first Africans arrived in Jamestown in 1619. They were indentured servants. They had to work without pay for a set number of years. After that, they were completely free. However, traders and plantation owners found that they could make money by enslaving people. Millions of Africans were brought to North and South America.

The system of slavery grew along with the demand for cotton. More land was needed for growing cotton. Enslaved people were put to work clearing this land. Then they plowed the fields and grew the cotton. The South came to believe that slavery was absolutely necessary. Many of its people were proud of their states and ways of life. They were proud of their system of slavery. They were even proud that few factories were built in the South.

☆☆☆

Connections

▲ James Madison

Many Americans worried about enslavement. People like Thomas Jefferson and James Madison felt this system was wrong. They felt that slave owners would become hard and cruel people. Enslaved people began to outnumber the free people in many areas. There were new fears of what could happen if the enslaved people turned against free people.

Some people in the South began to question the slavery system. The Virginia legislature held a special meeting in January, 1831. It talked about ways of ending enslavement. It was called the "Great Debate." Should enslaved people be freed? How would this be done? No answers were found. The legislature voted 74 to 58 to keep enslavement. Africans were still enslaved because of a difference of only 16 votes.

★★☆ CHAPTER REVIEW

Critical Thinking

Write your answers on a sheet of paper, or discuss in class.

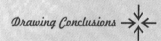 *Drawing Conclusions* →←

1. How did life change in the United States? Why?

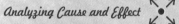 *Analyzing Cause and Effect*

2. How did immigration and slavery affect the country?

Cooperative Learning

LEARNING STYLE
Reading
Tactile

3. Work with a study partner or as part of a study group. Find out about the lives of enslaved people on cotton plantations. Build a model of a plantation. Include figures that show the kinds of work that enslaved people did. Share your models with other classes.

Write About It

Writing Portfolio

4. Find out about early trains. Imagine you have just seen the first train pass through your town. Write a story for your local newspaper. Remember to describe what you have seen and how people acted.

Chapter 33

Western Growth

GROWTH OF THE UNITED STATES (1783-1854)

- OREGON COUNTRY 1846
- LOUISIANA PURCHASE 1803
- THE UNITED STATES IN 1783
- THE ORIGINAL THIRTEEN COLONIES
- MEXICAN CESSION 1848
- TEXAS ANNEXATION 1845
- GADSDEN PURCHASE 1853
- FLORIDA 1819

Read about how Texas and California joined the United States. Why did the United States go to war with Mexico?

Key *Vocabulary*

expansion (ek SPAN shuhn) growth of a country by adding more land

Manifest Destiny (MAN uh fest • DEST uh nee) the idea that the United States needed to spread from the Atlantic Ocean to the Pacific

academy (uh KAD uh mee) a school where certain kinds of skills are taught

efficiently (i FISH uhnt lee) without mistakes or waste

persuade (per SWAYD) to talk someone into doing something

MAP ANALYSIS

★ **Ask** Was more land added before 1800 or after 1800?

★ **Organize** Make a table listing the sections of land. Also list the years they were added to the United States.

★ **Analyze** In which direction did the United States grow? Why was this?

★ **Answer** Do you think the number of people in the United States was growing or staying the same in the 1800s? Why?

Decoding Tip: Note that su makes the sound /sw/ in **persuade**.

ay	cake	ah	fall, cot	air	air
ee	tree	i	sit	oh	cold
or	cord	oy	toy	uh	above, hundred
a	ask	ar	hard	oo	book
e	yet	eye	nice	uhr	liar, fir, further, color
ow	cow	ooh	boot, true	yoo	you, few, cube

33.1　How did Texas become part of the United States?

Texas was controlled by Spain and then Mexico before becoming part of the United States. In 1821 Mexico broke away from Spain. Texas became part of the new Mexican republic. Mexico let Stephen F. Austin start an American colony in southeast Texas. It grew quickly, and others followed. By 1830, almost 30,000 Americans were living in Texas. Mexico feared it was losing control. It would not let in any more Americans. This move angered the Americans who were already there.

In 1834, Mexico's government fell to General Antonio López de Santa Anna. Americans in Texas fought against his rule. They defeated Mexican troops at San Antonio. In 1836, Santa Anna put together a large army and took back the city. The battle was fought at the Alamo, a Spanish church. Not one American fighter was left alive. But Americans in Texas would not give up. "Remember the Alamo!" became the Texas battle cry. In April 1836, Sam Houston led a small army to victory against Santa Anna. Texas had won its independence.

For 10 years, Texas was a separate nation. Most Texans wanted to join the United States. But two problems held things up. First, adding Texas to the United States might start a war with Mexico. Second, Texas allowed enslavement. Many in the North didn't want another slave state. Finally in 1845, Congress asked Texas to join the Union.

33.2　How did James K. Polk add the Oregon territory to the United States?

The Oregon territory was a large area in the American Northwest. It included what is now Oregon, Washington, Idaho, and parts of Montana and Wyoming. Britain controlled this land. However, in 1844 many Americans were talking about **expansion**. They wanted more land in the West.

▲ President James K. Polk

Thousands had already made the long wagon trip to Oregon. James K. Polk used this issue to win the 1844 race for President. He said the United States should take over both Texas and Oregon. This was a popular idea. Some called it "**Manifest Destiny**." They believed the United States was meant to spread from the Atlantic to the Pacific. Polk believed it, too. Taking land away from Native Americans was fine to those who believed in Manifest Destiny. Once in office, Polk took steps to keep his word.

One problem was where Oregon's north boundary line was. Polk claimed it was 54°40' north latitude. (See the map on page 196.) "Fifty-four Forty or Fight!" was Polk's slogan in the race. Others put the line farther south, giving the United States less land. Talks with Britain went nowhere. Finally Polk took action. He claimed "the whole of the Oregon territory" for the United States. Then he sent a message to Britain. He would accept the southern boundary line. Britain agreed. In 1848, Oregon territory was added to the United States.

33.3　What started the Mexican-American War?

▲ General Zachary Taylor

In the 1840s, Mexico and the United States were not on good terms. There were two sticking points: Texas and California. When Texas joined the United States, Mexico made threats to start a war. In 1845 President Polk set his sights on California. His offer to buy California made the Mexicans angry. Polk feared that Mexican troops might attack Texas. He sent General Zachary Taylor to an area north of the Rio Grande, a river in Texas. Both Mexico and the United States had claimed this land. Taylor's men were attacked. Three were

▲ Battle of Molino del Rey

killed. Polk used this to start a war with Mexico. He told Congress that Mexico had crossed into American land. In fact, no border had yet been agreed upon. Whigs in Congress were against the war. Most Americans, however, were for it.

33.4 Why did American troops have success against Mexico?

From the start, American troops did well. New Mexico fell to them without a shot being fired. They marched west to California. The United States Navy took San Francisco. American forces drove the Mexicans out of Los Angeles and San Diego. By the end of 1846, they had taken control of California. They also attacked in Mexico. There the war was harder, but the Americans kept on winning. Monterey, Veracruz, and Mexico City all fell to American troops. By September 1847 the war was over.

There were several reasons for the United States' success. American officers were well trained. Many came from the new military **academy** at West Point. Their men had better equipment than past American armies. For the first time, they all were given uniforms. Guns, cannons, and shells poured from American factories. The new telegraph sent words over wires. The army got what it needed faster and more **efficiently**. Also, President Polk took an active part in the war. He named generals and planned battles. He got Congress to spend $100 million a year for the war. However, Polk didn't discuss with Congress how to fight the war. He did whatever he felt was needed to win. Later presidents would also claim special powers during war.

33.5 Why did Congress delay the Treaty of Guadalupe Hidalgo?

After a year of talks, Mexico and the United States signed a peace treaty. It was called the Treaty of Guadalupe Hidalgo. Mexico gave up all claims to Texas. New Mexico and California became part of the United States. This was a huge amount of land. It is now the states of California, Texas, Nevada, and Utah. Parts of six other states also came from this land.

The terms were good for the United States. Yet some members of Congress were against the treaty. Some thought the war was wrong. They didn't want the country to gain land from such a war. Others wanted to hold out for all of Mexico. President Polk had to **persuade** Congress to vote for the treaty. It took effect in July 1848.

☆☆☆

SPEAKING OUT AGAINST THE WAR

Most Americans seemed in favor of the Mexican-American War. But some famous Americans spoke out against it. Abraham Lincoln was one of these. The young Illinois congressman questioned Polk's war. He wanted Polk to show the spot where Mexicans had shed American blood on American soil. Frederick Douglass, an African-American writer, also spoke out. He called the war "disgraceful" and "cruel." Another writer spent a night in jail for being against the war. Henry David Thoreau did not want his tax money used for fighting. He refused to pay. Thoreau's friends paid for him, against his will. Thoreau later wrote a famous piece about his actions, *Civil Disobedience*.

▲ Henry David Thoreau

 CHAPTER REVIEW

Critical Thinking

Write your answers on a sheet of paper, or discuss in class.

 *Making Inferences*

1. Why do you think so many Americans wanted the country to grow westward?

 *Drawing Conclusions*

2. Was the Mexican-American War necessary?

Cooperative Learning

 LEARNING STYLE *Visual*

3. Work with a partner. Trace a map of the United States. Then draw lines to show the territories of Texas, Oregon, and New Mexico-California. Use the map on page 196 to draw these lines. Use scissors to cut the sections apart. Then take turns placing each piece where it belongs on the map. As you place it, tell how it came to be added to the United States.

Write About It

 Writing Portfolio

4. Write an editorial about the Mexican-American War. An editorial is a piece of writing that tells what you think. Write your piece for or against the war. Use facts from this chapter to support your views.

Chapter 34

The Trail of Tears

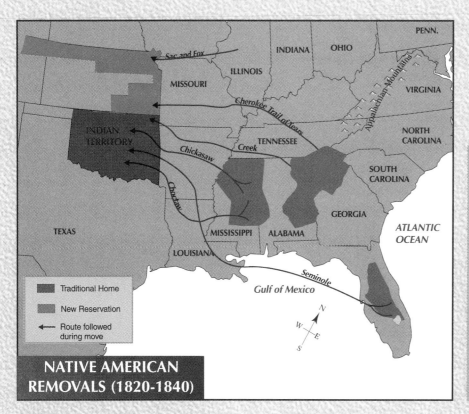

Traditional Home
New Reservation
← **Route followed during move**

NATIVE AMERICAN REMOVALS (1820-1840)

Read about how Native Americans were forced from their lands. What reasons did the United States give for moving them?

Key *Vocabulary*

policy (PAHL uh see)
a plan for how to deal with something

invent (in VENT)
to make up something that never existed before

authority (uh THOR uh tee)
the power to tell a person or group what to do

enforce (en FORS)
to carry out or put into action some law or ruling

truce (troos)
an agreement to stop fighting

MAP ANALYSIS

★ **Ask**   What states in the Southeast had Indian lands?

★ **Acquire**   Look at an up-to-date map of the United States. What state is where the Indian Territory used to be?

★ **Analyze**   In what direction did Native Americans go to reach Indian Territory?

★ **Answer**   Why do you think Americans were willing to let Native Americans have Indian Territory in exchange for their lands in the Southeast?

Decoding Tip: Note that *y* at the end of a word can make a long *e* sound.

ay	cake	ah	fall, cot	air	air
ee	tree	i	sit	oh	cold
or	cord	oy	toy	uh	above, hundred
a	ask	ar	hard	oo	book
e	yet	eye	nice	uhr	liar, fir, further, color
ow	cow	ooh	boot, true	yoo	you, few, cube

34.1 Why did the United States government want to move Native Americans out of the Southeast?

After the War of 1812, life changed for Native Americans. The British had helped them keep their ways of life. Now the British were not around. White people poured into Native American lands and took them. Between 1816 and 1848, 12 states joined the Union. During this time, Native Americans signed many treaties with the United States. They gave up most of their land east of the Mississippi River. Sometimes they did not realize they were losing the land. To Native Americans, land was for everyone's use. It couldn't be owned. They thought they could go on hunting on land they had signed away.

The United States government wanted Native Americans to move out so that white people could have the land. Native Americans would be moved west and given new land. Not all Americans agreed with this **policy**. They said it was unfair to Native Americans. Those closer to the Southeast favored the plan. Presidents from Jefferson to Jackson put the policy into effect.

34.2 Why did Native Americans in the Southeast take on some of the ways of white Americans?

In the early 1800s, there were five main nations of Native Americans living in the Southeast. These were the Choctaws, Chickasaws, Cherokees, Seminoles, and Creeks. These Native Americans hoped to keep their homelands. To do this, they had to live in peace with white Americans. They even took on some of the white people's ways. Their leaders urged them to learn English. They started farms and grain mills. They set up governments like that of the United States. Non-Indians called these groups the Five Civilized Tribes.

▲ The illustration above shows Sequoyah with the alphabet that he created.

The Cherokees led the way. Their chief, John Ross, worked hard for his people. Ross helped plan New Echota, the Cherokee capital. It was filled with large houses and shops. The Cherokees also had their own written language. Its written form was **invented** by a Cherokee named Sequoyah. He is the only person known to have started a new written language. Sequoyah hoped the new language would bring his people together. By 1828 a Cherokee newspaper was begun. The Cherokees also wrote their own constitution. In many ways, the Cherokee nation was ahead of the states around it. This only made those states angrier.

34.3 Why didn't the Supreme Court help the Cherokees?

In 1828, Georgia passed a new law. It placed Cherokees in that state under Georgia law. The Cherokees' constitution was ignored. Then gold was found in Cherokee country. Gold miners swept into Georgia and crossed over into Cherokee lands. The Cherokees asked for help from federal troops. But Georgia complained to President Andrew Jackson. Jackson took the troops out. The Cherokees then turned to the Supreme Court for help.

The Court sided with the Native Americans. Chief Justice John Marshall handed down the ruling. Georgia had no

authority over the Cherokees. Only the federal government could make laws for them. The Cherokees were joyful. At last they would get back their lands and laws. But Georgia ignored the ruling. And President Jackson would not help the Cherokees. "John Marshall has made his decision. Now let him **enforce** it," Jackson supposedly said. The Supreme Court had no means to enforce its decision. The Cherokees saw their hopes slipping away.

34.4   What did the Removal Bill of 1830 do?

Andrew Jackson believed that Native Americans had to move west. He said the move was for their own good. Out west they could live as they pleased. But many thought Jackson just wanted Native Americans out of the way. After the problems with the Cherokees in Georgia, Jackson pushed for a new law. This was the Removal Bill of 1830. The law had three main parts. First, Native Americans in the Southeast had to sell their lands at a cheap price. Second, they had to move west to new lands. The lands were called Indian Territory. These lands are now in Arkansas and Oklahoma. Third, the government promised to help Native Americans settle in their new homes.

The Removal Bill speeded up what was already happening. By 1830, some Native Americans groups had already moved west. They had made treaties to sell their lands. The Choctaws and Chickasaws left Mississippi. The Creeks made their way from Alabama to Indian Territory. Many Creeks were robbed and cheated. Horses and other belongings were taken from them. Some were packed onto old steamboats for the trip west. One of the boats sank, killing hundreds. The Seminoles were also forced to leave Florida. Some fought to keep their land. Their war with the United States lasted several years. In 1837, the Seminole leader Osceola wanted to talk peace. He and an American general met under a white flag of **truce**. The general ignored the flag. Osceola was caught and died in prison soon after.

34.5   What was the Trail of Tears?

The Cherokees became divided on the question of moving or staying. Their chief, John Ross, wanted to stay in Georgia. But others feared too much blood would be shed. In 1835, Major Ridge, another Cherokee leader, went to Washington. He signed a treaty with the United States. Cherokee lands were sold for five million dollars. Cherokees had three years to move west.

In 1838, General Winfield Scott went to Georgia to remove the Cherokees. He ordered his 7,000 troops to treat the people well. But many did not follow orders. Cherokees were rounded up at gunpoint. They waited in camps until it was time to go. As soon as a Cherokee house was taken, it was looted. Finally the forced march began. Most had to walk the whole way. They didn't have enough food, and many became sick. It took them six months to reach Indian Territory. Of about 18,000 who left, 4,000 died. The march became known as "the Trail of Tears."

☆☆☆

Yesterday & TODAY

Yesterday . . .

▲ A Mississippi Choctaw family on the porch of their home

The Choctaws were forced to leave their Mississippi home. Their march to Oklahoma was filled with pain and hunger. In 1847, they learned of problems in Ireland. Thousands were dying because of failing potato crops. The Choctaws remembered their own pain. They sent money to help the Irish.

. . . and Today

In 1995, the Republic of Ireland gave its official thanks. President Mary Robinson went to Durant, Oklahoma. There she met with leaders of the Choctaws. There were dances by Choctaw and Irish dancers. The Irish president spoke in her own language and in Choctaw. Robinson said she was "completing the circle" that began in 1847.

★★☆ CHAPTER REVIEW

Critical Thinking

Write your answers on a sheet of paper, or discuss in class.

Comparing and Contrasting

1. How did Native Americans and whites think differently about land use? Why did this lead to problems between them?

Making Inferences

2. What could have been done to prevent the Trail of Tears?

Cooperative Learning

LEARNING STYLE
Oral

3. Copy the names of Native American groups from this chapter. Look up each name to see how it sounds. Practice saying the names out loud. Then read sections 34.4 and 34.5 out loud. Make sure to say the names correctly.

Write About It

Writing Portfolio

4. Imagine you are a Cherokee in the Southeast. The year is 1830. You have learned English in school. Write a letter to President Andrew Jackson. Tell him what you think of his plan for Native Americans. Tell him what a better plan might be.

Unit 4 ★ REVIEW

Quiz

Number a piece of paper from 1–10. Write a, b, c, and d beside these numbers. Read the following sentence beginnings. Four endings follow each one. Choose the ending that best completes the sentence. On your paper, circle the letter that matches the letter of your answer. Be sure you mark your answer beside the correct number.

1. **The Whig party was started by people who . . .**
   a. supported Andrew Jackson and his ideas.
   b. wanted to stop Andrew Jackson and his ideas.
   c. wanted the United States to have a king or queen like Britain.
   d. wanted the United States' president to have more power.

2. **President Van Buren would not help the banks because . . .**
   a. he felt this power was not allowed by the Constitution.
   b. he felt they didn't need any help.
   c. all the bankers were Whigs who voted against him.
   d. all of the above.

3. **From 1807-1850, travel in the United States became easier because of . . .**
   a. steamboats.　　c. trains.
   b. airplanes.　　d. both a and c.

4. **The main reason that immigration to the United States increased was . . .**
   a. lack of large cities in Europe.
   b. problems in Europe such as war and lack of food.
   c. lack of factories in Europe.
   d. all of the above.

5. **Slavery grew along with the demand for . . .**
   a. iron.　　c. sugar.
   b. free trade.　　d. cotton.

6. **At one time, the state of Texas was . . .**
   a. controlled by Spain.
   b. controlled by Mexico.
   c. a separate nation.
   d. all of the above.

7. **Before 1848, Oregon territory was owned by . . .**
   a. the United States.
   b. France.
   c. Britain.
   d. Spain.

8. **The United States got the land that would become California by . . .**
   a. winning the battle at the Alamo.
   b. winning the Mexican-American War.
   c. buying the Oregon territory.
   d. buying it from Britain.

9. **When the Indian Removal Act was passed, the president was . . .**
   a. Thomas Jefferson.
   b. James Monroe.
   c. Andrew Jackson.
   d. Martin Van Buren.

10. **Native Americans in the Southeast were moved to what is now the state of . . .**
    a. Oklahoma.
    b. Texas.
    c. California.
    d. New Mexico.

ANALYZING CAUSE AND EFFECT

Add numbers 11–15 to your paper. Read the ideas below. The ideas on the left describe a cause, or something that makes a second event happen. The ideas on the right are effects, the events that are caused. Match these causes and effects. Write your answers beside the correct numbers on your paper.

11. To win its independence . . .
12. To beat the Democrats in the election of 1840 . . .
13. To add more land to the United States . . .
14. To ship goods faster and easier . . .
15. To provide more land for whites to live on . . .

a. the Erie Canal was built in New York.
b. the United States government moved Native Americans out of the Southeast.
c. many Americans followed the idea of Manifest Destiny.
d. Texas defeated Mexico's army.
e. the Whig party promised to end the depression.

Look over the things you wrote for these chapters. Choose one that you like the best. Add to your writing. For example, you wrote a news story about seeing a train. Write another story about seeing something else from these chapters. You might have seen a special person or something that happened. Use details to make your story interesting. Trade papers with a study partner. Read each other's work. Make a clean, neat copy of your paper. Put it in your portfolio.

Work alone or with a study partner. Make a poster showing important events from this unit. Think of the best way to show what happened. If you need to, use the encyclopedia for picture ideas. You might draw the events in order, from left to right. Or you might group them on a map of the United States. That way, you could show where they happened. When you are done, let the class see your poster. Have people tell what each drawing shows.

COOPERATIVE PROJECT: A DEBATE ON MANIFEST DESTINY

Work with a group. Divide the group into two teams. Hold a debate about Manifest Destiny. (Remember that Manifest Destiny was the idea that the United States should spread from coast to coast.) In a debate, two sides speak about some important issue. One team should speak in favor of this idea. The other team should speak against it. Give each speaker a time limit of two minutes. Work in the things from all the chapters in this unit. For example, what did Manifest Destiny mean for Native Americans? After the debate, talk about what was said. What were the best points made by each side?

Unit 5

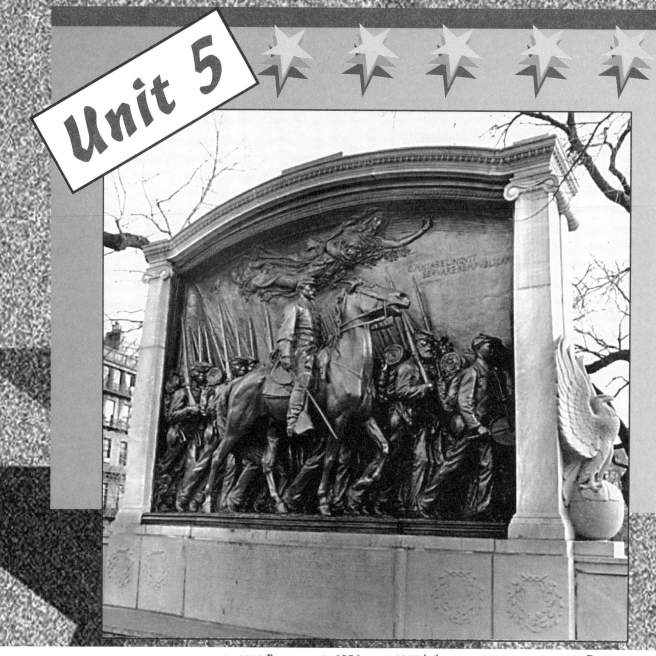

POLITICS

- **1850**-The Compromise of 1850 allowed territories gained from Mexico to settle the question of slavery for themselves.
- **1854** Kansas and Nebraska were allowed to decide about slavery for themselves.
- **1857**-In the Dred Scott case, the Supreme Court said that as a slave, Scott was property and had no rights.
- **1860** Abraham Lincoln was elected President. Seven states decided to leave the Union.
- **1861**-The Confederate States of America was formed. War broke out when Confederate troops fired on Fort Sumter on April 12.

CE   1850   1855   1860

CULTURE

- **1845** *The Autobiography of Frederick Douglass* told of Douglass's life as a slave and his escape to freedom.
- **1847** Frederick Douglass began his own newspaper, the *North Star*.
- **1848** The Seneca Falls Convention held as a call for women's rights.
- **1852**-Harriet Beecher Stowe's book *Uncle Tom's Cabin* sold over 300,000 copies and turned many Americans against slavery.
- **1858**-Slavery was the issue of the Lincoln-Douglas Debates, between Abraham Lincoln and Stephen Douglas in the Illinois race for the U.S. Senate.
- **1859** The oil business began with the drilling of the first oil well in Pennsylvania.

Civil War and Reconstruction 1850 - 1877

"I started with this idea in my head. There's two things I've got a right to... death or liberty.' "

— **Harriet Tubman**
former slave

Slavery became an issue that tore the country apart. Abraham Lincoln was elected President. Even though he supported abolition, he promised to leave slavery as it was in the South. Why did this part of the country decide to leave the United States? How did this lead to war?

1863
President Lincoln's Emancipation Proclamation freed those slaves held in Confederate states. The Confederates lost at Gettysburg. The war turned in favor of the Union.

1865
Confederate General Lee surrendered. The Union won the war. President Lincoln was assassinated. The Thirteenth Amendment ended slavery in Union states.

1868
The Fourteenth Amendment explained who could be citizens and what their rights would be.

1870
The Fifteenth Amendment was passed to ensure that African Americans could vote.

1876
Democrat Samuel Tilden won the Popular vote. Some Electoral votes were questioned. Congress chose Republican Rutherford B. Hayes to be President.

1877
Congress ended Reconstruction in order to please Democrats upset by the Election of 1876.

1865   1870   1875

1862
The first department store was opened in New York City.

1869
The Cincinnati Red Stockings became the first professional baseball team.

1876
Alexander Graham Bell invented the telephone. The United States celebrated its 100th birthday at the Centennial Exposition in Philadelphia. The fair grounds were lit with electric arc lights.

Chapter 35

Slavery

Read about people's changing ideas about slavery. Why did feelings run so high during the 1840s and 1850s?

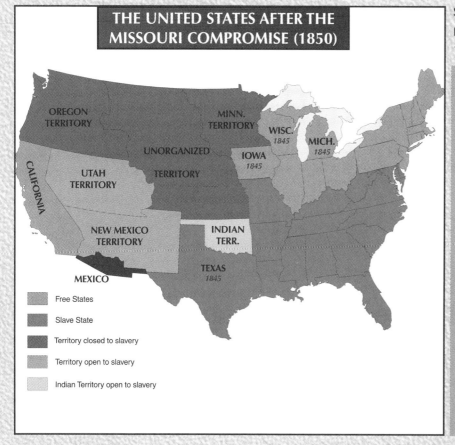

THE UNITED STATES AFTER THE MISSOURI COMPROMISE (1850)

OREGON TERRITORY

MINN. TERRITORY

WISC. 1845

MICH. 1845

IOWA 1845

UNORGANIZED

CALIFORNIA

UTAH TERRITORY

TERRITORY

NEW MEXICO TERRITORY

INDIAN TERR.

TEXAS 1845

MEXICO

Free States

Slave State

Territory closed to slavery

Territory open to slavery

Indian Territory open to slavery

Key *Vocabulary*

abolitionist
(ab uh LISH uh nuhst)
a person who works to end slavery

popular sovereignty
(PAHP yuh luhr • SAHV ruhn tee)
the freedom to choose whether or not to allow slavery

campaign (kam PAYN)
to perform the acts necessary to reach a goal, such as winning an election

education (edj uh KAY shuhn)
knowledge gained from schooling

Reteaching Vocabulary

compromise
(KAHM pruh meyez)
an agreement reached when the different sides each give up part of their demands

---

MAP ANALYSIS

★ **Ask**   What does this map show?

★ **Organize**   Make a table listing the different sections of the country. Tell what each was like.

★ **Analyze**   Which territories were open to slavery? Which were closed to slavery?

★ **Answer**   The government planned to make new states from the territories. How do you think it could form these states and still keep the Senate balanced?

Decoding Tip: Note that c makes the sound /k/ in **campaign**, **education**, and **compromise**.

ay	cake	ah	fall, cot	air	air
ee	tree	i	sit	oh	cold
or	cord	oy	toy	uh	above, hundred
a	ask	ar	hard	oo	book
e	yet	eye	nice	uhr	liar, fir, further, color
ow	cow	ooh	boot, true	yoo	you, few, cube

35.1 How did the issue of slavery affect the Election of 1848?

Heated arguments spread across the country when the Wilmot Proviso was sent to Congress. This law would have kept slavery out of western lands gained from Mexico. **Abolitionists** were people who worked to end slavery. They liked the Wilmot Proviso. However, they wanted all enslaved people to be set free. People in the South hated the Proviso. They wanted the number of free and slave states to be balanced. Then the slave states would have as many members in the U.S. Senate as the free states. Some people were caught in the middle. They wanted to end slavery, too. But they felt this should be done slowly. Then, they said, the country would not be hurt by arguing and fighting.

The House of Representatives was controlled by abolitionists, so the Wilmot Proviso passed. The Senate was balanced between free and slave states. There were not enough Senators to pass the bill.

The Whigs and Democrats decided to ignore the issue of slavery in 1848. The parties were afraid of making any group of voters angry. The Whigs chose General Zachary Taylor for the race. Democratic President Polk did not want a second term. The Democrats chose Senator Lewis Cass. Neither Taylor nor Cass would take a stand about slavery. Many abolitionists were angry with the parties. They formed their own party. It was called the "Free-Soil Party." They chose Martin Van Buren to run for another term as President. Van Buren took many votes from Cass. Taylor was elected President.

35.2 What caused California's amazing growth?

In 1848 gold was discovered at Sutter's Mill near Sacramento, California. The news spread throughout the territory. Many people from San Francisco rushed to the gold

▲ A community of miners posing in front of the claim they were working.

fields. The city was almost deserted overnight. The news quickly spread across the country and around the world. Thousands of Americans rushed west. Some traveled by wagon across the country. Others sailed around South America. Once in San Francisco, even the ships' crews went to the gold fields. Empty ships filled the harbor. People from other countries flocked to California. In China, the people called California the "land of the golden mountain." By 1849, over 100,000 people were living in California.

35.3   How did slavery become an issue in the vote to make California a state?

California was swamped with people and problems. Crime was out of control. California needed a strong government. The territory's leaders asked President Taylor for help. He suggested that they ask to become a state. They could then form their own government. He made this suggestion to New Mexico, too. He knew that Southerners would not like any more free states in the union. He felt that they would agree to let these territories decide the question for themselves. This freedom to choose on the issue of slavery is known as **popular sovereignty**.

Taylor's plan failed. The people of California asked to become a free state. The South angrily said that this was not possible. The Senate would be thrown out of balance. Like the House, the Senate would become controlled by abolitionists. The arguing became very heated. Some members even began taking guns into Congress.

35.4 How did President Taylor's death lead to the Compromise of 1850?

Henry Clay suggested a **compromise**. Each side would give up some of its goals. Then the issue could be settled peacefully. Clay's plan had four main points.

1. California would become a free state.

2. Two territories would be formed from the other lands gained from Mexico. The people would decide about slavery for themselves.

3. Slavery would continue in the District of Columbia. However, no more slaves could be sold there.

4. New laws would help capture runaway enslaved people. They would then be returned to their owners.

▼ Stephen A. Douglas

The compromise plan was held up in Congress for months. President Taylor did not like the plan. He fought against it. There were not enough votes to pass all the bills at once. Speeches for and against the plan rang through Congress. John C. Calhoun was dying. He had himself carried into the Senate. He gave a stirring speech against the plan. Stephen Douglas decided to steer the plan through Congress.

President Taylor died in July 1850. Vice President Millard Fillmore took office. He liked Clay's plan and worked with Douglas. All the points were presented as separate laws. The plan's supporters **campaigned** across the country. All the points were passed. The plan was called the "Compromise of 1850."

☆☆☆

Women's Rights

Slavery was not the only issue that involved people's rights. Women began working to make sure they had their rights as citizens, too. They also wanted **educations**. Their hard work paid off. A high school for women opened in New York in 1821. Oberlin College was in Ohio. It opened its doors to women in 1833. African Americans were admitted to Oberlin in 1835.

Women's rights joined slavery and abolition as issues in 1848. A special convention was held in Seneca Falls, New York, in that year. It had been organized by three important leaders who were working for women's rights. They were Elizabeth Cady Stanton, Lucretia Mott, and Martha Coffin Wright. Elizabeth Stanton read her Declaration of Sentiments to the large crowds of men and women. It was based on the ideas of the Declaration of Independence. The three women worked tirelessly for the Declaration. It was accepted by the convention.

Susan B. Anthony soon joined Elizabeth Stanton. They traveled the country to work for women's rights. They worked together as a team. Stanton wrote fiery speeches. Anthony used them to excite crowds about the rights of women. Both of them died before 1920. Women finally gained the right to vote in that year.

▲ Susan B. Anthony

 CHAPTER REVIEW

Critical Thinking

Write your answers on a sheet of paper, or discuss in class.

 1. Why did people become so angry with each other during the debates about slavery?

 2. Do you think the Compromise of 1850 was fair to both sides? Explain your answer.

Cooperative Learning

 3. Work with a partner. Find facts about slave owners and abolitionists. Talk about ways in which these people were alike. For example, both felt very strongly about their opinions. Then, talk about ways in which they were different.

Write About It

 4. Write a paragraph in support of the abolitionists. Write a sentence that tells your main opinion. Then, write at least two other sentences to complete your paragraph. These sentences should tell reasons why you hold this opinion.

Chapter 36

Abolition

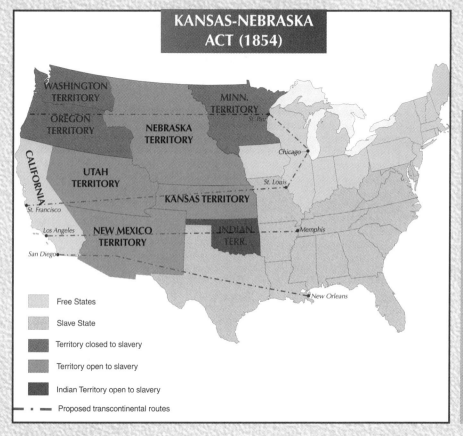

KANSAS-NEBRASKA ACT (1854)

WASHINGTON TERRITORY

OREGON TERRITORY

MINN. TERRITORY
St. Paul

NEBRASKA TERRITORY

Chicago

CALIFORNIA

UTAH TERRITORY

St. Louis

KANSAS TERRITORY

St. Francisco

Los Angeles

NEW MEXICO TERRITORY

INDIAN TERR.

Memphis

San Diego

New Orleans

- Free States
- Slave State
- Territory closed to slavery
- Territory open to slavery
- Indian Territory open to slavery
- - - Proposed transcontinental routes

Read about the growing fight over slavery. How was the government pulled into this fight? Why?

Key *Vocabulary*

fugitive (FYOOH juht iv)
a person who is running away from something

crime (kreyem)
an act that is against the law and that can lead to some kind of punishment

transcontinental
(TRANS kahnt uhn ENT uhl)
across a continent

unorganized
(uhn OR guh neyezd)
not yet established or arranged

autobiography
(aht oh beye AHG ruh fee)
the story of a person's life as told by that person

MAP ANALYSIS

★ **Ask**   What does this map show?

★ **Organize**   Make a table listing the four different routes for the transcontinental railroad. List the territories and states each would run through.

★ **Analyze**   Which territories were open to slavery? Which were closed to slavery?

★ **Answer**   How do you think each route would have affected the territories' votes on whether or not to allow slavery?

Decoding Tip: Note that both f and ph can stand for the sound /f/.

ay	cake	ah	fall, cot	air	air
ee	tree	i	sit	oh	cold
or	cord	oy	toy	uh	above, hundred
a	ask	ar	hard	oo	book
e	yet	eye	nice	uhr	liar, fir, further, color
ow	cow	ooh	boot, true	yoo	you, few, cube

The Compromise of 1850

The plan had four main points:

1	California would become a free state.
2	Two territories would be formed from the other lands gained from Mexico. The people would decide about slavery for themselves.
3	Slavery would continue in the District of Columbia. However, no more slaves could be sold there.
4	New laws would help capture runaway enslaved people. They would then be returned to their owners.

36.1   What was the purpose of the Fugitive Slave Act?

Sometimes enslaved people ran away. They were called **fugitives**. The Fugitive Slave Act was the fourth point of the Compromise of 1850. This act made it legal to catch runaway enslaved people. Then they could be returned to their owners. United States marshals were even sent to catch fugitives.

Often, the Africans were put in chains. People in the North were angry to see people being sent back into slavery. John McHenry was caught in Syracuse, New York, in 1851. There he was put in jail. A crowd of Abolitionists went to the jail. They rushed the building. They let McHenry go.

36.2   How did Abolitionists violate the Fugitive Slave Act?

Abolitionists worked to protect fugitives. Some states even joined the fight. They told their state officers not to carry out the Fugitive Slave Act. People in the South became angry that

▲ William Lloyd Garrison

▲ Horace Greeley

▲ Harriet Tubman

the act was not followed. They were afraid that the Abolitionists were taking over in the North.

Leading the Abolitionists were two newspaper editors. One was William Lloyd Garrison. The other was Horace Greeley. They wrote strong words calling for an end to slavery. Garrison started his paper, *The Liberator*, in 1831. He grew to hate the U.S. government because it permitted slavery. Garrison even wanted the North to break away from the Union. Greeley began the *New York Tribune* in 1841. His paper had strong ties to the Whig party. From the start, Greeley was against slavery. But as time went on, he became more angry. His demands to end slavery took on added fire. Both Garrison and Greeley got death threats for their words. The threats came from North and South alike.

Many Africans did break out of slavery. Most who escaped did so alone, by their own courage. A small number were helped by the Underground Railroad. There were no trains or tracks. Abolitionists ran this system. They helped fugitives move from one safe spot to another. Sometimes, the people were sent north into Canada. Others might go south into Mexico. The safe spots were called "stations." These stations were places like homes, barns, and basements. But most Africans who escaped had to use their own bravery and strength.

Free African Americans often helped run the Underground Railroad. They even led enslaved people on their trips. These trips were dangerous. Sometimes, the free African Americans were caught. They could then be sold back into slavery. This danger did not stop people like Harriet Tubman. She had run away from slavery. She made the trip all by herself. Over the years, she made 19 other trips. She helped over 300 people reach freedom.

36.3 What were the rights of free African Americans?

Over 4,000,000 African Americans were living in the United States by 1860. Only about 250,000 were free. These people had to live in free states. Slave states would let them stay for only so long. Then they could be enslaved again. African Americans in free states still had few rights. Only a few states would let them vote. African Americans could not get good jobs. They were very happy when they could find any kind of work. They would often work for less money just to get a job. Some people were afraid of losing their own jobs to African Americans. It even became a **crime** for African Americans to move into some free states.

36.4 What was the purpose of the transcontinental railroad?

A train route was needed across the country. It was called the **transcontinental** railroad. Transcontinental means "across a continent." Congress began talks about this kind of railroad. Trains already joined cities in lands east of the Mississippi River. Now, Congress talked about where the new line would begin. Four different plans came up in Congress.
1. From Chicago to St. Paul to Oregon
2. From Chicago to St. Louis to San Francisco
3. From Memphis to Los Angeles
4. From New Orleans to San Diego

36.5 Why did talks about a transcontinental railroad bring up the issue of slavery?

Most Americans agreed on one thing. Towns would have to be built in the **Unorganized** Territory. Then, the railroad could be built and run safely. People in free states feared a line running from Memphis or New Orleans. People from these states might bring slavery into the Unorganized Territory. People in the South wanted more slave states. This would keep the numbers of slave and free states the same. One side would not be stronger than the other.

36.6 How did the Kansas-Nebraska Act overturn the Missouri Compromise?

Stephen Douglas's plan for the Unorganized Territory caused fierce fighting about slavery. The Missouri Compromise of 1820 said this land would be for free territories. People in the South called for slavery to be allowed in it. Douglas's plan called for two territories. They would be the Kansas and Nebraska Territories. The people who lived there would then make up their own minds about slavery. His plan was passed in 1854. It was the Kansas-Nebraska Act. The Missouri Compromise had drawn a line between slave and free states. The new act did away with this line. People could begin slavery in any territory. Fighting over slavery grew worse than ever.

Biography

One of the country's great leaders was helped by the Underground Railroad. Frederick Augustus Washington Bailey had been born into slavery in 1817. Despite the law, this young man taught himself to read and write. He ran away from Maryland when he was 18. He was caught and went to jail for three years. In 1835, he reached New York and freedom. He did not want to be caught again. He changed his last name to Douglass.

Douglass wrote a book about his life in 1845. *The Autobiography of Frederick Douglass* sold very well. Now that he was famous, the danger of being caught grew. Douglass moved to England. He stayed for about two years. Then he returned to the United States in 1847. Douglass began his own newspaper. It was called the *North Star*. This was the star that fugitives followed in order to reach freedom. Douglass spent his life working for the rights of all African Americans.

▲ Frederick Douglass

★★☆ CHAPTER REVIEW

Critical Thinking

Write your answers on a sheet of paper, or discuss in class.

Comparing and Contrasting

1. How was the Underground Railroad like a real railroad?

Drawing Conclusions →✕←

2. Why would an Abolitionist hate the Kansas-Nebraska Act?

Cooperative Learning

LEARNING STYLE
Visual

3. Work with a partner. Make a poster about the Underground Railroad. Include pictures that tell what it was like. Draw pictures of people who helped make it work. Put the poster on the walls of the classroom.

Write About It

Writing Portfolio

4. Find out about Harriet Tubman and Frederick Douglass. Write a short report about these people. Share your report with the class. Add your reports to those of your class. Put them into a book. Name this book "Great African Americans."

Chapter 37

Political Battles

The Election of 1856

Candidate	Party	Popular Vote	Electoral Vote	Result
James Buchanan	Democratic	1,832,955	174	elected
John C. Frémont	Republican	1,339,932	114	
Millard Fillmore	Know Nothing	871,731	8	

Key *Vocabulary*

appoint (uh POYNT)
to choose someone for a job or office

violence (VEYE uh luhns)
the use of force against people

outbreak (OWT brayk)
a sudden burst of fighting

balance (BAL uhns)
having something to please all sides

Reteaching Vocabulary

candidate (KAN duh dayt)
one who runs for an office

CHART ANALYSIS

★ **Ask**   Who ran for the Republicans in the 1856 election?

★ **Organize**   Make a pie chart showing the popular vote. Draw a circle and divide it into three pieces. Each piece should show the size of one candidate's vote total in the race.

★ **Analyze**   Did any of the candidates get more than half of the popular vote?

★ **Answer**   In what ways does a strong third-party candidate affect the outcome of an election?

Decoding Tip: Note that the long *a* sound can be made by *ea* and by *ai*.

ay	cake	ah	fall, cot	air	air
ee	tree	i	sit	oh	cold
or	cord	oy	toy	uh	above, hundred
a	ask	ar	hard	oo	book
e	yet	eye	nice	uhr	liar, fir, further, color
ow	cow	ooh	boot, true	yoo	you, few, cube

37.1 How did slavery affect the way Kansas was settled?

▲ President Franklin Pierce

Kansas was fast becoming a battleground over slavery. President Franklin Pierce hoped the Kansas-Nebraska Act would end the fight over slavery. After it passed, Pierce started in to make it work. He **appointed** a man from the North as Kansas's governor. He named a southerner to govern Nebraska. But the South was not happy. They feared Kansas would become a free state. Proslavery people from Missouri sent in people with guns. They tried to bully the people who were living there. A group from the North sent in armed settlers also. Then a vote was held to send a Kansas representative to Congress. The southerners' man won, but with help. Armed people from Missouri crossed over to vote for him. Guns and money continued to pour into Kansas from North and South.

37.2 Why did Kansas have two territorial governments?

In October 1855, antislavery groups in Kansas met. They were called "Free Staters." They hated the present Kansas government because it allowed slavery. The Free Staters drew up the "Topeka Constitution." It made slavery against the law in Kansas. The Free Staters even chose their own governor. Kansas now had two governments. President Pierce was on the side of the first one. He called for Kansas to become a state. Also, he asked Congress to pass a special bill. Money would be needed for troops in Kansas.

37.3 What was "Bleeding Kansas"?

The Kansas problem spilled over into **violence**. The pro-slavery group struck first. In May 1856, the sheriff of Lawrence was shot. Soon the town of Lawrence was burned.

▲ John Brown

Then the antislavery people struck back. John Brown, a northerner, led a raid in which five people were killed. Fighting broke out all over Kansas. By the fall, 200 were dead.

President Pierce named another new governor. He had full rights to use government troops. The troops were able to end the fighting. Armed men from other states were stopped at the border. However, Americans still did not rest easy. They called the **outbreak** "Bleeding Kansas." It showed how ugly the fight over slavery could become.

37.4 What caused the end of the Whig Party?

In 1854, the Whig Party was already breaking apart. The Kansas-Nebraska Act finished it off. Whigs from the North and South could no longer work together. Slavery was the sticking point. It was tearing the whole country in two. The Whigs had been started in the 1830s to oppose Andrew Jackson. They had worked for high tariffs and a national bank. But now the most important fight was over slavery. Most Whigs left to join other parties. Southern Whigs who wanted slavery to continue became Democrats. Northern Whigs were against slavery. They left to join new parties. In the 1856 race for President, the Whigs played almost no part.

37.5 What new parties were formed before the election of 1856? Why?

The fight over slavery led to new parties being started. Whigs who wanted to end slavery met and talked. They saw the Kansas-Nebraska Act as an important test. When it passed, they decided to start a new party. On July 6, 1854, the Republican Party was born. At the time it did not have wide support. Few Southerners joined. Most of them wanted slavery to spread, not end. Lots of people in the North joined the Republican Party. But others in the North held back their support. They feared that strong voices against slavery would break up the Union.

Another new party was the American Party. Its members met in secret groups. When asked what they believed, they would say, "I don't know." They were called the "Know-Nothings." The American Party was against immigrants and the Roman Catholic Church. It wanted to stop the flow of immigrants into the country. Former President Millard Fillmore was their **candidate** in 1856.

37.6 Why did James Buchanan win the 1856 election?

The 1856 election showed how deeply the country was divided over slavery. John C. Frémont of California ran for the Republicans. Frémont campaigned against slavery. If he couldn't end it, he would try to roll it back. The Democrats picked James Buchanan. Buchanan had been in England during the "Bleeding Kansas" problems. He had not been hurt by them. He was against enslavement himself, but thought the South had rights too. Above all, Buchanan wanted to save the Union.

Many people were comfortable with Buchanan's **balanced** ideas. In a three-man race, Buchanan won less than half the votes. But he won easily in electoral votes. Buchanan touched on slavery in his first speech. He planned to let the Supreme Court decide the problem. Two days later, the Supreme Court did decide an important case. It was the Dred Scott case. And it only made things worse.

The Brooks-Sumner Affair

▲ Senator Charles Sumner

On May 22, 1856, angry words in the Senate ended in blows. The Kansas problem was on everyone's mind. Senator Charles Sumner of Massachusetts made an angry talk. Sumner attacked those who supported slavery. Senator Andrew Butler from South Carolina was his key target. Butler's nephew was a member of the House named Preston Brooks. Two days later, Brooks marched into the Senate. He began beating Sumner with a heavy cane. Taken by surprise, Sumner could do nothing. He was badly hurt. It took him three years to recover. Brooks' attack helped bring things in Kansas to a boil. On May 24, John Brown led his raid. The fighting in Kansas would go on for months.

 ## CHALLENGE REVIEW

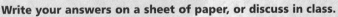

Critical Thinking

Write your answers on a sheet of paper, or discuss in class.

 Drawing Conclusions 1. Why wasn't Franklin Pierce able to keep fighting from breaking out in Kansas?

 Making Inferences 2. The Republican Party began as an antislavery party. Would a party based on one idea be strong or weak?

Cooperative Learning

LEARNING STYLE *Visual* 3. Work with a partner. Make a diagram to show how the Whig Party split on the slavery question. Write which party each group of Whigs joined. Draw arrows from the Whig party to the other parties.

Write About It

Writing Portfolio 4. Write a short speech about "Bleeding Kansas." Tell what you would do to stop the fighting.

Chapter 38

Closer to War

DRED SCOTT'S TRAVELS AS AN ENSLAVED AFRICAN (1834-1843)

Mississippi River

Wisconsin

Iowa

Illinois

Missouri

St. Louis

Free States

Slave States

←--- Dred Scott's Travels as an Enslaved Person

Read about the heated debate over slavery. Who wanted slavery to spread to new states? Why?

Key *Vocabulary*

property (PRAHP uhr tee) something that is owned

reaction (ree AK shuhn) a feeling or statement caused by some event

crisis (KREYE sis) a time of great danger or a turning point

debate (di BAYT) a public talk about issues between two or more people in a political race

weapon (WEP uhn) a gun, bomb, knife, etc.

MAP ANALYSIS

★ **Ask** What river did Dred Scott cross going from Missouri to Illinois?

★ **Acquire** In what three places did Dred Scott live?

★ **Analyze** Was Dred Scott ever in free territory? If so, where was it?

★ **Answer** Using this map, how would you argue that Dred Scott should be free?

Decoding Tip: Notice the two sounds for the vowel *i* in **crisis**.

ay	cake	ah	fall, cot	air	air
ee	tree	i	sit	oh	cold
or	cord	oy	toy	uh	above, hundred
a	ask	ar	hard	oo	book
e	yet	eye	nice	uhr	liar, fir, further, color
ow	cow	ooh	boot, true	yoo	you, few, cube

38.1 What were the facts of the Dred Scott case?

▲ Dred Scott

Dred Scott was an enslaved African American. Scott worked for an Army doctor named John Emerson. Emerson moved his family and workers from Missouri to Illinois. Missouri allowed slavery, while Illinois did not. By Illinois law, Scott could not be held as a slave there. Scott said nothing at the time. Emerson moved his family back to Missouri. In 1846, Emerson died. By Missouri law, ownership of Dred Scott passed to Mrs. Emerson's brother. However, Scott pointed out that he had lived in free territory. He should be a free man. Scott and his lawyer took his case to court.

The decision in the case was slow in coming. Several lower courts ruled on the matter. Some favored Scott and some didn't. At last the case reached the Supreme Court. In 1857, the Court ruled against Scott by 7 to 2. It made two key points. (1) As a slave, Dred Scott was not a citizen of the United States. (2) Enslaved people were like **property**. Congress could not pass laws to take property away from the people.

38.2 What effect did the Dred Scott decision have on the nation?

President James Buchanan hoped the Dred Scott case would end problems over slavery. Buchanan wanted people to accept the ruling and go on. He knew some Americans would not like it. But the angry **reactions** surprised him. Republicans in the North exclaimed against it. They promised to win control of the government. Then they would change the Supreme Court. The new Court would throw out the Dred Scott ruling. Congress was also angry. Was the Supreme Court taking away their right to make laws? They had passed laws against slavery in certain territories. Now those laws were struck down. Many in Congress believed slavery was a matter of politics. They believed the Supreme Court should stay out of it. Only the Southern Democrats liked the decision. But even they thought the Supreme Court had gone too far. Henry Clay spoke for many in the country. The Supreme Court should "solve our problems, not make them," he said.

38.3   Who was Abraham Lincoln?

As the country headed towards **crisis**, it looked for new leaders. One was Abraham Lincoln. Lincoln was born in 1809 in Kentucky. His first home was a log cabin. Yet he would become the 16th President of the United States. His strong leadership helped bring the country through a hard time.

As a boy, Lincoln worked hard on his parents' farm. He had little time for school. However, he learned many things by reading. He read by the fire at night. Neighbors saw him reading while plowing the fields. In 1830, the Lincolns moved to Illinois. Abraham studied law. He got into politics. He was against slavery from the start. In Illinois, he got his first taste of the bitter fight it could cause. He won a seat in Congress. His stand against the Mexican War showed he would fight for what he believed. Soon he was talked about as a man of promise. He was also known for his jokes and his rich use of words.

▲ Abraham Lincoln

▼ Stephen A. Douglas

38.4   Why were the Lincoln-Douglas debates important?

In 1858, Abraham Lincoln ran for the Senate in Illinois. Since he was against slavery, he ran as a Republican. His opponent was Democrat Stephen A. Douglas. Douglas had pushed the Kansas-Nebraska Act. The spread of slavery became the key to the race. Lincoln and Douglas met in seven **debates**. The whole country was interested in what they said.

Each debate had a circus air to it. Bands played and cannons roared. The two speakers were very different. At five feet four, Douglas was called "the Little Giant." Lincoln was a

foot taller. The talks were serious. But sometimes Lincoln used jokes to win over the people. At one point, Douglas called Lincoln "two-faced." Lincoln replied, "If I had another face to wear, do you think I would wear this one?"

The Lincoln-Douglas debates were important because they aired out the slavery question. Should slavery spread to new states? Douglas believed each state should decide for itself. Lincoln thought slavery was wrong no matter what. He didn't seek to end it in states that already had it. But he was against its spreading to other states. Lincoln lost the Senate race. But he won a following that would send him to the White House.

38.5 Why did the raid at Harpers Ferry shock most Americans?

In 1859, John Brown led a raid in Harpers Ferry, Virginia. Brown had already fought in "Bleeding Kansas." He was a northerner who hated slavery. Brown and his men tried to take **weapons** from the U.S. storehouse at Harpers Ferry. They planned to set up a country for African Americans. It would be a home for those who had run from slavery. Instead, Brown and his men were caught and put to death.

▼ Convicted by a Virginia court for insurrection, treason, and murder, John Brown is escorted from prison to his execution by hanging in Charlestown, VA, 1859.

Brown's raid shook the nation. It showed how dangerous the fight had become. The two sides were further apart than ever. Abolitionists in the North called Brown a hero. Churches were covered in black on the day of his death. However, many in the South were angry. They claimed the North was trying to start trouble. A new kind of talk began. The South might leave the Union. Jefferson Davis, a senator from Mississippi, said it plainly. Things were heading towards "civil war."

☆☆☆

In Their Own Words
THE LINCOLN—DOUGLAS DEBATES

In 1858, the slavery issue was on everyone's mind. This came through in the speeches of Abraham Lincoln and Stephen A. Douglas. Many of the things they said became well known.

Stephen A. Douglas—

"I believe [this government] was made by white men, for the benefit [good] of white men and their posterity [children] for ever."

"Why can [this country] not exist divided into free and slave states? . . . Why can it not exist on the same principles on which our fathers made it?"

"The great principle of this Government is, that each State has the right to do as it pleases on all these questions, and no other State, or power on earth has the right to interfere with us . . ."

Abraham Lincoln—

"'A house divided against itself cannot stand.' I believe this government cannot endure permanently [cannot last] half slave and half free. . . It will become all one thing, or all the other."

"Slavery is an unqualified [pure] evil to the Negro, to the white man, to the soil, and to the state."

"That is the real issue. That is the issue that will continue in this country when these poor tongues of Judge Douglas and myself shall be silent. It is the eternal struggle [fight] between these two principles—right and wrong—throughout the world."

★★☆ CHAPTER REVIEW

Critical Thinking

Write your answers on a sheet of paper, or discuss in class.

Drawing Conclusions →※←

1. Could any decision in the Dred Scott case have ended the fight over slavery? Explain your answer.

Making Inferences

2. Would you vote for someone based on how well he or she did in a debate?

Cooperative Learning

LEARNING STYLE
Tactile

3. Work with a partner or group. Make a diorama, or small scene in a box. Have it show one of the Lincoln-Douglas debates. Make the figures from papier-mache or clay. Paint the figures to look like Lincoln and Douglas. Paint the inside of the box to show people in the crowd. Make paper flags and signs to finish the scene. Tape record some of Lincoln and Douglas's words. Play the tape as you display the diorama.

Write About It

Writing Portfolio

4. Imagine that you are going to debate Lincoln or Douglas. Write notes for the debate. Write ten short points that you want to cover in your speech.

For the People, By the People

Chapter 39

The Future of the Nation

Read about the Election of 1860. How did this election pull the country apart? Why?

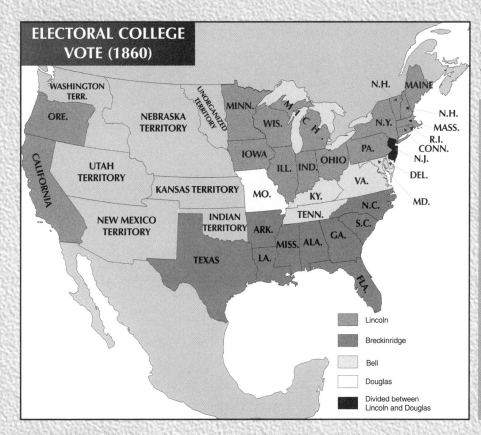

ELECTORAL COLLEGE VOTE (1860)

■	Lincoln
■	Breckinridge
☐	Bell
☐	Douglas
■	Divided between Lincoln and Douglas

Key *Vocabulary*

plank (plangk)
each idea of a party's plan for running government

platform (PLAT form)
all the ideas that make up a party's plan for running government

moderate (MAHD ur ruht)
a person who does not support extreme ideas

majority (muh JOR uht ee)
any number that is greater than one half

Reteaching Vocabulary

secession (suh SESH uhn)
the act of leaving or breaking away from a group or country

MAP ANALYSIS

★ **Ask**   What does this map show?

★ **Organize** Make a table listing the four candidates for President. List the states that each candidate won.

★ **Analyze**   Who won in the North and West? In the South? In states between the North and South?

★ **Answer**   How does this map show the factions that had formed in the country?

Decoding Tip: Note that both *s* and *c* stand for the sound /s/ in **secession**.

ay	cake	ah	fall, cot	air	air
ee	tree	i	sit	oh	cold
or	cord	oy	toy	uh	above, hundred
a	ask	ar	hard	oo	book
e	yet	eye	nice	uhr	liar, fir, further, color
ow	cow	ooh	boot, true	yoo	you, few, cube

39.1 Why did the Democrats choose two people to run for President in 1860?

Slavery issues blew the 1860 Democratic convention apart. Northern Democrats wanted the government to overlook the Dred Scott decision. Southerners were frightened by John Brown's raid on Harpers Ferry. Some even believed that Republicans were involved in the raid. They wanted harsh laws to keep strict controls on enslaved people. Northern Democrats refused to add such **planks** to the party's **platform**. A platform is a plan for running government. Each idea in the plan is called a "plank." Eight states marched out of this convention in Charleston, South Carolina. A second convention was held in Baltimore. Northern Democrats led the party to choose Stephen Douglas. Southern Democrats stormed out of this meeting, too. They knew that Douglas did not share their ideas about slavery. They chose Vice President John C. Breckinridge to run for President.

39.2 What were the planks of the Republicans and their candidate, Abraham Lincoln?

Republicans watched the Democratic fighting with glee. Now they saw their chance to take the White House. The Chicago convention chose Abraham Lincoln as the Republican candidate. The party built a platform with many kinds of planks. They wanted to please voters in all parts of

The Election of 1860

Candidate	Party	Popular Vote	Electoral Vote	Result
Abraham Lincoln	Republican	1,865,593	180	elected
John C. Breckinridge	Democrat	848,356	72	lost
John Bell	Constitutional Union	592,906	39	lost
Stephen Douglas	Democrat	1,382,713	12	lost

the country. They promised that free land would be given out in the Western territories. Building projects for things like roads were included in the platform. Northerners were pleased when Republicans supported a tariff to protect business interests. Republicans would not agree to let slavery into new territories. However, they did promise to continue slavery in states where it was already practiced. Republicans also took a stand against acts like the raid on Harpers Ferry.

39.3 How did a third party affect the Election of 1860?

Moderates formed a new party in hopes of keeping the country together. These people supported some changes, but would use compromise to keep the country going as it was. Some of the country's Whigs, Democrats, Know-Nothings, and Republicans shared these ideas. They formed the Constitutional Union Party. Its candidate was John Bell. The party wanted the Union and the Constitution to be protected. They called for all laws, like the Dred Scott decision, to be carried out. Almost 600,000 voters supported the party and John Bell.

39.4 How did the election's results divide the nation?

Secession became a threat during the election. Southern Democrats could not stand the idea of a Republican President. These states said they would leave the Union if Lincoln was elected. Lincoln won the Popular Election. He did not have a clear **majority** of votes, though. Lincoln would have lost if all the other votes had gone to just one candidate. But, Lincoln swept the Electoral College. He would have won even if there had been only one other candidate. Southern Democrats carried out their threat. South Carolina was the first state to vote for secession. Soon, seven other states had left the Union, too.

39.5   How did President Buchanan and the Senate try to keep the Union together?

President James Buchanan hoped to save the Union. He told the Southern states that they had no right to secession. However, he believed it was against the law to send troops to prevent such acts. He asked the Senate for a new law. The Missouri Compromise would be put back into effect. The line dividing slave and free states would be pushed west to the Pacific Ocean. Slavery would be allowed in all states and territories south of this line. Lincoln and the Republicans would not agree. This would create new lands for slavery. Buchanan's plan failed.

39.6   How was the Confederacy formed?

The seceding states wanted a new country. South Carolina, Georgia, Florida, Alabama, Mississippi, Louisiana, and Texas sent representatives to Montgomery, Alabama in February, 1861. They formed the Confederate States of America. Its government would be like that of the United States. The federal government would be much weaker, though. The President and Vice President were Jefferson Davis and Alexander Stephens. They would serve only one term each. However, the term would last six years. Slavery would be continued and protected. The new government took over all land and buildings in the South that had belonged to the United States. This included all forts and other military centers.

Biography

▲ Jefferson Davis

Jefferson Davis had helped lead the country until his state of Mississippi left the Union. He had attended West Point and entered the army. There he met General Zachary Taylor's daughter, Sarah. He left the army to marry her, but she died only three months later. He worked hard running his plantation on the Mississippi River. It made him rich. In 1845 he was elected to the House of Representatives. Later, he was elected to the Senate. During his years in Congress he always supported the idea of states' rights.

Davis left Congress for a while in 1846. He fought in the Mexican-American War. He was with General Zachary Taylor at Buena Vista. Davis's plans saved the battle for the United States. President Franklin Pierce asked Davis to be in his Cabinet. Davis was Secretary of War from 1853 to 1857. He built up the army and navy so they were stronger than ever.

Mississippi voted for secession in 1861, so Davis left the U.S. Senate. The first Confederate Congress elected him President. He would rather have led the army. He was not popular. Some people complained about the way he ran his office. After the Civil War, he traveled widely. He became much more popular with the former Confederates. After his death, Mississippi presented a statue of Davis for Congress's Statuary Hall.

 CHAPTER REVIEW

Critical Thinking

Write your answers on a sheet of paper, or discuss in class.

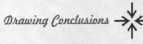 *Drawing Conclusions*

1. Why were planks in the Republican platform so hateful to Southern Democrats?

 Comparing and Contrasting

2. How were the Confederate government and the U.S. government alike and different?

Cooperative Learning

 LEARNING STYLE *Visual*

3. Work with a partner. Make a poster for one candidate in the Election of 1860. Be sure to include the candidate's ideas. Display your poster with others from your class.

Write About It

 Writing Portfolio

4. Abraham Lincoln had a wonderful sense of humor. Find books about Lincoln. Read about some of the funny things he said. Write a short paragraph about one of his sayings. Tell what happened to make him think of this funny thing to say.

Chapter 40

Battle Lines

The Union versus the Confederacy		
	United States	Confederate States
Number of States	24	11
Number of Territories	6	1
Number of People	22,000,000	9,000,000
Number of Factories	119,000	21,000
Number of Farms	1,400,000	690,000
Number of Trading Ships	150,000	17,000
Miles of Railroad Tracks	21,500	8,500
Money held in Banks	$111,000,000	$38,000,000
Money Earned from Exports	$175,000,000	$226,000,000

Read about the war that broke out between the United States' citizens. What did each side hope to achieve? Why?

Key *Vocabulary*

military (MIL uh tair ee) anything involved with the army, navy, air force, or marines

installation (in stuh LAY shuhn) a place where the military sets up full-time quarters, such as a fort or base

volunteer (vahl uhn TEER) a person who chooses to join the army, navy, air force, or marines

Reteaching Vocabulary

blockade (blah KAYD) the act of using ships on a country's coast to keep other ships from bringing in goods

CHART ANALYSIS

★ **Ask** What does this chart show?

★ **Organize** Which side had the most of each item?

★ **Analyze** How would each item help each side fight the war?

★ **Answer** Which side do you think was better able to win the war?

Decoding Tip: Note the different sounds that i can stand for.

ay	cake	ah	fall, cot	air	air
ee	tree	i	sit	oh	cold
or	cord	oy	toy	uh	above, hundred
a	ask	ar	hard	oo	book
e	yet	eye	nice	uhr	liar, fir, further, color
ow	cow	ooh	boot, true	yoo	you, few, cube

40.1 What message did Lincoln send to the South in his inaugural speech?

In his inaugural speech, Lincoln suggested ways of keeping the Union together. He did not want war. The South was asked to give up secession peacefully. In return, Lincoln promised to continue slavery in those states where it was already being practiced. However, he also took a stand on some issues. He would not allow any more "slave states" to be formed. If the South did not give up secession, he would use any means needed to bring those states back into the Union.

40.2 What crisis led to the attack on Fort Sumter?

Lincoln promised to support **military installations** in the South. Word arrived from Charleston, South Carolina, on the day after his inaugural speech. Fort Sumter needed more troops and supplies. The fort was built on an island in the bay. The Confederates warned the Union not to help this fort. They felt it belonged to the new Confederate country.

Lincoln thought about the problem for almost six weeks. Finally, he decided to send supplies. No troops would be sent.

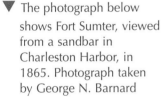

▼ The photograph below shows Fort Sumter, viewed from a sandbar in Charleston Harbor, in 1865. Photograph taken by George N. Barnard

This might help to keep the peace. The ship arrived in April 1861. The Confederates took it as an act of war. They attacked the fort on April 12. Now that fighting had broken out, Lincoln knew that peace was impossible. He asked for **volunteers** in order to build up the army.

40.3   How did the Confederacy plan to use foreign help against the North?

Cotton would be used as a weapon by the South. Europe needed the South's cotton. Their factories could not make cloth without it. The Confederate government wanted European help in exchange for shipments of cotton. It also wanted France and Britain to officially recognize the independence of the South. There were even hopes that these countries would fight for the South. The South depended on Europe in other ways. These states had always bought most of the goods they needed. Many of these goods had come from Europe.

40.4   How did the North hope that a blockade would affect the war?

General Winfield Scott was put in charge of the U.S. military. He sent ships to block Southern ports. This would keep cotton shipments from reaching Europe. European goods would be kept out of the South. At first, the U.S. Navy did not have enough ships to carry out this order. President Lincoln began a building program. Soon, the navy was cutting off the South from the world.

Blockade runners helped the South carry on. These ships were small and fast. They would slip past the U.S. Navy and sail to the Bahamas. This was English territory. They traded cotton for goods and sailed back with these supplies. The Confederacy built some ships, too. They even bought ships from Britain. Some of these ships tracked U.S. merchant

▲ Lt. General Winfield Scott

ships. They would capture these ships and take all the goods on board.

40.5 What was General Scott's "Anaconda Plan"?

General Scott planned to squeeze the South into surrendering. The anaconda is a snake that catches animals by squeezing them. Scott's plan became known as the "Anaconda Plan." The blockade had already cut the South off from the world. Next, Scott planned to take over the Mississippi River. This would cut the Confederacy off from its western states and territories. Then, Scott would lead Union troops south and east into the main body of the Confederacy. Scott knew that this would not make the South give up easily. It would have to be crushed.

40.6 What advantages did each side have in the Civil War?

The South had to buy everything it needed for the war. However, the Union could make everything it needed. Almost all of the country's factories were in the North. There were more railroads in Union states. This would make it easy to ship goods to the army. More people lived in the North, too. There would be more people to fight as soldiers. Union leaders felt that they would be able to destroy any idea that a state could secede.

▲ The photograph above shows the east front of Arlington Mansion, General Lee's home, with Union soldiers on the lawn on June 28, 1864

▲ Confederate General Robert E. Lee

Confederate leaders planned only one battle outside the South. They would move against Washington, D.C. They would not move against any Union states, though. They would only fight to defend themselves. Besides, some even felt they could win the war quickly and easily. The Confederates were determined to secede. Their leaders knew that many Northerners had no strong feelings about the secession. They hoped these people would grow tired of the war. Then, these Northerners would push the Union to recognize Confederate independence.

☆☆☆

Connections

▲ Mary Todd Lincoln

Not only the country was divided by the Civil War. Families took different sides, too. Mrs. Mary Todd Lincoln's family owned slaves. One of her brothers was an officer in the Confederate Army. Her other brother was a doctor in the Confederate Army. Mrs.Lincoln had three sisters. All three were married to Confederate soldiers. At one point, some Northerners said that Mrs. Lincoln was passing Union secrets to her family. President Lincoln appeared in Congress to stop these claims.

Many Southerners had links to great Americans. One example is Confederate General Robert E. Lee. Lee was the son of "Lighthorse" Henry Lee. Henry Lee had been an officer on George Washington's staff during the Revolutionary War. Lee was also related to Robert Henry Lee. He had called for the vote on independence from Britain during the Second Continental Congress of 1776. General Robert E. Lee married into George Washington's family. His wife was Mary Custis, great granddaughter of Martha Custis, who has married George Washington. Washington's adopted son built Arlington plantation outside Washington, D.C. The Robert E. Lees lived there after marrying in 1831. Union forces took over the home on April 22, 1861. Secretary of War Edwin M. Stanton's office had to set up cemeteries for those killed in battle. He ordered the dead to be buried on the lawn of Arlington in 1864. He said that the Lees would never want to live in the house again. Today, this place is Arlington National Cemetery. Thousands are buried there. They include people who fought in all U.S. wars. President John F. Kennedy was buried there in 1963.

 ## CHAPTER REVIEW

Critical Thinking

Write your answers on a sheet of paper, or discuss in class.

1. Why would fighting on their own ground and for their own homes make the Confederates even more determined to win?

2. How were the goals of the Confederacy and the Union alike and different?

Cooperative Learning

3. Work with a partner. Find out about Fort Sumter. Make a model of the fort. Put the model on a large piece of cardboard. Show the coast of South Carolina and the island where the fort was built. Make small trees and soldiers to make your model look real.

Write About It

4. Many Presidents of the late 1800s served in the Civil War. Find out about these Presidents. Write a short report that compares the ways in which they served the United States during this crisis.

Quiz

Number a piece of paper from 1-10. Read each question below. Read the answers that follow each question. Choose the answer for each question. Write the letter of the answer you choose beside the correct number on your piece of paper.

1. **What issue caused arguments when states like California and Missouri asked to join the Union?**
   a. tariffs
   b. slavery
   c. secession
   d. none of the above

2. **After the Kansas-Nebraska Act, who would decide whether or not new states would allow slavery?**
   a. Congress
   b. the Supreme Court
   c. the people living in those states
   d. the people of the whole country

3. **What does the term "Bleeding Kansas" refer to?**
   a. fighting in Kansas over the issue of slavery
   b. injuries in Kansas caused by tornadoes
   c. fierce arguments in Congress over making Kansas a state
   d. all of the above

4. **What new party was formed in 1856 in order to fight slavery?**
   a. the Republican party
   b. the Democratic party
   c. the American party
   d. the Know-Nothing party

5. **According to the Supreme Court, what was Dred Scott's place in the United States?**
   a. He was a visiting African.
   b. He was not a United States citizen.
   c. He was property and had no rights.
   d. both b and c

6. **What idea did the South begin discussing after the raid on Harpers Ferry?**
   a. abolition
   b. popular sovereignty
   c. secession
   d. none of the above

7. **Who was elected President in 1860?**
   a. Abraham Lincoln
   b. Stephen A. Douglas
   c. John Bell
   d. James Buchanan

8. **How did the South react to the election results?**
   a. It closed all its ports to Northern ships.
   b. It seceded and formed a new country.
   c. It called for the Supreme Court to decide the election.
   d. all of the above

9. **When did war break out between the North and the South?**
   a. the day of Lincoln's inauguration
   b. when Jefferson Davis became President of the Confederacy
   c. the day Fort Sumter fired on the city of Savannah, Georgia
   d. when Confederates fired on Fort Sumter to stop Lincoln's supply ships

10. **Which side had better resources for fighting a war?**
    a. the North
    b. the South
    c. neither side
    d. both were equal

ANALYZING CAUSE AND EFFECT

Add numbers 11–15 to your paper. Read the ideas below. The ideas on the left describe a cause, or something that makes a second event happen. The ideas on the right are effects, the events that are caused. Match these causes and effects. Write your answers beside the correct numbers on your paper.

11. Antislavery and proslavery groups both wanted to have more members in Congress.
12. People in the territories could decide about slavery for themselves.
13. There was no party that worked to end slavery.
14. Abraham Lincoln was elected President of the United States.
15. General Winfield Scott used a blockade to cut the South off from the world.

a. Seven Southern states seceded and formed the Confederate States of America.
b. The Republican Party was formed in 1854.
c. The Compromise of 1820 would no longer have any effect on the states.
d. Both groups tried to take control in new states.
e. The South could not use cotton sales to supply its war efforts.

Look over the writing you did for Chapters 36–40. Work with a study partner or group. Turn your work into a speech about the issue of slavery. Include facts about famous abolitionists such as Frederick Douglass and Abraham Lincoln. Be sure to give reasons to support your opinions about slavery. Exchange papers with a partner. Look for errors. Talk about the ideas in the speech. Are they clearly presented? Write out a clean copy of your speech. Present it to the class. Put your speech in your writing portfolio.

Work with a partner. Think about what happened in Chapters 36-40. Make a list of these important events. Note the date that each happened. Then, use the events to make a timeline for the chapter. Write a sentence for each date. Tell what happened on that date. Also tell why that date is important. Share your timeline with the class.

COOPERATIVE PROJECT: THE LINCOLN-DOUGLAS DEBATES

Work with a group. Find a book about the Lincoln-Douglas debates. Find important points that each man made in his speeches. Make a list of these points. Be sure to copy out the speaker's exact words. Then, choose two people to play Abraham Lincoln and Stephen A. Douglas. Give these people your lists. Have them act out a debate for the class. You may even wish to make costumes and present the debate for the whole school.

Chapter 41

The Struggle for Control

UNION AND CONFEDERATE STATES (1861)

WASHINGTON TERRITORY
OREGON
DAKOTA TERRITORY
WISC.
MINN.
MICH.
IOWA
NEV. TERR.
UTAH TERR.
NEBRASKA TERR.
COLORADO TERR.
CALIFORNIA
KANSAS
MO.
NEW MEXICO TERRITORY
INDIAN TERR.
ARK.
TEXAS
LA.
MISS.
ALA.
GA.
TENN.
KY.
IL. IND.
OHIO
PA.
N.Y.
VT. N.H.
MAINE
MASS.
R.I.
CONN.
N.J.
DEL.
Washington, D.C.
MD.
VA.
NC.
SC.
FL.

Original states to secede

States that seceded after Lincoln's call for troops

Union States

Territories and states not involved in the war

Read about some of the important ideas and events in the Civil War. How did each side plan to defeat the other?

Key *Vocabulary*

secede (si SEED)
to leave the Union

defeat (di FEET)
to beat, as in battle

Reteaching Vocabulary

blockade (blah KAYD)
the act of using ships on a country's coast to keep other ships from bringing in goods

MAP ANALYSIS

★ **Ask** Which states had seceded from the Union before the battle of Fort Sumter?

★ **Analyze** Why was battle in northern Virginia so dangerous for the Union capital?

★ **Answer** Locate the Mississippi River on the map. Work with a partner to explain why the Union needed to control the river to be successful in the war.

Decoding Tip: Notice the different spellings for the sound ee in the vocabulary words.

ay	cake	ah	fall, cot	air	air
ee	tree	i	sit	oh	cold
or	cord	oy	toy	uh	above, hundred
a	ask	ar	hard	oo	book
e	yet	eye	nice	uhr	liar, fir, further, color
ow	cow	ooh	boot, true	yoo	you, few, cube

▲ The photograph above shows a high-angle view toward the Capitol in 1862.

▲ Above is a photograph of the *White House of the Confederacy*, which was also Jefferson Davis's home.

▼ The photograph below shows a scene from the March in Manassas, Virginia, 1862.

41.1 Why did the Confederacy move its efforts and headquarters to Virginia?

When Fort Sumter was attacked, only seven states had **seceded**, or left the Union. After the attack, President Lincoln called for volunteers to fight. Jefferson Davis, president of the Confederacy, also called for soldiers.

When Lincoln called to form an army, four more southern states seceded to join the Confederacy. They were Tennessee, Arkansas, North Carolina, and Virginia.

The states of Delaware, Maryland, Kentucky, and Missouri were also slave states, but they chose not to secede. Forty-six counties of Virginia refused to secede. They formed the state of West Virginia.

Virginia was a very important state to the Confederacy. It had a large population. It also had a good economy. Both would be helpful in the war effort. Several experienced army officers also called Virginia home. Because Virginia was so important, the Confederacy moved its capital from Montgomery, Alabama to Richmond, Virginia.

41.2   How did the First Battle of Bull Run shock the Union?

On July 16, 1861, Union General Irvin McDowell decided to move his troops toward Richmond. They intended to capture the Confederate capital. No one thought the war would last more than three months. The Union army marched toward a little town in Virginia called Manassas. A little stream of water called Bull Run ran near the town.

On July 21, the Union troops met Confederate troops at Manassas. People from Washington, D.C. heard about the Union battle plans and rode in wagons and carriages to Manassas to watch the battle. Most people thought it would be like a sporting event. Some of them even brought picnic lunches.

▲ The photograph above shows the *U.S.S. St. Louis*, the first ironclad gunboat, renamed the *Baron de Kalb* in October 1862.

▼ The painting below shows a scene from the Battle of Gaines Mill, Valley of the Chickahominy, Virginia on June 27,1862. Painting by Prince de Joinville.

However, the South's General Pierre G.T. Beauregard and General Joeseph E. Johnston were better prepared than McDowell thought. The South stopped several attacks by the Union army. Then when the Union soldiers were tired, the southern generals began their own attack. The Union soldiers were **defeated**. They ran back toward Washington to get away from the southern army.

This early battle was a shock to the Union army. They had thought that the South could not possibly fight a war. They had predicted that the war would be over in three months. After the battle at Manassas, the northern army knew that the war would be a long and hard one.

41.3   Why was control of the Mississippi River vital?

Both sides wanted to control the Mississippi River. In February of 1862, Union General Ulysses S. Grant began a move to take control of the river. First, he took Fort Henry on the Tennessee River. Next, he took Fort Donelson on the Cumberland River.

In April of 1862, General Grant's troops defeated the Confederates at Shiloh and took control of the Mississippi River. The Union now controlled much of the western part of the Confederacy. They controlled land to the north and west of the Confederate states. To the east and south was the Atlantic Ocean. The North had placed a **blockade** on the coast. The Union was slowly surrounding the Confederacy.

41.4   Why was General McClellan not regarded as a suitable commander in 1862?

General George B. McClellan led the Army of the Potomac. President Lincoln ordered McClellan to take Richmond. McClellan moved the troops by water. Moving them was a slow process. In fact, they moved so slowly that General Robert E. Lee and the Confederate army were ready for them. The two armies fought for three months. The Union army was driven back to the coast. President Lincoln removed General McClellan as commander of the Army of the Potomac.

41.5   How did General Lee change the Confederacy's basic plans for war?

After Lee's Army of Northern Virginia defeated General McClellan, Lee changed his battle plans. Before, most of the battles had been on southern territory. Lee did not want to attack the Union. He only wanted to defend the South. Now Lee went into northern territory. He wanted England and France to see the Confederacy as separate from the Union. He was hoping that they would send money and other support for the cause of the Confederacy. ☆☆☆

Connections

Warfare today is different from warfare in the Civil War. However, the Civil War brought about some tools of war that are still used today. Our lives changed in other ways because of the war. Among the "firsts" that came about during the Civil War are:

INCOME TAX

U.S. SECRET SERVICE

U.S. MEDAL OF HONOR

A SUCCESSFUL SUBMARINE

THE SNORKEL, FOR BREATHING UNDER WATER

LAND-MINE FIELDS

HOSPITAL SHIPS

THE MACHINE GUN

NAVY TORPEDOES

WAR-TIME PRESS CORRESPONDENTS

PHOTOGRAPHY IN BATTLE

STEEL SHIPS

▲ Scene from the Civil War

★★☆ CHAPTER REVIEW

Critical Thinking

Write your answers on a sheet of paper, or discuss in class.

 *Making Inferences*

1. What could General McClellan have done to keep from being removed as commander by President Lincoln?

 *Drawing Conclusions*

2. From what you know about the war so far, why did General Lee want the support of France and England?

Cooperative Learning

LEARNING STYLE
Visual

3. Work with a partner. Beginning with the attack on Fort Sumter, draw a flow chart of the events and major happenings of the Civil War up to the point at which this chapter ends.

Write About It

Writing Portfolio

4. Imagine you are a soldier for the South at the battle of Bull Run, or Manassas. Write a letter home describing how people and soldiers ran away from the field of battle.

Chapter 42

The Union Advances

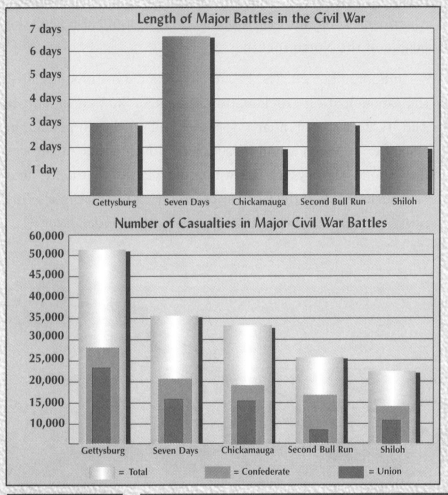

Length of Major Battles in the Civil War

(Bar graph showing days: Gettysburg 3 days, Seven Days 7 days, Chickamauga 2 days, Second Bull Run 3 days, Shiloh 2 days)

Number of Casualties in Major Civil War Battles

(Bar graph showing casualties by battle: Gettysburg, Seven Days, Chickamauga, Second Bull Run, Shiloh)

☐ = Total   ▨ = Confederate   ■ = Union

Read about some of the events that changed the Civil War. How did President Lincoln free the slaves?

Key *Vocabulary*

trench (trench)
a ditch dug into the ground in which soldiers hide and fire at the enemy

draft (draft)
the selection of people who will be forced to serve in the military

GRAPH ANALYSIS

★ **Ask**   Which battle lasted for the longest period of time?

★ **Acquire**   In which battle were the most people killed and injured?

★ **Analyze**   The battles of Chickamauga and Shiloh each lasted for two days.
How do the number of dead and injured compare for these two battles?

★ **Answer**   Which side seemed to have lost the most people in these battles?

Decoding Tip: Notice the short sound of the vowels in the vocabulary words.

ay	cake	ah	fall, cot	air	air
ee	tree	i	sit	oh	cold
or	cord	oy	toy	uh	above, hundred
a	ask	ar	hard	oo	book
e	yet	eye	nice	uhr	liar, fir, further, color
ow	cow	ooh	boot, true	yoo	you, few, cube

42.1 Why did President Lincoln issue the Emancipation Proclamation?

President Lincoln felt that he was fighting the Civil War to save the Union. He wanted all people to be free, but he did not consider slavery to be the cause of the war. He also did not want the slavery states, or border states, to leave the Union. However, he knew that freedom for enslaved African Americans would hurt the Confederacy. It would also keep the people of the North together.

On September 22, 1862, Lincoln signed a document called the Emancipation Proclamation. It was an announcement. It said that, as of January 1, 1863, all enslaved people in Confederate lands would be set free. This announcement was not about slavery in Delaware, Maryland, Kentucky, and Missouri, or any of the territories won back by the Union. This new freedom would only be in states in the Confederacy.

▼ The photograph below shows a dead Confederate sharpshooter in the Devil's Den in Gettysburg, Pennsylvania, July 1863.

▲ The photograph above shows dead soldiers after the Battle of Gettysburg in Pennsylvania in July 1863.

42.2 How did the Battle of Gettysburg change the course of the war?

For the second time during the war, General Lee decided to take his troops into northern land. This time he hoped to attack either Philadelphia, Baltimore, or Washington, D.C. He hoped that winning a battle in one of these places would make the Union army give up the war.

People in the North were worried. President Lincoln put General Joseph Hooker in charge of the Army of the Potomac. He told Hooker to stop Lee and his army. The Army of the Potomac outnumbered Lee's army by about 25,000 men.

The two armies met at Gettysburg on July 1, 1863. The battle raged for three days. On the third day, Confederate General George E. Pickett led a charge against the Union army. He led his troops up Cemetery Ridge, where they were forced to fall back. By the end of the battle, General Lee's army had lost more than 20,000 men.

Lee lost so many men at Gettysburg that the southern army was never the same. Never again was the Confederate army strong enough to attack the North in a major battle.

42.3 How did General Grant divide the Confederacy?

About the same time that General Lee was fighting at Gettysburg, General Grant was fighting in another part of the country. He was fighting near the town of Vicksburg, Mississippi.

For several months, Grant had tried to attack Vicksburg, but the ground north of it was low and marshy. He finally slipped past the Confederates during the night. The troops marched south of Vicksburg on the west side of the river. They then crossed the river and went north to Vicksburg.

The actual battle lasted six weeks. On July 4, the day after Lee lost Gettysburg, Grant defeated the Confederate army at Vicksburg. This defeat separated Arkansas and Texas from the rest of the South.

42.4 How did African Americans participate in the war effort?

As early as July 1862, African American men were accepted into the army. They worked as cooks, **trench** builders, and at other jobs within the camps. After the Emancipation Proclamation, whole troops were made up of African Americans. These troops were given guns and trained in how to fight. After the Proclamation was issued, almost 200,000 African Americans joined the Union army. Others joined the Confederate army.

The 54th Regiment, Massachusetts Volunteer Infantry was commanded by Colonel Robert Gould Shaw, a white colonel. The 54th Regiment showed outstanding bravery in the charge during the Battle of Fort Wagner. Colonel Shaw was killed and many of his men were wounded. Some were given awards for bravery. The movie *Glory* is based on the story of Colonel Shaw and the 54th Regiment. A monument to these men stands at the Boston Common in Boston, Massachusetts.

42.5 Why did draft laws make Lincoln unpopular?

When the Civil War first began, all soldiers were volunteers. People joined the army to fight for their cause. However, as the war dragged on, fewer and fewer people signed up to fight.

In 1862, the Confederate army came up with a solution for this problem. The Confederate congress passed a law creating the **draft**. A draft is government selection of people who will be forced to serve in the army. In 1863 the Union also started a draft.

▲ In July 1862, African Americans were able to participate in the war effort.

In the North the draft made President Lincoln unpopular. In both the Confederate and Union armies, people chosen for the draft could pay someone else to take their places. This idea was fine for the rich. Those who did not want to fight could buy their way out. But the poor had no choice. They had to fight. The poor felt that this was unfair. In 1863 in New York City, about 50,000 people rioted because of the draft. The Union army had to stop the riots.

☆☆☆

Biography

Martin R. Delaney was the first African American staff officer in the United States military. He was commissioned as a major in the 104th U.S. Colored Troops in 1865. Delaney was sent to South Carolina to help organize the 104th and 105th U.S. Colored Troops.

▲ Major Martin R. Delaney

Alexander T. Augusta was commissioned in 1863. He became an officer in 1865. Dr. Augusta was an army surgeon. Even though he was the second African American army officer, he held the highest rank. He was promoted to brevet lieutenant colonel.

 CHAPTER REVIEW

Critical Thinking

Write your answers on a sheet of paper, or discuss in class.

 1. Why do you think Lincoln's Emancipation Proclamation freed African Americans in Confederate states but not Union states?

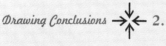 2. Why did it help the Union to cut off Arkansas and Texas from the other Confederate states?

Cooperative Learning

 3. Work with a group. Hold a round table talk about the Emancipation Proclamation. How would the North have felt about it? The South? African Americans? Give each person in the group a chance to talk.

Write About It

 4. Imagine you are a trusted friend of President Lincoln. Write a letter to Lincoln suggesting that more African American army units should be started. Use facts from section 42.4 in your letter.

Chapter 43

One Nation

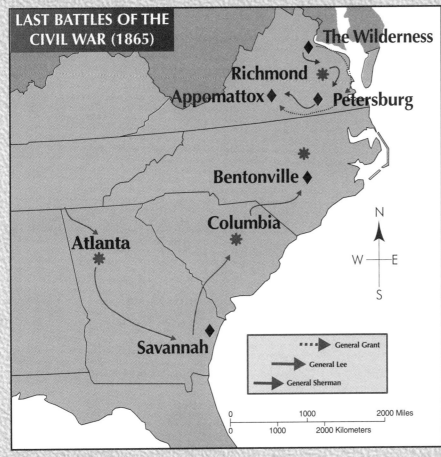

LAST BATTLES OF THE CIVIL WAR (1865)

The Wilderness
Richmond
Appomattox ◆ ◆ Petersburg
Bentonville ◆
Columbia
Atlanta
Savannah

N
W   E
S

- - - - ▶ General Grant
——▶ General Lee
━━▶ General Sherman

0   1000   2000 Miles
0   1000   2000 Kilometers

Read about the end of the Civil War. How did a new idea for war help the Union armies? Why did the South lose?

Key *Vocabulary*

confiscate (KAHN fuh skayt)
to take away a person's belongings for use by the government

cavalry (KAV uhl ree)
a group of soldiers who fight while riding horses

favorable (FAYV ruh buhl)
in one's favor or to one's advantage

treason (TREEZ uhn)
the crime of betraying one's country

Reteaching Vocabulary

surrender (suh REN duhr)
to quit or give up

MAP ANALYSIS

★ **Ask**   What does this map show?

★ **Organize**   List the states that fell to General Sherman. List the state over which Lee and Grant had fought.

★ **Analyze**   How would General Lee be affected by having a Union army to his north and another to his south?

★ **Answer**   Do you think it was wise for Lee to surrender rather than fight both Sherman's and Grant's armies?

Decoding Tip: Note that *c* can stand for the sound /k/.

ay	cake	ah	fall, cot	air	air
ee	tree	i	sit	oh	cold
or	cord	oy	toy	uh	above, hundred
a	ask	ar	hard	oo	book
e	yet	eye	nice	uhr	liar, fir, further, color
ow	cow	ooh	boot, true	yoo	you, few, cube

43.1 Why did the Confederacy think that the U.S. Election of 1864 might bring independence to the South?

Southerners hoped the Democrats would win the White House in 1864. They knew that Lincoln, the Republicans, and the War Democrats would never give up the war. However, many Northerners were tired of the war. They wanted peace even if the South would be lost to the United States. The Democrats pushed this idea in the Election of 1864. They chose General George B. McClellan to run for President. He promised to stop the war as soon as he took office.

43.2 How did General Sherman affect the war and the Election of 1864?

General William T. Sherman believed in total war. He did not fight against Southern soldiers only. He fought against all Southerners. Crops and animals were **confiscated** or destroyed. Homes, farms, towns, and cities were burned. Railroads were torn up. Sherman made it impossible for the people to care for themselves or their soldiers.

Sherman and other Union troops were very successful. Sherman pushed south into Tennessee. He took Atlanta in September 1864. General Philip Sheridan used Sherman's ideas to take Virginia's Shenandoah Valley. News of these wins thrilled people in the North. It helped President Lincoln, too. He won a second term in 1864.

▲ Major General William Tecumseh Sherman

▼ The top photograph below shows the ruins of Bull Run in Virginia, March 1862.

▼ The bottom photograph below shows the ruins seen from the Circular Church in Charleston, South Carolina in 1865.

▲ General John B. Hood

1864 ended with great Union victories. General John B. Hood led the Confederate Army of Tennessee. His army was broken in a December battle near Nashville. Lee led the only major Confederate army left in the war. Sherman burned Atlanta. Then he moved toward the Atlantic coast. He burned everything in his path. He took Savannah on December 20.

43.3 How did Generals Grant and Sherman trap General Lee's army?

Sherman and Grant both moved toward Lee's army. Grant pushed south into Virginia. His army had terrible losses. However, Grant kept pushing farther south. Lee had to stretch out his line all the way from Richmond to Petersburg. In the meantime, Sherman moved north from Savannah. He marched his troops into the Carolinas. Sherman left a strip of scorched land behind him. It was 60 miles wide. Sherman kept pushing north. Sherman and Grant planned to pin Lee between their two armies.

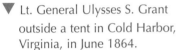

▼ Lt. General Ulysses S. Grant outside a tent in Cold Harbor, Virginia, in June 1864.

43.4 Why did General Lee decide to surrender?

Lee held out against Grant for several months. Then Grant punched through Lee's lines in April, 1865. Lee pulled back. Grant took Richmond. A Union **cavalry** troop made up of African Americans led the army into the city. The Confederate government moved to Danbury, Virginia. General Lee moved the last of his troops to the town of Appomattox Court House on April 8. It was a cloudy evening at Appomattox. Lee's army built camp fires. They shone against the clouds. Lee saw Union fires shining against the clouds, too. He saw that he was blocked on three sides.

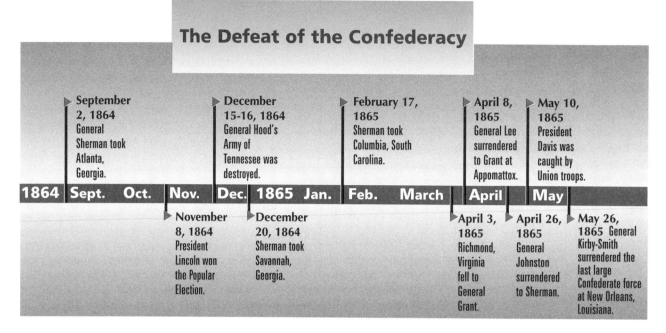

The Defeat of the Confederacy

September 2, 1864 General Sherman took Atlanta, Georgia.

December 15-16, 1864 General Hood's Army of Tennessee was destroyed.

February 17, 1865 Sherman took Columbia, South Carolina.

April 8, 1865 General Lee surrendered to Grant at Appomattox.

May 10, 1865 President Davis was caught by Union troops.

| 1864 | Sept. | Oct. | Nov. | Dec. | 1865 | Jan. | Feb. | March | April | May |

November 8, 1864 President Lincoln won the Popular Election.

December 20, 1864 Sherman took Savannah, Georgia.

April 3, 1865 Richmond, Virginia fell to General Grant.

April 26, 1865 General Johnston surrendered to Sherman.

May 26, 1865 General Kirby-Smith surrendered the last large Confederate force at New Orleans, Louisiana.

Lee decided that he could not win another battle. He sent word to Grant. They agreed to meet the next morning. They chose the McLean house for their meeting. The McLean family had fled to Appomattox after the Battle of Bull Run in 1861. That was the first battle of the war. It had been fought on the McLeans' farm near Bull Run. Lee arrived at Appomattox on April 9. Grant was waiting for him. Lee **surrendered** to Grant in the McLeans' parlor. It took several weeks for the news to reach all the soldiers. But the war was finally over.

43.5   What happened to the South after Lee surrendered?

Grant was kind in his dealings with Lee. He made the Confederate troops give up their rifles and cannon. But he let them keep their pistols, horses, and mules. Grant knew that the animals would be needed for farming. Food was very hard to find in the South. Many of the people were starving. Grant

The photograph to the right shows the McLean house, where General Lee surrendered and finally put an end to the war. The house was in a little town called Appomattox Court House, Virginia.

knew the soldiers were hungry, too. He ordered that food be handed out to the Confederates.

President Jefferson Davis did not believe that the Union's leaders would be so easy. He and other government leaders fled west. Davis ordered other Confederate troops to carry on the fighting. He wanted the North to grow so tired of the war that it would give **favorable** terms to the South. However, General Joseph Johnston decided to surrender to Sherman on April 26. Davis was caught on May 10. The last large Confederate force was led by General Edmond Kirby-Smith. The war had long been over when this group surrendered at New Orleans on May 26.

Some Union leaders took a hard stand against the Confederates. President Davis and Vice President Stephens were arrested. They were sent to Washington, D.C. They were chained up in an army prison. They were held on charges of **treason**. This is the crime of betraying one's country. The army had moved the two men to Washington in a coach. They were brought through Augusta, Georgia. A nine-year-old boy watched them pass by his home. He was Woodrow Wilson. Wilson became President of the United States in 1912.

▲ General Joseph E. Johnston

☆☆☆

Biography

▲ Clara Barton

Many women took part in the Civil War. They worked in factories, grew food, and made uniforms and bandages. Before this time, most nurses had been men. Now, there were not enough men to work as nurses. President Lincoln turned to Dorothea Dix. She had worked for years to make hospitals better places. Lincoln put Dix in charge of the government's nursing department. It trained hundreds of women as nurses. Clara Barton had been the first woman ever hired to work in a U.S. government office. When the war began, she worked as a nurse, too. She helped other women become nurses. Many supplies were not reaching the army. Barton collected money and began shipping supplies herself. Often, she and her wagons were the first to arrive where the army was fighting.

Mary Walker was a doctor who wanted to help wounded soldiers. Many of the men doctors did not believe that she could handle the work. Dr. Walker worked so hard that she finally became an army doctor. She traveled with the army to battle. She was caught by the Confederates in 1864. She was held in prison for four months. Dr. Walker was given the Congressional Medal of Honor in 1865. She is the only woman to have received the military's highest honor.

Women worked as spies for both sides. Belle Boyd and Rose O'Neal Greenhow worked for the South. They gathered important information. This helped the Confederates win several battles. Elizabeth Van Lew lived in Richmond but worked for the North. She had freed her slaves after her father's death. During the war, she gathered information for the North. She hid Union soldiers who were escaping from Confederate prisons. She hired African Americans to carry her information. Elizabeth Bowser had been one of her slaves. Van Lew got Bowser a job in Jefferson Davis's home. Bowser was then able to spy on the Confederate President.

★★☆ CHAPTER REVIEW

Critical Thinking

Write your answers on a sheet of paper, or discuss in class.

Identifying Main Idea

1. How did Sherman's way of fighting affect the South's limited resources?

Making Inferences

2. Why did General Lee decide to surrender rather than lose the war by being beaten in battle?

Cooperative Learning

LEARNING STYLE
Verbal
Visual

3. Work with a partner. Talk to each other about Sherman and total war. Think about what the countryside must have looked like after Sherman's army left. Describe what you might have seen if you had been there. Draw a picture of what you describe. Display your pictures for the class.

Write About It

Writing Portfolio

4. Make up a secret code. Reread the part about Grant and Lee at Richmond and Petersburg. Pretend that you are a Union spy in Richmond. Write a message with news that General Grant could use against General Lee. Put the message in code. Trade messages and codes with someone in the class. Decode each other's messages.

Chapter 44

Aftermath

Bringing the South Back into the Union

Lincoln's Plan		Johnson's Plan	
Demand to be met:	**Then:**	**Demand to be met:**	**Then:**
(1) Confederates must take an oath to support the Constitution and the Union; (2) Military and government leaders must apply for special pardons.	Confederates would receive pardons.	(1) Confederates must take an oath of loyalty to the United States; (2) No oaths could be taken by Confederates or other people who were worth at least $20,000.	Confederates would receive pardons.
10% of those who could vote in 1860 had to take the oath.	These people could form new state govern-ments.	Part of those who could vote in 1860 had to take the loyalty oath.	(1) Temporary governors would be chosen by President Johnson; (2) Governors would run elections for state conventions.
New states must protect freedom for African Americans.	States would be recognized by the federal government.	Conventions had to (1) refuse to pay Confederate debts; (2) totally reject secession; (3) ratify the 13th Amend-ment; (4) write new state constitutions.	President would (1) end rule by Union armies; (2) allow the states back into the Union.

Read about the United States after the Civil War. How did Lincoln's death affect the South? Why?

Key *Vocabulary*

assassination
(uh sas uh NAY shuhn)
the killing of a person for political reasons

former (FOR muhr)
at one time in the past

loyalty (LOY uhl tee)
being faithful to a person, group, or government

radical (RAD i kuhl)
being in support of extreme measures or changes

alien (AY lee uhn)
being part of another country

CHART ANALYSIS

★ **Ask** — What does this chart show?

★ **Organize** — Which plan has the fewest number of demands that the South had to meet?

★ **Analyze** — Which plan seems to be the simplest? Why?

★ **Answer** — Which plan do you think the Southern states would have liked better? Why?

Decoding Tip: Note the different sounds *a* can stand for.

ay	cake	ah	fall, cot	air	air
ee	tree	i	sit	oh	cold
or	cord	oy	toy	uh	above, hundred
a	ask	ar	hard	oo	book
e	yet	eye	nice	uhr	liar, fir, further, color
ow	cow	ooh	boot, true	yoo	you, few, cube

Civil War Deaths			
	Union	Confederate	Total
Killed in battle	110,000	94,000	204,000
Died of illness	250,000	164,000	414,000
Total	360,000	258,000	618,000

NOTE: These numbers are estimates. Records are incomplete. Records were not often kept during the war.

44.1 What losses did each side suffer in the Civil War?

More Americans were killed in the Civil War than in any other U.S. war. Even the losses in both World Wars were less. Families were left without fathers, sons, and brothers. Many civilians had died, too. Thousands of soldiers were missing. Families were desperate for news of them. President Lincoln asked the famous nurse Clara Barton for help. She received letters from people throughout the country. Her group found over 20,000 missing soldiers. Most had been killed, but their graves had not yet been marked.

Southern states were almost destroyed by the war. It has been estimated that Sherman's army alone caused $100 million in damage. Salmon P. Chase was Chief Justice of the United States. He was sent on a tour of the South. He listed the damage and ruin that he saw. Union armies had burned away crops, homes, and towns. There were few places to live. Food was hard to find. People could not get jobs. Rebuilding the South and its economy would take a

▼ The photograph below shows dead Confederate soldiers after the Battle of Chancellorsville, in Fredericksburg, Virginia in May 1863.

For the People, By the People

great deal of work. The task would last for years. First, the states had to be joined back together into one country. This would be a great task, too.

44.2 What were President Lincoln's ideas about accepting the South back into the Union?

Lincoln felt there had been only one reason to fight the war—to keep the Union together. He had no thoughts about punishing the Confederates. In 1863, the President made plans for dealing with the South after the war. He simply wanted to put the Union back together. The country should be the way it was before the war started. However, slavery would not be allowed. The Emancipation Proclamation had freed those people enslaved in the South. Slavery was still practiced in some Union states. Congress set up the 13th Amendment in February 1865. All enslaved people became free when it was ratified by the states. After Appomattox, Lincoln could begin putting his plan into effect.

▲ Above is a photograph of Abraham Lincoln taken in 1863 by Mathew B. Brady.

44.3 How did Lincoln's administration come to an end?

President Lincoln never had a chance to enjoy the peace for which he had fought so hard. He was killed only five days after Lee's surrender at Appomattox. The President and his wife had taken time to relax. They went to a play at Ford's Theatre on the evening of April 14. John Wilkes Booth, a Southerner, was in the play. He sneaked into Lincoln's box at the theater. He shot Lincoln in the head. Booth escaped by jumping to the stage. He broke his leg in the fall. Lincoln was carried to a nearby house. He died in the early hours of the morning. The

▲ Shown above is the box in Ford's Theatre where Lincoln was assassinated.

▼ John Wilkes Booth

entire country was shocked. Even people in the South were outraged by this crime. President Lincoln's body was taken to his home in Springfield, Illinois. Thousands of people lined the tracks as the special train passed.

Vice President Andrew Johnson became the new President. It was Johnson's job to deal with the South and the **assassination**. Ten people were involved in the plan to kill the President. Booth was to kill the President. But Lincoln was not the only target. The plan called for killing both Vice President Johnson and Secretary of State William Seward. None of the plotters was able to get near these two men. Most of the plotters were quickly arrested. However, Booth was on the run for 12 days. On April 26, the army surrounded a barn where Booth was hiding. Booth was shot and killed. Booth may even have shot himself. One of the plotters was freed. Four were hanged. Four were put into prison.

44.4 What were President Johnson's ideas for the South?

Johnson wanted to continue most of Lincoln's ideas. This shocked many Republicans. Johnson was a Southern Demo- crat from Tennessee. However, he had refused to secede with his state. And unlike Lincoln, he had made harsh statements about how the South's leaders should be treated. He felt that they had tricked their people into this terrible war. As President, Johnson wanted to punish these leaders. Still, many Republicans felt that his plan was too easy on their **former** enemies.

▲ Secretary of State
William H. Seward

Confederate leaders had to follow strict steps to become citizens again. They had to write special letters to President Johnson. Some Confederates refused. Former Confederate President Jefferson Davis would not write one of these letters. He never became a U.S. citizen again. However, Robert E. Lee disagreed. He wrote a letter to Johnson. He wanted to show the Confederates that becoming U.S. citizens was their only hope for the future. Johnson refused to give Lee his rights as a citizen. Lee had not included a signed **loyalty** oath with his letter. Lee signed and mailed an oath. He never heard anything about his request. A government worker found Lee's signed oath in 1970. Congress voted to give Lee full citizenship in 1975.

44.5 How did the Radical Republicans feel about the South?

Many Republicans hated the Confederates. They called for harsh punishment of these people. After all, the Confederates had caused the war. These Republicans became known as "**Radical** Republicans." The South had seceded from the Union. It had insisted that it was a separate country. The Radical Republicans agreed. The South had lost the war. Now it should be treated as an **alien** nation. As aliens, the Confederates had no rights as citizens. The Radical Republicans began fighting with President Johnson. They felt that Congress should deal with the South. They also wanted Congress to take back some of the power that Lincoln had taken as President. Radical Republicans took over Congress after the elections of 1866. As a result, the South would face some very hard days.

☆☆☆

Connections

▲ Native American fighting in the Civil War

Native Americans in Indian Territory took part in the Civil War, too. Many of them had cotton plantations. Enslaved Africans worked the fields just as they did in the South. At first Native Americans wanted to stay out of the Civil War. In 1861 Jefferson Davis sent General Albert Pike to the five nations. These were the Choctaw, Cherokee, Creek, Chickasaw, and Seminole nations. He talked the nations into signing treaties with the Confederacy. However, the war divided Native Americans just like it did the people of the United States. Each nation sent troops to fight. Some fought for the South. Others fought for the Union.

General Stand Watie led the Cherokee Confederates. Chief John Ross led those Cherokee people who supported the Union. General Watie joined the Creek troops led by Colonel Dan N. McIntosh. They beat the Creeks who supported the Union. Later, Watie and McIntosh joined forces with Confederates in Arkansas. They lost the Battle of Pea Ridge. However, Watie was a hero of the battle. He led his troops in other battles of the war. His were among the last forces to surrender in 1865.

The Radical Republicans wanted to punish the five nations for their part in the war. Native American leaders like Reverend Allen Wright went to Washington. Wright even coined the name for the territory—"Oklahoma." "Okla" is the Choctaw word for "people." "Homa" is the word for "red." These leaders signed new treaties with the United States. They had to free their enslaved people. These people were to receive the same rights as other members of the nations. Each nation lost land. This land would be given to other Native Americans who were forced to leave their homes.

★★☆ CHAPTER REVIEW

Critical Thinking

Write your answers on a sheet of paper, or discuss in class.

Making Predictions

1. How might President Lincoln's death have affected the treatment of the South after the war?

Analyzing Cause and Effect

2. Why did President Johnson's plan call for harsher punishment of the South's leaders than for its soldiers?

Cooperative Learning

LEARNING STYLE
Reading
Tactile

3. Work with a partner or group. Reread the part about Lincoln's assassination. Work out a short skit about the killing. Choose parts for the skit. Present the skit for the class.

Write About It

Writing Portfolio

4. Pretend that you are putting out a newspaper at the time of the Civil War. Write a short story about the President's assassination. Think up a headline for your story. Put this material together for the front page of your paper. Display your paper for the class.

Chapter 45

Reconstruction

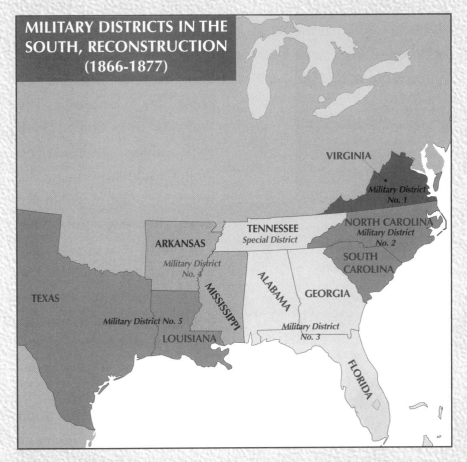

MILITARY DISTRICTS IN THE SOUTH, RECONSTRUCTION (1866-1877)

VIRGINIA

Military District No. 1

TENNESSEE
Special District

ARKANSAS

Military District No. 3

NORTH CAROLINA
Military District No. 2

SOUTH CAROLINA

TEXAS

Military District No. 5

MISSISSIPPI

ALABAMA

GEORGIA

Military District No. 3

LOUISIANA

FLORIDA

Read about
Reconstruction in the South. Who took charge of Reconstruction plans? Why?

Key *Vocabulary*

pardon (PAR duhn)
an official act that forgives some crime or activity

impeach (im PEECH)
to charge a public official with crimes in office

carpetbagger (KAR puht BAG uhr)
a person from the North who came to the South to make money after the Civil War

scalawag (SKAL i wag)
a person in the South who helped the North's Reconstruction government for gain

sharecropper (SHAIR krahp uhr)
a person who farms land owned by someone else and earns a share in the money made

MAP ANALYSIS

★ **Ask**   What states are in Military District No. 3?

★ **Acquire**   Find out what year each state was let back into the Union. Use an encyclopedia or other book.

★ **Analyze**   Think of how important Virginia was to the old South. Why do you think it was in a military district by itself?

★ **Answer**   Which district do you think would be hardest to govern? Why?

Decoding Tip: Note the different sounds for *ar*. In **sharecropper**, the *ar* sounds like *air* because of the *e* that follows.

ay	cake	ah	fall, cot	air	air
ee	tree	i	sit	oh	cold
or	cord	oy	toy	uh	above, hundred
a	ask	ar	hard	oo	book
e	yet	eye	nice	uhr	liar, fir, further, color
ow	cow	ooh	boot, true	yoo	you, few, cube

45.1 Why were the Reconstruction Acts hated in the South?

In 1865 Andrew Johnson followed through on his hopes for Reconstruction. He gave a **pardon** to all Confederate rebels. He tried to make it easy for Southern states to rejoin the Union. In his first year, things went well.

However, Radical Republicans hated Johnson's ideas. They wanted to punish the South. A group of Radicals met to plan a different Reconstruction. At first, their laws were vetoed, or turned down, by Johnson. But in 1866, more Republicans won races for Congress. The Radicals went ahead with their plans. Johnson no longer could stop them. The tough new laws were known as the Reconstruction Acts. The South was divided into five parts. Each part was run by a U.S. Army general. Soldiers kept watch over the South. States in the South had to meet stiff rules to get back in the Union. Still, there were lots of good things done. Free schools were started for all children. Hospitals, roads, and railroads were built. African Americans were given the right to vote.

The Radical Republicans wanted to make sure that they stayed in power. To do this, they took away certain rights from white men in the

▼ President Andrew Johnson

For the People, By the People

South. Men who had sworn to uphold the Constitution and then had fought for the Confederacy could not vote or hold office. Many other whites also lost the right to vote. Meanwhile, thousands of African Americans could vote for the first time. They voted for Republican candidates. Most Southern whites were Democrats. Their party won few offices. The Republicans ran the Southern states and the country. The tough Reconstruction laws made many whites in the South hate the North.

45.2 Why was Andrew Johnson tried for impeachment?

The Radical Republicans' ideas for Reconstruction undid the work of Abraham Lincoln and Andrew Johnson. The Radicals continued to pass new laws. Reconstruction was done their way. They wanted the new laws to be hard on the South. Johnson kept trying to stop such laws. But the Republicans in Congress were too strong. Also, Johnson had many enemies among the Radicals. Thaddeus Stevens of Pennsylvania was one of the most bitter. "The Republican Party and it alone can save the Union," Stevens said.

Finally the Radicals decided to get rid of Johnson. In 1867 they passed the Tenure of Office Act. It kept the President from firing anyone in the Cabinet without Congress's OK. Johnson broke this law. He got rid of Secretary of War Edwin Stanton. Stanton had lied to Johnson and lost his trust. On February 24, 1868, the House voted to **impeach** Johnson. Johnson had only 10 days to prepare his defense.

Hundreds came to watch the trial in March 1868. However, Johnson stayed at the White House. For two weeks, both sides made their cases with ringing speeches. The final vote came in May. Thirty-five senators went against Johnson. This was one less than needed to impeach. President Johnson had kept his job by one vote.

45.3   Who were the carpetbaggers and scalawags?

Reconstruction needed many people to make it work. Northerners rushed into the South to take jobs. They helped carry out Congress's plan. Some were honest and did their best. However, others were only out for themselves. They cheated and stole from Southerners. They often paid African Americans to vote a certain way. Many of them came to the South with cheap bags made from old pieces of carpet. For this reason, they were called **carpetbaggers**. The South also had its own crooks and cheats. These people were called **scalawags**. They would sell out their neighbors for a few dollars. Working with Northerners, they tricked people out of land and goods. Anything of worth they took. The once proud South was being torn apart.

▼ The photograph below shows the excavation for Devereux Station of the Orange and Alexandria Railroad. The "General Haupt" is the name of the engine pulling the train. It was named for General Hermann Haupt, Chief of Construction and Transportation, U.S. Military Railroads.

45.4 How did life change for African Americans in the South?

Radical Republicans in Congress took special steps to help African Americans in the South. They passed three amendments to the Constitution. These made sure that African Americans would be free and could vote. Republicans counted on these votes. The black vote would keep their party strong. Many African Americans won seats in Congress. Most worked to make things better for all people in the South. African Americans felt a new hope. It was not to last.

The new laws failed in an important way. African Americans still were not treated as equals. They were promised "40 acres and a mule." Instead of getting their own land, they went to work for whites. Many African Americans went back to picking cotton as field hands. Some became **sharecroppers**. This meant working for a share of what the crops sold for. It was hardly better than slavery. After a few years, the North seemed to lose interest in African Americans. The war had been won, but not much had changed.

In the South, hate groups were started. Their goal was to keep African Americans from having a place in society. One group was the Ku Klux Klan. It began in 1866. Its members wore white robes and masks. They wanted African Americans to believe they were ghosts of Confederate soldiers. Riding at night, they burned African Americans' houses. They beat the owners or hanged them. Many African Americans feared for their lives.

Connections

After the Civil War, Radical Republicans passed the Civil Rights Act of 1866. African Americans could vote for the first time. However, most of them could not read or write. There had been laws against teaching enslaved blacks.

Some African Americans had been able to teach themselves to read. A few had gone to school in the North or in Canada. From among these

▲ Hiram Revels

came the first African Americans in Congress. Hiram Revels of Mississippi was the first African American elected to Congress. Revels entered the Senate in 1870. The first African American in the House of Representatives was Joseph Rainey. Before long, there were several African Americans in state and national offices.

A few years later, these gains melted away. Southern states made their own voting laws. The laws were supposed to keep African Americans from voting. Force and threats also kept them away. Things

went on like this for a long time. In 1965 the Voting Rights Act was passed. It kept states from charging fees for voting. State voting laws had to be fair to all races. African Americans in the South began to vote in large numbers. Once again African Americans won seats in Congress. Since then, the government has worked to protect the voting rights of African Americans.

▲ Joseph H. Rainey

★★☆ CHAPTER REVIEW

Critical Thinking

Write your answers on a sheet of paper, or discuss in class.

Comparing and Contrasting

1. Why did Andrew Johnson have more problems with Congress than Lincoln did?

Drawing Conclusions →⧓←

2. Were African Americans in the South better off after the Civil War? Explain your answer.

Cooperative Learning

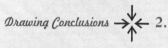

LEARNING STYLE
Auditory Verbal

3. Work with a group to play a quiz game using words and names from this chapter. Pick teams of three or four. Pick another person to ask the questions. One question might be "Who was Hiram Revels?" Each team gets 10 points for a correct answer. If a team cannot answer a question, the other team gets a try. Play until both teams have been asked 10 questions.

Write About It

Writing Portfolio

4. You are going to be called to speak at President Andrew Johnson's impeachment trial. Write notes about Johnson for your own use. List good and bad points about him.

Chapter 46

Deal Making

Important Events during Grant's two terms as President

1865   1870   1875   1880

1868
Grant elected
President

1869
First railroad
across the country
completed

1870
The 15th Amendment
passed; race could
not be used to keep
someone from voting

1870-71
Force Bills passed;
government could use
force to support the
voting rights of
African Americans

1872
Grant re-
elected
President

1872
Yellowstone
made the
first national
park

1873
Panic of 1873

1876
Battle of Little
Big Horn; Native
Americans
defeat General
Custer

1875
Congress looks
into the Whiskey
Ring

Read about the end
of Reconstruction. Who
ended it? Why?

Key *Vocabulary*

scandal (SKAN duhl)
disgrace caused by doing
something that offends people
or is against the law

finance (FEYE nans)
to pay money to support
something

reform (ri FORM)
the act of making changes to
clean up or improve something

betray (bi TRAY)
to fail someone in time of need

annual (AN yoo uhl)
happening once a year

TIMELINE ANALYSIS

★ **Acquire**   Look up one of these events in the chapter and in the encyclopedia. Tell
the class what you find.

★ **Analyze**   Which of Grant's terms saw the most action on African American voting
rights?

★ **Answer**   Which event would have been most important to a person living
in these years? Why?

Decoding Tip: Note that an *a* followed by *n* and a consonant usually has a short sound.

ay	cake	ah	fall, cot	air	air	
ee	tree	i	sit	oh	cold	
or	cord	oy	toy	uh	above, hundred	
a	ask	ar	hard	oo	book	
e	yet	eye	nice	uhr	liar, fir, further, color	
ow	cow	ooh	boot, true	yoo	you, few, cube	

46.1 What problems did the Grant Administration have?

In 1868 Ulysses S. Grant won the race for President. It was an easy win. Some said Grant could have won for either party. As it was, he ran as a Republican.

Grant was not prepared to be President. He knew little about the Constitution and almost nothing about the law. Also, the country was changing. Big business was taking the place of small shops. Some men with money were willing to do anything to get more. Grant needed to pick his friends with care. As a war leader, Grant was a good judge of people. But in the White House, he made mistakes. He trusted the wrong people. He took gifts from those who wanted something in return.

The list of problems was long. Grant's head of the Navy made money selling contracts illegally. The head of Public Works took 17 million dollars. Then there was the Whiskey Ring. Large whiskey companies paid off government officials so the companies wouldn't have to pay taxes. One of Grant's close friends was part of the ring. With Grant's help, the friend went free. A **scandal** with the Union Pacific Railroad hit Vice-President Schuyler Colfax.

Even with all these problems, Grant won a second term. But he was not a leader. His White House years hurt his name. The great General Grant was a poor President.

46.2 How did the Panic of 1873 affect people's ideas about Reconstruction?

Making money seemed easy right after the war. Many people thought good times would continue. Then the stock market began to fall. Farm prices dropped. A large bank had to close its doors. It was the same bank that had **financed** the war and the Northern Pacific Railroad. The news shook everyone. People took their money out of banks, which hurt more banks.

▲ The 1880 illustration above is called *Great Railroad Station at Chicago— Departure of a Train*. The platform is crowded with departing passengers, including several Native Americans.

Factories shut down. Many people lost their jobs. Bread lines stretched for blocks. The Panic of 1873 had the whole country worried.

Money problems in the North became more important than Reconstruction. People began to ask why so much money was going to the South. Why pay for soldiers to keep the South in line? That money was needed in other places. Many people believed it was time to let the South take care of itself. Reconstruction was coming to an end.

46.3   How did Rutherford B. Hayes become President?

The 1876 race for the White House was strange in many ways. It was very close. There was lots of cheating. And for months, no one knew who had won. It was decided by a secret agreement at the last minute. The election left bad feelings on both sides.

Running for the Republicans was Rutherford B. Hayes of Ohio. Hayes was not well known outside his home state. Democrat Samuel Tilden ran on the idea of **reform**. He promised to clean up Washington, D.C. "Throw the rascals out!" his people shouted in the streets. Tilden edged Hayes in the popular vote. But the electoral count was too close to call. The problem was in three states. South Carolina, Florida, and Louisiana would decide the race.

Both Democrats and Republicans sent people South to count the returns. There had already been cheating. The Ku Klux Klan had kept many African Americans from taking part. Boxes were filled with fake votes. Republicans and Democrats

▲ President Rutherford
B. Hayes

came up with different numbers. An Electoral Commission was set up to decide who had won. The Republicans had one more on this board than the Democrats. Hayes was named President.

There was more. The House of Representatives still had to make the official count. Democrats planned to take their time. After March 4, 1877, the country would have no President. No one knew what might happen. To settle things, Republicans made an offer. All federal troops would leave the South. Money would be spent on Southern problems. The Democrats went along. Hayes had won at last.

46.4 Why did the new constitutions in the South limit voting rights?

President Hayes kept his word. Troops were pulled out of the South. Hayes hoped that whites in the South would be grateful. Perhaps they would work with the North to protect African Americans' rights. Hayes thought both parties would be strong in the new South. Hayes even took a trip to the South. He wanted to see how things were going. People cheered him. They seemed to like what he said. Hayes thought his plan was working.

The truth was quite different. Several states wrote new constitutions. Special rules in them kept most African Americans from voting. Threats were also used. All this let Southern white Democrats take over. They were angry about Reconstruction and the end of slavery. They saw to it that African Americans had no voice in government. The Republican party lost its following in the South. Democrats were sure to win every race. African Americans felt **betrayed**. The promises of Reconstruction would have to wait for 100 years.

Biography

▲ Lucy Webb Hayes

Lucy Webb Hayes, the wife of Rutherford B. Hayes, had a number of "firsts." She was the first President's wife to be called "the First Lady." She was also the first President's wife to have gone to college. Her ideas had a great effect on her husband. Lucy hated slavery. In time, Rutherford came to be against it, too.

She may have talked to her husband about a new law. In 1879, Rutherford signed a law helping women lawyers. It let them practice before the Supreme Court.

Mrs. Hayes held many parties in the White House. But she did not serve alcohol drinks. The press made fun of her.

They called her "Lemonade Lucy." Still, her parties and dinners were very beautiful. Another first was the White House Easter Egg Roll. Lucy started it when Congress would not hold it on the Capitol lawn. Children were invited to the White House for this **annual** event.

 CHAPTER REVIEW

Critical Thinking

Write your answers on a sheet of paper, or discuss in class.

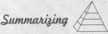 *Summarizing*

1. Republicans and Democrats did not trust each other in the 1876 Presidential race. Why?

 Analyzing Cause and Effect

2. Why did Hayes's plans for the South fall through?

Cooperative Learning

LEARNING
STYLE
Oral
Listening

3. Work with the group. Hold a Presidential election in class. Pick two people or more to run. Work together to make signs for the candidates. Let each person who is running make a short speech. Then hand out slips of paper to the whole group. Tell them to vote by writing one candidate's name on the paper. Pick three people to count the votes. Have the person who wins make an "acceptance speech."

Write About It

Writing
Portfolio

4. Imagine you are an African American in the South. The year is 1878. Write a letter to President Rutherford B. Hayes. Tell him what you think should be done about Reconstruction.

Quiz

Number a piece of paper from 1–10. Write a, b, c, and d beside these numbers. Read the following sentence beginnings. Four endings follow each one. Choose the ending that best completes the sentence. On your paper, circle the letter that matches the letter of your answer. Be sure you mark your answer beside the correct number.

1. To beat the South, the Union's generals at first planned to . . .
   a. take the Mississippi River and move east toward Richmond.
   b. capture Richmond, the Confederate capital.
   c. push Europe into fighting against the South.
   d. none of the above.

2. General Lee pushed the war into Union territory in order to . . .
   a. capture Washington, D.C., the Union capital.
   b. push Union citizens into calling for an end to the war.
   c. push England and France into helping the South.
   d. none of the above.

3. Fighting at Gettysburg turned the war in favor of . . .
   a. the North.
   b. the South.
   c. the Confederacy.
   d. both b and c.

4. Both the North and the South gained more soldiers by . . .
   a. giving bonuses to volunteers.
   b. accepting African Americans.
   c. setting up the draft.
   d. both b and c.

5. Total war made it impossible for the South to . . .
   a. win battles.
   b. continue slavery.
   c. get help from Europe.
   d. supply its people or soldiers.

6. After Lee's surrender, Jefferson Davis wanted the war to continue so he could . . .
   a. get better terms from the North.
   b. pull England and France into the war.
   c. bring troops from the West to help Richmond.
   d. all of the above.

7. Lincoln and Johnson's easy peace terms were not put into place after Congress was controlled by . . .
   a. Radical Republicans.
   b. Union Democrats.
   c. Southern Republicans.
   d. Know-Nothing party members.

8. Reconstruction was the Radical Republicans' plan to . . .
   a. weaken Union control of the North.
   b. form the South into states that would fit back into the Union.
   c. punish the South for causing the war.
   d. both b and c.

9. In exchange for naming Hayes as President, Republicans promised to . . .
   a. elect a Democrat as Vice President.
   b. pull all federal troops out of the South.
   c. weaken rules against slavery.
   d. allow all Southerners to run for office.

10. In spite of Hayes's work, African Americans in the South lost the right to . . .
    a. hold office.
    b. move to the North.
    c. vote in elections.
    d. none of the above.

CLASSIFYING

Add numbers 11–15 to your paper. Read the names of the groups listed below. Some of these groups worked against slavery and for rights for African Americans. Write A on your paper for these groups. Other groups worked for slavery and against rights for African Americans. Write B on your paper for these groups.

11. Union Supporters
12. Radical Republicans
13. Confederates
14. Southern Democrats
15. Ku Klux Klan

Look over the things you wrote for these chapters. Choose one that you like the best. Add to your writing. For example, you wrote a newspaper article about the Civil War. Turn your other writings about the Civil War into newspaper articles. Put them together so they look like a newspaper. You may wish to include drawings or illustrations in your paper. Trade papers with a study partner. Check each other's work. Make a clean, neat copy of your newspaper. Put it in your portfolio.

Write the headings **Cause** and **Effect** on a piece of paper. Think about something that happened in the first chapter. Did it make something else happen? If so, list it under the heading **Cause**. Did an earlier event make it happen? If so, list it under the heading **Effect**. List two causes and effects for each chapter.

COOPERATIVE PROJECT: CIVIL WAR DIORAMA

Work with a group. Choose a battle of the Civil War. Make a list of what happened during the battle. Check a map of the battle to see where the troops were placed and how they fought. Make your own map out of clay. Be sure to show hills, streams, rivers, and forests. Let the clay dry. Paint the map. Make small buildings, fences, and people for your map. Put them in their correct places. Display your map for the class or the school. Take turns with members of your group in telling what the battle was like.

Unit 6

POLITICS

1865
The 13th Amendment ended slavery.

1875
Congress passed the Civil Rights Act in order to protect African Americans.

1882
Congress passed laws keeping Chinese immigrants from entering the country.

1883
The Pendleton Act allowed the Civil Service Commission, not politicians, to hire people for jobs in the federal government.

CE   1860   1870   1880

CULTURE

1862
Congress gave out free land to help settle the Great Plains and built the transcontinental railroad.

1868
The first practical typewriter was patented in the United States.

1875
Alexander Graham Bell invented the telephone.

1876
General Custer's troops were killed during one of the battles that led to all Native Americans having to live on reservations.

Thomas Edison invented the phonograph.

1879
Thomas Edison built the first successful electric light.

1880
Immigration went up in great numbers. The U.S.A. led the world in making steel and many other goods.

Industrial Development in the U.S.
1870 - 1900

"The life of the nation is secure only while the nation is honest, truthful, and virtuous."

— **Frederick Douglass**, *from a speech dated April 1885, celebrating the 23rd anniversary of Lincoln's Emancipation Proclamation*

After the Civil War, the United States changed. People's ideas did, too. People worried about what government's job should be. People like Frederick Douglass began calling for a change in government. They wanted truth, honesty, and goodness in government. What had happened to make people feel this way? Why?

1887
The Dawes Act said Native Americans would have to live like U.S. citizens.

1892
The Populist Party wanted reform and picked James Weaver to run for President.

1896
Populist ideas were picked up by both the Democratic and Republican parties. The Populist Party ended.

The Supreme Court decided that segregation was not against the Constitution.

1901
Congress made all Native American citizens.

1890

1900

1881
Booker T. Washington started the Tuskegee Institute in Alabama.

1886
The first American movie to be projected on a screen was presented in a music hall in New York City by Thomas Edison.

1888
George Eastman introduced the Kodak box camera, the first camera designed to be used by the general public.

1889
Scott Joplin wrote "Maple Leaf Rag." Ragtime, a mix of African and European ideas about music, became popular across the country.

1900
Over 14 million immigrants had arrived in the United States since 1861.

Chapter 47

Expansion by Railroad

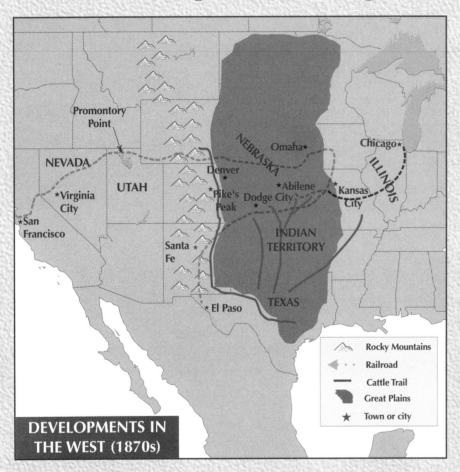

DEVELOPMENTS IN THE WEST (1870s)

Map labels: Promontory Point, NEVADA, UTAH, Virginia City, San Francisco, Denver, NEBRASKA, Omaha, Chicago, ILLINOIS, Pike's Peak, Abilene, Kansas City, Dodge City, Santa Fe, INDIAN TERRITORY, El Paso, TEXAS

Legend:
- Rocky Mountains
- Railroad
- Cattle Trail
- Great Plains
- ★ Town or city

Read about

building railroads in the United States after the Civil War. How did trains change the country? Why?

Key *Vocabulary*

mine (meyen)
a hole dug in order to remove metals buried in the soil

plain (playn)
a place that is fairly flat, covered with grass, and has few trees

homestead (HOHM sted)
a piece of land given away by the government in exchange for living on the land and turning it into a farm

desert (DEZ uhrt)
a place where there is so little water that hardly anything can grow

irrigate (IR uh gayt)
to bring water to dry land so that plants can be grown

MAP ANALYSIS

★ **Ask**   What does this map show?

★ **Acquire**   What does the legend tell you?

★ **Organize**   Make a chart that shows which states have mines, which have railroads, and which have ranches.

★ **Analyze**   What did Kansas towns have that ranchers in Texas wanted to reach?

★ **Answer**   How could these Kansas towns help ranchers?

Decoding Tip: Note the different sounds *e* stands for in the vocabulary words.

ay	cake	ah	fall, cot	air	air
ee	tree	i	sit	oh	cold
or	cord	oy	toy	uh	above, hundred
a	ask	ar	hard	oo	book
e	yet	eye	nice	uhr	liar, fir, further, color
ow	cow	ooh	boot, true	yoo	you, few, cube

47.1 How did mining affect the West?

Americans poured into the West from the eastern part of the U.S. They wanted to get rich. Gold was found in Colorado in 1859. Miners rushed to this spot near Pike's Peak. Silver was found that year, too. This place was called the "Comstock Lode." It made Virginia City in Nevada rich. Iron and copper were also found. People mined for them, too. Most people worked the mud at the bottoms of rivers. Some **mines** were dug. They were small. Most were worked by just one person.

Many mining towns were built, but not all of them lasted. The gold or silver would all be mined. Sometimes, the minerals could not be reached. They were too far down in the ground. The miners would move away. Many towns disappeared. Others were just empty. They are called "ghost towns." Miners searched other places. Sometimes the searches paid off. Then new towns would be built.

▲ Miners in the West during the gold rush

Mining helped the country. The miners needed goods. Some people became rich by selling these goods. Levi Strauss made pants out of canvas. They were tough. Miners liked the pants. They did not wear out easily. Levi's pants became known as jeans. He became as rich as some miners. People built mining companies. They built mines to reach metals that were deep in the ground. All the metal was used to make goods. More factories were needed. Gold and silver became coins. Copper was used for pipes, pots, and pans. All these new riches helped the country to grow.

47.2 How did the Homestead Act of 1862 change Americans' ideas about the Great Plains?

Congress gave away the land of the Great **Plains**. Many people wanted good farm land. They did not want the land in the Great Plains, though. They thought that good farm land would have big trees growing on it. Few trees grew on the Plains. Grass covered most of this land. Few Americans would move there. Congress set up the **Homestead** Act of 1862. Congress wanted Americans to live on the Plains. Each person could claim 160 acres. They had to live on the land for five years. They had to farm the land, too. Some land was free. Sometimes, small fees were charged. This paid for filing the claims. People learned to farm the Plains. Wheat, a kind of grass, grew very well on the Plains. The Great Plains became known as the country's bread basket.

Congress changed the Homestead Act several times. Some places were very dry. Farmers could not earn their livings. They needed more than 160 acres. Congress let each person claim another 160 acres in these places. These were called tree claims. The people had to plant at least 40 acres of trees. The Southwest United States was a **desert**. People could have 640 acres of this land. They had to **irrigate** this land to keep it. Americans moved to almost all parts of the West.

Some people took advantage of Congress's land acts. They paid others to claim the land. Then they bought the land for very little money. Other people used another plan. First they would claim some land. Then they would plant just a few trees. They would build only shells of homes. These people had followed the law. However, they did not build real farms. After five years, the people owned the land. They could then sell it. Sometimes, they could claim even more land.

47.3 What was the purpose of the Pacific Railroad Act of 1862?

Congress wanted trains to run all across the country. It passed the Pacific Railroad Act in 1862. This law gave land to railroad companies. Tracks could be laid on this land. The companies could use trees from government land, too. They were used for ties and bridges. The companies were also given land beside some of the tracks that they laid. This land was sold. The money was used to pay for building the railroad.

Railroads spread throughout the West. The Central Pacific built east from San Francisco. The Union Pacific built west from Omaha, Nebraska. They met at Promontory Point in Utah. The last spike was driven in 1869. It was made of gold. Trains now ran from shore to shore. Land was given to other railroads, too. Congress's railroad acts ended in 1871. Almost 200 million acres of land was given to 29 companies.

Many people found jobs because of the railroads. Workers helped lay the tracks. Bridges had to be built, too. Workers helped to make engines, cars, and tracks. Towns and cities were built. People needed more goods. New factories opened. There were more jobs than ever before. There were not enough workers to do them. People came to the United States from other countries to work. Most came from Europe. News about the jobs reached China. Thousands of Chinese people sailed to California. Most of the people who built the Union Pacific Railroad were Chinese.

47.4 Why were buffalo so important to the railroads?

Americans became rich from the buffalo. These animals lived on the Great Plains. Blankets and leather were made from their hides. Hunters spread across the Plains. They killed and skinned millions of buffalo. All the hides had to be shipped to market. Some were carried by wagons. Most were shipped by train. Railroads made a lot of money by shipping these hides. Some buffalo meat was used to feed the people who were building the railroads in the West. However, most of the meat was wasted. It was left to rot in the sun. At one time, over 15 million buffalo lived on the Plains. By 1900, less than one hundred were left.

47.5 How did the railroads affect ranching and farming?

Americans loved to eat beef. Railroads helped people get this food. Texas was filled with cattle ranches. After the Civil War, people wanted more beef. Texas cattle could be sold for high prices. However, the cattle had to reach the East. Some were shipped by boat. This took a long time. It also cost a lot of money. Then railroads reached Kansas. Ranchers moved their cattle north. They crossed Indian Territory to reach Kansas. They sold their cattle in Abilene and Dodge City. They were called "cow towns." People would buy the cattle. Then railroads carried them across the country. Chicago, Illinois became an important city. New factories were built there. These plants turned the cattle into food.

Indian Territory made money from the cattle, too. Cattle are sold by the pound. The cattle lost weight on the walk from Texas. Indian Territory was part of the Great Plains. There was plenty of grass for cattle. Cattle drives would stop just short of Kansas. The cattle would feed on the grass and gain weight. Native Americans charged money to let the cattle eat this grass. Then the cattle were driven on to the cow towns.

Railroads made shipping cattle easy. It was cheap, too. Ranches spread throughout the Plains and other places in the West. Some ranches were very large. They might cover 100,000 acres or more. Often, ranchers only owned small pieces of land. These were next to rivers or streams. They would not let other people use the water. No one else could use the land next to the ranches. The ranchers would let their cattle eat the grass on this land. Terrible winters hit the Plains in 1885 and 1886. Ranchers lost eight out of ten head of cattle. Most of the large ranches went broke. The land was divided into many small ranches.

Connections

▲ Sandra Day O'Connor

Sandra Day O'Connor is on the Supreme Court. She is the first woman to hold such a job. President Ronald Reagan chose her for the Court in 1981. She comes from an old ranching family. The ranch is in Arizona and New Mexico. She now owns the ranch. It covers more than 155,000 acres.

 CHAPTER REVIEW

Critical Thinking

Write your answers on a sheet of paper or discuss in class.

Identifying Main Idea
1. Why were railroads so important to the United States after the Civil War?

Recognizing Details
2. What changes happened because of the railroads?

Cooperative Learning

LEARNING STYLE
Verbal

3. Work with a partner or group. Talk about railroads. Think about the kinds of things they carried. Remember, they helped miners, farmers, and ranchers. What kinds of things might these people ship by train? What kinds of things might trains bring to them? Make a chart of the things you talk about. You might use the following heads.
   - Things Shipped by Farmers
   - Things Needed by Farmers
   - Things Shipped by Miners
   - Things Needed by Miners
   - Things Shipped by Ranchers
   - Things Needed by Ranchers

Write About It

Writing Portfolio

4. Imagine that you have taken a train trip through the West. What might you have seen on the Plains? In Texas? In Colorado? In Kansas? In Indian Territory? Write a letter to a friend. Tell about your trip. Tell about the things you have seen and done.

Chapter 48

African & Asian Americans

The Fight for Civil Rights

Jim Crow Laws	Supreme Court	Response
Laws were passed to segregate races in:	States' rights to pass Jim Crow laws were upheld in:	The push for equality of all races was led by:
➤ trains ➤ schools ➤ hospitals ➤ theaters ➤ restrooms ➤ water fountains ➤ neighborhoods	➤ Slaughterhouse case (1873) ➤ *Plessy* vs. *Ferguson* (1896) ➤ *Mississippi* vs. *Williams* (1898) ➤ *Cummings* vs. *County Board of Education* (1899)	➤ Booker T. Washington's 1895 "Atlanta Compromise"—work for financial success rather than civil rights ➤ Niagara Movement—begun in 1905 by African Americans to fight for civil rights ➤ National Association for the Advancement of Colored People (NAACP)—Niagara Movement formed new group in 1910 that included whites in the fight for civil rights

Read about African Americans in the late 1800s. What important rights did they still not have? Why?

Key *Vocabulary*

prejudice (PREJ uh duhs)
senseless hatred of a person or group

status (STAYT uhs)
place or rank in society

receipt (ri SEET)
a piece of paper that proves something was done or paid for

segregate (SEG ruh gayt)
to keep one group separate or set apart from another

Reteaching Vocabulary

immigrant (IM i gruhnt)
a person who moves to another country in order to live there

CHART ANALYSIS

★ **Ask** What does this chart show?

★ **Acquire** What does each column tell you?

★ **Organize** Work with a partner to discuss the facts included in each column.

★ **Analyze** How did African Americans seem to feel about Jim Crow laws and the decisions of the Supreme Court?

★ **Answer** Why do you think African Americans joined forces with white Americans in the fight for civil rights?

Decoding Tip: Note the different letters that can make the schwa sound (uh) - u in **prejudice**, e in **segregate**, and i in **immigrant**.

ay	cake	ah	fall, cot	air	air		
ee	tree	i	sit	oh	cold		
or	cord	oy	toy	uh	above, hundred		
a	ask	ar	hard	oo	book		
e	yet	eye	nice	uhr	liar, fir, further, color		
ow	cow	ooh	boot, true	yoo	you, few, cube		

48.1   How did life change for African Americans from 1865 to 1890?

After the Civil War, African Americans thought life would get better. In 1868, the 13th Amendment ended slavery. Reconstruction seemed to offer a new life for African Americans in the South. Republicans in Congress passed laws to help them. They promised to protect their rights. Schools, churches, and small businesses were started. For a few years, African Americans saw real changes. They began to take part in the life of the country as never before. The road ahead looked brighter.

▲ W.E.B. DuBois was an African American leader in the late 1890s and early 1900s. He urged African Americans to speak out for civil rights. In 1909 DuBois helped start the National Association for the Advancement of Colored People (NAACP).

But the changes didn't last. Many whites in the South were afraid of change. They did all they could to keep African Americans down. Black voters were tricked. Some were beaten. The Republican drive for Reconstruction began to slow down. The Civil Rights Act of 1875 was the last important Reconstruction act.

For the rest of the 1800s, African Americans lost ground in their fight. In the South, things got worse. Most blacks still worked in the fields. Their lives were not much better than under slavery. African Americans began to leave the South. Some moved west to Arkansas, Louisiana, and Texas. Others headed for cities in the North. By 1890, life for African Americans was still hard. Most whites would not give them a chance. **Prejudice** was now their biggest problem.

48.2   What was the purpose of the Civil Rights Act of 1875?

Since 1865, Congress had made some changes to help African Americans. It passed laws to give them full citizenship. How could the **status** of African Americans in the South be changed? One way was to protect their rights by law.

The Civil Rights Act of 1875 was passed to do this. The act had three parts. (1) All people had the same rights to use public places. This meant places like trains and stores. African Americans could not be kept out. (2) All people could serve on juries. Race or color did not matter. (3) The above two rules were backed by United States law. Keeping any person from enjoying these rights was a crime. Republicans in Congress thought the new law would protect African Americans. It would give them a chance. They could live and work among whites. But the states found ways around the law. And in 1883 the Supreme Court said the law went against the Constitution.

48.3   How did whites in the South keep African Americans from voting?

Many towns in the South had more African Americans than whites. Black votes could decide important races. Whites wanted to stop African Americans from doing this. U.S. soldiers were no longer watching the South. Reconstruction was at an end. Southern whites were free to make their own laws. These laws would hold back African Americans for almost 100 years.

One law set up a Poll Tax. People had to pay to vote. Sometimes the money had to be paid months ahead of time. The payment dates were kept secret from African Americans. Or their **receipts** would be the wrong color. All these actions were tricks to keep them from voting.

Another law set up special tests. African Americans had to answer trick questions. How many bubbles in a bar of soap? How high is up? There were no right answers.

The Grandfather Clause was another law. When had someone in the family last voted? If it was before 1867, no tests were needed. Of course, almost no African Americans had voted before 1867. That was the point.

48.4 What idea was upheld in *Plessy* vs. *Ferguson*?

Homer Plessy was an African American in Louisiana. One day he tried to take a seat on a train. He was told he could not sit with whites. Plessy was told to sit in the **segregated** car. This was a car for African Americans only. Plessy believed he had the right to sit where he wanted. His case went all the way to the Supreme Court. *Plessy* vs. *Ferguson* (1896) set out an important rule. The Court said it was all right for African Americans to be kept apart. But their train cars and restrooms had to be as good as those for whites. This rule was called "separate but equal."

One man on the Supreme Court did not like it. Justice John Harlan wrote against the rule. "Our Constitution is color blind," he said. "All citizens are equal before the law." However, the rule now was the law of the land. The races lived side by side. But they were not living together. African Americans had their own places. But they were almost never as good as those for whites. New laws in the South made certain that African Americans were separated from whites. These laws were called "Jim Crow" laws. (Jim Crow was a black-face character in minstrel shows.)

48.5 In what ways were laws for Asian immigrants different from those for other immigrants?

In the late 1800s, great numbers of new people entered the United States. These people were **immigrants**. They came from Italy, Russia, Poland, and other countries. Many lived in large Eastern cities. They worked in mines and shops. Even their children worked. Life in their new country was hard. But with luck they could get by.

One group had special problems. The Chinese had come to the West Coast. They worked laying track for the new railroad.

Hard times hit in the 1870s. Jobs were few. Whites blamed the Chinese for taking their jobs. Sometimes angry groups would start fights with the Chinese. The Workingman's Party of California asked for a new law. They wanted a law against giving jobs to the Chinese. (The head of the party was from Ireland himself.) In 1882, the U.S. government went along. Chinese could no longer enter the country. People born in China could not become U.S. citizens. Those Chinese already in the country had few rights. Japanese and other Asians had the same problems.

Biography

In 1895 Frederick Douglass died. Douglass had been a strong leader for years. Now who would lead African Americans? One person who appeared ready was Booker T. Washington. He was born enslaved. He had worked to better himself. In 1881, he started the Tuskegee Institute in Alabama. It was a school that taught trades to African Americans. Washington believed the answer for African Americans lay in hard work. Too much worry about social problems was bad. In 1895, Washington made a talk in Atlanta. In it, he set out his ideas. He said blacks could live separately from whites. His talk was called the Atlanta Compromise.

Not all African Americans thought the same. W.E.B. DuBois was one. DuBois had a Ph.D. from Harvard. He wrote *The Souls of Black Folk* about African American life.

DuBois wanted his people to fight for their rights. He felt Washington's way was too slow. Change was called for now. DuBois was quick with words. Young African Americans were eager to hear him. Washington had a softer voice. But both men had important things to say.

▲ Booker T. Washington

"It seems to me," said Booker T.,
"That all you folks have missed the boat
Who shout about the right to vote
And spend vain days and sleepless nights
In uproar over civil rights.
Just keep your mouths shut, do not grouse,
But work, and save, and buy a house."

"I don't agree," said W.E.B.,
"For what can property avail
If dignity and justice fail?
Unless you help to make the laws,
They'll steal your house with trumped-up clause.
A rope's as tight, a fire as hot,
No matter how much cash you've got.
Speak soft, and try your little plan,
But as for me, I'll be a man."

—from "Booker T. and W.E.B."
by Dudley Randall

★★ CHAPTER REVIEW

Critical Thinking

Write your answers on a sheet of paper or discuss in class.

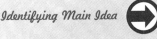

1. Southern states wanted to keep African Americans from voting. Why?

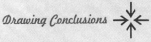

2. What is wrong with the idea of "separate but equal"?

Cooperative Learning

LEARNING STYLE
Visual

3. Work with a group to make a large picture. Draw important people from this chapter. Show changes in African American life before 1900. See if others can name the people and events.

Write About It

Writing Portfolio

4. Write two short pieces about *Plessy v. Ferguson*. Write one from Booker T. Washington's point of view. Write the other from that of W.E.B. DuBois.

Chapter 49

My Native Land

INDIAN TERRITORY (1830-1880s)

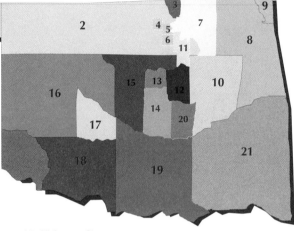

1. **No Man's Land**
2. **Cherokee Outlet**
3. Kaw
4. Nez Percé, Tonkawa
5. Ponca
6. Oto and Missouri
7. Osage
8. **Cherokee**, Munsee, Stockbridge, Delaware
9. **Ottowa Area**
   Cahokia, Cayuga, Chippewa, Conestoga, Eel River, Erie, Illinois, Kaskaskia, Miami, Michigamea, Modoc, Moingwena, Mohawk, Ottawa, Peoria, Piankashaw, Quapaw, Seneca, Shawnee, Tamaroa, Tuscarora, Wea, Wyandotte
10. **Creek**, Yuchi, Natchez, Tuskegee, Apalachicola, Koasati, Alabama, Hitchiti
11. Skidi, Pawnee
12. Sac and Fox
13. Iowa
14. Kickapoo, Shawnee, Pottawatomie
15. Unassigned Lands
16. Arapaho, Cheyenne
17. Wichita, Tawakoni, Waco, Anadarko, Caddo, Hainai, Kichai
18. Comanche, Kiowa, Lapan, Kiowa-Apache, Apache
19. **Chickasaw**
20. **Seminole**
21. **Choctaw**, Catawba

Note: *Native Americans of the southeastern United States were moved to Indian Territory in 1830. Their names are in red. Later, other Native Americans were moved to Indian Territory. Their names are in regular type.*

Read about Native Americans and the Great Plains. How did these people lose their land? Why?

Key *Vocabulary*

troops (troops) members of the armed forces

unassigned (uhn uh SEYEND) not given out or claimed

Reteaching Vocabulary

reservation (rez uhr VAY shuhn) land set aside for a group of people to live on

frontier (fruhn TEER) land that is still wild and has few people living there

---

MAP ANALYSIS

★ **Ask**   What does this map show?

★ **Acquire**   Read the note. What happened to some Native Americans living in the southeastern United States?

★ **Organize** Make a list of other Native Americans who lived on Cherokee, Creek, and Choctaw lands.

★ **Analyze**   "Unassigned Lands" means *lands not given out.* What do you think these places and *No Man's Land* were like?

★ **Answer**   Why do you think other Native Americans were moved not only to open lands but also to lands owned by people like the Cherokee?

Decoding Tip: Note the sound that oo stands for in **troops**.

ay	cake	ah	fall, cot	air	air
ee	tree	i	sit	oh	cold
or	cord	oy	toy	uh	above, hundred
a	ask	ar	hard	oo	book
e	yet	eye	nice	uhr	liar, fir, further, color
ow	cow	ooh	boot, true	yoo	you, few, cube

▲ The artwork above shows a scene of Blackfoot Native Americans chasing buffalo.

49.1 What was life like for early Native Americans who lived on the Great Plains?

Buffalo covered the Great Plains. Native Americans lived there, too. Some of these people were the Comanche, Wichita, and Cheyenne. They hunted buffalo. No part of the animal was wasted. The people ate buffalo meat. The hides were used for clothes. Tents were made from the hides, too. Bones were made into tools. Water bags were made from the stomachs. The buffalo did not stay in one place. They moved around looking for grass. Native Americans followed the buffalo, hunting them in large parties. There were no horses. Dogs worked for the people. Sticks were used to make frames. The frames were loaded with goods. Dogs would pull the frames. The people walked beside the dogs.

Horses changed life for Native Americans. Spanish people lived in Mexico. They visited the Plains. They brought horses. Some of the horses ran away. Groups of horses soon dotted the land. The Wichita are the first Native Americans known to have caught horses. Native Americans became great riders. They put the horses to work. Horses helped them hunt buffalo. Horses took over work from dogs, too. Now the people could make long trips. It was easier to follow the buffalo.

49.2 How did life change on the Great Plains after 1700?

Many Native Americans moved to the Plains. Europeans moved into North America. They built towns on the east and west shores. They pushed many Native Americans off their lands. These people had to move to the Great Plains. Some Native Americans fought each other. The Sioux lived near the Great Lakes. They had fights with the Chippewa. The French traded guns with the Chippewa in the early 1700s. The Chippewa were able to push the Sioux off their land. The Sioux moved west to the Plains.

More and more Native Americans were pushed to the Plains. The British were defeated by the United States in the Revolutionary War. Some Native Americans had fought on the British side. The Americans made these tribes move off their lands. They had to move out of the United States. They moved west of the Mississippi River. There was nowhere to go but the Plains.

In 1803 France sold land to the United States. It included most of the Plains. Americans began to move west of the Mississippi River themselves. More Native Americans lost their land. They gave up their ways of life. They began following and hunting buffalo.

49.3 How did Congress's plan for reservations fail?

Congress set up **reservations** for Native Americans on the Plains. Americans entered the Plains in the late 1840s. They were looking for gold, silver, and farming land. They began killing buffalo for their hides. The Native Americans fought the Americans. They wanted to save their way of life. Congress tried to keep the two groups apart. It began setting up reservations. The Native Americans would give up some of their lands. The rest would become reservations. The Native

Americans were not to leave the reservations. Congress would give them food, money, and other goods. However, the government did not always pay what it owed. Sometimes, the food was bad. Sometimes, government workers just kept the money and goods.

Fierce fighting broke out on the Plains in the 1860s. The Civil War was going on in the East. Most of the U.S. Army had been pulled out of the Plains. A few **troops** stayed. They could give little help. Colorado began fighting Native Americans in 1864. The Cheyenne and Arapaho were led by Black Kettle and Left Hand. They did not want war. The U.S. Army sent these people to Sand Creek, Colorado. It said they would be safe there. Colorado sent its own troops to Sand Creek. The Native Americans raised a white flag to surrender. But Colorado's troops opened fire anyway. They killed between 400 and 500 Native Americans. Congress and the U.S. Army were shocked. Land in Indian Territory was traded to Black Kettle and others who had lived.

49.4 Why did the United States and some Native Americans go to war?

Full war broke out between the Native Americans and the United States. The Civil War had ended in 1865. Americans poured onto the Plains. The Native Americans fought back. The U.S. Army returned to the Plains in force. It tried to protect Americans. Some Cheyenne had fought the people of Kansas in 1868. Now, the Cheyenne went to Indian Territory.

General George Custer was sent to punish them. Custer found the wrong group. Black Kettle's camp was attacked. He was killed. Over 100 of his people were killed, too. About 50 lived through the fight. Custer's men killed all the horses and burned the camp.

These wars lasted until 1890. Many in the army were African Americans. The Native Americans called them

"Buffalo Soldiers." Their skins were like the color of buffalo hides. The U.S. Army did not always win. Sitting Bull and Crazy Horse led the Sioux. General Custer went to Montana and the Dakotas. Gold had been found there. He helped keep the miners safe. The Sioux moved against Custer. Custer and all his men were killed. They died in Montana in 1876.

However, the U.S. Army was too strong. Like other Native Americans, the Sioux finally had to give up. Most of the wars were over by 1886. Small fights went on until 1890. The Native Americans lost most of their lands. Reservations were set up all across the West. However, most Native Americans were moved to Indian Territory.

49.5 What was the effect of the Dawes Act of 1887?

Life became hard for Native Americans. The buffalo had been killed off. The people had to live on smaller reservations. The U.S. government did not pay enough money and food. Many Native Americans died. Helen Hunt Jackson was a writer. She learned about the Native Americans' problems. She wrote *A Century of Dishonor*. She told what had happened to the Native Americans. It shocked many Americans. Some began calling for changes. Congress passed the Dawes Act of 1887. It pushed the Native Americans to live like white Americans.

The government took over the lives of most Native Americans. Some children were taken away from their families. They were sent to schools. They could talk only in English. They had to wear American clothes. They had to eat American food. They had no freedom of religion. The Dawes Act tried to set up the Native Americans as farmers. Most reservations were broken up. Land was handed out to each family. However, much of the land was bought by the government. It was sold to white Americans.

Even Indian Territory began to change in 1889. The **Unassigned** Lands were owned by the Seminoles and the Creeks. They did not live on these lands. Congress bought the land. It became Oklahoma Territory. Americans lined up at the edges of this land.

On April 22, 1889, a gun was fired. The people rushed in. Each person claimed a spot. By that night, over 50,000 people were living there. Oklahoma Territory grew. Soon, it covered the west half of what had been Indian Territory. Only the east part was Indian Territory. Its reservations were broken up in 1893. Again, some land was given out to Native American families. Congress bought the land that was left over. These lands were then sold. The days of the **frontier** were over.

1867 Nebraska became a state.

1889 Land in Indian Territory was sold to Americans.

1890 The Census Bureau stated that the frontier was closed. All the land had been divided up.

1912 Arizona and New Mexico became states.

1865 1875 1885 1895 1905 1915 1925

1876 Colorado became a state.

1889 Montana, North Dakota, and South Dakota became states.

1890 Wyoming became a state.

1896 Utah became a state.

1907 Indian Territory and Oklahoma Territory became the state of Oklahoma.

1924 All Native Americans were made citizens of the United States.

49.6 What happened to the Plains?

The Plains became different states. The deserts of the Southwest became states, too. Congress passed a special law in 1924. All Native Americans became citizens of the United States. They were to have the same rights as all other Americans. Indian Territory asked to become a state on its own. It wanted the name "Sequoyah." Sequoyah was a Cherokee. He had made up a way of writing for the Cherokee. Congress would not agree to the new state. Oklahoma Territory and Indian Territory worked together. They became the state of Oklahoma in 1907. Arizona and New Mexico became states in 1912. There were 48 states. The United States now stretched from the Atlantic to the Pacific. It filled the land between Canada and Mexico.

☆☆☆

Connections

Native Americans fought for the United States in World War II. Over 250,000 fought in this war against Japan and Germany. The troops used radios to keep in touch. They wanted their plans to be secret, though. The Japanese and Germans were often listening. Very few people speak Native American languages. Native Americans, such as the Navajo, took over the radios. They kept the troops in touch. The Germans and Japanese never knew what was said. All the American plans were kept very secret.

▲ Ira H. Hayes, a Pima, at age 19, ready to jump during Marine Corps Paratroop School in 1943

▲ Lt. Woody J. Cochran, a Cherokee bomber pilot who earned the Silver Star, Purple Heart, Distinguished Flying Cross, and Air Medal during World War II

★★☆ CHAPTER REVIEW

Critical Thinking

Write your answers on a sheet of paper or discuss in class.

Identifying Main Idea

1. Why did many Native Americans give up hunting to become farmers?

Making Inferences

2. How well did the government keep its promises to Native Americans?

Cooperative Learning

LEARNING STYLE
Reading Verbal

3. Work with a partner or group. Copy the names used in this chapter. Look up each name. See how it sounds. Say the names out loud. Then read the chapter out loud. Make sure to say the names correctly.

Write About It

Writing Portfolio

4. Choose one group of Native Americans. Find out about these people. Make notes about them. How did they live in the 1700s and 1800s? Where did they live? What happened to them? Were they moved to reservations? Do any of these people still live on reservations? What are their lives like today? Write a short report. Share your report with the class.

Chapter 50

A Recipe for Growth

UNITED STATES MINERAL RESOURCES (1870)

Legend:
- Oil
- Natural Gas
- Coal
- Oil Shale
- Iron

Read about the changing ways Americans earned their livings. How did factories change jobs? Why?

Key *Vocabulary*

industry (IN duhs tree)
all the work done by a country's factories

computer (kuhm PYOOT uhr)
a machine that can deal with facts by handling electric currents

Reteaching Vocabulary

immigrant (IM i gruhnt)
a person who moves to another country in order to live there

resource (REE sors)
something that can be sold and/or used to make an item that can be sold

---

MAP ANALYSIS

★ **Ask**   What does this map show?

★ **Acquire**   What does the legend tell you?

★ **Organize** Make a chart of your state and its neighbors. List the resources found in each of these states.

★ **Analyze**   Which areas do not have many mineral resources?

★ **Answer**   How might having mineral resources affect a state?

Decoding Tip: Note the different sounds u stands for in the words **industry** and **computer**.

ay	cake	ah	fall, cot	air	air
ee	tree	i	sit	oh	cold
or	cord	oy	toy	uh	above, hundred
a	ask	ar	hard	oo	book
e	yet	eye	nice	uhr	liar, fir, further, color
ow	cow	ooh	boot, true	yoo	you, few, cube

50.1 How did the Civil War affect factories?

Factories were a part of the Civil War. They filled the North. There were few in the South. Factories had given the Union an edge. It was able to win the war. Great numbers of goods were used in the war. Factory owners became rich. Many new factories opened up. With the war over, the country grew. New states were added to the Union. Trains reached all parts of the country. They carried the factories' goods. Soon American goods were being shipped to other countries, too.

▲ The illustration above shows men and women working in a factory making cartridges. Illustration by Theo R. Davis, from *Harpers Magazine,* 1877

50.2 What resource did immigrants provide for factories?

Immigrants had long been coming to the United States. After the Civil War, their numbers continued to grow. They found work in factories. More and more factories were opening. There were many new jobs. However, there were not enough American workers. Immigrants helped the factories. They took factory jobs. They helped the country to grow. It was like a circle. Now, more people lived in the United States. They all needed goods. More goods needed to be made. More factory jobs opened up. More immigrants came to the United States to take these jobs. They needed goods, too. Even more goods needed to be made. Owners continued to build factories. By 1890, the United States was making more goods than any other country.

▶ The photograph to the right shows the interior of a cloth-making factory in 1900.

50.3 Why were coal, oil, and iron important American resources?

American **resources** helped the country grow. Coal was used in many ways. It was burned to warm houses. It was burned for cooking. It was burned to heat water and make steam. Steam made machines run. Steam ran trains, ships, and factories. The United States was rich in oil, too. It kept machines working. Their moving parts were oiled. Oil made them slide easily as they worked. Oil could be turned into gas, too. People soon learned how to use gas to run machines.

Iron was mined in many places. It was very important to the growing country. Trains were made of iron. Native Americans even called them "Iron Horses." Tracks and bridges were made of iron, too. During the Civil War, people began using iron for ships. Iron was turned into fences, horseshoes, and

The photo to the right shows a group of miners posing for a photograph around 1900.

many kinds of machines. Making iron became one of the country's biggest businesses.

50.4 Why did steel replace iron?

People wanted goods made of steel. Iron was not as strong as steel. It could be made into steel, though. Steel goods did not wear out as easily as iron ones. However, making steel took a lot of money. Iron ore was never perfect. Unneeded things were mixed with the iron. This kept the iron from being strong. Once the unneeded things were taken out, steel could be made. Two men worked on this problem. Each one came up with the same idea. Cold air was used in melting the iron. Only perfect iron was left behind. Now it could be turned into steel very easily. Steel could be made for less money, too.

Steel became important to the United States. It soon took the place of iron for many goods. Giant steel plants were set up. Their owners became some of the world's richest people. Steel helped **industry** to grow. Industry kept growing throughout the late 1800s. Industry changed the country and its people.

☆☆☆

Yesterday...

Steam engines did heavy work. They could do work that people had once done. Some people lost jobs to steam engines. The song "John Henry" was about this lost work. John Henry was an African American. He and his group helped lay train tracks. They drove spikes to hold the rails to the ties. Then a steam engine began doing this work. John Henry wanted to show that he could work as well as the engine. A race was held.

John Henry drove his spikes. The engine worked beside him. John Henry won the race. He had worked too hard, though. He died from the work. Steam engines took over many jobs. However, people had to run these engines. New jobs opened up.

▲ Joseph Cugnot's engine, built in 1969

Today...

Some machines take over jobs even today. **Computers** are the newest of these machines. There are many kinds of jobs in banking. It used to take many people to keep a bank's books. Now, one computer can hold all of a bank's books. Only one person is needed to run the computer. This person has to know a lot about computers. Computers are used in all kinds of companies. Knowing how to use a computer is important for today's workers.

CHAPTER REVIEW

Critical Thinking

Write your answers on a sheet of pape, or discuss in class.

 Identifying Main Idea

1. How did America's resources change the country and its people?

 Making Inferences

2. Why might it be important to protect the country's resources?

Cooperative Learning

 LEARNING STYLE *Oral*

3. Work with a partner or group. Find old songs like "John Henry." They should tell about people's work. One old song was about digging the Erie Canal. Play these songs. Talk about the songs and the jobs they tell about.

Write About It

 Writing Portfolio

4. What resources are near you? How are they used? Where are they sold? Find out about these resources. Use these facts in a paragraph. Read your paragraph aloud. Put your paragraph into a class book. Call the book "Our State's Resources."

Chapter 51
Corporate America

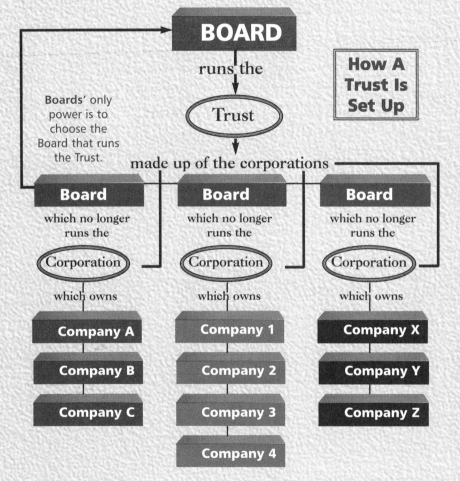

BOARD

runs the

Trust

How A Trust Is Set Up

Boards' only power is to choose the Board that runs the Trust.

made up of the corporations

Board	**Board**	**Board**
which no longer runs the	which no longer runs the	which no longer runs the
Corporation	Corporation	Corporation
which owns	which owns	which owns

Company A	**Company 1**	**Company X**
Company B	**Company 2**	**Company Y**
Company C	**Company 3**	**Company Z**
	Company 4	

Read about the ways in which companies change. How did companies grow? Why?

Key *Vocabulary*

profit (PRAHF uht)
the money left over after all costs have been paid

corporation
(kor puh RAY shuhn)
a business owned by two or more people and set up under the laws of a certain state

trust (truhst)
corporations that have joined together so that they do not compete with one another

monopoly (muh NAHP uh lee)
total control of all the parts of a certain kind of business, such as all parts of the oil business

CHART ANALYSIS

★ **Ask** What does this chart show?

★ **Organize** List the parts of a trust. Tell what each part does.

★ **Analyze** How much power does each board in a trust have?

★ **Answer** Think about the people on the board of each corporation. Why might these people want to be on the board that runs the trust?

Decoding Tip: Note the different sounds o stands for in the vocabulary words.

ay	cake	ah	fall, cot	air	air	
ee	tree	i	sit	oh	cold	
or	cord	oy	toy	uh	above, hundred	
a	ask	ar	hard	oo	book	
e	yet	eye	nice	uhr	liar, fir, further, color	
ow	cow	ooh	boot, true	yoo	you, few, cube	

51.1 What were companies like before the Civil War?

Early factories were owned by one person or just a few people. One person or family might own a factory. Sometimes, two or more people might become partners. These people ran the factory. They knew all the workers. They also kept all the **profits**. Each factory was fairly small. However, the Civil War had used great numbers of goods. Factories needed to grow. This could take a lot of money. Owners did not always have this money. A means had to be found so that factories could grow.

51.2 Why did corporations become important in the United States?

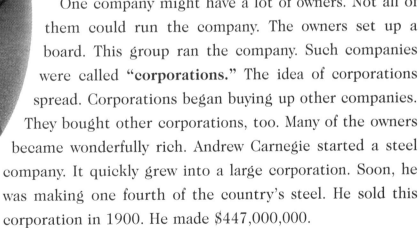

▲ Andrew Carnegie

Companies were set up to run the factories. Parts of the company were sold. Different people bought these parts, or shares. A lot of money was raised. Factories could grow. They could spread to many places. The companies made money. All the owners were given part of this money.

One company might have a lot of owners. Not all of them could run the company. The owners set up a board. This group ran the company. Such companies were called "**corporations.**" The idea of corporations spread. Corporations began buying up other companies. They bought other corporations, too. Many of the owners became wonderfully rich. Andrew Carnegie started a steel company. It quickly grew into a large corporation. Soon, he was making one fourth of the country's steel. He sold this corporation in 1900. He made $447,000,000.

51.3 How did mass production and assembly lines affect industry?

Eli Whitney made the first cotton gin in the late 1700s. Cotton became important to the South. Factories in the

North bought the cotton. They turned it into cloth. Whitney had another idea. It changed the way factories worked. It was called "mass production." This is a special way of making parts for goods. The parts are exactly like each other. Each part will fit any one of the goods. The final goods are exactly like each other, too. Workers can make the goods more quickly. The goods can be made for less money, too.

▲ "Mule spinners," automated cotton-spinning equipment, in a Lowell, Massachusetts, cotton mill

Factories changed again. Assembly lines were set up. They are still used today. One person does not build all of one good. People have different jobs. Parts are sent down a line. Each person adds one part to the good. The next worker adds another part. When the good reaches the end of the line, it is finished. Some factories made trains. One person or group would build the engine. The next person or group would add the wheels. Another would paint the train. Trains could be made very quickly. Less money was spent making the goods. Companies earned more money.

51.4 How did trusts and monopolies affect business?

Sometimes, corporations joined together. A group of corporations was called a "**trust**." It was run by a board, too. They came from the boards of the corporations. The trust would run all the corporations. A trust could earn more money than the corporations could earn by themselves. Each corporation would then take part of the money that was earned. This money would go to the owners of that corporation.

Trusts even took over whole businesses. John D. Rockefeller began an oil company in Ohio. He bought other oil companies. His company had to buy goods, too. These goods kept his company running. Rockefeller began buying up these companies, too. Other companies joined him in a trust. The trust took over almost all the oil companies in the United States. It had a **monopoly**. It charged anything it wanted. People had to pay. There was no place else to buy these kinds of goods. The trust even told companies what it would pay for goods. Oil was shipped by train. Rockefeller told these companies what he would pay. They always gave in. The trust was too strong to fight. Other trusts became monopolies, too.

The United States helped American business. The Bill of Rights gave everyone rights as owners. Congress carried out this idea. It passed few acts about business. It left businesses alone. The country grew. It became very rich. But by the late 1890s, some people's ideas began to change. Many people felt that trusts and monopolies were not fair. They felt these companies were too strong. These ideas began to change government, too.

Biography

Sarah Breedlove was born in 1867. She was an African American who lived in Louisiana. Her mother and father had been enslaved. She had problems with her hair. Some would fall out. Then her hair would be very thin. She began making goods to help take care of hair problems. One of them saved her hair. She opened her own company in 1905. It was in Indianapolis, Indiana. She only had $1.50. She went by the name of Madame C.J. Walker. Her company grew. It made her a millionaire.

Marjorie Merriwether Post became a millionaire, too. Her father was C.W. Post. He began a company in 1897. It made breakfast foods. It was called Postum Cereal Company. He trained his daughter to run the company. She took over the company when he died. She bought other companies. Her new company became General Foods Corporation. She was one of the richest people in the United States.

▲ Majorie Merriwether Post

★★☆ CHAPTER REVIEW

Critical Thinking

Write your answers on a sheet of paper or discuss in class.

Comparing and Contrasting

1. How are corporations and trusts alike?

Making Inferences

2. Why was business important to the United States?

Cooperative Learning

LEARNING STYLE
Reading
Tactile

3. Work with a partner or group. Look over the facts about businesses. Make lists about corporations, trusts, and monopolies. Put these facts in a chart. Use the name "Industry in the United States."

Write About It

Writing Portfolio

4. Think of something you buy because you like it. Find out the name of the company that makes it. This can be found on the package. The address should be there, too. Write a letter to this company. Tell why you like this thing.

Chapter 52

A New Way of Life

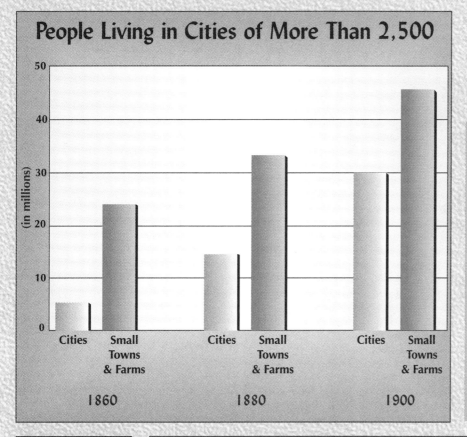

People Living in Cities of More Than 2,500

(y-axis: (in millions) — 0, 10, 20, 30, 40, 50)

1860
Cities / Small Towns & Farms

1880
Cities / Small Towns & Farms

1900
Cities / Small Towns & Farms

Read about inventions in the United States in the late 1800s. What changes did they bring about? Why?

Key *Vocabulary*

combine (KAHM beyen) a machine that handles every step of harvesting grain

slaughterhouse (SLAH tuhr hows) place where animals are butchered for meat

urban (UHR buhn) having to do with cities

tenement (TEN uh muhnt) a building divided into small rooms for family dwellings

suburb (SUHB uhrb) an area or town with neighborhoods of houses located outside a large city

GRAPH ANALYSIS

★ **Ask** For this graph, how many people make up a city?

★ **Acquire** How many people lived in cities in 1900?

★ **Analyze** What happened to the number of people living in cities between 1860 and 1900?

★ **Answer** Imagine that the graph also lists the year 1920. How do you think the two bars would compare for that year?

Decoding Tip: Note the /uhr/ sound that ur makes in **urban** and **suburb**.

ay	cake	ah	fall, cot	air	air
ee	tree	i	sit	oh	cold
or	cord	oy	toy	uh	above, hundred
a	ask	ar	hard	oo	book
e	yet	eye	nice	uhr	liar, fir, further, color
ow	cow	ooh	boot, true	yoo	you, few, cube

52.1 How did inventions affect farming in the 1880s?

In the 1880s, people continued moving to the West. The great promise was owning land. The Homestead Act gave everyone a chance to own 160 acres. They only had to do two things. First, they had to pay a small fee. Second, they had to live on the land for five years. Most people bought land to become farmers. Making a farm pay off was not always easy. American farm prices had gone down. But European markets needed lots of grain. Most new farmers could get by.

▲ Men working in a steel factory

Farmers could make better money if they had more land. Family farms began to grow. To farm large fields, new machines were needed. Two had been in use before the Civil War. Cyrus McCormick had made the first machine that cut grain. John Deere's steel plow could turn the hard ground of the Great Plains. Several new machines appeared from 1876 to 1880. McCormick made one called a **combine.** It could handle every step of bringing in wheat. It cut it and even put it in bags. Another machine could separate cream from milk. Large machines were made to plow large fields. The new machines saved lots of work. Less people were needed to run a farm. The number of acres used for farming grew from 500,000,000 to almost 900,000,000.

52.2 How did cheap steel affect life in America?

In 1859, Henry Bessemer, an Englishman, found a new way to make steel. William Kelly, an American, discovered the same thing. The new way cost less money. It also saved time. What used to take a day now took about 15 minutes. Also, rich fields of ore were found. They were around Lake Superior in Michigan. This was mined to make steel.

By the 1880s, tons of steel were being made in the United States every day. Things made with steel cost less. Steel was also strong. It lasted longer than iron. It was perfect for making railroad tracks. Hundreds of other things were made from steel. Some, like beams for buildings, were large. Others, like needles, were small. All could now be made in great numbers like never before. Trains, towers, plows, bridges, and ships were made. People had more things to buy. Cities grew quickly, helped by the new steel. It was so important that some called this time the Age of Steel.

52.3 How did inventors make large modern cities possible?

The late 1800s were a time of great change. New ideas were changing the face of America. No longer was it a country of farms and small towns. People were gathering in large cities. Inventors were dreaming up things that helped cities grow. In 1879, Thomas Edison made the first electric light. Candles became a thing of the past. Cities were not dark at night. Streets and signs were lighted with electricity. Power lines were built. They sent light and power all over the new cities. People used to get around in wagons pulled by horses. Now there were electric streetcars. Trains were run on tracks above the street. In 1875, Alexander Graham Bell made the telephone. By 1900, there were more than 1,300,000 in the country. Telephone lines let people talk over great distances.

People in cities needed lots of things to live. Food had to be marketed in new ways. Animals were no longer brought in for food. The meat was cut in **slaughterhouses.** It was loaded on trains. The meat was then shipped to cities. People working all day on jobs had no time to make clothes. New machines made

▲ A slaughterhouse

cloth fast. The cloth was then made into suits and dresses. Stores sold these clothes to working people. Clothes and other things were made in large numbers. Because of mass production, these clothes cost less.

52.4 Why did people move to cities in such large numbers?

As industry grew, so did cities. After the Civil War, cities were the best places to find jobs. Factories were started in cities. Shipping went on there. Growing companies needed lots of people. Cities grew up near rivers. Some were near important resources, such as trees or cattle. Large cities offered lots of ways to make money. Chances seemed better there than on farms. **Urban** life seemed more exciting to some. There were plays, shows, and games to go to. By 1900, many more people worked in cities than on farms.

People coming to the United States from other countries moved into cities. They lived in New York, Boston, and Chicago among others. Few went to the Great Plains. Prices for land were going up. Also, things were strange to these new people. Many needed help. They moved into neighborhoods with others from their country. Sometimes these neighborhoods became closed off. A neighborhood would be all Irish or Italian. Most couldn't afford their own houses. They lived in small rooms in **tenements.** They worked long hours in factories. Often their dream was to make it out of the neighborhood.

☆☆☆

Connections

In the late 1800s, many cities were growing too fast. They were not comfortable places to live. People longed to have more room. They wanted to see grass and trees. Towns were started outside cities. These were called suburbs. People could take streetcars to work and back. They could have the best of both worlds. They could have a good job in the city. They could also enjoy a quiet house with grass and flowers. Only some people could pay for this, however. For those who could, life got better.

Suburbs continued to grow. City streets became empty at night. Many places in the city closed down. People were afraid of crime. In the 1980s, some cities began trying to get people back. They worked on new plans. They built comfortable places to shop and eat. Often these places were made out of old warehouses. New lights went up. Parking was added. Baltimore, Maryland, had the Inner Harbor.

There was the West End in Dallas, Texas. People began to stay in these cities after work. The new places were bringing the cities back to life.

▲ Baltimore Harbor, Maryland, in 1885, now the site of an inner-city mall.

★★☆ CHAPTER REVIEW

Critical Thinking

Write your answers on a sheet of paper or discuss in class.

Drawing Conclusions

1. Many machines take the place of people. Is this always a good thing? Why or why not?

Making Inferences

2. What problems might new Americans have faced living in a large city?

Cooperative Learning

LEARNING STYLE
Auditory Verbal

3. Read this chapter again. This time work with a friend. Take turns reading out loud. Help each other with any words you don't know.

Write About It

Writing Portfolio

4. Imagine you are living in the late 1800s. You live in a large city. Today they put electric lights in your neighborhood. Write about this special day in your diary.

Quiz

Number a piece of paper from 1–10. Write a, b, c, and d beside these numbers. Read the following sentence parts. Four answers follow each one. Choose the answer that best completes the sentence. On your paper, circle the letter that matches the letter of your answer. Be sure you mark your answer beside the correct number.

1. **Americans moved to the middle of the country because . . .**
   a. railroads were built.
   b. Congress gave away free land.
   c. mining and ranching could earn big money.
   d. all of the above

2. **Of the following, only _____?_____ did NOT help African Americans gain rights.**
   a. the 13th Amendment of 1865
   b. *Plessy* vs. *Ferguson* (1896)
   c. the Civil Rights Act of 1875
   d. none of the above

3. **Congress passed an act in 1882 that did not allow_____?_____to become citizens.**
   a. African Americans
   b. Native Americans
   c. people from China
   d. people from Southwestern Europe

4. **In return for land, Native Americans agreed to live . . .**
   a. on reservations.
   b. in Canada.
   c. on army posts.
   d. all of the above

5. **After passing the Dawes Act of 1887, the government . . .**
   a. pushed Native Americans to live like other Americans.
   b. took over Native Americans' lives.
   c. divided most reservation land among Native Americans and sold the rest.
   d. all of the above

6. **Factories grew because . . .**
   a. the world wanted factory goods.
   b. American immigrants wanted factory jobs.
   c. plenty of resources, such as iron, could be found in the United States.
   d. all of the above

7. **Before the Civil War, most companies were . . .**
   a. giant organizations.
   b. owned by one or just a few people.
   c. set up as corporations, trusts, and monopolies.
   d. none of the above

8. **Some trusts took over so many companies that . . .**
   a. Congress made such giants against the law.
   b. they went broke trying to pay all their workers.
   c. they took over whole lines of work, such as the oil business.
   d. all of the above

9. **Because of inventors and their ideas, . . .**
   a. the country's farms covered over 900,000,000 acres.
   b. steel became a main good used all across the country.
   c. cities could grow and spread out.
   d. all of the above

10. **By 1900, most people worked . . .**
    a. in cities.
    b. on farms.
    c. on the country's two coasts.
    d. none of the above

ANALYZING CAUSE AND EFFECT

Add numbers 11–15 to your paper. Read the ideas below. The ideas on the left describe a cause, or something that makes a second event happen. The ideas on the right are effects, the events that are caused. Match these causes and effects. Write your answers beside the correct numbers on your paper.

11. Congress wanted a transcontinental railroad, . . .
12. Some Southerners wanted to take away African Americans' rights, . . .
13. In order to build up the Great Plains, . . .
14. Resources, workers, and money increased after the Civil War, . . .
15. Congress passed few acts about business because . . .

a. so they set up poll taxes, Jim Crow laws, and grandfather clauses.
b. Congress moved Native Americans to reservations and gave out free land.
c. so it gave large amounts of land to railroad companies.
d. it felt that the Bill of Rights gave everyone rights as owners.
e. so business and factory owners became very important to the country.

Look over the things you wrote for these chapters. Choose one that you like the best. Add to your writing. For example, you wrote a letter to a friend as if you were riding on the transcontinental railroad. Write the friend's answering letter. Trade papers with a study partner. Check each other's work. Make a clean, neat copy. Put it in your portfolio.

Write the headings **Cause** and **Effect** on a piece of paper. Think about the years between 1865 and 1890. How did the country change? How did people change? What happened to people's rights? Make a list of things that happened. Did one make something else happen? If so, list it under the heading **Cause**. Did an earlier event make it happen? If so, list it under the heading **Effect**. Look at the chart in Chapter 51. Make a chart with these causes and effects. Use arrows to show how some things led to other happenings.

COOPERATIVE PROJECT: MAP OF ILLUSTRATIONS

Work with a partner or group. Get a large piece of paper. Draw a big map of the United States. Show all the states except Alaska and Hawaii. What happened during 1870-1900? Where did these things happen? Draw pictures of these happenings. Draw them on the correct spots on the map. Hang your finished map for the whole school to see.

Chapter 53

Immigrants and Industry

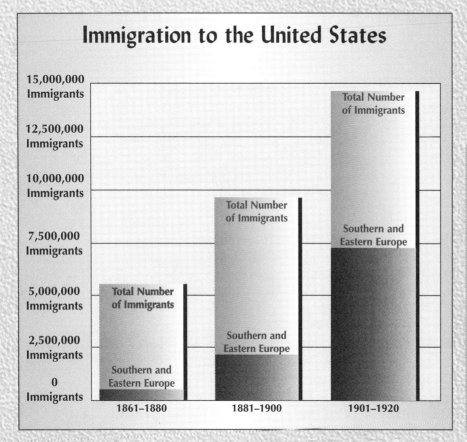

Immigration to the United States

15,000,000 Immigrants

12,500,000 Immigrants

10,000,000 Immigrants

7,500,000 Immigrants

5,000,000 Immigrants

2,500,000 Immigrants

0 Immigrants

1861–1880
Total Number of Immigrants
Southern and Eastern Europe

1881–1900
Total Number of Immigrants
Southern and Eastern Europe

1901–1920
Total Number of Immigrants
Southern and Eastern Europe

Read about people who came to the United States. How did they change the country? Why?

Key *Vocabulary*

immigration
(im uh GRAY shuhn)
the act of moving to another country in order to live there

exclusion (iks KLOO zhuhn)
keeping someone or something out

liberty (LIB uhrt ee)
the state of being free or able to do what one wants

Reteaching Vocabulary

immigrant (IM i gruhnt)
a person who moves to another country in order to live there

GRAPH ANALYSIS

★ **Ask**   What is this graph about?

★ **Acquire**   Why is part of each bar colored gray?

★ **Organize**   List the number of immigrants who arrived in each time period. How many were from Southern and Eastern Europe?

★ **Analyze**   How did the number of immigrants change for each time period?

★ **Answer**   What might have caused so many people to leave their homes in order to come to the United States?

Decoding Tip: Note the sounds of tion in **immigration** and sion in **exclusion**.

ay	cake	ah	fall, cot	air	air
ee	tree	i	sit	oh	cold
or	cord	oy	toy	uh	above, hundred
a	ask	ar	hard	oo	book
e	yet	eye	nice	uhr	liar, fir, further, color
ow	cow	ooh	boot, true	yoo	you, few, cube

53.1 How did the Homestead Act of 1862 affect immigration?

Congress began giving out free land. It had passed the Homestead Act in 1862. People could have land in the Great Plains. They had to live on the land. They had to begin farms. After five years, the land was theirs. If they left before five years, they lost the land.

Immigrants came to the United States for free land. They had heard about the Homestead Act. Not only Americans could have the land. Immigrants could have the land, too. Most immigrants came from Northern Europe. They came from countries like the Netherlands and Germany. Scandinavia is in Europe's far north. Norway, Sweden, and Denmark are countries in Scandinavia. People from these countries poured onto the Plains. They built farms in places like Minnesota, Wisconsin, and Nebraska. Trains helped them reach their new homes.

▲ The photo above is of the Statue of Liberty, a gift from France to the United States in honor of the 100th anniversary of the signing of the Declaration of Independence on July 4, 1776. In later years it became a symbol of hope and freedom for millions of immigrants who saw it upon arriving by ship in New York Harbor.

53.2 Why did most immigrants settle in cities?

Reaching free lands took money. Immigrants had to take ships to the United States. They had to pay for these trips. Ships carried them to places along the East Coast. Immigrants entered the country through cities like Boston, New York, and Baltimore. Many used all their money reaching the United States. They could not move to the Plains. They

▲ The photograph above shows a recent view of the New York City skyline where immigrants from many different countries live and work and call themselves Americans.

had to stay in the cities. Most of these cities were in the North. The North was full of factories. Many new jobs were opening up in these plants. Most immigrants were glad to take these jobs. They kept the factories running. The factories kept the country growing.

53.3 Why did some Americans want to stop immigration?

After 1880, **immigration** went up in great numbers. The United States let most of these people in. Hard times had hit Europe. Wars had broken out. Many Europeans were very poor. They saved their money. Then they could pay to reach the United States. Some only came for a little while. They found jobs and saved money. Then they went back to Europe. Most stayed in the United States. They became Americans.

Immigrants changed after 1880. Many were coming from Southern and Eastern Europe. They were very different from the people of Northern Europe. People in the North were often Protestants. Most people in the South and East followed a different religion. Many were Catholics. Others were Jewish. All these people had different ways of living, too. Most early Americans had come from Northern Europe. There were worries about these new immigrants. Would they change the United States?

Soon, there were more workers than jobs. Immigrants needed work badly. They would even work for less money just to get jobs. Some companies fired their workers. They gave the jobs to immigrants. The companies saved money. The owners could keep this money as profits. Hard feelings grew up between some Americans and the new immigrants.

▼ The photograph below shows immigrants coming into the United States by way of Ellis Island.

53.4 Why were new laws passed to cut down on immigration to the United States?

"America for the Americans" became a popular saying. Groups were set up to fight immigration. They pushed for new laws. These laws were made by different cities and states. They kept immigrants from getting certain kinds of jobs. Often, immigrants were not given the same rights as Americans. Fighting sometimes broke out. People were hurt.

The United States Congress took action. It passed the Chinese **Exclusion** Act in 1882. Chinese immigrants had poured into the United States. They lived in Hawaii and along the Pacific Coast. Congress's act stopped all immigration from China and Asia. The law was to last for 10 years. Other acts were passed by Congress. Immigration was slowed. A certain number of immigrants was set for each country. Only that number could enter the United States each year. Even today, Congress sets the number of immigrants who can enter the country.

Connections

▲ Statue of Liberty

France and the United States are old friends. France helped the United States win the Revolutionary War. The United States was 100 years old in 1876. France gave the country a special gift. It was the Statue of **Liberty.** Frédéric Auguste Bartholdi came up with the idea. The people of France paid for the work. The people of the United States had to raise money, too. They bought some land for the Statue of Liberty. They paid for the base it stands on. It was completed in New York Harbor in 1884.

Emma Lazarus wrote a poem about the Statue of Liberty. It is printed on the stand. Its words are very special. It is about the immigrants who came to the United States.

. . . Give us your tired, your poor,

Your huddled masses yearning to breathe free, . . .

Ships sail past the Statue of Liberty every day. It was often the first thing most immigrants saw of the United States. Today, it stands as a sign of our country. It is a sign of liberty found in the United States and France. It is a sign that all Americans come from immigrants. Even Native Americans are immigrants in a way. They too came to the Americas from another land—Asia.

★★★ CHAPTER REVIEW

Critical Thinking

Write your answers on a sheet of paper or discuss in class.

Identifying Main Idea

1. Why is it often said that the United States is a country of immigrants?

Drawing Conclusions

2. How did immigrants change the United States?

Cooperative Learning

LEARNING STYLE
Tactile

3. Work with a partner or group. Find a picture of the Statue of Liberty. Cut out this picture, or draw one of your own. Put the picture on poster board. Find the poem "The New Colossus" by Emma Lazarus. Copy this poem onto your poster. Hang your poster in the room.

Write About It

Writing Portfolio

4. Imagine you are an immigrant of the 1880s. You have just reached the United States. What city are you in? What do you see? What is the city like? How do you plan to live? Write a letter to a friend back home. Tell this person about the United States.

Chapter 54
Cities and Their Problems

Read about the way in which American cities grew. How did they change the country? Why?

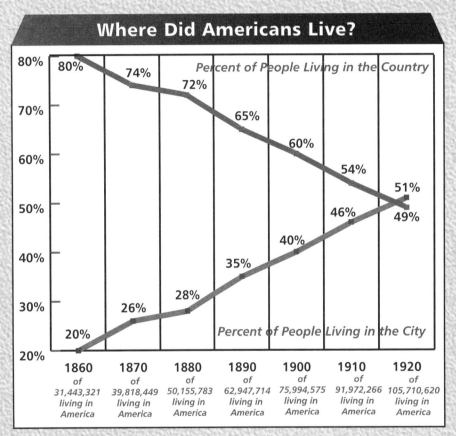

Where Did Americans Live?

Percent of People Living in the Country

80% — 80%
74%
72%
70%
65%
60%
60%
54%
51%
50%
46%
49%
40%
40%
35%
30%
28%
26%
20%
20%

Percent of People Living in the City

1860	1870	1880	1890	1900	1910	1920
of 31,443,321 living in America	of 39,818,449 living in America	of 50,155,783 living in America	of 62,947,714 living in America	of 75,994,575 living in America	of 91,972,266 living in America	of 105,710,620 living in America

Key *Vocabulary*

slum (sluhm) a part of a city that is very crowded, poor, and dirty

sewer (SOO uhr) a set of drain pipes that carry off water and waste material

elevated (EL uh vayt uhd) placed or built above the ground

subway (SUHB way) a train that runs through a set of tunnels that have been dug under a city

Reteaching Vocabulary

crime (kreyem) 1. an act that is against the law and that can lead to some kind of punishment 2. all these acts that government must deal with

GRAPH ANALYSIS

★ **Ask** What does this graph tell you?

★ **Acquire** What does the blue line tell you?

★ **Organize** List the percent of people who were living in cities for each year. List the total number of people living in the country.

★ **Analyze** How did population change in the cities and the country?

★ **Answer** What might have caused so many people to leave the country and move to cities?

Decoding Tip: Note the sound of *u* in **slum** and **subway**.

ay	cake	ah	fall, cot	air	air
ee	tree	i	sit	oh	cold
or	cord	oy	toy	uh	above, hundred
a	ask	ar	hard	oo	book
e	yet	eye	nice	uhr	liar, fir, further, color
ow	cow	ooh	boot, true	yoo	you, few, cube

54.1 Why did so many people leave their farms and move to cities?

Factories were usually found in cities. They needed workers. After the Civil War, even more factories opened. There were not enough workers. One factory might even try to take workers from other factories. It would give the workers higher pay. Immigrants helped keep the factories working. Soon, farmers began looking for these jobs, too.

Many people left their farms after the Civil War. They needed work in the factories. Farmers had not usually made a lot of money. Most farms were small. Farmers raised all their own food. They made most of the things they needed. Sometimes farmers did have a few crops to sell. But they made only a little money. Life was often very hard on farms. Factory jobs gave people a chance for better lives.

Many farmers became poor during the late 1800s. New machines had made farm work easier. They cost a lot of money, though. Many farmers bought these machines. They took out loans to pay for the machines. Then hard times hit in 1873, 1882, and 1893. Many farmers could not pay back their loans. They lost their farms. They took their families to cities.

However, factories had changed. Many immigrants had poured into the country. There were now too many workers. Factory owners cut workers' pay to save money. Then hard times hurt the factories, too. Workers were paid even less. This did not stop cities from growing. People still needed jobs. Factory jobs were still the best to be found.

54.2 What are slums?

Housing was a problem in most cities. Hundreds of people might arrive in a day. There were not enough homes for them all. Some people built large apartment buildings. They were often poorly made. The owners still charged high rents. People filled these buildings. There were no other homes for them. Many of these buildings were in poor shape. There were few lights. Often there was only one sink on each floor. There was little heat in the winter. Often, the buildings were not kept up. They fell apart. These neighborhoods were very crowded and dirty. They became known as "**slums**."

54.3 Why was city life often dangerous?

Cities faced many problems. Garbage was piled in the streets. It was not picked up very often. Chicago's slum streets were piled six feet high. Rain would wash some of the garbage away. It would pour into rivers and lakes. Even **sewers** emptied into this water. City water turned bad, too. Many people became sick. Sicknesses spread quickly in the crowded cities. Hundreds of people could die in a short time.

Crime became worse as the cities grew. Slums were very crowded. Most of the people were very poor. Other parts of the cities were much better. There, people earned more money. They had larger homes. Their homes were filled with nice things. Some people were very rich. Their homes were like palaces. But for some people living in the slums, stealing became a way of life. There were even gangs in those days. Children sometimes set up their own gangs, too.

54.4 What was it like to work in a factory in the late 1880s?

People were glad to have factory jobs. However, factories had their problems, too. Lights were poor. There was little running water. There were few windows to let in fresh air. Workers were crowded together. They often worked beside powerful machines. The workers were often hurt. The crowding made fire a problem. No plans were made for fires. Many people could die in one factory fire. One New York City factory caught fire in 1911. One hundred forty-five women died in the fire.

▲ The photograph above shows an example of a growing city. The trolley shares the street with a horse-drawn produce wagon and an open automobile.

▼ The photograph below shows New York City's Sixth Avenue elevated railway.

Men, women, and children worked in factories. Families were very poor. Everyone had to work. Many families still did not have enough money to live on. Children of all ages went to work. They did not go to school. They did not have time to play or have fun. Factories liked child workers. Children could be paid less money than their mothers and fathers. Besides, their small fingers could reach tight places. Many children picked over rags. They put the rags into different groups. The rags were then made into things like paper. Dust filled the air while the children worked. These children often got sick from breathing this dust. Some children worked in mines. All the miners breathed dust, too. Many of them died from breathing this dust.

54.5 How did cities handle their problems?

Cities faced giant problems. They grew too quickly. The problems grew just as fast. Cities could not keep up. Their governments did try. Special offices were set up. They had different jobs. Some worked to clean up the cities. They wanted to cut down on sicknesses that were spreading. Others tried to set up better housing for the poor. More police were put to work. As problems kept growing, cities could not usually keep up.

▲ The photograph above shows city officials inspecting a subway car.

Getting from one place to another was another problem in most cities. Many people walked. By the Civil War, buses were pulled by horses. Cities spread out. People needed new ways to get to work and to stores. Buses helped. Trains also became more important. New York City built a new kind of train in 1870. Its tracks were really bridges. These bridges went over streets and beside buildings. They were called "**elevated** trains." These trains were built in many other cities, too. Richmond, Virginia began using a new kind of train in 1887. It did not run on steam, but on electricity. It helped keep the city clean. Soon, most city trains were run by electricity. Steam engines were still better for going between cities, though. In 1897, Boston took its city trains one step further. They ran under the ground. Boston had the first **subway** in the United States.

☆☆☆

Biography

▲ Jane Addams

Jane Addams spent her life helping the poor. Her family had not been poor. She had even gone to college. She visited Europe in the 1880s. Europe's poor were helped by settlement houses. Jane Addams took the idea to Chicago. She opened Hull House in 1889.

Workers at Hull House did many things. They ran a school for children. They even set up rooms for day care. They held special classes. People learned about cooking, music, and art. Lists of job openings were posted at Hull House. Jane Addams kept everything running. She spent all her own money. She then had to spend much of her time raising more money. News about Hull House spread. Soon, other cities had their own settlement houses, too.

Jane Addams hated the idea of war. She joined groups that worked for peace. One group was the International League for Peace and Freedom. It had many offices around the world. Jane Addams became its President. She worked very hard for peace. She was given the Nobel Peace Prize in 1931.

 CHAPTER REVIEW

Critical Thinking

Write your answers on a sheet of paper or discuss in class.

Drawing Conclusions 1. Why did people move to cities even after they knew that factory owners were now paying less?

Analyzing Cause and Effect 2. What caused all the changes in cities? How did cities change as they grew?

Cooperative Learning

LEARNING
STYLE
Verbal

3. Work with a partner or group. Find out more about slums. Hold a talk about slums. What were they like? Who lived in them? Where did all the people come from? What problems did they cause?

Write About It

Writing
Portfolio

4. Many people and groups worked to help the poor. Find out about people like Jane Addams and Lillian D. Wald. Lillian Wald built Henry Street Settlement in New York. You might find out about groups like the Salvation Army, the YMCA, and the YWCA. Write a short report. Read your report to the class.

Chapter 55

Honesty and Change

Year	Result of this Election
1868	Republican Ulysses S. Grant elected President.
1872	Ulysses S. Grant reelected President.
1876	Democrat Samuel J. Tilden won the Popular Election for President. The Electoral College tied. The House of Representatives chose Republican Rutherford B. Hayes as President. Democrats agreed in exchange for all U.S. troops being pulled out of the South. This ended Reconstruction.
1880	Hayes did not want a second term as President. Republican James A. Garfield won the office. He was shot and killed in the summer of 1881. Vice President Chester A. Arthur became President.
1884	Republicans dumped Arthur because of his ideas about reform. They picked James G. Blaine. He lost because of his past as a political boss. Some Republicans wanted reform. They joined with the Democrats. Grover Cleveland became President. He was the first Democrat to be President since James Buchanan left office in 1861.
1888	Cleveland took stands on risky issues. Even with weak support, he won the Popular Election. However, the Electoral College chose the Republican, Benjamin Harrison. He was the grandson of President William Henry Harrison.
1892	Harrison let lobbyists and other special interests have too much power. Cleveland ran against Harrison and won the race for President.

Read about the problems in government after the Civil War. How did some people break the law? Why?

Key *Vocabulary*

lobbyist (LAHB ee uhst) a person whose only job is trying to influence government into passing laws that are good for the people that he or she works for

favor (FAY vuhr) an act or gift done in exchange for another act or gift

politician (pahl uh TISH uhn) a person who tries to affect or control government decisions

Reteaching Vocabulary

scandal (SKAN duhl) disgrace caused by doing something that offends people or is against the law

political (puh LIT i kuhl) trying to affect or control government decisions

TABLE ANALYSIS

★ **Ask**　　　*What events are shown in this table?*

★ **Acquire**　*Who won each race?*

★ **Organize**　*Make a chart from these facts: which Presidents served only one term? which served two terms? which lost reelection? which became President because of death?*

★ **Answer**　*How did special deals affect the elections?*

Decoding Tip:　Note the different sounds for o in the vocabulary words.

ay	cake	ah	fall, cot	air	air
ee	tree	i	sit	oh	cold
or	cord	oy	toy	uh	above, hundred
a	ask	ar	hard	oo	book
e	yet	eye	nice	uhr	liar, fir, further, color
ow	cow	ooh	boot, true	yoo	you, few, cube

55.1 How did business and government feel about each other?

Most people had strong beliefs about government and business. They felt that government should leave business alone. It should work in its own way. Government acts would just hurt business. Workers and the country would be hurt, too.

In fact, business often wanted government help. Some business leaders wanted Congress to pass special acts. These would help them make more money. Some of these acts gave free land to train companies. This helped spread trains across the country. However, some companies took much more land than they needed. They became rich just by selling this land.

Companies sent workers to talk with Congress. They pushed Congress to pass special acts. They often talked in the lobbies of Congress. These workers became known as **"lobbyists."** Lobbyists still work with Congress today. It has often been felt that they cause problems. Some people want lobbyists stopped. They feel that Congress spends too much time on lobbyists' special interests.

55.2 What problem did lobbyists cause?

Sometimes lobbyists broke the law. They took their work too far. They got Congress to give too much to their companies. Some members of Congress took money for these **favors**. Sometimes they were given shares in the companies. They earned the money by passing certain acts. These people were working for their own interests. They were not working for the good of the country. Crédit Mobilier was a building company. It did building for the government. It was owned by the Union Pacific Railroad. Its lobbyists gave away money and shares to certain people in all parts of government. Even Grant's Vice President, Schuyler Colfax, took part.

55.3 How did these problems affect President Grant?

Other money **scandals** happened, too. Many of the people worked for President Grant. He had been a great war leader. But he was not good at picking people. He had to pick people for different jobs. These were special jobs in the President's branch of government. Many ended up breaking the law. His own secretary and some people in his Cabinet took part. Some took millions of dollars in tax money. This news spread across the country. Grant was very hurt by what had happened. He would not run for President a third time. He left the White House in 1877.

55.4 What problems happened with state and city governments?

Business people bought favors from states and cities, too. Some train companies paid for special laws. **Political** machines were sometimes set up. A machine was a group of **politicians**. They would win different offices. Then they would take over the city or state. Machine leaders were called "bosses." Boss Tweed ran the machine in New York City. Millions of dollars were stolen or wasted. Often, machines helped immigrants get jobs. They would help them find homes. The people would then help the machines. They would vote for people in the machine. Sometimes, people would break the law by voting more than once. They would vote in different places. Machines became very strong. Cities and states lost a lot of money. Needed work was not done. Cities became dirty and run down.

55.5 What did the Mugwumps want?

Some people hated what was happening. They wanted to fight crime in government. They wanted changes in the way things were run. One group was the Mugwumps. This is a

Native American word that means "big chief." These people were Republicans. They wanted new laws. They wanted to set up a new way to fill jobs. Jobs would not be handed out for favors. People would take tests. A special board would pick workers from among those who passed.

Jobs for favors brought about the killing of a President. James A. Garfield became President in 1881. He was shot by Charles J. Guiteau on July 2. Guiteau had wanted a government job. President Garfield picked someone else. Garfield was making a trip outside Washington, D.C. Guiteau waited at the train station. He shot the President twice. Doctors took out one bullet. They could not find the second one. President Garfield died on September 19.

▲ President James A. Garfield
1831-1881

Vice President Chester A. Arthur became President. He pushed the Pendleton Act of 1883. It set up the Mugwumps' testing plan. The Civil Service Commission was set up. The President still filled some jobs. But most were handed out by the Civil Service Commission. This plan cut down on handing out jobs for favors. The Civil Service Commission still handles government jobs today.

55.6 Why did President Arthur have only one term?

President Arthur made some Republicans angry. They belonged to machines. Arthur had helped set up the Civil Service Commission. He vetoed acts that these people liked. They led the Republicans against Arthur. The party picked James G. Blaine to run for President. He was part of a machine, too. The Mugwumps worked with the Democrats. The Democrats picked Grover Cleveland. He was the governor of New York. He had fought Boss Tweed's machine in New York City. The race for President was close, but Cleveland won. The people showed they wanted honest government.

▲ This political cartoon shows one of Boss Tweed's friends with money in place of brains. Tweed's New York political machine often paid for votes. This cartoon was done in 1871 by Thomas Nast.

☆☆☆

Biography

▲ Ulysses S. Grant

President Grant had no job after leaving the White House. He took his family to Europe and on other trips. He had many friends in his home of Galena, Illinois. They gave him a house there. Grant had saved about $100.000. He used the money to start a bank in New York City. His partner stole the money. The bank closed in 1884. General Grant was left with no money. He was sick and knew that he would soon die. He wrote a book. It was about his life, the Civil War, and his years as President. Mark Twain was the greatest American writer of the time. He put out the book soon after President Grant died in 1885. The book made $500,000. This money cared for the President's family. Grant was buried in New York City.

CHAPTER REVIEW

Critical Thinking

Write your answers on a sheet of paper, or discuss in class.

Identifying Main Idea ➡ 1. How did lobbyists go against people's beliefs about government?

Analyzing Cause and Effect 2. Today, many people still run for office. By law, they must tell about their business dealings. What caused this kind of law?

Cooperative Learning

LEARNING STYLE *Visual Tactile*

3. Work with a partner or group. Look over the chapter. Find things that happened. Did they cause something else to happen? What effect did these things then have? Use a piece of poster board. Make a chart about these happenings. Tell which things are causes. Tell which things are effects.

Write About It

Writing Portfolio

4. Imagine you live in a city of the 1880s. It is run by a machine. Write a letter to your newspaper. Tell about the machine. What does it do? Why is it bad? What should be done? Read your letter aloud to the class.

Chapter 56

Labor

Number of Strikes in the U.S.A.

1881	1883	1885	1887	1889	1891	1893	1895	1897	1899
477 Strikes	506 Strikes	695 Strikes	1,503 Strikes	1,111 Strikes	1,786 Strikes	1,375 Strikes	1,255 Strikes	1,110 Strikes	1,838 Strikes

Note: Business went bad in the United States at three different times during these years. They were the years 1884-1886, 1893-1894, 1895-1897.

Key *Vocabulary*

union (YOOHN yuhn)
a group of workers that is set up to work for the good of the members

skill (skil) something that a person has learned to do well

labor (LAY buhr)
workers

strike (streyek)
the act of walking off a job until certain terms are met

Reteaching Vocabulary

boycott (BOI kaht)
the act of refusing any dealings with a person or group until certain terms are met

---

GRAPH ANALYSIS

★ **Ask**   What events are shown in this graph?

★ **Acquire**   What does the note tell you?

★ **Organize** There were three periods of hard times in the 1880s and 1890s. List the number of strikes for each of these times.

★ **Answer**   Does the number of strikes seem to go up or down during a period of hard times? Explain why the number of strikes might go up or down during a period of hard times.

Decoding Tip: Note that the *k* in **skill** and **strike** and the *c* in **boycott** make the sound /k/.

ay	cake	ah	fall, cot	air	air
ee	tree	i	sit	oh	cold
or	cord	oy	toy	uh	above, hundred
a	ask	ar	hard	oo	book
e	yet	eye	nice	uhr	liar, fir, further, color
ow	cow	ooh	boot, true	yoo	you, few, cube

56.1 What was it like for workers after the Civil War?

Most factory workers were not well paid. Companies paid $8 to $10 per week. Few people could live on this pay. Everyone in a family had to work. Also, women earned less than men. African Americans worked for less than women. Children earned less than anyone. Companies often cut pay. Yet, people worked long hours, too. Most spent 10-12 hours on the job each day. They worked six days a week. For most workers, Sunday was their only day off.

Often, factories were not nice places in which to work. There was little light. Most buildings had few windows. Getting fresh air was always a problem. All kinds of dust filled the air. People breathed the dust. It made them sick. Miners had to breathe all kinds of dust. Sometimes it slowly killed them. Many people were hurt in accidents. They worked with or near dangerous machines. Few steps were taken to keep workers safe. Factory fires were always a problem. Mines often fell in. The number of accidents grew all through the late 1880s.

Getting hurt on the job was just one problem. It could put people out of work. No one helped pay any doctor bills. Sometimes a person would be badly hurt. The person could not work. But the job was not kept open. Someone else was brought in to take the job. Workers had little say about what went on. They were usually just glad to have jobs.

56.2 What is a labor union?

Some workers joined special groups. They would work together. Then, things might be changed. These groups are called **unions**. Most early unions were not open to all workers. Each was open to people in one line of work. The people had to have certain **skills**. They might work in printing, plumbing, or with electricity. Each union helped train these workers.

They kept their numbers low. Companies paid them higher wages. They were glad to have such skilled workers.

Other workers saw the good that unions could do. They set up their own unions. However, most workers did not have special skills. It did not take much training to learn most jobs. Unions could not keep these numbers low. Companies could always find people willing to take these jobs. Unions did not work very well for workers without skills.

56.3 How did unions try to make changes?

Unions sometimes joined together. They turned into very large groups. They often covered the whole country. These large groups were stronger than the small unions. They had better luck in working for change. One of the first was the National **Labor** Union. It pushed for a working day of eight hours. It wanted higher pay. It wanted men, women, and African Americans to earn the same pay. Perhaps it had too many goals. It won very few of them.

The first Unions often did little good. They tried to talk with company owners. They asked for changes. But early unions had problems setting up these meetings. Owners saw no need. Unhappy workers could just quit their jobs. The owners would then find new workers. Some unions called for **boycotts**. They asked people to stop buying a company's goods. If the owners agreed to talks, the boycott would end. Walking off the job could bring a problem into the open. However, most early unions did not like these **strikes**. The workers could earn no money. Owners could just find new workers. Owners kept lists of people in unions. They shared these lists. These people would have trouble finding jobs.

56.4 What happened to early unions?

Hard times hit the country in 1873. Many farmers lost their land. People in the South had the hardest time. African

Americans were hurt the most. They had always been among the poorest people. Hard times just made things worse. Many people moved from farms to cities. Most were in the North. People wanted factory jobs. However, factories were cutting back, too. They laid off some workers. They cut the pay of those who stayed. People were hungry for jobs. They would work for low pay. Unions could do very little to help. Many unions closed. The National Labor Union closed in 1873.

The Knights of Labor wanted many kinds of changes. It had opened in 1869. It wanted to help workers. However, it also pushed for large changes in the country. It wanted Congress to make very large changes. For example, it did not like the way trains were run. The Knights wanted the government to run all trains. Most Americans did not believe in such changes. They felt that most things about the country were sound. Only a few changes were needed. Still, the Knights did grow. It became very large after hard times hit again in 1884. This union did not believe in strikes. Without strikes, it reached few of its goals. Some of its member unions did go on strike. They even won a few of these strikes. But the changes did not last very long. The Knights almost disappeared after 1887.

One successful union was the AF of L. This stands for "American Federation of Labor." Its president was Samuel Gompers. It was happy with the country as it was. It only wanted changes for workers. Gompers believed strikes could bring change. And some of its strikes did reach the AF of L's goals. Gompers had problems, though. His union was for skilled workers. Other workers could not join. The AF of L spoke for a small part of the country's workers. It could not make lasting changes in all work places.

▲ Samuel Gompers

56.5   How did the Haymarket Riot hurt unions?

The AF of L called for a great strike on May 1, 1886. It wanted the strike to cross the country. All people were asked

to walk off their jobs. They would return to work, though. The AF of L wanted companies to shorten the work day to eight hours. Many workers did go out on strike. Strikes fired up all over the country.

A strike was already happening in Chicago on May 1. Workers wanted changes at the McCormick Harvester Company. They met in Chicago's Haymarket Square. The police tried to stop the meeting. A bomb went off. No one knows who threw it. It killed seven police officers and 67 other people. The police then opened fire. They killed four more people. Hundreds were hurt in the fight.

News of the Haymarket Riot spread across the country. Most Americans were shocked. They blamed unions for the trouble. Newspapers came out against unions, too. All unions lost members. Some closed down. The AF of L did go on. People remembered the Haymarket Riot for years. Now troops were often sent in to stop strikes. Unions lost ground for years.

▲ The illustration above shows a scene from the Haymarket Riot on May 4, 1886.

56.6 What did unions achieve?

Unions did reach some of their goals. Congress passed on a work day of eight hours. It paid for its own building projects. Beginning in 1868, all these jobs lasted for eight hours a day. All government workers had eight-hour days after 1892. States passed laws for the work place, too. They made companies take steps to keep workers safe. However, few of these laws were carried out.

Biography

Many women took part in unions. Leonora Barry O'Reilly belonged to the Knights of Labor. She had worked as a teacher in New York. She gave up her job when she married. She felt mothers should stay at home. She also felt that mothers should work when the family needed money. Her husband died in 1881. Mrs. Barry had to go to work. She took a job in a factory. The job paid only 65 cents a week. None of the other women would act. They had not been raised to speak out. Barry wanted workers to be treated fairly. She joined the Knights of Labor. She became president of her city's union. Soon, she was working for the national union. Few women of the late 1800s took part in unions. This made Barry unhappy. She kept up her work for them. Later, she married again. Now she was known as Leonora Barry O'Reilly. She held to what she believed, though. She quit her work for the Knights. She stayed at home with her family.

★★★ CHAPTER REVIEW

Critical Thinking

Write your answers on a sheet of paper or discuss in class.

Comparing and Contrasting

1. How strong were unions and company owners?

Drawing Conclusions

2. Do you think there was a need for unions in the late 1800s? Why or why not?

Cooperative Learning

LEARNING STYLE
Visual Tactile

3. Work with a partner or group. Make a large picture. Draw important people from this chapter. Show changes in American life before 1900. See if others can name the people and events.

Write About It

Writing Portfolio

4. Look through your city's newspaper. Are there stories about unions? What is happening in these unions? What kinds of things do they want? Write a report about these unions. Read it aloud.

Chapter 57

Populism

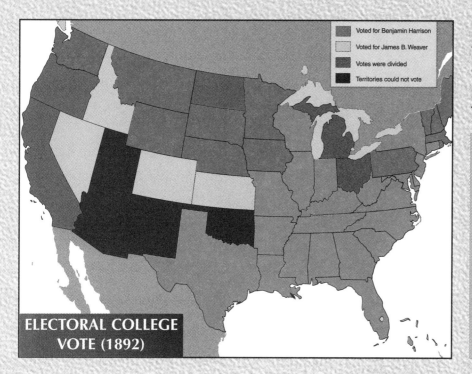

Voted for Benjamin Harrison
Voted for James B. Weaver
Votes were divided
Territories could not vote

ELECTORAL COLLEGE VOTE (1892)

Read about the part farmers took in government. What problems did farmers face? Why?

Key *Vocabulary*

market (MAR kuht)
all the buying and selling that goes on in one certain country or area

regulate (REG yuh layt)
to use laws to control some kind of action or actions

Reteaching Vocabulary

alliance (uh LEYE uhns)
two or more people or groups working for a common goal

MAP ANALYSIS

★ **Ask**   What does this map show?

★ **Acquire**   What does each color tell you?

★ **Organize** Make a list of the three candidates. List the areas in which each person won. Who won in the Southeast? in the Northeast? the Mississippi River states? the Plains states? the Mountain states? the Pacific Coast states?

★ **Answer**   People in the territories could not vote for the President. Who do you think they would have voted for?

Decoding Tip: Note the silent *e* in **regulate** and **alliance**.

ay	cake	ah	fall, cot	air	air
ee	tree	i	sit	oh	cold
or	cord	oy	toy	uh	above, hundred
a	ask	ar	hard	oo	book
e	yet	eye	nice	uhr	liar, fir, further, color
ow	cow	ooh	boot, true	yoo	you, few, cube

57.1 Why did some Americans want to break up monopolies and trusts?

Companies became very strong. Their leaders even set the course of the country. Most Americans felt this was a good plan. The country was becoming very rich. Few other countries were as rich as the United States. Some companies became giants. They took over whole lines of work. Their leaders set up monopolies and trusts.

However, some people came to fear giant companies. They felt these companies were hurting the country. Many small companies had to close. They could not keep up. Giant companies could keep prices high. Farmers had a very hard time in this kind of **market**. Their food sold for less and less. They had to pay a lot of money for the goods they needed. Some Americans felt that the giants had too much power. Giants also had a strong voice in government. Everyday people seemed to have no say. Some people felt this was unfair. Wasn't the U.S. set up to be a government of its people?

57.2 Why did regulation of companies fail?

A few states did try to **regulate** companies. Railroad companies were a chief target. They were very rich. They charged anything they wanted. They gave other giant companies special favors. Small companies and farmers paid much more. Some states set up new laws. They set the prices that railroads could charge.

At first, the Supreme Court agreed. Then new people took seats on the Court. The states' laws were thrown out. The Supreme Court said that the states did not have such rights. Only Congress could pass such acts. And Congress showed no interest in doing so. Some acts did stay on the books. But they were not carried out very often. Most Americans still held to one chief idea. Government should stay out of people's lives. This meant leaving companies alone too.

57.3 Why was the Populist Party formed?

Farmers had tough times in the late 1800s. Farming had changed. Food sold for less money. To make more money, farmers had to grow more food. New machines helped. They cost a lot of money, though. Most farmers had to borrow money to keep going. They did grow more food. But Americans could not use all this food. Food prices dropped again. Farmers were making less money. They could not pay back what they had borrowed.

Unions were started by farmers. One was the Grange. It worked for new laws. Some farm states passed these laws. Some laws set what railroads could charge farmers. Others kept prices down for storing food that farmers could not sell. The Grange even started its own companies. They sold goods to farmers. Farmers were able to save money. However, these companies closed in the 1870s. The Grange lost ground, too.

Another farmers' group was known as the Southern **Alliance**. It began in Texas. Soon, it spread through the South. African Americans started the National Colored Farmers' Alliance. These two groups worked together. People in the North started a group, too. It was the Northern Alliance. Over 2,000,000 people joined these groups in the 1880s.

The Alliances worked. They helped get laws passed. They picked people to run for office. They won many of these races. Soon, labor unions joined in the work. Together these groups started their own party. They became the Populist Party. It ran against the Democrats and the Republicans.

57.4 What did the Populists want?

Populists tried to put someone in the White House. They held a meeting in Omaha, Nebraska, in 1892. James B. Weaver was picked for the race. The party wanted government to follow a new idea. It should be involved with the country and its companies. Government should work so that people

Presidential Race of 1892

Candidate	Party	Popular Vote	Electoral College Vote
Grover Cleveland	Democrat	5,555,000	277
Benjamin Harrison	Republican	5,182,000	145
James Weaver	Populist	1,029,000	22

had better lives. Populists asked for other things, too. People had usually voted in front of each other. Sometimes they felt pushed to vote in certain ways. Populists wanted all people to vote in secret. Then they could vote as they pleased. Populists agreed with the income tax. All people paid taxes on what they earned. Populists wanted a change. Some people earned a lot of money. Populists thought they should pay higher taxes. Populists wanted government to put more coins and paper money in circulation. This would probably push prices up. But earnings might go up, too.

Weaver did not become President. He did get 22 votes in the Electoral College. Usually Democrats and Republicans got all these votes. They had not lost one since 1865. Now, Populists were cutting into their ground. Populists took some seats in Congress. They were in state governments, too. Change was blowing across the United States.

▲ President Grover Cleveland

☆☆☆

Biography

Mark Twain was probably America's best writer. His books are all about America. He talked about its problems. However, he poked fun at most things. He wanted people to laugh. This would help them understand their problems. *Huckleberry Finn* was about problems with race. Jim was an enslaved African. He was running away from his owners. Huck Finn helped him. Some of their adventures were very funny. Jim's terrible problems were very clear, though.

In the late 1800s, the country was torn between different ideas. Twain could not make up his mind either. It was a time of change. People wanted changes in government. How much change was needed? What kinds of things should it do? The answer was hard to find. Twain moved back and forth from one idea to another. His books showed this problem. Americans could not agree either.

Times were hard from the 1870s to the 1890s. Farmers lost their land. Many people went broke. Twain did too. He had begun several companies. One put out President Ulysses S. Grant's book. It told the story of his life. Twain lost his companies. To make money, he took a trip around the world. He gave shows in almost every country. He talked about his books. He also talked about the United States. Twain earned his fortune back. He paid off everything he owed. The country came back from the hard times, too.

▲ Mark Twain

★★☆ CHAPTER REVIEW

Critical Thinking

Write your answers on a sheet of paper, or discuss in class.

Analyzing Cause and Effect

1. How did companies and farmers affect each other?

Making Predictions

2. What things do you think might happen in the United States if the Populists did take over?

Cooperative Learning

LEARNING STYLE *Verbal*

3. Work with a partner or group. Read the names in this chapter. Look in the back of the book. Find out how to say these names. Practice saying these names aloud.

Write About It

Writing Portfolio

4. Think about the Populists. Who were they? What kinds of people were part of this group? What did they want? How did they work? Imagine that you are a Populist. You are running for office. Make a poster for the race. Be sure to tell about your ideas.

Chapter 58

Reform

Read about the push for changes in government. What problems brought these ideas about? Why?

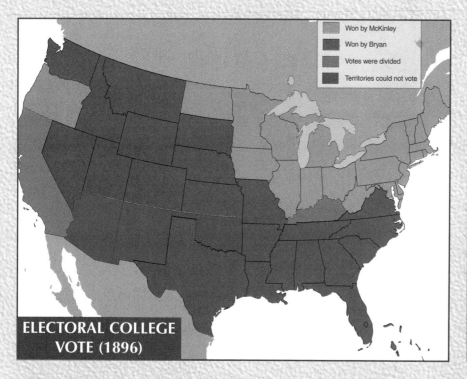

Won by McKinley
Won by Bryan
Votes were divided
Territories could not vote

ELECTORAL COLLEGE VOTE (1896)

Key *Vocabulary*

suffrage (SUHF rij) the right to vote

Reteaching Vocabulary

trust (truhst) a group of corporations that have joined together so that they do not compete with one another

monopoly (muh NAHP uh lee) total control of all the parts of a certain kind of business, such as all parts of the oil business

militia (muh LISH uh) a state or local army made up of regular citizens

reform (ri FORM) the act of making changes to clean up or improve something

---

MAP ANALYSIS

★ **Ask**   What does this map show?

★ **Acquire**   What does each color tell you?

★ **Organize**   Write the names of the candidates. List the areas in which each person won. Who won in the Southeast? in the Northeast? the Mississippi River states? the Plains states? the Mountain states? the Pacific Coast states?

★ **Answer**   One candidate won the most states. Why do you think the other candidate became President?

Decoding Tip: Note that the letters *ti* make the sound /sh/ in **militia**.

ay	cake	ah	fall, cot	air	air
ee	tree	i	sit	oh	cold
or	cord	oy	toy	uh	above, hundred
a	ask	ar	hard	oo	book
e	yet	eye	nice	uhr	liar, fir, further, color
ow	cow	ooh	boot, true	yoo	you, few, cube

For the People, By the People

58.1 What problems was America facing in the 1890s?

Life in the United States could be very good for some people. Factories had made the country rich. There were many opportunities for Americans. There were three main groups of people. The smallest group was the rich. They owned the large companies. They had a very strong voice in government. Another group was the poor. Most workers, some farmers, and many other Americans belonged to this group. The largest group was not poor. It was not rich either. It was between the other two groups. These people were known as the "middle class."

▲ The picture above shows an example of the wealth in the United States during the late 1800s. This house was owned by Commodore Vanderbilt.

By the 1890s, America's rich were very rich. The poor were very poor. There was a giant difference in the way they lived. Caught between them was the middle class. They feared the power of **trusts** and **monopolies**. They felt badly for the poor. They felt that something should be done to help the poor. However, they hated the fighting that seemed to come with union work. Problems between the rich and the poor were growing.

Fighting sometimes broke out between companies and their union workers. Workers went out on strike. Companies would bring in new workers. Fights broke out when the new workers arrived. States sent **militias** to end strikes. Sometimes, the President would step in. The U.S. Army would be sent to end the strikes. The middle class hated this fighting. They worried that the country could be destroyed.

▲ The picture above shows the poverty suffered by Americans in the late 1800s as residents stand in front of their dilapidated frame house in Kansas City.

58.2 What seemed to be the answer to these problems?

Old ideas about the country did not seem to be working. Many people still believed that change was not needed. Things were as they should be. There had always been a gap between the rich and poor. However, the gap was very big by the 1890s. Some people felt it was dangerous for the country. These people wanted **reform**, or change. Government should work to make people's lives better. Then, the middle class and the rich would have nothing to fear. Many people believed in this idea. It caused farmers to set up the Populist Party.

58.3 What reforms did women and churches want?

Women in America had never had many rights. Single women could own property. But this changed when they married. The property then belonged to their husbands. Now, schools and colleges were opening for women. By the 1890s, many women had finished school. They wanted rights, too. After all, they were Americans. The **suffrage** movement grew stronger. Women worked to have all the rights held by men.

Many churches wanted changes, too. This was a new idea. Many church leaders had followed older ideas. They believed

▼ The picture below shows two officials inspecting a cluttered basement living room in 1900.

that people were rich because they were good. Others were poor because they were bad. By the 1890s, many church leaders turned against this idea. The rich and the poor could be good people. There were bad ones in each group, too. Church leaders now wanted to reach all parts of society. They felt this would make all people's lives better.

58.4   Who were the muckrakers?

Some writers told about America's problems. They did not want to shame the country. They wanted reform. If no one knew about the problems, they would just go on. Once people were shown what was wrong, answers could be found. The writers became known as "muckrakers." They raked up the bad things for people to see.

Different people wrote about different problems. Their stories were in papers and in books. Ida M. Tarbell did a book about John D. Rockefeller. She told about the ways in which his oil company worked. It did not always work fairly. Sometimes it even broke the law. Lincoln Steffens wrote about political machines that ran cities. People in these groups ran for office. They took over many cities. Then they stole and wasted the cities' money. The Tammany Hall machine ran New York City. It stole over $100 million. Other stories told about meat companies and train companies. Upton Sinclair wrote *The Jungle*. It told about Chicago's meat companies. Their meat often went bad. They would sell it anyway. Americans were alarmed by these stories. The calls for reform grew.

58.5   How did money affect the 1896 race for the White House?

Money had become an American problem. Congress set up the country's money. The U.S. Mint made the coins and paper money. Paper money had come out during the Civil War. There was too much money on hand. Prices kept going up. People's pay did, too. Congress began pulling back some of the paper money. People took the money to banks. They got gold and silver coins in return. Congress set the price of gold and silver. One ounce of gold could be bought for 16 ounces of silver. Companies liked this idea. Prices stayed steady. They could pay workers less money. Then, many silver mines opened in

1896 Presidential Race

Candidate	Party	Popular Vote	Electoral College Vote
William McKinley	Republican	7,035,638	271
William Jennings Bryan	Democrat/Populist	6,467,946	176

the West. The price of silver dropped. The government lost money buying silver at the old price. Congress stopped the use of silver for coins. Now, there was too little money. Prices and pay dropped.

Money became the chief issue in the race to be President. Hard times had hit the country in 1893 and 1894. Populists wanted more silver coins. Prices would go up. However, most people could then earn more money. Many Democrats and Republicans liked the idea, too. However, the Republicans picked William McKinley for the race. He was against the idea. The Democrats picked William Jennings Bryan. He spoke for more silver coins. He wanted people to make more money. The Populists backed him, too. However, unions would not back him. This hurt Bryan and helped McKinley. McKinley said that the silver idea was bad. Higher prices could only hurt the country. Then, good times returned during the race. This helped McKinley, too. He became President.

58.6 Why did the Populist Party end?

Populists both won and lost in 1896. They did not take the White House. They won some state offices. However, the Republicans and Democrats had taken on some of their ideas. There was no longer a great need for the party. It ended. But its ideas went on. The rights of Americans had always been important. Now, the kind of lives they would lead was government business, too.

☆☆☆

                    For the People, By the People

Biography

Elizabeth Cochrane Seaman believed in women's rights. She lived in Pittsburgh, Pennsylvania. She sent a letter to the city's paper. It was about women's rights. She was a very good writer. She got a job on the paper. She was only 18 years old. Later, she took the name Nellie Bly. She went to work in New York City. Her stories were in *The World*.

Nellie Bly turned her adventures into stories. She pretended to be different people. Once she said she was a thief. She went to jail. Her story was about the way women were treated by the police. Sometimes, husbands wanted their wives out of the way. It was simple to do. They signed special papers. They stated that the wives had lost their minds. The wives were then locked away. Nellie Bly had someone sign a paper for her.

She went into the hospital. She found out the real story. People became angry after reading it in *The World*. New laws were passed. After that, only a court and a doctor could decide such things.

A trip around the world was Nellie Bly's biggest story. Jules Verne had put out the book *Around the World in Eighty Days*. Nellie Bly wanted to beat this time. *The World* paid for her trip. She went by train and ship. She used carts and horses. She sent stories back about her trip. It took 72 days, 6 hours, and 11 minutes.

▲ Elizabeth Cochrane Seaman, also known as Nellie Bly

CHAPTER REVIEW

Critical Thinking

Write your answers on a sheet of paper or discuss in class.

Analyzing Cause and Effect

1. Why might some Democrats and Republicans have taken over Populist ideas of reform?

Identifying Main Idea

2. Why did the Populists not need to pick someone for the 1896 race for President?

Cooperative Learning

LEARNING STYLE
Reading

3. Work with a partner or group. Get a copy of your city's paper. Look at its stories. Are any of them about problems that need answers? Do the stories suggest answers? Make a list of problems. List possible answers for each one. Read your list aloud. Hold a vote about which answer seems to be the best for each problem.

Write About It

Writing Portfolio

4. Look over this chapter. Make a list of things that happened. What made each thing happen? Each of these is called a "cause." Did one of them cause something else to happen? If so, it is called an "effect." Write "cause" or "effect" beside each thing on your list.

REVIEW

Quiz

Number a piece of paper from 1–10. Read each question below. Read the answers that follow each question. Choose the answer for each question. Write the letter of the answer you choose beside the correct number on your piece of paper.

1. **Before 1880, where did most immigrants to the United States come from?**
   a. Northern Europe
   b. Western Europe
   c. Southern Europe
   d. both a and b

2. **After 1880, where did most immigrants come from?**
   a. Northern Europe
   b. Southern Europe
   c. Eastern Europe
   d. both b and c

3. **What caused people to move to cities?**
   a. wars with Native Americans
   b. jobs in factories
   c. acts of Congress
   d. none of the above

4. **Which of the following was NOT a problem in cities of the late 1800s?**
   a. power outages
   b. slums
   c. crime
   d. sicknesses

5. **How did Congress work to affect the growth of business?**
   a. It set rules that companies had to follow.
   b. It passed laws setting the sizes of most companies.
   c. It let companies work and grow as they pleased.
   d. none of the above

6. **Which of the following caused some government officers to break the law?**
   a. lobbyists
   b. political machines
   c. government jobs handed out for favors
   d. all of the above

7. **Who worked to make changes in the work place?**
   a. unions
   b. owners
   c. government
   d. all of the above

8. **Why did most Americans feel that unions were bad for the country?**
   a. Unions ran companies out of business.
   b. Union strikes sometimes ended in fighting and riots.
   c. Union leaders were often sent to jail.
   d. all of the above

9. **How did farmers work to end problems caused by hard times?**
   a. by leading strikes against Congress
   b. by boycotting train companies
   c. by setting up special groups like the Populist Party
   d. none of the above

10. **Which of the following was NOT a goal of people who wanted reform?**
    a. voting rights for all citizens
    b. better lives for the poor
    c. breaking the power of trusts and monopolies
    d. all of the above

CLASSIFYING

Add numbers 11–15 to your paper. Read the ideas listed below. Is it something a Populist would like? Is so, write P on your paper. Is it something the owner of a company would like? If so, write O on your paper. Is it something a union member would like? If so, write U on your paper.

11. government ownership of train companies
12. no laws limiting business activities
13. strikes to make changes in companies
14. better prices for crops
15. lobbyists to get special favors from government

Look over the people who are described in these chapters. Choose one person who interests you. Find out more about this person. Write a short report about this person. Trade papers with a study partner. Check each other's work. Make a clean, neat copy. Put it in your portfolio. You may also wish to combine your report with those of your classmates. Put them in a book called "People Who Have Influenced America."

You may wish to work with a study partner. Make a set of flash cards. Think up questions about this chapter. Answer these questions, too. Use 3 x 5 index cards. Write one question on the front of each card. Write the answer on the back. Put the cards in a stack. Make sure all the questions are on the top sides of the cards. Place the stack of cards on a table. Take turns drawing the cards and asking the questions. Each correct answer earns five points. After all the cards have been used, total the scores.

COOPERATIVE PROJECT: PANEL DISCUSSION

Hold a panel discussion about the late 1800s. Divide into groups. Have each group take the roles of a company owner, a worker, a Populist, a union leader, a person in the suffrage movement, an African American, a Chinese immigrant, and a muckraker. Each group should choose a person to be on the panel. Help these people learn important ideas they should know. Have the panel members sit at the front of the room. Each person should describe himself or herself. Then, open the floor to questions. Members of each group can help their panel members answer these questions. After the discussion, talk about how well each group did its work.

Unit 7

POLITICS

1898
The U.S.A. gained lands in the Pacific and Caribbean after the Spanish-American War.

1914
Europe went to war after Austria's Archduke Franz Ferdinand and his wife were killed.

1917
The U.S. entered War I i

Commu over in and for Soviet

CE   1890   1900   1910

CULTURE

1903
In the first World Series, Boston of the American League defeated Pittsburgh of the National League.

1907
Lee De Forest, an American inventor, patented a vacuum tube that made radio signals stronger. This led to the growth of the electronics industry.

1908
Henry Ford introduced the Model T, the first low-priced car.

1909
Leo H. Baekeland, an American chemist, invented Bakelite, one of the first kinds of plastic.

1911
The first movie studio in Hollywood, California, was built by the Nestor Company.

1912
Jim Thorpe won gold medals in the pentathlon and decathlon at the Olympics in Stockholm, Sweden.

The Emergence of Modern America 1890-1930

"The history of every country begins in the heart of a man or a woman."

—**Willa Cather**, from her book O Pioneers! (1913)

P eople work to make their hopes and dreams come true. Americans moved to the West searching for better lives. American ideas changed greatly from 1890 to 1930. How did these changes reflect people's hope and dreams? Why?

1918
The U.S.A and the Allies won World War I in November.

1919
It was against the law to make, sell or use alcoholic drinks under the 18th Amendment.

1920
The U.S. Senate turned down the League of Nations and the Treaty of Versailles.

The 19th Amendment gave the vote to all adult women.

1921
Germany and the other Central Powers agreed to treaties with the U.S.A.

1929
The Great Depression hit the U.S.A.

1920

1930

1918-1919
27 million people around the world died of influenza.

1920
This Side of Paradise by F. Scott Fitzgerald was one of the first books to describe the new ideas of youth during the Jazz Age.

1925
Klan leader David C. Stephenson went to jail on murder charges. By 1930, the Klan had fallen from 4 million members to only 9,000.

1926
Langston Hughes' poetry, in *The Weary Blues*, made him the leader of African American writers who were part of the Harlem Renaissance.

1927
Jazz trumpet player Louis Armstrong recorded "Potato Head Blues."

1930
Vannevar Bush, an American engineer, built the first reliable computer.

Chapter 59

Out into the World

LANDS GAINED BY THE UNITED STATES (1867-1899)

Arctic Ocean

RUSSIA

ALASKA

ASIA

Bering Sea

Gulf of Alaska

CANADA

MIDWAY ISLAND
1898

USA

PHILIPPINE
ISLANDS
1898

JAPAN
1898

GUAM
1898

HAWAII

PUERTO RICO
1898

Gulf of
Mexico

MEXICO

Caribbean Sea

SOMAO
1899

SOUTH
AMERICA

Indian Ocean

South Pacific Ocean

AUSTRALIA

NEW ZEALAND

United States

Lands owned by the United States

Read about the push for lands outside North America. How did Americans achieve this goal? Why?

Key *Vocabulary*

base (bays) a place where the military sets up full-time operations

port (port) a body of water that is protected by land, such as a harbor or bay, where ships can dock safely and stand at rest

foreign (FOR uhn) not belonging to one particular country; coming from outside that country

Reteaching Vocabulary

population (pahp yuh LAY shun) all the people who live in a specific area

---

MAP ANALYSIS

★ **Ask**   What does the title tell you?

★ **Acquire**   Where are most of these places found?

★ **Organize**   Draw a line from the United States to Hawaii to Guam to the Philippines. What is the first place you would reach by sailing west from the Philippines?

★ **Answer**   Why do you think Americans would want to sail back and forth between the United States and Asia?

Decoding Tip: Note the sound of or in **port** and **foreign**.

ay	cake	ah	fall, cot	air	air
ee	tree	i	sit	oh	cold
or	cord	oy	toy	uh	above, hundred
a	ask	ar	hard	oo	book
e	yet	eye	nice	uhr	liar, fir, further, color
ow	cow	ooh	boot, true	yoo	you, few, cube

59.1 What idea did William Seward suggest for the United States?

William Seward followed a new idea. He was the Secretary of State. His job was handling government business with other countries. He worked for Presidents Abraham Lincoln and Andrew Johnson. He wanted the country to grow. Russia had taken over Alaska. It was known as "Russian America." By the middle 1860s, Russia needed money. It wanted to sell Alaska. Seward jumped at this chance. He took the idea to the United States Senate. It agreed.

The United States bought Alaska on March 30, 1867. It paid $7.2 million for Alaska's 586,412 square miles. Seward felt that Alaska could help the U.S. trade with the Pacific. He wanted the Navy to set up **bases** there. They could protect American ships in the Pacific Ocean. In 1869, Seward acted again. He helped the country take over Midway Island in the Pacific. Many Americans made fun of him. They felt that the United States was big enough.

59.2 Why did Seward's ideas become popular?

Asia was very important to the Americas. Europeans had reached the American continents in the 1400s and 1500s. They had been searching for China and Japan. The United States would not have been started without this search. Then Americans began trading with Asia. The China trade began in 1844. Commodore Matthew Perry took the Navy to Japan in 1853. He opened its **ports** to American trading ships.

Seward's ideas spread in the 1890s. The Census Bureau counted the **population** every 10 years. In 1890, it found that Americans lived in all 48 states and territories. It said that there was no more frontier. Many European countries had been taking lands around the world. They built colonies all around the world. They might even be dangerous to the United States. President Monroe had issued the Monroe

Doctrine in 1823. It said that Europe should stay out of the Western Hemisphere. This would keep the United States safe, too. The United States had helped drive the French out of Mexico after the Civil War had ended.

By the 1890s, most Americans wanted to do more than just keep the Western Hemisphere safe. They wanted America's shipping and trade throughout the world to grow. China had lost a war to Japan in 1895. Japan and some European countries took over different Chinese port cities. Each country ran the trade in that city. The United States feared that its China trade would be hurt. John Hay was President McKinley's Secretary of State. He sent letters to Japan, Great Britain, Russia, France, and Italy. He suggested that each country open its Chinese ports to other countries. Trade would be open to all. This plan was called the "Open Door Policy." It went into effect in 1900.

59.3 Why was the U.S. Navy involved with America's traders?

The U.S. Navy helped protect American trade and shipping. Bolivia and Peru went to war with Chile in 1881. It was called "The War of the Pacific" in the United States. The United States found that Chile's navy was more powerful than its own. How could the U.S. protect its ships all over the world? Congress decided to build up the navy. It began carrying out this plan in 1890. By 1900, the United States had one of the greatest navies in the world. The government decided it now needed Navy bases throughout the Pacific.

59.4 How did the United States gain lands in the Pacific?

President Ulysses S. Grant also helped the country to grow. He sent Americans to set up a base in Samoa in 1878. However, Great Britain and Germany wanted bases there, too.

The three countries came up with a special plan in 1889. They would set up bases to protect Samoa. The Samoans were supposed to govern themselves. The three countries often stepped in, though. By 1899, the three countries could not agree. They set up a new plan. Great Britain pulled out of Samoa. Germany and the United States each took over a part of Samoa. In return, Germany pulled out of some areas of Africa. Britain's power grew in Africa.

Hawaii was considered a good spot for bases, too. Americans had moved to these islands in the 1820s. Growing sugar became very important to Hawaii. Most of these farms were owned by Americans. The United States needed its sugar. At first, Congress did not charge taxes on **foreign** sugar. But it ended this favor in 1890. People could buy sugar grown in the U.S. for less money. Congress even paid farmers to grow sugar in the United States. Sales of Hawaiian sugar dropped. Many Hawaiian sugar farms went broke.

▲ The illustration above shows Queen Liliuokalani.

Americans in Hawaii wanted to join the United States. They wanted to take advantage of the new law, too. These Americans moved against the Hawaiian government. U.S. Marines helped them take over the islands in 1893. Queen Liliuokalani lost her throne. A new government was set up. It asked that the United States take over Hawaii. President Grover Cleveland would not agree. He worked to return Queen Liliuokalani to her throne. His plan failed. Cleveland finally had to recognize the new government. William McKinley became President in 1897. He led the United States in taking over Hawaii. It became an American territory in 1898.

59.5   How did the Cuban Revolution pull the United States into war with Spain?

Sugar also caused problems in Cuba. Spain had lost most of its holdings in the Americas. Revolutions had spread through these lands in the early 1800s. However, the people of Cuba had been loyal to Spain until 1868. That year the Cubans lost a revolution against Spain. Sugar farming was as important in Cuba as it was in Hawaii. Congress's laws against foreign sugar hurt Cuba. Many Cubans became very poor. The people started a new revolution against Spain in 1895.

Spain's actions during the revolution alarmed people all over the world. Spain treated the Cubans very badly. Stories of what was happening shocked Americans. Spain set up special camps. These were for prisoners of the war. Newspaper stories told about the poor state of the camps. Almost 200,000 of the prisoners died. Newspapers helped make feelings worse. Some of their stories made things seem worse than they were. Some of the stories were even false. Americans began calling on their government to help the Cubans. The Navy was sent to protect Americans in Cuba. The *U.S.S. Maine* sailed to Havana Harbor. It blew up on February 15, 1898. No one was sure what had really happened. However, most Americans called for war with Spain. Congress voted for war on April 25.

59.6 What happened during the Spanish-American War?

Spain could not stand up to the United States. Its navy was larger, but its ships were old and out of date. The U.S. Navy wanted to protect the West Coast from attack. It sent some of its ships to the Philippines. The Navy destroyed all the Spanish ships in Manila Bay. None of the American ships were lost. By August, the U.S. Army had taken over all the islands of the Philippines.

Cuba soon fell to the United States, too. The U.S. Army landed in late June. It marched across Cuba. It took El Caney and San Juan Hill. Then it moved toward Santiago. The U.S. Navy fought the Spanish Navy in Santiago Bay on July 3. Spain's navy fell in only four hours. Then the Army quickly took the city of Santiago. General Nelson A. Miles had led the Army in its wars against the Native Americans. He also led troops in the Spanish-American War. His troops had little trouble taking the island of Puerto Rico from Spain. Fighting went on for a few more weeks. Spain gave up the fight on August 12.

59.7 What did the United States gain from the war?

The United States now owned the Philippines, Guam, and Puerto Rico. Governments were set up in the Philippines and Puerto Rico. Americans became part of each government. The people of the islands had a voice, too. The people of the Philippines were not happy, though. They had fought to become independent. However, President McKinley decided that the U.S. should keep the islands. Navy bases would be set up in all three places.

Spain lost Cuba, too. The U.S. Army ran the government for a few years. The Cubans wrote their own Constitution in 1901. It followed the ideas in the U.S. Constitution. The U.S. Army would be pulled out of Cuba. First, Cuba had to agree to four special points:

- Cuba could not do anything to hurt its citizens' rights or liberties.

- The Cuban government could not spend more than it collected in taxes.

- Land would be given to the United States for Navy bases.

- Cuba would let the United States return if trouble broke out.

Cuba agreed to these points. The U.S. Army left in 1902. The Cubans tried democracy for themselves.

☆☆☆

Biography

▲ Theodore Roosevelt

One of the American heroes of the Spanish-American War was Theodore Roosevelt. Roosevelt's family had become rich from trading and shipping. They had worked in the China trade for many years. He had been President McKinley's Assistant Secretary of the Navy. Roosevelt quit this job when war broke out with Spain. He joined the army and became part of a group called the "Rough Riders." Roosevelt led their charge up San Juan Hill. This story was printed in all American newspapers. Roosevelt became very popular in the United States. President McKinley ran for a second term in 1900. He picked Roosevelt to run with him on the ticket. Roosevelt became Vice President in 1901.

Other Americans became popular during the Spanish-American War. President McKinley picked William Howard Taft as governor of the Philippines. Mr. and Mrs. Taft loved their time on these Pacific Islands. McKinley was shot by an anarchist on September 6, 1901. Anarchists fight against any kind of government. McKinley later died. Roosevelt became President. Roosevelt ran for office in 1904. He picked Taft to be his Vice President. Taft was elected President after Roosevelt finished his term. Mrs. Nellie Taft filled the White House with the things she had bought in the Philippines. She even changed the look of Washington, D.C. She had loved the cherry trees that grew in Japan. She brought some of these trees to Washington. They were planted on the banks of the Potomac River. They are a beautiful sight when they bloom each spring.

★★☆ CHAPTER REVIEW

Critical Thinking

Write your answers on a sheet of paper, or discuss in class.

Analyzing Cause and Effect

1. How did countries use their armies and navies to help them reach their goals?

Identifying Main Idea

2. Why did countries want to take over lands in the Americas and in Asia?

Cooperative Learning

LEARNING STYLE
Verbal
Tactile

3. Work with a partner or group. Copy the map at the start of this chapter. Place it on a table. Play a map game. Take turns tossing a paper clip on the map. Name the place where it lands. Tell one fact about this place. Did it have any effect on the United States? Each correct answer earns 10 points. Let everyone take three turns. Then total the scores.

Write About It

Writing Portfolio

4. Look over this chapter. Pick a person or place talked about in this chapter. Find out about this person or place. Write a paragraph about your topic. Read the paragraph to the class. Put all the class's paragraphs into a booklet. Hold a class discussion. Decide on a title for the booklet. Put the booklet in the class library.

Chapter 60

The Progressives

Read about the effect Theodore Roosevelt had on the country. How did he help Progressives to reach their goals? Why?

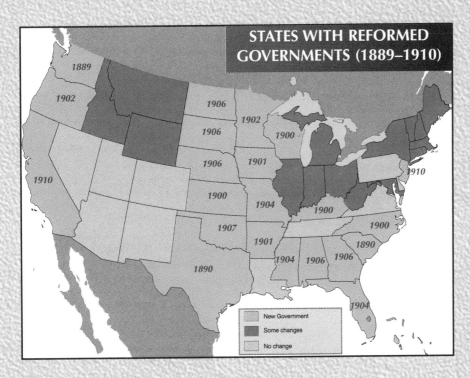

STATES WITH REFORMED GOVERNMENTS (1889–1910)

1889
1902
1906
1902
1906
1900
1906
1901
1910
1906
1910
1900
1904
1900
1907
1900
1901
1890
1904 1906 1906
1890
1904

New Government
Some changes
No change

Key *Vocabulary*

progress (pruh GRES) to grow or become better

free enterprise (free • ENT uhr preyez) the right to run a business in open competition with others and with only that government control needed to protect the public

environment (in VEYE ruhn muhnt) the weather, living things, and geography that make up a place and that depend upon each other

Reteaching Vocabulary

petition (puh TISH uhn) a paper written to ask that something be done

---

<table>
<tr><td rowspan="5">MAP
ANALYSIS</td></tr>
<tr><td>★ Ask</td><td>What does the title tell you?</td></tr>
<tr><td>★ Organize</td><td>Write these heads on a piece of paper: No Change, New Government, Some Changes in Government. Look at the map. Check the key. List the states under the correct heads.</td></tr>
<tr><td>★ Analyze</td><td>When were most of the new governments set up?</td></tr>
<tr><td>★ Answer</td><td>What kinds of problems do you think would make Americans want to replace their state governments?</td></tr>
</table>

Decoding Tip: Note that the *o* in **progress** and **environment** stands for the /uh/ sound.

ay	cake	ah	fall, cot	air	air
ee	tree	i	sit	oh	cold
or	cord	oy	toy	uh	above, hundred
a	ask	ar	hard	oo	book
e	yet	eye	nice	uhr	liar, fir, further, color
ow	cow	ooh	boot, true	yoo	you, few, cube

60.1 How were the Progressives like the Populists?

President Theodore Roosevelt stood for change. America was a rich country. Many people were poor, though. The gap between the rich and poor was very wide. Unions had pushed for change. Fighting often broke out. The U.S. Army was often sent to stop the fighting. Many people worried about the country. It might be pulled apart. Populists had called for change. They were mostly concerned with farmers and their problems. Their acts were peaceful. People saw that change did not have to be bad. Reform became a popular idea. People who called for reform came from many different groups. They were workers, farmers, company owners, rich people, poor people, Democrats, and Republicans. They became known as "Progressives." Roosevelt was a leading Progressive in the Republican Party. He wanted the country to change so that it could grow, or **progress**.

60.2 What changes did Progressives want in government?

Progressives called for an old idea. People should have power over the government. This was why the Revolutionary War had been fought, they said. Progressives wanted honesty in government. They felt that some people with money had taken too much control over government. Bribery had bought them special favors. Government must be reformed, said the Progressives. When it was honest, all people would have a voice in government.

Some cities tried new forms of government. Cities would not be run by politicians. Politicians would be elected to a city council. The council would set guidelines. Then a city manager would be hired. This person would run the city. The guidelines would have to be followed. If not, the council would find a new city manager. Other cities followed a plan begun in

Galveston, Texas, in 1900. Galveston had been almost destroyed by a hurricane. Rebuilding was a giant job. The city elected boards. Each person on the board handled one kind of job. This plan worked very well. Soon, other cities set up these boards. One member might handle the police department. Another might handle the street department.

States changed, too. Progressives set up new laws and even whole new state governments. Party leaders no longer picked people to run for office. Direct primaries were held. People signed up to run for different offices. Then a special election was held. Republicans chose a candidate for each office. Democrats did too. State legislatures still made laws, but so could the people. They could sign **petitions**. Once a set number of signatures was reached, the law could be voted on by the people. Also, the people could use petitions and a special election to remove people from office. All this gave the people a strong voice in their government.

60.3 What changes did Progressives want in people's rights?

Progressives worked for equal rights. They wanted voting rights for all adults. All men and women should be able to vote, they said. Women should also have power over their money. They should be able to make their own wills. Few jobs were open to women. Progressives wanted women to be able to work at any jobs they wished. Many women had worked in settlement houses for the poor. They often became Progressives. They saw first hand the problems that needed to be solved.

African Americans who lived in the South still were having very hard times. President Roosevelt once invited Booker T. Washington to the White House. Many Southerners complained that this was not proper. This pointed out the problems of African Americans to many Progressives. Some began calling for change. However, very little was done to help

African Americans gain their rights.

60.4 What changes did Progressives want in people's lives and in business?

Not all Americans had good lives. The poor often lived and worked in very bad conditions. Progressives pushed for better housing. They wanted higher pay for workers. Children should not have to work, they said. They should go to school. Progressives helped bring about new laws. Only people 14 or older could get jobs in most states. Many states made it against the law for children under 16 to miss school. Progressives helped workers, too. Many workers were hurt while at their jobs. Workers' Compensation laws were set up. Company owners had to buy this kind of insurance. Then injured workers would get money to

▲ Women marching in support of woman's suffrage. They are carrying a sign quoting President Wilson as supporting the movement.

help pay their bills.

Theodore Roosevelt led Progressives in their work against trusts and monopolies. These giant companies had too much power. Progressives felt they kept **free enterprise** from working. Laws against trusts and monopolies had been passed. Businesses had brought cases against these laws. The Supreme Court ruled against the laws. Then, President Roosevelt called for a case to be brought against Northern Securities Company. It owned three huge railroads. Roosevelt said that this went against the Sherman Anti-Trust Act. In 1904, the Supreme Court agreed that the law had been broken. The railroads had to be run by different owners. They would have to compete against each other. This would help people and business, too. The free enterprise system would be working as it should, said Progressives. Roosevelt won 25 other cases against trusts and monopolies.

60.5 How did Roosevelt work to protect the country's resources and consumers?

President Roosevelt wanted the government to help protect the people. As consumers, people bought the goods that companies made. Sometimes, these goods were bad. For example, some meat packing companies would sell spoiled meat. Roosevelt set up new government offices. The Department of Labor and Commerce opened in 1903. It worked with problems faced by workers and people in trade. The Bureau of Corporations was set up, too. It spread news about big businesses. Roosevelt hoped that this would make all companies follow the law. New cases might not have to be brought under the Sherman Anti-Trust Act. The Interstate Commerce Commission was given power to control prices set by railroads. Now these companies would have to treat all their customers as equals. The Food and Drug Administration was set up in 1906. It worked to make sure that food and medicines did not hurt people.

American lands were important to Roosevelt, too. He loved the outdoors. He loved to camp, fish, and hunt. However, land was being destroyed. Whole forests were cut down. No trees were left in some places. No one planted new ones. Mining companies left some land unusable. Roosevelt pushed for the government to take over some lands. Forests would be saved for use in the future. Coal and oil fields were set aside, too. Some lands would never be used. They became National Parks. Roosevelt wanted the country's **environment**, resources, and beauty to last forever.

☆☆☆

Connections

▲ classroom in the United States

Puritans who began Massachusetts Bay colony believed in learning. All children had to go to school. They needed to know how to read the Bible for themselves. The colony collected taxes. This money paid for the schools. Since they were paid for by the public, they were known as "public schools."

People like George Washington and Thomas Jefferson believed in schools, too. The people would be running the country. They needed educations so they could handle this job. As the years went by, more people pushed for public schools. President Andrew Jackson led the idea that all people should take part in government. Public schools were part of this idea. Public schools spread while Jackson was in the White House. By 1900, public schools were in all the states. Only 57% of children were in school in 1870. The number had climbed to 72% in 1900. There were only 160 public high schools in 1870. By 1900, there were over 6,000. Progressives like Theodore Roosevelt supported public schools. They felt that all Americans should have educations. That way, they would be equal to each other. They would all have the same chances.

CHAPTER REVIEW

Critical Thinking

Write your answers on a sheet of paper or discuss in class.

 Analyzing Cause and Effect

1. What did Progressives think would happen to the country if changes were not made?

 Identifying Main Idea

2. How did Progressives feel that life could be made better?

Cooperative Learning

 LEARNING STYLE *Verbal*

3. Work with a partner or group. Play a question game. Write these words on different pieces of paper: business, women, African Americans, workers, and government. Put the papers in a box. Take turns drawing these papers from the box. Read each name. Think up a question about this person or group. The question should ask about changes that Progressives wanted. The person who gives the correct answer earns five points. Then put the paper back in the box. Continue until all players have had two turns. Total the scores.

Write About It

 Writing Portfolio

4. Look over this chapter. Make a list of the Progressives' goals. List the ways in which these goals were reached. Use these facts to make a chart about the Progressives. Exchange charts with a study partner. Check each other's work.

Chapter 61

Roosevelt's Foreign Policy

Read about the effect Theodore Roosevelt had on the world. How did this show his goals as a Progressive? Why?

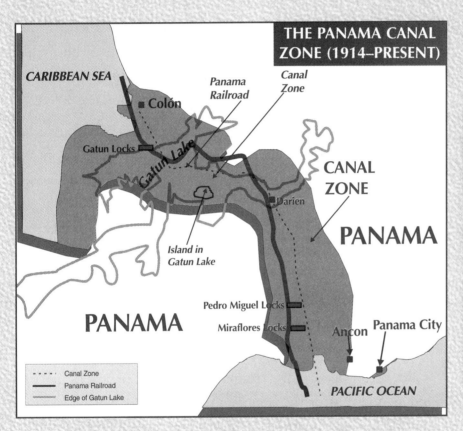

THE PANAMA CANAL ZONE (1914–PRESENT)

CARIBBEAN SEA

Colón

Panama Railroad

Canal Zone

Gatun Locks

Gatun Lake

Darien

CANAL ZONE

Island in Gatun Lake

PANAMA

Pedro Miguel Locks

Miraflores Locks

PANAMA

Ancon   Panama City

PACIFIC OCEAN

- - - - Canal Zone
——— Panama Railroad
——— Edge of Gatun Lake

MAP ANALYSIS

★ **Ask**   What is this map about?

★ **Organize**   List the parts that make up the Panama Canal. How do these parts help ships sail between the Caribbean and the Pacific?

★ **Analyze**   How did the railroad probably help in building the canal?

★ **Answer**   Why do you think cities grew up along the canal?

Decoding Tip: Note the sound of short *a* in the words **ambassador** and **canal**.

ay	cake	ah	fall, cot	air	air
ee	tree	i	sit	oh	cold
or	cord	oy	toy	uh	above, hundred
a	ask	ar	hard	oo	book
e	yet	eye	nice	uhr	liar, fir, further, color
ow	cow	ooh	boot, true	yoo	you, few, cube

61.1 How did Roosevelt use the "big stick policy" to end the crisis in Venezuela in 1902?

Theodore Roosevelt felt that the United States should take part in world affairs. Roosevelt was President of one of the world's strongest countries. The Spanish-American War had showed this power to all the world. Roosevelt wanted the United States to help solve the world's problems. He said that the United States would not be afraid to use its Army and Navy. "Speak softly and carry a big stick" was a saying from Africa. Roosevelt often used it in his speeches. This helped him explain how the United States should act in handling world problems. This idea became known as the "big stick policy."

Roosevelt used his ideas in Latin America. Venezuela and the Dominican Republic owed money to European countries. They were not paying this money back. The Europeans sent troops to collect this money. Roosevelt worried that the Europeans wanted more than money. They might try to take over Venezuela and the Dominican Republic. The Monroe Doctrine said that the United States would stop such actions. Roosevelt called for talks in Europe. He said that the United States would protect its Latin American neighbors. Europe backed down. Ways of paying the debts were set up.

Roosevelt also sent troops to Cuba. Cuba had become independent after the Spanish-American War. Voting was held in 1906. Some people felt that it was a fixed vote. Fighting broke out. Roosevelt wanted democracy to continue in Cuba. U.S. troops were sent to stop the fighting. A new vote was held. After the new government took over, U.S. troops left Cuba. The United States kept its bases there, however.

61.2 Why was a canal in Central America so important to the United States?

Keeping up the U.S. Navy cost the country a lot of money. Ships were needed in both the Atlantic and Pacific Oceans. It was too far to sail around South America. The Spanish-American War was almost over before Pacific ships could reach the Caribbean. The United States had to pay for two **fleets**. A shorter route between the two oceans was needed. The United States would need fewer ships. Money could be saved.

Some countries wanted a **canal** cut through Central America. Great Britain joined the United States in making some plans in 1850. Nothing came of these plans, however. After the Spanish-American War, the idea became more important than ever. Where should the canal be built?

61.3 How did Panama become the site of the canal?

President William McKinley set up a board to bring about the canal. It chose land in Nicaragua. However, France had begun a canal in Panama. It was the same company that had built the Suez Canal. It had joined the Red Sea with the Mediterranean. The French company began working in

▼ The illustration below shows the construction of the Panama Canal.

Panama in 1881. The work was too great. The company went broke in 1889. It said that it would sell its interests in Panama to the United States. The United States agreed. However, Panama was part of Colombia. Terms needed to be reached with the government of Colombia. A treaty was worked out with Colombia's **ambassador**. But the government in Colombia did not like the terms. It refused to let the canal be built.

Panama became an independent country. Its people had long been unhappy with the way Colombia ran the government. They wanted the canal to be built in their area. People from the French canal company helped them plan and

The United States' Involvement in Latin America

Country	Involvement	Years
Cuba	✦ under American protection ✦ troops sent in	1898-1934 1898-1902 1906-1909 1912 1917
Puerto Rico	✦ given to the U.S. by Spain	1898
Panama	✦ under American protection ✦ leased Canal Zone ✦ troops sent in	1903-1938 1903 1903 1918 1921
Dominican Republic	✦ under American protection ✦ troops sent in	1905-1941 1916-1934
Nicaragua	✦ under American protection ✦ troops sent in	1911-1933 1912-1933
Mexico	✦ troops sent in	1914 1916-1917
Virgin Islands	✦ bought from Denmark	1916
Haiti	✦ under American protection ✦ troops sent in	1916-1941 1915-1934

fight a revolution. Some people in the United States were also involved. The war had even been planned in New York City. The United States sent the *U.S.S. Nashville* to sail off the coast of Panama. Panama began its revolution the next day — November 3, 1903. Colombia was afraid this ship might fight if it tried to stop the revolution. Panama quickly won the war. It set up its own government.

Panama agreed to the United States' canal plan. The United States would buy out the French company. It would then **lease** a strip of land 10 miles wide. It would pay to build the canal. Panama would get $10 million. It would then be paid $250,000 each year. The United States promised that the canal would be open to all countries. Work began in 1904. The canal was finished in 1914. It cost $365 million.

61.4 Why did Roosevelt win the Nobel Peace Prize in 1906?

Roosevelt also helped bring peace to parts of the world. France wanted to take over Morocco in North Africa. Other countries wanted it, too. France talked Italy, Spain, and Great Britain into giving up their claims to Morocco. In return, France gave up its claims to other parts of Africa. But Kaiser Wilhelm II would not give up Germany's claim. The Kaiser asked President Roosevelt for help in settling the problem. Roosevelt set up talks between France and Germany. France was given Morocco. The United States promised to send troops to carry this out if necessary. The Senate agreed. However, it wanted to stay out of future European affairs. U.S. troops would only be sent to help Europe when American interests were involved.

China became a problem for the world in 1900. The Open Door Policy let many countries rule different places inside China. The Chinese wanted all foreign powers out of their country. They began a war to take back their country. Many Europeans and Americans were killed. The United States

▲ Generals and soldiers during the Russo-Japanese War in Manchuria

Europeans and Americans were killed. The United States helped other countries end this war. However, the United States wanted some independence for China. China must become free. Trade would continue. All but Russia agreed with this plan. Russia would not leave the Chinese land known as Manchuria.

A new war broke out in Manchuria. Japan and Russia both wanted control there. These two countries went to war in 1904. Roosevelt felt that the Open Door in China might be hurt by the war. He asked Japan and Russia to end the fighting. They would not agree. Japan won many great battles. However, it was too much of a drain on Japan. Finally, the two countries asked Roosevelt to help them reach peace terms. Talks were held in Portsmouth, New Hampshire. The war ended on September 5, 1905. Japan would take over part of Manchuria. It would also own part of Sakhalin Island and part of the Liaotung Peninsula. Russia would not be asked to help pay Japan's war debts. Roosevelt was honored for his work for peace. He was given the Nobel Peace Prize in 1905.

61.5   What was the Gentlemen's Agreement?

Japan became angry with California in 1906. San Francisco began setting up **segregated** schools. Asian children would not be allowed to go to school with other children. Japan learned about this plan. The Japanese government sent an angry letter to President Roosevelt. There was even a danger that war could break out. Roosevelt held talks with the San Francisco School Board. It agreed not to carry out these plans. In return, the United States would cut back on immigration from Asia. It would not accept immigrants who did not have passports for the United States. Japan agreed not to give out these passports to immigrants leaving Japan. Immigration from Japan stopped. This became known as the "Gentlemen's Agreement." There was no real law, only an agreement between countries. Each country also promised to work together in other ways. They would keep things as they were in lands along the Pacific. This would keep Japan and its territories safe from other countries. It would also keep the Philippines safe from Japan.

Connections

▲ Dr. Walter Reed

Canals are an old idea. The Suez Canal is 91 miles long. It runs from the Mediterranean through Egypt to the Red Sea. However, today's canal is just the latest one to be dug in this spot. Ships sailed through a canal dug in the Suez desert almost 4,000 years ago. Africans had dug the canal to help them in their shipping and trade. The sand and wind did not help the canal. It slowly filled in with sand. It was rebuilt several times. Then the French dug the current canal in the late 1800s. It was still a great achievement.

Digging the Panama Canal was a great achievement, too. At almost any time, over 40,000 people were working on the project. Almost three-fourths of the people were Africans. They were descendants of enslaved Africans brought to Latin America. The work was very dangerous. Accidents did happen. Sickness was a terrible problem. Yellow fever and malaria killed many of the workers. So many died that work had to stop after only one year. Colonel William Gorgas knew how to help. He was not only a soldier, but also a doctor. The U.S. Army sent him to Panama. Mosquitos were spreading the sicknesses. They live in still puddles, pools, ponds, and lakes. Gorgas led the work to drain swamps and other bodies of standing

water. The number of mosquitos fell. Fewer people were getting sick. The work could go on.

The Spanish-American War had taught people how to fight these sicknesses. Yellow fever and malaria had been problems in Cuba during the war. More soldiers died from these sicknesses than in battle. One of Cuba's doctors was Carlos Juan Finlay. He was the first person to suggest that mosquitos caused these sicknesses. The U.S. Army sent Dr. Walter Reed to Cuba in 1900. He led the work to fight these sicknesses. He learned about Finlay's ideas. After finishing some experiments, he proved that Dr. Finlay was right. Then Colonel Gorgas was sent to Cuba. He led the fight against the mosquitos.

★★☆ CHAPTER REVIEW

Critical Thinking

Write your answers on a sheet of paper or discuss in class.

Analyzing Cause and Effect

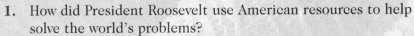

1. How did President Roosevelt use American resources to help solve the world's problems?

Making Inferences

2. How do you think people in Asia and Latin America might have felt about what the United States was doing in these years?

Cooperative Learning

LEARNING STYLE
Tactile

3. Work with a partner or group. Look at the map of the Panama Canal. Use clay to make a model of the Canal Zone. Be sure to include high spots as well as low ones. Let the map dry. Place it in a bowl or tub. Add water so that you can see how it flows through the canal. Look at the places where locks were built. Why is it necessary to pump water to the locks?

Write About It

Writing Portfolio

4. Find out more about the Panama Canal. How long did the work take? How many locks were built? What building problems did the workers face? Why was it necessary to build lakes as well as locks? Write a report about the Panama Canal. Share your findings with the class.

Chapter 62

Problems: Foreign & Domestic

Read about the changes that government and business went through in the early 20th Century. How did Progressive ideas help change the country? Why?

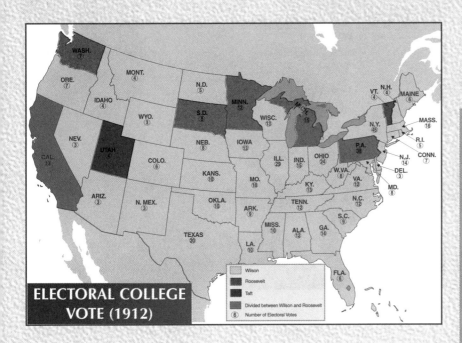

ELECTORAL COLLEGE VOTE (1912)

Wilson
Roosevelt
Taft
Divided between Wilson and Roosevelt
⑥ Number of Electoral Votes

Key Vocabulary

income tax (IN kuhm ● tax) a part of a person's earnings taken for government use

diplomacy (duh PLOH muh see) the act of handling affairs between countries

conservation (kahn suhr VAY shuhn) the act of controlling a resource in order to protect it, such as stopping people from cutting down forests

Reteaching Vocabulary

economy (i KAHN uh mee) the system through which the people and companies of a certain area make their livings

---

MAP ANALYSIS

★ **Ask**   What does the number listed for each state tell you?

★ **Organize** The size of a state's population determines its number of electoral votes. Write these heads on a piece of paper: **Less than 5 Votes, Less than 10 votes, Less than 20 Votes,** and **20 or More Votes**. List the states under the correct heads.

★ **Analyze** The size of a state's population determines its number of electoral votes. Where are the states with the largest populations?

★ **Answer**   Why do you think some states had larger populations than others?

Decoding Tip: Note that different vowels may stand for the /uh/ sound.

ay	cake	ah	fall, cot	air	air
ee	tree	i	sit	oh	cold
or	cord	oy	toy	uh	above, hundred
a	ask	ar	hard	oo	book
e	yet	eye	nice	uhr	liar, fir, further, color
ow	cow	ooh	boot, true	yoo	you, few, cube

▶ President Theodore Roosevelt

62.1 How did President Taft carry out Progressive ideas?

Theodore Roosevelt's second term as President ended in 1908. He worked to see that his ideas would still be carried out. He picked William Howard Taft to run for the Republicans. The Democrats picked William Jennings Bryan for the third time. Both men were Progressives. Roosevelt's influence helped Taft. He became President in 1909. Roosevelt was very pleased. Taft promised to carry out Roosevelt's ideas.

Taft did push for Progressive ideas concerning America and its businesses. He broke up even more trusts and monopolies than Roosevelt. One was the Standard Oil Company. It was

John D. Rockefeller's giant oil business. At one time, it had controlled almost all U.S. oil.

Taft worked for other business laws, too. Some helped keep workers safe. Taft also started the Children's Bureau. It worked to see that America's children were healthy and received educations. The Constitution was changed while Taft was President. Two amendments were added. With the 16th Amendment, the country began collecting **income taxes**. U.S. Senators had always been elected by state legislatures. The 17th Amendment gave this power to the people of each state.

Taft helped in the fight for women's rights. He had set up the Children's Bureau. Taft picked Julia C. Lathrop to run the Children's Bureau. She became the first woman to head a federal department. This was an important achievement. In 1912, most American women could not vote. Thanks to President Taft, however, a woman was helping to run the government.

62.2 What was Taft's dollar diplomacy?

Taft handled problems with other countries. European companies were building railroads in China. Russian and Japanese companies joined in. Taft pushed for American companies to build some, too. Taft also worried that foreign countries might take over parts of China. The United States wanted China to rule itself. Then its trade would be open to all countries. Taft and Congress agreed to loan China money. It would be used to buy the railroads. However, Russia and Japan would not sell. They ended up by dividing Manchuria between themselves. The U.S. loan was never made. Taft's use of money to handle this world problem failed.

Taft had more success in Latin America. Some of these countries had problems with their debts. Most of this money was owed to European banks. Taft worried that Europe would take over these countries. He decided to carry out the Monroe

Doctrine. Taft used the idea of dollar **diplomacy** again. He pushed American banks to take over these loans. Troops were sent to Nicaragua and other countries. They collected the countries' taxes. Some was given to the countries' governments. The rest was used to pay off the debts to American banks. Later Presidents also followed this plan. After the debts were paid, U.S. troops were brought home.

62.3 Why did Taft lose the support of many Progressives?

Taft did not always please the Progressives. They wanted lower tariffs. They hoped that this would lower prices. The bill was sent to Congress. However, the Senate would not agree. One Senator added almost 200 amendments to the bill. These would keep the tariffs high. Taft worked with the Senate on the bill. Some tariffs did go down. Others did not. The Progressives felt that Taft had turned against them. President Roosevelt had set aside land for National Parks and Forests. Some was for future use. Taft's Secretary of the Interior decided to sell some of this land to businesses. The Chief of the Forestry Service called for the sales to stop. Taft was angry with this attack on his Cabinet. He fired the Forestry Chief. Progressives were very angry. They felt that Taft did not care about **conservation** and the environment. Roosevelt also turned against Taft.

62.4 How did Roosevelt and Taft split the Republican Party?

Four people ran for the White House in 1912. Roosevelt was unhappy with Taft. He felt that Taft had broken his promise to carry out Roosevelt's ideas. Roosevelt decided to take the White House from Taft. In February he said that "his hat was in the ring." He was the first to use this phrase. Progressive Republicans pushed for Roosevelt. However, Taft's supporters took over the party's convention. Taft was picked by the Republicans.

Roosevelt then set up his own Progressive Party. He said that he felt "as strong as a bull moose." Some people began calling his party the "Bull Moose Party." This party put Roosevelt into the race. The Democrats picked Woodrow Wilson. He had been President of Princeton University, then governor of New Jersey. Eugene V. Debs ran for the White House, too. He was the candidate of the Socialist Party. Roosevelt and Taft split the Republican vote. Only 42% of the people voted for Wilson. Still, this was more than any other candidate. Wilson became President in 1913.

62.5　How were people's ideas about government and business different?

The race for President showed three different ideas about government and business. Debs wanted the government to take over all American companies. Few Americans agreed with this idea of the Socialist Party. Roosevelt and Taft had fought for Progressive ideas. They had managed to control some trusts and monopolies. Many were broken up. However, some were still in business. For example, many companies supplied gas, water, electricity, and telephone services. Building these systems cost a lot of money.

Taft and Roosevelt wanted to make sure that these services reached all Americans. These companies were given monopolies in different areas. However, President Wilson did not agree. He felt that there should be no trusts and monopolies. They were bad for competition, he said. Competition was good for the country and for businesses. Democrats had taken over Congress in 1913, too. They agreed with many of Wilson's ideas. Together, Congress and President Wilson passed many new laws to regulate business in the United States.

62.6 What economic programs did Wilson put in place?

Wilson set up programs to regulate banking. 1907 had been a very bad year for the **economy**. There was not enough money on hand. Most people used cash. Few checks were written. The government could not keep up with this sudden demand for coins and dollar bills. Banks began making loans only to their biggest customers. The poor and people in the middle class were suffering. Wilson pushed a new idea.

The Federal Reserve Act was passed in 1913. The government set up 12 banks of its own. Each one works for a different area of the country. They hold money for the banks in that area. They also handle any checks that are written in the area. All these banks are ruled by a board in Washington, D.C. It has seven members. Each is picked by the President and approved by the Senate. The board makes plans so that there will always be enough money. The Federal Reserve Banks also make loans to banks in each area. This gives the board power over interest rates, too. The Federal Reserve Banks and board still do this work today.

Business and farming are still affected by Wilson's ideas. Strict laws were set up. Now, only certain business practices would be allowed. Companies could not hold secret meetings with their competitors. Usually, these meetings were held to make sure all the companies charged the same prices. Often, the prices were very high. Wilson said this destroyed the American idea of competition in business. Unions and labor groups were supported by Wilson, too. New laws made it harder for companies to use courts against unions. More and more people began joining unions. Farmers received help, too. Wilson and Congress set up 12 more banks. These banks still make loans to farmers. Only low interest rates are charged. Farmers face less risk of losing their farms during bad times.

Biography

American athletes have amazed the world in Olympic Games. Jim Thorpe, a Native American, was a member of the Sac and Fox tribe. His family lived in Oklahoma. Thorpe was taken from his family. He was sent to the Carlisle Indian Industrial School in Pennsylvania. Thorpe made his mark in sports. He became a star on the football and baseball teams. The United States put him on its team for the 1912 Olympics.

In Stockholm, Sweden, Thorpe won two gold medals. One was for the pentathlon. This is a set of five track and field events. Then Thorpe amazed the world, again. He won the decathlon, too. This is a set of ten events. The King of Sweden presented the medals to Thorpe. The king said that he had never seen such a wonderful athlete. However, Thorpe

had his medals for only a month. He had once played baseball for a small salary. The Olympic Committee only allowed amateur, or unpaid, athletes in the games. They took his medals away.

After the Olympics, Jim Thorpe continued in sports. He was a professional, or paid, athlete. He began professional baseball in 1913. From 1915 to 1919, he was paid to play baseball in the summer and football in fall. After 1919, he stuck with football. Thorpe was one of the greatest football players ever. He became the National Football League's first president in 1920. He was elected to the National Football Hall of Fame in 1951. Thorpe died in 1953. For years, people had pushed the Olympic Committee to return Thorpe's Olympic medals. Finally, the

Committee gave in. These medals were given back to his family in 1982.

▲ Jim Thorpe

★★☆ CHAPTER REVIEW

Critical Thinking

Write your answers on a sheet of paper or discuss in class.

Drawing Conclusions →✦←

1. Why did all the presidential candidates of 1912 want to control the way companies do business?

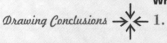
Comparing and Contrasting

2. How were Roosevelt, Taft, Wilson, and Debs alike and different?

Cooperative Learning

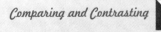

LEARNING STYLE
Verbal

3. Work with a partner or group. Imagine that it is the race for President in 1912. You are working for one of the four candidates. Tell why your candidate should be President. Remember to tell about the person's ideas and plans. Tell why you think this would be good for the country.

Write About It

Writing Portfolio

4. Find out more about the early Olympics. Why is this a very old idea? Why were the games brought back in 1896? How did U.S. athletes surprise the world in the 1896 games? Who besides Jim Thorpe won medals in the 1912 games? Share your findings with the class.

Chapter 63

The World Goes to War

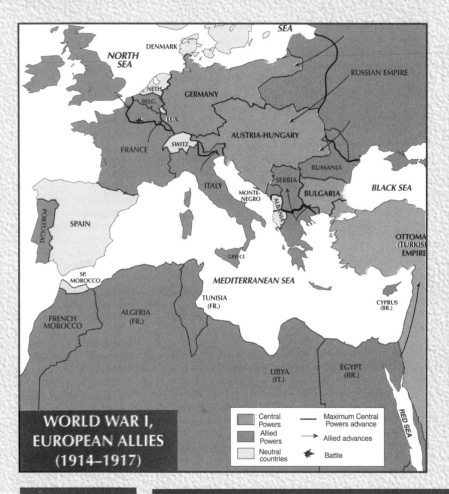

WORLD WAR I,
EUROPEAN ALLIES
(1914–1917)

Central Powers		──	Maximum Central Powers advance
Allied Powers		→	Allied advances
Neutral countries		✦	Battle

Read about Europe. How did a war between two European countries spread? Why?

Key *Vocabulary*

neutral (NOO truhl) refusing to take sides in some sort of disagreement

communist (KAHM yuh nuhst) a person or country following the idea that government should own everything, that a central group should make all decisions, and that the people work for the good of the government

Reteaching Vocabulary

empire (EHM peyer) a nation that is made up of many areas and people; ruled by a king or queen known as an emperor or empress

alliance (uh LEYE uhns) two or more people or groups working for a common goal

assassination (uh sas uhn AY shuhn) the killing of a person for political reasons

---

MAP ANALYSIS

★ **Ask**   What does this map show?

★ **Acquire**   What do the colors tell you?

★ **Organize**   Write these heads on a piece of paper: **Central Powers**, **Allied Powers**, and **Neutral Countries**. List the countries under the correct heads.

★ **Answer**   Britain, Germany, France, and Italy had colonies in Africa, Asia, and the Pacific. How do you think the war might affect these colonies?

Decoding Tip: Note that double consonants stand for one sound as in **communist** and **assassination**.

ay	cake	ah	fall, cot	air	air	
ee	tree	i	sit	oh	cold	
or	cord	oy	toy	uh	above, hundred	
a	ask	ar	hard	oo	book	
e	yet	eye	nice	uhr	liar, fir, further, color	
ow	cow	ooh	boot, true	yoo	you, few, cube	

For the People, By the People

63.1 Why had the countries of Europe formed such complicated alliances?

War had been used to create the countries of Europe. Early cities had been small kingdoms in themselves. Neighboring cities fought wars against each other. One would take over another. Soon, larger kingdoms were formed. By the 1500s, the countries of England, Scotland, Spain, France, and Denmark had been formed. There were other countries like the Netherlands, Switzerland, and many small German and Italian kingdoms. Spain, France, and England pushed west across the Atlantic Ocean. They took over the Americas.

Europe's countries changed and grew during the 1700s and 1800s. Great Britain was made up of Scotland, England, and Wales. It also owned Ireland, Australia, Canada, and parts of Africa and Asia. France also wanted an **empire**. It competed with Britain for lands in Africa and Asia. Austria had its own empire. It had taken over Hungary and countries like Bosnia and Serbia on the Balkan Peninsula. Russia's empire was ruled by the Tsar. It had taken Finland, Poland, and other lands along the Baltic Sea. The Russian Empire also wanted lands in the Middle East. These lands were part of the Ottoman Empire. By the late 1800s, the German and Italian kingdoms became united. Germany and Italy wanted empires of their own. Germany had even taken over parts of France.

Europe was filled with strong and dangerous countries. They were afraid of each other. Many began building up their armies and navies. They wanted to protect themselves. This arms race made things even more dangerous. Soon, countries were banding together. They wanted friends. These friends would help them in case of attack. Germany, Austria, and Italy promised to help each other. Russia, France, and Britain lined themselves against the Germans, Austrians, and Italians. The smaller countries also set up their own **alliances**. Sometimes, large countries would promise to help small countries. The web of alliances and agreements was very complicated.

63.2 Why was the Austrian archduke assassinated?

▲ The photograph above shows the Archduke of Austria, Franz Ferdinand, with his wife, Sophie.

Independence had long been an important idea in Europe. Different groups wanted their own countries. The Netherlands had fought for independence from Spain. Sweden had freed itself from Denmark. Norway had broken away from Sweden. Belgium was formed from lands that had once belonged to France and the Netherlands. Austria's empire was very uneasy. Some lands had been part of Italy. Many people in the Balkans were also ruled by Austria. Some were Christians. Others were Muslims. They were people of different races. They spoke different languages. They also had different customs. Serbia had become free. However, many Serbs lived in Bosnia and other parts of Austria. Many of these groups wanted to form their own independent countries.

Assassination became a tool of some who fought against Europe's governments. Emperor Franz Josef had ruled Austria-Hungary since 1848. In 1898, his wife was walking in a garden in Switzerland. A man jumped over the wall. He rushed up to the Empress and seemed to shove her. He was caught as he ran away. The Empress and her friends began to walk away. However, the Empress fell dead. She had been

▲ Kaiser Wilhelm II of Germany (1859-1941)

stabbed through the heart with a hat pin. The assassin had killed her because he wanted Bosnia to be free. The next in line to the throne was the Emperor's nephew, Archduke Franz Ferdinand. On June 28, 1914, he made a trip to the city of Sarajevo. He and his wife rode through the streets in an open car. A man in the crowd shot and killed them both. He was a student attending college in Bosnia. He wanted Bosnia to be free. The student was a Serb. Austria blamed Serbia for causing the killings. It declared war on Serbia.

63.3 How did the European alliances turn this fight into a world war?

Europe's alliances brought other countries to the side of Austria and Serbia. Russia declared war on Austria. It said that it wanted to protect Serbia. Now, Austria was in real danger from such a large country. Germany came to Austria's help. They became known as the "Central Powers." They forced France to take a stand. France went to war against the Central Powers. On August 3, 1914, Germany marched through Belgium toward France. Great Britain had an alliance with Belgium. It declared war on Germany on August 4. Italy decided to fight against Austria. It hoped to take back the lands it had lost to the Austrian Empire. France, Britain, Italy, and other countries were the Allied Powers. Bulgaria and the Ottoman Empire joined Germany and Austria. They wanted to protect themselves from Russia. Then Japan entered the war. It declared war on Germany, too. It hoped to take some of its colonies in the Pacific. Europe's colonies even became involved. Germans and Britains fought in Africa. Soon people were calling the fight the "Great War." Now it is called "World War I."

63.4 How did the United States react to the war?

War in Europe was not something most Americans cared about. The United States had helped keep Morocco from Germany. However, the U.S. Senate had said that the country would not get involved in any more European affairs. The United States felt it had nothing to gain from entering this war. Europe should solve its own problems. The United States decided to remain **neutral** in the war. Even some European countries stayed out of the fighting. The war was being fought over issues that did not affect them. Neither the United States nor the other neutral countries wanted to risk their independence for such issues.

Connections

War and the killing of innocent people is going on in the Balkans today. After World War I, Yugoslavia was separated from Austria. This new country governed many different groups of people. It became a communist country. The Soviet Union fell apart in 1992. Europe's communist countries began to change, too. Yugoslavia was divided into the countries of Croatia and Bosnia-Herzegovina. However, Bosnia was made up of both Serbs and Croats. A new war began. Each group fought to take over the country. Serbia helped the Bosnian Serbs. Croatia helped the Bosnian Croats. Troops shelled cities and villages. Thousands of men, women, and children have been killed in the fighting. The United States and the United Nations have made some attempts to stop the war. However, both sides seem determined to continue the war no matter what the cost.

▲ A Croat soldier cries by comrade's graveyard

★★☆ CHAPTER REVIEW

Critical Thinking

Write your answers on a sheet of paper, or discuss in class.

Identifying Main Idea 1. Why were European countries so afraid of each other?

Making Inferences 2. What do you think might cause the United States to get involved in this war?

Cooperative Learning

LEARNING STYLE
Verbal

3. Work with a partner or group. Look at the map at the beginning of the chapter. Choose a country shown on the map. Tell the class about this country. Why is it fighting in this war? Is it an Allied or Central Power? Is the country neutral? How did the country get involved in the war?

Write About It

Writing Portfolio

4. Imagine you are a reporter on the streets of Sarajevo on June 28, 1914. Write a news story about the assassination of Franz Ferdinand and his wife. Remember to answer the questions Who? What? When? Where? Why? and How?

Quiz

Number a piece of paper from 1-10. Read each question below. Read the answers that follow each question. Choose the answer for each question. Write the letter of the answer you choose beside the correct number on your piece of paper.

1. **What lands were bought so that the United States could set up Navy bases in the Pacific?**
   a. Alaska
   b. Hawaii
   c. Wake Island
   d. both a and c

2. **How did the United States take over Puerto Rico, Guam, and the Philippines?**
   a. It bought them from Germany.
   b. It took them from Cuba.
   c. It won a war with Spain.
   d. both a and b

3. **What ideas did Theodore Roosevelt and the Progressives support?**
   a. honesty in government
   b. equal rights
   c. some control over business
   d. all of the above

4. **How did President Roosevelt help the country's environment?**
   a. by setting aside resources for future use
   b. by setting up the first national parks
   c. by setting up laws limiting mining and lumbering
   d. none of the above

5. **Why did the United States send troops to different countries in Latin America?**
   a. to help these countries pay their debts
   b. to stop civil wars in these countries
   c. to stop Spain's blockade of their ports and harbors
   d. all of the above

6. **What country declared independence so that it could sign a treaty with the U. S. allowing it to build a canal across Central America?**
   a. Venezuela
   b. Panama
   c. Nicaragua
   d. Haiti

7. **Why did Roosevelt turn against President Taft?**
   a. because Taft joined the Democrats
   b. because Taft used dollar diplomacy to solve problems with other countries
   c. because Taft broke his promise to follow Roosevelt's ideas
   d. all of the above

8. **What was the goal of laws that were set up under President Wilson?**
   a. to control business practices
   b. to help unions and farmers
   c. to control banking
   d. all of the above

9. **Why did so many European countries go to war over a problem in Austria?**
   a. because of the complicated secret agreements between these countries
   b. because anarchists assassinated so many important people in these countries
   c. because Germany used the war as an excuse to invade Great Britain
   d. because Austria attacked Pacific lands owned by other European countries

10. **What was the United States' position on the war in 1914?**
    a. It sided with the Central Powers.
    b. It fought with the Allied Powers.
    c. It wanted to stay neutral.
    d. none of the above

RECOGNIZING DETAILS

Add numbers 11–15 to your paper. Read the two lists below. People are listed on the left. What the people did are listed on the right. Match the people with the things that they did. Write your answers on your paper.

11. Theodore Roosevelt
12. Woodrow Wilson
13. Eugene V. Debs
14. William H. Taft
15. Julia C. Lathrop

a. Republican who formed the Bull Moose Party
b. President who followed the idea of dollar diplomacy
c. first woman to head a federal department
d. President who set up the Federal Reserve banking system
e. Socialist who ran for President

Look over the things you wrote for these chapters. Choose one that you like the best. Add to your writing. For example, you wrote about the goals of the Progressives. You may wish to write about the goals of other groups, such as the Socialists, the Central Powers, and anarchists. You also wrote a news story as if you were a reporter who saw the killing of Franz Ferdinand. You may wish to write stories about the Panama Canal or the use of submarines in World War I. Trade papers with a study partner. Check each other's work. Make a clean, neat copy. Put it in your portfolio.

You may wish to work with a study partner. Make a map that shows where American troops were sent between 1890 and 1920. Look over the chapter for these facts. Make up a key for the map. It should tell what your colors stand for. For example, green could show where the Spanish-American War was fought. Write a short label for each country that was involved. Paste these labels on your map. Hang your map in the classroom.

COOPERATIVE PROJECT: OUR STATE AND PRESIDENTIAL ELECTIONS

Work with a partner or group. When did your state join the Union? What Presidential Elections have been held since that year? Make a chart that shows how your state voted in each election. Use the following headings: **Candidate, Party, Number of Votes, Number of Electoral Seats Won,** and **Person Who Became President.** Find these facts for each Presidential Election. Show your chart to the class. Discuss it with the class. Did your state vote for the national winner each time?

Chapter 64

World War I

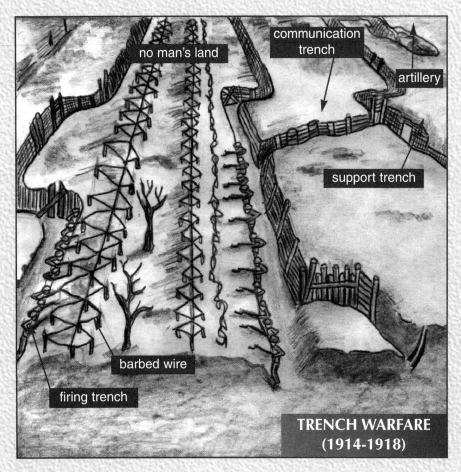

no man's land

communication trench

artillery

support trench

barbed wire

firing trench

TRENCH WARFARE (1914-1918)

Read about the First World War. How did the United States affect the result of the war? Why?

Key *Vocabulary*

atrocity (uh TRAHS uht ee) an act that is considered to be terribly wicked or cruel

pacifist (PAS uh fuhst) a person who believes that war should never be used to settle disagreements

diplomat (DIP luh mat) a person who handles dealings between governments

discrimination (dis krim uh NAY shuhn) the act of treating a person or group badly because of the mistaken idea that the group is inferior

Reteaching Vocabulary

merchant (MUHR chuhnt) used in buying goods and selling them for a higher price, or profit, in order to make a living

---

DIAGRAM ANALYSIS	★ **Ask**	*What does this diagram show?*
	★ **Organize**	*Make a list of the things that make up each side's trench system. Tell what each part is for.*
	★ **Answer**	*How successful do you think charges across no man's land would be?*

Decoding Tip: *Note that all vowels can stand for the /uh/ sound.*

ay	cake	ah	fall, cot	air	air
ee	tree	i	sit	oh	cold
or	cord	oy	toy	uh	above, hundred
a	ask	ar	hard	oo	book
e	yet	eye	nice	uhr	liar, fir, further, color
ow	cow	ooh	boot, true	yoo	you, few, cube

64.1 Why was it so hard for the United States to stay neutral?

Americans felt different pressures during the war. The United States was a country that had been started by English people. Many of its ideas and customs were based on those of Britain. The country felt strong ties to France, too. The French had helped the United States win the Revolutionary War. However, the United States was a land of immigrants. Millions of people had ties to Germany, Austria, Russia, and the Balkan countries. There were strong feelings for both the Allied and Central Powers.

Britain pushed to get the United States into the war. It spread war news in the United States. These stories told about terrible happenings in Europe. Many Americans were angered and shocked by these happenings. Germany was blamed for **atrocities**. The British even made up stories about German actions.

Britain used trade as a weapon in the war. The British Navy took a great part in the war. It set up a blockade against the Central Powers. These countries could not trade for the things they needed during the war. It became harder for them to fight the Allies. Britain kept trade flowing to its shores. The United States had always traded with Europe. Its trade with Allied Powers had been five times larger than trade with the Central Powers. After 1914, trade with the Central Powers dropped from about $170 million to $2 million. However, trade with the Allies increased from almost $800 million to over $3 billion. Britain hoped the increase in trade would push the United States to support the Allied war effort.

64.2 How did the Central Powers work against the British blockade?

A new weapon helped Germany fight the British blockade. German submarines could sneak up on British ships. They sank ships in the British Navy. They also sank **merchant** ships. This angered people around the world. Germany was not giving warnings to merchant ships. When these ships were sunk, the people on board went down. Many were killed. Warnings were called for by international law. However, Germany felt that such warnings put its submarines at risk. Soon, German submarines were sinking many merchant ships.

Germany sank ships from neutral countries, too. This kept goods from reaching the Allied Powers. Sometimes, passenger ships like the *Lusitania* were sunk, too. Americans were killed in some of these attacks. President Woodrow Wilson sent angry letters to Germany. Germany did not want the United States in the war. It decided to stop attacks on passenger and merchant ships. However, these attacks started again in 1915. Wilson went to Congress. He said that further attacks could not happen. The United States would break off all contact with Germany. Germany agreed to stop this second round of attacks.

64.3 How did the Zimmerman Note bring the United States into the war?

Divisions among Americans grew during the war. By 1916, two groups had been formed. Some wanted the country to be ready for war. They wanted to build up the army and navy. If war did come, the United States would be prepared. The other group worked for peace. The **Pacifists** said that war was not the answer to any problem. They wanted the United States to stay out of the war. Henry Ford was a Pacifist. He led a group to Sweden. They asked the other neutral countries for help. Perhaps these countries could use their influence to stop the fighting. Ford's group failed. The war went on.

Different ideas about the war were shown in the race for the White House in 1916. President Wilson had worked to keep the country at peace. He said that this had been done with honor. He had gained important points by dealing carefully with both sides. Many Democrats used the slogan, "He kept us out of war." However, Wilson did not like this slogan. He was not sure that the United States could stay out of the war permanently.

The Republicans picked Charles Evans Hughes. Hughes was Chief Justice of the Supreme Court. He believed in preparedness. Theodore Roosevelt and others pushed this idea, too. The race was very close. The two men divided the states evenly. California became the key. Late on election night, the results showed that Hughes would win California. He went to sleep believing he was President. During the night, the final results had arrived. Wilson won California by about 3,000 votes. Wilson stayed in the White House. He still believed in peace. The country had to be safe, though. He asked that Congress build up the U.S. Army and Navy.

Germany ended up pushing the United States into the war. In January, 1917, it said that submarine attacks would begin again. This time the Germans would not back down. American goods were helping the Allies too much. Germany wanted this trade stopped. In February, the United States found out about a letter to a German **diplomat** in Mexico. It had been written by Germany's foreign minister, Arthur Zimmerman. The letter set out plans for Mexico to enter the war on Germany's side. In return, Mexico would take over the states of Arizona, New Mexico, and Texas. Mexico never agreed. However, this caused great anger throughout the United States. Many people began calling for war. In March, Germany sank four American ships. President Wilson went to Congress on April 2. He asked Congress to declare war on Germany. Congress agreed. War was declared on April 6, 1917.

64.4 What new weapons made the war last so long and become so destructive?

The Central Powers were forced to fight the war on different fronts. The Germans and Austrians fought the Allies in France and Belgium. This was the Western Front. They also fought Russia on the Eastern Front. On the Southern Front, Germany and Austria faced Italy. The Ottoman Empire and Bulgaria fought the Allies in the Middle East. The war bogged down on all sides. The Allied and Central Powers each dug trenches along the fronts. These countries had built arms to defend themselves. Each could hold its trenches. However, these countries were not as well prepared for carrying out attacks. The war had begun in August, 1914. By September, the war was being fought on no man's land between the trenches.

New weapons helped keep the war going. Trench warfare was a new idea. New weapons were needed for this kind of war. Fire from machine guns and cannons could keep the enemy down inside their trenches. This fire would stop at a predetermined time. Then, troops could dash toward the enemy trenches. Often, they had not run very far when the enemy opened fire. Thousands could be killed in a single charge. Trenches did change hands many times. However, this usually made little difference in the war.

Tanks were developed by the British for the war. These vehicles were covered with armor. They could cross land damaged by bombs. Tanks could also fight enemy trenches. Enemy fire had little effect on them. Poison gas was used in the war. Bombs carrying the gas were shot at enemy lines. The gas injured and killed thousands. Some soldiers suffered permanent lung damage. The danger was great for both sides. If the wind changed, the gas might be blown back on the troops that had fired these bombs.

Air ships were important in the war, too. Hot air balloons were used to drop bombs. They were dropped on troops and

▶ The photograph to the right shows Russian demonstrators being machine-gunned in Petrograd by police in 1917.

cities. London was bombed by German balloons. Usually, the balloons caused little damage. Planes dropped some bombs, too. They were used to blow up roads, trains, and bridges. Dogfights between planes made heroes of many pilots.

64.5   How did the war end?

Russia was important to the war. It had kept Germany and Austria fighting on two fronts. However, millions of Russians had died. The country was being drained of money and resources. The people turned against their government. Tsar Nicholas II was driven from the throne in 1917. The new government did not last long, though. V. I. Lenin and the Communists took over in October, 1917. Lenin ordered troops to kill the Tsar and his family. The Communists promised that all Russian land and property would be shared equally. Lenin wanted peace while he rebuilt Russia into a Communist country. He set peace terms with Germany. Then Lenin strengthened his hold on Russia. Soon, he had total control of the country and its government. Not even the Tsar had held such power. The peace terms closed down the Eastern Front in 1917. Italy was defeated in the fall of 1917. Germany and Austria could put all their might on the Western Front. The Ottoman Empire continued to fight the Allies in the Middle East. For help, the Allies turned to their new friend—the United States.

The United States made the difference. The Allies were worn out by the war. They needed fresh troops. Some American troops were sent to Europe in the summer of 1917. However, the U.S. Army was small. There had not been enough volunteers. Congress began drafting men into the armed forces. Time was needed to train the new soldiers. America sent about 270,000 troops by May, 1918. However, one million were promised to be in Europe by the end of the year.

▲ The photograph above shows Lt. Douglas Cambell, the first American-trained pilot to shoot down a German plane in World War I.

Germany decided to make its move before all these troops arrived in Europe. It began a major attack. Fierce fighting broke out in the summer of 1917. It continued into 1918. American troops helped push the Germans and Austrians back to their own trenches. American pilots helped fight the air war. The U.S. Navy helped fight in the Mediterranean. Allied troops were fighting the Ottoman Empire in the deserts of the Middle East, too.

American strength helped end the war. In September, 1918, there were one million U.S. troops in Europe. These fresh troops turned the war in favor of the Allies. U.S. General John J. Pershing and France's Marshal Ferdinand Foch began pushing the Germans out of France. By November, these troops broke the German lines. Germany was worn out. Its money and resources were spent. President Wilson received word from Germany on November 6. It believed that Wilson could talk the Allies into offering easy terms. Germany asked President Wilson to help set up these terms for peace. The other Allied leaders would not set any terms. Wilson told Germany that only complete surrender would be accepted. Terms would be set by the Allies after the war was over. The Germans had no choice but to agree. At 11:00 A.M. on November 11, 1918, the war came to an end.

Connections

▲ African American soldier during World War I

World War I changed the U.S. economy. Trade went up during the war. More goods were manufactured for Europe. New jobs opened up in factories. However, the high demand for goods pushed up prices. Companies were earning record profits. Wages did not keep up. It became harder and harder for workers to pay their bills. Millions of Americans began joining unions. Some Pacifists said that business leaders only wanted the United States in the war so that companies could keep earning huge profits. However, the Zimmerman Note and submarine attacks of March, 1917, changed many people's ideas about entering the war. The economy changed even more after the U.S. declared war on Germany. The U.S. Army and Navy needed more goods than ever. Factories geared up to make these goods. Wages increased dramatically after the U.S. entered the war. Farmers made more money than ever for their crops, too.

Workers changed after 1917, too. So many men went to war that there were not enough workers. Factories began hiring women. They showed that they could do jobs that most people had believed only men could handle. They not only worked in factories. Some drove buses. Others worked as police officers directing traffic. The U.S. Post Office even hired women to deliver the mail. African Americans benefited, too. Factories hired African Americans for jobs that only white Americans had held. Over half a million African Americans moved from the South to take work in Northern factory cities.

Women and African Americans served in Europe, too. African Americans entered the Army and the Navy. Women worked as nurses, secretaries, and ambulance drivers. Over 11,000 women saw service in Europe during World War I. Almost 400,000 African Americans were sent to Europe. However, they faced discrimination in the services. African Americans became officers only after W.E.B. DuBois and the National Association for the Advancement of Colored People (NAACP) complained to the government. African American units fought with honor during the war. The 369th Infantry fought for 191 days without relief. It never lost a trench. It did not retreat either. None of its troops was ever captured during the fighting. No other unit ever matched this record.

★★☆ CHAPTER REVIEW

Critical Thinking

Write your answers on a sheet of paper, or discuss in class.

Identifying Main Idea

1. How did resources and industry affect World War I?

Making Inferences

2. President Wilson and Europe's leaders had different ideas about surrender terms. How do you think these differences might affect talks on peace terms?

Cooperative Learning

LEARNING STYLE
Verbal

3. Work with a partner or group. Choose some events in World War I, such as the first American troops marching into Paris. Imagine you were there. Tell what you have seen. Tell how it made you feel. If possible, tell what event happened next.

Write About It

Writing Portfolio

4. Work with a partner or group. Look over the facts about World War I. What decisions were made by the Allied and Central Powers? What effect did these decisions have? Did they cause other things to happen? Make a chart of these causes and effects. Use arrows to show how one event led to another.

Chapter 65

A World at Peace

Read about the treaty talks after World War I. How did President Wilson work for democracy? Why?

EUROPE AND THE MIDDLE EAST AFTER WORLD WAR I (1919)

- Russian Empire
- Austria-Hungary
- German Empire
- Ottoman Empire

ICELAND

Norwegian Sea

NORWAY   SWEDEN   FINLAND
Oslo★   Helsinki★   ★St. Petersburg
Stockholm★   ESTONIA
North Sea   LATIVA   ★Moscow
DENMARK   U.S.S.R.
Copenhagen★   LITHUANIA
North Atlantic Ocean
IRELAND   GREAT   NETHERLANDS
Dublin★   BRITAIN   Berlin★   POLAND
London★   GERMANY   ★Warsaw
BELGIUM   RHINELAND
Paris★   LUX.   Prague★   CZECHOSLOVAKIA
FRANCE   Vienna★   ★Budapest
Bern★   AUSTRIA   HUNGARY
SWITZ.   BOSNIA   ROMANIA
★Belgrade   ★Bucharest   *Black Sea*
PORTUGAL   ITALY   YUGOSLAVIA
★Lisbon   ★Madrid   ★Rome   BULGARIA
SPAIN   Tirana★   ★Sofia   Constantinople   PERSIA
ALBANIA   GREECE   TURKEY
★Athens   SYRIA   IRAQ
MOROCCO   LEBANON
Mediterranean Sea   PALESTINE TRANSJORDAN
TUNISIA
ALGERIA   LIBYA   EGYPT   Cairo★   SAUDI ARABIA

Key *Vocabulary*

general assembly (JEN uh ruhl • uh SEM blee) a group elected to set rules and laws for the people or countries who have elected them

normalcy (NOR muhl see) a time when things work in patterns that people believe are regular and acceptable

influenza (in floo EN zuh) a virus that attacks a person's lungs, making it hard to breathe

refugee (ref yoo JEE) a person who tries to escape a place where battles are happening

Reteaching Vocabulary

compromise (KAHM pruh meyez) an agreement reached when the different sides each give up part of their demands

MAP ANALYSIS

★ **Ask**   *What does this map show?*

★ **Organize**   *Write these headings on a piece of paper:* **Germany, Austria-Hungary, Russia,** *and* **The Ottoman Empire.** *Look at the map. Note the new countries that were formed from these four nations. List the new countries under the names of the nations to which they had once belonged.*

★ **Answer**   *Why do you think the new borders would make some countries happy while making others angry?*

Decoding Tip: Note that both *c* and *s* can stand for the /s/ sound, as in **assembly** and **normalcy**. *C* can also stand for the /k/ sound and *s* can stand for the /z/ sound as in **compromise**.

ay	cake	ah	fall, cot	air	air
ee	tree	i	sit	oh	cold
or	cord	oy	toy	uh	above, hundred
a	ask	ar	hard	oo	book
e	yet	eye	nice	uhr	liar, fir, further, color
ow	cow	ooh	boot, true	yoo	you, few, cube

President Woodrow Wilson

65.1 How did the League of Nations illustrate President Wilson's ideas for peace?

President Woodrow Wilson blamed the war on greedy government leaders. Germany's Kaiser, Austria's Emperor, and the Ottoman's Sultan had misled their people. These men had fought for more land and power. Their people were the ones to suffer.

Wilson spelled out his plans for peace nearly a year before the war ended. He pushed for freedom. New countries should be formed. They should be countries that practiced the American form of democracy. He even said that the war had been fought to "make the world safe for democracy." All the world's countries should agree to freedom of the seas. Trade should be carried out freely, too.

One goal was most important to Wilson. He wanted a **general assembly** of all countries. This group would be made up of people from all the countries of the world. It would work to settle problems between countries. He believed that this League of Nations would make sure no world war ever happened again.

▼ Palace of Versailles, France, where the peace treaty was signed

65.2 What were the terms of the Treaty of Versailles?

Peace talks were held at the French Palace of Versailles. It had been the home of France's kings and queens. Now it would be the spot where Wilson would try to carry out his plans. Wilson pushed for his plan for a League of Nations. Most of the countries were more interested in punishing Germany and Austria-Hungary. Wilson had not wanted such terms. But he could not get his League without agreeing to

The photograph to the right shows President Woodrow Wilson with his secretary Joseph P. Tumulty.

some of them. An agreement was reached in February, 1919. Wilson returned to present his plan to the U.S. Senate. According to the Constitution, any treaty had to be approved by the Senate.

In Washington, President Wilson found that his agreement was in trouble. He had long fought with the Republican Party. It was led by Senator Henry Cabot Lodge. Bitter disputes had often broken out between Lodge and the President. Lodge led a fight against the League of Nations. Like many Americans, Lodge wanted the country to return to **normalcy.** He wanted the country to avoid getting involved in the world's problems. He felt that the League might pull the country into new wars.

Almost one-third of the Senate asked for changes in the plan for the League. Wilson knew that his plan would not be approved. He returned to France for further talks. He had to agree to tough terms for the Central Powers. In return, the Allies agreed to the changes that the Senate wanted.

Germany signed the Treaty of Versailles on June 28, 1919. This was exactly five years after the assassination of Archduke Franz Ferdinand and his wife, which had started the war. Under the peace terms, Germany had to:

- give up all its arms.

- admit that it was responsible for causing the war.

- give back some territory to France and other European countries.

- pay the Allies $56 billion so they could pay their war debts.

Austria, Bulgaria, and the Ottoman Empire all signed similar treaties. Wilson hoped that the changes in the League would make the Treaty of Versailles acceptable to the Senate.

65.3 Why did some members of the Senate still object to the treaty?

Many people worked against the Treaty of Versailles. They hated the idea of the League of Nations. Senator Lodge had hoped that the Allies would not agree to the changes he and the Republicans had requested. However, the treaty included the League plan with Lodge's changes.

Other Senators and many Americans did not like the treaty's terms. Many German-Americans felt it was too tough on Germany. Other Americans felt that more new countries should have been formed. For example, Irish-Americans

▲ The photograph above shows soldiers fighting in the trenches during World War I.

wanted all of Ireland to be independent. However, Northern Ireland still belonged to Great Britain. Italian-Americans felt that Italy had not gained enough territory for helping to win the war.

Three groups were formed in the Senate. Some Senators liked the Treaty of Versailles as set up by the Allies. Another group was led by Senator Lodge. This group was called the "reservationists." They had reservations, or concerns, about the treaty. They set up 12 new terms for the treaty. If these terms were accepted, they would vote for the treaty. One term would not allow the League to settle U.S. problems. Another term set the Senate's powers. Only the Senate, but not the President, could agree to any decisions made by the League. The third Senate group was the irreconcilables, or people who said they would never accept the League of Nations.

65.4 Why did the United States reach separate peace terms with Germany and the other Central Powers?

President Wilson decided to fight for the Treaty of Versailles. He would not accept any more changes in its terms. Some Democrats felt they could work with the reservationists. They believed that terms could be found that both sides would like. Wilson refused all the **compromises** worked out by the Democrats. He took his idea to the people.

Traveling by train, Wilson made over 40 speeches in September 1919. He asked the people to elect only Democrats to the Senate in the November elections. The work was too much for Wilson. The peace talks in France had worn him out. He was ill when he began his speeches. Wilson collapsed in Pueblo, Colorado. He returned to Washington. In October, he had a stroke. At first, Wilson could not speak or move.

▶ The photograph to the right shows Frank Luke, Jr., of the 27th Squadron standing in front of his plane, which he used to shoot down a German fighter.

While he was sick, the Republicans won many elections. They took over both houses of Congress. The Republican Senate turned down the Treaty of Versailles.

Wilson recovered from his stroke. But he was not able to lead the country again. Wilson's wife, Edith, had helped him greatly in his work as President. After the stroke in 1919, Mrs. Wilson rushed the President back to Washington. She kept all reporters and members of Congress from the White House. They never knew how sick the President had been.

Wilson almost lost the office of President. There were rumors that the President was in a coma. Some members of Congress called for the Vice President to take over as President. Mrs. Wilson had President Lincoln's great bed set up in one bedroom. The President was dressed and propped up in this imposing bed. Several members of Congress were allowed to meet with President Wilson. They saw that he was much better and that he had full control of his mind. Wilson served out his term.

Mrs. Wilson helped him carry out all necessary duties. Some people even believed that Mrs. Wilson made all his decisions. Others did not believe such stories. However, President Wilson was not able to push his plans for the country. Congress carried out the business of finding peace with Germany.

The United States signed its own treaties with each of the Central Powers. Peace terms with Germany were not reached until 1921. Many of the terms of the Treaty of Versailles were included. The treaties recognized the new countries that had been formed. The Central Powers had to help pay U.S. war debts. However, the United States never joined the League of Nations. Without the world's strongest nation, the League was always a weak organization.

Connections

World War I was a very costly war. The United States alone spent about $1 million an hour to fight the war. The war cost the United States almost $32 billion. Together, the Allied Powers spent almost $400 billion. Over 10 million soldiers died. The United States lost 116,516 soldiers in the war. The other Allied Powers lost 5,116,272 soldiers. Germany and the Central Powers lost 3,947,945 soldiers. Millions of civilians were also killed in this war.

Even more deaths were caused by **influenza**. A passenger ship from Norway docked in Brooklyn in August 1918. The flu had broken out on board. Four people had died. One more died after leaving the ship. This disease spread quickly through the whole United States. In one day, more than 500 people died in Philadelphia. Suddenly in July 1919, the disease went away. By that time, 548,000 Americans had died. The flu had killed over 27 million people around the world.

The war may even have caused the spread of this disease. Soldiers training in Kansas came down with the flu in March 1918. It was not a bad attack. These troops were sent to France. French people near their camp also came down with the flu. No one knows why the disease became so deadly. Troops and **refugees** spread the disease throughout Europe. From Norway, it traveled back to the United States. Many soldiers became sick. Nearly one-third died after catching the disease. President Wilson thought of stopping all troop shipments to Europe. However, the Allies begged for fresh troops. Wilson allowed the ships to continue taking Americans to the war.

▲ Allied troops fighting in Verdun during World War II

★★☆ CHAPTER REVIEW

Critical Thinking

Write your answers on a sheet of paper, or discuss in class.

 Identifying Main Idea

1. How do you think the Germans felt about the peace terms that were set?

 Comparing and Contrasting

2. How were the reservationists' and irreconcilables' ideas like the ideas held by the Allied leaders in Europe? How were they different?

Cooperative Learning

LEARNING STYLE
Visual

3. Work with a partner or group. Choose an event that happened during the war. It could have happened in Europe or the United States. Think about what happened. What did the people look like? How did they act? What was the result of this event? Draw four pictures that tell what happened. Make up a title for your drawings.

Write About It

Writing Portfolio

4. Look over the ideas in this chapter. Different people held different ideas and opinions before, during, and after the war. Make notes of these people and their ideas. Use your notes to make a chart about the end of World War I. Write sentences that tell the people's ideas.

Chapter 66

Boom Times

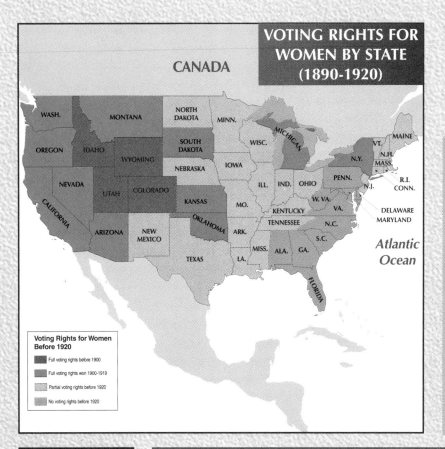

VOTING RIGHTS FOR WOMEN BY STATE (1890-1920)

CANADA

WASH.
MONTANA
NORTH DAKOTA
MINN.
MICHIGAN
MAINE
OREGON
IDAHO
WYOMING
SOUTH DAKOTA
WISC.
VT.
N.H.
MASS.
NEBRASKA
IOWA
N.Y.
NEVADA
UTAH
COLORADO
KANSAS
ILL.
IND.
OHIO
PENN.
N.J.
R.I.
CONN.
CALIFORNIA
MO.
W. VA.
KENTUCKY
VA.
DELAWARE
MARYLAND
ARIZONA
NEW MEXICO
OKLAHOMA
ARK.
TENNESSEE
N.C.
S.C.
Atlantic Ocean
TEXAS
MISS.
ALA.
GA.
LA.
FLORIDA

Voting Rights for Women Before 1920
- Full voting rights before 1900
- Full voting rights won 1900-1919
- Partial voting rights before 1920
- No voting rights before 1920

Read about the changes in the United States after World War I. How did Presidents Harding and Coolidge represent people's ideas? Why?

Key *Vocabulary*

controversial (kahn truh VUHR shuhl) causing heated quarrels or disagreements

boom (boohm) a time when business grows quickly throughout an area or country

Reteaching Vocabulary

normalcy (NOR muhl see) a time when things work in patterns that people believe are regular and acceptable

ballot (BAL uht) the time when a vote is held

scandal (SKAN duhl) disgrace caused by doing something that offends people or is against the law

---

MAP ANALYSIS

★ **Ask**　　What does this map show?

★ **Acquire**　　In which region did women first gain the right to vote: the East, the West, the North, or the South?

★ **Organize**　　Look at the key for the map. Read the labels. Copy them as headings on a piece of paper. List the states under the correct headings.

★ **Analyze**　　Which area had newly formed states with newly written constitutions?

★ **Answer**　　Why do you think that the newer states would be the first to give women the rights to vote?

Decoding Tip:　　Note that c can stand for the /k/ sound, as in **controversial** and **scandal**.

ay	cake	ah	fall, cot	air	air
ee	tree	i	sit	oh	cold
or	cord	oy	toy	uh	above, hundred
a	ask	ar	hard	oo	book
e	yet	eye	nice	uhr	liar, fir, further, color
ow	cow	ooh	boot, true	yoo	you, few, cube

66.1 What factors helped Warren Harding become President in 1921?

Most Americans were tired of world problems. They just wanted **normalcy.** They were tired of the changes that had come with the war. They had made many sacrifices during the war. Americans had cut back on eating meat. The food was needed for the troops. They had collected metal goods. These goods were used to make weapons and other items needed by the soldiers. Now the war was over. Americans were tired of these sacrifices. They wanted things to be the way they had been before the war.

Republicans took over government after World War I. In 1919, the people returned Congress to the Republican Party. In 1920, it was time to elect a new President. The Democrats continued the push for change. They wanted to carry on the ideas begun by the Populists and Progressives. They picked Ohio Governor James M. Cox for President. For Vice President, they wanted President Wilson's Assistant Secretary for the Navy, Franklin D. Roosevelt. The Republicans looked for a candidate who would promise not to make great changes in government and the country.

Deal-making helped put a little-known candidate into the White House. The Republican Convention was in Chicago. Several **ballots** were held on the first day. The Republicans could not settle on one of the three leading candidates. Late that night, the party's leaders met in a Chicago hotel.

Warren G. Harding was not one of the leading candidates. However, his campaign manager kept pushing his name to the party leaders. Late that night, they called Harding to the meeting. After a short talk, they decided to back Harding. He was a Senator from Ohio. He was popular in his home state. He was not well known outside Ohio. However, he did not have any enemies.

Harding had taken no strong stands on the issues. This was a good sign. American voters wanted a President who would not be **controversial.** Harding promised not to support major change. The leaders presented his name at the Convention. Harding was chosen to run for the White House. The Republicans chose Governor Calvin Coolidge of Massachusetts to run for Vice President. The plan worked. Harding and Coolidge won the race.

66.2   How was the Election of 1920 different from all earlier Presidential Elections?

Women's right to vote had been won in 1920. Congress had passed the 19th Amendment to the Constitution. However, three-fourths of the states now had to approve the Amendment. The necessary 36 states finally approved the 19th Amendment in the summer of 1920. When the people went to the polls in November, women voted, too. Warren G. Harding became the first President elected by both men and women.

▲ The photograph above shows President Warren G.Harding, on the left, with Vice President Calvin Coolidge.

Women's right to vote had been called for in the early years of the country. Abigail Adams had urged her husband John Adams to work for women's rights. He was in the Second Continental Congress, which was drafting the Declaration of Independence in 1776. Suffragettes had fought for these rights for many years. They were led by people such as Susan B. Anthony and Elizabeth Cady Stanton. It took almost 150 years after the birth of the United States before women earned the right to vote.

66.3 What happened to the United States economy after World War I?

Things slowed down after the war. Company profits had soared during World War I. Americans had produced more goods than ever before. Wages had reached all-time highs. So many men went to war that women took factory jobs.

After the war, the demand for goods dropped. Factories needed fewer workers. Most factories fired their women workers. They hired men who were returning from the war. There still were not enough jobs. Companies cut wages, too. Many people were angry with these changes.

Unions grew after the war. However, the majority of Americans still worried that unions might hurt the country. Union workers wanted the high pay of the war years. They wanted shorter hours, too. They had joined unions in order to get what they wanted. Workers joined unions in record numbers. They were still only a small part of the American working force, though. The main weapon of unions is calling a strike. In 1919 there were over 4,000 strikes in the United States. Fighting often broke out. Troops were used to stop not only the fighting but also the strikes. Calvin Coolidge was the governor of Massachusetts in 1919. He sent the state militia to stop a strike being held by the police in Boston. Union work was still seen as dangerous by most Americans.

There were problems throughout the 1920s. Most Americans were very happy with life, though. The war was over. Wages had dropped, but most people had jobs. Prices were lower, too. New products like radios and automobiles made life easier. People had time to travel. There were shows and movies to see. Sports became wildly popular. Baseball had athletes like Babe Ruth and Ty Cobb. Bobby Jones thrilled people with his golf game. Tennis fans were electrified by the playing of Helen Wills Moody. Gertrude Ederle broke all records in swimming the English Channel. She took two hours off the men's and women's record for this swim from England to France. Americans played sports, too. The demand for sporting goods created a new industry. Americans had saved their money. The were investing it as well. People bought stocks in all kinds of companies. The country was experiencing real "**boom** times."

66.4   How did scandals affect President Harding?

Warren G. Harding was a good man who wanted good things for the country. He had promised to put the "best minds" of the country to work in the White House. He had picked Andrew Mellon as Secretary of the Treasury. Secretary Mellon had led Congress to pass laws to help business. Tariffs were raised. This cut down on competition from foreign businesses. The country's war debt was greatly reduced. Taxes were cut for the wealthy. His ideas were so popular that he was Secretary of the Treasury not only for Harding, but also for Presidents Coolidge and Hoover.

▲ Andrew W. Mellon, Secretary of the Treasury

Scandals over money hurt President Harding. Like President Ulysses S. Grant, Warren G. Harding had trouble with his friends and associates. The Director of the Veterans Bureau stole thousands of dollars. When this news broke, the director shot himself. Jesse Smith was a friend of Attorney General Harry M. Daugherty. Smith shot himself, too. Before his death, he had burned many of his papers. They contained proof that Daugherty and he had also stolen government money. There was even a rumor that the Attorney General had shot his friend. Albert M. Fall was Harding's Secretary of the Interior. Past Presidents had set some of the country's resources aside. They would be for future use. Oil reserves at Teapot Dome in Wyoming were to be used by the Navy. However, two businessmen bribed Secretary Fall. He put these reserves up for sale. But he did not accept bids from any other companies. Secretary Fall was put on trial. He was the first member of a President's Cabinet to go to jail.

President Harding never learned of Fall's crimes. The earlier scandals had rocked his faith in his friends. President Harding became ill. He took a vacation. He made a trip through the West and into Alaska in the summer of 1923. During the trip, Harding had a heart attack. He died on board ship while sailing back from Alaska. Vice President Calvin Coolidge took over the White House. Coolidge began working to restore honesty in government.

▲ President Calvin Coolidge

66.5 Why did President Coolidge disapprove of the Progressives' ideas?

Unlike the Progressives, Coolidge supported the idea of limited government. He believed that people should solve their own problems. Coolidge made sure that his staff worked for his ideas. Progressive ideas concerning reform and controlling trusts were not carried out. The government took very little action in regulating business. Coolidge even helped businesses stop strikes. He believed that strikes kept companies from operating freely.

Coolidge pointed to the country's strong economy. He said that freedom from regulation had allowed businesses to create this strong economy. He said that "the business of government is business." He meant that government should work to help businesses. They would become successful. This would then help the people. Workers would have jobs. President Coolidge believed that businesses could run the country well and make the people happy.

☆☆☆

Connections

▲ Suffragettes working for women's rights

The women of Wyoming Territory were the first to win the right to vote. Esther Morris and her family moved to Wyoming in 1869. She was a Suffragette who worked for women's rights. Wyoming Territory was setting up its first legislature. H. G. Nickerson and William Bright were running for office from Mrs. Morris's district. She invited both men to her home. She made them promise to work for voting rights for women. Bright won the election. He kept his promise to Mrs. Morris. The Wyoming Legislature passed his act giving women the right to vote. Today, a statue of Esther Morris stands in the U.S. Capitol's Statuary Hall. It was a gift of the people of Wyoming.

Tennessee became the state to give all American women the right to vote in 1920. Congress had passed the 19th Amendment. However, 36 states had to ratify the Amendment before it could become law. Only 35 states had ratified this Amendment by the middle of 1920. Now the bill went before the Tennessee Legislature. Suffragettes wore and handed out yellow roses. People who were against the Amendment used red roses. The Amendment came to a vote on August 18, 1920. No one knew how the vote would go. The Suffragettes saw that Harry Burn was wearing a red rose. They were shocked. He had promised his help. After voting, the Legislature was tied. During the second vote, Burn changed his vote. This put the Suffragettes over the top. Now, women had the right to vote. People asked Burn why he changed his vote. He showed them a letter he had received from his mother. She had advised him to vote for the 19th Amendment.

CHAPTER REVIEW

Critical Thinking

Write your answers on a sheet of paper, or discuss in class.

Identifying Main Idea 1. What did Americans want out of life after World War I?

Comparing and Contrasting 2. How did President Coolidge's ideas conflict with the ideas of Presidents Theodore Roosevelt, William H. Taft, and Woodrow Wilson?

Cooperative Learning

LEARNING STYLE
Verbal

3. Work with a partner or group. Read the vocabulary words aloud. Discuss the meanings of these words. Look through the chapter. Practice saying the names you read. Find words that are unfamiliar. Say these words aloud. Look up their meanings in the glossary or classroom dictionary. Discuss these meanings with your partner or group.

Write About It

Writing Portfolio

4. Imagine you are a reporter covering the Tennessee Legislature. You are watching on August 18, 1920, when the Legislature votes for the 19th Amendment. Write a story about the day. Remember that your story should answer these questions: **Who? What? When? Where? Why?** and **How?** Share your story with the class.

Chapter 67

The Roaring Twenties

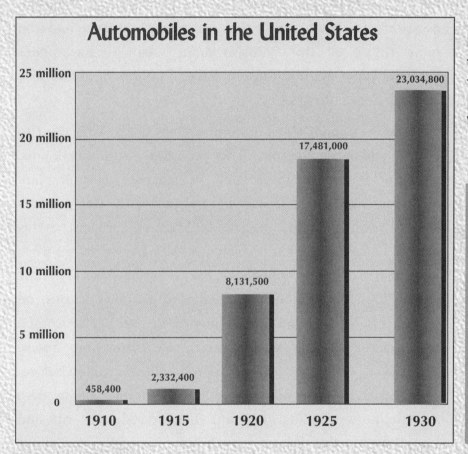

Automobiles in the United States

25 million					23,034,800
20 million				17,481,000	
15 million					
10 million			8,131,500		
5 million		2,332,400			
0	458,400				
	1910	**1915**	**1920**	**1925**	**1930**

Read about life in the United States during the 1920s. How did people's lives change? Why?

Key *Vocabulary*

style (steyel) a specific way in which something is made, such as writing a book or creating clothing

society (suh SEYE uht ee) a group of people who form a state or country and follow similar traditions

process (PRAHS es) the steps in which some activity is completed

GRAPH ANALYSIS

★ **Ask**   What does this graph show?

★ **Organize**   Point to the top of each bar on the graph. See how many cars were in the United States during that particular year. Make a list of these numbers by year.

★ **Answer**   The price of cars dropped greatly after 1916. How might this fact explain the growth in the number of cars in the United States?

Decoding Tip: Note that *c* can stand for the /s/ sound, as in **society** and **process**.

ay	*cake*	ah	*fall, cot*	air	*air*
ee	*tree*	i	*sit*	oh	*cold*
or	*cord*	oy	*toy*	uh	*above, hundred*
a	*ask*	ar	*hard*	oo	*book*
e	*yet*	eye	*nice*	uhr	*liar, fir, further, color*
ow	*cow*	ooh	*boot, true*	yoo	*you, few, cube*

67.1 How did women's roles change during the 1920s?

Women set new goals for themselves in the 1920s. In the past, most women had married and had families. A few women did work. Some were doctors and lawyers. Most worked as teachers and nurses. For the most part, husbands had complete control over their wives. Until the late 1800s, husbands owned a family's property. A wife could make no decisions that would hold up in court. Slowly, women had won more rights. In the 1920s, women began to have more choices. Some might choose marriage. Others might choose careers. Some might choose both.

There were many signs of women's new goals. They went to college and earned degrees. They took different kinds of jobs. Margaret Bourke White became a magazine photographer. She specialized in photos of industry at work. Her pictures showed people making steel or building skyscrapers. **Styles** changed to show women's new ideas. Women had always worn long hair. Now, they bobbed, or cut, their hair in very short styles. Their dresses became shorter, too. For centuries, no woman would show her feet in public. In the 1920s, women wore dresses that only reached their knees. Some women were arrested for doing things that women had never done before. They could be arrested for smoking in public. Some were arrested for wearing bathing suits that showed their arms and legs. However, this did not stop the spread of new ideas about women and their place in **society**.

67.2 What effect did radio and the automobile have on people's lives?

Radio had a great influence on Americans' lives. Early radios were simple head sets. Soon, cabinet models were made for home use. People listened to radio for entertainment. Singers, bands, and actors put on radio shows.

The photograph to the right shows *Pickwick Stages*, counterparts of modern day buses, outside Union Station, Los Angeles, awaiting passengers bound for southern California in 1920.

Companies put ads on radio, too. Sales for many products skyrocketed.

Radios also helped spread the news. Reporters took radio trucks on the road. Live reports could be heard as events happened. The news could reach people very quickly. Sports were reported on the radio, too. Games were broadcast all over the country. Fierce competition grew up between radio stations and newspapers. Americans learned more about each other. They learned how similar many of their interests and ideas really were.

Assembly lines changed automobiles. Ransom Eli Olds lost his automobile factory in a fire. In building a new one, he followed a new plan. Some workers put the cars together. Other workers brought the parts that they needed. This assembly line could make cars much more quickly. Olds saved money. He sold the cars for less. More people could afford cars.

This photo shows early automobiles on a busy street in Chicago, 1917.

Henry Ford also changed the assembly line idea. The car actually moved on a long belt. Each worker added another part to the car. When it reached the end of the belt, the car was finished. It took 12 1/2 hours to build a car with Olds' system. Ford's moving assembly line cut the time to only 1 1/2 hours. The price of a Ford Model T dropped from about $900 in 1908 to about $400 in 1916. By the 1920s, Ford made half the cars sold in the United States.

Buying a car changed many Americans' lives. Families began taking trips across the country. Hotels and restaurants did booming business. States hired people to build new roads and bridges. Farmers used Ford's Model T, also. They could buy a kit to turn a Model T into a truck. The trucks carried crops to market. The truck engines helped run some farm machines. These machines milked cows, cut wood, and lifted heavy bales of hay. The automobile and other machines made work faster and easier. Americans gained more free time.

67.3 How did art and music change during this period?

Artists followed new ideas during the 1920s. Women were breaking with the past. Artists' styles did, too. Painters might work to show the way ordinary people lived. Some artists worked with shapes. Works of art sometimes did not look much like real objects. Authors wrote about the problems of the poor and the rich. Happy endings did not always happen in real life. Now, they did not have to happen in plays or stories either. Artists hoped their works would make people see themselves and their lives in new ways.

African Americans had a great influence on music. Most musicians had followed European styles. Enslaved people from Africa had a strong history of music. Their ideas were mixed with those of Europe. By the late 1800s, America had its own styles of music. Scott Joplin

▼ The picture below shows a painting called *Power Plant, Harlem* by African American artist Aaron Douglas.

▲ The picture above shows King Oliver's Creole Jazz Band, Chicago, May 1923. L-R: Baby Dodds, drums; Honore Dutry, trombone; King Oliver, cornet; Louis Armstrong, cornet; Bill Johnson, bass and banjo; Johnny Dodds, clarinet; Lil Hardin, piano

began a style called "ragtime." It swept the country. New dances were created for this kind of music. W. C. Handy used these ideas to create another new style—the blues. Blues and jazz music from New Orleans became popular all over the world. Count Basie, Duke Ellington, and Louis Armstrong took their bands to many American cities. Often, they had to stay in people's homes. There might be no hotels that would accept African Americans as guests. Many clubs and theaters wanted to hire jazz bands. But some did not want African American bands. Whites formed their own jazz bands. This kept African Americans from reaching all audiences. African Americans had a long way to go in receiving equal rights.

67.4 Why are the movies considered to be an American art form?

Americans developed most movie-making **processes**. Movies had been invented in France. However, the best camera was invented by a worker in Thomas Edison's workshop. Edison wanted to control the movie business. He hired actors, writers, and directors who worked in theaters. They made the earliest movies. These were silent movies. There was not yet a way of matching sound with the movement on the film. Most movies were very short. They were played inside a machine. It cost a nickel to stand at the machine. One person at a time could watch the movie. Then people found ways of showing movies on screens. Now groups of people could see the same movie in one theater. Movie theaters were sometimes called palaces. They were often huge and grand.

Other people got copies of Edison's camera. One early director was D. W. Griffith. His cameraman was Billy Bitzer.

▲ The picture above shows one of the great jazz musicians of all time, Duke Ellington.

They invented such things as the fade out, the close up, and long story movies. Griffith made a movie that was about two hours long. Most people said that Americans would not sit still that long just to watch a movie. However, the movie was a huge success. It was controversial, too. Griffith was the son of a Confederate soldier. His movie was called *The Klansman*. It was about the way the Ku Klux Klan had worked in the South after the Civil War. Its members were shown as heroes. Many Americans were angered by the movie. They knew the harm that the Klan had done to African Americans. Griffith renamed his movie. It became known as *Birth of a Nation*. This did not stop the controversy.

The movie business grew up in California. Los Angeles had sunny weather. This helped light the movies. It was near the ocean, mountains, and a desert. These settings could be used in all kinds of movies. Hollywood became known all across the world. More movies were made in the United States than in any other country. People began copying the actors and ways of life shown in the movies. American styles appeared in many other countries. American stars could even be mobbed in these countries. Lillian Gish, Douglas Fairbanks, Mary Pickford, and Buster Keaton were famous movie stars. Movies made them rich.

People from other countries became stars in America, too. Rudolph Valentino was from Italy. Charlie Chaplin and Stan Laurel came from England. Greta Garbo came from Sweden. Directors, writers, and actors came from other countries, too. Sound movies took over after 1927. Many stars could not speak English. This had not mattered in silent movies. Other actors did not have good speaking voices. Voices were important in talking movies. Many actors became writers and directors. Others left the movie business. However, the business continued to grow through the 1920s and into the 1930s. It influenced the United States and the world.

☆☆☆

Connections

▲ Pancho Villa

Pancho Villa led a revolution against the government of Mexico. In 1913, he defeated the Mexican Army and took over part of northern Mexico. Newspapers all over the world carried stories about the war. Villa often took money and land from rich people. He gave it to the poor. He became a hero to many people. Hollywood even decided to put him into the movies.

General Villa was paid $25,000 to make a movie for the Mutual Film Company. The company also agreed to pay him half of the movie's profits. In return, camera crews would follow him through Mexico during the spring of 1914. Early movie cameras could not make pictures at night. Villa agreed to fight his battles only during the day. Sometimes the crews did not like the film they shot. Then, General Villa had his troops play out the battle for the cameras. The movie was called *The Life of General Villa*. It was shown in the United States and Canada in May, 1914. It was also shown in those parts of Mexico controlled by Villa. The movie was a huge success. Villa gained more than fame and money. He used the story to show people about his ideas. He hoped more people would support his fight.

★★★ CHAPTER REVIEW

Critical Thinking

Write your answers on a sheet of paper, or discuss in class.

Identifying Main Idea
1. How did styles show the changes that were happening in American life?

Making Inferences
2. How could movies and radio be used to help spread ideas?

Cooperative Learning

LEARNING STYLE
Reading Verbal

3. Work with a partner or group. Look through the chapter. Look at the names of people you read about. Find these names in the Gazetteer in the back of the book. Practice saying these names.

Write About It

Writing Portfolio

4. Make a list of the changes that happened in the 1920s. Think about the ways in which these changes are alike. How are they different? Divide the changes into groups. Use these groups to make a chart about the 1920s. Put your chart on a large piece of paper or poster board. Hang your poster in the classroom.

Chapter 68

Cracks in the Seams

Where Did the Immigrants Come From?

Year	Number of Immigrants	Northern & Western Europe	Southern & Eastern Europe
1921	800,000	16%=128,000	41%=328,000
1925	300,000	26%=78,000	4%=12,000
1930	240,000	29%=69,600	12%=28,800
Year	Number of Immigrants	Central Europe	Latin America
1921	800,000	22%=176,000	15%=120,000
1925	300,000	19%=57,00	48%=144,000
1930	240,000	18%=43,200	36%=86,400
Year	Number of Immigrants	Asia	Others
1921	800,000	3%=24,000	3%=24,000
1925	300,000	1%=3,000	2%=6,000
1930	240,000	1%=2,400	4%=9,600

Read about problems faced by the United States during the 1920s. How did changes in people's lives help bring about these problems? Why?

Key *Vocabulary*

Prohibition (proh huh BISH uhn) a law making it a crime to make, sell, or use alcoholic drinks

embassy (EM buh see) the home of a person who lives in one country in order to represent his or her country's government

value (VAL yooh) a belief or action that is held to be good and worthwhile

traditional (truh DISH nuhl) in a manner that follows a long accepted pattern; customary

deport (di PORT) to force a person to return to his or her own country

CHART ANALYSIS

★ **Ask**   What does this chart show?

★ **Acquire**   How did the total number of immigrants change from 1921 to 1930?

★ **Organize**   The United States set limits on the number of immigrants from each area. Which areas increased during this time? Which areas decreased?

★ **Answer**   Until the 1860s, most immigrants had come to the United States from Northern and Western Europe. How might this fact explain the cuts in the numbers of immigrants allowed into the United States during the 1920s?

Decoding Tip: Note that more than one letter can stand for the sound /uh/.

ay	cake	ah	fall, cot	air	air
ee	tree	i	sit	oh	cold
or	cord	oy	toy	uh	above, hundred
a	ask	ar	hard	oo	book
e	yet	eye	nice	uhr	liar, fir, further, color
ow	cow	ooh	boot, true	yoo	you, few, cube

68.1 Why did farmers not take part in the boom times of the 1920s?

Farmers sold their goods for less money in the 1920s. Earlier, Europe had needed lots of food during World War I. In the 1920s, Europeans were able to grow their own food again. Food sales to Europe dropped. Farmers were still growing lots of food. There was more than the United States could use.

Farmers could not sell everything they grew. Prices fell. Farmers were earning less. Farm machines had helped farmers. They saved time and money. Each farmer could grow more food. However, the machines cost a lot of money. During the good years, farmers borrowed money. Then they bought the new farm machines. In the 1920s, low prices brought bad times. Many farmers could not pay back their loans. Sometimes, these farmers even lost their land.

68.2 How did Prohibition lead to more crime?

Many Americans fought against the use of alcohol. Drinking had ruined many lives. Groups were formed to fight the sale and use of alcohol. These groups pushed for new laws. Selling or using alcohol would be a crime. By 1917, 19 states had set up these laws. Congress passed the 18th Amendment in 1917. It was ratified in 1919. Starting in 1920, alcohol would be against the law. No drink could have more than one-half percent alcohol.

The 18th Amendment did not stop drinking. Drinking was too much a part of American life. Many people drank. Most of them did not have problems with alcohol. They saw no need to follow this law. New businesses sprang up. People broke the law by smuggling alcohol into the country. Others made their own alcohol. Many people broke the law by buying this alcohol.

Carrying out **Prohibition** was the job of the Bureau of Internal Revenue. Revenue agents raided many clubs where

▲ The photograph above shows the Detroit police inspecting equipment found in a secret underground brewery during the Prohibition era.

these drinks were served. These clubs were called "speakeasies." 200,000 speakeasies could be found in the United States by 1920. People who made and smuggled alcohol were called "bootleggers." Revenue agents went after these people, too. But so many people were breaking the law that the law was failing.

Not even the White House went along with Prohibition. Other countries had **embassies** in the United States. These buildings and lands were not under U.S. law. Drinks could be served legally in these places. Some people bought alcohol from embassies. President Harding sent White House workers to the embassies. They smuggled alcohol into the White House.

Big money was made on illegal alcohol. Gangs took over most of this business. Fighting for money and power often led to killings. Gangsters bribed city and state officials, too. Then the illegal business could be carried on in the open. It became dangerous to live in some cities.

68.3 How did the idea of traditional values affect the United States in the 1920s?

Many Americans worried about the country in the 1920s. They did not like the changes that were happening. These people felt that the country was losing its way. It should return to the **values** that had helped form the country.

▲ The photograph above shows the bodies of two gangsters and bullet-riddled cars following a gun battle with police in the 1920s.

Religion had always been important in the United States. Most of the English colonies had been based on freedom of religion. Religious leaders had led the fight against alcohol. They had pushed for the 18th Amendment. In the 1920s, they called for an end to crime. It was as much a danger as alcohol, they said. Many religious leaders did not like the new ideas for women. They wanted women to follow **traditional** ideas. Women should marry and have families. Mothers should not work. This would destroy families they said. And family life was a strong part of American life.

Some religions followed fundamentalist ideas. These ideas are based on a strong belief in the Bible. Some ideas in the U.S. seemed to go against the Bible, fundamentalists said. Fundamentalists would not follow these ideas. Fundamentalist leaders did not like some of the ideas taught in schools. They had strong feelings against Charles Darwin's Theory of Evolution. His idea was that people had evolved, or developed, from apelike creatures. This went against the ideas found in the Bible. Fundamentalists brought cases against teachers who talked about evolution. They often won these cases in the 1920s.

68.4 What ideas were followed by the Ku Klux Klan?

The Ku Klux Klan had started up again in the 1910s. Like many Americans, its members worried about race, crime, and other "problems." However, the Klan took matters into its own hands. They took on the job of carrying out the law. A member might accuse someone of a crime. The Klan would visit the person at night. It might start by burning a cross in the person's yard as a warning. Later, the KKK might beat the person or even kill him.

All the Klan's members were Protestants. People in the Klan did not like Catholics and Jews any more than African Americans. Many Catholics and Jews were immigrants. Some of their ideas were not the traditional ones practiced in the United States. Immigrants became a chief target of the Klan.

▼ The photograph below shows the Ku Klux Klan as they march down Pennsylvania Avenue in Washington, D.C., in 1928.

African Americans had the most to fear from the Klan. The Klan was strongest in the South. However, it had groups in all parts of the country. It had only 16 members when it began in 1916. By 1922, there were 400,000 members. By 1924, over four million were members. The Klan worked to keep African Americans especially from having equal rights. Many African Americans were hanged by the Klan. Over 400 African Americans were lynched, or hanged, in the Klan's first seven years.

African Americans wanted protection from the Klan. The National Association for the Advancement of Colored People (NAACP) pushed for new laws. They wanted the government to protect African Americans' lives and rights. Fighting often broke out. Race riots sometimes broke out.

Many cities were hit by riots in 1919. All this fighting hurt the Klan. The leader of the Klan was called the "Grand Dragon." He was David C. Stephenson. He went to jail on murder charges in 1925. Many Klan members were shocked. They had not wanted fighting and murder. Other Americans were also shocked by these happenings. New laws were passed. Only 9,000 members were left in the Klan by 1930.

68.5 Why did problems in Russia lead to new U.S. immigration laws?

Russia's government fell during World War I. At first, people hoped a democratic government would be set up. However, the Bolsheviks took over and formed the Communist Party. It was led by V. I. Lenin. Communists do not believe in private property. The government owns everything. The people work for the government. It gives them the things it feels they need. Everyone is supposed to be equal under Communist rule.

However, this was not the case in Russia. The party was run by the Central Committee. Lenin ran the Central Committee.

His word was law. People who did not agree were arrested. Some were sent to jail. Others were killed. Joseph Stalin took over after Lenin died. His rule was even harder. Millions were sent to camps. Most of them died.

One Communist idea frightened other countries. Communists hoped to bring down all the world's governments. They wanted their ideas in place. Many revolutions did break out. Many governments cracked down on Communists. They were arrested. They were not always Russians. Many were sent to Russia, though. In 1919 this scare came to the United States. Mail bombs were sent to 36 people. Some worked in state government. Others worked in the federal government. One was sent to the Chief Justice of the Supreme Court. Only one bomb went off. One person was hurt. The Communists were blamed.

The U.S. government moved against the Communists. More bombs had been sent in the mail. One went to the home of A. Mitchell Palmer. It blew up inside his home. A person on the sidewalk was killed. Palmer was the U.S. Attorney General. He asked Congress for money. With the money, he opened a new office in the Justice Department. It arrested Communists and other people who wanted to bring down the government. Over 6,000 people were arrested. Palmer tried to **deport** them. Many had been born in the United States. They could not be deported. Often, Palmer had no proof against these people. They were set free. Congress decided to stop Communists from entering the country. It set limits on the number of immigrants. Few people from Communist countries were now allowed into the United States.

Connections

▲ Carry Nation

Women often led the fight against alcohol. One of these leaders was Carry Nation. Her first husband died of alcoholism. She joined the Women's Christian Temperance Union (WCTU). This group pushed for Prohibition. Nation took the fight from words to blows. She lived in Kansas. Kansas had Prohibition in 1900. She heard a voice tell her to smash up bars. She gathered a load of rocks. She threw the rocks inside three illegal bars in Kiowa, Kansas. The bars were almost destroyed. Soon, Nation gave up the use of rocks. She used a hatchet instead. News of her fight spread across the country. Other women followed her lead. Many people were shocked. But the news about alcoholism spread. Prohibition became a national idea when the 18th Amendment was passed. However, Carry Nation would be shocked today. The 18th Amendment was ended in 1933. Today, there are legal bars in Nation's home town of Medicine Lodge, Kansas.

★★☆ CHAPTER REVIEW

Critical Thinking

Write your answers on a sheet of paper, or discuss in class.

Classifying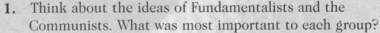

1. Think about the ideas of Fundamentalists and the Communists. What was most important to each group?

Identifying Main Idea

2. Why were the problems of the 1920s so frightening to some people?

Cooperative Learning

LEARNING STYLE *Reading*

3. Work with a partner or group. Look through the chapter. Note the questions. What do they tell you about the chapter? Look at the chart and any pictures. What do you think you will be reading about? Read the vocabulary words. Talk about their meanings.

Write About It

Writing Portfolio

4. Make a list of the groups you read about. Who were the people in these groups? Write a sentence telling about the people in each group. Find out about these groups. What were their ideas? Write a sentence describing each idea. Use your sentences to write a paragraph about each group. Put your paragraphs together to make a report. Give your paper a name.

Quiz

Number a piece of paper from 1-10. Write a, b, c, and d beside these numbers. Read the following sentence parts. Four answers follow each one. Choose the answer that best completes the sentence. On your paper, circle the letter that matches the letter of your answer. Be sure you mark your answer beside the correct number.

1. **The United States entered World War I because Germany . . .**
   a. used submarines to sink American merchant ships.
   b. attacked Puerto Rico, which was owned by the United States.
   c. forced Russia into forming a Communist government.
   d. none of the above

2. **World War I ended because . . .**
   a. the United States and its resources entered the war.
   b. Russia's new Communist government signed peace terms with Germany.
   c. Germany, its people, and its resources were worn out by the war.
   d. all of the above

3. **The U.S. Senate would not approve the Treaty of Versailles because . . .**
   a. they felt it did not punish Germany.
   b. they did not like the part about the League of Nations.
   c. they wanted one treaty with all the Central Powers, not just one with Germany.
   d. none of the above

4. **Setting treaties with Germany and the Central Powers was carried out by . . .**
   a. President Woodrow Wilson.
   b. the U.S. Senate.
   c. the House of Representatives.
   d. the Secretary of State.

5. **Harding became President because . . .**
   a. Americans wanted a return to normalcy.
   b. Americans wanted a candidate who would not make great changes.
   c. Americans, both men and women, voted together for the first time.
   d. all of the above

6. **Even though wages dropped, people were happy in the 1920s because . . .**
   a. most people had jobs.
   b. prices were lower.
   c. many people had money to invest in stocks.
   d. all of the above

7. **New ideas changed styles for . . .**
   a. women.
   b. art.
   c. music.
   d. all of the above

8. **America's different industries were NOT affected by . . .**
   a. assembly lines.
   b. radio advertising.
   c. voting rights for women.
   d. the invention of movies.

9. **Violence was often caused by all of the following EXCEPT . . .**
   a. farmers protesting prices.
   b. gangs bootlegging whiskey.
   c. Ku Klux Klan members taking the law into their own hands.
   d. people who sent mail bombs as a way of overthrowing the government.

10. **Low prices during the 1920s caused hard times for . . .**
   a. workers.
   b. business owners.
   c. farmers.
   d. small businesses.

RECOGNIZING DETAILS

Add numbers 11–15 to your paper. Read the two lists below. People are listed on the left. What each person might say is listed on the right. Match the people with the things that they may have said. Write your answers on your paper.

11. Bootlegger
12. Pacifist
13. Fundamentalist
14. Communist
15. Klan member

a. I strongly support the ideas in the Bible.
b. I do not believe in private property.
c. I support only the rights of white people in the United States.
d. I smuggle alcohol into the United States during Prohibition.
e. I do not believe that war is the answer to any problem.

Writing Portfolio

Look over the things you wrote for these chapters. Choose one that you like the best. Add to your writing. For example, you made a chart about decisions made during World War I. Make a companion chart about the decisions made in the United States during the 1920s. Trade papers with a study partner. Check each other's work. Make a clean, neat copy. Put it in your portfolio.

Alternative Assessment

You may wish to work with a partner. Make a list of things that happened in the United States. Work with the years from 1917 to 1930. Put these events in order. List the year in which each happened. Use these events to make a timeline. Share your timeline with the class.

COOPERATIVE PROJECT: HISTORY CONCENTRATION GAME

LEARNING STYLE
Visual Tactile

Work with a partner or group. List people and groups from this unit. Think of sentences that tell about these people and groups. Write each name on a 3 x 5 index card. Write each sentence on other cards. Use a pencil to number the backs of these cards. Place the cards in rows on a table or desk. Make sure that only the numbers show. Pick someone to start the game. Each player must choose two cards to turn over. The player must match a name with the correct sentence. If a match is made, the player earns five points. Leave the cards turned up. If a match is not made, turn the cards back over. Continue playing until all the cards have been matched. To play another game, carefully erase the pencil numbers. Shuffle the cards. Write new pencil numbers on the backs.

Unit 8

POLITICS

1922
Mussolini and the Fascists took over Italy.

1932
President Franklin Roosevelt increased the federal government's power as a way of fighting the Great Depression.

1934
Hitler and the Fascists took over Germany.

CE   1920   1930   1935

CULTURE

1929
The Great Depression reached the United States.

1931
Drought caused the Dust Bowl, and many farmers lost their land.

1933
Fourteen million Americans had no jobs.

1935
Philadelphia played Cincinnati in the first nighttime baseball game. The Phillies beat the Reds by a score of 2-1.

1936
Benny Goodman, a white jazz clarinet player, formed the first great integrated jazz band. African Americans Teddy Wilson (piano) and Lionel Hampton (vibraphone) became stars in the band.

The Great Depression and World War II 1929-1945

> "You must do the thing you think you cannot do."
>
> — **First Lady Eleanor Roosevelt**, *from her book* You Learn by Living

Work can be hard and difficult, especially the work of solving problems. The 1930s and 1940s brought great and terrible events. Eleanor Roosevelt knew that people can achieve things that seem impossible. How did suffering become a world problem in these years? Why?

1939
Germany and the Soviet Union divided Poland. Britain and France declared war on Germany.

1941
France fell to Germany. The U.S.A. joined World War II after the Japanese attack at Pearl Harbor.

1943
The Allies took islands close enough to begin regular bombing raids on Japan.

1944
The Allies invaded France.

1945
Germany surrendered on May 8.

Atomic bombs were dropped on Hiroshima and Nagasaki, forcing Japan to surrender on August 12.

The United Nations was formed on June 26.

1940

1945

1939
The Grapes of Wrath by John Steinbeck told about the hardships of an Oklahoma family who lost their farm during the Dust Bowl.

1945
The Detroit Tigers won the World Series. It was the last World Series to feature replacement players for those who were fighting in the war.

1947
Scientists at Bell Telephone Laboratories made the first transistors. These made electronic devices portable.

Chapter 69

The Crash

Read about the United States economy during the 1920s. How did prices and the stock market affect people's lives? Why?

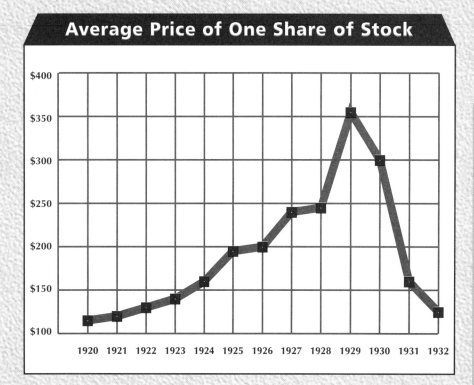

Average Price of One Share of Stock

Key *Vocabulary*

stock market (stahk • MAR kuht) a place where shares in a company are bought and sold

interest (IN truhst) 1. the fee paid by banks for money they keep as people's savings 2. the fee charged for lending money to someone

Reteaching Vocabulary

profit (PRAHF uht) the money left over after all costs have been paid

depression (di PRESH uhn) a time when the economy slows and people are put out of work

---

GRAPH ANALYSIS	
★ **Ask**	What does this graph show?
★ **Acquire**	How did the price of a share of stock change from 1920 to 1932?
★ **Organize**	List the years in which shares increased in price. List the years in which they decreased.
★ **Analyze**	When were stock prices the lowest?
★ **Answer**	Why do you think times were so bad in 1932 even though stocks were not at an all-time low?

Decoding Tip: Note that *ck* in **stock** stands for one sound, /k/, and that *ss* stands for /sh/ in **depression**.

ay	cake	ah	fall, cot	air	air
ee	tree	i	sit	oh	cold
or	cord	oy	toy	uh	above, hundred
a	ask	ar	hard	oo	book
e	yet	eye	nice	uhr	liar, fir, further, color
ow	cow	ooh	boot, true	yoo	you, few, cube

69.1 How did the booming economy help Herbert Hoover become President?

▲ President Herbert Hoover

Most Americans were happy with life under the Republicans during the 1920s. Times had been good for most people. Farmers had problems with low crop prices. However, this kept food prices low. Families liked the bargains in stores. There were new goods for people to buy. Radios, cars, refrigerators, and other goods made life easier.

Herbert Hoover promised to follow Republican ideas. Government would do what it could to help businesses. Businesses would make sure that the country kept making money. The voters wanted these ideas to continue. Hoover had no trouble winning the White House in 1928.

69.2 Why were people so eager to buy stocks in the 1920s?

Becoming rich was a chief goal of many people during the 1920s. There was a big gap in the way some Americans lived. Some people were very rich. Others were very poor. The middle class fell between these two groups. Very rich people were often business owners. Americans were saving money in the 1920s. Some used this money to become business owners.

Other Americans bought shares in companies. Shares in businesses were sold on the **stock market**. People earned money by owning shares. When a business made **profits**, it was divided among the owners. The prices of shares went up all during the 1920s. Many people learned to play the stock market. They would buy stocks. They did not wait for the company profits to be paid. The stocks would be held until their prices went up. Then the people would sell the shares and make a profit. Sometimes, this earned more money than waiting for profits to be divided up. It was often more than could be earned in interest from banks.

69.3 What happened to sales and building by 1927?

Business owners noticed something bad was happening late in the 1920s. They were making more goods than ever. Many people had bought cars, radios, and other factory goods. By 1927, however, most people who could afford these things had already bought them. Sales of these goods were dropping across the country. Many people had also bought land and homes cheaply. They sold these to make profits. Sales in land and homes were dropping now, too. Fewer new homes were being built. Florida's land prices had gone sky high during the early 1920s. Many people entered the market. Some became very rich. In 1927 land prices started dropping, too.

Many Americans were worried about the country in 1927. Business leaders pointed to dropping sales. They said that factories were making goods faster than Americans could afford to buy them. These leaders saw that factories would have to slow down. They would not need as many workers. People would lose their jobs. Businesses would not be making as much money. There would be less profit to divide among owners. The economy would probably slow down. Some people saw that bad times were ahead. President Calvin Coolidge shared this idea. He could think of no way to keep this from happening. He decided not to run for President in 1928.

69.4 Why did the stock market crash in 1929?

Most people were playing the stock market in risky ways. They made down payments on their stocks. The rest of the price was borrowed from the stock broker. A stock broker is a person who sells stocks. Usually, stock brokers would borrow this money from banks. They would pay **interest** to the banks. Then they would charge higher interest rates to their buyers. The buyers often did not make payments on these loans. They would sell the stock before the first payment was due. The

▲ The photograph above shows people gathering in front of the Treasury Building in New York City during the stock market crash of 1929.

broker would keep what was owed, including any interest. The buyer would keep the rest of the profit.

However, problems could come up. A bank might call in a loan. The broker would have to pay off this loan immediately. Then the broker would have to call the owner. If the owner could not pay, then the stock would be sold. It might even be taken by the bank. Many times, there was no money left for the owner. The owner would lose the profit. The money used as a down payment would also be lost. But this did not happen often in the 1920s.

Things changed on the stock market in 1929. Stock prices went up and up. Most of these prices were too high. The companies simply were not worth that much money. After all, their sales were dropping. They were making less money.

By fall, people began noticing the drop in sales. They worried that stock prices might drop. They began selling record numbers of shares. This pushed stock prices down. Prices dropped about $30 per share on Thursday, October 24. Business leaders spent huge sums of money buying stocks that afternoon.

Prices shot back up. President Hoover said the worst was over. However, the plan did not work. On Tuesday, October 29, stock prices collapsed. Banks called in their loans. Brokers called the owners. No one could pay the debts on stock sales. In the next few years, thousands of people went broke. Terrible times hit the country. Companies shut down. Hundreds of banks went out of business. It was the start of the Great **Depression**.

P l a n

- Taxes on the rich were cut. The rich would build more factories. More people would be put to work.

- Fewer loans were made to other countries.

- Tariffs were raised so foreign companies would not take sales away from American businesses.

- Laws against trusts and monopolies were not enforced.

How Well Did the Government's Ideas Work?

R e s u l t

- The rich put more money into the stock market and into land deals. Few new jobs were created.

- These countries could not buy as many American goods.

- (a) American businesses had no competition. They could keep their prices high. (b) Trade with other countries dropped.

- Trusts and monopolies could charge any price they wanted. People could not pay these prices. Sales dropped.

69.5 How did the federal government help slow down the economy?

Republican Presidents and Congresses had worked for businesses throughout the 1920s. They tried to help American businesses. They cut taxes on the rich. They loaned less money to other countries. They set up high tariffs to keep out foreign goods. They did not carry out the laws against trusts and monopolies. These ideas did help businesses for a while. However, they hurt the country in the long run. These ideas put more money into the stock market. They also kept prices high so people were not able to buy as many goods. Trade with other countries dropped off, too.

All this kept the economy from growing. As the economy dropped, businesses shut down and workers lost their jobs. In 1929, the country's businesses and workers earned almost $88 billion. By 1933, this had dropped to about $40 billion. Some people said that helping businesses had not been good for the country. They began calling for government to help the people instead.

The Dust Bowl

Even nature seemed to turn bad during the 1930s. The Great Plains was a farming area. Most of this land was turned into ranches and farms after the Civil War. Many of the ranches were huge. However, the farms were small. By the 1910s and the 1920s, new farm machines had been invented. Each farmer could now handle more land. Each could grow more crops and make more money. Much of the Plains was plowed up. Then in 1931, the rains stopped. This drought lasted for about 10 years.

The drought dried out much of the Great Plains. Worse times came when the winds blew. The wind picked up the soil and blew it away. The sky filled with great clouds of this dust. It seeped into every crack. Homes filled with dust. Dust covered food inside refrigerators. The affected states were known as the "Dust Bowl." Crops could not be grown. Even the grass and trees died. Farmers could not pay back their loans. Banks took over their land. Many of the people moved away. Most went to the West Coast. They looked for jobs. However, the Great Depression made this very difficult. The drought ended in 1940. By then, the population of the Dust Bowl states had dropped by one-third.

▲ A farm family during the Dust Bowl in Oklahoma

 ## CHAPTER REVIEW

 Identifying Sequence

 Identifying Main Idea

 **LEARNING STYLE** *Visual*

Writing Portfolio

Critical Thinking

Write your answers on a sheet of paper, or discuss in class.

1. What events helped cause the Great Depression?

2. Why did the Depression cause a radical change in people's ideas?

Cooperative Learning

3. Work with a partner or group. Choose an event, such as the Dust Bowl or the stock market crash. Draw what might have happened during this event. Add your picture to the others done by the class. Hang the pictures on a wall to make a mural. Think of a title. Cut out letters for the title. Put them on the wall above the mural.

Write About It

4. Choose one of the states in the Dust Bowl. Find out about this state. What happened there during the Dust Bowl? How were the people affected? How did they try to stop the effect of the wind? Use the facts you find to write a paragraph or two about this time. Share your writing with the class.

Chapter 70

The Great Depression

Read about the effect of the economy's crash. How did people's lives change during the 1930s? Why?

Changes from 1920 to 1933

Item	Drop	Increase	Amount
Profits paid on stocks	x		57%
Banks that had to close		x	769%
Wages for factory workers	x		60%
Wages for other workers	x		40%
People who had no jobs		x	1,750%

Key *Vocabulary*

homeless (HOHM luhs) having no place to live

auction (AHK shuhn) a sale in which people bid against each other until a price is reached that only one person is willing to pay

unemployment (uhn im PLOY muhnt) the state of having no job

Reteaching Vocabulary

radical (RAD i kuhl) being in support of extreme measures or changes

veteran (VET uh ruhn) a person who has served in the armed forces.

CHART ANALYSIS

★ **Ask**   *What does this chart show?*

★ **Organize** *What parts of the economy increased? What parts of the economy went down?*

★ **Answer**   *How do you think people felt as these changes happened?*

Decoding Tip: Note that the vowels au stand for the sound /ah/ in **auction**.

ay	cake	ah	fall, cot	air	air
ee	tree	i	sit	oh	cold
or	cord	oy	toy	uh	above, hundred
a	ask	ar	hard	oo	book
e	yet	eye	nice	uhr	liar, fir, further, color
ow	cow	ooh	boot, true	yoo	you, few, cube

70.1 How did the crash affect workers and their lives?

After the crash, businesses tried to keep going. They promised President Hoover that they would not cut wages. Many kept this promise. However, some had to cut the number of hours each person worked.

Things did not get better. In fact, they became worse. United States Steel had to cut wages in October 1931. Workers were now paid ten percent less. Many other companies followed this lead.

Soon, even wage cuts were not enough to keep the companies open. Almost every American company let workers go. Many were able to stay open. However, thousands of companies closed. In 1931, about 800,000 people did not have jobs. By 1933, that number was 14 million. The hard times of the 1930s became known as the "Great Depression."

▼ The photograph below shows the unemployed lining up outside a Depression soup kitchen in 1931.

Life became very hard for many Americans. Things like cars, refrigerators, and homes had been bought with loans. Now, many people did not have jobs. They could not pay back these loans. They lost everything they owned. They had to live on the streets. Soon, breadlines were formed in cities across the country. Private groups handed out food to **homeless** people. Sometimes, they opened soup kitchens for the needy.

By 1931, over one million Americans were homeless. Homeless people got by on free meals from soup kitchens. They built shacks in parks or on empty land outside cities and towns. These areas were often called "shantytowns." Crime went up, too. Some people stole the things they needed. Often, the police were sent to tear down the shantytowns. The people were driven away. But this did not last. Soon, more homeless people arrived.

70.2   Why were banks hit so hard by the crash?

Banks lost money on the loans they had made. The stock market crashed on October 29, 1929. Few people could pay back the loans they had used in buying stocks. Banks took over these stocks. However, stock prices had dropped. Often, the stocks could not bring enough money to earn back the

▶ Police break up the Shanty towns of the Bonus Marchers during the Depression in Washington, D.C..

banks' money. Many times, the stocks were for companies that had closed. These stocks could not be sold at all. Many banks went out of business, too.

As the Great Depression grew worse, more banks failed. People had borrowed money for cars, homes, and farms. Now these people had no jobs. They could not pay back their loans. Banks took these goods from the people. Once again, the goods could not be sold for enough money to pay off the loans. More and more banks began to fail each year. Over 500 banks closed in October 1931 alone.

Some Americans began working against banks. They were angry that banks were not helping them. They felt that banks should give people a break. As things became better, people could pay back their loans. The banks would get their money back. People could keep their homes. Farmers were the strongest supporters of this plan. But most banks did not share this idea. They needed money to pay their bills, too. Sometimes, people banded together. They would go to bank **auctions**. Real buyers would be driven away. No one would bid for the goods. The bank would make no money. At other auctions, people would bid for the goods. However, they would only bid a few cents. Later, the people would give these things back to their owners. These actions caused some banks to go out of business.

70.3   How did President Hoover deal with the Depression?

President Hoover and business leaders believed their ideas would turn the country around. These ideas had brought the 1920s boom, they said. The government had no business interfering in people's lives. The crash was a terrible problem. However, they felt the economy was just straightening itself out. Things would soon get better. Badly run businesses would close. Well-run businesses would be stronger than before.

Hoover even said that good times were near. To help Americans, Hoover set up the President's Committee on **Unemployment** Relief. Over 3,000 offices opened across the country. None of these offices was run by the government. Private individuals and companies pitched in to help the homeless.

As times became worse, President Hoover changed his ideas. People needed help. However, Hoover was afraid that giving people direct payments would only hurt Americans. They would come to depend on the government. They would not want to work for their livings. Hoover decided that he would help businesses. This help would work its way down to the people.

As businesses improved, more people would be put back to work. Hoover set up the Reconstruction Finance Corporation (RFC). It would make loans to businesses. They would build back up. They would hire more workers. These workers would buy more goods. More workers would be needed to make these goods. Then even more goods would need to be made.

Hoover's plan for business failed. Businesses did borrow money from the government. Most of the money went to the country's largest companies. Small businesses had a hard time getting these loans. Most big companies did not use this money to build up business. They did not hire new workers. The government charged less interest than banks. Big companies used government loans to pay off bank loans. The companies saved money this way. Very little of the money reached the workers of the United States.

▲ President Herbert C. Hoover

70.4 How did the Great Depression affect President Hoover?

Many Americans turned against President Hoover and his ideas. They were suffering. They wanted direct help from the government. Most felt that he only cared about businesses and their owners. Hoover himself saw that his ideas were not working as he hoped. Soon, he set up new programs. The government loaned money to cities and states. They used the money to build things like roads and bridges. This did create new jobs.

However, millions of people still needed work. President Hoover set up the first law to give direct payments to the unemployed. He felt that the states could handle this work better than the federal government. Over $30 million was loaned to the states. They set up ways of handing out money to people who had no jobs. As quickly as Hoover worked, things continued to get worse. Soon people were blaming the Depression on President Hoover. Shantytowns were called "Hoovervilles." Newspapers were called "Hoover blankets."

The country began calling for new ideas and a new leader. Business seemed to be out of control. It had created good times in the 1920s. But in the 1930s most business people did not seem to know how to keep things going. So many people were unemployed and homeless that they could not help themselves.

A new idea began to spread. Government had always tried to stay out of people's lives. To many, this idea seemed to have failed. Now it was time, they said, for government to step in. Each state and territory had its own problems. Their governments were struggling, too. Many people felt that problems had to be handled by the federal government. Only it was large enough and strong enough to turn the country around, they said. Many of the old ideas came from the Republicans. Republican Presidents and Congresses had run the country through the 1920s. People began looking to the Democrats to carry out these **radical** new ideas.

The Bonus Army

In 1932 veterans marched on Washington, D.C. They had no jobs and wanted their bonus payments from the government. Congress had set up these payments in 1925. The payments would not be made until 1945. Each veteran of World War I would receive extra money. One dollar and twenty-five cents would be paid for each day a veteran had served in Europe. Each veteran would receive one dollar for each day he had served in the United States. Now, the Depression was raging. The veterans wanted the payments to be made in 1932. This "Bonus Army" went to Washington to push Congress into making the payments. The House of Representatives passed a law to go ahead and make the payments. Nothing could be paid until the Senate passed the law, too.

As many as 20,000 veterans and their families were living in shantytowns around Washington in the summer of 1932. The vote on the bonus payments came up in the Senate on June 17. It failed by a vote of 62 to 18. Congress set up a fund of $100,000. This would pay for the Bonus Army to go home. Few left Washington. Instead, they began marching through the city each day. They marched past the White House and the Capital.

City leaders decided to clear the Bonus Army out of Washington. The police were sent in. Shooting broke out. Two marchers were killed. President Hoover sent the Army to close down the camps. The effort was led by men who would play important parts in World War II. General Douglas MacArthur was in charge. Major George S. Patton led a cavalry group. Major Dwight D. Eisenhower worked with the police. The Army and police closed ranks. They marched against the camps. The Bonus Army had no choice. It had to back away. Other troops fired tear gas. People began running from the Army. MacArthur pushed the Bonus Army into Maryland. They were not allowed back into Washington, D.C.

▲ General Douglas MacArthur

★★☆ CHAPTER REVIEW

Critical Thinking

Write your answers on a sheet of paper, or discuss in class.

1. How did the Great Depression make some people lose faith in old ideas about business and government?

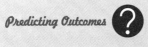

2. Why were the Democrats willing to take on the radical idea of giving direct help to the people?

Cooperative Learning

3. Work with a partner or group. Think about the Great Depression. Take the part of a rich person, an average person with a job, or a homeless person. What might this person believe? Tell your partner about your life and ideas.

Write About It

4. Make an outline of this chapter. Turn each section question into a sentence. Use Roman numerals to put the sentences in order. Write sentences that tell about each section. Use capital letters A, B, C, and so on to list them in order under the correct section heads. Trade papers with a partner and check each other's work.

Chapter 71

The New Deal

Read about the effect President Franklin Roosevelt had on the country. How did he change people's ideas about government? Why?

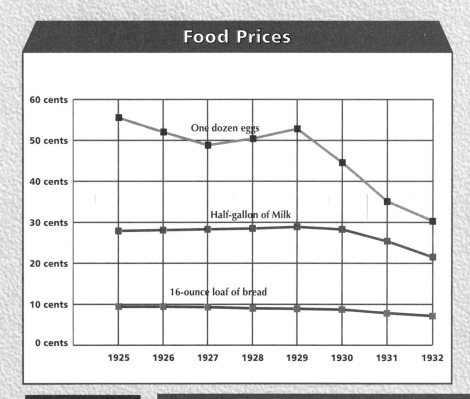

Food Prices

One dozen eggs

Half-gallon of Milk

16-ounce loaf of bread

60 cents
50 cents
40 cents
30 cents
20 cents
10 cents
0 cents

1925 1926 1927 1928 1929 1930 1931 1932

GRAPH ANALYSIS

★ **Ask** — What does this graph show?

★ **Organize** — Make a list of the years in which prices went down. List the years in which prices went up. List the years in which some prices went up and some went down.

★ **Analyze** — What happened to prices after the Great Depression began in 1930?

★ **Answer** — How do you think farmers and unemployed workers felt about the low prices in 1930?

Decoding Tip: Note that *a* followed by a consonant and an *e* stands for the sound /ay/ in **regulate**.

ay	cake	ah	fall, cot	air	air
ee	tree	i	sit	oh	cold
or	cord	oy	toy	uh	above, hundred
a	ask	ar	hard	oo	book
e	yet	eye	nice	uhr	liar, fir, further, color
ow	cow	ooh	boot, true	yoo	you, few, cube

71.1 Why did President Hoover lose the White House in 1932?

Republican ideas cost Herbert Hoover a second term in the White House. The party and its President believed in their ideas. However, few Americans still liked Hoover. They felt that Hoover could not end the Great Depression.

The people turned to the Democrats. This party promised new ideas and an end to hard times. The party picked Franklin Delano Roosevelt for the race. He had been Assistant Secretary of the Navy. He had also been governor of New York. He had led New York's government to help the people directly. This seemed to be helping. The people believed that Hoover's ideas of helping business were failing. Hoover won only five states.

People had great hopes for Roosevelt as the new President. He called for a new kind of plan for government. Roosevelt said that all Americans would get a new deal from Washington. His whole plan became known as the "New Deal." He sent 15 bills to Congress. All of them were passed in 100 days. Today, people look at each President's first 100 days. They hope that this will give them an idea of what the President will be able to do for the country.

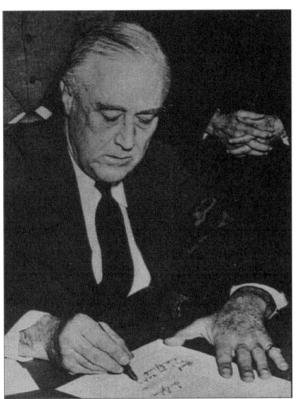

▲ President Franklin D. Roosevelt

71.2 What idea was the basis of Roosevelt's plans?

Roosevelt decided to follow the ideas of John Maynard Keynes. Keynes said that the **economy** was affected by three things. Businesses make money by producing goods and services. People earn money by working for businesses. Government takes money out of the economy. It collects this money as taxes. However, the government also puts money back into the economy. It pays its workers. They buy goods and services, too. Government uses the rest of the money to buy the goods and services it needs.

Keynes also explained the Great Depression. Businesses were not spending enough money. They were earning profits and not building up their companies. By keeping wages low, they were keeping the people from buying as many goods and services. The Depression had begun. Now, it was even more difficult for either businesses or people to restart the economy. That left only government to help. Roosevelt believed in Keynes' ideas. He would push government to spend money. This would turn the economy around, he said.

71.3 Why was Roosevelt worried about the country's banks?

Many banks had closed since the Depression had started. When the banks closed, people lost the money they had on deposit. By 1932, there was a general rush on banks. People were taking out their money. In February 1933, almost 2 billion dollars was removed from banks. States began calling bank holidays. The banks were closed until calm returned. Roosevelt wanted banks to succeed. He took action on March 4, his first day as President. Banks were closed from March 6 through March 9. New laws were passed. When banks opened again, they would be **regulated** by the government.

Banks did get better. Three-fourths of the banks did reopen. The others went out of business. The new laws made banks pay special taxes. This money paid for the work government did for banks. It paid for the work of armored cars. It gave banks insurance. Now, if a bank closed, the people would get back their money. A limit of $5,000 for each person was set.

People took Roosevelt's word that banks would now be safe. They began depositing their money again. Roosevelt also called for the government to cut some of its spending.

Government workers took pay cuts. This helped Roosevelt balance the government's **budget**. It was not spending more than it took in as taxes. This kept the government from borrowing money from banks. Instead, this money could be loaned so businesses could build up. Loans could be made so people could buy cars and other goods.

71.4   How did Roosevelt's ideas help the country?

Roosevelt set up unemployment payments and other plans to help the people. People without jobs could get weekly sums from the government. However, Roosevelt did not want people to depend on the government. They should earn their money. He asked Congress to set up work projects. The government hired many people. They built bridges, roads, public buildings, parks, and many other things. Photographers, artists, and writers were put to work, too. They made a record of what was happening for history. One project involved people who had been enslaved. Many older African Americans had been born under slavery. Over 5,000 African Americans were interviewed about slavery and its effects. Today, this record helps writers and historians understand what slavery was really like.

▼ Some small businesses did well even during the Depression, as shown below in this refreshment stand in 1932.

Businesses gained from these projects, too. The government had to buy goods for these projects. It bought steel, cement, bricks, and paper. All these goods were bought from businesses. The workers were also buying food, clothes, and other goods. Their wages were paid to stores and to businesses. This helped the economy to grow. Roosevelt helped unions, too. Millions of people had joined unions since 1929. They hoped unions would be able to help them. Roosevelt and Congress set up new laws. Businesses and unions would have to follow strict rules. Unions gained more power. Companies could not fire workers just for joining a union.

Farmers were helped by the government. They had been growing more food than people could buy. This kept prices low. Growing less food would bring prices up. However, farmers would have less to sell in order to earn money. Roosevelt set up a plan to pay farmers. In order to get this money, they had to agree to cut back. Now they could afford to grow less food. Prices went up. Companies that canned and packaged crops paid a new tax. The money was used to pay farmers. The government also took over many farm loans. It charged lower interest than banks. Farmers faced less risk of losing their lands. This also helped business. Farmers who earned more money could buy new farm machines and more goods for themselves.

▲ Farmers went through changes in the United States in the early 1930s with the help of Roosevelt.

Things did get better for many people. However, some were worried. Was the government becoming too powerful? Did it have too much control over people's lives? Were President Roosevelt's ideas good for the country in the long run?

☆☆☆

Connections

▲ President Franklin Delano Roosevelt giving a speech over the radio

Many banks failed during the Great Depression. By the time President Roosevelt became President, over 10,000 banks had closed. Most people did not get their deposits back. Roosevelt set up new banking laws when he took office in March 1933. During Roosevelt's first year as President, about 60 banks went under. The crisis was over. From this time on, banks would pay special taxes. This money would be used to make sure people would get back their deposits.

Another banking crisis happened in the 1980s. Banks had been making risky loans. Some bankers even broke the law in making loans. From 1981 to 1990, almost 1,200 banks and savings and loans went out of business. Most deposits were insured for up to $100,000. Banks and savings and loans had not paid enough taxes for this kind of coverage. The government still gave back people their covered deposits. This cost the government over $500 billion. It did not have this money on hand. The money was borrowed from banks and by selling bonds. Now, the government pays interest. No one knows how much the crisis will end up costing the federal government.

CHAPTER REVIEW

Critical Thinking

Write your answers on a sheet of paper or discuss in class.

 Making Inferences

1. Why were many people so anxious for Roosevelt to be President?

 Making Predictions

2. How would people feel about Roosevelt if his ideas really worked?

Cooperative Learning

 LEARNING STYLE *Tactile*

3. Work with a partner or group. Choose one of Roosevelt's programs. What is it about? How is it supposed to help people? Make a poster about this program. Share your poster with the class.

Write About It

 Writing Portfolio

4. Most of Roosevelt's programs were known by initials. For example, the government set up insurance for bank deposits. The group that handles this is the FDIC. The letters stand for "Federal Deposit Insurance Corporation." Find out the names of other programs. Make a chart about these programs. Tell what each does. Give its name. Include the initials by which each was known. Tell if the program is still working.

Chapter 72

A Social Experiment

Read about the conflicts over President Roosevelt's ideas. How did the government affect people's lives? Why?

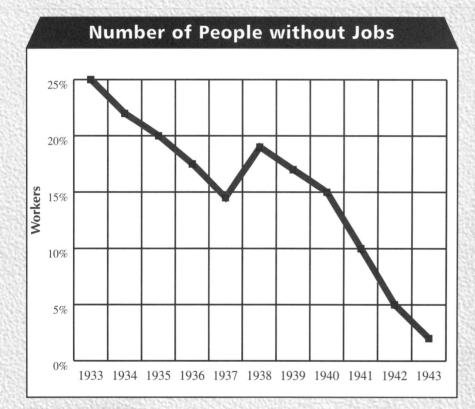

Number of People without Jobs

(Y-axis: Workers — 0%, 5%, 10%, 15%, 20%, 25%)
(X-axis: 1933, 1934, 1935, 1936, 1937, 1938, 1939, 1940, 1941, 1942, 1943)

Key *Vocabulary*

conservative (kuhn SUHR vuht iv) a person who wants to keep things as they are or have been

dictator (DIK tayt uhr) a person who has total rule over a country

capitalism (KAP uht uhl izm) a system in which people and companies decide what to buy and what to sell

mandate (MAN dayt) the voters' approval of a candidate's ideas and plans

society (suh SEYE uht ee) all the people of a country, including their ideas, relationships, and problems

GRAPH ANALYSIS

★ **Ask** *What does this graph show?*

★ **Organize** *Make a list of the years in which the percentage of people without jobs went down from the year before.*

★ **Analyze** *What happened to unemployment after Franklin Roosevelt became President?*

★ **Answer** *How well did Roosevelt's ideas seem to work?*

Decoding Tip: Note that *c* can stand for /k/, as in **conservative**, **dictator**, and **capitalism**. It can also stand for /s/, as in **society**.

ay	cake	ah	fall, cot	air	air
ee	tree	i	sit	oh	cold
or	cord	oy	toy	uh	above, hundred
a	ask	ar	hard	oo	book
e	yet	eye	nice	uhr	liar, fir, further, color
ow	cow	ooh	boot, true	yoo	you, few, cube

72.1 Why did some Americans work against Roosevelt and the New Deal?

Roosevelt's ideas were changing the shape of American government. Many people were afraid these changes would end up hurting the people and the country. Most of these people were **conservatives**. They wanted to conserve, or save, the government as it had been. Conservatives could be found in all groups. They were Republicans, Democrats, rich people, poor people, men, and women. Some did not want the government to hand out money. They did not like some of the work projects. They felt that some projects were not necessary. Roosevelt was just making work so people could get government money. Charity was the job of the people, not the government, these people said. Others were afraid that Roosevelt was taking too much power as President. They feared he would become a **dictator**. Many business leaders did not like Roosevelt's plans. He had raised taxes on rich people and big businesses. They believed that government should

▼ President Franklin D. Roosevelt

help businesses. Businesses would then create new jobs, they said. The country and its economy would grow.

People with opposite ideas also did not like Roosevelt's New Deal. Some were Communists. They believed the Depression showed that **capitalism** was wrong. They wanted things left alone in order to bring down the government. Then a Communist government like the one in Russia could be set up. Other people on the left wanted Roosevelt to keep the rich out of government. They felt that the rich were too powerful. These special interests were getting favors from government. This was causing the Depression and hurting the country, they said.

Huey Long changed the idea of taxing the rich. He was a U.S. Senator from Louisiana. He wanted the government to take money from the rich. It would be shared among all the people. He called for government to put heavy taxes on the rich. The money would be given to the poor. Each family would get $5,000 each year. Since everyone would have money, they could always buy food and other goods. Factories could keep working.

Senator Long was very popular. Some thought he might become President in the 1936 election. Long died in 1935. The Republicans chose Alf Landon for the race. However, Roosevelt and his ideas were much more popular. The President won over 60% of the votes. In the Electoral College, he won 46 of the 48 states.

72.2   How did the Supreme Court rule on Roosevelt's new laws?

The Supreme Court struck down several of the New Deal programs. Cases against these laws had been brought by businesses. They reached the Supreme Court in 1935. It said these laws went against the ideas in the Constitution. President Roosevelt was very angry. He said that the Justices were not reading the Constitution correctly. He felt that these laws did fit the ideas of the Constitution. Roosevelt believed the Justices were simply following old-fashioned ideas about business and government.

Roosevelt won a **mandate** in the November election of 1936. The country showed that it truly believed in what he was doing. The President decided it was time to change the Supreme Court. The nine Justices could not be fired. Roosevelt asked Congress for a new law in 1937. He wanted there to be 15 Justices. He would choose six new ones. They would be people who followed his ideas. Most people were shocked by this plan. The Constitution had been set up to balance the powers of the three branches. If this law passed, the President would have too much power.

Even though the law failed several times, Roosevelt had a great effect on the Supreme Court. The Supreme Court began to uphold some New Deal programs in 1937. Many of the Justices began to retire. Roosevelt was able to appoint new people to the Court. By 1941, Roosevelt had appointed seven of the Court's nine members. The new members were strong Roosevelt supporters. Most Presidents since Roosevelt have made Supreme Court appointments. Each President has hoped to change the Court so that it will follow his own ideas. However, there are still only nine members. All of them still serve life terms.

72.3 Why were some of Roosevelt's plans called "social experiments"?

Roosevelt decided that government should help **society** with its problems, too. Older Americans needed help. Many were unable to work. They could not earn a living. Some people had physical problems that made work impossible. Roosevelt asked Congress to set up the Social Security program. Workers pay this tax. Their employers must pay the same amount as a tax. This money is used to make monthly payments to people who are retired or have physical problems. When workers retire, they begin receiving the payments, too.

At first African Americans did not support President Roosevelt. Most of them were Republicans. The Republican Party under President Lincoln had ended slavery. Roosevelt did not push for the rights of African Americans. He wanted the support of white Southerners. African Americans actually lost land and became poorer under Roosevelt's first farm programs. Then African Americans found that they could get jobs in Roosevelt's work programs. They began switching their support to Roosevelt and the Democrats. Roosevelt asked for help from African American leaders. They helped him make plans for fighting discrimination.

One of these leaders was Mary McLeod Bethune. She had begun a school in Daytona, Florida. She felt that education was the key African Americans could use in improving their lives. President Roosevelt made her the head of one branch of the National Youth Administration (NYA). This office ran job and school projects for African American children. Even things at the White House changed because of Mrs. Bethune.

▲ Mary McLeod Bethune

Only white reporters had been allowed into the President's press conferences. Mrs. Bethune asked the President to include African American reporters, too. President Roosevelt was quick to agree. He said that Mrs. Bethune was a great woman who only worked for others, not for herself. Since Roosevelt's time, African Americans have usually been strong supporters of the Democratic Party.

Native Americans saw their lives change under President Roosevelt. Before his time, they were pushed to live like white Americans. They had had to give up more and more of their lands. Roosevelt helped set up new laws in 1934. Work projects were set up. Native Americans were hired to complete projects on reservations. Each tribe was given the right to form its own government. This government would handle all the tribe's finances. The law allowed Native Americans to choose the ways in which they would live. It encouraged them to protect their own customs. Almost three-fourths had accepted the laws by 1936.

72.4 Why did Roosevelt turn away from some of his ideas in 1937?

Things went well for the country and its President. The economy was growing. People were going back to work. Roosevelt's ideas seemed to be working very well in 1937. But all of his projects had pushed the government into deficit spending. Many of his advisors suggested that it was time to cut back. The government could balance its budget. It would spend less. Business and workers were doing well. They would not be hurt. Roosevelt agreed. However, the plan failed. The Depression became worse without government spending. Roosevelt asked for more spending than before. Soon, the economy was growing again. Some people even began to say that these ideas would always work. There would never be another Great Depression. Even so, millions still did not have jobs. The Depression did not truly end until the military buildup of World War II.

Roosevelt was so popular that he broke tradition. Every President had followed George Washington's lead. They left the White House after two terms. However, Roosevelt was elected to a third term in 1940. He won a fourth term in 1944. Some people began to worry that he really did want to become a dictator.

▼ Orson Welles

72.5 How did American life change during the Great Depression?

Times were so hard that people looked for things to ease their minds. They found this relief in entertainment. Radio shows became wildly popular. Radios played music and also carried other programs. Radio plays made people laugh, cry, and even become afraid. Orson Welles did a show on Halloween night in 1938. It was *War of the Worlds,* from a novel by Jules Verne. It was done as if radio reporters were covering a real attack by beings from Mars. Some people did not hear the announcer say that it was only a story. People all over the country fled cities in panic. The show made Welles famous. He went to Hollywood and began making movies.

For the People, By the People

▲ Margaret Mitchell

Making movies became one of the country's largest businesses. It cost only 10¢ to see a movie. People could spend time in a theater and forget their troubles. Many of the most popular movies were about people who were rich. People liked seeing that life could be free of cares. Americans copied the clothes and hairstyles of the actors in these movies. Movies changed people's ideas about other kinds of styles as well. Some movies showed how people could overcome their troubles. Shirley Temple was a favorite star. Her most popular movies were about little girls facing hard times. They always had happy endings, though.

Margaret Mitchell wrote the book *Gone with the Wind*. It came out in 1936. It is one of the best-selling books of all time. People loved this story about a young woman who overcame the terrible hardships of the South after the Civil War. If she could make it, they could, too. It became a movie in 1939. It cost $1.00 to see this movie. Even with such a large price, millions of people went to see it. By the late 1930s, movies were more popular than ever. Most people were back to work. Only good times seemed to be ahead.

☆☆☆

Connections

▲ Eleonor Roosevelt

Both President Franklin and Mrs. Eleanor Roosevelt were from a President's family. Theodore Roosevelt was Eleanor's uncle. He was Franklin Roosevelt's cousin. Franklin and Eleanor Roosevelt were cousins, too. Eleanor Roosevelt followed her uncle in supporting Progressive ideas. Her family was rich. She went to finishing school in Europe. She was a debutante in New York society in 1902. However, she took a job that year. She was a social worker in New York City's slums. She met her cousin Franklin for the first time that year. She took him to visit the slums. This helped begin Roosevelt's interest in helping the poor.

Eleanor Roosevelt changed during her years as Franklin Roosevelt's wife. She had stayed at home with her children. Roosevelt and his mother made most decisions. Then, Roosevelt caught polio in 1921. Eleanor Roosevelt nursed him through the sickness. He still lost the use of his legs. Roosevelt wanted to continue in public office. He could not make trips to give speeches. Mrs. Roosevelt had to go in his place. She had always been shy and afraid in public. It took a lot of work, but she soon was doing the job well. She went on traveling after Roosevelt became President. These trips took her to the Dust Bowl and into factories and coal mines. They helped the President know what people were thinking and saying.

The First Lady took stands for people's rights. Marian Anderson was an African American singer. She had been in many operas in Europe. She planned a concert in Washington. However, the building was owned by the Daughters of the American Revolution (DAR). They would not let African Americans into the building. They called the concert off. Mrs. Roosevelt belonged to the DAR. The news forced her to give up her membership. Marian Anderson did give her concert. Thousands, including Mrs. Roosevelt, attended. The concert was given on the steps of the Lincoln Memorial.

 CHAPTER REVIEW

Critical Thinking

Write your answers on a sheet of paper or discuss in class.

Identifying Main Idea

1. Why did Roosevelt and his ideas remain so popular?

Drawing Conclusions

2. What might have happened to Roosevelt and the Democrats if Roosevelt's ideas had failed?

Cooperative Learning

LEARNING STYLE
Verbal

3. Work with a partner or group. Imagine you have been invited to the White House by the Roosevelts. Tell about the people you might have met. What ideas might these people talk about? What things might you see? Share your ideas with the class.

Write About It

Writing Portfolio

4. Find out more about President and Mrs. Roosevelt's work for African Americans and Native Americans. What programs were set up? Which leaders worked with the President? What kinds of work had these people been doing? How successful were the President's programs? Use these facts in a report. Read your report to the class.

Quiz

Number a piece of paper from 1-10. Read each question below. Read the answers that follow each question. Choose the answer for each question. Write the letter of the answer you choose beside the correct number on your piece of paper.

1. **What helped Herbert Hoover both win and lose the White House?**
   a. the state of the economy
   b. the effect of World War I
   c. the state of civil rights
   d. all of the above

2. **Why did the stock market fail, marking the beginning of the Great Depression?**
   a. Sales dropped.
   b. Building slowed down.
   c. Stock prices were too high.
   d. all of the above

3. **How did the Depression affect the country?**
   a. Unemployment increased.
   b. Banks failed.
   c. Businesses closed.
   d. all of the above

4. **Under Hoover's plans, who should be helped to restart the economy?**
   a. unemployed people
   b. the homeless
   c. businesses
   d. people with jobs

5. **According to Roosevelt and Keynes, which of the following is NOT one of the three main parts of the economy?**
   a. people
   b. businesses
   c. government
   d. unions

6. **Under Roosevelt's plans, who should be helped to restart the economy?**
   a. people
   b. businesses
   c. government
   d. all of the above

7. **Which group did NOT receive help from Roosevelt's plans?**
   a. workers
   b. banks
   c. federal government
   d. farmers

8. **What plan did conservatives want to see used in place of Roosevelt's?**
   a. plans like Hoover's that help businesses
   b. no plans at all; the government should fall
   c. plans like Huey Long's promise of government wages for all people
   d. none of the above

9. **Which group did NOT work against Roosevelt's plans?**
   a. conservatives
   b. minorities
   c. Communists
   d. the Supreme Court

10. **What happened when Roosevelt cut government spending in 1937?**
    a. The Depression ended.
    b. Interest rates dropped.
    c. The Depression became worse.
    d. Republicans took over Congress.

CLASSIFYING

Add numbers 11–15 to your paper. Read the names below. If a person would support President Hoover's ideas, write H. If a person would support President Roosevelt's ideas, write R.

11. conservative
12. worker
13. union member
14. business leader
15. member of a minority

Writing Portfolio

Look over the things you wrote for these chapters. Choose one that you like the best. Add to your writing. For example, you wrote about the effects of the Dust Bowl. You may wish to write about the effects of the Depression and Roosevelt's plans. Trade papers with a study partner. Check each other's work. Make a clean, neat copy. Put it in your portfolio.

Alternative Assessment

Work with a study partner. Think of an idea from this chapter. Ask a question about this idea. Have your partner answer the question. If the answer is not correct, tell the right answer. Then, ask another question about this idea or another one. If your partner's answer is correct, then the partner should think of an idea and a question about it. Continue until you have each correctly answered five questions.

COOPERATIVE PROJECT: DEPRESSION BUILDINGS IN MY COMMUNITY

LEARNING STYLE
Writing Listening

Work with a partner or group. Talk with people in your community. Did they work on a government project during the Depression? What did they build? Is it still a part of your community? What is it used for? How has it changed over the years? Prepare a booklet about your community's projects built during the Depression. Add photographs if possible. You may wish to share your booklet with the local newspaper. Display the booklet in the classroom.

Chapter 73

The World of the 1930s

U.S.S.R.

Outer Mongolia

MANCHURIA

NORTH KOREA

CHINA   SOUTH KOREA   JAPAN

Shanghai

Hong Kong

INDIA   TAIWAN

PACIFIC OCEAN

PHILIPPINES
SEA   GUAM (U.S.)   MARSHALL
ISLANDS

PHILIPPINES

BRUNEI   PALAU
MALAYSIA   MICRONESIA   Gilbert
Islands
(Br.)

SOLOMON
ISLANDS (Br.)

NEW GUINEA

EUROPEAN AND
AMERICAN
COLONIES IN ASIA
(1930s)

CORAL SEA   VANUATU

AUSTRALIA   NEW CALEDONIA

Key:
- Japan
- Britain
- The Netherlands
- United States
- France

Read about other countries in the 1930s. How did the Great Depression and dictators affect them? Why?

Key *Vocabulary*

fascist (FASH uhst) a person or group who follows a dictator and believes that each person is less important than the country and its main race of people

minority (muh NOR uht ee) a group that is a small part of a country's population

ghetto (GET oh) a city section in which only Jewish people must live

Reteaching Vocabulary

resource (REE sors) something that can be sold and/or used to make an item that can be sold

MAP ANALYSIS

★ **Ask**   What does this map show?

★ **Organize**   Look at the key. What countries owned parts of Asia? Make a chart to show which parts of Asia were owned by these countries.

★ **Analyze**   What Asian country had taken over parts of China and some Pacific islands?

★ **Answer**   Why do you think this country might be dangerous to Europe and the United States?

Decoding Tip: Note that *sc* can stand for /sh/ in **fascist**.

ay	cake	ah	fall, cot	air	air
ee	tree	i	sit	oh	cold
or	cord	oy	toy	uh	above, hundred
a	ask	ar	hard	oo	book
e	yet	eye	nice	uhr	liar, fir, further, color
ow	cow	ooh	boot, true	yoo	you, few, cube

73.1 How did Japanese influence spread during the 1930s?

The Great Depression did not begin in the United States. Most of the world was having problems before the American stock market crash of 1929. Many countries were still suffering from World War I. Others had been poor for many years. Hard times became worse in the late 1920s. It did not take long for the Depression to affect the whole world. Then it reached the United States.

Japan is an island country. This had caused Japan some problems. The people wanted industry. However, the land had few natural **resources**. For hundreds of years, Europe had controlled the resources of Japan's neighbors. Japan was especially interested in China.

By the 1920s, Japan had taken over part of the Chinese state of Manchuria. Now it was moving against the rest of the country. Japan used Chinese resources for itself. Japanese leaders hoped this would help business and industry.

Still, the country was going through very hard times. The people and the Japanese Army blamed the government for these problems. In 1932, the Army moved to take over the rest of Manchuria. Then it attacked the city of Shanghai. The Japanese people then turned to the Army. It took control of Japan and the government in 1936. The Japanese Army planned to take over more Asian lands in the next few years.

The world did little to stop the Japanese. Japan not only took land, it killed thousands of people. The Chinese were enslaved. They were put to work for the Japanese Army. The United States sent angry messages about Japan's actions in China. Japan ignored these messages. It even ignored messages from the League of Nations. No troops were being sent against them. The Japanese Army leaders saw no reason to change their plans.

73.2 What was Italy's government like under Mussolini?

Allied countries owed huge debts after the war. Italy tried to pay its debts. But it was rebuilding from the war. Times were very hard. Italy soon fell behind in making payments.

Benito Mussolini formed a new party, the **Fascist** Party. Mussolini said he would return Italy to the greatness of the Roman Empire. This empire had fallen almost 1,500 years before. The Fascists promised to fight the country's enemies. Some enemies were other countries, Mussolini said.

Some government leaders spoke out against Fascist ideas. Mussolini said they must be enemies, too. The Fascists won seats in the government, but not enough to take control.

▲ Benito Mussolini, on the left, with Adolf Hitler

In 1922, the King of Italy asked Mussolini to lead the government. Mussolini called for new elections in 1924. Fighting broke out as the Fascists made sure that Mussolini won easily. Now the Fascists had strong control over the government and the country.

Under Mussolini, many changes were made. Newspapers could print only Fascist ideas. People could be jailed for speaking out against the Party. Children were sent to camps to learn Fascist ideas.

73.3 How did the Nazis gain power in Germany?

Central Powers from World War I had agreed to help the Allies pay their war debts. Germany faced hard times after the war. It fell behind in its war payments. The Allies lowered the debt and interest payments. Germany fell behind again.

To keep up, the German government printed more money. Soon, the money lost most of its value. By the middle 1920s,

▲ The photograph above shows Adolf Hitler, middle, in Paris, 1940.

it took a wheelbarrow full of money to buy a loaf of bread. Money was even burned for cooking and for heat.

Adolf Hitler followed Mussolini's lead. He formed a fascist party, the Nazis. Germany's government fell in 1923. Hitler and the Nazis moved to take over. They failed. Hitler went to jail until 1924. The Depression made things worse. Like Mussolini, Hitler blamed other countries. He also blamed some Germans. He was a strong speaker. Germans flocked to his support. By 1934, Hitler had control of the country.

73.4 What effect did Hitler's racist ideas have on minorities?

Hitler turned his people against German **minorities**. He talked about the Aryan race as the master race. This was a group of people from old legends. They were blond. They had blue eyes. Hitler said that true Germans were their children. These people should keep their blood pure. Every German was tested. Most were given cards saying they were pure Aryans.

Many "minority" people failed the test. This included Gypsies, Africans, and many other minorities in Germany. The largest group, though, were the Jewish people. Hitler talked about a false idea from the late 1800s. He claimed that this lie was true. He said that all Jewish people were trying to destroy Germany and all other countries. They were controlling the world's banks. They were causing the Depression. When each country fell, it would be taken over by Jewish people, said Hitler.

New laws were passed by the Nazis. All minorities had to wear special patches. For example, Jewish people had to wear yellow Stars of David on their clothes. Soon, the Nazis included people with handicaps as a group to be hated. People with mental illnesses were included, too. All these people were rounded up. Some were sent to prison camps. Special parts of cities were set aside for Jewish people. They could live nowhere else. Each Jewish **ghetto** was circled by a wall. There was only one way into and out of each ghetto. At first, Jewish people could leave ghettos only to go to their jobs. Soon, it was against the law to buy things in Jewish shops. Jewish books were burned. It was against the law to hire Jewish workers. Jewish people became prisoners in the ghettos.

73.5 Why did Hitler and his ideas become popular in other countries?

Hitler also hated Communists. Joseph Stalin had become the dictator of the Soviet Union. Stalin followed Communist ideas. All property belonged to the government. It ran all factories and farms. It told people what work they would do. Everyone in government followed Stalin's orders. Like Mussolini and Hitler, he had complete control of the country. Stalin broke off ties with the world. In secret, he sent agents to other countries. They worked to bring down other governments. The hope was that Communist governments would be set up. Stalin would control them all.

Most governments worked against the Communists. Hitler passed laws against Communist ideas. German Communists were sent to prison. This helped Hitler become popular with some people in other countries who feared the Communists. Hitler helped spread news about the Soviet government. People learned that Stalin was arresting and killing millions of his people. Stalin claimed these people were enemies of his government. News of Hitler's treatment of Jewish people and other minorities did not spread as widely.

Connections

Americans helped show up Hitler's ideas about Aryans during the 1936 Olympics. These games were held in Berlin. Hitler saw the games as a wonderful chance. His specially trained athletes would prove that Aryans were better than any other group of people. However, German athletes failed to win as many medals as Hitler hoped. American athletes took many of these medals. Some of the best athletes were African Americans. Ralph Metcalf, Eddie Tolan, and Jesse Owens won medals in track.

The medals were handed out at special services. The top three finishers in each event received medals. A German band then played the national anthem of the winner's country. "The Star Spangled Banner" was played four times for Jesse Owens. He won four gold medals at these Olympics. Hitler was very upset with these results. He would not watch the medals being handed out. He left the stands until the services were over. Owens, Metcalf, and Tolan proved that Hitler's ideas were wrong.

▲ Jesse Owens in the long jump, 1936 Olympic games, Berlin

★★☆ CHAPTER REVIEW

Critical Thinking

Write your answers on a sheet of paper, or discuss in class.

 Identifying Main Idea

1. Why did the Great Depression hurt the move toward democracy in some countries?

 Analyzing Cause and Effect

2. How might bad times cause people to look for enemies in their own countries?

Cooperative Learning

LEARNING STYLE
Reading Verbal

3. Work with a partner or group. Look through the chapter. Find words and names that you do not know. Check them in the dictionary or gazetteer in the back of this book. How are they pronounced? What do they mean? Take turns making up sentences for these words. Say the sentences aloud. Were the words used correctly?

Write About It

Writing Portfolio

4. Write these headings on a piece of paper: **Japan, Italy, Germany**, and the **Soviet Union**. Look through the chapter. Find out facts about these countries. List them under the correct heads. Use the facts to make a chart about these countries. Show your chart to the class. Talk about how these countries were alike and were different in the 1930s.

Chapter 74

The March to War

Germany

Areas in other countries where Germans were a majority

Area taken from Germany after World War I

MIDDLE EUROPE (1938)

Read about the goals of the 1930s dictators. How did they plan to change the world? Why?

Key *Vocabulary*

blitzkrieg (BLITZ kreeg) a surprise attack by land and air forces which carefully work together

premier (pri MEER) the leader of a country's government

appeasement (uh PEEZ muhnt) the act of giving up one's demands so that a bullying power will not attack

nonaggression agreement (nahn uh GRESH uhn • uh GREE muhnt) a promise made between two or more countries not to attack each other

Reteaching Vocabulary

neutral (NOO truhl) refusing to take sides in some sort of disagreement

---

MAP ANALYSIS

★ **Ask**   What does this map show?

★ **Organize** Look at the key. Make a list of the countries where Germans lived.

★ **Analyze**   What country might these people want their lands to be a part of?

★ **Answer**   Why do you think Hitler's Germany might be a danger for the other countries of Middle Europe?

Decoding Tip: Note that two vowel letters can stand for one sound in each of these words.

ay	cake	ah	fall, cot	air	air
ee	tree	i	sit	oh	cold
or	cord	oy	toy	uh	above, hundred
a	ask	ar	hard	oo	book
e	yet	eye	nice	uhr	liar, fir, further, color
ow	cow	ooh	boot, true	yoo	you, few, cube

74.1 How did the Spanish Civil War affect Europe and the United States?

Spain's Fascists moved to take over the country in 1936. General Francisco Franco led the Spanish Army in Morocco. Spain owned part of this land in North Africa. He moved almost 60,000 troops against Spain. Most of the Spanish Army joined his side. The Spanish King had been forced out of the country in 1931. A democratic government was then set up. Many people still supported this government. They were the Loyalists. The two sides went to war. There seemed to be little hope for the Loyalists. France and Mexico did send some help to the Loyalists. Then the Soviet Union joined the fight. It sent arms to the government's troops. These arms evened up the two sides. The war lasted almost three years.

▲ General Francisco Franco in Guelgamuros giving a dedication address for a war monument.

Most other countries stayed out of the war. Some Europeans and Americans hated Fascist ideas. About 15,000 went to Spain to fight for the Loyalists. Many others hated the Communists. They did not want the Loyalists to win. They knew that the Soviet Communists would then take over.

Franco turned to Hitler and Mussolini for help. Thousands of German and Italian troops were sent to Spain. Both Hitler and Mussolini had built up their armies. Now they could try them out. German and Italian planes and tanks spread across the country. Germany's Air Force carried out the first **blitzkrieg**. A blitzkrieg is a time when the Army and Air Force attack at the same time. Tons of bombs are dropped by planes. Tanks and troops roll across the countryside. Every part of the city of Guernica was hit by bombs. The city was almost completely wiped out. Thousands of troops and civilians were killed. This help turned the war in Franco's favor. By 1939, he had total control of Spain and its government. Over one million people died in the war.

74.2   How did Hitler break the Treaty of Versailles?

Hitler and most Germans hated the Treaty of Versailles. They felt it punished Germany too much for World War I. In 1933, Hitler took Germany out of the League of Nations. He would not follow its ideas any more. Hitler broke its terms by building up the German Army. Germany had lost the Rhineland after World War I. It was run by the Allied Powers. Hitler sent his Army into the Rhineland in 1936. It became part of Germany once more.

Hitler had broken the Treaty of Versailles once again. But none of the Allied Powers moved to stop him. They did not want to get into a war. Later that year, Hitler signed treaties with Italy and Japan. These three Fascist countries would support each other. They would also fight against Communism. Japan moved to take over lands in Asia and the Pacific.

Germany also moved against Austria. The Austrian people spoke German. Austria's customs and ideas were German, too. Austria had fought with Germany during World War I. A Nazi party was set up in Austria. The Nazis killed the country's **Premier** in 1934. However, they failed in taking over the government. Many Germans and Austrians wanted the two countries to join together. Austria's government called an election for March 13, 1938. The Austrians would decide whether or not to join Germany.

Hitler did not wait for the election. He sent troops into Austria on March 12. They took over the country. German troops ran the election. Austria lost its independence. It became another German state.

74.3   Why did other countries follow ideas of appeasement in dealing with Hitler?

Most of the Allied Powers let Hitler break the Treaty of Versailles. World War I had been a terrible experience. Few countries wanted to get into another war like it. The League of Nations was weak. The United States had never joined. Other countries did not give it strong support. The League had made some decisions. It had recognized Japan's claims in Asia. However, it had no troops of its own. It could not force Hitler to give up the lands he had taken.

Britain's Prime Minister was Neville Chamberlain. He followed the idea of **appeasement**. This idea called for working with Hitler. There would be no need to go to war.

▲ A Sudeten women cries as she dutifully salutes Hitler, unable to hide her misery as Hitler becomes more powerful.

Hitler lied to Chamberlain and other European leaders. He said he was only interested in lands where Germans lived. That was why he had taken back the Rhineland. In 1938, he said he would take over the Sudetenland. It was part of Czechoslovakia. Its people were German, though. Both countries sent troops to the border between Germany and the Sudetenland. War was close to breaking out.

British and French leaders worked to end this crisis. They met with Hitler in Munich. Hitler signed an agreement. Germany could have the Sudetenland. Hitler promised he would leave the rest of Europe alone. France and Britain forced Czechoslovakia to agree. Many of the British and other Europeans were happy. It was a small price, they said, for avoiding war. Chamberlain said it would lead to "peace for our time." Some Americans supported appeasement, too. Ambassador Joseph P. Kennedy was one American who felt that Hitler could be trusted.

However, Hitler knew that Britain and France had let their armed forces become weak. They had given in to his promises. He felt that they would not stand in his way no matter what he did. Europe watched Hitler break his Munich promise when he took over the rest of Czechoslovakia in March, 1939.

74.4　How did Germany's interest in Poland lead to World War II?

After the fall of Czechoslovakia, Britain and France finally decided to stand up to Hitler. Germany now wanted parts of Poland. Many Germans lived there. Britain and France sided with Poland. They promised war if Hitler attacked Poland. The British and French asked Joseph Stalin for help. They wanted the Soviet Union to keep Poland free. Stalin wanted lands in Europe in return for his help. Britain and France would not agree.

▼ German troops parade through Warsaw, Poland, in September 1939.

Stalin turned to Hitler. They signed a **nonaggression agreement**. Neither country would attack the other. They would split Poland between themselves. The world was shocked to see the Fascists and Communists working together. Some Fascists and Communists in other countries even left these parties in anger.

Germany attacked Poland on September 1, 1939. Britain and France went to war with Germany on September 3. Soon, Europe was taking sides. World War II was underway. As it had at the beginning of World War I, the United States decided to stay **neutral**.

☆☆☆

Connections

▲ Conference of the Big Three at Yalta—Winston Churchill, Franklin Roosevelt, and Joseph Stalin, in 1945

During his time in jail in 1923 and 1924, Adolph Hitler wrote *Mein Kampf*. The title means "my struggle." The book told of Hitler's ideas. He wrote about his plans for taking over Germany. He explained how he would take over not only Europe but also the whole world. The book even had all the details of how he would fight this war. One member of Britain's Parliament was Winston Churchill. He had studied Hitler's book. Churchill was not popular during the 1920s and 1930s. People did not listen to his warnings about Hitler. They did not agree with his plans of building up the Army and Navy. After the war broke out, Chamberlain's government lasted only a few months. It fell in 1940. Chamberlain had lost all favor with the British people. He died a few months later. The Conservative Party formed the country's new government. Churchill became Prime Minister. His government carried out the fight with Germany. Churchill always seemed to know what Hitler was thinking. He even predicted how long Hitler would try to invade the British Isles. Many people wondered how he did this. Churchill always told them just to read *Mein Kampf*. All of Hitler's ideas were there.

CHAPTER REVIEW

Critical Thinking

Write your answers on a sheet of paper, or discuss in class.

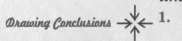

1. Why do you think that offering appeasement might make a country and its people look weak?

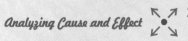

2. How did having strong armed forces affect the different dictators' goals?

Cooperative Learning

3. Work with a partner or group. Look through the chapter. Make notes about the events of the 1930s. Clear the floor of the classroom. Use masking labels for the countries of Europe. Place them so that the floor is like a map of Europe. One person should stand on the label for Germany. Use the notes to help the person talk about Germany in the 1930s. What did Germany do? What countries did it attack? Have the person move from label to label as you talk about these countries.

Write About It

4. Imagine you are an American reporter in Europe during the 1930s. Choose an event from this time. Write a news story about this event. Remember to answer the questions **who**, **what**, **when**, **where**, **why**, and **how**. Read your story to the class.

Chapter 75

Fascist Victories

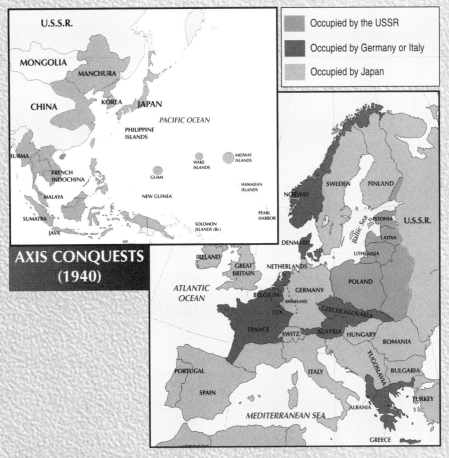

Occupied by the USSR

Occupied by Germany or Italy

Occupied by Japan

AXIS CONQUESTS (1940)

Read about the first months of World War II. How did the Axis Powers affect the world? Why?

Key *Vocabulary*

radar (RAY dar) a machine that uses radio waves to track moving objects, such as planes and ships

occupy (AHK yuh peye) to use troops to control a foreign country

concentration camp (kahn suhn TRAY shuhn • kamp) a camp where people are held prisoner

resistance (ri ZIS tuhnts) a group that fights in secret against foreign troops that have taken over their country

Reteaching Vocabulary

invade (in VAYD) to attack another country by crossing its borders

MAP ANALYSIS	★ **Ask**	What does this map show?
	★ **Organize**	Look at the key. Make a chart to show the places taken by Germany, Italy, and Japan.
	★ **Analyze**	How do you think people in these places might feel about the Axis troops that had taken over their countries?
	★ **Answer**	How do you think these people might affect the war?

Decoding Tip: Note that *a* stands for the long sound when it comes at the end of a syllable as in **radar** and **concentration** and when it is followed by a consonant and silent *e* as in **invade**.

ay	cake	ah	fall, cot	air	air
ee	tree	i	sit	oh	cold
or	cord	oy	toy	uh	above, hundred
a	ask	ar	hard	oo	book
e	yet	eye	nice	uhr	liar, fir, further, color
ow	cow	ooh	boot, true	yoo	you, few, cube

75.1   Why did early Allied efforts fail?

Britain and France planned to keep the Germans inside Germany. France had built a strong line of bunkers. It had cost $500 million. It stretched all along the border between France and Germany. The French felt that the Maginot line would keep the Germans out of France. British troops were sent to hold this line.

Hitler sent troops to the border, too. Nothing happened during the fall of 1939 and the winter of 1940. Some people began to hope that the Germans might back down. However, fighting did happen. The Soviet Union took over Finland. Germany supported this move by its Russian ally, Joseph Stalin.

Spring changed the face of the war. Hitler began a blitzkrieg across Europe. In April, Germany moved against Norway and Denmark. These countries could not stand against the Germans. In May, the Netherlands, Luxembourg, and Belgium fell to Germany. Germany was just too strong for the Allies. June brought the Germans into France. They had passed around the Maginot Line. As they had done many times in the past, they simply marched through Belgium and into France. Mussolini then brought Italy into the war. The Italians marched into Southern France. Italy, Germany, and Japan became the Axis Powers. Japan moved against Europe's colonies in Asia. Britain's Army was pushed to Dunkirk on the English Channel. They were trapped on the beach there.

75.2   What was the Battle of Britain?

Britain promised it would not give up the fight. The British Army had to be saved. It was trapped between the Germans and the sea. The British Navy did not have enough ships for all the troops. Hundreds of British people took to the sea. They used sailboats, rowboats, fishing boats, and small motor boats. They sailed across the English Channel. They picked up most of the troops and brought them to England. Almost 350,000 troops were saved. Many of the civilians were killed. However, the Army was saved. Now it was time to save Britain itself.

Hitler promised to take over Great Britain. His Air Force was the *Luftwaffe*. It began bombing the British Isles. Thousands of buildings were destroyed. Thousands of people died in these raids.

▲ Sir Winston Churchill

Churchill promised the British people that the Germans would not win. No one had **invaded** England for almost 900 years. British fighter planes fought the *Luftwaffe*. They had fewer planes than the Germans. However, they did have a new invention—**radar**. This helped them shoot down German bombers. Churchill told the Royal Air Force to hang on. Hitler was following the plans from his book *Mein Kampf*. It told Churchill how many days the battle would last.

Churchill was right. Britain hung on, and Hitler gave up. The invasion was called off. Hitler did not know that Britain had only had a few fighter planes left. However, he needed his fighters and bombers.

Hitler had broken with Stalin. In June 1941, Germany attacked the Soviet Union. Now this Communist country joined the Allies.

75.3 How did German victories affect the people of Europe?

German Nazis took over the governments of **occupied** countries. The royal families of most countries fled. Many were related to England's King George VI. The British took them in. Some troops also made it to the British Isles. They joined the Royal Army, Navy, and Air Force. In the occupied countries, German laws were set up. One man, a member of the Nazi Party, was chosen from each country to be the country's leader. Germany really made all decisions, though.

Laws against minorities were put in place. Jewish people, Gypsies, handicapped people, homosexuals, and others lost any rights they may have had. Many of these people were hidden by friendly people. However, most were rounded up. They were shipped east to Poland and Czechoslovakia. People who helped them were arrested and shipped east, too.

The people went to two kinds of **concentration camps**. Some went to work camps. They helped build roads, arms, and goods that were used to fight the war. Most of the prisoners went to extermination camps. They were killed in many different ways. Many were left to die of hunger. Some were shot. Children were often hanged. Others were used in medical experiments. They were not given anything to stop the pain. Many people were put into showers. Poison gas instead of water came out of the faucets. The bodies were burned. Millions of men, women, and children died in the camps. The killing of Europe's Jews by the Nazis is called the Holocaust.

Things were different in Denmark. The royal family was captured. However, the King and the government kept some control of the country. All the occupied countries' Jewish people were told to wear yellow Stars of David. In Denmark, the Germans saw something unusual. Everyone was wearing these patches. The Germans were afraid to punish anyone. The whole country might turn against them. Most of Denmark's Jewish people were smuggled into Sweden and safety.

Hitler kept control of Denmark and most of Europe. However, many brave Europeans began working in the

resistance. They not only fought against the Germans. They spied for the Allies, too.

75.4 How did the United States help the Allies?

President Roosevelt worked to keep the United States neutral. He wanted the country to be prepared, though. He asked Congress for extra money in 1938. It was used to build up the U.S. Armed Forces. Roosevelt took secret actions, too. He wrote secret letters to Britain's Prime Minister Winston Churchill. He felt that protecting Great Britain was important to the safety of the United States. Together, Roosevelt and Churchill worked out plans to help the Allies in their fight against Germany. At this time Britain began an office called G2. The United States had the Office of Strategic Service (OSS). Both groups gathered news about the Axis powers and their spies in Allied countries. Some Axis spies were even caught working in the United States. After World War II, the OSS became the Central Intelligence Agency (CIA).

When war broke out, most Americans hoped the Allies would win. But they did not want to get into the war. Roosevelt agreed to sell arms to the Allies. American troops were not sent to Europe. American ships were not allowed to sail to areas in the war. Americans supported President Roosevelt. He won a third term as President in 1940.

American plans changed after France fell in 1940. Roosevelt had been loaning goods to Britain. Most of them were things the U.S. would no longer need. In return, Britain gave land for eight bases in the Atlantic and Caribbean. Later, Roosevelt asked Congress for a new law. It agreed.

The United States began loaning and selling Britain anything it needed. Prime Minister Churchill promised no American soldiers would be needed. With the loan of these goods, Britain would beat Germany. Roosevelt moved to prepare the United States for war. Money was spent to build

▲ A view of Pearl Harbor attack, taken from Hickam Field at Pearl Harbor, Hawaii.

up the Armed Forces. A draft law was passed. More Americans would be called into the services. They would be trained so that America could be protected.

75.5 What brought the United States into the war?

Trouble with Japan boiled over in 1941. Japan had moved against lands in Asia. Its troops were fighting to take China and islands in the Pacific. Many people worried that Japan would move against America's Philippine Islands. The American trade treaty with Japan ran out in 1940. However, President Roosevelt would not set up a new one.

Then Japan took over Indochina. Roosevelt ordered them to give up these lands. Until then, he said, no new treaty could be set up. The Japanese were very angry. They needed American steel and gasoline. The Japanese and Americans had money in each other's banks. Neither country would let the other get to this money. Roosevelt called the National

▲ The photograph above shows the explosion of the *USS Shaw* during the raid on Pearl Harbor, Hawaii, December 7, 1941.

Guard of the Philippines into service. A Japanese attack was feared. Then Roosevelt closed the Panama Canal to all Japanese ships.

General Tojo took over Japan's government on October 18, 1941. He set up new talks with the United States. Tojo said that Japanese demands had to be met. If not, he planned to attack the United States. Roosevelt sent a message to Japan's Emperor Hirohito on December 6. Roosevelt wanted the emperor to help pull Japan out of Indochina. The Japanese sent a message to their people in Washington. It took the Japanese officials until December 7 to decode it. The message told the Japanese officials to let Roosevelt know that the two countries were at war. By that time, Pearl Harbor and other bases in Hawaii were already under attack.

The Japanese attack at Pearl Harbor brought the United States into the war. 2,400 people were killed. Almost 200 planes were destroyed. 19 ships were sunk. Roosevelt went to Congress on December 8. He asked for war with Japan. It took only one hour for Congress to say yes. Three days later, Germany and Italy called for war against the United States.

75.6 What happened in the first months after Pearl Harbor?

American forces were driven out of bases in the Pacific. They lost Guam and Wake Island. General Douglas MacArthur had to give up the Philippines. Over 60,000 American and Filipino troops were taken prisoner. The Japanese cared little about their lives. Over 7,000 died while marching to prison camps at Bataan.

Thousands of European colonists and Asians were sent to these camps. They were enslaved and put to work for the Japanese. They had little food. Many of them died. The Japanese had made no plans for a women's camp on Sumatra. The women and children were marched from place to place. No camp would take them in. They died by the hundreds. Finally, even their Japanese guards died. Only a few women were left alive. One village took them in. They worked in the rice fields. In return, they were given food and homes. It would be a great struggle to beat Japan and the other Axis Powers.

Connections

Some heroes helped the Jewish people and other minorities during World War II. In the Netherlands, Corrie Ten Boom and her family hid Jewish people in their homes. This was very dangerous. If the Jewish people were found, their helpers could be arrested, too. The Ten Booms were arrested. But the Germans never caught the Jewish people that had been hiding in their homes. Corrie's father, sister, and other members of her family died in prison or extermination camps. Corrie, however, lived through the war. She wrote The Hiding Place about her experiences.

Oskar Schindler was a factory owner. He was a German from the Sudetenland. At first he supported the Nazis. He even bought a factory they had taken. It made pots, pans, and other kitchen goods. The Nazis used their prisoners as slave labor. Many of them were sent to factories. Thousands died even in the factories. However, Schindler was shocked at what he saw in the camp where his workers lived. He built his own camp at the factory. He bought food and other things for the workers. At the end of the war, he bought his workers from the Germans. The factory was moved to the Sudetenland. But his plan did not go well. All his people were named on a list. They were supposed to get safe passage. However, some men and all of the women and children were sent to Auschwitz. It was the largest of all the extermination camps. Schindler bribed the Germans to let his people go. He saved over 1,000 people from death. Stephen Spielberg made a movie about Oskar Schindler. It was called Schindler's List. This movie was named best picture in 1993.

▲ Oskar Schindler

★★☆ CHAPTER REVIEW

Critical Thinking

Write your answers on a sheet of paper, or discuss in class.

Identifying Main Idea

1. What do you think was the goal of Hitler's Germany and Tojo's Japan?

Analyzing Cause and Effect

2. How did people suffer under the laws set up by the Germans and Japanese?

Cooperative Learning

LEARNING STYLE
Reading
Tactile

3. Work with a partner or group. Find out about concentration camps. What buildings were set up? What happened in these places? What did they look like? Think about the facts you find. Draw a map or picture of one of the camps. Show your picture to the class. Talk about the camp and what happened there.

Write About It

Writing Portfolio

4. Many people died at the hands of the Japanese in World War II. Find out about the Bataan Death March, the building of the Asian Railroad, or how the Chinese and Koreans were treated. Use these facts to write a short report. Read your report to the class. Put all the reports into a class book. Give the book a title. You may wish to store the book in the class or school library.

Chapter 76

Fighting the War at Home

Read about the war effort in the United States. How did life change? Why?

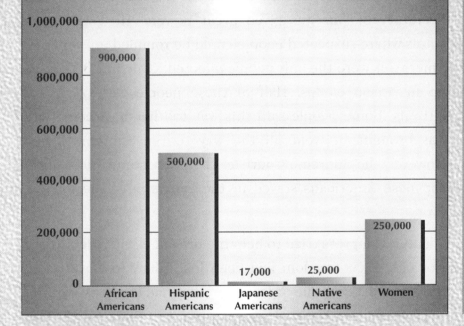

15 Million Americans Served in the Armed Forces during World War II

Women and Minorities Included:

African Americans	900,000
Hispanic Americans	500,000
Japanese Americans	17,000
Native Americans	25,000
Women	250,000

GRAPH ANALYSIS

★ **Ask**   What does this graph show?

★ **Acquire**   What groups were in the U.S. Armed Forces?

★ **Organize**   List the groups in order from the largest group to the smallest group.

★ **Analyze**   What group was probably the largest in the whole population of the United States?

★ **Answer**   How do you think discrimination might have affected minorities in the Armed Forces?

Decoding Tip: Note that *tion* stands for /shuhn/ in **inflation** and **discrimination**.

ay	cake	ah	fall, cot	air	air
ee	tree	i	sit	oh	cold
or	cord	oy	toy	uh	above, hundred
a	ask	ar	hard	oo	book
e	yet	eye	nice	uhr	liar, fir, further, color
ow	cow	ooh	boot, true	yoo	you, few, cube

76.1   How did the war affect Japanese Americans?

After Pearl Harbor, most Americans feared another attack. Japanese submarines were seen off California. One was even sunk. Cities and towns ordered **blackouts**. Many people turned against Americans who had German, Italian, or Japanese ancestors. American Fascists were kept under watch. Some were arrested. However, the strongest feelings were against Japanese Americans. People said there could be spies among them. People on the West Coast were especially worried.

Japanese Americans ended up in prison camps. In January 1942, President Roosevelt signed an **Executive Order**. The Secretary of War was given great powers. He could name states where suspected people could be rounded up. Japanese Americans were the only people affected. Over 112,000 ended up in prison camps. Half of these people were American citizens. Some people said this was too harsh. A court case was brought. It went all the way to the Supreme Court. However, the Supreme Court let the order stand. Most of the Japanese Americans stayed in the camps until the war was over.

Later, Congress tried to help the prisoners with their losses. Not only their freedom had been lost. Many lost everything they owned. When the order came, they had to sell everything. They could take only a few suitcases to prison camp. They were given less than two days to get ready. Buyers took advantage. They would pay only small prices. Sometimes, Japanese Americans burned things rather than sell at such losses. In 1988, Congress passed a new law. It said the U.S. government had been wrong. Prisoners who were still alive would be paid. Each would receive $20,000. Over 60,000 Japanese Americans were paid. It cost the government over $1 billion.

76.2 How were other American minorities affected?

Discrimination against African Americans led to some changes. A new draft law was set up in 1940. African American leaders fought for special wording in the bill. Discrimination in the U.S. Armed Forces was now against the law. However, discrimination did not end. Most African Americans were still segregated on base and in the field. Few ever became officers. Some were even beaten by other American troops. President Roosevelt's efforts to help them often had little effect. One exception was Benjamin O. Davis. He had been the first African American to graduate from West Point. In his years there, no other student ever spoke to him. He still succeeded. He became the first African American to become a U.S. general.

President Roosevelt signed Executive Order 8802 early in the war. This banned discrimination among government workers. This included workers in defense plants. Many factories were making goods for the war. There were not enough workers. Roosevelt set up a board to make sure his order was followed. Over two million African Americans and Hispanics were able to get these jobs. However, some other Americans became angry with their success. Rioting often broke out. Fighting in Detroit involved African American workers. Fights in California involved sailors and Hispanics. Some people died in these fights.

76.3 What effect did the war have on women?

Ideas about the place of women changed because of the war. Women helped the country carry out its war plans. About 250,000 joined the Armed Forces. They served as typists, nurses, file clerks, and ambulance drivers. Many served on bases here at home. They helped make sure that all military work went well. However, thousands went to work in factories.

About 15 million men were in the Armed Forces. That left fewer men to work in the factories. This kind of work had almost always been for men. However, winning the war was now more important.

People changed their ideas, and women went to work. They built planes, tanks, ammunition, and ships. However, they were paid less than men. Some women even became flyers. They flew new planes to Europe and the Pacific. Many women served near the front lines. Some nurses and other women in the Armed Forces were killed in the line of duty. Overall, women proved that they could handle these jobs. Some people decided that the old ideas about women should be changed for good.

76.4 Why did the economy change during World War II?

▼ The photograph below shows women war workers of Marinship Corporation in 1942.

Millions of tons of goods were needed for the war. Congress set up the War Production Board (WPB). The WPB helped the **Pentagon** decide what goods were needed. Then it went to factories to order these goods. At first, things were a real mess. Some business people even tried to cheat the government. President Roosevelt picked the head of the WPB. He was Donald M. Nelson. Only the President had more power in making decisions about war goods. Through Nelson's work, things turned around. Nelson could tell factories what to make. He could set the amount of goods needed. The factories made money, and war work was carried out successfully.

Americans had to cut back on the goods they bought. Too many things were needed for the war. Cars, sewing machines, and other goods were not being made anymore. The plants were turning out planes and tanks. Meat and other foods were hard to

This photo shows Americans on line trying to buy sugar that is being rationed during World War II. ▶

find. Meals without meat were planned. People began their own gardens. They were called "victory gardens." Americans even gathered things for the war effort. They collected old metal and paper. Most Americans were glad to pitch in. They wanted to help win the war as quickly as possible.

President Roosevelt had to step in to help the economy. One out of every three dollars was being spent for the war. There were fewer goods for people to buy. People were making good money, though. Prices shot up. **Inflation** was a terrible problem. People with more money bought the goods. Others had to do without. Roosevelt set up guides for controlling prices. He even set up a rationing plan. Families received tickets for things like butter, meat, and shoes. The tickets had to be turned in when each good was bought. Goods were now sold more fairly. The plan did lead to crime, though. Some people printed fake tickets. Others stole such goods and secretly sold them for high prices. Even so, inflation dropped. Prices still went up, but not as quickly. Through their efforts, Americans showed they would do anything to win the war.

☆☆☆

Connections

Japanese Americans did serve in the U.S. Armed Forces. They had been sent to prison camps. Most were American citizens. They had to follow draft laws, too. About 17,000 Japanese Americans were in the Armed Forces. About half were drafted. But the other half volunteered. Many even served in the Pacific. At first, the government worried about sending them to fight against Japan. Would they be loyal? These fears turned out to be wrong. At the beginning of the war, the United States broke the Japanese Army's secret code. Japan never learned about this success. Japanese

Americans then translated all Japan's messages. Thousands of Japanese American troops helped translate for the Armed Forces.

▲ Members of the 442 Regiment Combat Team during WWII

Most Japanese Americans were in the 442nd Regimental Combat Team. No other U.S. brigade had as many members killed in the war. No other brigade won as many medals, either. Their efforts in Italy and France helped make sure that the Allies beat Germany and Italy. Among other medals, the 442nd won:

➤ *5 Presidential Citations*

➤ *4,500 Purple Hearts for being wounded*

➤ *65 Distinguished Service Crosses*

★★☆ CHAPTER REVIEW

Critical Thinking

Write your answers on a sheet of paper, or discuss in class.

Making Inferences

1. Why do you think Americans were willing to do without certain goods during the war?

Making Predictions

2. With the success of Executive Order 8802, what might happen in the fight against discrimination after the war?

Cooperative Learning

LEARNING STYLE
Writing/ Verbal

3. Work with a partner or group. Does anyone in your family or community remember World War II? Ask these people what life was like then. What did they give up? What work did they do? Were they in the Armed Forces? Did they lose anyone in the war? Take notes as you talk. Share what you learn with the class.

Write About It

Writing Portfolio

4. Imagine that you are in school during World War II. Think about your life. What is it like? Pretend you are keeping a diary of the war years. Write a paragraph about one particular day. Tell what happened and how it made you feel. Read your paragraph to the class.

Chapter 77

War in Europe

WORLD WAR II IN EUROPE (1942-1945)

Neutral Country

Area held by Allies

Areas still in Axis hands in May 1945

ICELAND

NORWAY

SWEDEN

FINLAND

ESTONIA

LATVIA

LITHUANIA

U.S.S.R.

IRELAND

GREAT BRITAIN

DENMARK

NETHERLANDS

BELGIUM

GERMANY

POLAND

FRANCE

SWITZ.

AUSTRIA

CZECHOSLOVAKIA

HUNGARY

ROMANIA

YUGOSLAVIA

BULGARIA

ITALY

PORTUGAL

SPAIN

GREECE

TURKEY

IRAN

SYRIA

IRAQ

LEBANON

MOROCCO

ALGERIA

TUNISIA

PALESTINE

TRANSJORDAN

LIBYA

EGYPT

Read about the fight against the Axis Powers. How did American resources affect the war? Why?

Key *Vocabulary*

rocket (RAHK uht) a metal tube that is pushed into flight by burning gas

atom (AT uhm) the smallest part of each kind of element, all of which combine to form everything that exists

Reteaching Vocabulary

surrender (suh REN duhr) to quit or give up

MAP ANALYSIS

★ **Ask**   What does this map show?

★ **Organize**   List the areas held by the Axis Powers in May 1945, those held by the Allies, and those that were neutral.

★ **Answer**   Why would the seas around Europe cause problems for the Allied push into Germany and Italy?

Decoding Tip: Note that ck stands for /k/ in **rocket**.

ay	cake	ah	fall, cot	air	air
ee	tree	i	sit	oh	cold
or	cord	oy	toy	uh	above, hundred
a	ask	ar	hard	oo	book
e	yet	eye	nice	uhr	liar, fir, further, color
ow	cow	ooh	boot, true	yoo	you, few, cube

77.1 Why did the United States put most of its strength in fighting the war in Europe?

Of all the Axis Powers, Germany was the strongest. Pearl Harbor had made the United States angry. But Allied leaders decided that beating Japan would not end the war. Beating Germany would save Europe and the Soviet Union. All these countries could then help fight Japan. Besides, bad news had reached the Allies. Germany was working on terrible new weapons. If their tests were successful, even the United States could be in danger from Germany. The Allies did stand up to Japan. Fighting went on in the Pacific. However, the main effort was in Europe. American factories met every need. During the war, they made three times the goods of all the Axis Powers.

German scientists helped Hitler fight the war. They were making new kinds of weapons. Huge new tanks were built. They were very heavy. They were an important part of the blitzkrieg. Germany's big guns were very accurate. They kept the Allies on the defensive. Real fear was caused by **rockets**. German rockets were fired from Germany to bomb London. By the end of the war, Germany had built an even stronger rocket. It could have flown from Germany all the way to New York City.

▲ The photograph above shows a V-1 rocket in flight in London in 1944.

Many of Germany's scientists had left the country. They were Jewish. They had lost their rights and property. One was Albert Einstein. He sent a message to President Roosevelt. He talked about the work in Germany. Germany had found out how to split **atoms** in 1939. This could be used for a terrible bomb. No other weapon would be as strong. Einstein said the United States should work to make this bomb, too. Roosevelt agreed. Hundreds of scientists went to work. It was all top secret. Einstein and scientists from other countries helped. They all wanted the Allies to win.

77.2   Why were North Africa and Sicily important to the Allies?

Americans led the Allies in the war by 1942. The U.S. Pentagon wanted to move against Germany itself. They called for an invasion of France and Western Europe. British leader Winston Churchill said that Germany was too strong in these areas. The Pentagon decided he was right. Germany also had pushed deep into the Soviet Union. If the Germans took this country, most of the world would be in Hitler's hands. A flood of American goods was shipped to the Soviet Union.

▲ The photograph above was taken as American troops moved forward to storm a North African beach in 1944.

The Allies decided to bomb German targets. Italy became the Allies' main goal. It was not as strong as Germany. If it fell, Germany would have to fight on another front. To reach Italy, the Allies decided to go through North Africa. They landed in North Africa on November 8, 1942. By May 1943, North Africa belonged to the Allies. Next, the Allies moved against Sicily.

It took the Allies one month to take Sicily. They moved into Italy in September. The King of Italy worked with other Italians against Mussolini and the Fascists. Mussolini was put in jail. The Fascist Party was outlawed. On September 8, Italy **surrendered**. However, the Germans moved south into Italy. Germany took over Rome. Mussolini was freed. He took over the Italian government again. Italy came back into the war. But in June 1944, Rome fell to the Allies. The Allied plan was working. The Germans were too spread out. Slowly, German troops were being pushed back into Germany.

77.3   What was the purpose of D-Day?

Finally, it was time to invade Western Europe. Millions of troops were ready. Tons of goods were set. The American and British navies would carry them to France. On June 6, 1944, the Allies landed on France's Normandy beach. The Germans were taken by complete surprise. However, the fighting was terrible. Thousands died on the beach. Many were killed in German bombings of their landing craft. Among the dead was Theodore Roosevelt, Jr. The son of this President had become a General. He received the Medal of Honor for his part in the battle. Even with the loss of life, the Allies pushed into France. Over one million Allied troops had landed by July. They took Paris from the Germans in August. Belgium and then Luxembourg were freed in September.

77.4 Why did the Allies lose ground in December 1944?

Hitler and Germany did not give up. However, some Germans began turning against Hitler. Some of his generals even tried to kill him. They failed, though. Hitler made new

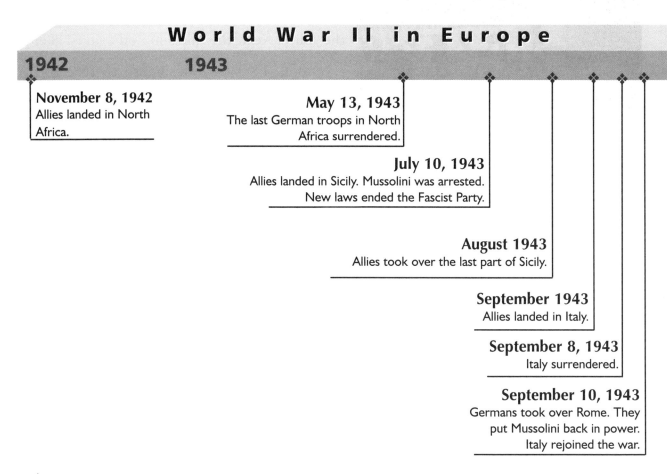

World War II in Europe

1942 **1943**

November 8, 1942
Allies landed in North Africa.

May 13, 1943
The last German troops in North Africa surrendered.

July 10, 1943
Allies landed in Sicily. Mussolini was arrested. New laws ended the Fascist Party.

August 1943
Allies took over the last part of Sicily.

September 1943
Allies landed in Italy.

September 8, 1943
Italy surrendered.

September 10, 1943
Germans took over Rome. They put Mussolini back in power. Italy rejoined the war.

plans. A huge attack was begun in December 1944. It caught the Allies by surprise. Once again, the Germans moved toward France through Belgium. American troops held the city of Bastogne. The Germans took lands around the city and behind it. The Americans were cut off from the Allied Army. They spent Christmas Day in one of the worst battles in all of Europe.

Things turned against the Germans in spite of their attack. Allied troops at Bastogne held out until help arrived. Generals George Patton and Omar Bradley pushed the Germans back past Bastogne. There had been a terrible loss of life. The 101st Airborne Division had been completely cut off. It was almost wiped out. However, it did not give up the city of Bastogne. As a group, the 101st won the Medal of Honor. The push did not end at Bastogne. The Allies rolled toward Germany. In the south, the Allies had pushed the Germans almost out of Italy. Hitler was losing in the East, too. Soviet troops had pushed the Germans out of Russia. The Soviets had taken Poland and the countries along the Baltic Sea. Now, they were marching toward Germany, too. Everyone believed that the end of the war was near.

☆☆☆

1944

January 1944
American General Dwight D. Eisenhower took over all Allied Forces in Europe. He began planning the invasion of Europe.

June 6, 1944
Eisenhower's plan took effect. D-Day was launched. The Allies successfully invaded France.

June 1944
Allies took Rome and began pushing north to the German border.

July 1944
Over one million Allies were fighting the Germans in France.

August 25, 1944
Allies freed Paris from the Germans

December 1944
Soviets pushed Germans out of Russia, the Baltic, Romania, Bulgaria, Hungary and eastern Poland. Four German armies attacked the Allies in Western Europe. They pushed 50 miles into Belgium. After four weeks, the German push was stopped.

September 1944
Allies attacked Germany on land for the first time.

Connections

▲ Benjamin O. Davis

African Americans helped the Allies win battles in Europe. Almost one million were in the war. Some began training as flyers. They became officers in the Army Air Corps. They had learned to fly at the Tuskegee Institute in Alabama. Even there, discrimination was a problem. Once they were trained, the flyers were not sent on to the war. President Roosevelt heard of the problem. His wife had taken a large part in his work. Eleanor Roosevelt visited Tuskegee. She demanded to know why these flyers were not being used in the war. Because of her efforts, the Tuskegee Airmen were sent to North Africa in 1943. They were led by Benjamin O. Davis. He became the first African American General. In the air, these men proved they were a match for any other flyers.

The move against Italy and Germany was helped by the Tuskegee Airmen. They flew fighter planes. These planes protected bombers like the B-29. Once in Europe, the Tuskegee Airmen took part in over 3,000 missions. 66 gave their lives in the fight. However, they never lost a single bomber in any of these missions. Davis and 87 Tuskegee Airmen won the Distinguished Flying Cross. 450 Tuskegee Airmen won medals. In all, they won 850 medals. No other fighter group had as good a record.

 CHAPTER REVIEW

Critical Thinking

Write your answers on a sheet of paper, or discuss in class.

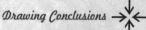 *Drawing Conclusions*

1. How did American resources help the Allies fight the war?

 Making Predictions

2. What do you think the Allies will have to do to Germany in order to make this country surrender?

Cooperative Learning

LEARNING STYLE
Reading Tactile

3. Work with a partner or group. Choose one of the countries of Europe. What happened to this country during the war? How were the people treated? When was it freed from the Germans? What did its flag look like? Make a drawing of the flag. Show it to the class. Talk about what the country went through during World War II.

Write About It

Writing Portfolio

4. There were different plans by some Germans to kill Hitler. Find out about these plans. Why did these people turn against Hitler? How was Hitler to be killed? Why did the plan go wrong? What happened to the planners? Write a short report. Share the facts with the class.

Chapter 78

Approach to Peace

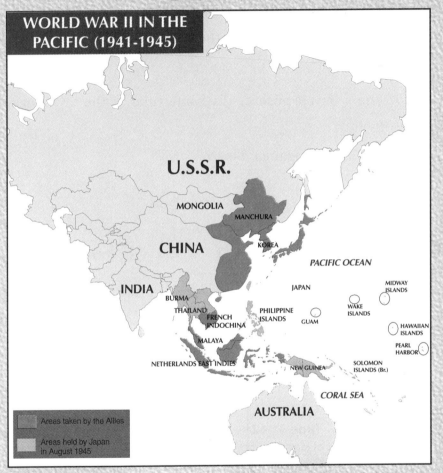

WORLD WAR II IN THE PACIFIC (1941-1945)

U.S.S.R.

MONGOLIA

MANCHURA

CHINA

KOREA

INDIA

PACIFIC OCEAN

BURMA

JAPAN

MIDWAY ISLANDS

THAILAND

WAKE ISLANDS

FRENCH INDOCHINA

PHILIPPINE ISLANDS

GUAM

HAWAIIAN ISLANDS

MALAYA

PEARL HARBOR

NETHERLANDS EAST INDIES

NEW GUINEA

SOLOMON ISLANDS (Br.)

CORAL SEA

AUSTRALIA

Areas taken by the Allies

Areas held by Japan in August 1945

Read about the fight against Japan. How did the United States use planes against the Japanese? Why?

Key *Vocabulary*

term (tuhrm) 1. the length of time a person is elected to hold an office 2. the details set up in order to reach an agreement or goal

bunker (BUNG kuhr) an underground shelter used to protect people during war

radiation (rayd ee AY shuhn) the energy released when an atom is split; poisonous for most living things

Reteaching Vocabulary

occupy (AHK yuh peye) to use troops to control a foreign country

MAP ANALYSIS

★ **Ask** What is this map about?

★ **Organize** Make a chart about the war in the Pacific. Show which lands were held by Japan in August 1945. Show the lands held by the Allies.

★ **Analyze** What branch of the U.S. Armed Forces would be needed for an ocean war?

★ **Answer** Why would planes be helpful in fighting from island to island?

Decoding Tip: Note that the *y* at the end of **occupy** stands for the long sound of *i*.

ay	cake	ah	fall, cot	air	air
ee	tree	i	sit	oh	cold
or	cord	oy	toy	uh	above, hundred
a	ask	ar	hard	oo	book
e	yet	eye	nice	uhr	liar, fir, further, color
ow	cow	ooh	boot, true	yoo	you, few, cube

78.1 What agreements were made by the Americans, British, and Soviets?

Allied meetings set up plans for the war. They also set up plans for after the war. American, British, and Soviet leaders made these decisions. Roosevelt and Churchill often went to these meetings. Stalin had sent members of his government. Finally, Stalin went to the meeting at Yalta in November 1943. Many decisions were made at these meetings:

- to invade Normandy in 1944

- to time a Soviet push at the same time as the invasion of Normandy

- to push harder against Japan

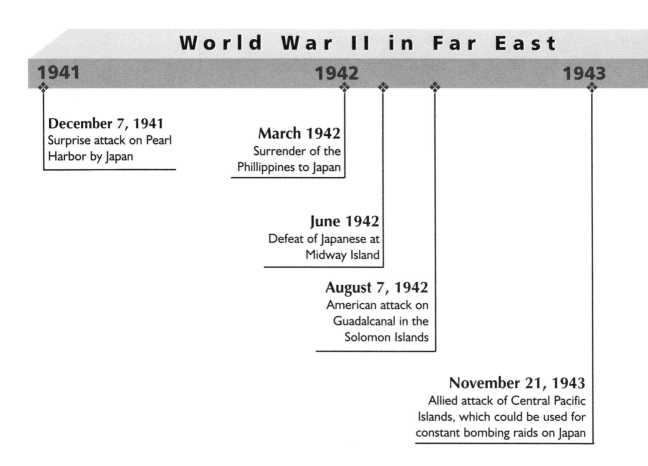

World War II in Far East

1941

December 7, 1941
Surprise attack on Pearl Harbor by Japan

1942

March 1942
Surrender of the Phillippines to Japan

June 1942
Defeat of Japanese at Midway Island

August 7, 1942
American attack on Guadalcanal in the Solomon Islands

1943

November 21, 1943
Allied attack of Central Pacific Islands, which could be used for constant bombing raids on Japan

- to set up an international organization to replace the failed League of Nations

- to include China and France in planning this new organization

- to give the Soviets some rule over Manchuria, Mongolia, and the Koreas in return for its declaration of war against Japan

- to hold elections in that part of Poland held by the Soviets

- to divide Germany into four parts, each to be ruled by the United States, Britain, France, and the Soviet Union

- to divide Berlin in the same way

- to open a planning meeting for the United Nations on April 25, 1945

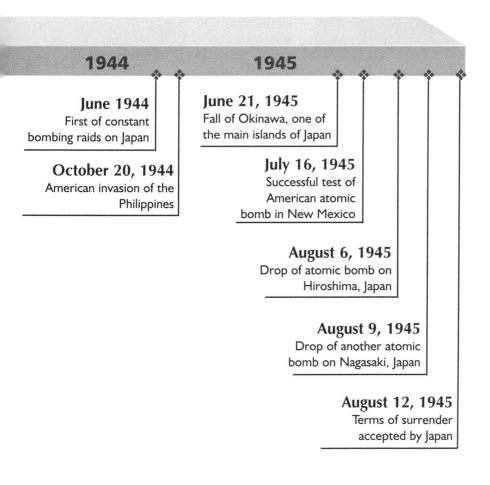

1944

June 1944
First of constant bombing raids on Japan

October 20, 1944
American invasion of the Philippines

1945

June 21, 1945
Fall of Okinawa, one of the main islands of Japan

July 16, 1945
Successful test of American atomic bomb in New Mexico

August 6, 1945
Drop of atomic bomb on Hiroshima, Japan

August 9, 1945
Drop of another atomic bomb on Nagasaki, Japan

August 12, 1945
Terms of surrender accepted by Japan

▲ The photograph above shows President Truman with General Eisenhower in 1945 on the *USS Augusta* during Truman's trip to the Big Three meeting with Churchill and Stalin.

78.2 Why did the Allies turn to the fight against Japan in May 1945?

President Roosevelt died on April 12, 1945. The country went into shock. He had just begun his fourth **term**. No other President had served as long. Roosevelt had been visiting Warm Springs, Georgia. His body was taken to Washington by train. Crowds lined the tracks. Special services were held in Allied countries. Vice President Harry S Truman became President. Truman followed Roosevelt's plans. Germany was falling apart.

The war in Europe ended on President Truman's birthday. Germany gave up on May 8, 1945. Hitler had never stopped fighting. The Soviets fought all the way to Berlin. At last, they reached Hitler's **bunker**. He had killed himself the day before. Italy's freedom fighters captured and shot Mussolini. Now the Allies could turn their might against Japan. Truman and Churchill had a new hope. Maybe Stalin would finally declare war on Japan.

78.3 How had the Allies stopped the Japanese in the Pacific?

An ocean war was hard to fight. Slowly, the Allied Navies had pushed back the Japanese. Planes helped make the difference. Navy carriers sent their planes against the Japanese. They bombed Japanese islands. After that, the Marines would land. The Allies kept pushing to get closer to Japan. They even took Okinawa. Japan was a country of islands. Okinawa was one of

its main islands. 50,000 Americans died in this fight. Over 100,000 Japanese died. Bases were set up on Okinawa. Now bombs easily could be dropped on Japan. Even so, the U.S. Pentagon knew the invasion of Japan would be hard. It believed that as many as one million Americans would die. Almost five million Japanese would be killed.

Bombing raids brought Japan to its knees. This plan had worked in Europe. Cities and factories were destroyed. Fires then sprang up. This made the destruction even worse. Now Tokyo and other Japanese cities went through the same thing. Hundreds of thousands of people died. Still, the Japanese held out.

▲ The photograph above shows a mushroom shaped cloud of smoke rising over the Japanese port of Nagasaki on August 9, 1945.

▼ The photograph below shows Hirohito visiting New York City three decades after the war ended.

78.4 Why did the Japanese surrender?

Most Japanese leaders knew the war was lost. However, the Army would not give up. Japan had never been invaded. They did not want this to happen now. They were willing for everyone to die. Women and children learned how to fight. Often, they had only sticks and rocks. The Japanese Emperor had other ideas. Hirohito sent members of his family to meet Stalin. They asked him to help set peace **terms** with the United States. Stalin would not agree. The Japanese Army found out about these plans. They called Hirohito's family enemies. Some tried to capture the Emperor. They wanted to free him from these enemies. Their plan failed. Still, the Army would not give up.

The photograph to the right is of the Task Force 58 raid on Japan with guns firing aboard *USS HORNET* in February 1945 during WWII.

Work on the atomic bomb succeeded. A test was held at Los Alamos, New Mexico on July 16, 1945. The results were even bigger than expected. Truman decided to use the bomb against Japan. An invasion would not be needed. Thousands would still die. But millions might be saved by ending the war so soon. Hiroshima was bombed on August 6. It had many war plants. It was a main base for the Japanese Navy. Nothing was heard from Japan. After many promises, the Soviets went to war with Japan on August 8. Another atomic bomb was dropped on Nagasaki on August 9. Emperor Hirohito led the Japanese to surrender. The Japanese asked for one thing. Could they keep the Emperor? Truman agreed. However, U.S. Armed Forces would **occupy** Japan. They would rule the country. On September 2, 1945, peace terms were signed. After six long years, World War II was over.

☆☆☆

Connections

▲ U.S. planes dropping bombs over Japan in July 1945

Atomic bombs caused great death and ruin. Almost 100,000 were killed in the Hiroshima blast. Almost 70,000 died in Nagasaki. Things were worst at the place where the bomb hit. Heat reached as high as 540,000° F. Buildings disappeared. People turned into air. Rocks melted. Terrible fires broke out. In Hiroshima it began to rain. The drops were black. They were filled with radiation. It poisoned the living. Thousands more died from this sickness. People around the world were shocked. Only a few scientists had some idea what the effects might be. No one expected all that really happened. American troops and doctors were rushed to Hiroshima and Nagasaki. Some of the Japanese were even sent to American hospitals. Using atomic bombs is a frightening idea. In the United States, only the President can decide if they will be used.

★★☆ CHAPTER REVIEW

Critical Thinking

Write your answers on a sheet of paper, or discuss in class.

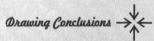
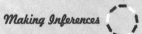

1. Why was planning so important for the Allies?

2. How might the people of Japan and Germany now feel about the idea of war?

Cooperative Learning

3. Work with a partner or group. Make a poster about the war. When did it end? How did it end? What plans had been made for the future? Work these ideas into your poster.

Write About It

4. Think about Emperor Hirohito, Hitler, Roosevelt, and Churchill. What were some of their ideas? Write sentences about these ideas. Write two sentences for each man. Read your sentences to the class. See who can name the man who would have each idea.

Chapter 79

Aftermath

Troops Lost During World War II

Country	Dead	Wounded	Missing and Prisoners
ALLIES			
Belgium	11,240	Unknown	198,321
Britain and its colonies	271,370	284,049	236,242
China	1,324,518	1,761,924	130,172
France	200,240	429,600	1,798,543
Soviet Union	7,500,000	unknown	unknown
United States	405,399	670,846	139,709
AXIS POWERS			
Austria	247,000	unknown	unknown
Bulgaria	10,000	unknown	unknown
Finalnd	51,808	47,500	6,445
Germany	2,916,000	5,240,000	1,858,000
Hungary	140,000	unknown	unknown
Italy	159,957	unknown	unknown
Japan	2,144,507	247,229	unknown
Romania	200,000	unknown	unknown

Total Dead:	55,000,000 troops and civilians
	6,000,000 Jewish people dead in extermination camps
	6,000,000 other people dead in extermination camps
Cost:	About $1,500,000,000,000

Read about the world after World War II. How had the United States changed because of the war? Why?

Key *Vocabulary*

humanity (hyoo MAN uht ee) all people

persecute (PUHR si kyooht) to bring about suffering for a person or group

evidence (EV uhd uhnts) proof

collaborate (kuh LAB uh rayt) to cooperate, especially with enemy forces occupying one's own country

isolationism (eye suh LAY shuh niz uhm) the idea of avoiding dealings with other countries

---

CHART ANALYSIS

★ **Ask** What is this chart about?

★ **Organize** List the countries that knew the number of people that were missing or taken prisoner. List the countries that did not know.

★ **Answer** Why would it be so hard for some countries to come up with these numbers?

Decoding Tip: Note that the *u* stands for the sound /yooh/ in **humanity** and **persecute**.

ay	cake	ah	fall, cot	air	air
ee	tree	i	sit	oh	cold
or	cord	oy	toy	uh	above, hundred
a	ask	ar	hard	oo	book
e	yet	eye	nice	uhr	liar, fir, further, color
ow	cow	ooh	boot, true	yoo	you, few, cube

79.1 How great was the cost of World War II?

Much of the world is still paying for World War II. Large parts of Europe and Asia were destroyed. Almost 55 million people were killed during the war. The Soviets lost 7.5 million soldiers. However, almost 14 million of its civilians also died. The people of China died by the millions, too. Over a trillion dollars was spent fighting the war. Some countries are still trying to pay off these debts. Almost three billion dollars worth of buildings were destroyed. Europe's scientists guessed it would take 16 years just to pick up the rubble. Some of the work is still going on today.

American losses were not as high as some countries'. Pearl Harbor and some spots in Alaska were damaged. Most of the country was never touched. However, the loss of life was very high. Everyone in the country was affected by these deaths. Family members and friends had been killed. From 1775 to 1940, the U.S. Congress had spent $160 billion. About four years of World War II had cost the United States twice that much. Even with this cost, the United States was still the richest country in the world.

79.2 Why were war crimes trials held after World War II?

Terrible things happened in the countries occupied by Germany and Japan. The Allies learned about some of these events. President Roosevelt spoke out about the terrible things that were happening. Seventeen Allied countries formed the United Nations War Crimes Commission in 1943. The Allies promised to punish any guilty people once the war was over. In 1945 the Allies reached Germany's concentration camps. The sights shocked even hardened troops. The news shocked the world. It was hard to believe such horrible things had happened. Japan had also killed millions of people. Prisoners of war and civilians in occupied countries had died.

▲ The photograph above was taken during the Nuremberg Trials in 1945-1946.

They had been enslaved by the Japanese Army and Navy. In 1945, the Allies set up plans for trials. People would be tried for these war crimes. Three kinds of war crimes were established:

1. Crimes against peace—planning and waging war that broke treaties

2. War crimes—killing people and prisoners outside battle, pushing citizens out of occupied lands, stealing personal property, mistreating prisoners, and destroying property outside battle

3. Crimes against humanity—killing or enslaving citizens of occupied lands, **persecuting** minorities while committing other war crimes

Thousands of people were tried and convicted in war trials from 1945 to 1949. Most of the trials were held in Nuremburg, Germany and Tokyo, Japan. Many of Germany's and Japan's top leaders went to trial. Government and Armed Forces leaders were convicted of many of these crimes. Members of Germany's Nazi Party and Gestapo were also tried. The concentration camps had been run by Germany's SS. Many people from the SS were tracked down and put on trial. Some of the people were hanged. Some were put in prison for life. Others were put in prison for 10-20 years. Still others were set free. There was not enough **evidence** against them.

▲ This victim of Nazi inhumanity still rests in the position in which he died, attempting to rise and escape his horrible death. He was one of 150 prisoners savagely burned to death by Nazi SS troops.

Occupied countries held their own trials. Some of their own people had **collaborated** with the Germans and the Japanese. In Europe, a native Nazi leader was put in charge of each occupied country. After the war, these people were arrested. Most of these leaders were executed. Some went to prison for life. Thousands of other people went on trial. Today, the hunt for these criminals goes on. From time to time, someone is caught. The person might have been a guard at a prison camp. These trials make the news all over the world.

79.3 What organization replaced the League of Nations?

A new international organization was called for. The United States never joined the League of Nations. The League had always been weak. The League had not been able to deal with Germany after World War I. Hitler and the Nazis had then brought on World War II. During this war, Roosevelt, Churchill, and other Allied leaders called for a new organization. The first planning meeting was held in San Francisco on April 25, 1945. 50 countries were at the meeting. They set up the United Nations (UN). This time the United States did join the international organization. The UN has six main parts:

▲ United Nations building, New York City

- **Secretariat**—handles everyday business; led by the Secretary-General of the UN

- **General Assembly**—sets the ideas the UN will follow; all countries are members; each country has one vote

- **Security Council**—handles disputes among the member countries; Britain, China, France, the Soviet Union, and the United States are always members; six other seats are rotated among the other member countries

- **Economic and Social Council**—works with people's rights and well being; UNICEF is run by the Council

- **International Court of Justice**—settles legal problems among the member countries

- **Trusteeship Council**—works with the world's colonies; helps them prepare for independence

79.4   How had the war changed the United States' role in the world?

After the war, the United States was the world's most powerful country. Most of Europe and Asia were badly damaged. These countries had huge debts to pay. The United States had to pay war debts, too. However, it was also the world's richest country. Its economy was booming. Little damage had been done to American cities and factories. The Great Depression was a thing of the past. Only the United States had the atomic bomb. No other country could match its might. American ideas were different, too. After World War I, most Americans wanted a return to **isolationism**. Things were different in 1945. Most Americans knew that no other country could lead the world successfully. The United States would have to shape the future.

☆☆☆

Connections

Many people who feared war crimes trials tried to escape. Germany's SS set up escape plans during the war. This group had run the concentration and extermination camps. It had tried to close down many of the camps. They were destroyed. The SS wanted no evidence left behind. But some of the camps were just too big to wipe away. The world found out about the terrible work of the SS. Many SS members had become rich. They had taken the property of people sent to the camps. Even gold teeth had been removed from bodies. This money helped SS members escape. Many went to South America, where some people still supported Nazi ideas. ODESSA is a secret group. Its members still help the SS hide from the world.

Bringing in war criminals became the work of the Jewish Documentation Center of Vienna. It was set up in 1961 by Simon Wiesenthal. Wiesenthal had been in the camps himself. Most of his family had been killed. He has spent his life tracking down war criminals. His Center gathers evidence against these people. It even finds the people so they can be arrested. Over 1,100 criminals have been brought to trial because of the Center's work. In 1960, Wiesenthal found Adolph Eichmann. He was living under a new name in Argentina. Eichmann was a leader of the SS. He led the office that sent all Jewish people to the camps. Agents from Israel kidnapped Eichmann. They took him to Israel. He was put on trial. Eichmann was hanged in 1962. Wiesenthal's work still continues today.

▲ Adolph Eichmann

CHAPTER REVIEW

Critical Thinking

Write your answers on a sheet of paper, or discuss in class.

Drawing Conclusions

Comparing and Contrasting

1. What do you think is the main goal of the United Nations?

2. Why were American ideas different after this war than they had been after World War I?

Cooperative Learning

LEARNING STYLE
Verbal

3. Work with a partner or group. Look through the chapter. Find words that you do not know. Put them in a list. Talk about how words can be found in the glossary or in a dictionary. Look up words on your list. How do you say these words? What do they mean?

Write About It

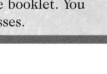
Writing Portfolio

4. Find out about the work of Simon Wiesenthal's Center or about the capture of other war criminals. Write a short report. Share this information with the class. Put all the reports into a booklet. Think of a title for the booklet. You may wish to share the booklet with other classes.

Quiz

Number a piece of paper from 1–10. Write a, b, c, and d beside these numbers. Read the following sentence parts. Four answers follow each one. Choose the answer that best completes the sentence. On your paper, circle the letter that matches the letter of your answer. Be sure you mark your answer beside the correct number.

1. In the 1930s, Fascist governments were set up in . . .
   a. Japan.
   b. Italy.
   c. Germany.
   d. none of the above.

2. Germany broke World War I's Treaty of Versailles by . . .
   a. taking back the Rhineland.
   b. taking over Austria.
   c. taking over the Sudetenland and Czechoslovakia.
   d. all of the above.

3. Britain stopped appeasement and went to war with Germany when Hitler invaded . . .
   a. Britain.
   b. Poland.
   c. Czechoslovakia.
   d. the Soviet Union.

4. Germany took over most of Europe by using all of the following EXCEPT . . .
   a. radar.
   b. the blitzkrieg.
   c. the *Luftwaffe*.
   d. armed troops.

5. To protect lands it had taken in Asia and the Pacific, Japan attacked . . .
   a. Australia.
   b. the Soviet Union.
   c. Pearl Harbor.
   d. Los Angeles.

6. In order to win World War II, Americans . . .
   a. took jobs they had usually not held.
   b. cut back on the goods they bought.
   c. rationed the food people could buy.
   d. all of the above.

7. By 1944, Germany was fighting different armies in . . .
   a. France.
   b. the Soviet Union.
   c. Italy.
   d. all of the above.

8. Allied planes had beaten Germany, then they . . .
   a. flew on to bomb the Soviet Union.
   b. attacked German troops in Poland.
   c. dropped two atomic bombs on Japan.
   d. all of the above.

9. Even before winning the war, 50 Allied countries set up the . . .
   a. United Nations.
   b. Second League of Nations.
   c. World Bank.
   d. new Constitution of Germany.

10. After the war, thousands of Germans, Japanese, and people living in occupied countries . . .
    a. killed themselves rather that surrender.
    b. were put on trial for war crimes.
    c. rushed to safety in the Soviet Union.
    d. all of the above.

RECOGNIZING DETAILS

Add numbers 11–15 to your paper. Read the two lists below. Things and ideas are listed on the left. A description of each thing or idea is listed on the right. Match the things and ideas with the correct description. Write your answers on your paper.

11. concentration camp
12. atomic bomb
13. blitzkrieg
14. extermination camp
15. discrimination

a. A surprise attack by land and air forces which carefully work together
b. A weapon that causes high levels of heat and radiation
c. Bad treatment of a person or group because of the mistaken idea that the group is inferior
d. A place where prisoners are put to death.
e. A place where prisoners are enslaved and put to work

Look over the things you wrote for these chapters. Choose one that you like the best. Add to your writing. For example, you made a chart about the dictators in Europe and Asia. Make a companion chart about the leaders of the Allied countries. You wrote a news story as if you had seen the beginning of the war. Write another story about the battles of war or the surrenders of Germany and Japan. Trade papers with a study partner. Check each other's work. Make a clean, neat copy. Put it in your portfolio.

Work with a partner. Write these names on different slips of paper: Winston Churchill, Benito Mussolini, Adolf Hitler, Joseph Stalin, Emperor Hirohito, General Tojo, and President Franklin Roosevelt. Place the papers in a box. Take turns drawing a paper. Think of a sentence about the person. Ask your partner if this sentence is correct. If either of you is unsure, check the facts in Chapters 73-79. Take turns drawing the slips until a sentence had been formed for each person.

COOPERATIVE PROJECT: WHO CAN HANDLE THE PROBLEM?

Work with a partner or group. List the six parts of the United Nations (UN). Take turns telling about the duties of each part. Work with your partner or group in making a list of problems that a country or countries might face. Decide which part of the UN would handle this problem. Keep these answers on a separate list. Take turns with other pairs or groups in asking your questions of the class. The first group to answer the question correctly earns five points. Continue until all the questions have been asked and answered. Total the scores to find out which pair or group has won.

Unit 9

POLITICS

1947 Truman Doctrine was set up to stop the spread of Communism.

1950 The U.N. sent troops to South Korea to fight against Communist North Korea. China later joined North Korea.

July 1953 The Korean War ended. North Korea and South Korea remained separate countries.

April-June 1954 Senator Joseph McCarthy held television hearings to look for Communists in America.

1957 Congress passed the first civil rights act since the Civil War.

1962 President Kennedy forced the Soviet Union to pull its missiles out of Cuba.

November 22, 1963 President Kennedy was killed in Dallas, Texas.

CE   1950   1960

CULTURE

1946 The American birth rate jumped greatly. The "baby boom" lasted through the 1950s.

1950 Three million Americans owned TV sets.

1952 Ralph Ellison's *Invisible Man* helped bring about the civil rights movement.

1955 "Rock Around the Clock" by Bill Haley and the Comets helped make American rock music popular around the world.

1956 The U.S. began building about 42,000 miles of interstate highways.

1959 Hawaiian Hiram L. Fong became the first Asian American to take a U.S. Senate seat.

1960 Over 50 million TV sets had been sold in the United States.

1962 Rachel Carson's book *Silent Spring* described the danger bug sprays cause for the environment.

Postwar United States

1945 to early 1970s

M artin Luther King led the fight for civil rights. The Civil War had done little to end discrimination. How did the Civil Rights Movement and a world-wide push for democracy affect the United States? Why?

"Injustice anywhere is a threat to justice everywhere."

—Reverend Martin Luther King, Jr., *from a letter written in the Birmingham jail (August 1963)*

April 1965 President Johnson sent the first .U.S. troops to fight in Vietnam.	**1964-1966** Riots broke out across the country as African Americans continued to push for civil rights.	**January 30, 1968** North Vietnam's Tet Offensive totally surprised South Vietnam and the U.S. Peace Talks began.	**August 1968** Student riots broke out around the hall in Chicago where the Democrats were holding their convention.	**November 1968** Richard Nixon was elected President.	**1972** Nixon set up agreements on trade and limits on atomic weapons with China and the Soviet Union.	**1973** Nixon signed a treaty ending the Vietnam War.

1965   **1970**   **1975**

1963 *The Feminine Mystique* by Betty Friedan helped begin the women's movement.

January 1967 The first Super Bowl game was played.

July 20, 1969 Americans Neil Armstrong and Buzz Aldrin were the first people to land on the moon.

1971 Romana Acosta Bañuelos became the first Hispanic American to reach high public office when President Nixon chose her to head the Treasury Department.

Microprocessors, or "computer chips," were introduced. These would be used in video games, digital watches, and microwave ovens.

Chapter 80

Leading the World

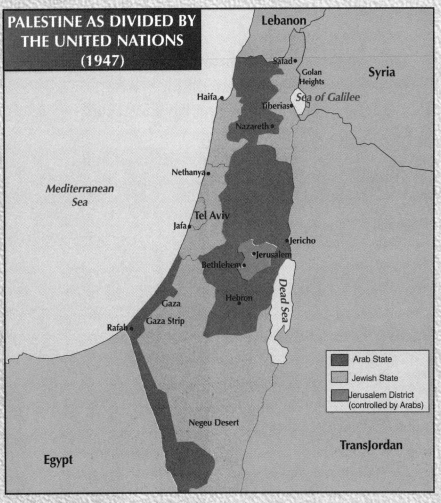

PALESTINE AS DIVIDED BY THE UNITED NATIONS (1947)

Lebanon

Safad

Golan Heights

Syria

Haifa

Sea of Galilee

Tiberias

Nazareth

Mediterranean Sea

Nethanya

Tel Aviv

Jafa

Jericho

Jerusalem

Bethlehem

Hebron

Dead Sea

Gaza

Gaza Strip

Rafah

Negeu Desert

TransJordan

Egypt

Arab State

Jewish State

Jerusalem District (controlled by Arabs)

Read about the years just after World War II. What was most important to Americans in these years? Why?

Key *Vocabulary*

proclaim (proh KLAYM) to declare the beginning of something

sacrifice (SAK ruh feyes) the act of giving up enjoyable things in order to do a job

commentator (KAHM uhn tay tuhr) someone who talks or writes about the news

execute (EKS uh kyoot) to put to death as punishment for a crime

armistice (AR muh stuhs) a short-term agreement not to fight

MAP ANALYSIS

★ **Ask**   *What does this map show?*

★ **Organize** *Make a table about this map. List at least three Jewish cities. List at least three Arab cities.*

★ **Analyze**   *Which side appears to get more land?*

★ **Answer**   *What are the weak points of this plan?*

Decoding Tip: Note the different sounds for ice in **sacrifice** and **armistice**.

ay	cake	ah	fall, cot	air	air
ee	tree	i	sit	oh	cold
or	cord	oy	toy	uh	above, hundred
a	ask	ar	hard	oo	book
e	yet	eye	nice	uhr	liar, fir, further, color
ow	cow	ooh	boot, true	yoo	you, few, cube

80.1 What problem did the United States face in the Middle East?

In 1947 Great Britain decided to pull out of Palestine in the Middle East. The British had ruled there since World War I. Now Palestine would be turned over to the United Nations. The UN voted to make it into two countries. One would be for Jews and one for Arabs. Jews had been moving to Palestine since the late 1800s. They wanted to make a safe place for Jewish people. But both Jews and Arabs claimed Palestine as their homeland. Fighting soon broke out between them.

▲ President Harry S Truman

President Truman supported the idea of a Jewish state. Jews who had been through the Holocaust needed a place to go. But Truman also wanted to stay friends with Arab countries. Their oil was important to the U.S. On May 14, 1948, Great Britain gave up Palestine. Jews **proclaimed** the new country of Israel. At once the U.S. recognized Israel. The next day, five Arab countries attacked Israel. By year's end, Israel had stopped the Arabs. Half the land the United Nations had set aside for Arabs now belonged to Israel. The rest went to other Arab countries. Arabs from Palestine felt they were without a home. These people are called Palestinians. The U.S. tried to be friends with both Israel and its Arab neighbors. But fighting continued between the old enemies.

80.2 Why did most Americans dislike Truman's Fair Deal program?

As the war ended, the United States' economy was strong. Still, President Truman saw hard times ahead. Americans would be coming home and looking for jobs. Demand would be great. But it would take time to make the things people wanted. Prices might rise quickly. To protect the country, Truman came up with a new program. It was called the "Fair Deal" after Roosevelt's "New Deal." The plan included the following:

- higher minimum wage

- money for schools

- more money for people without jobs

- public and private housing

- raises in farm income

- raises in Social Security

- national health insurance

- equal job opportunities for all races

Few people liked Truman's Fair Deal. The country had just been through four years of **sacrifice**. Now business was going strong. Most Americans wanted to enjoy life. The Republican Congress refused to pass the new laws. Many were not passed until Lyndon Johnson became president. That was more than 25 years later.

80.3 Why was Truman's victory in the 1948 election a surprise?

In 1948, Harry S Truman ran for president. Few thought he could win. Truman had a strong record in foreign affairs. But his record at home was disappointing. The Republican Congress would not work with him. Truman wanted government to do more for people. But many Americans wanted to be left alone. Truman's plans seemed out of touch with the country. The Republicans picked New York Governor Thomas E. Dewey to run. Dewey prepared for a big win.

Truman refused to give up. He went by train to cities and small towns. He gave more than 700 speeches. Truman told people that Congress was the problem. He called them the "Do-Nothing Congress." His words began to get through. People would clap and yell "Give 'em hell, Harry!" Most **commentators** still thought Dewey would win. But Election Day brought a surprise. Truman won. A Chicago paper made a famous mistake. Its front page said *DEWEY DEFEATS TRUMAN*. Pictures showed Truman holding up the paper. He wore a big smile.

80.4 Why did Truman's Fair Deal still not pass?

In 1949, Truman and his party seemed to be riding high. Not only had Truman won the White House, Democrats had also won control of Congress. Again Truman tried to pass his Fair Deal laws. Again most were not passed. Democrats from the South joined with Republicans. They worked against Truman. Americans were not ready for big changes in government.

80.5 What did Truman do to fight Communism in the United States?

A new problem appeared. There were fears about Communists in the United States. Were they in Washington, D.C.? Were they giving secrets to the Soviet Union? The Soviet Union had become the United States' enemy. Alger Hiss was found to have passed secrets. Ethel and Julius Rosenberg were put on trial. They were accused of giving Russia secrets about making an atom bomb. Not all people thought they did it. But the Rosenbergs were **executed**. Truman tried to stop Communism at home. He set up a special board. It looked into people who worked for the government. Top people in the American Communist Party were charged. Most of Truman's second term was spent fighting Communism.

Biography

▲ Ralph Bunche

One man who worked for peace in the Middle East was Ralph Bunche. Bunche was an African American. He had a Ph.D. from Harvard. President Truman named him to work at the United Nations. Bunche and Count Folke Bernadotte from Sweden worked together. They tried to start talks between Arabs and Israelis. Then Bernadotte was killed by an Israeli group. Bunche took over the job. He used all his skill as a diplomat. He had to overcome hate on both sides. Months of talks paid off at last. In 1949, Bunche set up an **armistice**. The two sides stopped fighting. For his work, Bunche won the Nobel Peace Prize in 1950. He was the first African American to win it. Bunche continued to work at the U.N. His whole life was spent helping people live together.

★★ CHAPTER REVIEW

Critical Thinking

Write your answers on a sheet of paper, or discuss in class.

Comparing and Contrasting

Making Inferences

1. Why did Truman's Fair Deal do less well than the New Deal?

2. What strong points helped Truman beat Dewey?

Cooperative Learning

LEARNING STYLE
Tactile
Verbal

3. Work with a friend. Role-play talks between Arabs and Israelis. What does each side want? What is most important to each side? First play one side, then the other. Talk about how the fighting could be stopped.

Write About It

Writing Portfolio

4. Headlines give the news in easy words. Read again the headline about Truman in Section 80.3. Then write your own headlines. Write one for each section in this chapter. Remember to keep them short. Share your headlines with the class.

Chapter 81

The Cold War

THE SOVIET UNION'S SATELLITE COUNTRIES (1947)

ICELAND

Satellite Countries

NORWAY SWEDEN FINLAND

IRELAND

DENMARK U.S.S.R.

GREAT BRITAIN NETHERLANDS EAST GERMANY POLAND

BELGIUM WEST GERMANY CZECHOSLOVAKIA

FRANCE SWITZ. AUSTRIA HUNGARY ROMANIA

YUGOSLAVIA BULGARIA

PORTUGAL ITALY GREECE

SPAIN

AFRICA

Read about growing hostility between the United States and the Soviet Union. What did each side want? Why?

Key *Vocabulary*

exile (EG zeyel) a punishment; being sent far away or out of the country

purge (puhrj) the act of getting rid of people thought to be enemies

satellite (SAT uh leyet) a country that is controlled by another country

containment (kuhn TAYN muhnt) the act of preventing the growth or spread of something

solidarity (sahl uh DAIR uh tee) a feeling of oneness, of working together for the same goal

MAP ANALYSIS

★ **Ask** What is the subject of this map?

★ **Acquire** Look up the red countries in an encyclopedia. Find out what year each one became a Soviet satellite.

★ **Analyze** Find West and East Germany. How do the satellite countries protect the Soviet Union from future German attack?

★ **Answer** Why was Greece important to both the Soviet Union and the West?

Decoding Tip: Note the sound of *x* in *exile*.

ay	cake	ah	fall, cot	air	air
ee	tree	i	sit	oh	cold
or	cord	oy	toy	uh	above, hundred
a	ask	ar	hard	oo	book
e	yet	eye	nice	uhr	liar, fir, further, color
ow	cow	ooh	boot, true	yoo	you, few, cube

81.1 What was Communist rule in the Soviet Union like under Stalin?

After World War II, the United States had a new enemy. It was the Soviet Union. The U.S.S.R. also had fought against Germany. Many Russian lives were lost. The Russians were proud of having won. But the world was beginning to see the true U.S.S.R. It was not a pretty picture.

▲ Joseph Stalin

Joseph Stalin took over the U.S.S.R. after Lenin died. He forced Russians to make changes. All farms were taken over by the government. Many farmers refused to give up their land. Millions of families were sent into **exile**. Millions more died hungry. The state also decided what things to make. Machines and farm equipment were important. Clothes and house goods were not. At last the economy began to grow. But the cost in human lives was high.

Stalin used his secret police against his enemies. And Stalin saw enemies everywhere. Millions were shot for imagined crimes. Neighbors were told to spy on each other. Children were told to spy on their parents. Most people lived in fear. No one could speak out against Stalin. Books and papers were controlled by the state. Even members of the Communist Party were shot. Stories of Stalin's **purges** were slow to reach the West. Only years later was the real story known.

81.2 How did the Iron Curtain come about?

As the war ended, the United States and the Soviet Union were working together. Beating Germany was the important thing. But cracks in the partnership started to appear. The Soviets set up their own kind of government in Poland. Poland would be a shield against German attacks. Roosevelt and

Churchill wanted Poland to be free. Stalin promised free elections there. They never happened. Stalin's armies covered Eastern Europe. He used them to set up Communist states. These **satellites** took orders from the Soviet Union. Among them were the following countries:

- Bulgaria

- Czechoslovakia

- East Germany

- Hungary

- Poland

- Romania

- Yugoslavia

In 1946, Stalin was cutting off ties to the West. But many Americans still thought well of the Soviet Union. It was a friend and an ally. Then Winston Churchill made a speech in Missouri. Truman was also there. Churchill said an "Iron Curtain" had come down across Europe. Behind it were the countries Stalin had taken. Churchill wanted the U.S. and Great Britain to team together. Only then could they stop the Soviets from taking more countries. Some people thought Churchill and Truman were turning against a friend. But others saw the real picture. This war was not yet a shooting war. It was a war of careful moves. It was soon being called "the Cold War."

81.3   What was containment?

In 1947, the Soviet Union made new threats. It now wanted Greece and Turkey. Great Britain could no longer defend these countries. It lacked money. The United States had to step in. On March 12, President Truman told Congress about his new plan. He asked for $400 million to protect Greece and Turkey. The money would be used for military help. Truman also made a promise. The United States would help free people stay free. It would fight Communism anyplace in the world. America would not stand by while the Soviets took over countries. Soviet power would be held in check. This plan was called the Truman Doctrine. It was also called **containment**.

81.4 How was the Marshall Plan used to keep Communism from spreading?

A big part of the Truman Doctrine was the Marshall Plan. It was named for Truman's Secretary of State, George C. Marshall. The Marshall Plan was a giant aid package for Europe. More than $17 billion was spent in four years. The money helped European countries rebuild after the war. The Marshall Plan did two good things:

▲ General George C. Marshall

1. It slowed down local Communism. Communists were gaining ground in some European countries. People were tired and angry. Communists promised them a better life. Communists were using hard times as a chance to gain power. The Marshall Plan helped people get jobs and money. Not as many people listened to Communist promises.

2. It gave the U.S. new markets. Lots of the money was used to buy American goods. The American economy grew.

The Marshall Plan had one bad effect. It split Europe even more. The money was to be spent on Europe as a whole. Stalin wanted it spent on single countries. He wanted to decide how to spend the money in Eastern Europe. He refused to let Eastern Europe join the plan. The Soviet Union came up with its own plan. There was no trade between the two sides. Europe was now like two enemy camps.

☆☆☆

Connections

▲ Mikhail Gorbachev

In 1946 the Iron Curtain was a new fact of life. By the 1950s it seemed permanent. Eastern Europe was cut off from the West. Most people thought it would always be that way. In 1956, Hungary tried to gain some small freedoms. Soviet tanks rushed in to stop them. The same thing happened in Czechoslovakia in 1968. The Soviet Union would never give up its satellite countries.

The next country to rise up was Poland. In 1980, Polish workers went on strike against the government. The workers had true **solidarity**. In fact, that's what they called their new trade union. But a year later the union was broken up. Its leader, Lech Walesa, was put in jail. People in the West saw it as the same old story. The Soviets would never allow freedom in Eastern Europe. However, two things were different. Pope John Paul II, the head of the Catholic Church, was from Poland. He continued to speak out against Soviet control. Also, in 1985, a new leader appeared in the Soviet Union. Mikhail Gorbachev loosened the government's grip on the people. In August 1989, the Communist government in Poland fell. Gorbachev did not send in tanks to take over. With Poland free, the other satellite countries followed. Only Romania saw violent change. In October, the Berlin Wall came down in Germany. The Iron Curtain had been built with feelings of fear and hate. It came down to wild cheers and feelings of joy and hope.

CHAPTER REVIEW

Comparing and Contrasting

Drawing Conclusions

Critical Thinking

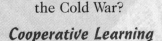
Write your answers on a sheet of paper, or discuss in class.

1. What American rights did people in the Soviet Union lack?

2. Why was the struggle between the U.S. and the Soviets called the Cold War?

Cooperative Learning

LEARNING STYLE
Visual

3. Make word webs about Stalin and Truman. Draw a circle. Write "Joseph Stalin" inside it. Then think of words or phrases that tell about him. Write these around the circle. Next, do the same for "Harry S Truman." Talk about your word webs to a partner.

Write About It

Writing Portfolio

4. Think about the reasons behind the Marshall Plan. What was it made to do? Pretend you are working for President Truman. Write a short speech about the plan. Explain why all Americans should back the Marshall Plan.

Chapter 82

New Alliances

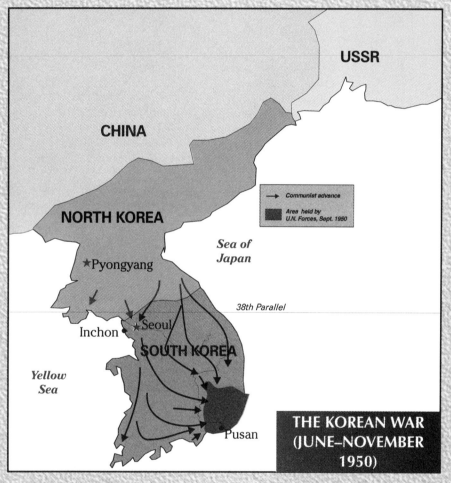

CHINA

USSR

NORTH KOREA

★Pyongyang

Sea of Japan

Communist advance

Area held by
U.N. Forces, Sept. 1950

38th Parallel

Inchon ● ★Seoul

SOUTH KOREA

Yellow Sea

Pusan

THE KOREAN WAR
(JUNE–NOVEMBER 1950)

Read about the threat of Communism. How did the spread of Communist ideas bring the United States into a new war? Why?

Key *Vocabulary*

Communism (KAHM yuh niz uhm) the idea that government should own everything, that a central group should make all decisions, and that the people should work for the good of the government

corrupt (kuh RUHPT) filled with people who break the law by such acts as stealing and taking bribes

defense (di FENTS) the act of protecting or rescuing

Reteaching Vocabulary

alliance (uh LYE uhns) two or more people or groups working for a common goal

---

MAP ANALYSIS

★ **Ask**   *What is this map about?*

★ **Acquire**   *What is the dividing line between North and South Korea?*

★ **Organize**   *List the countries shown. What country is north of North Korea?*

★ **Answer**   *Why do you think it might be hard for the UN to turn back the North Korean Army?*

Decoding Tip: Note that the u stands for the sound /yoo/ in **humanity** and **persecute**.

ay	cake	ah	fall, cot	air	air
ee	tree	i	sit	oh	cold
or	cord	oy	toy	uh	above, hundred
a	ask	ar	hard	oo	book
e	yet	eye	nice	uhr	liar, fir, further, color
ow	cow	ooh	boot, true	yoo	you, few, cube

82.1   Why did the Berlin Blockade fail?

Strong stands by the United States helped stop the spread of **Communism**. The Allies began plans for setting up a new German government. The Soviet Union did not want to lose its share of Germany. If Germany remained divided, it would always be weak. It could not start another war. Stalin wanted to stop the Allied plan. He decided to push the Allies out of West Berlin. Soviet troops blocked all roads, rails, and rivers around the city on June 23, 1948. Nothing could get into or out of Berlin. President Truman wanted to save West Berlin. He talked the Allies out of going to war. Instead, planes would carry goods into the city. One plane landed every three minutes for the next year. Truman's idea was a success.

West Berlin was saved. Stalin and the Soviet Union backed down. Truman and the Allies set up the Federal Republic of Germany in May, 1949. It became known as West Germany. Stalin set up the Democratic Republic of Germany, or East Germany. It was a Communist country. It was controlled by the Soviet Union. West Germany would rule itself. It would have close ties with Europe and the United States. Truman began looking for a new way to keep the Soviet Union and Communism contained.

82.2   What was the purpose of the North Atlantic Treaty Organization (NATO)?

Truman decided an **alliance** was needed with the countries of Western Europe. The first President, George Washington, had warned against such agreements. However, he saw the Atlantic and Pacific Oceans as the best protection for the United States. Sending an army across these oceans would cost too much. Most countries of the 1700s and 1800s could not pay this price. The United States was safe from European and Asian attacks. However, weapons of the 1940s included atomic bombs and rockets. They were a terrible danger for all countries. They could cross the oceans easily. Soviet actions in Germany showed the world what a threat Stalin and the Soviet Union could be. Truman felt that strength could come in numbers. The United States should join with other countries. Talks were held in 1949.

In April, 1949, the United States and Western Europe set up the North Atlantic Treaty Organization (NATO). Its members were the United States, Britain, France, the Netherlands, Belgium, Italy, and Iceland. Each promised to help another member who was being attacked. The U.S. Congress quickly approved the treaty. American troops were sent to NATO bases in Europe. General Dwight D. Eisenhower had led the Allies to victory in World War II. Now he was in charge of NATO's troops. The idea kept the Soviet Union in check. The Soviet Union set up its own organization. Its members included the new Communist countries in Eastern Europe.

82.3 How did China become a Communist country?

Communists had fought the Chinese government before World War II. Then they had worked together to fight the Japanese. Once Japan was beaten, the Communists again tried to take over China. Truman tried to work with the groups to set up peace terms. Neither side was interested. Truman sent American officials to China. They returned to Washington with bad news. Chiang Kai-shek was in trouble. His troops were weak. The people did not support his government. It was very **corrupt**. However, no one else had a

▲ Mao Zedong

better chance of stopping the Communists. Truman did not want all-out war. He sent arms and other aid to Chiang Kai-shek. The plan failed. By 1949, Mao Zedong and the

Communists had won. Chiang Kai-shek and his followers escaped to the Chinese island of Formosa. They set up a new country called Taiwan.

82.4 Why did the United Nations become involved in Korea?

At the end of World War II, Japanese rule ended in Korea. Soviet troops took over in the north. U.S. troops moved into the south. The Korean Peninsula was divided into two countries. The United States and the United Nations (UN) set up a new government in South Korea. A Communist government was set up in North Korea. Like other Communist countries, North Korea wanted to take over new lands. It wanted all the lands of the Peninsula. It attacked South Korea on June 25, 1950. The Soviet Union approved the attack.

▲ UN troops are welded into a single force with one purpose: to prevent other Koreas from happening.

The United Nations came to the **defense** of Korea. The Security Council voted to send UN troops to help South Korea. With its vote, the Soviet Union could have vetoed this plan. But the Soviet Union missed the vote. It had stopped attending Council meetings. It said it would return when Communist China was allowed on the Council. Since the Soviet Union was absent, the plan passed.

President Truman and the United Nations took a stand in Korea. Communist countries must leave other countries alone. American troops and ships were sent to South Korea. The UN decided to send more troops to protect the country.

▲ Troops involved in battle during the Korean War

Soldiers from 16 other countries would be sent to South Korea. They would drive out the North Koreans. Truman did not go to Congress to ask for war. He was afraid this would push Soviet troops into war with the United States and Europe. It took time to put the UN plan to work. By September 1950, North Korea had taken all but one corner of the Peninsula. UN troops and arms began flooding into this area. Most of the soldiers were American and South Korean. The United States was fighting a Communist country for the very first time.

☆☆☆

Connections

▲ Renovations of the White House

President Truman did not spend all his years as President in the White House. In 1948, the building was in sad shape. People noticed that the ceilings and floors were sagging. Congress approved a plan to rebuild the White House. It was taken apart. Steel and concrete were used for its new frame. Then the parts were put back in their proper places. The White House was finished in 1952. During this time, Truman and his family lived in Blair House. This is now the official home of the country's Vice President.

In the fall of 1950, problems came up in Puerto Rico. This island in the Caribbean had become U.S. property after the Spanish-American War. Its people were not happy. Truman helped them gain their rights as American citizens. For the first time, a Puerto Rican was chosen as governor. However, some Puerto Ricans wanted to be free of the United States. On November 1, 1950, Oscar Collazo and Giselio Torresola went to Blair House. Guards stopped them on the front steps. The two men opened fire. The guards fired back. One guard and Torresola were killed. Guards inside Blair House protected Truman and his family. They were not hurt. Collazo was tried and given a death sentence. However, President Truman used his power as President to change this to a life sentence. Collazo spent almost 30 years in prison. President Jimmy Carter used his power as President to set Collazo free in 1979.

CHAPTER REVIEW

Critical Thinking

Write your answers on a sheet of paper, or discuss in class.

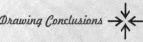 *Drawing Conclusions*
1. Why was the Soviet leader Stalin so interested in other countries?

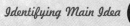 *Identifying Main Idea*
2. How did the Korean War illustrate the United States' plan to keep the Soviet Union's power in check?

Cooperative Learning

LEARNING STYLE
Oral

3. Work with a partner or group. Look through the chapter. Find the names of the people who are described. List facts about these people. Choose a person to play. Hold a panel discussion. Each role player should sit at the front of the class. Each person should tell about his or her ideas. Explain how you think your character would feel about the other's ideas. Answer questions from the class.

Write About It

Writing Portfolio

4. Think about the major events included in this chapter. Pretend you own a newspaper. Write the headline you would run for each of these events. Remember to include only the most important facts. Share your headlines with the class.

Chapter 83

The Korean War

NORTH
KOREA

★Pyongyang

November 1950

July 1953

Panmunjom
Inchon ★ Seoul

January 1951

SOUTH
KOREA

September 1950

• Pusan

Yellow Sea

CHINA

USSR

Sea of Japan

Demilitarized Zone (DMZ)

38th Parallel

N
W—E
S

→ Farthest North Korean Advance
→ Farthest UN Advance
→ Farthest Chinese-North Korean advance
---» Armistice Line
→ Communist advance

THE KOREAN WAR (SEPTEMBER 1950-JULY 1953)

Read about the fight to save South Korea. How did the Chinese affect the war? Why?

Key *Vocabulary*

civilian (suh VIL yuhn) not being part of any armed forces

demilitarized zone (dee MIL uh tuh reyezd • zohn) an area where armed forces are not allowed

Reteaching Vocabulary

blockade (bloc AYD) to surround an area so its people are cut off from the outside world

military (MIL uh tair ee) anything involved with the army, navy, air force, or marines

MAP ANALYSIS

★ **Ask**   What is this map about?

★ **Organize**   Look at the key. It helps you understand who was involved in the war. List these three groups.

★ **Analyze**   Who seemed to be winning on September 15, 1950? on November 25, 1950? on January 24, 1951?

★ **Answer**   Why do you think the United Nations had trouble holding on to the lands it had won?

Decoding Tip: Note that the vowels *o* and *a* in **demilitarized zone** and **blockade** are long vowels because each is followed by a consonant and silent e.

ay	cake	ah	fall, cot	air	air
ee	tree	i	sit	oh	cold
or	cord	oy	toy	uh	above, hundred
a	ask	ar	hard	oo	book
e	yet	eye	nice	uhr	liar, fir, further, color
ow	cow	ooh	boot, true	yoo	you, few, cube

83.1 How did General MacArthur change the course of the Korean War?

General Douglas MacArthur helped stop the North Korean Army. He had led the Allies against Japan during World War II. After the war, he stayed in Japan. He actually ran the country for a few years. In 1951, Japan was allowed to form its own government. However, the United States kept bases in Japan. MacArthur used these bases and their troops in Korea. On September 15, 1950, he landed a force at Inchon. They pushed east and took the center of the Korean Peninsula. It was cut in two. Most of the North Korean Army was trapped in South Korea. MacArthur pushed into North Korea in October. By November, most of the Peninsula was controlled by the United Nations.

83.2 Why did China enter the war?

President Truman and the United Nations had a plan for the two Koreas. MacArthur had pushed the Communist North Koreans to the Chinese border. Now, all of the Peninsula would become one country. The new country would not have a Communist government. President Truman flew to Wake Island. He held meetings with MacArthur about the war. MacArthur gave his ideas about China and the Soviet Union. They would stay out of the fight, he said.

MacArthur's ideas proved to be wrong. China was a Communist country. It liked having North Korea as a Communist neighbor. China acted to keep North Korea from being wiped out. It sent an army of over 300,000 into North Korea on November 26, 1950. This army was too strong for the UN forces. They were pushed back out of North Korea. Icy roads and a blizzard made the retreat even worse. Many troops died because of the weather. American troops called the road "Nightmare Alley." It began to look as if China might take over all of South Korea, too.

83.3 Why did President Truman fire General MacArthur?

Truman and MacArthur now had different goals for the war. Truman felt it would be impossible to do away with the North Korean government. Now he was interested only in saving South Korea. However, MacArthur did not agree. He still felt the UN forces could win the war. This meant attacking China. He sent the details of his plan to Truman:

- bomb places north of the Yalu River

- bomb places inside China itself

- **blockade** China by sea

- bring Chiang Kai-shek's Army of Taiwan onto the UN side

Truman and MacArthur were now at odds. Truman talked with the Chairman of the Joint Chiefs of Staff. This officer is in charge of the Pentagon and all the Armed Forces. General Omar Bradley was afraid of what MacArthur's plan could cause. It would certainly anger China and the Soviet Union. A huge war might break out. If the United States dropped bombs on China, the Soviet Union might enter the war against the United States. Truman did not want World War III to break out. He did not approve MacArthur's plan.

MacArthur turned against the President. He spoke openly against Truman's ideas. He sent a letter to Congress. He asked Congress to overturn Truman's decision. The U.S. Constitution gives the President control over the **military**. The Founders of the country wanted the Armed Forces under **civilian** control. Truman felt that MacArthur was going against this idea. He felt he had to protect the Constitution. He fired MacArthur. General Matthew Ridgway took his place. Many people supported MacArthur. He returned to the United States as a hero. Congress asked

▲ General Douglas MacArthur

him to make a speech to both Houses. Later, a special committee in Congress checked into MacArthur's firing. It decided that President Truman had done the right thing.

83.4   How did the Korean War end?

▲ President
Dwight D. Eisenhower

North Korea agreed to talk with members of the UN. The war had been fought to a draw. Neither side could get the upper hand. Fighting went on for about two years as the talks were held. However, the front line of the war changed little. It was about where the old border between North and South Korea had been. What should happen to the prisoners taken by each side? This question held up the peace talks. All the UN prisoners wanted to go home. But, over 40,000 North Korean soldiers wanted to stay in South Korea. North Korea said they must return if the war was to end.

1952 Presidential Race			
Candidate	**Party**	**Popular Vote**	**Electoral College Vote**
Dwight D. Einsenhower	Republican	33,936,234	442
Adlai E. Stevenson	Democrat	27,314,992	89

Peace was won after Dwight D. Eisenhower became President in 1953. Eisenhower had led the Allies to victory in Europe during World War II. Then he had led the forces of NATO. Truman had decided not to run again. Firing MacArthur had cost him much of his popularity. The Democrats chose Adlai E. Stevenson for the race. Eisenhower ran for the Republicans. During the election, Eisenhower promised to find a way to end the war. Eisenhower became the first Republican President since Herbert Hoover.

▲ The photograph above is from the Korean War peace talks. Major General Lee signs the agreement for the POW exchange at Panmunjom conference.

Conditions changed after Eisenhower became President. Stalin died in 1953. New leaders took over the Soviet Union. That country needed peace to solve its own problems. It began pushing North Korea to find a way to peace. Eisenhower threatened to allow Chiang Kai-shek's troops to attack China. The United States would begin bombing China, too. A treaty was signed in July, 1953. North and South Korea would be two different countries. Prisoners could decide where they wanted to live.

83.5 What was the result of the Korean War?

The cost of the war had been high. Almost 35,000 Americans died in the war. Over 100,000 had been hurt. 415,000 South Koreans were killed. North Korea lost about 520,000 soldiers. China lost over 1 million. This was too great a cost to let another war break out. The peace treaty set up a **demilitarized zone**. This was a strip of land about 2 miles wide. It would separate North Korea and South Korea. China and the United States help guard this border even today.

The Korean War reached the goal of containment. The fighting had stopped the spread of Communism. South Korea would remain a democracy. North Korea would stay out of other Asian countries. It had been a limited war. Limits had been set by both sides. This had kept the war from spreading to other countries. World War III had not broken out. From now on, fights in the Cold War would be limited wars. The risk of all-out war was just too great a danger for the world.

☆☆☆

Connections

▲ Kim Il Sung with Former President Jimmy Carter

Kim Il Sung was the Communist dictator of North Korea. Like Stalin and Mao Zedong, he ruled for life. A new problem broke out on the Korean Peninsula in the 1990s. Many people were afraid that North Korea wanted atomic bombs. They felt that Kim Il Sung had ordered the work to begin. In 1993, President Bill Clinton pointed out that North Korea had signed a special treaty. It had agreed not to build such weapons. Kim Il Sung would not admit his program. He even said he would pull out of the treaty. Things became very tense.

President Clinton sent a former President to North Korea. Jimmy Carter began talks with Kim Il Sung in 1994. Things seemed to get better. Carter asked Sung to allow UN leaders into North Korea. They would check bases and plants for work on atomic bombs. However, Sung would not agree. Then, he suddenly died on July 15, 1994. His son Kim Jong Il was set to take over the country. He announced that he was the new leader. However, things in North Korea were not clear. Little news has reached the world. Was Kim Jong Il in charge? Would talks continue? Would any new leader in North Korea let the UN check for atomic weapons?

 CHAPTER REVIEW

Critical Thinking

Write your answers on a sheet of paper, or discuss in class.

 Analyzing Cause and Effect

1. How did the United States and China affect the war between North and South Korea?

Making Inferences

2. Why might some people feel that the war between North and South Korea was a mistake?

Cooperative Learning

LEARNING STYLE
Reading/ Verbal

3. Work with a partner or group. Look through the chapter. Find names and words that you do not know. Look them up in the glossary or gazetteer in the back of the book. You might also find these words in dictionaries. How do you say each word? What does it mean? Does it name a person, a place, a thing, or an idea? Is it a word that describes an action someone or something might take?

Write About It

Writing Portfolio

4. Write Cause and Effect at the top of a piece of paper. Think about what happened in the Korean War. What caused it to happen? Did it bring about an effect of its own? List these causes and effects under the heads on your paper. Check your work with a partner. Are you not sure about some events? Hold a class discussion to decide whether they are causes or effects.

Chapter 84

The 1950s

Read about the United States in the 1950s. How did American life change? Why?

1956 Presidential Race

Candidate for President	Popular Vote	Electoral College Vote
Dwight D. Eisenhower (R)	35,590,472	457
Adlai E. Stevenson (D)	26,314,992	73

Note: R= Republican
D= Democrat

Congress	Total Seats	Number of Republicans	Number of Democrats
House	431	199	232
Senate	96	47	49

Key *Vocabulary*

ethnic origin (ETH nik • OR uh juhn) the culture and traditions of the country or group from which a person or family comes

censure (SEN chuhr) to place blame for doing something that is wrong or bad

Reteaching Vocabulary

population (pahp yuh LAY shun) all the people who live in a specific area

inflation (in FLAY shuhn) a time when prices continue to go up

transportation (trans por TAY shun) the way in which something is moved from one place to another

CHART ANALYSIS

★ **Ask** — What facts are included in these charts?

★ **Acquire** — What three kinds of candidates were elected in 1956?

★ **Organize** — List which party won the Presidential race, the most House seats, and the most Senate seats.

★ **Answer** — Why might the President have trouble in getting Congress to follow his ideas?

Decoding Tip: Note that c can stand for /k/ in **ethnic origin** and /s/ in **censure**.

ay	cake	ah	fall, cot	air	air
ee	tree	i	sit	oh	cold
or	cord	oy	toy	uh	above, hundred
a	ask	ar	hard	oo	book
e	yet	eye	nice	uhr	liar, fir, further, color
ow	cow	ooh	boot, true	yoo	you, few, cube

84.1 How did the U.S. population change during the 1950s?

"Baby boom" was a term formed in the late 1940s and early 1950s. More and more babies were being born. The number of people in the United States grew tremendously. New medicines had affected the **population**, too. People were living longer, healthier lives. There were about 151 million Americans in 1950. The country had 179 million people in 1960. Fewer people became immigrants to the United States.

Congress still limited the number of immigrants. The largest number came from Northern and Western Europe. Americans grew to share many of the same ideas. They were becoming more and more alike. Differences because of **ethnic origin** were often frowned upon. Everyone wanted to share in the good life that the 1950s had brought.

84.2 What was the U.S. economy like during the 1950s?

America's economy boomed during the 1950s. Prices jumped after World War II ended. However, Presidents Truman and Eisenhower followed ideas to keep **inflation** in check. There were plenty of jobs. Wages were higher, too. About 25 percent of American workers belonged to unions. However, new laws strictly controlled their actions. Few strikes were called. The federal government sometimes stepped in to settle the strikes that were called. Corrupt practices in some unions led to even tougher laws controlling union activities.

Eisenhower did not want government to limit businesses. He felt that they were running themselves successfully. This was making the country rich. Government and business even depended on each other. For example, buying for the Armed Forces affected the whole country. The U.S. government was the biggest customer served by the country's largest companies.

84.3 How did Senator McCarthy affect the Cold War?

The Cold War was the struggle to stop the spread of Communism. Some people began to fear Communist activities in the United States. Americans were even caught spying for the Soviet Union. These people wanted the U.S. government to fall. They felt the country should have a Communist government instead.

Both Truman and Eisenhower set up special boards. They checked to make sure government workers were loyal to the United States. Many people felt this program was hurting the constitutional rights of citizens to have different opinions. Others, including Truman and Eisenhower, felt that the country must be protected. New laws were set up. Belonging to the Communist Party became a crime.

▲ Joseph McCarthy with subpoena from Senate Investigating Committee, 1954.

Senator Joseph McCarthy called for the arrest of all Communists in government. He was a Republican member of the U.S. Senate from Wisconsin. McCarthy claimed that the State Department was filled with Communists. Soon, a special Senate committee was set up. It was led by Millard Tydings, a Senator from Maryland. The committee investigated the charges. It said that its findings proved that McCarthy was wrong. McCarthy then said that Tydings was a Communist himself. Tydings lost his seat during that year's elections.

Fear of McCarthy gave this Senator much power. He took over the committee to investigate the government. Soon, every branch of the government was being checked. Thousands of people were said to be Communists. McCarthy urged people to turn in their friends and family members. The committee then began checking American businesses, such as the movie industry. Many people lost their jobs. Some changed their names to begin new lives. Others left the

For the People, By the People

▲ Lucille Ball and Desi Arnaz of the *I Love Lucy* show

country. Some even killed themselves. McCarthy ruined the lives of many people.

84.4 What effect did television have on the country?

Television took the country by storm during the 1950s. It had been invented in the 1930s. Programs had even been shown in Britain. British television was showing a Krazy Kat cartoon when World War II broke out. It shut down its work in the middle of the show. After the war, the station went back on the air. The first program to be shown was the end of that Krazy Kat cartoon. By the 1950s, there were three networks in the United States. Over three million Americans had televisions in 1950. People loved programs starring Milton Berle, Lucille Ball, and Bob Hope. By 1960, over 50 million television sets had been sold in the United States.

The government was deeply affected by television. General Eisenhower ran the first television ads in a race for President in 1952. Senator McCarthy began holding committee hearings about Communists in the U.S. Army. Generals and other officers attended these hearings. They were shown on television. The hearings lasted from April to June, 1954. Americans were fascinated by the hearings. They watched Senator McCarthy at work. They saw how badly he treated the Army officers. Soon, it became obvious that most of McCarthy's evidence had been faked. McCarthy ruined his own reputation. Even Congress turned against him. The Senate voted to **censure** McCarthy for the way he had behaved. People still worried about Communist spies. However, the huge hunts through people's records were cut back. Only those people involved in government were to be checked now.

84.5   Why were suburbs and interstates developed?

Eisenhower called for a national highway plan. During the 1930s, he had been ordered to take troops and gear across the country. He saw that some of the country's roads were very bad. Better roads would improve **transportation** of both people and the goods they needed. Congress set up a plan in 1956. It would pay for about 42,000 miles of highways. They would link all of the United States' biggest cities. Almost 8,000 miles had been built by 1961. Taking vacations by car became an American pastime. Trucks began carrying goods to every part of the country. Trains began to lose their importance in the American economy.

With good roads, people could escape the problems of city life. By the 1950s, most Americans were working in cities. The baby boom had hit. People looked for other places in which to raise their families. Cities were crowded and often dirty. Crime was another problem of city life. With good roads, people began buying homes in areas around the cities. These communities are known as suburbs. People live, shop, go to school, and attend church in suburbs. Most of them actually work in cities. Driving to work is still a major part of most people's lives.

Highways helped people move to different parts of the country. Large companies set up offices in many cities. They could transfer workers from one place to another. Family members might move thousands of miles from one another. Often, people decided on their own to make such moves. They went to places like California where they felt opportunities would be better. The problems of war and depression were over. Most Americans felt life in the 1950s was very good.

Connections

▲ Family viewing television in 1950

Like many Americans, the television industry moved across the country in the 1950s. Most early television shows were made in New York City. Studios broadcast these shows as they were performed. Theaters where plays had been performed became centers for the television industry.

Hollywood and the film business brought television to California. Lucille Ball and Desi Arnaz were Hollywood stars. Both had made movies. Arnaz was also a popular band leader from Cuba. In the early 1950s, CBS asked them to star in their own television show. However, the couple did not want to leave their life in California. Arnaz arranged to have their show filmed as if it were a short movie. Movies are filmed with only one camera. The camera has to be moved in order to do closeups and other shots. This takes time and money. Arnaz worked with photographers in setting up three cameras. All the kinds of shots could be filmed at once. *I Love Lucy* became one of the most popular shows CBS ever had. It is still shown in reruns today. However, CBS made a mistake. Arnaz asked for the rights to the films. CBS wanted each program for only one showing. It agreed. Now, each time a program is rerun, Lucy's and Desi's families still earn money.

The idea of filming shows took over the television industry. Hollywood was the natural place for filming the programs. By the 1960s, most shows were being made in Hollywood. Desi Arnaz and Lucille Ball even set up their own studio. They bought RKO. They named it Desilu. It made shows like *The Untouchables* and *Star Trek*. In the middle 1960s, Desilu was sold to Paramount. It has continued making similar shows. *The Untouchables* became a popular movie in the 1990s. Four other *Star Trek* shows and even movies have made billions of dollars for Paramount.

★★★ CHAPTER REVIEW

Critical Thinking

Write your answers on a sheet of paper, or discuss in class.

Comparing and Contrasting

1. How were the 1930s and 1940s different from the 1950s? How were they alike?

Making Inferences

2. Why do you think President Eisenhower was so popular with most Americans?

Cooperative Learning

LEARNING STYLE
Oral
Tactile

3. Work with a partner or group. Talk about the 1950s. What was the country like? How did the population change? What were people's lives like? How did Americans feel about Communism? Think about your answers to these questions. Make a poster that displays facts about the United States in the 1950s. Hang your poster in the classroom.

Write About It

Writing Portfolio

4. Choose a topic from this chapter. You might choose the McCarthy hearings, the development of television, America's new highways, President Eisenhower, or others. Find out about your topic. Use your notes to write a short report. Trade papers with a partner. Read and talk about each other's report.

Chapter 85

The Rights of Citizens

Three Main Political Viewpoints

	Liberal	Moderate	Conservative
Belief	open to all kinds of changes	wants only limited changes	Wants to keep things as they have been
Synonym	left wing	centrist	right wing
1950s position on Civil Rights	supported any government actions to promote and protect civil rights	supported guarantees of civil rights, but feared giving government unlimited power	supported the established system of allowing states to determine what rights people can hold
Supporters	➤ President Harry S Truman ➤ Martin Luther King, Jr. ➤ Earl Warren, Chief Justice of the Supreme Court ➤ Ernesto Galarza, consultant to the U.S. House of Representatives	➤ President Dwight D. Eisenhower, who later saw the actions of Governor Faubus as disgraceful and took a liberal stand in sending troops and other officials to enforce civil rights	➤ Governor Orval Faubus of Arkansas ➤ Governor J. Strom Thurmond of South Carolina ➤ Senator Richard Russell of Georgia

Note: One person may hold liberal views on one issue, such as civil rights. But the person may hold moderate and conservative views on other issues.

Read about great changes during the 1950s. How were African Americans affected? Why?

Key *Vocabulary*

segregation (seg ri GAY shuhn) the act of closing membership to some people or groups

integration (int uh GRAY shuhn) the act of opening membership to all people

unconstitutional (uhn kahnt stuh TOOH shuh nuhl) not following the ideas of the U.S. Constitution

civil rights (SIV uhl • reyets) all the privileges held by the citizens of a city, state, or country

Reteaching Vocabulary

boycott (BOY kaht) to refuse any dealings with a person or group until certain terms are met

---

CHART ANALYSIS

★ **Ask**   What facts does this chart show?

★ **Acquire**   What three groups are compared?

★ **Organize**   Talk about these groups with a partner. Share your knowledge of any of the people listed.

★ **Analyze**   Which person in the list fits the facts in the note?

★ **Answer**   What things might help change a person's ideas and views?

Decoding Tip: Note that *a* stands for the long sound when it comes at the end of a syllable as in *segregation* and *integration*.

ay	cake	ah	fall, cot	air	air
ee	tree	i	sit	oh	cold
or	cord	oy	toy	uh	*above*, hundred
a	ask	ar	hard	oo	book
e	yet	eye	nice	uhr	liar, fir, further, color
ow	cow	ooh	boot, true	yoo	you, few, cube

85.1 What effect did a 1954 Supreme Court decision have on segregation?

Chief Justice Earl Warren led the Supreme Court in an unexpected direction. President Eisenhower had thought the California governor was more conservative. That is why he selected Warren for the court. However, Chief Justice Warren led the court in making liberal decisions. Many of these decisions helped do away with **segregation**.

Brown vs. *Board of Education of Topeka* came to the Supreme Court in 1954. The court's decision did away with segregation in schools. An African American had tried to enter his daughter into an all-white school in this Kansas city. He was refused. Oliver Brown decided to sue the city's Board of Education. This case went all the way to the Supreme Court. Early courts had supported segregated schools. They said such schools only had to be equal. However, Brown won his case. The Warren Court pointed out that segregated schools had rarely been equal. African American schools had little money from their Boards of Education. In 1955, the Court ordered the country's schools to begin **integration.**

▼ Dr. Martin Luther King, Mrs. Rosa Parks, and David Boston at a freedom march rally, June 1963.

85.2 How did Rosa Parks and Martin Luther King, Jr., bring about the civil rights movement?

Another form of segregation was brought down by Rosa Parks. She was returning home from work on December 3, 1955. She found a seat on one of Montgomery, Alabama's city buses. It soon became full. More people got on the bus. Mrs. Parks broke the law by not giving her seat to a white man. The bus stopped and Mrs. Parks was arrested. A Montgomery

▲ Dr. Martin Luther King, Jr.

court ordered her to pay a fine for breaking the law. The city's African Americans decided to take a stand against segregation.

Martin Luther King, Jr., was picked to lead the fight in Montgomery. He was an African American minister at one of the city's Baptist churches. Dr. King called on people to **boycott** city buses. All African Americans and some of Montgomery's other citizens agreed. The boycott went on for a year. Ticket sales on city buses dropped by almost two-thirds. The Supreme Court settled the boycott in December, 1956. It said that segregation on buses was **unconstitutional**. Montgomery ended segregation on its city buses. Dr. King's boycott ended in success.

The push for **civil rights** was now led by Dr. King. He set up the Southern Christian Leadership Conference (SCLC). Dr. King's organization led protests against segregation. These peaceful protests were held in cities across the country. Dr. King and the SCLC believed change could come without violence.

Their goal was ending all forms of segregation. Boycotts, demonstrations, and marches helped spread their ideas. Sit-ins began in February, 1960. Restaurants and lunch counters were segregated in many cities. Four black students sat down at a lunch counter in Greensboro, North Carolina. They ordered food, but were refused service. They did not leave until they had eaten their meals. The fight for civil rights brought support from liberals and moderates. Civil rights became one of the main issues of the 1960s.

85.3 What was the Civil Rights Act of 1957?

Voting rights had not been protected after the Civil War. The Supreme Court and Congress followed the idea of states' rights. On certain issues, states had more power than the

▲ The photograph above shows Lyndon Johnson signing the Civil Rights Act of 1957. Standing behind Johnson is Dr. Martin Luther King, Jr.

federal government. Some states passed laws making it impossible for African Americans to vote. Many of these were Southern states. Their laws gave voting rights only to certain people. They had to be able to read. They had to pay special taxes. Their grandparents could not have been enslaved. Few African Americans could meet all these tests. Those who could were often afraid to vote. These people were often attacked and sometimes killed.

World War II changed people's ideas. President Truman tried to end discrimination in the Armed Forces. Discrimination was not allowed in hiring people for government jobs. African Americans had fought for the country. Now they insisted on having their rights as citizens. Congress acted on this idea. Senator Lyndon B. Johnson of Texas steered the Civil Rights Act through Congress in 1957. The Justice Department was to use the courts to make sure that all African Americans were allowed to vote.

The Civil Rights Act of 1957 was only a beginning. African Americans wanted more than voting rights. They wanted all the rights held by other American citizens. Segregation in any form should be done away with, they said. This idea was spread by such leaders as Martin Luther King, Roy Wilkins, Thurgood Marshall, and A. Philip Randolph. They found supporters of all races and classes. Hispanics, Asian Americans, and Native Americans had also experienced discrimination. By the late 1960s, they were part of the civil rights movement, too.

85.4 How did President Eisenhower support civil rights?

Congress could change laws, said President Eisenhower. But how could it change people's hearts? Eisenhower believed that the laws could be enforced. But discrimination would not end until people's attitudes were changed. Civil rights was not one of his top issues. However, as President he had the duty of carrying out the law. Eisenhower did not give up this duty. He ordered all government offices to follow the laws.

The first real test of these laws came in Arkansas. Central High School was in Little Rock. The courts had begun integration there in 1957. However, some people in the state tried to stop this from happening. Governor Orval Faubus supported these people.

To keep African American students out of Central High School, Governor Faubus sent in the Arkansas National Guard. This was the state's own branch of the Armed Forces. President Eisenhower talked the Governor into pulling the National Guard away from the school. Angry crowds then surrounded the school. Eisenhower was angered by news reports about these events. Americans were able to watch what was happening on television.

Eisenhower sent the U.S. Army to make sure the students could go to school. The next spring, Ernest Green became the first African American to graduate from Central High School. Since that time, the federal government has made civil rights one of its top issues.

Connections

▲ Justice Thurgood Marshall

Thurgood Marshall helped lead the fight for civil rights. He became a lawyer in 1933. In 1938, he became the chief lawyer for the National Association for the Advancement of Colored People (NAACP). He held this post for over 20 years. During these years, he brought cases in the fight for civil rights. He spoke out against discrimination in schools, the Armed Forces, and all parts of American life. He won the Spingarn Medal in 1946.

Marshall led the lawyers who brought the case of *Brown* vs. *Board of Education of Topeka* to the Supreme Court. With its decision, the Supreme Court said that segregation was unconstitutional. Marshall became known as a great African American leader. President John F. Kennedy chose him as a judge for the U.S. Court of Appeals in 1961. In 1967, President Johnson picked him to be the first African American justice on the Supreme Court. From there, he was able to do much to help the cause of civil rights. Marshall retired from the court in 1991 and died in 1992.

 CHAPTER REVIEW

Critical Thinking

Write your answers on a sheet of paper, or discuss in class.

Comparing and Contrasting

1. How would liberal, moderate, and conservative opinions about the Civil Rights Act of 1957 be alike? How would they be different?

Making Inferences

2. Why do you think civil rights became such an important issue in the 1950s?

Cooperative Learning

LEARNING STYLE
Verbal

3. Work with a partner or group. Look through the chapter. Find names and other words that you do not know. Find these words in the glossary and gazetteer in the back of the book. They can also be found in most dictionaries. How do you say these names and words? What are the words' meanings? Can you use the names and words in sentences?

Write About It

Writing Portfolio

4. Choose a person discussed in this chapter. Find out about this person. Use your notes to write sentences about the person. Copy these sentences onto 3 x 5 cards. Draw or find a picture of this person. Hang the picture in the classroom. Display the note cards under the picture. Tell the class about this person. Talk about the important things the person accomplished.

Quiz

Number a piece of paper from 1-10. Read each question below. Read the answers that follow each question. Choose the answer for each question. Write the letter of the answer you choose beside the correct number on your piece of paper.

1. What was President Truman's plan to keep the economy strong as soldiers looked for jobs after World War II?
   a. New Deal
   b. Fair Deal
   c. New Federalism
   d. none of the above

2. Why did Truman's plan fail in Congress?
   a. Americans wanted lower prices.
   b. Americans wanted higher wages.
   c. Americans wanted few changes in government.
   d. none of the above

3. What was the U.S. plan to stop the spread of Communism called?
   a. solidarity
   b. containment
   c. concentration
   d. all of the above

4. Who had the job of protecting the West from attack by the Soviet Union?
   a. the United States
   b. Europe
   c. SEATO members
   d. NATO members

5. Why was Korea not reunited as one country?
   a. South Korea lost the war.
   b. Atomic bombs were dropped on China.
   c. The United States did not want to risk a war with China.
   d. all of the above

6. What demand did North Korea make that slowed down the peace talks?
   a. to force all North Korean prisoners to return to their country even if they wanted to stay in South Korea
   b. to be allowed to keep all its South Korean and American prisoners
   c. to set up a Communist government in South Korea
   d. to buy atomic bombs from the United States and the Soviet Union

7. What terms ended the Korean War in July 1953?
   a. keeping the two separate countries of North and South Korea
   b. allowing prisoners to decide where they wanted to live
   c. setting up a demilitarized zone between North and South Korea
   d. all of the above

8. Which of the following affected American life in the 1950s?
   a. inflation's effect on the U.S. economy
   b. McCarthy's hearings about Communists in the United States
   c. growth of suburbs, television, and interstate highways
   d. all of the above

9. Which of the following helped stop some forms of segregation?
   a. *Brown* vs. *Board of Education of Topeka*
   b. Montgomery bus boycott
   c. government forced integration of schools
   d. all of the above

10. Which of the following people did NOT support civil rights for African Americans?
    a. Martin Luther King, Jr.
    b. Governor Orval Faubus
    c. Thurgood Marshall
    d. President Dwight Eisenhower

CLASSIFYING

Add numbers 11–15 to your paper. Read the two lists below. People are listed on the left. Things that the people believe are listed on the right. Match the people with the things that they believe. Write your answers on your paper.

11. liberal
12. moderate
13. conservative
14. left wing supporter
15. right wing supporter

a. wants to keep things as they have been
b. open to all kinds of changes
c. wants only limited changes

Look over the things you wrote for these chapters. Choose one that you like the best. Add to your writing. For example, you made a display with pictures and note cards about people in the civil rights movement. You may wish to add to this display with pictures and note cards about people involved in the Cold War. You also wrote sentences that matched the causes and effects of the Korean War. You may wish to add to that list with sentences about the Cold War and the civil rights movement. Trade papers with a study partner. Check each other's work. Make a clean, neat copy. Put it in your portfolio.

You may wish to work with a study partner. Write these three headings on a piece of paper: **Cold War, Korean War**, and **The Civil Rights Movement**. Discuss these ideas with your partner. List facts under each heading. Share your ideas with other pairs or groups. Are your facts correct? Did you put them under the correct headings? Use these facts to make a chart about the years from 1946-1960. Hang your chart in the classroom.

COOPERATIVE PROJECT: A PICTURE TIMELINE

Work with a partner or group. Make a list of important events that happened during the years that Truman and Eisenhower were President. Write a sentence for each event. Tell why the event was important. Draw a picture for each event, or copy a photograph that shows what happened. Cut a long strip of white paper. Paste the pictures on the paper. Make sure that they are in the correct order. Copy your sentences under the pictures. Remember to add the date for each event. Draw arrows to show how one event may have led to another. Hang this picture timeline on the wall in the hallway so other classes can study it.

Chapter 86

Only 90 Miles Away

Course of Soviet Ships
U.S. aircraft carriers
U.S. naval blockade
Soviet missile sites
U.S. air bases
Bay of Pigs (1961)

Gulf of Mexico

Cape Canaveral
FLORIDA
Miami
Key West

Atlantic Ocean

Havana
CUBA
Guantanamo
Haiti
Dominican Republic
Puerto Rico (U.S.)

Caribbean Sea

```
0        180          360 Miles
0    90       270
```

THE CUBAN MISSILE CRISIS (1962)

Read about how close the United States came to war during the 1960s. How was Cuba involved? Why?

Key *Vocabulary*

missile (MIS uhl) a rocket fired as a weapon

communicate (kuh MYOOH nuh kayt) to speak and write in order to share ideas

Reteaching Vocabulary

debate (di BAYT) a public talk about issues between two or more people in a political race

depression (di PRESH uhn) a time when the economy slows and people are put out of work

mandate (MAN dayt) the voters' approval of a candidate's ideas and plans

---

MAP ANALYSIS

★ **Ask**   What is this map about?

★ **Acquire**   What does the key tell you?

★ **Organize** Look at the legend. It shows how to figure distances. Use a ruler to find out what length stands for 90 miles. Decide what country is 90 miles from Cuba.

★ **Answer**   Why might this country worry about a Communist government running Cuba?

Decoding Tip: Note that e at the end of a syllable can stand for the sound /i/ as in **debate** and **depression**.

ay	cake	ah	fall, cot	air	air
ee	tree	i	sit	oh	cold
or	cord	oy	toy	uh	above, hundred
a	ask	ar	hard	oo	book
e	yet	eye	nice	uhr	liar, fir, further, color
ow	cow	ooh	boot, true	yoo	you, few, cube

▲ John F. Kennedy with Dwight D. Eisenhower

86.1 How did religion and television affect the race for President in 1960?

Religion became an issue in 1960. Richard M. Nixon had been Eisenhower's Vice President. Eisenhower's two terms were ending in 1960. Nixon was chosen for the race by the Republicans. The Democrats chose John F. Kennedy. Massachusetts had sent Kennedy to the U.S. House and Senate. Kennedy was a Roman Catholic. Some people worried he might be more loyal to the Catholic leader—the Pope in Rome.

Kennedy said he would follow the U.S. Constitution. It set up the separation of church and state. Nixon never attacked Kennedy because of his religion. Any worries seemed to die down. However, the race was still very close.

Television seems to have turned the race to Kennedy. It carried news reports about both men's ideas. Candidates had often held **debates**. Now, for the first time, debates were carried by television. Nixon talked about how strong the country was. He promised to keep the United States as a world leader. Kennedy said he would end the small **depression** that had broken out in 1957. Nixon was well known to the people. But he did not come across as well as Kennedy. The television debates helped people get to know Kennedy. The results were very close. Kennedy won the race by about 115,000 popular votes.

▼ The photograph below shows John F. Kennedy giving a speech as his wife Jacqueline Kennedy sits to his right.

1960 Presidential Race

Candidate	Party	Popular Vote	Electoral College Vote
John F. Kennedy	Democrat	34,227,096	303
Richard M. Nixon	Republican	34,108,546	219
Harry F. Byrd	Democrat	Unknown	15

86.2 Why did Kennedy support an invasion of Cuba?

The photograph below shows the debate between Kennedy and Nixon in 1960.

Cuba's government was not liked by its people. It was led by Fulgencio Batista. The United States had given him strong support. But the Cubans hated the way he had been taking away their freedoms. A revolution began in 1953. Fidel Castro led the fight. Batista was forced out of the country in 1959.

▲ Fidel Castro

Castro took over. At first, Americans seemed to like Castro. He promised democracy.

Castro led his country to Communism. This turned most Americans against him. They did not want a Communist country so close to the United States. In 1960, Castro formed close ties with the Soviet Union. President Kennedy decided to help bring down Castro and the Communists.

Kennedy's plan for Cuba failed. The Central Intelligence Agency (CIA) had the job of gathering news about other countries. It made the plans to bring down Castro. It worked with Cubans who hated Castro. They had come to the United States. Kennedy agreed to support their invasion plans. However, no American troops would be used. Kennedy did not want war with the Soviets. The invasion took place on April 17, 1961. The invaders used American guns and ships. They landed at Cuba's Bay of Pigs. Castro's troops stopped the invasion. It took only a few days for Castro to win. Many of the invaders were put in jail.

86.3 Why did the issue of Communism in Cuba affect the world?

Nikita Khrushchev decided to arm Cuba in 1962. He became head of the Soviet Union after Stalin died. He wanted to spread Communism to other countries. Khrushchev put atomic **missiles** in Cuba. They could be fired at places 1,000 miles away. President Kennedy would not stand for that danger to the United States. He ordered the missiles to be

ERECTOR ON LAUNCH PAD
MISSILE READY BLDGS
OXIDIZER VEHICLES
PROB HYDROGEN PEROXIDE TANKS
MISSILE READY BLDGS
FUELING VEHICLES
TENTS
ERECTOR ON LAUNCH PAD
MISSILE ON TRAILER

▲ Cuban missile bases

removed. Khrushchev sent ships with more arms. Kennedy ordered the U.S. Navy to blockade Cuba. He promised an atomic attack on the Soviet Union if Cuban missiles were fired at the United States. People all over the world worried that World War III would break out. At the last minute, Khrushchev ordered the ships to turn around.

86.4 What was the result of the Cuban Missile Crisis?

Both sides won in 1962. The missiles were taken out of Cuba. The Soviet Union showed it did not want an atomic war. Neither did the United States. The Soviet Union kept its weapons away from the United States. However, the United States did stop working against Castro. It would not allow Americans to visit Cuba. American goods could not be sold there either. Cuba remained a Communist country. Khrushchev and Kennedy began **communicating** more closely. A special phone connected the White House with Moscow. The American President could reach the Soviet Premier in a few moments. However, the Cold War was far from over.

☆☆☆

Connections

▲ John F. Kennedy

▲ Richard M. Nixon

Voting in 1960 was not always honest. California and Illinois had problems. Their votes were very close. Some political leaders had broken the law. They had ordered officials to add false votes to the results. This news reached papers and television. Cases were even brought in court. These cases could have changed the winner in each state. However, the courts decided to leave the results as they were. California's Electoral votes stayed with Nixon. Kennedy kept the ones from Illinois.

Some people still believe a false idea about the race. They say that the race was stolen from Nixon. The courts should have given Illinois's Electoral votes to Nixon. Then he would have become President instead of Kennedy. But this is not true. Kennedy won 303 Electoral votes. Nixon won 219. What if the Illinois votes had been changed by the courts? Its 32 Electoral votes would have given Nixon 251 total votes. Kennedy would still have had 271. Kennedy would still have become President.

 CHAPTER REVIEW

Critical Thinking

Write your answers on a sheet of paper, or discuss in class.

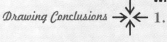 *Drawing Conclusions* →

1. What problems did Kennedy face in having a Communist country so close to the U.S.?

Identifying Main Idea →

2. Why would a world war in the 1960s probably have been worse than World War I or World War II?

Cooperative Learning

LEARNING STYLE
Verbal

3. Work with a partner or group. Some voting results are not even close. One candidate may get far more votes than another. People say the winner has a **mandate**. They mean that the voters really seem to agree with the winner's ideas. They expect the ideas to be carried out. Think about the race between Kennedy and Nixon. How many Americans voted for Kennedy? How many popular votes did Nixon win? Did Kennedy win a mandate in 1960?

Write About It

Writing Portfolio

4. Find out about John F. Kennedy, Fidel Castro, or Nikita Khrushchev. Who was this person? How did he become the leader of his country? What happened to his country while he was the leader? How long did this man keep power? Write a report that answers these questions. Share these facts with the class.

Chapter 87

Exploring Space

The Space Race		
Event	**United States**	**Soviet Union**
First satellite sent to orbit Earth	Explorer I January 30, 1958	Sputnik I October 4, 1957
first living thing sent into space	Able and Baker (monkeys) May 28, 1959	Laika (dog) November 3, 1957
first person sent into space	Alan B. Shepard, Jr. Mercury-Redstone 3 May 5, 1961	Yuri A. Gagarin Vostok I April 12, 1961
first person to orbit the Earth	John H. Glenn, Jr. Mercury-Atlas 6 February 20, 1962 3 Orbits	Yuri A. Gagrin Vostok I April 12, 1961 1 Orbit
first woman sent into space	Sally Ride Challenger April 4-9, 1983	Valentina V. Tereshkova Vostok 6 June 16-19, 1963
first person to walk in space	Edward H. White II Gemini-Titan 4 June 3-7, 1965	Aleksei A. Leonov Voshkod 2 March 18, 1965
first ship to reach the moon	Ranger IV April 23, 1962	Luna 2 September 12, 1959
first ship to land on the moon	Surveyor V September 8, 1967	Luna 9 February 3, 1966
first people to fly to the moon	Frank Borman; James A. Lovell, Jr.; William A. Anders Apollo-Saturn 7 October 26-30, 1968	
first people to land on the moon	Neil A. Armstrong; Edwin E. Aldrin, Jr., Michael Collins Apollo-Saturn 11 July 16-24, 1969	

Read about people who actually left the planet Earth. What two countries led the way? Why?

Key *Vocabulary*

space (spays) the area between planets and other heavenly bodies; contains no gravity or air

satellite (SAT uh leyet) a machine sent into space so it can circle a planet or moon and help send radio and television signals

astronaut (AS truh naht) someone who travels into space

Reteaching Vocabulary

explore (ik SPLOR) to search the unknown in order to find facts

---

CHART ANALYSIS

★ **Ask**   What does this chart compare?

★ **Organize**   Compare the facts. Decide which country had the most firsts.

★ **Answer**   Which word describes how well these two countries were getting along: **friends** or **competitors**?

Decoding Tip: Note that e at the end of a word is silent as in **space**, **satellite**, and **explore**.

ay	cake	ah	fall, cot	air	air
ee	tree	i	sit	oh	cold
or	cord	oy	toy	uh	above, hundred
a	ask	ar	hard	oo	book
e	yet	eye	nice	uhr	liar, fir, further, color
ow	cow	ooh	boot, true	yoo	you, few, cube

87.1 What began the space race between the United States and the Soviet Union?

Shocking news reached the United States in 1957. The Soviet Union had fired a rocket into **space**. Soon, it was sending more rockets. They even carried passengers. A dog named "Laika" was the first living thing from Earth to go into space. The Soviets did not bring this ship back, though. The dog died in space. Soviet space rockets were something to worry about for the United States. Would the Soviets arm them with atomic weapons? President Eisenhower did not want the Soviets to have this edge. He pushed the government to set up a space program. Congress agreed.

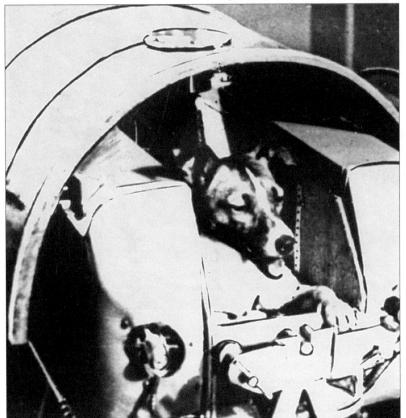

▲ The photograph above shows Laika, the world's first space traveller, aboard the Sputnik II in 1957.

The U.S. Congress set up the National Aeronautics and Space Administration (NASA). It still runs America's space program. Congress also set up a special committee. It checks all the work done by NASA. This committee was first led by Senator Lyndon B. Johnson. NASA's plans worked very well. By the middle 1960s, the United States led the Soviet Union in **exploring** space.

Many American and Soviet rockets carried **satellites**. These machines were set to orbit, or circle, Earth. Today, satellites are very important. Radio, telephone, and television signals can be sent to the satellites. They bounce the signals to all parts of the world. Wires are no longer needed for people to communicate with each other. Without satellites, there would be no pagers, cellular phones, and television shows played live all over the world.

▶ John Glenn

87.2 What were the Mercury and Gemini programs?

NASA set up two special programs. Mercury was the push to put a person into space. Each Mercury rocket carried just one person. The program proved that such trips were possible. The first Mercury **astronauts** were from the United States Armed Forces. These men not only reached space. They orbited the world in Mercury ships.

Gemini ships carried two people. These ships proved that people could work in space. Special tests were held. One person would fly the ship. The other person would step out into space. Special suits were needed for these walks in space. There is no air in space. Only a gold rope was strong enough to keep the person from floating away. The Mercury and Gemini programs showed that long space trips were possible.

87.3 How did the Apollo program reach President Kennedy's goals?

President John F. Kennedy continued the push into space. He asked Congress for more money. Billions of dollars were spent. The United States kept up with the Soviets in the space race. President Kennedy promised that Americans would walk on the moon by 1970.

NASA's Apollo program sent Americans to the moon. Each Apollo ship carried three people. According to plans, a ship would fly to the moon. One person would stay on board. The other two would fly a landing craft down to the moon. But was such a trip possible? Apollo 7 flew to the moon in October 1968. It did not land. It made orbits around the moon. The flight was a success. But was a landing possible?

Americans walked on the moon in 1969. Apollo 11 carried Neil Armstrong, Edwin Aldrin, and Michael

▲ The photograph above shows one of the astronauts of the Apollo II walking on the moon.

Collins. Collins stayed on Apollo 11. Armstrong and Aldrin flew the landing craft, the *Eagle*. It landed on the moon on July 20. Armstrong left the *Eagle*. He was the first person to set foot on the moon. At that moment, he said, "That's one small step for man, one giant leap for mankind."

☆☆☆

Connections

▲ Splashdown of Apollo 13

Six trips were made to the moon. All but one went well. Apollo 13 had problems. An air tank blew up. Apollo 13 could not be flown or controlled. The astronauts did not try to land on the moon. Instead, they used the landing craft in a new way. It flew Apollo 13 back to Earth. Then it was released into space. Apollo 13 fell through Earth's atmosphere. It splashed down into the ocean. The three astronauts were saved. The story of Apollo 13 became a movie in 1995. This movie was a big hit in the summer season. People were fascinated by the story. The special effects looked very real. NASA helped in the making of the movie. The astronauts from Apollo 13 said the movie told the true story of what had happened. The movie *Apollo 13* helped people see just how dangerous the return trip had been.

★★★ CHAPTER REVIEW

Critical Thinking

Write your answers on a sheet of paper, or discuss in class.

Recognizing Details

1. Why was the United States worried about the Soviet Union's space program?

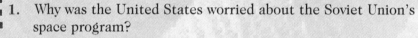
Making Inferences

2. How do you think having total control of space would affect a country?

Cooperative Learning

LEARNING STYLE
Visual
Tactile

3. Work with a partner or group. Find photographs of early American and Soviet space trips. Use these pictures to make a poster about the space race. Hang your poster with those made by others in your class. Add labels to explain what is happening in each poster. Display them in a hallway for the whole school to see.

Write About It

Writing Portfolio

4. Imagine you are a reporter. You are covering one of the events listed in the chart. Write a report about this event. Tell what people might have seen. Remember to answer **who**, **what**, **when**, **where**, **why**, and **how**. Work with others in your class. Put all the stories together. Create a "Space Race" newspaper. Share the paper with other classes.

Chapter 88

Violence in America

Civil Rights and President Kennedy

Right	Date	President's Action
jobs	March 1961	Executive order created the Equal Employment Opportunity Commission to make sure defense factories gave jobs to African Americans
education	June 1962	Used National Guard and U.S. troops to make sure African Americans were allowed into the University of Mississippi
voting	August 1962	Supported the 24th Amendment, to make poll taxes illegal; ratified by the states in 1964
housing	November 1962	Executive order made discrimination illegal in tax-supported housing
education	June 1963	Used National Guard and U.S. troops to make sure African Americans were allowed into the University of Alabama

Read about problems in the 1960s. How did these problems cause fighting? Why?

Key *Vocabulary*

protest (PROH test) an act held to show that people disagree or oppose some plan or idea

Reteaching Vocabulary

violence (VEYE uh luhns) the use of force against people

civil rights (SIV uhl • reyets) all the privileges held by the citizens of a city, state, or country

CHART ANALYSIS

★ **Ask**   What is this chart about?

★ **Organize**   What facts are listed in each column?

★ **Answer**   How did President Kennedy seem to feel about the rights of African Americans?

Decoding Tip: Note that c stands for the /s/ sound in **violence** and **civil rights**.

ay	cake	ah	fall, cot	air	air
ee	tree	i	sit	oh	cold
or	cord	oy	toy	uh	above, hundred
a	ask	ar	hard	oo	book
e	yet	eye	nice	uhr	liar, fir, further, color
ow	cow	ooh	boot, true	yoo	you, few, cube

▲ Jacqueline and John F. Kennedy

John Connally with Mrs. Connally

88.1 Why did violence break out in the civil rights movement?

Pushing for civil rights led to **violence**. This push had begun with President Franklin D. Roosevelt. Each President who followed also worked for **civil rights**. John F. Kennedy did not push civil rights during his first year as President. He felt that Congress would not agree with his ideas. He set up Executive Orders instead. These helped African Americans gain many rights. For example, the government began hiring more African Americans. However, it was a slow process. Kennedy's orders only affected the federal government. The rest of the country did not have to follow these orders.

African Americans began holding more **protests**. People in the marches were often attacked. Riots broke out across the country. Kennedy decided to go to Congress. He asked for a new Civil Rights Act. The government would lead the fight. It would make sure that African Americans had their rights.

▼ The photograph below shows Mrs. Kennedy about to enter the motorcade to the burial of her husband, assassinated President John F. Kennedy.

However, Congress would not pass the act. More riots then broke out.

88.2 How did the Kennedy Presidency end?

President Kennedy was killed on November 22, 1963. The President and Mrs. Kennedy were visiting Texas. They went to Dallas. They were riding in an open car. Texas Governor John Connally and his wife were with them. About noon, shots rang out. The President and Governor Connally were hit. They were rushed to a hospital.

Connally pulled through. But the President died less than an hour after the shooting. *Air Force I* flew the President's body back to Washington, D.C. Mrs. Kennedy, Vice President Lyndon Johnson, and Mrs. Johnson went on the plane, too. During the flight, Johnson took the oath of office. The country now had a new President.

▲ The photographs above of Lee Harvey Oswald were taken from the Warren Commission.

88.3 What were the results of the Warren Commission?

Soon after the shooting, Lee Harvey Oswald was arrested. He had shot a Dallas police officer near his home. Oswald was caught in a movie theater. A rifle had been found in the Texas School Book Depository. Oswald worked there. The FBI learned that the rifle was Oswald's. The police kept him in jail for two days. Then they decided to move him. During the move, shots rang out again. Oswald was killed. The police saw the shooting. Most Americans did, too. The move was being shown live on television. Everyone saw the police arrest Jack Ruby for this shooting.

A special board was set up to study Kennedy's killing. President Johnson picked its members. It was led by Earl

▲ The photograph above shows flowers scattered about the site of the President's assassination.

Warren, the Chief Justice of the Supreme Court. Its report came out in September 1964. It said there had been no big plot. Yes, Oswald was a Communist. Yes, he had lived in the Soviet Union. However, the Warren Commission said that the Soviets had nothing to do with killing the President. Oswald had acted alone. Ruby had also acted alone, the Commission said. Ruby was put on trial. He was to be put to death. However, he died in jail on January 3, 1967.

☆☆☆

Connections

Arlen Specter worked for the Warren Commission as a lawyer. Specter later became a Senator from Pennsylvania. Specter came up with an idea to explain the killing of President Kennedy. Three shots had been fired. Two bullets had reached Kennedy's car. Specter said one bullet had hit Kennedy in the neck. Then it had flown out of his body. It had next hit Governor Connally. The Commission agreed with this idea. Some people said this finding was wrong.

Congress put out its own report in 1978. Many books had been

▲ Ted, Jacqueline and Robert Kennedy at President Kennedy's Funeral

written since the killing. They said other people had helped Oswald.

Finally, the U.S. House looked into the killing. It said that other people probably had helped kill the President. No people were named, though. Congress ordered the Justice Department to study this idea. Some people said this was a waste of time and money. The Warren Commission was right, they said. The Justice Department has not started its study yet. What really happened on November 22, 1963? No one may ever know for sure.

★★☆ CHAPTER REVIEW

Critical Thinking

Write your answers on a sheet of paper, or discuss in class.

Recognizing Details

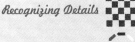
Making Inferences

1. How did violence affect the United States in the 1960s?

2. Why do you think people have been so interested in Kennedy's killing?

Cooperative Learning

LEARNING STYLE
Tactile

3. Work with a partner or group. Pretend you are a TV reporter. You are in Dallas on November 22, 1963. You have seen the shooting. Now you have to give a live TV report. Think about what you will say. Remember to tell **who, what, when, where, why,** and **how.** Give your report to the class.

Write About It

Writing Portfolio

4. Choose a person from Chapter 88. Find out about this person. Write five sentences about this person. Add your sentences to those written by the class. Use the sentences to make a chart about President Kennedy. Put the chart in a display on the bulletin board.

Chapter 89

Controversial Ideas

CHINA

VIETNAM
Dien Bien Phu
Hanoi★   •Haiphong

LAOS

Gulf of
Tonkin   HAINAN

Vientiane   •Vinh

THAILAND   Khe Sanh   Quang Tri Hue
Hue
Da Nang
Tam Ky
Chu Lai
Kontum

Bangkok   Pleiku

CAMBODIA   Quinhon
Ban Me
Thuot   Tuy Hoa
Phnom Penh
Tay Ninh   Da Lat   Nha Trang
Phuoc Binh   Cam Ranh Bay
Long Binh
Can Tao   Mekong Delta   SOUTH VIETNAM
Quan Long   Khanh Hung

N
W   E
S

South
China
Sea

▲ Tet Offensive, Jan. 1968
■ United States Base
☐ South Vietnam
☐ North Vietnam

0   1000   2000 Miles
0   1000   2000 Kilometers

**THE VIETNAM WAR
(1968)**

Read about Lyndon Johnson's years as President. How did he try to carry out President Kennedy's ideas? Why?

Key *Vocabulary*

offensive (uh FENT siv)
an attack against an enemy during war

pollution (puh LOO shuhn)
those things that make land, water, or air dirty and dangerous

Reteaching Vocabulary

adviser (uhd VEYE suhr)
a person who shares knowledge or facts in order to be of help

environment (in VEYE ruhn muhnt) the weather, living things, and geography that make up a place and that depend upon each other

MAP ANALYSIS	★ **Ask**	What is this map about?
	★ **Acquire**	What Communist country was a neighbor of North Vietnam?
	★ **Organize**	Make a chart of the countries shown in the map. List which countries had U.S. bases.
	★ **Analyze**	In what parts of Vietnam did Communist attacks take place in 1968?
	★ **Answer**	Why do you think it might be hard for the United States to keep South Vietnam independent?

Decoding Tip: Note the long sound of *i* in **adviser** and **environment**.

ay	cake	ah	fall, cot	air	air
ee	tree	i	sit	oh	cold
or	cord	oy	toy	uh	above, hundred
a	ask	ar	hard	oo	book
e	yet	eye	nice	uhr	liar, fir, further, color
ow	cow	ooh	boot, true	yoo	you, few, cube

89.1 What was President Johnson's plan to create a Great Society?

Few other Presidents were as successful in getting their ideas carried out as Lyndon Johnson. President Johnson felt he should carry out Kennedy's ideas. After all, he was filling out Kennedy's term. Johnson pushed Congress to pass Kennedy's programs. Besides, Johnson had been in both the U.S. House and Senate. He knew how Congress worked. He knew its members well. This knowledge helped Johnson get new laws passed.

▲ President Lyndon B. Johnson

Johnson was elected President in 1964. The Republicans had chosen Barry Goldwater for the race. He promised to cut back on federal government. It was too powerful, he said. He wanted government to take less action in people's lives. Goldwater said people had the right to do what they pleased. He said they had the right to segregate themselves. Government had no business working to end discrimination.

The people did not agree with Goldwater. Johnson beat Goldwater by about 16 million votes. Democrats also took over most of the seats in Congress. They helped Johnson carry out his plans.

The President said he wanted to create a Great Society. Everyone would be equal. Opportunity would be open to all. Government would work to make sure that no one was poor. Johnson called this a "War on Poverty." New laws set up these programs. Kennedy's Civil Rights Acts were passed. Voting rights would be guaranteed by the federal government. No one could discriminate in selling or renting a home. Johnson pushed his own ideas, too. The United States government began building homes for the poor. More money was spent on schools. Government even helped with health issues. Medicare and Medicaid were set up. Medicare helps the elderly pay hospital and doctor bills. Medicaid helps the poor with these bills.

89.2 Why were the people of Vietnam fighting a war?

Like Korea, Vietnam was a divided country. Communists ruled North Vietnam. South Vietnam had a democratic government. However, it was very corrupt. Government leaders stole most of the tax money. Little was left to pay for government services. Many South Vietnamese became Communists. They were known as the "Vietcong." They received help from North Vietnam. The Vietcong began a war to take over the country in 1960.

President Kennedy sent **advisers** to help South Vietnam. These people were members of the U.S. Armed Forces. They helped train the South Vietnamese Army. They helped make war plans. Kennedy was carrying out the promise of the Southeast Asia Treaty Organization (SEATO). Like NATO, this was a group of countries. They promised to help each other in case of attack. Both the United States and South Vietnam were members. North Vietnam increased its support for the Vietcong. However, Kennedy would not send American soldiers to help fight the war.

89.3 How did the United States become deeply involved in the Vietnam War?

Even with some U.S. help, the war went badly for South Vietnam. The South Vietnamese Army decided to take over the government in 1963. General Nguyen Van Thieu later became President of South Vietnam. The government was still corrupt. However, the United States did not want Communists to win the war. It supported Thieu's government.

▲ American soldier in Vietnam

Congress gave Johnson special powers. He could do anything to help South Vietnam in its fight against Communism. President Johnson decided to send more advisers to South Vietnam in 1964. In early 1965, the United States sent planes to bomb North Vietnam. In April, U.S. troops arrived to fight in the war. North Vietnam sent more and more troops and arms to the Vietcong. By July, almost 200,000 American soldiers were in the war. Over 1/2 million Americans were in the fight by 1968.

The Tet **Offensive** changed the war. North Vietnam and the Vietcong had agreed to a short truce. The Vietnamese were celebrating their new year. The Vietcong broke the truce on January 30, 1968. All parts of South Vietnam were attacked. South Vietnam and the United States were taken by complete surprise. They fought to hold onto the country. The North Vietnamese and the Vietcong lost lots of soldiers. But the American people saw that the war had no end in sight. The Communists seemed stronger than ever. Bombing of North Vietnam was stopped. Johnson called for peace talks. They began in May 1968.

☆☆☆

Connections

▲ Rachel Carson

In the 1960s, people began to worry about the **environment**. They were afraid of what was happening to animals and plants in the United States. Rachel Carson wrote about this problem. Her book *Silent Spring* came out in 1962. It talked about all the sprays people used to kill bugs.

Farmers used sprays to protect their crops. People used sprays to save their homes and lawns. However, *Silent Spring* showed that bugs have an important place in nature. Sprays were dangerous in other ways. Some seeped into foods. People ate the sprays with their food. These sprays could make people sick. Some people wanted to protect the environment. They asked the U.S. government to pass new laws against dangerous sprays.

Other kinds of **pollution** began to worry Americans. Cleaning up the country became one of the nation's chief goals. First Lady Lady Bird Johnson began a special program. It was called "Keep America Beautiful." She urged Americans to stop littering the countryside. For over

▲ Lady Bird Johnson

30 years, she has helped set up groups around the country. They plant wildflowers along roads and in parks. Picking up trash and planting flowers was only one answer. Recycling, or reusing, old paper and metals also helps the environment. Today, there are recycling programs in almost every American city and town.

★★☆ CHAPTER REVIEW

Critical Thinking

Write your answers on a sheet of paper, or discuss in class.

Identifying Main Idea

1. What two main problems did President Johnson work to solve?

Making Inferences

2. How did American voters seem to feel about President Johnson and his ideas?

Cooperative Learning

LEARNING STYLE
Reading Oral

3. Work with a partner or group. Think about the facts in Chapter 89. Make up a question about one fact. Ask the question of your partner or group. If no one knows the answer, show where it can be found. Have your partner or other member of the group ask a question. Continue until each person has asked three questions.

Write About It

Writing Portfolio

4. Look over Chapter 84 about the Korean War. How was it like the Vietnam War? Use facts from Chapters 84 and 89 to make a chart. Compare the Korean and Vietnam Wars. Make sure you use complete sentences in your chart. Compare your chart with those of other people in your class.

Chapter 90

People Power

African Americans Who Were Registered to Vote			
State	Percent Registered in 1960	Percent Registered in 1966	Change
Alabama	15.2%	48.9%	+33.7%
Arkansas	37.6%	54.0%	+16.4%
Florida	34.7%	62.1%	+27.4%
Georgia	29.3%	43.2%	+13.9%
Louisiana	30.4%	42.3%	+11.9%
Mississippi	5.2%	27.8%	+22.6%
N. Carolina	31.3%	49.0%	+17.7%
S. Carolina	15.7%	45.1%	+29.4%
Tennessee	58.9%	71.7%	+12.8%
Texas	34.9%	44.0%	+20.2%

Read about the push for civil rights during the 1960s. How did different groups try to gain their rights? Why?

Key *Vocabulary*

feminism (FEM uh niz uhm) the idea of complete equality between the sexes

generation (jen uh RAY shuhn) a group of people born about the same time and sharing the same experiences

demonstration (dem uh STRAY shuhn) an event staged to show people's beliefs and ideas

Reteaching Vocabulary

inflation (in FLAY shuhn) a time when prices continue to go up

slum (sluhm) a part of a city that is very crowded, poor, and dirty

CHART ANALYSIS

★ **Ask**   What is this chart about?

★ **Acquire**   What does each column and row tell you?

★ **Organize** Write these headings on a piece of paper: **Less than 33%, Between 34% and 66%,** and **Over 66%.** List the states under each heading for 1960. Then make a similar list for 1966.

★ **Analyze**   What state made the biggest gain in registering African Americans to vote? Which state made the smallest gain?

★ **Answer**   Why might the numbers have been low in 1960 and higher in 1966?

Decoding Tip: Note that tion stands for /shun/ in **generation, demonstration,** and **inflation.**

ay	cake	ah	fall, cot	air	air
ee	tree	i	sit	oh	cold
or	cord	oy	toy	uh	above, hundred
a	ask	ar	hard	oo	book
e	yet	eye	nice	uhr	liar, fir, further, color
ow	cow	ooh	boot, true	yoo	you, few, cube

90.1 What was the women's rights movement?

Inflation grew because of President Johnson's programs. The government was spending money at home and around the world. Fighting in Vietnam cost a lot of money. Much of this money was used to buy goods. This made prices go up. Wages did not go up at the same rate. Most workers were men. By the late 1960s, it was hard for one person to earn enough money to support a family. Many women began working, too.

Working women faced problems. Some jobs were not open to them. They pushed to get jobs as lawyers and doctors. Some women took construction jobs. They helped put up buildings. It took years, but most jobs opened up to women. There were other problems, though. A woman was often paid less for doing the same job as a man.

Many women began calling for equal rights. They wanted the same rights as male workers. They also wanted equal rights in all areas of American life. This idea is called **feminism**. They were led by people like Betty Friedan and Gloria Steinem. By the late 1960s, women had formed their own political groups. The largest was the National Organization of Women (NOW).

▼ The photo below shows Dr. Martin Luther King delivering his famous "I Have a Dream" speech.

90.2 What groups pushed for civil rights?

Equal rights were demanded by many minorities. Laws had set up segregation in some states in the South. However, segregation and discrimination happened in all states, even where they were against the law.

Martin Luther King led African Americans in pushing for equal rights. King would not let his followers use

▲ Malcolm X

violence, though. Some African Americans were not happy. Rights were not being gained fast enough.

Some African Americans began to follow the teachings of Elijah Muhammad. He led the Black Muslims. They wanted equal rights. They also wanted complete separation from whites in America. Malcolm X was a powerful Black Muslim leader. As the years passed, Malcolm X felt that separation was not possible. He began calling for integration of African Americans into all parts of American life. He was killed in 1965. Many people believe that he was killed by Black Muslims for going back on Black Muslim ideas.

Native Americans wanted their treaty rights. For hundreds of years, Native Americans had lost their lands and rights. New government plans were often set up. But things never seemed to get much better. In the 1960s, Native Americans were seeking stronger tribal governments. The National Congress of American Indians pushed for civil rights. The tribes did have some victories. The government honored some old treaties. Lands were given to Native Americans in states like New Mexico and Alaska. However, things moved slowly.

▲ Cesar Chavez

Hispanic Americans formed their own civil rights groups. Cesar Chavez led one of the largest groups. He pushed for the rights of migrant workers. Most of these people had come from Mexico. They moved from place to place. They picked farmers' crops. Chavez's United Farm Workers helped bring about better living conditions on the farms. They pushed for higher wages, too. Almost 1/2 million Hispanics had come to the United States from Puerto Rico. Most moved to New York. They were already U.S. citizens. However, they were often segregated into **slums**. Most could find only the lowest paying jobs. They began calling for their rights as citizens, too.

90.3   Why did young people begin protests?

Young people in the 1960s turned against the corruption they saw in America. Many were worried about the Vietnam

▲ The photograph above shows young people protesting the Vietnam War during the 1960s.

War. The government had brought back the draft. Most of the people called into the Armed Services were 18 years old. Some went to bases in Europe and other parts of the world. However, most were sent to Vietnam.

Many young people felt the war was being fought out of greed. Communism was not being beaten. Clearly, thousands of people were dying in Vietnam. But the government was spending billions of dollars. The Armed Forces needed uniforms, arms, planes, and other goods for the war. Factories were turning out these goods in record numbers. Factory owners were becoming richer than ever. They would lose money if the war ended, said some Americans. College students seemed to be especially upset at this idea. These students began protests against the war. Protests were held at colleges all across the country. Young people pushed for another new idea. They wanted to be able to vote. In 1971, the

Constitution was changed. The 26th Amendment lets all citizens vote when they turn 18.

Students rebelled in other ways, too. They pointed to a "**generation** gap." The older generation did not understand new ideas, some young people said. These young people turned against anything supported by the older generation. Students at the University of California at Berkeley were among the strongest student leaders. They let their hair grow long. They wore wild clothing. Even their music was very different. Wild colors were popular. Some young people studied new religions. Asian religions were followed. However, the youth movement had a dark side. Many young people tried different drugs. During the 1960s, problems with drugs grew.

90.4   Why did violence break out during the 1960s?

Violence grew in the civil rights movement. New African American groups were formed. Stokely Carmichael took over as leader of the Student Non-Violent Coordinating Committee (SNCC). He formed the idea of black power. African Americans should demand equal rights. They should take control of their own lives. However, like Martin Luther King, Jr., Carmichael opposed violence.

Another group, the Black Panthers, followed the idea of black power. However, they used all forms of violence to reach this goal. The move toward civil rights was very slow. Many African Americans became

▼ The photograph below shows the National Guard taking action during a violent period in the suburb of Watts in Los Angeles, California, in August 1965.

frustrated at this slowness. Rioting broke out in several American cities in 1964–1966.

Other civil rights groups caused violence, too. The American Indian Movement (AIM) sometimes used violence to push for its demands. Once again, the National Guard was used to keep law and order. Many Native Americans did not like this violence. It even slowed the push for civil rights. Students led protests and demonstrations across the country. These events often turned into riots. Many colleges were hit by student riots and **demonstrations**. Student groups became some of the most dangerous. The Weathermen and Students for a Democratic Society (SDS) called for an overthrow of the United States government.

90.5 How did the government try to stop the violence?

President Johnson sent the National Guard to stop the riots. It stopped riots in Watts, California in 1965. Twenty-eight African Americans were killed in the fighting.

The violence of racism killed Martin Luther King, too. He was visiting Memphis, Tennessee in 1968. He was shot on April 4. James Earl Ray was sent to prison for killing King. King did not believe in violence. However, his death caused more rioting by African Americans.

The National Guard was sent to stop almost every riot and protest. On May 4, 1970, students were protesting at Kent State University. The National Guard opened fire. Four students were killed. The whole country was shocked. Most people felt the killings should never have happened. A few felt the students had been out of control. The killings had a deep effect on the country. The violence began to stop. Few riots broke out after the killings at Kent State.

Connections

Everything seemed to be changing in the 1960s. Music also changed. Rock music was everywhere. To many young people, rock music was more than just fun. It was an important part of their lives. And no group was more important than the Beatles.

The Beatles were from Liverpool, England. They started out playing simple rock and roll songs. Their heroes were American singers like Chuck Berry and Elvis Presley. By 1964, the Beatles were the top group in the world. Young people grew their hair long like the Beatles. The group played to large crowds in the United States. They appeared on TV on "The Ed Sullivan Show." It seemed like everyone was watching. The Beatles' first songs were simple and fun. But like everything in the 1960s, the Beatles were changing fast.

By 1967, the Beatles' music had grown more complicated. John Lennon and Paul McCartney wrote many different kinds of songs. Some were playful and some were dark. Fans listened closely for hidden meanings. With *Sgt. Pepper's Lonely Hearts Club Band* (1967), the Beatles reached a new peak. Their songs spoke to young people in new ways. They wrote about drugs and revolution. Then as the 1960s came to an end, the Beatles broke up. The hopes of the 1960s seemed to crash in war protests and race riots. But the Beatles' music still sounds fresh today.

▲ The Beatles

★★☆ CHAPTER REVIEW

Critical Thinking

Write your answers on a sheet of paper, or discuss in class.

Identifying Main Idea

1. Why were some groups unhappy with American life in the 1960s?

Making Inferences

2. How did people become divided over the issues of the 1960s?

Cooperative Learning

LEARNING STYLE
Writing
Tactile

3. Work with a partner or group. Look through books and magazines for facts about the 1960s. Copy some of the ideas you find. Draw pictures to illustrate these ideas. Use the words and pictures to make a poster about the 1960s.

Write About It

Writing Portfolio

4. Think about the "generation gap." What might an older person have believed in the 1960s? What ideas were held by some young people? Write three sentences for each of these two groups. The sentences should express their ideas. Read your sentences aloud. Ask volunteers to name the group that would support each idea.

Chapter 91

New Directions

CHINA

VIETNAM

Dien Bien Phu

Hanoi★ •Haiphong

LAOS

Gulf of Tonkin HAINAN

Vientiane •Vinh

N

W E

S

Quang Tri Hue

THAILAND Khe Sanh •Hue

•Da Nang

Tam Ky

•Chu Lai

Kontum

Bangkok

Pleiku

CAMBODIA Ban Me •Quinhon
Thuot •Tuy Hoa

Phnom Penh Da Lat •Nha Trang
Tay Ninh Phuoc Binh Cam Ranh Bay
Long Binh

Can Tao Mekong Delta **SOUTH VIETNAM**

Quan Long •Khanh Hung

South China Sea

	United States Base
	North Vietnames sanctuary
◄···	North Vietnamese supply routes
	South Vietnam
	North Vietnam

0 1000 2000 Miles
0 1000 2000 Kilometers

THE VIETNAM WAR (1973)

Read about
President Richard Nixon. How did he change the course of the country? Why?

Key *Vocabulary*

convention (kuhn VEN chuhn) a meeting held to choose a party's candidates for office

Reteaching Vocabulary

debt (det) money owed to another

term (tuhrm) the details set up in order to reach an agreement or goal

treaty (TREE tee) a written agreement reached by two or more countries

MAP ANALYSIS

★ **Ask** What is this map about?

★ **Acquire** What countries are neighbors of North and South Vietnam?

★ **Organize** Look at the key. Make a list of the countries that supported North Vietnam. Make a list of the countries that supported South Vietnam and the United States.

★ **Answer** Why do you think the United States might move against countries like Cambodia and Laos?

Decoding Tip: Note that *ea* stands for the long sound of *e* in **treaty**.

ay	cake	ah	fall, cot	air	air
ee	tree	i	sit	oh	cold
or	cord	oy	toy	uh	above, hundred
a	ask	ar	hard	oo	book
e	yet	eye	nice	uhr	liar, fir, further, color
ow	cow	ooh	boot, true	yoo	you, few, cube

91.1 How did violence and the Vietnam War affect the race for President in 1968?

Anti-war protests became a major issue in the 1968 race for President. Most of the protests were against the war. Some were also against President Johnson. Many people felt he was creating too much **debt**. Johnson's War on Poverty was costing a lot of money. The President decided he was too unpopular to run again.

The Democrats needed to pick a new candidate for President. They held their **convention** in Chicago. Vice President Hubert Humphrey was chosen for the race. He promised to carry out Johnson's ideas for the Great Society. However, he did not support Johnson's ideas in Vietnam.

Terrible rioting broke out in Chicago during the Democratic Convention. Student protesters filled the streets outside the convention hall. They called for equal rights and an end to the war. Mayor Richard Daley sent the Chicago police to stop the protests. Fighting broke out. Hundreds of people were hurt in the fight. Even some innocent people on the sidewalks were hurt. All of it was shown on television. The country was shocked and angered by the violence of the government against citizens using their right of free speech.

A third party was formed in 1968. George Wallace had been the governor of Alabama. He had tried to stop integration in his state. He set up the racist American Party. It called for an end to the civil rights movement. States would be allowed to pass laws setting up segregation. Many states in the South voted for Wallace. However, few other states followed his ideas.

Richard Nixon promised to bring back law and order to the country. He also promised to pull U.S. troops out of Vietnam. He said South Vietnam would not be abandoned. He talked about a secret plan that would bring "peace with honor." After the events in Chicago, people worried about the

▲ Americans were divided in the 1960s. The top photograph shows demonstrations in favor of the Vietnam War, and the bottom photograph shows a scuffle with police during a protest of the war.

▲ The photograph above is of soldiers and civilians in the streets of Hue, Vietnam.

Republican Convention in Miami. However, it was peaceful. The Republicans chose Nixon as their candidate.

The race was close. Nixon won less than half of all the votes. But this was enough for Nixon to become President.

91.2 How did President Nixon plan to pull U.S. troops out of Vietnam?

"Vietnamization" was the name of Nixon's plan for Vietnam. American troops would be brought home in groups.

1968 Presidential Race			
Candidate	Party	Popular Vote	Electoral College Vote
Richard M. Nixon	Republican	31,785,480	301
Hubert H. Humphrey	Democrat	31,275,166	191
George C. Wallace	American	9,906,473	46

▲ The photograph above is from the war in Vietnam.

The war would not end. South Vietnam would carry on the fight. Its troops would be trained and armed by the United States. The first American troops were pulled out of Vietnam in August 1969. This plan would be used around the world, said Nixon. The United States would help protect other countries. Arms and supplies would be sent. However, no American troops would fight in any of these wars.

Nixon knew that South Vietnam would have trouble with the war. He ordered planes to bomb parts of Cambodia and Laos. The Vietcong and North Vietnamese had bases in these countries. Nixon wanted to push them back into Vietnam. Then the Communists would have trouble winning without outside help.

Peace **terms** were reached in early 1973. The United States promised to pull out of Vietnam. Thousands of Americans had been killed in the Vietnam War. Nothing had been won. In

Americans in Vietnam	
Number who served	8,744,000
Killed in Battle	47,369
Others Killed	10,799
Wounded	153,303
Missing	about 2,500

1973 less than 25,000 American soldiers were still in Vietnam. All American prisoners were to be set free by North Vietnam. North Vietnam promised to leave South Vietnam alone. Elections would be held in South Vietnam to set up a democratic government.

However, when U.S. troops left, the war went on. In late 1974, North Vietnam began a huge attack on South Vietnam. On April 30, 1975, the North won the war and took over the South. Vietnam became one country with a Communist government. Many South Vietnamese fled the country. They crowded onto small boats. Most of them came to the United States.

The United States had few dealings with Vietnam until 1995. In that year, President Bill Clinton recognized the country of Vietnam. The two countries now have full and open dealings with each other. However, many Americans were angered by President Clinton's actions. Some American prisoners were still missing. Many Americans wanted Vietnam to tell what had happened to these prisoners. Only then should the United States deal with Vietnam, they said.

91.3 Why were President Nixon's dealings with other countries so successful?

Nixon hoped to slow down the Cold War. The two main Communist countries were China and the Soviet Union. However, these two countries did not get along. China did not like the way the Soviets tried to control its affairs. China supported North Korea. The Soviet Union supported North Vietnam. Nixon worked to make friends with Communist China. If that happened, the Soviet Union would have less

For the People, By the People

▲ The photograph above shows Richard Nixon at the Great Wall of China during a trip while he was President.

support in the world. It might be more willing to talk. It might stop trying to take over other countries.

New agreements were reached with China in 1972. Trade was opened up between the United States and China. The United States promised to help China get into the U.N. Nixon said that Taiwan should stay in the U.N., too. However, the U.N. did not agree. Taiwan's seat was taken away. It was given to Communist China. A Washington, D.C., office was opened by China. The United States set up one in Peking.

Friendship with China changed U.S. dealings with the Soviet Union. Each side feared atomic war. They now agreed to limit their atomic weapons. They agreed not to sell these weapons to other countries, either. A **treaty** was written. It was called the SALT Treaty. President Nixon went to Moscow to sign the treaty in May 1972. In August, the U.S. Senate

▲ The photograph above is a section of the Vietnam Veterans Memorial, which was built in the 1980s and inscribed with the names of all American soldiers killed in the Vietnam War.

approved this treaty. Other agreements were also reached. The two countries would work together in trade and space exploration. The Soviet Union needed food. The United States agreed to sell $750 million of wheat to the Soviets.

✩✩✩

Biography

▲ Shirley Chisholm

Shirley Chisholm spent her early working years as a teacher. She taught nursery school in the late 1940s and early 1950s. At the same time, she worked on her Master's Degree. Then she took jobs running day care centers in Texas and her home state of New York. Ms. Chisholm worked in the Civil Rights Movement, too.

Winning public office became one of Ms. Chisholm's goals. Being able to vote is one civil right.

Another is the right to hold public office. Ms. Chisholm was elected to the New York State Assembly in 1964. She worked for laws to help African and Hispanic Americans get college degrees. She won a federal office in 1968. She became the first African American woman ever elected to the U.S. House of Representatives. In 1972, she even ran for President. After many years in Washington, Ms. Chisholm retired. Now she is a college professor.

 # CHAPTER REVIEW

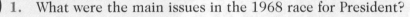

Critical Thinking

Write your answers on a sheet of paper, or discuss in class.

Identifying Main Idea

1. What were the main issues in the 1968 race for President?

Comparing and Contrasting

2. How did Nixon's agreements with Vietnam, China, and the Soviet Union succeed? How did they fail?

Cooperative Learning

LEARNING STYLE
Verbal

3. Work with a partner or group. Look through this chapter. Find names and words you do not know. Look them up in the glossary and gazetteer in the back of this book. They can also be found in most dictionaries. How do you say these words? What do they mean? Think of a sentence for each word. Tell your sentences to your partner or group.

Write About It

Writing Portfolio

4. Choose a person from this chapter. Find out about this person. Where was the person born? Did the person go to college? What kind of work did the person do? How did the person affect history? Write a short report. Share your report with the class.

Quiz

Number a piece of paper from 1-10. Write a, b, c, and d beside these numbers. Read the following sentence beginnings. Four endings follow each one. Choose the ending that best completes the sentence. On your paper, circle the letter that matches the letter of your answer. Be sure you mark your answer beside the correct number.

1. **Because of a Communist takeover in Cuba, President Kennedy . . .**
   a. approved the Bay of Pigs invasion.
   b. forced the Soviet Union to take its atomic missiles out of Cuba.
   c. cut off all trade with China and the Soviet Union.
   d. both a and b.

2. **The first rocket to reach space was launched by . . .**
   a. the United States.
   b. the Soviet Union.
   c. Europe.
   d. both a and b.

3. **Running the U.S. space program became the job of . . .**
   a. Congress.
   b. the Apollo program.
   c. NASA.
   d. none of the above.

4. **Spending on the space race programs helped President Kennedy end . . .**
   a. the arms race.
   b. Soviet missile programs.
   c. a small depression.
   d. all of the above.

5. **Lyndon Johnson became President . . .**
   a. when President Kennedy was shot and killed.
   b. after the Election of 1960.
   c. when President Kennedy died in a plane crash.
   d. while peace talks were being held about the Vietnam War.

6. **President Johnson pushed American involvement in . . .**
   a. his plan for a Great Society.
   b. the war on Poverty.
   c. the Vietnam War.
   d. all of the above.

7. **After the Tet Offensive, all sides in the Vietnam War agreed to . . .**
   a. ban the use of atomic weapons.
   b. begin peace talks.
   c. stop all fighting until terms could be reached.
   d. all of the above.

8. **Peaceful protests for civil rights were held by all of the following EXCEPT the . . .**
   a. women's movement.
   b. Student Non-Violent Coordinating Committee (SNCC).
   c. Students for a Democratic Society (SDS).
   d. the followers of Martin Luther King.

9. **Violence broke out during . . .**
   a. student demonstrations.
   b. civil right movement.
   c. the 1968 Democratic Convention.
   d. all of the above.

10. **President Nixon worked for world peace by . . .**
    a. ending the Vietnam War.
    b. recognizing and dealing with Communist China.
    c. signing the SALT Treaty with the Soviet Union.
    d. all of the above.

ANALYZING CAUSE AND EFFECT

Add numbers 11–15 to your paper. Read the two lists below. The ideas on the left describe a cause, or something that makes a second event happen. The ideas on the right are effects, the events that are caused. Match these causes and effects. Write your answers beside the correct numbers on you paper.

11. Fear of Soviet atomic weapons in space . . .
12. Stopping the Communist threat led to . . .
13. Anti-war feelings among students . . .
14. Discrimination happened not only in the South, . . .
15. Nixon's dealings with China and the Soviet Union . . .

a. brought about riots at colleges and the 1968 Democratic Convention.
b. slowed down the Cold War.
c. the Cuban missile crisis and the Vietnam war.
d. so marches and race riots happened in different cities from 1964-1966.
e. caused the U.S. to begin a space program.

Writing Portfolio

Look over the things you wrote for these chapters. Choose one that you like the best. Add to your writing. For example, you wrote a news report about the space race. Write reports about the Bay of Pigs invasion, the Cuban missile crisis, the beginning or end of the Vietnam War, the push for civil rights, and/or student demonstrations in the late 1960s. Trade papers with a study partner. Check each other's work. Work with a partner to put your reports into a newspaper titled "The 1960s." Make a clean, neat copy. Put it in your portfolio.

Alternative Assessment

Work with a partner. Write these names on different slips of paper: Fidel Castro, Lyndon Johnson, Nguyen Van Thieu, Martin Luther King, Stokely Carmichael, Betty Friedan, American Indian Movement (AIM), Cesar Chavez, the Weathermen, the Students for a Democratic Society (SDS), Hubert Humphrey, and Richard Nixon. Place the papers in a box. Take turns drawing a paper. Think of a sentece about the person or group. Ask your partner if this sentence is correct. If either of you is unsure, check the facts in Chapters 73-79. Take turns drawing the slips until a sentence has been formed for each person and group.

COOPERATIVE PROJECT: GEOGRAPHY AND HISTORY

LEARNING STYLE
Visual Tactile

Work with a partner or group. Find out about the land that makes up Vietnam. Are there jungles? Are there mountains? What rivers flow through these countries? Is either country near the ocean? What is the weather like? Use clay to make a map of Vietnam. Be sure to show mountains as high areas. Show where the land is low. Let the map dry. Paint jungles and marshes green. Paint the sea coasts brown. Paint the rivers blue. Talk about these features. How would these features affect a war? Would they have helped or hurt troops for the United States and North Vietnam? Share your map and ideas with other classes.

Unit 10

WELCOME
BACK TO
FREEDOM

POLITICS

June 17, 1972
The Watergate Scandal began.

Oct. 1973
First Arab oil embargo began.

Aug. 9, 1974
Richard Nixon resigned as President.

March 26, 1979
President Carter helped set up a peace treaty between Egypt and Israel.
November 4, 1979
Iranian radicals made hostages of American embassy workers in Tehran.
Dec. 1979
The Soviet Union invaded Afghanistan.

January 20, 1981
Ronald Reagan became President. A few minutes later, Iran finally honored its promise to free its U.S. hostages.

CE   1970   1975   1980

CULTURE

1969
The U.S. Air Force opened ARPANET, the first form of today's Internet.

1972
Ray Tomlinson invented a computer program with the first form of e-mail.

July 4, 1976
The United States celebrated its 200th birthday.

1977
Toni Morrison's book *Song of Solomon* described African American women's feelings and ideas.

1980
The U.S. did not attend the Moscow Olympics. Many countries joined the protest of the Soviet takeover of Afghanistan.

June 18, 1983
Sally K. Ride became the first American woman to travel into space.

Contemporary United States 1968 to Present

"The future of mankind lies waiting for those who will come to understand their lives and take up their responsibilities to all living things."

— **Vine Victor Deloria, Jr.**
Native American writer, from his book God Is Red *(1973)*

*C*hange has always been a part of American life. The colonists broke away from Britain and tried a new kind of government. Later, the people turned away from farming. They turned to work in factories and businesses. People moved from the country to the cities. Government changed itself to deal with the Great Depression, two world wars, and the threat of Communism. Now, people are developing new ideas. How are these ideas changing the federal government? Why?

March 11, 1985 Soviet leader Mikhail Gorbachev began doing away with many Communist ideas.

February 1989 A bad economy forced the Soviets to pull out of Afghanistan.

June 4, 1989 Communist China crushed student demonstrations for democracy.

Aug. 2, 1990 Iraq invaded Kuwait.

Aug. 7, 1990 The U.S. and its allies set up bases around Iraq.

Jan. 16, 1991 Iraq missed a U.N. deadline for leaving Kuwait. Air attacks began.

Feb. 21, 1991 A ground war to free Kuwait was fought.

Feb. 27, 1991 Iraq pulled out of Kuwait.

November 1994 Republicans took over both houses of Congress for the first time since 1952.

1990 — 1995

1985 Rock musicians held TV concerts in Philadelphia and London. "Live Aid" raised money to buy food for starving people in Africa.

1986 The space shuttle *Challenger* blew up on takeoff. Eight Americans were killed, including school teacher Christa McAuliffe and the first Asian American astronaut, Ellison S. Onizuka.

1987 Stock prices went through a major crash in October.

1992 The Corporation for Research and Educational Network opened the World-Wide Web.

Chapter 92

Scandal in the White House

The Watergate Scandal

Date	Event	Result
June 17, 1972	Five men were caught trying to bug the Democratic National Committee's offices in the Watergate Building.	The burglars were found to be working for Nixon's Committe to Reelect the President (CREEP).
January 30, 1973	The five burglars and two members of CREEP were sentenced. James W. McCord read a special letter. It said there had been a cover-up.	The U.S. Senate set up a special committee to look into what had really happened.
April 30, 1973	Nixon ordered the Justice Department to look into McCord's charges.	Archibald Cox was chosen as Special Prosecutor to do this job.
May 17, 1973	Sam Ervin's Senate Committee began hearings on Watergate.	John Dean said White House officials lied about the cover-up.
July 1973	The Senate learned that all conversations in the Oval Office had been recorded.	Judge John Sirica agreed with Cox that the tapes should be handed over. However, Nixon refused.
October 10, 1973	Vice President Spiro Agnew resigned after being sentenced for not paying taxes in 1967. Other charges, including bribery, were dropped.	Gerald R. Ford was chosen by Nixon to be the new Vice President. Congress agreed. He took office on December 6.
October 19, 1973	Nixon said he would give written summaries of the tapes. Cox refused. He said he wanted the tapes themselves.	Richardson and his deputy resigned rather than fire Cox on Nixon's orders. Solicitor General Robert Bork then fired Cox.
	New Special Prosecutor Leon Jaworski also demanded the tapes.	Nixon refused.
April 1974	All nine Supreme Court Justices ordered Nixon to give up the tapes.	The tapes showed Nixon ordered the cover-up on June 23, 1972.
July 1974	The House voted three charges in order to impeach President Nixon.	Nixon resigned on August 9. Ford became the new President.

Read about

President Richard Nixon. How did he leave the office of President of the United States? Why?

Key *Vocabulary*

ticket (TIK uht) the two people chosen by a party to run for President and Vice President

landslide (LAND sleyed) a win in which one candidate takes far more votes than anyone else

investigation (in ves tuh GAY shuhn) a check or examination to find out facts

Reteaching Vocabulary

impeach (im PEECH) to charge a public official with crimes in office

CHART ANALYSIS

★ **Ask**   What is this chart about?

★ **Organize** List the people who were involved in the scandal. List the people who looked for the truth.

★ **Analyze**   What was the purpose of the cover-up?

★ **Answer**   Why do you think people might have become involved in such things as the burglary and cover-up?

Decoding Tip: Note the long sound of i in **landslide**.

ay	cake	ah	fall, cot	air	air
ee	tree	i	sit	oh	cold
or	cord	oy	toy	uh	*above, hundred*
a	ask	ar	hard	oo	book
e	yet	eye	nice	uhr	liar, fir, further, color
ow	cow	ooh	boot, true	yoo	you, few, cube

92.1 What ideas did Nixon carry out after winning a second term?

Richard Nixon won a second term in 1972. He ran against Democrat George McGovern. McGovern said that the peace talks were taking too long. He promised to bring all American troops home from Vietnam. He planned to do this as soon as he became President. However, Nixon's Secretary of State made a surprising announcement. Henry Kissinger said that peace talks were almost over. McGovern lost ground in the race. He lost more ground because of his ticket. He had picked Senator Thomas Eagleton to be Vice President. Reporters told about Eagleton's visits to a psychiatrist. Eagleton left the **ticket**. President Kennedy's brother-in-law took his place. Sergeant Shriver did not help McGovern make any gains. Nixon won the race by a **landslide**.

1972 Presidential Election			
Candidate	**Party**	**Popular Vote**	**Electoral College Vote**
Richard M. Nixon	Republican	47,165,234	520
George McGovern	Democrat	29,170,774	17

Many conservatives did not like the way Nixon was handling his office. Other Presidents had used executive orders. They are like laws. But they do not have to be passed by Congress. Nixon put out more than any other President. Nixon took more powers in other ways. They were:

- impoundment—refusing to spend money that Congress had set aside for different purposes. Nixon used this as a way of getting around acts he did not like.

- executive privilege—refusing to give information to the people or to Congress because its release might be dangerous for the country.

Some Americans were worried about the office of President. It was becoming more powerful. Congress was losing power.

The photograph to the right shows President Nixon leaving the White House after his resignation on August 9, 1974.

Nixon used his powers to run the Vietnam War. However, the Constitution gave war powers only to Congress. Conservatives and other Americans called for limits to any President's power. They felt the Constitution should be followed as it was written. Congress passed the War Powers Act in 1973. The President could use troops for only 60 days without approval from Congress. Congress also set limits on the use of impoundment in 1974.

92.2 What scandal involved President Nixon?

Scandal hit the Nixon White House in 1973. During the 1972 race for President, there had been a crime. Five men had broken into the Democrats' offices in Washington, D.C. They were caught in the Watergate building by a guard on June 17, 1972. Reporters from the *Washington Post* followed the story. Bob Woodward and Carl Bernstein wrote stories telling what had happened. Two of Nixon's campaign officers had helped plan the break-in. They had lied about their knowledge. Other stories pointed to White House employees. There was one big question. What did President Nixon know about this event?

92.3 How did Congress affect the Watergate scandal?

The U.S. Senate looked into the break-in. A special committee was set up. Senator Sam Ervin was put in charge. It called witnesses. Most were White House employees. Many said they had not taken part in the break-in. Nor had they tried to cover up what had really happened.

▲ White House Counsel John Dean testifying during the Watergate scandal.

However, John Dean told what he knew. Dean was Nixon's White House Counsel, or lawyer. According to Dean's story, many of the White House employees had lied. Few of them had anything to do with the break-in. But they had helped cover up the crime. Dirty tricks had been played on other candidates for President. Millions of dollars had been collected illegally for the President. The White House kept lists of Americans whom Nixon felt were his enemies. The CIA had helped keep these people under watch. It had also worked to keep the FBI from finding out what had really happened. John Dean said that President Nixon had helped in the cover-up. But was Dean telling the truth?

92.4 Why did Congress decide to impeach President Nixon?

Surprising news brought the case to a head. Nixon had recording gear in the White House. All talks in the Oval Office were on tape. Congress sent orders for the White House to turn over the tapes. Nixon would not agree. He claimed

▲ The photograph above shows Gerald Ford taking the oath as President of the United States.

executive privilege. He said the tapes held state secrets. The Justice Department had been helping in the **investigation**. Special Prosecutor Archibald Cox got Judge John Sirica to send a court order for the tapes. Nixon told Attorney General Elliot Richardson to fire Cox. Richardson and his assistant both refused. They resigned instead. Solicitor General Robert Bork was now the acting Attorney General. He fired Cox and other Justice Department employees.

The Supreme Court ended the disagreement. It ordered the tapes to be turned over. Congress found blank spaces on the tapes. Parts had been erased. The tapes also held another surprise.

One tape proved that Nixon had known everything. He had ordered a cover-up six days after the break-in. A House committee voted to **impeach** the President. He would be removed from office. Nixon decided to resign on August 9, 1974. Vice President Gerald Ford became President. Ford said, "Our long national nightmare is over." One month later, President Ford pardoned Nixon. He could never be tried for any crimes he may have committed while serving as President.

☆☆☆

Biography

▲ Judge Robert Bork

As acting Attorney General, Robert Bork fired Archibald Cox on orders from President Nixon. In 1987, Bork became the center of another political fight. Lewis F. Powell, Jr., retired from the Supreme Court. President Ronald Reagan wanted to nominate someone who shared his conservative ideas. He nominated Bork to this seat. Reagan had appointed Bork as a judge on the U.S. Court of Appeals in 1982. However, the Senate became involved in a fight over Bork's nomination in 1987. The Senate has the duty of approving all people nominated to the Supreme Court.

The Senate looked hard at Judge Bork and his ideas. Many of the Senators felt he was more than a conservative. They said he held radical, or extreme, ideas. Others felt that Bork's ideas were being twisted by his foes. Months of investigations and angry words in newspapers and on television followed. In October 1987, the Senate refused to confirm Judge Bork to the Supreme Court. President Reagan said that the Senate had punished Judge Bork out of spite, not because of his ideas. He promised to find another judge who shared these ideas. Judge Anthony Kennedy finally took this seat on the Supreme Court. He was less conservative than Bork, however.

★★☆ CHAPTER REVIEW

Critical Thinking

Write your answers on a sheet of paper, or discuss in class.

Drawing Conclusions →

Making Inferences ⟲

1. Why do you think President Nixon decided to resign?

2. One duty of the President and the Executive Branch is to enforce the laws passed by Congress. How well did President Nixon's staff carry out this duty?

Cooperative Learning

LEARNING STYLE
Prereading
Verbal

3. Work with a partner or group. Look at the chart at the beginning of this chapter. Talk about the facts in the chart. What people are named in the chart? What years are covered? Why did the break-in happen? How did the scandal end?

Write About It

Writing Portfolio

4. Look up information about Watergate. For example, Bob Woodward and Carl Bernstein wrote a book called *All the President's Men*. It was turned into a movie. Find the book, the movie or another book about Watergate. Write a short summary of the facts. Share your summary with the class.

Chapter 93

At 200 Years of Age

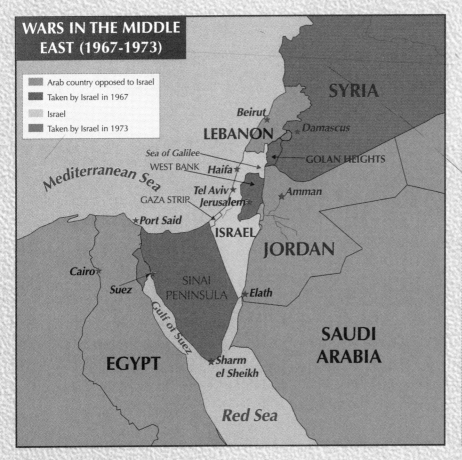

WARS IN THE MIDDLE EAST (1967-1973)

- Arab country opposed to Israel
- Taken by Israel in 1967
- Israel
- Taken by Israel in 1973

SYRIA

Beirut
Damascus

LEBANON

Sea of Galilee
WEST BANK Haifa
GOLAN HEIGHTS

Mediterranean Sea

Tel Aviv
GAZA STRIP Jerusalem
Amman

Port Said

ISRAEL

JORDAN

Cairo
Suez
SINAI PENINSULA
Elath

Gulf of Suez

SAUDI ARABIA

EGYPT
Sharm el Sheikh

Red Sea

Read about the United States in the late 1970s. How did the Middle East affect the United States? Why?

Key *Vocabulary*

recession (ri SESH uhn) a time when the economy slows and people are put out of work

stagflation (stag FLAY shuhn) a time when both inflation and a recession or a depression are happening

balance of trade (BAL uhnts • uhv • trayd) the difference between the value of goods sold to other countries and the value of the goods bought from them

embargo (im BAHR goh) an order to stop a kind of trade

MAP ANALYSIS

★ **Ask**   What does this map show?
★ **Organize** List Israel's neighbors who are its enemies.
★ **Answer**   Why might Israel face constant war?

Decoding Tip: Note that a stands for /a/, /uh/, and /ay/ in **balance of trade**.

ay	cake	ah	fall, cot	air	air
ee	tree	i	sit	oh	cold
or	cord	oy	toy	uh	above, hundred
a	ask	ar	hard	oo	book
e	yet	eye	nice	uhr	liar, fir, further, color
ow	cow	ooh	boot, true	yoo	you, few, cube

93.1 How had the U.S. economy changed since the late 1960s?

Inflation caused many problems for the U.S. economy. Prices kept going up. President Nixon believed in conservative ideas. Interest rates should be pushed up. Then people would borrow less money. They would spend less, too. Demand for goods would drop. Then prices would fall.

However, companies did not drop prices. They cut back on making as many goods. They kept prices high so they would make more money by selling fewer goods. This caused a small depression. Since this time, a small depression has been called a **recession.** Both inflation and a recession were happening at the same time. This became known as **stagflation.** In 1971, Nixon set up a board to freeze prices and wages. Some companies broke the rules. But things did get better for a while. When the freeze was taken off, prices jumped. The President then turned to Roosevelt's ideas from the Great Depression. He urged Congress to spend more money. The country would go into debt. But the economy would get better as more goods were bought. The recession did slow down. But inflation became an even bigger problem.

Money left the country, too. Americans sold goods to other countries. They bought goods from other countries as well. By the early 1970s, more goods were being bought than sold. Nixon lowered the value of the dollar. Other countries would get more dollars with their money. They could buy more American goods than before. It would also take more dollars for Americans to buy their goods. It was hoped this would change the **balance of trade.** However, the plan failed. The balance of trade grew worse.

93.2 Why did issues in the Middle East affect the United States?

Oil is important to the United States. It is used to produce power across the country. The United States produces oil. But these supplies are not enough. By the early 1970s, the United States was buying much of its oil from other countries. Some came from Mexico and South American countries. But most of the oil came from Arab countries in the Middle East. This area was not at peace. Most Arab countries hated Israel. They wanted Israel's land returned to the Palestinians. Several wars were fought to take over Israel. However, the country had survived. The United States was a strong supporter of Israel. This caused some Arab countries to turn to the Soviet Union.

Date	Event	Result
May 14, 1949	State of Israel was declared.	War broke out with the Palestinians, Egypt, Jordan, Syria, Lebanon, Iraq, and Saudi Arabia.
1949	Peace terms were reached with the Arab countries.	Jordan took the West Bank of the Dead Sea. Egypt took the Gaza Strip. They would not allow the Palestinians to rule themselves.
October 29, 1956	Egypt was attacked by Israel, Britain, and France to stop terrorist raids on Israel and to open up the Suez Canal.	Israel took the Gaza Strip from Egypt. The U.N. set up a peace that lasted until 1967. It sent troops to keep the peace.
May 19, 1967	U.N. troops left the area.	Egypt took back the Gaza Strip and closed the Gulf of Aqaba.
June 5-10, 1967	Six-Day War between Israel and Egypt broke out.	Israel took back the Gaza Strip. It took the Sinai Peninsula and Old Jerusalem.
October 6, 1973	Egypt and Syria carried out a surprise attack on Israel. It became known as the "Yom Kippur War."	Soviets supplied Egypt and Syria. The United States supplied Israel.
	11 other Arab countries then joined the war against Israel. They also began an embargo by refusing to sell oil to the United States.	Israel pushed the Syrian Army out of Israel, took the west bank along the Suez Canal from Egypt, and took the West Bank along the Dead Sea from Jordan.
October 24, 1973	Peace terms were arranged.	Israel gave up the west bank of the Suez Canal.

▲ The photograph above shows Israeli soldiers in the old city of Jerusalem during the Six Day War.

93.3 Why did problems in the Middle East affect economies around the world?

In 1973, Egypt and Syria attacked Israel by surprise. This was the Yom Kippur War. Arab countries also began an oil **embargo**. They quit selling oil to countries that were supporting Israel. The embargo was aimed chiefly at the United States. When it stopped helping Israel, the embargo would be lifted. The United States needed oil to keep its economy moving. A cease-fire was arranged. The Yom Kippur War came to an end. The Arab countries agreed to stop the embargo.

The Yom Kippur War taught the Arab countries a lesson. They set up an organization of countries that produce oil. Most were from the Middle East and South America. It was named "OPEC." OPEC began other embargoes. It cut back on the amount of oil its members would produce. Then it set high prices for oil. If countries wanted this oil, they would have to pay. The cost of oil shot up. OPEC countries became extremely rich. The United States could not get the oil it needed. High oil prices caused other prices to go up. Inflation became worse than ever.

President Nixon called on all Americans to solve this energy crisis. The oil embargo was hurting the country. Nixon asked Congress for new laws. It passed them quickly. One allowed oil companies to drill on federal lands in Alaska. A special pipe line was built to carry this oil. Nixon called on Americans to save energy. This would decrease the need to buy oil from the Arab countries. They would have less power over the U.S.

This photograph shows a gas station with no gas during the oil crisis in the United States.

economy. Nixon resigned in 1974. President Ford followed Nixon's ideas in dealing with the energy crisis.

93.4   What was the Bicentennial?

America reached its 200th birthday in 1976. It was called the Bicentennial. The Revolutionary War broke out in 1775. The country was formed when independence was declared on July 4, 1776. President Ford led the country in celebrating this important day. Ford attended a special event in Boston in 1975. It was held in the Old North Church. Lights from its tower had signaled Paul Revere's ride and the beginning of the Revolutionary War. For the next year, special events were held across the country. Countries from all over the world sent special messages and gifts. On July 4, 1976, huge parties and fireworks helped Americans celebrate 200 years of freedom.

☆☆☆

Connections

▲ Alaskan Pipeline

Alaskan oil helped ease the energy crisis. Wells supply millions of gallons of oil each day. This oil is piped about 600 miles to the Alaskan coast. It is then pumped onto tankers and shipped to California. Plants in California turn the oil into gasoline and other fuels. Many Americans were worried about the wells and pipeline. What if they caused a spill? What would happen to the unspoiled land where they had been built?

A spill has never happened at the wells or on the pipeline. However, the largest spill happened in 1989. A tanker called the *Exxon Valdez* was sailing through Prince William Sound. On March 24, it hit a reef. Over 11 million gallons of oil spilled into the water. Within a month, the oil had spread for miles. The Alaskan coast was coated with oil for 800 miles. Oil floated on 1,600 square miles of ocean. President George Bush decided to let Alaska and the Exxon Company handle the spill. No help was sent from the federal government. Hundreds of thousands of animals were killed. The fishing industry lost millions of dollars. Exxon spent billions of dollars cleaning up the mess. Much of the oil now lies at the bottom of the ocean. No one knows how it will affect Alaska in the years to come.

CHAPTER REVIEW

Critical Thinking

Write your answers on a sheet of paper, or discuss in class.

Making Inferences

Analyzing Cause and Effect

1. Why were Arab goals not achieved in the Middle East?

2. How did Arab actions affect other countries around the world?

Cooperative Learning

LEARNING STYLE
Reading Verbal

3. Work with a partner or group. Copy the names used in this chapter. Look up each name. See how it sounds. Say the names out loud. Then read the chapter out loud. Make sure to say the names correctly.

Write About It

Writing Portfolio

4. Talk to family members and others in your community. What was the oil embargo? What was the energy crisis? How did it affect people in the United States? What was life like in your community during this time? How did people save energy? Compare your facts with those gathered by others in your class.

Chapter 94

World Conflicts

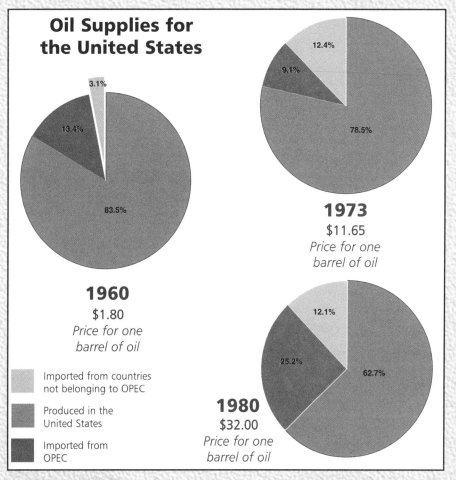

Oil Supplies for the United States

1960
$1.80
Price for one barrel of oil

3.1%
13.4%
83.5%

1973
$11.65
Price for one barrel of oil

12.4%
9.1%
78.5%

1980
$32.00
Price for one barrel of oil

12.1%
25.2%
62.7%

Imported from countries not belonging to OPEC

Produced in the United States

Imported from OPEC

Read about the United States in the late 1970s. How did the United States and the Soviet Union once again come into conflict? Why?

Key *Vocabulary*

nomination (nahm uh NAY shuhn) the state of being chosen by a political party to run for an office

primary (PREYE mer ee) an election held to choose the people whom a state's political parties will send to the parties' national conventions

foreign aid (FOR uhn • ayd) money and goods given to help another country

Reteaching Vocabulary

dictator (DIK tayt uhr) a person who has total rule over a country

---

CHART ANALYSIS

★ **Ask**   *What do the pie charts show?*

★ **Acquire**   *Where did the United States get its oil?*

★ **Organize**   *The United States had three sources for oil. List the source that began to supply less oil each year. List the sources that began to supply more oil.*

★ **Analyze**   *What happened to the price of oil during this time?*

★ **Answer**   *Why might Americans want to start using less oil?*

Decoding Tip: Note that *i* can stand for /eye/ at the end of a syllable, as in **primary**.

ay	cake	ah	fall, cot	air	air
ee	tree	i	sit	oh	cold
or	cord	oy	toy	uh	above, hundred
a	ask	ar	hard	oo	book
e	yet	eye	nice	uhr	liar, fir, further, color
ow	cow	ooh	boot, true	yoo	you, few, cube

94.1 What new plan helped Jimmy Carter become President?

President Gerald Ford was not sure of his **nomination** in 1976. He had not been elected either Vice President or President. He had taken over as Vice President from Spiro Agnew. Agnew had resigned. He had been sentenced for crimes while he was Maryland's governor. Then Nixon resigned because of the Watergate scandal. Ford was the first man to become President without ever having been elected to either office of the Executive Branch.

One month after taking office, Ford pardoned former President Nixon. Many people said a deal had been made. Nixon would make Ford the President. Then Ford would pardon Nixon. Both men said this was not true. Ford decided to run for President in 1976. Ronald Reagan entered the race, too. He had been governor of California. Voting was close at the Republican Convention. But Ford won the nomination.

A new President took office after the race of 1976. The Democrats chose Jimmy Carter. He had been governor of Georgia. He used the **primary** system to win the nomination. Each state voted for members to go to the Democratic Convention. Carter pushed to have his supporters elected in each state. His plan worked. Only one vote was held at the convention. Carter won easily. Since 1976, all candidates for President have followed this plan. Voting was close between Ford and Carter. The result was not known until late at night. Carter won the race by about two million votes.

1976 Presidential Election

Candidate	Party	Popular Vote	Electoral College Vote
Jimmy Carter	Democrat	40,828,929	297
Gerald Ford	Republican	39,148,940	240

94.2 How did inflation and the energy crisis affect the country?

OPEC countries continued raising the price of oil. American oil companies went along. They were all becoming very rich. But the U.S. economy was hurting. Everyone had to pay more for oil and gas. Factories were spending more. Companies had to raise their prices. These increases were passed on to buyers. Inflation had already been a problem. The energy crisis made inflation much worse. Sales dropped. Companies kept raising prices to make up for the money they were losing. Sales dropped even more. Soon, factories and other businesses began letting some workers go. The economy fell into a deep recession.

Carter hoped to end the recession by stopping the energy crisis. Oil prices would be controlled. New taxes would be charged on automobiles. The money would be used to find new energy sources. Gasoline would have a higher tax. People would use less gasoline. The United States would save energy. Then it would need less oil from OPEC. OPEC's sales would drop. It would have to lower its prices in order to sell more oil.

▼ The photograph below shows President Jimmy Carter with President Anwar Sadat of Egypt and Prime Minister Menachem Begin of Israel as they prepare to sign the Egyptian-Israeli Peace Treaty at the White House in 1979.

However, Congress passed only part of Carter's plans. Oil companies did not want to follow government controls. Automobile companies did not want to pay higher taxes. Neither did the American people. The country did save some energy. However, oil prices continued to go up.

94.3 Why did Latin America cause problems for the United States?

Communist countries brought danger to Latin America. Many of these countries were ruled by **dictators**. The people had few rights and little freedom. President Carter pushed for civil rights in these countries. He asked the dictators to hold free elections. Carter stopped sending **foreign aid** to some of these countries. Some of them became involved in civil wars. The Soviet Union helped supply the rebels.

Carter did not want the countries to become Communist. But he did not want to help the dictators either. The United States did little to help stop the wars. Nicaragua became a Communist country. It began helping rebels in other civil wars. President Carter decided to send aid to these countries. If they were richer, their governments might stand. Free elections might be held. However, this did not happen.

Carter's plan for the Panama Canal caused anger among many Americans. He set up a new treaty with Panama. Carter called for Panama to take over the canal in 1999. The U.S. would always be allowed to use the canal. The U.S. Army would protect the canal in case of war. Still, many Americans were concerned. Building the Panama Canal had been a great feat. Giving up the canal seemed dangerous. The Navy might need to use the canal in time of war. However, the Navy's ships had grown very large. Few of them would fit through the Panama Canal. That is why the United States had built two fleets. One sailed in the Pacific Ocean. The other sailed the Atlantic. Democrats and moderate Republicans supported Carter. The U.S. Senate approved the treaty.

94.4 What success did President Carter have in dealing with the Middle East?

President Carter also pushed for peace in the Middle East. He said the Palestinians should have their own country. They should rule themselves. However, the United States would still support Israel. President Anwar Sadat wanted peace for Egypt. Spending on the army was breaking his country. The money

▲ The photograph above shows President Jimmy Carter with President Anwar Sadat of Egypt during a meeting to discuss peace in the Middle East in 1978.

▼ The photograph below shows President Jimmy Carter with Israeli Prime Minister Menachem Begin at the White House in 1979.

was needed to build up the economy. Sadat even went to Israel. He met with Prime Minister Menachem Begin. But the talks soon broke down.

Peace between Israel and Egypt was finally arranged with Carter's help. He invited Sadat and Begin to the United States. They met at Camp David. This is a country home near Washington, D.C. It is for the President's use only. Carter kept the talks going. They were held in secret. They lasted for 13 days. Peace terms were reached. They were called the "Camp David Accords." Egypt agreed that Israel had a right to be a country. Israel agreed to return the Sinai Peninsula to Egypt. Both sides agreed to work for a country for the Palestinians. A treaty was finally signed on March 26, 1979.

Carter's work was a success. Sadat and Begin shared the Nobel Peace Prize. Still, many Arab countries felt that Sadat had betrayed them. Carter worked to calm these feelings. Some people in Egypt shared these feelings. Sadat was shot and killed by some of his own troops in 1981. However, the new Egyptian President continued Sadat's work for peace.

☆☆☆

Connections

▲ President Jimmy Carter

Jimmy Carter had been an unusual governor for Georgia. He showed how the South was changing. Other Georgia governors had fought against civil rights. Carter fought for these rights. His wife Rosalynn worked to improve hospitals and clinics for people with mental illnesses. Both worked to protect the environment. Carter was the first person from the Deep South to become President since the Civil War. People saw that the South and its ideas were changing. It became known as the "New South."

Weather in the South and Southwest helped the economies in these areas in the 1970s. Oil prices went up in the 1970s. Companies began moving to the South and Southwest. These areas are known as the "Sun Belt." They are warm most of the year. Heating is not needed as often as in the North. Companies can use less oil. They can save money. Workers in the North lost jobs as factories moved away. Many followed their companies to the Sun Belt. These states have been growing ever since.

California, Texas, and Florida have populations that are always growing. They have some of the largest populations in the whole country.

Population growth has changed Congress, too. A state's population sets its number of seats in the U.S. House. California, Texas, and Florida have gained many seats. Other states have lost seats. Some Americans worry that large states may be able to control the U.S. House. Others point out that things are balanced by the U.S. Senate. Each state has only two seats in the Senate. And its power equals that of the House. The U.S. Constitution was written to take care of this problem.

★★★ CHAPTER REVIEW

Critical Thinking

Write your answers on a sheet of paper, or discuss in class.

Comparing and Contrasting

1. Why did different Arab countries have different goals in the Middle East?

Making Inferences

2. How did its problems show that the United States was a world leader?

Cooperative Learning

LEARNING STYLE
Reading Verbal

3. Work with a partner or group. Choose a part of the chapter to read aloud. You may wish to record your readings. Check the vocabulary list. See what these words mean. Note how to say these words. Other words might be found in the back of this book. Remember, the names can be found there, too.

Write About It

Writing Portfolio

4. Make a chart about the problems caused by the Middle East. Take out a piece of paper. Divide the paper into two columns. List these headings at the tops of the columns: **Israel** and **Arab Countries**. Find out facts about these places. You may wish to check books in the school or community library. Find answers to questions like the following. What countries supported each side? What were their goals? Why did Israel and the Arabs go to war with each other? How did each side gain or lose after each war? List these facts in the correct columns of your chart. Show your chart to the class. Discuss how the chart helps you see how the two sides were alike and how they were different.

Chapter 95

The Cold War Heats Up

Read about the United States and the Soviet Union at the end of the 1970s. How did their work toward arms control break down? Why?

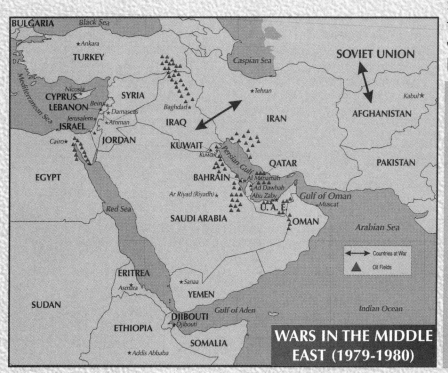

WARS IN THE MIDDLE EAST (1979-1980)

Key *Vocabulary*

hostage (HAHS tij) a person who is held as a prisoner until certain demands are met

Reteaching Vocabulary

ratify (RAT uh feye) to approve

boycott (BOY kaht) to refuse any dealings with a person or group until certain terms are met

radical (RAD i kuhl) a person who supports extreme measures or changes

diplomat (DIP luh mat) a person who handles dealings between governments

---

MAP ANALYSIS

★ **Ask**   *What does this map show?*

★ **Organize**   *Make a chart. List the countries that have oil fields. List the ones that have no oil fields.*

★ **Analyze**   *What countries were fighting in wars?*

★ **Answer**   *How might these wars affect how well the countries are able to produce and sell oil?*

Decoding Tip: Note that o can stand for the sound /ah/ as in **hostage** and **boycott** and the sound /uh/ as in **diplomat**.

ay	cake	ah	fall, cot	air	air
ee	tree	i	sit	oh	cold
or	cord	oy	toy	uh	above, hundred
a	ask	ar	hard	oo	book
e	yet	eye	nice	uhr	liar, fir, further, color
ow	cow	ooh	boot, true	yoo	you, few, cube

95.1 Why did many Senators disagree with the SALT II Treaty?

SALT talks were held to prevent a nuclear war. Presidents Nixon, Ford, and Carter each took part in these talks. The United States and the Soviet Union wanted to cut back on their atomic weapons. The world would become much safer. President Nixon and the Senate set up the SALT Treaty in 1972. Each country promised to make fewer weapons. They also got rid of some of their old weapons. President Carter worked with Premier Leonid Brezhnev. They agreed to the SALT II Treaty in 1979. More limits would be set on atomic weapons. Now the Senate had to **ratify** this treaty.

Many Senators felt that the new treaty would not work. The United States had cut back on its weapons. The Soviets said they had, too. However, there was no way for the United States to tell if this was the truth. The treaty did not allow Americans to visit weapons areas in the Soviet Union. Talks were held on the SALT II Treaty. No one was sure if it would pass.

95.2 How did Afghanistan affect U.S. and Soviet relations?

Afghanistan became a Communist country in 1979. The Soviet Union invaded the country. It set up a Communist government in December. The Soviets said that Afghanistan's Communists had asked for this help. However, the United States and most other countries disagreed. They said that the Soviet Union simply wanted to rule Afghanistan.

There were fears that the Soviets next would move against Iran. Other oil-rich countries might fall to the Soviets. The Soviet Union could become rich by controlling these oil fields. This would be dangerous for the United States. The whole world would also be affected deeply.

President Carter worked with world leaders. They wanted the Soviets out of Afghanistan. The U.N. called for the Soviets to leave. Carter set up a plan for this problem. The United States would not fight in Afghanistan. That might lead to World War III. Instead, the United States would send aid to Afghanistan's neighbors. Carter asked the Pentagon to train special troops. They could be sent to problem areas at any time. Carter even brought back the draft. All men from the ages of 18-20 had to register.

Steps were also taken against the Soviet Union itself. The President asked the Senate to put aside the SALT II Treaty. All trade with the Soviets was stopped. The Summer Olympics were to be held in Moscow in 1980. Carter said that the United States would **boycott** the games. For the first time since the games began in the 1890s, the United States did not go to the Olympics.

Most Americans supported the President. However, some disagreed. Farmers would lose money if grain was not sold to the Soviets. Some companies would lose sales that had already been set up. Many other people hated the idea of mixing politics and the Olympics. But Carter felt a hard line had to be taken against the Soviet Union.

95.3   What was the Iranian hostage crisis?

The Shah of Iran fell in 1979. He had ruled Iran for many years. Under him, people had few freedoms or rights. Many Iranians were strong believers in the Muslim religion, and wanted Muslim leaders to run the government. Riots broke out in January 1979. Many of the Shah's troops turned against him. He left the country. Ayatollah Ruhollah Khomeini, a Muslim leader, took over. The United States worked to make friends with the new government. But Khomeini's government was just as harsh as the Shah's. Everything changed that fall. The Shah was ill, and wanted to go to an American hospital. President Carter agreed.

For the People, By the People

▲ The photograph above shows a scene from the Iranian Civil War in January 1979. Supporters of Ayatollah Ruhollah Khomeini overturned the Shah's government and set up an Islamic state.

Radicals in Iran were furious. They stormed the American embassy on November 4, 1979. America's **diplomats** did not want a war. They told the Marine guards not to shoot. The radicals took 65 Americans prisoner. They wanted the United States to send the Shah back to Iran. He would be put on trial. President Carter would not agree. The President ordered the Navy to send ships to the Persian Gulf. Talks were held. Iran let 13 prisoners go. They freed all the women, all the African Americans, and one other man who was sick. The other 52 were held as **hostages.** The world supported the United States. Its backers included the UN, NATO, and the International Court of Justice. However, Iran stood firm. Carter broke all ties with Iran on April 1. Its diplomats were forced to leave the United States. Trade was blocked. Only food and medicine could be sold to Iran. Carter also froze all money that Iran had in American banks.

Carter agreed to a Pentagon plan to rescue the hostages. A special team met in the desert of Iran. But before the rescue could begin, two helicopters ran into each other. Eight men were killed. Iranian troops took the bodies. They were carried through the streets of Tehran. Huge crowds chanted, "Death to America," and "Death to Carter." Americans and people all over the world were shocked. Many Americans began to turn against President Carter. They felt he was not handling the hostage crisis well enough.

95.4 What was the result of the Presidential Election of 1980?

Ronald Reagan beat Jimmy Carter and became President. The two men had very different ideas. Carter called for the United States to continue to work for peace. Reagan wanted to spend more for the military. He thought it had become too weak. He pointed to troubles in Afghanistan and Iran. Armed forces might be needed there. Reagan also promised to cut regulations on businesses. The federal government was too powerful, he said. The ideas used to fight the Great Depression now were hurting the country. Businesses should run themselves. Inflation and unemployment were too high. Taxes should also be cut, said Reagan. Then people would have more money to spend. Reagan said this would turn the economy around.

► President Ronald Reagan

Many Americans liked Reagan's ideas. Reagan easily won the race in November 1980. He took office on January 20, 1981.

President Carter had finally made a deal with Iran. War had broken out between Iran and Iraq in September 1980. Iran needed arms. It needed the money that was frozen in American banks. Algeria's diplomats handled secret talks between the United States and Iran. The talks began two days before the Presidential Election. Terms were set.

1980 Presidential Race

Candidate	Party	Popular Vote	Electoral College Vote
Ronald Reagan	Republican	43,899,248	489
Jimmy Carter	Democrat	35,481,435	49
John Anderson	Independent	5,719,437	0

▶ The photograph to the right shows one of the American hostages during the Iranian Hostage Crisis.

But Iran refused to sign until a few minutes after Reagan was inaugurated as President. The hostages were set free and flown to an American base in Germany. President Reagan sent Jimmy Carter to greet the hostages. They had been held as hostages for 444 days.

☆☆☆

Connections

▲ Winter Olympics in Lake Placid

Canada gave great help to the United States during the hostage crisis. Four Americans were not in the building when radicals stormed the embassy. They managed to reach the Canadian embassy. The Canadians hid these Americans until January 1980. They were given false papers. The papers said that the Americans were really Canadian diplomats. The Canadians took them to the airport and flew them to Canada. The news flashed around the world. The Ayatollah was angry. He forced Canada to pull its diplomats out of Iran.

Celebrations were held all across the United States. The Winter Olympics were held in Lake Placid, New York. They began shortly after the four Americans reached home. A special march opens each set of games. Each country's athletes enter the games by marching in as groups. The Canadian athletes marched into the arena. The stands were filled with Americans and Canadians. They all stood to cheer the Canadian team. The world saw how grateful the United States was to Canada.

★★☆ CHAPTER REVIEW

Critical Thinking

Write your answers on a sheet of paper, or discuss in class.

Comparing and Contrasting

Drawing Conclusions →↓←

1. How were American and Soviet goals different in the Middle East?

2. Why did President Reagan's election show that Americans' ideas were changing?

Cooperative Learning

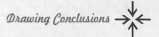
LEARNING STYLE
Visual Oral

3. Work with a partner or group. Look at the map that begins this chapter. Read the names on the map. Point out Afghanistan, the Soviet Union, Iraq, and Iran. Slide your finger from the Soviet Union to Iran. Then show how to reach the oil fields in Iran and Iraq. Talk about the danger that the Soviets caused for these oil fields.

Write About It

Writing Portfolio

4. Think about the Iranian hostage crisis. Reread the paragraph about the marches in Tehran. Imagine you are attending a march in the United States. What messages would you like to send to Iran? Use these ideas to make posters and banners that might be carried in your march.

Quiz

Number a piece of paper from 1-10. Read each question below. Read the answers that follow each question. Choose the answer for each question. Write the letter of the answer you choose beside the correct number on your piece of paper.

1. **What scandal happened during the race for President in 1972?**
   a. the fall of South Vietnam
   b. the Watergate break-in
   c. a civil rights riot in Watts, California
   d. all of the above

2. **Who caused this scandal?**
   a. the Committee to Reelect the President (CREEP)
   b. the Democratic Party
   c. the Republican Party
   d. none of the above

3. **Why did President Nixon resign?**
   a. so he could enter the hospital for serious health problems
   b. because the U.S. Senate had removed him from office
   c. because the U.S. House voted to impeach him for covering up crimes
   d. both a and b

4. **What caused stagflation in the United States?**
   a. inflation
   b. recession
   c. balance of trade
   d. both a and b

5. **Who was involved in wars in the Middle East?**
   a. Israel and the Arab countries
   b. the Soviet Union
   c. the United States
   d. all of the above

6. **How did Jimmy Carter plan to become President?**
   a. by using the primary system
   b. by running as both a Democrat and a Republican
   c. by running as an independent candidate
   d. both a and b

7. **How were President Carter's plans for the Middle East and Latin America different?**
   a. Only the plan for the Middle East involved the U.S. Army.
   b. Only the plan for Latin America involved the U.S. Navy.
   c. Middle East plans succeeded, while Latin American plans failed.
   d. Middle East plans failed, while Latin American plans succeeded.

8. **How did United States and Soviet peace plans fall apart?**
   a. The Soviet Union invaded Afghanistan.
   b. The United States and the Soviet Union took sides about Palestine.
   c. Nicaragua gave up Communism and signed a treaty with the United States.
   d. all of the above

9. **Who stormed an American embassy and took its Americans as hostages?**
   a. the Shah's government in Iran
   b. the Ayatollah's followers in Iran
   c. the followers of the President of Iraq
   d. the people of Algeria

10. **How did the hostage crisis affect President Carter?**
    a. It took the President 444 days to set up terms to free the hostages.
    b. Carter lost the 1980 race for President.
    c. A rescue attempt ordered by President Carter failed and eight Americans were killed.
    d. all of the above

IDENTIFYING MAIN IDEA

Add numbers 11–15 to your paper. Read the two lists below. People, ideas, and countries are listed on the left. Facts about them are listed on the right. Match the people, ideas, and countries with the appropriate facts. Write your answers on your paper.

a. stagflation
b. the Bicentennial
c. the Middle East
d. Latin America
e. the U.S. House of Representatives

11. I voted to impeach President Nixon for covering up the Watergate scandal.
12. I caused an economy that slowed down and cost people their jobs.
13. I was the United States' 200th birthday.
14. I am an area troubled by Communists fighting against dictators.
15. I am an area troubled by problems between Jews and Muslims.

Writing Portfolio

Look over the things you wrote for these chapters. Choose one that you like the best. Add to your writing. For example, you made a chart comparing problems between Israel and the Arab countries of the Middle East. You may wish to add other columns that tell how the United States and the Soviet Union became involved with these problems. You also wrote a report about interviews you held concerning the energy crisis of the 1970s. You may wish to add a report about an interview with people in your community about the hostage crisis in Iran. Trade papers with a study partner. Check each other's work. Make a clean, neat copy. Put it in your portfolio.

Alternative Assessment

You may wish to work with a study partner. Write these five headings on a piece of paper:

Watergate	Stagflation	the Middle East	Afghanistan	Latin America
Cause:	Cause:	Cause:	Cause:	Cause:
Effect:	Effect:	Effect:	Effect:	Effect:

Discuss these ideas with your partner. List facts under each heading. Make sure you tell a cause and an effect for each topic. Share your ideas with other pairs or groups. Are your facts correct? Did you put them under the correct headings? Use these facts to make a chart about the years from 1973-1980. Hang your chart in the classroom.

COOPERATIVE PROJECT: HISTORY CONCENTRATION GAME

LEARNING STYLE
Visual Tactile

Work with a partner or group. List people and groups from this unit. Think of sentences that tell about these people and groups. Write each name on a 3 x 5 index card. Write each sentence on other index cards. Use a pencil to number the backs of these cards. Place the cards in rows on a table or desk. Make sure that only the numbers show. Pick someone to start the game. Each player must choose two cards to turn over. The player must match a name with the correct sentence. If a match is made, the player earns five points. Leave the cards turned up. If a match is not made, turn the cards back over. Continue playing until all the cards have been matched. To play another game, carefully erase the pencil numbers. Shuffle the cards. Write new pencil numbers on the backs.

Chapter 96

New Federalism

United States Budget Deficits

Budget Deficits

Date	Money Taken In	Money Spent	Deficit
1970	$193.8 billion	$194.9 billion	$1.1 billion
1975	$281.0 billion	$324.6 billion	$43.6 billion
1980	$520.0 billion	$579.6 billion	$59.5 billion
1985	$734.0 billion	$945.9 billion	$211.9 billion
1990	$1.031 trillion	$1.251 trillion	$220.4 billion
1993	$1.153 trillion	$1.408 trillion	$254.9 billion

National Debt

Date	Total Debt	Interest Paid	% of Budget as Interest
1970	$370.1 billion	$19.3 billion	9.9%
1975	$533.2 billion	$32.7 billion	9.8%
1980	$907.7 billion	$74.9 billion	12.7%
1985	$1.823 trillion	$178.9 billion	18.9%
1990	$3.233 trillion	$264.8 trillion	21.1%
1993	$4.351 trillion	$292.5 trillion	20.8%

Read about the United States during the 1980s. How did President Reagan's ideas change the country? Why?

Key *Vocabulary*

deregulate (dee REG yuh layt) to remove rules and laws that control some group or activity

homelessness (HOHM luhs nuhs) the state of having no place to live

deficit (DEF uh suht) the money government must borrow to pay those bills not covered by tax money

Reteaching Vocabulary

debt (det) money owed to another

CHART ANALYSIS

★ **Ask** — What does this chart show?

★ **Acquire** — List the columns that tell about budget deficits. List the columns that tell about the national debt.

★ **Organize** — Have the deficits, debt, and interest payments gone up or down since 1970?

★ **Analyze** — How has the interest payment affected how much the government has to spend each year?

★ **Answer** — Why might the interest payments make it harder to pay off the national debt?

Decoding Tip: Notice the different sounds *e* stands for in the vocabulary words.

ay	cake	ah	fall, cot	air	air
ee	tree	i	sit	oh	cold
or	cord	oy	toy	uh	above, hundred
a	ask	ar	hard	oo	book
e	yet	eye	nice	uhr	liar, fir, further, color
ow	cow	ooh	boot, true	yoo	you, few, cube

96.1 Why did President Reagan want to change the role of the federal government?

Like most conservatives, Ronald Reagan did not believe in big government. It had too much power over people's lives, he said. As President, Reagan promised to cut back on the power held by the federal government. He called this idea "New Federalism." Too many people had come to depend upon welfare, unemployment, and other payments from government programs. These programs had been set up to help poor people without jobs.

President Reagan said that government payments kept people poor. They had no reason to get jobs. They could get money without working. Reagan called for cuts in these kinds of programs. Only those who truly needed help would get payments. Others would have to go to work. They would become responsible for their own lives. They would be better off. The country would, too. Or so Reagan and the conservatives said.

96.2 What was President Reagan's view of the Supreme Court?

President Reagan pushed to change the Supreme Court. Since Eisenhower's days, the Court had been liberal. Some of its decisions had included orders. One of these orders set up busing in schools to end segregation. Many people believed the Supreme Court was really making laws. The Constitution said it should only tell what laws mean. It should decide if laws go against the Constitution. Making laws was a power given to Congress by the Constitution.

Under Reagan, the Supreme Court became more conservative. Different seats opened up on the Supreme Court. Reagan chose conservative judges for these spots. He named the first woman to the Supreme Court, Sandra Day O'Connor. Democrats and Republicans did not always agree about Reagan's choices. But the Republicans controlled the Senate for the first time since the 1930s. Most of Reagan's choices were approved. All the open seats were finally filled with conservatives. The Supreme Court began taking a conservative turn in its decisions.

96.3   What was "Reaganomics"?

The President set up plans to end stagflation. Laws about business would be less strict. Some businesses were **deregulated**. They had fewer government rules to follow. It was hoped they would work better. They would make more

▼ President Ronald Reagan

money. More jobs would open up. Reagan also called for Congress to cut its spending on social programs. Congress did cut spending on some of them. But the cuts were not as deep as President Reagan wanted.

Reagan increased spending on defense. He wanted to build up the military. This would keep the country safe.

Reagan called for tax cuts, too. People would keep more of their pay checks. They could spend more money. This would help businesses. They would grow. More jobs would open up. Since these ideas affected the economy, they were known as "Reaganomics."

Cuts in federal spending at first caused the recession to get worse. Many people lost their jobs. Some businesses closed. Banks failed. Some people lost their homes. Instead of economic growth, the early 1980s saw an increase in **homelessness**. Some people began living on the streets. By the middle 1980s, things began to improve. However, unemployment was still high. President Reagan asked Congress to increase unemployment payments to help people who had no jobs. Some taxes were raised. Reaganomics was getting mixed results. Many Americans felt that it helped only the rich.

96.4 How did the federal budget change during the 1980s?

Deficit spending had happened at different times. President Nixon asked Congress to use deficits to help end inflation. Every President since that time has used deficit spending. President Reagan called for a balanced budget. He said the government should not spend more than it takes in. But with Reagan's tax cuts, the government was taking in less money. The deficits grew larger each year. Reagan called for Congress to cut its spending.

▼ A homeless man begging

Deficits continued during the Reagan years. The President's staff sends a budget plan to Congress each year. President Reagan's staff always asked for some cuts. But their plans always included huge deficits. Democrats controlled the House. Republicans controlled the Senate from 1981-1987. They often disagreed with each other. They often disagreed with the President, too.

Congress usually changed the budget plan. Most members sup-

supported social programs for the poor. Congress did not cut these programs as deeply as the President wanted. Even with the economy growing, the deficits remained.

To pay for deficit spending, the government must borrow money each year. Congress sells bonds and uses other ways of borrowing money. Each year's deficits have raised the national **debt**. By 1996, the United States had borrowed over $5 trillion. Each year, the government must pay interest as well as its other bills. A large part of each budget goes to pay the interest owed on the national debt. This has many Americans worried.

96.5 What happened to the economy during the 1980s?

After 1982, the economy began to get better. By Reagan's second term, it was doing very well. Inflation was down. Unemployment was down. Many businesses grew tremendously. The 1980s also was a time of business takeovers. One company would buy out another. These purchases were often made with borrowed money. Sometimes the buyer would sell off parts of the company that had been taken over. This money helped pay off some of the money that had been borrowed. Corporations became larger than ever before. Stock prices rocketed. In fact, they rose too fast. In October 1987, there was a major crash. Still, it was the longest time of growth during peace the American economy had ever seen.

☆☆☆

Connections

▲ President Franklin Delano Roosevelt

Many Americans wanted to change the Constitution during the 1980s. Some called for an end of the 22nd Amendment. It had been passed in 1951. Many people had become upset during Franklin Roosevelt's years in the White House. He had won four terms. It was not against the law. But some people felt that this was too long for one President to serve. However, President Reagan was very popular. He easily won a second term in 1984. Some people wanted him to serve even longer. Nothing came of this call.

A second idea gained more support. Many people called for a balanced budget amendment. This would require Congress to have a balanced budget each year. It could not spend more than it collects in taxes. The national debt grew throughout the 1980s and well into the 1990s. A vote on this proposed amendment was held in Congress in 1995. The U.S. House passed the amendment. But it failed in the U.S. Senate. The amendment's supporters promise to continue the fight.

★★☆ CHAPTER REVIEW

Critical Thinking

Write your answers on a sheet of paper, or discuss in class.

 Comparing and Contrasting

1. How were the ideas of conservatives different from ideas that the government had been following?

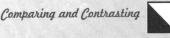 *Identifying Main Idea*

2. Why did the economy change during the Reagan years?

Cooperative Learning

 LEARNING STYLE *Reading Oral*

3. Work with a small group. Sit in a circle. Read over the chapter again. Then take turns telling about parts of the chapter. Make sure to tell the important points. After each person speaks, talk about what was said. Was everything covered? Do some in the group have different thoughts? Continue until all have had a chance to speak.

Write About It

 Writing Portfolio

4. Look through Chapters 71 and 72. They tell how President Roosevelt used government spending to fight the Great Depression. Compare his ideas with those of President Reagan. Write sentences about their ideas. Use these sentences to make a chart comparing Roosevelt's New Deal with Reagan's New Federalism.

Chapter 97

The U.S. and the World

Legend

- Communist Country giving arms and money to rebels in other countries
- Ruled by Army Dictators
- Retaken by Great Britain from invading troops from Argentina
- Communist Rebels fighting a civil war

0   1000   2000 Miles
0   1000   2000 Kilometers

FIGHTING IN LATIN AMERICA (1980s)

Read about the world during the 1980s. How did its problems affect the United States? Why?

Key *Vocabulary*

perestroika (pair uh STROY kuh) a plan for changing the Soviet Union's Communist government

glasnost (GLAS nohst) openness, or the grant of freedoms and rights to the Soviet people

terrorist (TAIR uhr uhst) a person who uses violence and fear to gain his or her demands

apartheid (uh PAR tayt) the South African word for segregation

immunity (im YOO nuht ee) an agreement to drop charges if a person will confess a crime, especially while working as a witness

MAP ANALYSIS		
★ **Ask**	What does this map show?
★ **Acquire**	What does the legend show?
★ **Organize**	Make a chart. List the countries that have Communist governments. List the countries where Communists are working to take over the governments. List the countries that are ruled by dictators.
★ **Analyze**	Why did a European country become involved in Latin America?
★ **Answer**	Why do you think the United States was worried about what was happening in Latin America?

Decoding Tip: Note that a, e, i, and o can all stand for /uh/ in the vocabulary words.

ay	cake	ah	fall, cot	air	air
ee	tree	i	sit	oh	cold
or	cord	oy	toy	uh	above, hundred
a	ask	ar	hard	oo	book
e	yet	eye	nice	uhr	liar, fir, further, color
ow	cow	ooh	boot, true	yoo	you, few, cube

97.1 What were things like between the United States and the Soviet Union in the 1980s?

At first, President Reagan called the Soviet Union the "Evil Empire." He pushed hard to win the Cold War. The United States spent more money on its military. It was the biggest build-up in a time of peace. Some Americans said that arms should be cut. Then peace talks could reach their goals. However, Reagan said the United States should be strong. Only then would the Soviets be willing for peace talks to succeed. The Soviets did respond. They spent more money on their military, too. The arms race was on again.

▲ Mikhail Gorbachev

The Soviet Union gained a new leader in 1985. Mikhail Gorbachev wanted to change the country. Its government would work differently. There would be more opportunities for business. He called this plan *perestroika*. He also called for *glasnost*, or openness, in Soviet life. More freedoms and rights would be given to the people.

Reagan's arms build-up helped get the Soviets to talk. Gorbachev knew his country could not win an arms race. The United States and the Soviet Union began to work together. The two countries became better friends. Reagan and Gorbachev met together four times. New treaties were set up. For the first time, the Soviets would allow Americans to check Soviet weapons areas. The Americans could see that the Soviets were following the treaties. However, Afghanistan was still under Soviet control. President Reagan increased help to the Afghan rebels. The Cold War was not yet over. But it was coming to an end.

97.2 Why were Central America and the Middle East trouble spots?

President Reagan worked against Communists in Central America. Sometimes he supported dictators who were fighting Communist rebels. The Contras were people in Nicaragua who were fighting against their Communist government. Reagan sent money to help the Contras. But many in Congress did not like giving out money to the Contras.

The United States could not be sure how the money was being used. Reports also reached the United States about **terrorist** acts. Both sides were killing innocent people. This began to happen in many countries of Latin America. Congress voted to stop sending money to the Contras. New laws said that the President must get approval from Congress before helping troops in other countries.

Terrorists also caused problems in the Middle East. The Palestinian Liberation Organization (PLO) had bases in Lebanon. They were fighting to take back land from Israel. Other Muslim groups worked for countries like Libya and Iran. They had taken many Westerners as hostages. The hostages were held in Lebanon. Some hostages were from the United States. The groups said that Western countries should force Israel to meet their demands. If not, the hostages would be killed. President Reagan worked to bring peace to the Middle East. American troops were sent to stop the fighting between Israel and the PLO in Lebanon. In October 1983, a truck bomb blew up outside the U.S. Marines' main offices in Beirut, Lebanon. 241 Marines were killed. Peace talks broke down. President Reagan pulled American troops out of Lebanon in 1984.

97.3   How did OPEC affect the U.S. economy?

War broke out between Iran and Iraq in 1980. President Reagan sent the U.S. Navy to the Middle East. U.S. ships sailed with oil tankers. Most belonged to countries in the Middle East. But many Middle East countries were in business with American companies. The tankers were shipping oil to countries like the United States and Japan. Reagan wanted to make sure the tankers got through safely. There were dangers. Iraq attacked the *U.S.S. Stark* in May 1987. 37 sailors were killed. The work was too important to stop. Besides, Iraq was friendly with the United States. The attack was a mistake.

As in the 1970s, OPEC affected the United States during the 1980s. Oil prices were very high. Oil companies were making record profits. People in other states were losing jobs because of company takeovers. Many of these people moved to Texas, Oklahoma, and Louisiana. They wanted high-paying jobs with oil companies. Soon, there were too many people. No jobs were left. Some people had to live in their cars. Soup kitchens were started to feed these people. Groups were set up to help them move to places where they might find jobs.

OPEC hurt the oil business in the middle 1980s. Its members began arguing among themselves. Their plans to keep oil prices high fell apart. Oil prices dropped through the middle and late 1980s. Oil companies had been through takeovers, too. Many had heavy debts. Lower prices caused lower profits. Many oil companies began to fail. This also hit banks very hard. Many people in oil businesses lost their jobs.

97.4   What was the Iran-Contra Affair?

News of a scandal broke out in 1986. These reports said that President Reagan's staff had been selling arms to Iran. In return, American hostages were to be set free. Profits were being given to the Contras in Nicaragua. This was against the law. Congress began checking into the reports. They were true. Arms were sold to Iran. Millions of dollars went to the Contras. Much of the money was missing. Only one hostage had been set free. Some White House members went on trial. President Reagan said he knew nothing about the scandal. No charges were ever brought against the President. However, some White House members were sentenced to jail.

97.5 How did *apartheid* in South Africa affect the United States?

▼ Nelson Mandela

Segregation in South Africa affected the United States. It was known as ***apartheid***. No Black South African was allowed a voice in government. Americans began protesting *apartheid*. Some American companies sold their shares in South African businesses. Many broke off deals with South Africa. Black South African leaders like Nelson Mandela were being held in prison. Mandela was one of the leaders of the African National Congress. That group was working to gain power for Black South Africans. Mandela was sentenced to life in prison for several bombings at government sites. Soon, protests demanded that these leaders be set free. Some Americans said that the United States should not interfere. The South African government might punish Black South Africans for these protests. However, the protests went on.

☆☆☆

▲ Segregation on an escalator in South Africa

Connections

▲ Lt. Col. Oliver North

Lt. Col. Oliver North helped in the Iran-Contra Affair. He worked in the White House. Like all White House members, he had taken an oath. He promised to obey the U.S. Constitution. North had helped sell arms to Iran. He had helped send the profits to the Contras in Nicaragua. Congress asked North to tell what he knew. He agreed. But first, Congress had to give him **immunity**. North would not be punished for anything that he confessed. Congress agreed. North told all about the scandal. He named the people involved. He said that President Reagan had known everything. However, he also said that he had done everything because he loved the United States. He wanted the country to be safe. He blamed Congress. It should never have cut off money used to fight Communism. Many Americans called him a hero. Others said that North and others in the scandal had broken their oaths of office. They had gone against the Constitution and broken the law.

Lt. Col. North was sentenced to jail. This sentence was thrown out of court, though. The main proof had been his speeches in Congress. He had been given immunity. The speeches should not have been used as proof. North never went to jail. Neither did others in the scandal. On December 24, 1992, President George Bush pardoned everyone involved.

 CHAPTER REVIEW

Critical Thinking

Write your answers on a sheet of paper, or discuss in class.

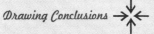 Drawing Conclusions

 Making Inferences

1. Why was the world a dangerous place in the 1980s?

2. How might President Reagan and Gorbachev have helped make the world safer?

Cooperative Learning

LEARNING STYLE
Reading
Tactile

3. Work with a partner or group. Make a large picture. Draw important people from this chapter. Show changes in Soviet life. Show things that happened in Latin America and the Middle East. See if others can name the people and events.

Write About It

Writing Portfolio

4. At this time, Americans and Soviets' lives began to change. Imagine how they felt about change. What was most important to them? What were they losing? What were they gaining? Write what you think in a poem or in a paragraph.

Chapter 98

The Changing World Map

THE FALL OF THE SOVIET UNION (1989)

1. Estonia
2. Lativa
3. Lithuania
4. Byelarus
5. Czech
6. Slovakia
7. Austria
8. Hungary
9. Romania
10. Switzerland
11. Slovenia
12. Croatia
13. Bosnia
14. Serbia
15. Bulgaria
16. Montenegro
17. Albania
18. Macedonia
19. Georgia
20. Armenia
21. Azerbaijan
22. Turkmenistan
23. Uzbekistan
24. Kyrgyzstan
25. Tajikistan
26. Belgium
27. Netherlands
28. Denmark
29. Moldova

Soviet States that became Independent Countries

Russia

Countries that Became Free of Soviet Control

Read about the ways in which the world map changed. How did governments change, too? Why?

Key *Vocabulary*

protest (PROH test) 1. an act or statement that shows disagreement or opposition 2. to disagree or oppose

foreigner (FOR uhn uhr) a person who comes from outside the country he or she lives in

Reteaching Vocabulary

economy (i KAHN uh mee) the system through which the people and companies of a certain area make their livings

invest (in VEST) to use money so that profits are earned

democracy (duh MAHK ruh see) a kind of government in which people rule themselves

MAP ANALYSIS

★ **Ask**   What does this map show?

★ **Acquire**   What does the legend show?

★ **Organize**   Make a chart. List the new countries that had been states of the Soviet Union. List the countries that had been under Soviet control.

★ **Analyze**   Which of the new countries had Communist governments?

★ **Answer**   What do you think might have made these people turn against Communism?

Decoding Tip: Note that c stands for /k/ in **economy** and /k/ and /s/ in **democracy**.

ay	cake	ah	fall, cot	air	air
ee	tree	i	sit	oh	cold
or	cord	oy	toy	uh	above, hundred
a	ask	ar	hard	oo	book
e	yet	eye	nice	uhr	liar, fir, further, color
ow	cow	ooh	boot, true	yoo	you, few, cube

98.1 How did economic problems affect the federal government in the late 1980s?

Economic problems hit in the late 1980s. President Reagan's ideas had worked for several years. The **economy** did grow. Then things changed. Prices began to drop. The economy began to slow down. Many companies began to go under. Oil companies, airlines, and others were hit hard. They had borrowed money. It was used to buy up other companies. Now, some could not pay back these loans. This put banks and savings and loans in trouble.

Some Americans lost their jobs. They had borrowed money, too. It was used to buy homes. Now they were falling behind in their payments. Land prices began to drop. People and companies had borrowed money to **invest** in land deals. Now, these loans were bad, too. Many banks and savings and loans began to go under. Things were almost as bad as the Great Depression for banks and savings and loans.

The government bailed out the banking business. George Bush had been Reagan's Vice President. He was elected President in 1988. President Bush asked Congress to help. Many banks and savings and loans had closed. What about the people's money? The government paid most of it back. This kept the banking business from breaking down. Congress spent over one-half trillion dollars. This added to budget deficits. The country's debt grew, too. Most Americans became worried. How could the United States pay off the debt? Future Americans might have to pay bills from the past.

1988 Presidential Election

Candidate	Party	Popular Vote	Electoral College Vote
George H. W. Bush	Republican	48,881,221	426
Michael S. Dukakis	Democrat	41,805,422	111

98.2   Why did the Cold War end?

Afghanistan helped bring down the Soviet Union. The war went badly. The cost was too great. Soviet spending on the military had always been high. By the late 1980s, the country could not pay these bills. It began cutting back. The Soviet Army was pulled out of Afghanistan in February 1989. Gorbachev's ideas were changing the Soviet economy. But things were moving slowly.

Communist countries saw a special chance. In August 1989, Poland elected a new government. It was Poland's first free vote since World War II. The Communists were thrown out. Of course, other Communist countries had tried to break from the Soviets. They had always been crushed. But things had changed in the Soviet Union. Gorbachev did not try to stop the new Polish government. Soon other Communist countries decided to become free. All these countries gave up Communism. They wanted American **democracy**. In November 1989, the Berlin Wall came down. The news was almost too good to be true.

▲ The photograph above shows people on top and around the Berlin Wall before it came down in 1989.

Two years later, the Soviet people moved away from Communism. Gorbachev's plans had been slowly changing the Soviet Union. Many Communist ideas were being given up. But some Communist leaders were afraid of losing power. They moved against Gorbachev in August 1991. He was held prisoner. However, the Soviet Army would not go along. Boris Yeltsin led the people. Gorbachev was set free.

Elections were held. Most Communists were thrown out of office. Yeltsin became head of the new government. He pushed for democracy. The Soviet Union fell apart. Several states broke away. They became new countries. All worked for democracy. The country's name was even changed. The old name "Russia" was brought back. The Cold War came to an end.

Communists fought back in 1993. They tried to take over the government again. They locked themselves into the Russian White House. Russian troops had to shell the building. Finally, the Communists gave up.

The Russian economy has troubles still. Some people are very poor. Some even long for the Communist days. The government took care of them. But others are learning how to build their own businesses. Time will tell how Russia deals with its new freedom.

▼ The photograph below shows a demonstration by Chinese students in Tienanmen Square in Peking in 1989. The students demanded that the Communist government allow democracy for the country.

98.3 How did the Communist governments in China and Cuba change?

In 1989, Chinese students pushed for democracy. Thousands of students marched through Beijing. The government did not say or do anything. The students gathered in Tienanmen Square. They were shown on television. Some held pictures of the Statue of Liberty. The news went all over the world. This worried China's leaders. On June 4, they moved against the students. Troops marched into the square. The people fought back. Some stood in the way of tanks. But this did little good. Many people were killed. Many more were hurt. The world saw it all. Television carried these pictures. **Protests** flooded into the country. The Communist government did not back down. Many Americans called for the United States to break ties with China. President Bush refused. He decided that China was too important to be ignored.

Cuba changed after the fall of the Soviet Union. It had always been a strong friend of the Soviets. Castro's Communist government remained in place. However, the Cuban economy got worse. The Soviet Union had pumped money into Cuba. The new country of Russia had to stop these payments. Cuba has become very poor. Castro has opened up the country to some outside businesses. He wants to help the economy. Western companies have built hotels and vacation spots. But Cubans can only work in them. They cannot visit these places. The country may have more money. But the people are still very poor. Many Cubans eat only once a day.

98.4   Why did South Africa change?

South Africa's government changed in 1994. Many countries had **protested** its ideas. *Apartheid* had given few rights to Black South Africans. The United States worked to bring change. Congress passed a special act in 1986. American companies could not deal with South Africa. Its economy suffered. Black South Africans were given rights in 1990. Nelson Mandela and other Black South African leaders were set free. Elections were held in 1994. Mandela became the new President on May 10. Now the country is working toward democracy. All people will have rights and freedoms.

☆☆☆

Connections

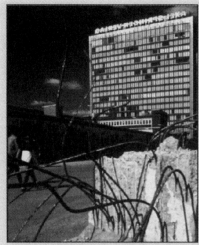

▲ Berlin Wall after it was torn down

Germany has gone through great changes. It became two countries after World War II. East Germany was Communist. This changed in 1989. The Soviet Union began to fall apart. Poland and other Communist countries broke free. East Germany followed. East Germans cut holes in the Berlin Wall. They moved back and forth to the West. In November, the people of Berlin tore down the wall. It was torn apart with tools and people's hands. The world watched on television. Germans danced and sang. The Iron Curtain had come down.

Germany became one country again in 1990. However, things have not always been good. The East was very poor. It had not been completely rebuilt after the war. Its companies fell apart. People needed jobs. The West is spending money to help it grow. The German economy has slowed. Some East Germans are angry with waiting. Some groups followed Nazi ideas. They blame others for these problems. They point to **foreigners** who live and work in Germany. These people have even been attacked. But most Germans have strong feelings for democracy. They are working with the government to stop these acts.

★☆☆ CHAPTER REVIEW

Comparing and Contrasting

Identifying Main Idea

Critical Thinking

Write your answers on a sheet of paper, or discuss in class.

1. How were the ideas of Communist leaders and their people alike? How were they different?

2. Why might money troubles cause problems for the new countries of the world?

Cooperative Learning

LEARNING STYLE
Verbal

3. Work with a study partner or as part of a study group. Write these words on separate pieces of paper: **debt, Communist, democracy, the Soviet Union, Russia, China, Cuba,** and **Afghanistan.** Put the papers in a box. Take turns drawing pieces of paper from the box. Read the word or name you have drawn. Tell what this person, country, or idea is like.

Write About It

Writing Portfolio

4. Imagine you were in Berlin in November 1989. You are watching the Berlin Wall come down. Think about what you are seeing. How are the people acting? How are they feeling? Why is this happening? What does this mean for Germany? Write a report about this special night.

Chapter 99

Storm Clouds

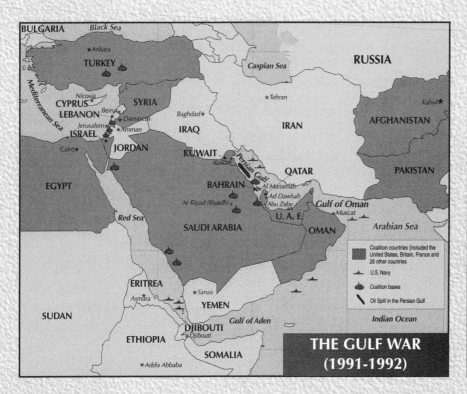

**THE GULF WAR
(1991-1992)**

Read about conflicts around the world. How did the United States become involved? Why?

Key *Vocabulary*

fanatic (fuh NAT ik) a person who so strongly believes in certain ideas that they become more important than anything else

loot (looht) to steal great quantities of goods, especially during a time of war or violence

Reteaching Vocabulary

embargo (im BAR goh) an order to stop a certain kind of trade

missile (MIS uhl) a rocket fired as a weapon

MAP ANALYSIS	★ **Ask**	What does this map show?
	★ **Acquire**	What does the legend show?
	★ **Organize**	Make a chart. List the countries that sided with the United States. List the countries that sided with Iraq.
	★ **Answer**	What do you think Iraq wanted from Kuwait?

Decoding Tip: Note the /ooh/ sound of oo in **loot**.

ay	cake	ah	fall, cot	air	air
ee	tree	i	sit	oh	cold
or	cord	oy	toy	uh	above, hundred
a	ask	ar	hard	oo	book
e	yet	eye	nice	uhr	liar, fir, further, color
ow	cow	ooh	boot, true	yoo	you, few, cube

99.1 Why did the United States support Iraq in its war with Iran?

▲ Ayatollah Ruholla Khomeini

Iran had turned against the United States in 1979. The Shah's government had been very friendly. However, this government fell in 1978. Many of his people were Muslim **fanatics**. They were led by the Ayatollah Khomeini. They took the American embassy by storm. Its staff was held prisoner for 444 days. After that, Iran carried out terrorists acts in many parts of the world. Most were directed at the United States and other Western countries.

War broke out in the Middle East in 1980. The United States helped Iraq in this war with Iran. Iran was still ruled by the Ayatollah. It was still carrying out terrorist acts. Iraq and Iran were neighbors. Iraq was ruled by Saddam Hussein. He was a dictator. He did not stand for people who disagreed. These people had to leave the country or be killed. Both Iran and Iraq were Muslim countries. However, the people of Iraq followed a different kind of Islam. The war dragged on for years. Millions were killed. Finally, the two countries ended the war in 1989.

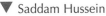
▼ Saddam Hussein

99.2 Why did the world turn against Iraq?

After the war, Iran and Iraq needed money. Their economies were in trouble. Too much money had been spent on the war. The United States was still leading an **embargo** of oil from Iran. In 1990, Iraq decided to invade another of its neighbors, Kuwait. It is a small country. But it is one of the richest in the world. Iraq said that Kuwait was stealing its oil. Saddam Hussein also claimed that Kuwait was not really a country. It had always been part of

A convoy of U.S. army helicopters flies over burning oil fields in Kuwait, March 1991

Iraq, he said. His troops took over Kuwait on August 2. The world rushed to protest this act. Even Russia worried that Iraq would move against more of its neighbors. It might take over all the oil in the Middle East. The UN called for an embargo of Iraq, too. Not only oil was affected. No trade would be allowed.

Saudi Arabia asked President Bush and the United Nations for help. The king worried that his country was next on Hussein's list. By August 7, all parts of the U.S. military were arriving in the Middle East. It was called "Operation Desert Shield." The Navy sailed along all the coasts. U.S. troops set

▲ An aerial view of the Kuwait Al Wafre oilfield set ablaze by Iraqi forces, January 1991.

up bases in the area. By November, things did not look good. Hussein still seemed very sure of himself. The UN called for a new plan. Iraq had until January 15, 1991, to get out of Kuwait. If not, it might be forced out. Iraq refused to leave.

On January 16, the United States and other allied troops attacked Iraq. The plan was called "Operation Desert Storm." Bombs and **missiles** hit all parts of Iraq. The U.S. shelled Iraq's bases in Kuwait. In return, Iraq shelled Saudi Arabia and Israel. Scud missiles were fired on these Allied countries. However, most were shot down with American Patriot missiles. The attack on Israel had a special goal. Most Arab countries hated Israel. They might have gone to Iraq's side if Israel had entered the war. However, this didn't happen. President Bush kept all the Allied countries together. On February 24, Bush

▲ Iraqi soldiers stand on their Soviet-made tank on the premises of Abu-Fadel al Abbas mosque in the holy city of Karbala in Southern Iraq, April 1991.

ordered ground attacks. These lasted until February 27. Iraq's troops gave up. The Gulf War was over. Kuwait was a free country again.

99.3 What happened after Operation Desert Storm?

Desert Storm succeeded. Iraq pulled its troops out of Kuwait. 293 U.S. troops died during Desert Storm. But Kuwait was free. The country was in a mess, though. It had been **looted**. Bomb damage was everywhere. Kuwait's oil fields were on fire. Iraq's troops had blown them up. They had opened the

▲ This photograph shows Iraqi troops surrendering to allied forces during Operation Desert Storm.

country's pipe lines. Millions of gallons of oil spilled into the Persian Gulf. It took a year and over $1-billion to put out the oil fires. The cleanup is still going on. Over 400,000 refugees returned to Kuwait from Saudi Arabia. It will take years for the country to recover.

Iraq is still being punished. Its oil is still under an embargo. Other trade is now allowed. However, no one can sell weapons to Iraq. UN teams check Iraq's bases. They make sure that Hussein is not rebuilding his military. The United States and the Allies are keeping troops in the Middle East. They will be ready if war breaks out again. Some people think that Hussein may be using terrorist acts against the Allied countries.

President Bush visited Kuwait in April 1993. The country held special ceremonies for him. Its people wanted to thank

▲ President George Bush addresses U.S. troops during the Persian Gulf War, November 1992.

Bush and the United States for their help. Kuwait arrested 14 people. They were sentenced for planning to kill Bush during this trip. Evidence showed that Hussein was behind the plan. President Bill Clinton ordered a bombing raid against Iraq on June 26, 1993. Iraq's military and spy offices were bombed.

Kurds live in northern and southern Iraq. Thy do not support Saddam Hussein. Iraq brok U.N. rules and attacked northern Kurds in September 1996. President Clinton had to take armed action against Hussein again. As long as Hussein controls Iraq, the danger will go on.

☆☆☆

Biography

▲ General Colin Powell

▲ General Norman Schwarzkopf

Chairman of the Joint Chiefs of Staff in 1989. He became the leader of all the U.S. Armed Forces. Only the President has a higher rank. General Powell handled the Pentagon during Operation Desert Storm. General Norman Schwarzkopf led the troops in the Middle East. Powell and Schwarzkopf often spoke on television during the war. The American people learned what able leaders the two men were.

Powell served as Chairman until 1993. Then he retired from the military. Many people began pushing him to run for the White House. For a while, he did think about the 1996 race. But he decided it was not for him. His wife did not want the problems of a Presidential Election. Since the 1970s, candidates have had little peace of mind. News reports dig into each candidate's life and past.

General Colin Powell led the Pentagon during Operation Desert Storm. He had served three tours of duty during times of war. One term was in Korea. The other two were served in Vietnam. He became a two-star general in 1982. President George Bush chose him as

Mean and nasty things are often said during the race. General Powell told the country that he knew he could handle the office of President. But he did not want his family to have to go through the strain of the race. What about the future? General Powell left that idea open.

 CHAPTER REVIEW

Critical Thinking

Identifying Main Idea

Write your answers on a sheet of paper, or discuss in class.

1. Why was Iraq's invasion of Kuwait a world problem?

Drawing Conclusions

2. How do you think Saddam Hussein has kept power even after losing the Gulf War?

Cooperative Learning

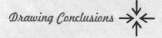 LEARNING STYLE
Visual
Tactile

3. Make a timeline of the Gulf War. Show the important events of the war. These may be battles and other events. Study your timeline to see how one event led to another.

Write About It

 Writing Portfolio

4. Choose one of the events from Operation Desert Storm. Write a song about it. Use strong images, as in "The Star-Spangled Banner." If you wish, make up a tune for your song. You might even sing it for the class.

Chapter 100

The Federal Debate

1996 Presidential Race			
Candidate	Party	Popular Vote	Electoral College Vote
William J. Clinton	Democrat	45,338,197	379
Robert Dole	Republican	37,689,108	179
H. Ross Perot	Independent	7,824,902	0

Read about new ideas in the United States. How did they affect the federal government? Why?

A Changing Congress

		1992 Elections	1994 Elections	1996 Elections
Senate	Democrats	56	47	45
	Republicans	44	53	55
	Total	100	100	100
House	Democrats	256	204	208
	Republicans	178	230	225
	Independents	1	1	2
	Total	435	435	435

Key *Vocabulary*

gridlock (GRID lahk) a situation in which arguments become so heated that nothing is achieved

health care (helth • kair) the system a country follows in treating its people's illnesses

Reteaching Vocabulary

reform (ri FORM) the act of making changes to clean up or improve something

candidate (KAN duh dayt) one who runs for an office

majority (muh JOR uht ee) any number that is greater than one half

CHART ANALYSIS

★ **Ask** What do these two charts show?

★ **Organize** List the party that won the Senate, the House, and the Presidency.

★ **Analyze** Why might the President and Congress not get along?

★ **Answer** Why do you think the people voted for such a big change in the members of Congress?

Decoding Tip: Note how *e* at the end of a syllable affects a vowel's sound, as in **health care** and **candidate**.

ay	cake	ah	fall, cot	air	air
ee	tree	i	sit	oh	cold
or	cord	oy	toy	uh	above, hundred
a	ask	ar	hard	oo	book
e	yet	eye	nice	uhr	liar, fir, further, color
ow	cow	ooh	boot, true	yoo	you, few, cube

100.1 How did a third candidate affect the Presidential Election of 1992?

Presidential Race

Candidate	Party	Popular Vote	Electoral College Vote
William J. Clinton	Democrat	44,908,254	370
George H.W. Bush	Republican	39,102,343	168
H. Ross Perot	Reform	19,741,065	0

Differences in ideas separate America's political parties. Republicans ask an important question. Why should government help run businesses and people's lives? Democrats ask another important question. What is wrong with government programs that work to help people and businesses? However, the people have an even more important question. What kind of government is best for the United States?

Gridlock has made many Americans angry. Congress had been controlled by the Democrats from 1952 to 1981. The Senate had gone to the Republicans from 1981 to 1987. However, the Democrats took the Senate back in the 1988 elections. Presidents Reagan and Bush were Republicans. Huge disagreements had broken out between the White House and the Democratic Congress. Each fought for very different ideas. Many Americans became disappointed in government. Were the parties fighting to help the government? Or were they just fighting to see which side would win? In 1992, the Republicans chose President Bush to run for a second term. The Democrats chose Governor Bill Clinton of Arkansas. Both men were strong supporters of their parties' ideas. H. Ross Perot, a rich businessman, also ran in the 1992 Presidential Election. He talked about changing Washington, D.C. The people were tired of the fighting, he said. They wanted **reform**. The government should be run smoothly. Big government was too wasteful.

▼ The photograph below shows H. Ross Perot speaking to supporters during the 1992 Presidential Race.

▲ President and Mrs. Bush visit American troops in the Middle East, November 1990.

Waste should be cut out. Then government could become smaller. But it could still carry out most of its programs. Most important, taxes could be cut. Many people cheered these ideas. However, Perot had other ideas that were not as popular. He wanted a tax of $5 on each barrel of oil. People would begin saving oil. The United States would begin buying less oil from other countries. But many Americans thought that the tax would also hurt the country's economy. Perot won More votes than any third-party **candidate** in

The photograph to the right shows President George Bush speaking to Congress in 1990.

history. But he did not win the Electoral Votes in any one state. He did take votes away from the other candidates. Like Nixon in 1968, Clinton did not win a **majority**. But he had the most votes. He became President.

100.2 What ideas caused conflict in government during the 1990s?

The argument over big government or smaller government took over in the 1990s. President Clinton's plan for **health care** showed the argument clearly. Clinton called on the federal government to set up a system for all Americans. This would help make sure that all people could afford to see doctors or be treated in hospitals. Most Americans turned against the idea. They did not want the government making these decisions for them. Besides, the program would be one

▲ The photograph above shows Democratic Presidential candidate Bill Clinton speaking in Los Angeles after the LA riots, in September 1992.

of the government's largest. Many thought it would cost too much money. The government was already deeply in debt. The plan was soundly beaten in Congress.

Clinton also asked for higher taxes to lower the deficit. However, he had promised a tax cut during the Presidential Election. Democrats in Congress passed the tax bill by just one vote. Many Americans began talking about "government as usual." The elections of 1992 had clearly shown that the people wanted reform.

100.3 How did ideas for reform change government in the 1990s?

New ideas affected the race for Congress in 1994. Newt Gingrich of Georgia led the Republicans in the House. He set

▲ The photograph above shows 1996 Presidential candidate Bob Dole resigning from the U.S. Senate to campaign full-time against President Clinton.

up the Contract with America. If the Republicans took control of the House, its ten ideas would be discussed. They involved such things as:

- allowing each member of Congress to serve only 10 years

- adding a balanced budget amendment to the Constitution

- creating a budget that was balanced by the year 2002

- cutting back on government regulations for businesses

- doing away with the Departments of Commerce, Education, and Energy

Democrats pointed to the Republicans' ideas. They asked questions like:

- Why should the people not be able to vote for someone just because the person had already served 10 years?

- How would the country be hurt if spending were cut too much in order to balance the budget?

- What would happen to commerce, education, and energy ideas if the departments were shut down?

Republicans and Democrats fought a hard race. The American people voted for change and reform. Republicans took over both Houses of Congress for the first time since 1952. Things were clear. The people were unhappy with government as usual.

Even with a Republican Congress, many people felt gridlock was still a problem. In 1995 and 1996, President Clinton upset many Democrats by supporting some Republican ideas.

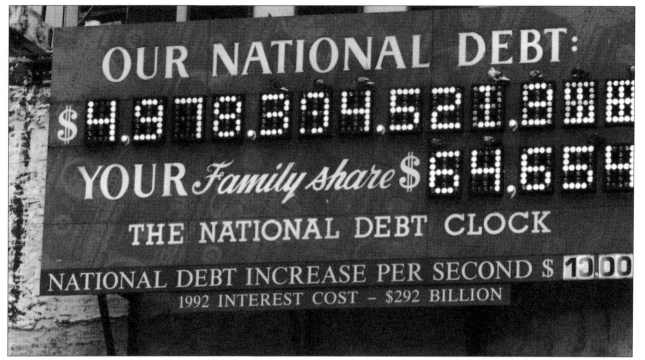

OUR NATIONAL DEBT:
$4,978,804,520,808
YOUR *Family share* $64,664
THE NATIONAL DEBT CLOCK
NATIONAL DEBT INCREASE PER SECOND $ 13,00
1992 INTEREST COST – $292 BILLION

▲ A National Debt clock continues to rise as politicians in Washington continue to debate the merits of a balanced budget bill.

However, he called for fewer changes and smaller cuts in spending. Disagreements between Congress and President Clinton held up many bills for government spending. The federal government was forced to shut down three times in 1995. Republicans called for a new President who would support their ideas. In the Election of 1996, Kansas Senator Bob Dole ran for the Republicans. He called for a large tax cut and an end to some federal programs and departments. Americans seemed to support President Clinton's ideas about limited reform. He won a second term as President. After taking office in 1997. President Clinton and Congress began looking for a way of reforming government without making broad new changes.

☆☆☆

Terror from Within

▲ Damage to the World Trade Center

Terrorism has been a world problem for years. Some people want Northern Ireland to leave Great Britain and join Ireland. Palestinians want to break away from Israel and form their own country. Some Muslims in Iran want all Muslims to follow their ideas. Arab leaders like Muammar al-Qaddafi and Saddam Hussein want more land to rule. Some of these people use terrorist acts in trying to reach their goals. They often kill innocent people. Sometimes these people live in other countries. But often, they kill their own people. Prime Minister Yitzhak Rabin led Israel to find peace with the Palestinians. He even set up terms for them to have their own country. Some Israeli radicals hated him for these ideas. Rabin was shot and killed by one of these people in November 1995.

These acts hit the United States in the 1990s. Arab radicals bombed the World Trade Center in New York. The 1994 bombing killed six people. The radicals were later caught and sentenced.

In 1995, Americans learned that the country has its own radicals. There are many groups in the United States. Some work against the government. FBI and ATF agents raided a camp at Waco, Texas, in 1993. The raid went bad. The camp was surrounded. After a few months, the FBI and ATF attacked. The camp caught fire and over 80 people died. This angered some Americans. A few were members of other radical groups. They are filled with hate for the federal government. They want to bring the government down and replace it. On April 19, 1995, the Murrah Federal Building was bombed in downtown Oklahoma City. 168 people died in the bombing. Americans were shocked. Then they were horrified by the FBI's findings. It seemed Americans had set off the bomb. Two men were charged. Both hate the federal government. Now the country has a new worry. Are other Americans so angry that this can happen again?

★★★ CHAPTER REVIEW

Critical Thinking

Write your answers on a sheet of paper, or discuss in class.

Analyzing Cause and Effect
1. Why might people want to make changes in their government?

Drawing Conclusions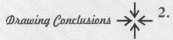
2. What ideas about government do Republicans and Democrats share? What ideas do they disagree about?

Cooperative Learning

LEARNING
STYLE
Reading
Tactile

3. Work with a study partner or group. Write the following on a sheet of paper. Write Democrats, Republicans, the people, and radical groups. Leave space between them. Circle each one. Draw three small circles around each one. In each small circle write a fact from this chapter. The fact should tell about the term. Draw lines from the fact circles to their main terms. Can you think of more facts? Write them also. Use your fact circles to learn about this chapter.

Write About It

Writing
Portfolio

4. Write a paragraph in support of one idea from this chapter. Write a sentence that tells your main opinion. Then write at least two other sentences to complete your paragraph. These sentences should tell reasons why you hold this opinion and why you think this opinion is correct.

Quiz

Number a piece of paper from 1-10. Write a, b, c, and d beside these numbers. Read the following sentence beginnings. Four endings follow each one. Choose the answer that best completes the sentence. On your paper, circle the letter that matches the letter of your answer. Be sure you mark your answer beside the correct number.

1. **As a conservative, President Reagan believed in . . .**
   a. cutting back the power of the federal government.
   b. a Supreme Court that did not make laws.
   c. tax cuts and deregulation to end stagflation.
   d. all of the above.

2. **During the 1970s and 1980s, federal budgets always included . . .**
   a. deficits.
   b. cuts in defense.
   c. tax increases.
   d. all of the above.

3. **The United States and Soviet Union became friendlier after . . .**
   a. the Soviets freed their American hostages.
   b. Mikhail Gorbachev began changing Soviet ideas.
   c. Afghanistan's rebels drove out Soviet troops.
   d. all of the above.

4. **A scandal broke out when it was believed that . . .**
   a. some people in the White House were selling weapons to Iran.
   b. money from the Iran arms sales was being given to Contra rebels in Nicaragua.
   c. OPEC was controlling the high prices charged for oil.
   d. both a and b.

5. **By the late 1980s, the U.S. economy was affected by . . .**
   a. dropping prices.
   b. bad loans.
   c. bank failures.
   d. all of the above.

6. **The switch from Communism to democracy in Eastern Europe and the Soviet Union was caused by . . .**
   a. too much spending on the Soviet military.
   b. the people refusing to support a Communist move against Mikhail Gorbachev in 1991.
   c. Soviet plans to take over Western Europe.
   d. both a and b.

7. **Operation Desert Shield was brought about by the invasion of . . .**
   a. Afghanistan by the Soviet Union.
   b. Iran by Iraq.
   c. Kuwait by Iraq.
   d. Nicaragua by the Contras.

8. **War broke out between Iraq and the United States and its allies when . . .**
   a. Iraq missed the U.N. deadline for removing its troops.
   b. Iraq carried out a surprise bombing raid of Israel.
   c. Iraq was proved to be supporting terrorists.
   d. all of the above.

9. **Gridlock caused by the Democrats and Republicans led the people to . . .**
   a. push for laws banning political parties.
   b. elect a third-party candidate as President.
   c. vote for candidates who promised to reform government.
   d. all of the above.

10. **Today, the main point being discussed by Congress is . . .**
    a. how big or small government should be.
    b. President Clinton's plans for health care.
    c. how to deal with terrorism at home.
    d. both a and b.

CLASSIFYING

Add numbers 11-15 to your paper. Read the ideas below. They are ideas supported by America's political parties. If an idea is held by the Democrats, write D beside the number. If the idea is held by the Republicans write R.

11. setting up special government programs to regulate businesses
12. deregulating businesses
13. making government smaller
14. doing away with the Departments of Commerce, Education, and Energy
15. keeping programs to help people with things like health care

Look over the things you wrote for these chapters. Choose one that you like the best. Add to your writing. For example, you made a chart comparing the ideas of Presidents Roosevelt and Reagan. Add the ideas of Presidents Bush and Clinton. You wrote a report about the fall of the Berlin Wall. You might want to write a report about the bombings of the World Trade Center or the Murrah Federal Building. Trade papers with a study partner. Check each other's work. Make a clean, neat copy. Put it in your portfolio.

Write the headings **Cause** and **Effect** on a piece of paper. Think about something that happened in Chapter 96. Did it make something else happen? If so, list it under the heading **Cause**. Did an earlier event make it happen? If so, list it under the heading **Effect**. List two causes and effects each for Chapters 96-100.

COOPERATIVE PROJECT: DESERT STORM DIORAMA

Work with a group. Think about Operation Desert Storm. Make a list of what happened during the war. Check a map of the war to see where the troops were placed and how they fought. Make your own map out of clay. Be sure to show hills, rivers, and roads. Let the clay dry. Paint the map. Make small buildings, fences, and people for your map. Put them in their correct places. Display your map for the class or the school. Take turns with members of your group in telling what the war was like.

RUSSIA

ASIA

MONGOLIA

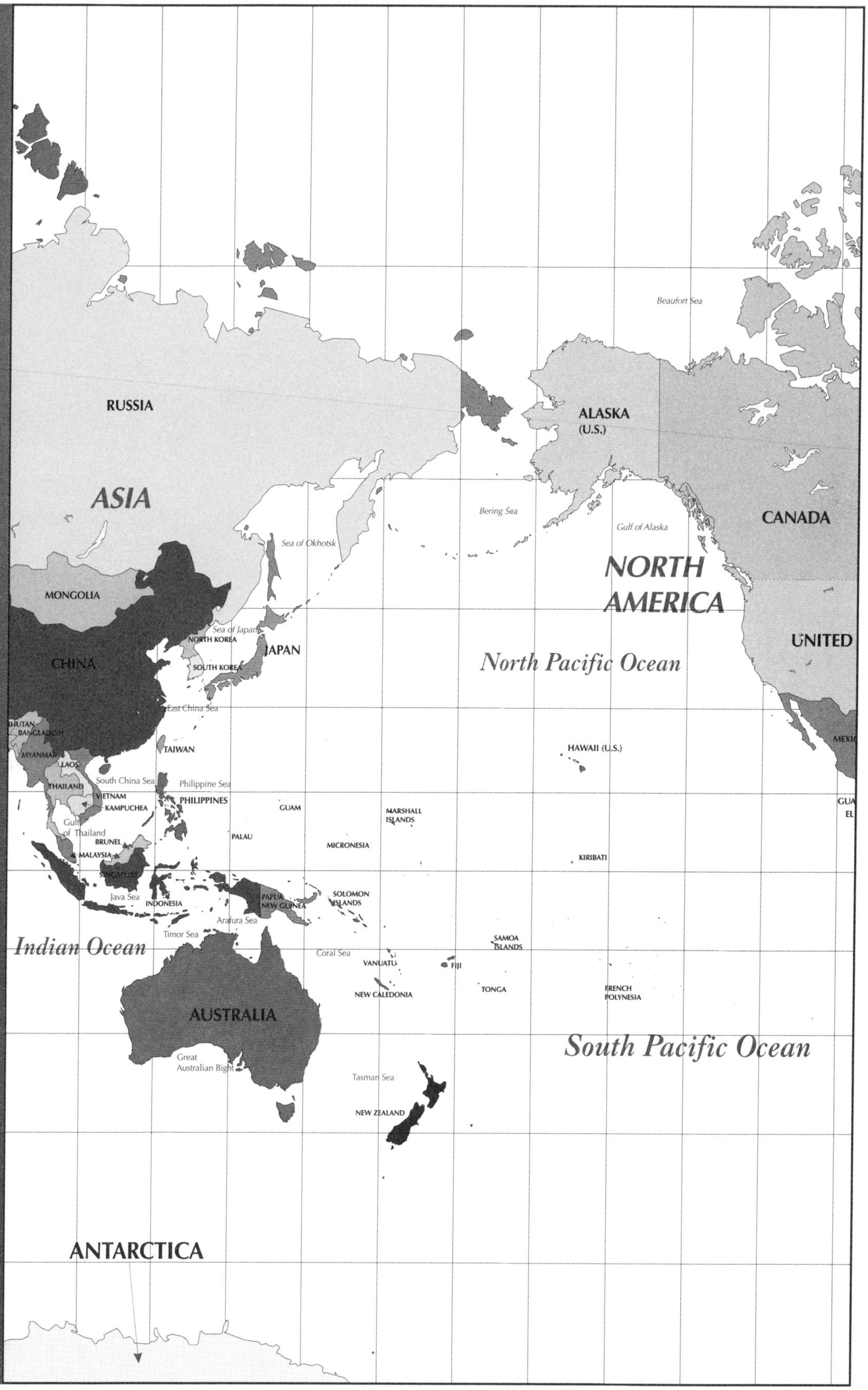

CHINA

BHUTAN
BANGLADESH
MYANMAR
LAOS
THAILAND
VIETNAM
KAMPUCHEA
Gulf
of Thailand
BRUNEI
MALAYSIA
SINGAPORE

NORTH KOREA
Sea of Japan
SOUTH KOREA
JAPAN

East China Sea

TAIWAN

South China Sea
Philippine Sea
PHILIPPINES

Java Sea
INDONESIA

Timor Sea

Sea of Okhotsk

Bering Sea

Beaufort Sea

ALASKA
(U.S.)

Gulf of Alaska

CANADA

NORTH
AMERICA

North Pacific Ocean

UNITED

MEXI

HAWAII (U.S.)

GUA
EL

GUAM

MARSHALL
ISLANDS

MICRONESIA

PALAU

KIRIBATI

Indian Ocean

PAPUA
NEW GUINEA
Arafura Sea

Coral Sea

AUSTRALIA

Great
Australian Bight

Tasman Sea

NEW ZEALAND

SOLOMON
ISLANDS

VANUATU

FIJI

NEW CALEDONIA

TONGA

SAMOA
ISLANDS

FRENCH
POLYNESIA

South Pacific Ocean

ANTARCTICA

For the People, By the People

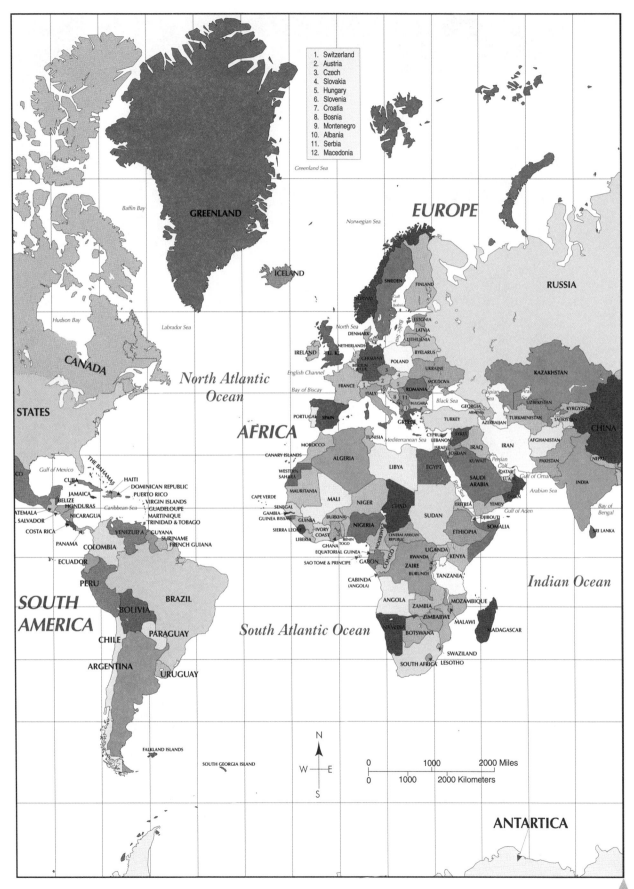

NORTH AMERICA

Bering Sea

Arctic Ocean

GREENLAND

ICELAND

ALASKA
(U.S.)

Labrador Sea

Great Slave
Lake

Lake
Athabasca

Hudson
Bay

NORTH
AMERICA

Canada

Lake
Winnipeg

Gulf of
St. Lawrence

Lake
Superior

Lake
Huron

Ottawa

Lake Ontario

Lake
Michigan

Lake Erie

New York

San Francisco

United States

Washington D. C.

Atlantic Ocean

MEXICO

Gulf
of
Mexico

Houston

New Orleans

BAHAMAS

CUBA

DOM. REP.

PUERTO RICO

JAMAICA

Pacific Ocean

*Mexico City

HAITI

BELIZE

GUATEMALA

HONDURAS

Caribbean Sea

EL SALVADOR

NICARAGUA

N

W   E

S

COSTA RICA

PANAMA

0		1000		2000 Miles

0		1000		2000 Kilometers

For the People, By the People

CANADA

MAINE
Augusta
MASS.
Boston
RHODE ISLAND
CONNECTICUT
NEW JERSEY
DELAWARE
MARYLAND
VT.
Montpelier N.H.
Concord
Albany
NEW YORK
Hartford
Trenton
Philadelphia
New York
PENN.
Harrisburg
Baltimore
Washington, D.C.
Norfolk

Atlantic Ocean

N
E
W
S

L. Ontario
Buffalo
Lake Erie
Cleveland
Pittsburgh
OHIO
Columbus
W. VA.
VIRGINIA
Charleston
Richmond
Raleigh
NORTH CAROLINA
Charlotte
Columbia
SOUTH CAROLINA

Lake Huron
MICHIGAN
Lansing
Detroit
Lake Superior
Lake Michigan
INDIANA
Indianapolis
Louisville
KENTUCKY
Frankfort
Nashville
TENNESSEE
Atlanta
GEORGIA
Montgomery
ALABAMA
Tallahassee
FLORIDA
Jacksonville
West Palm Beach
Miami
Tampa

WISCONSIN
St. Paul
Madison
Ames
Des Moines
IOWA
Chicago
ILLINOIS
Springfield
St. Louis
MISSOURI
Jefferson City
Kansas City
Memphis
MISSISSIPPI
Jackson
Birmingham
Baton Rouge
New Orleans
LOUISIANA
Houston

Gulf of Mexico

400 Miles
400 Kilometers
0
0

MINNESOTA
Minneapolis
Lincoln
Omaha
NEBRASKA
Topeka
KANSAS
Little Rock
ARKANSAS
Oklahoma City
OKLAHOMA
Dallas
Austin
San Antonio
TEXAS

NORTH DAKOTA
Bismarck
SOUTH DAKOTA
Pierre

MONTANA
Helena
WYOMING
Cheyenne
Denver
Boulder
COLORADO
Santa Fe
NEW MEXICO

Great Salt Lake
Salt Lake City
UTAH
IDAHO
Boise
Spokane
WASH.
Seattle
Olympia
Vancouver
Portland
Salem
OREGON

Carson City
NEVADA
Las Vegas
ARIZONA
Phoenix
Tucson

Sacramento
San Francisco
Oakland
CALIFORNIA
Los Angeles
San Diego

Pacific Ocean

MEXICO

HAWAII

ALASKA

UNITED STATES

NORTHEASTERN STATES

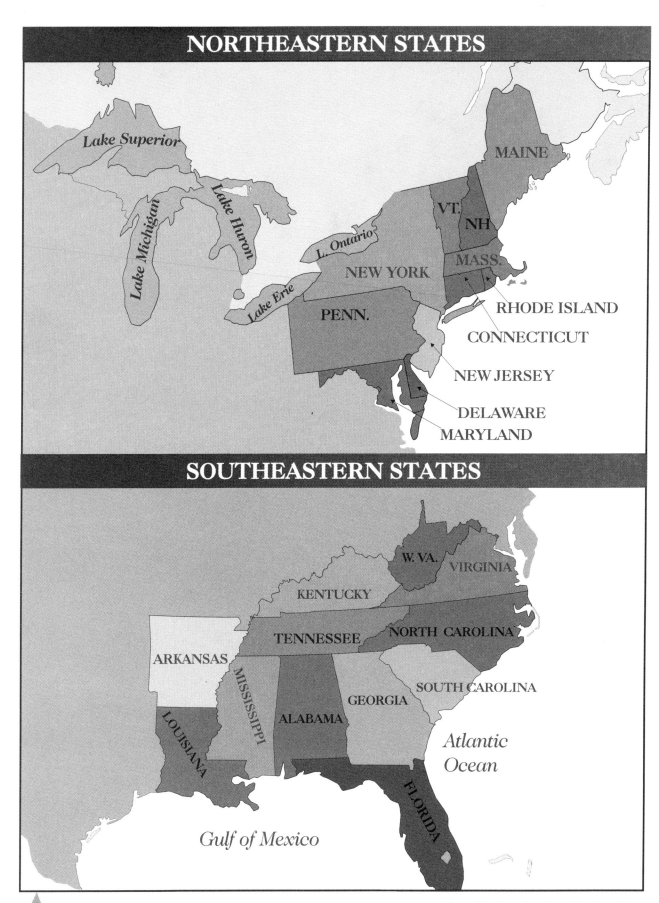

Lake Superior

Lake Michigan

Lake Huron

L. Ontario

Lake Erie

MAINE

VT.

NH

MASS.

NEW YORK

PENN.

RHODE ISLAND

CONNECTICUT

NEW JERSEY

DELAWARE

MARYLAND

SOUTHEASTERN STATES

W. VA.

VIRGINIA

KENTUCKY

TENNESSEE

NORTH CAROLINA

ARKANSAS

MISSISSIPPI

SOUTH CAROLINA

GEORGIA

ALABAMA

LOUISIANA

FLORIDA

Atlantic Ocean

Gulf of Mexico

For the People, By the People

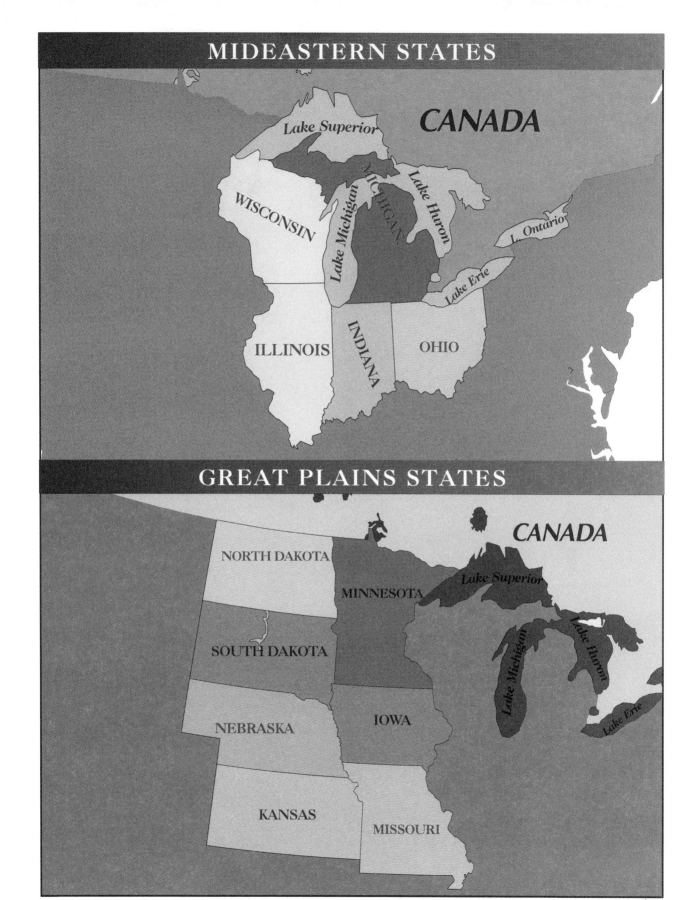

MIDEASTERN STATES

CANADA

Lake Superior

WISCONSIN

MICHIGAN

Lake Michigan

Lake Huron

L. Ontario

Lake Erie

ILLINOIS

INDIANA

OHIO

GREAT PLAINS STATES

CANADA

NORTH DAKOTA

MINNESOTA

Lake Superior

SOUTH DAKOTA

Lake Michigan

Lake Huron

NEBRASKA

IOWA

Lake Erie

KANSAS

MISSOURI

MOUNTAIN STATES

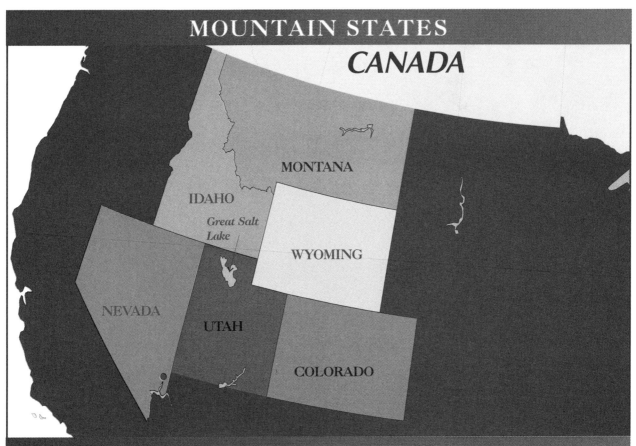

CANADA

MONTANA

IDAHO

Great Salt
Lake

WYOMING

NEVADA

UTAH

COLORADO

SOUTHWESTERN STATES

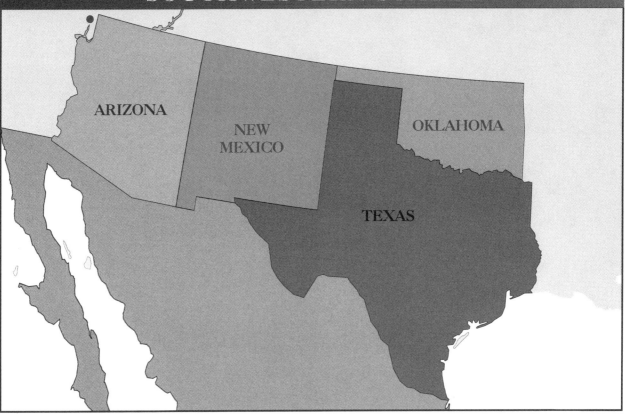

ARIZONA

NEW
MEXICO

OKLAHOMA

TEXAS

For the People, By the People

WEST COAST AND PACIFIC STATES

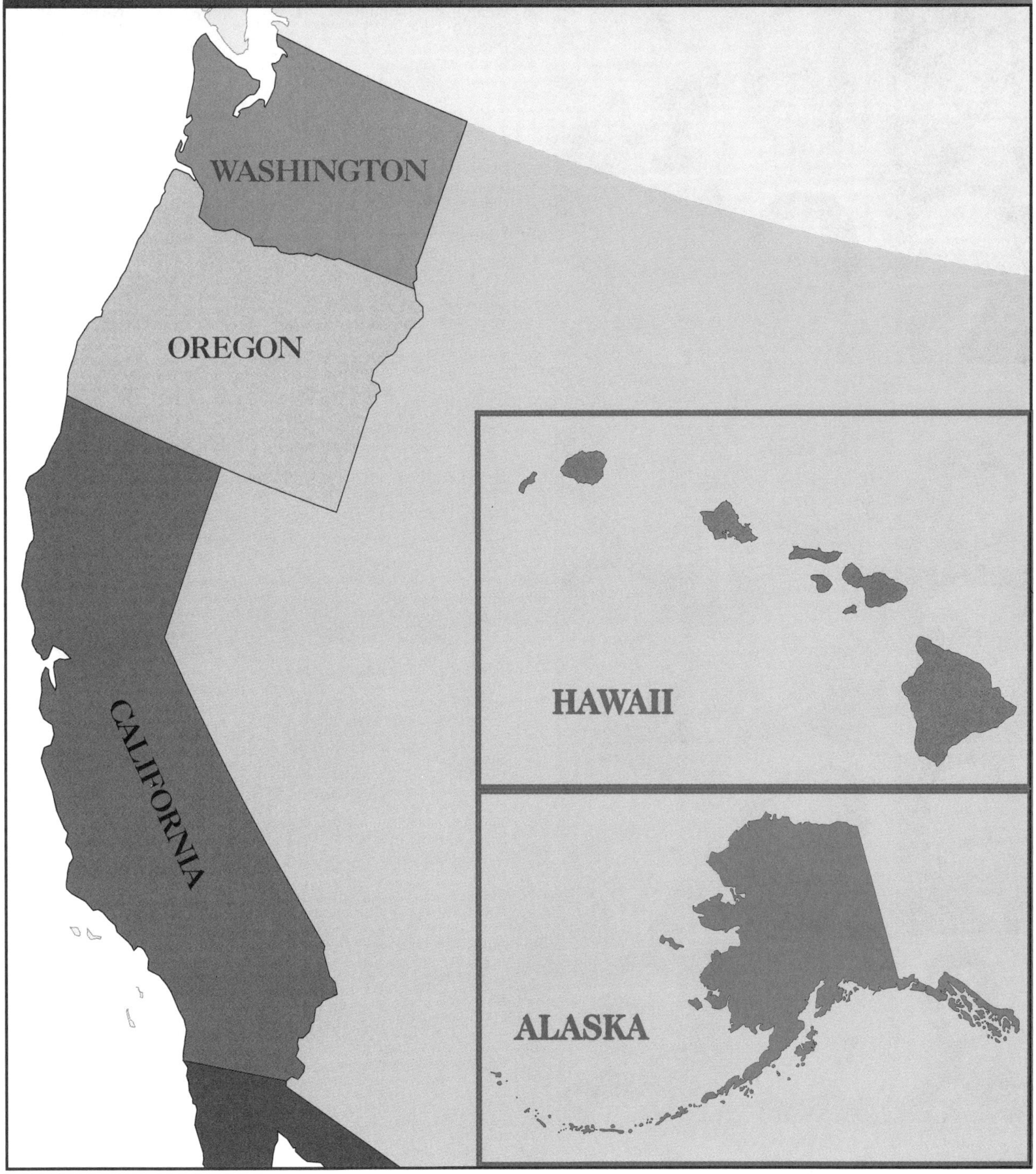

WASHINGTON

OREGON

CALIFORNIA

HAWAII

ALASKA

Presidents of the United States

1st George Washington (1732-1799)
Years in Office: 1789-1797
Party: None
State: VA
Vice Pres.: John Adams (MA)

2nd John Adams (1735-1826)
Years in Office: 1797-1801
Party: Federalist
State: MA
Vice Pres.: Thomas Jefferson (VA)

3rd Thomas Jefferson (1743-1826)
Years in Office: 1801-1809
Party: Democratic-Republican
State: VA
Vice Pres.: Aaron Burr (NY)
George Clinton (NY)

4th James Madison, Jr. (1751-1836)
Years in Office: 1809-1817
Party: Democratic-Republic
State: VA
Vice Pres.: George Clinton (NY)
Elbridge Gerry (MA)

5th James Monroe (1758-1831)
Years in Office: 1817-1825
Party: Democratic-Republic
State: VA
Vice Pres.: Daniel B. Thompkins (NY)

6th John Quincy Adams (1767-1848)
Years in Office: 1825-1829
Party: National Republic
State: VA
Vice Pres.: John C. Calhoun (SC)

7th Andrew Jackson (1767-1845)
Years in Office: 1829-1837
Party: Democratic
State: TN
Vice Pres.: John C. Calhoun (SC)
Martin Van Buren (NY)

8th Martin Van Buren (1782-1862)
Years in Office: 1837-1841
Party: Democratic
State: NY
Vice Pres.: Richard M. Johnson (KY)

9th William H. Harrison[1] (1773-1841)
Years in Office: 1841-
Party: Whig
State: OH
Vice Pres.: John Tyler (VA)

10th John Tyler (1790-1862)
Years in Office: 1841-1845
Party: Whig
State: VA
Vice Pres.: None[2]

11th James K. Polk (1795-1849)
Years in Office: 1845-1849
Party: Democratic
State: TN
Vice Pres.: George M. Dallas(PA)

12th Zachary Taylor[1] (1784-1850)
Years in Office: 1849-1850
Party: Whig
State: LA
Vice Pres.: Millard Fillmore (NY)

13th Millard Fillmore (1800-1874)
Years in Office: 1850-1853
Party: Whig
State: NY
Vice Pres.: None[2]

14th Franklin Pierce (1804-1869)
Years in Office: 1853-1857
Party: Democratic
State: NH
Vice Pres.: William R.D. King (AL)

15th James Buchanan (1791-1868)
Years in Office: 1857-1861
Party: Democratic
State: PA
Vice Pres.: John C. Breckenridge (KY)

16th Abraham Lincoln[1] (1809-1865)
Years in Office: 1861-1865
Party: Republican
State: IL
Vice Pres.: Hannibal Hamlin (ME)
Andrew Johnson (TN)

17th Andrew Johnson (1808-1875)
Years in Office: 1865-1869
Party: Democratic
State: TN
Vice Pres.: None[2]

18th Ulysses S. Grant (1822-1885)
Years in Office: 1869-1877
Party: Republican
State: IL
Vice Pres.: Schuler Colfax (IN)
Henry Wilson (MA)

19th Rutherford B. Hayes (1822-1893)
Years in Office: 1877-1881
Party: Republican
State: OH
Vice Pres.: William A. Wheeler (NY)

20th James A. Garfield[1] (1831-1881)
Years in Office: 1881-
Party: Republican
State: OH
Vice Pres.: Chester A. Arthur

21st Chester A. Arthur (1830-1886)
Years in Office: 1881-1885
Party: Republican
State: NY
Vice Pres.: None[2]

22nd S. Grover Cleveland (1837-1908)
Years in Office: 1885-1889
Party: Democratic
State: NY
Vice Pres.: Thomas a. Hendricks (IN)

23rd Benjamin Harrison (1833-1901)
Years in Office: 1889-1893
Party: Republican
State: IN
Vice Pres.: Levi P. Morton (NY)

24th S. Grover Cleveland (1837-1897)
Years in Office: 1893-1980
Party: Democratic
State: NY
Vice Pres.: Adlai E. Stevenson (IN)

25th William McKinley, Jr.[1] 1843-1901
Years in Office: 1897-1901
Party: Republican
State: OH
Vice Pres.: Theodore Roosevelt (NY)

26th Theodore Roosevelt (1858-1919)
Years in Office: 1901-1909
Party: Republican
State: NY
Vice Pres.: None[2]
Charles W. Fairbanks (IN)

27th William H. Taft (1857-1930)
Years in Office: 1909-1913
Party: Republican
State: OH
Vice Pres.: James S. Sherman (NY)

28th T. Woodrow Wilson (1856-1924)
Years in Office: 1913-1921
Party: Democratic
State: NJ
Vice Pres.: Thomas R. Marshall (IN)

29th Warren G. Harding[1] (1865-1923)
Years in Office: 1921-1923
Party: Republican
State: OH
Vice Pres.: J. Calvin Coolidge (MA)

30th J. Calvin Coolidge (1872-1933)
Years in Office: 1923-1929
Party: Republican
State: MA
Vice Pres.: None[2]
Charles G. Dawes (IL)

31st Herbert C. Hoover (1874-1964)
Years in Office: 1929-1933
Party: Republican
State: CA
Vice Pres.: Charles Curtis (KS)

32nd Franklin D. Roosevelt[1] (1882-1945)
Years in Office: 1933-1945
Party: Democratic
State: NY
Vice Pres.: James N. Garner (TX), Henry A. Wallace (IA), Harry S Truman (MO)

33rd Harry S. Truman (1884-1972)
Years in Office: 1945-1953
Party: Democratic
State: MO
Vice Pres.: None[2] for the first term
Alben W. Barkley (KY)

34th Dwight D. Eisenhower (1890-1969)
Years in Office: 1953-1961
Party: Republican
State: NY
Vice Pres.: Richard M. Nixon (CA)

35th John F. Kennedy[1] (1917-1963)
Years in Office: 1961-1963
Party: Democratic
State: MA
Vice Pres.: Lyndon B. Johnson (TX)

36th Lyndon B. Johnson (1908-1973)
Years in Office: 1963-1969
Party: Democratic
State: TX
Vice Pres.: None[2]
Hubert H. Humphrey (MN)

37th Richard M. Nixon[3] (1913-1994)
Years in Office: 1969-1974
Party: Republican
State: NY
Vice Pres.: Spiro T. Agnew[2] (MD)
Gerald R. Ford, Jr. (MI)

38th Gerald R. Ford, Jr. (1913-
Years in Office: 1974-1977
Party: Republican
State: MI
Vice Pres.: Nelson A. Rockefeller (NY)

39th James E. Carter, Jr. (1924-
Years in Office: 1977-1981
Party: Democratic
State: GA
Vice Pres.: Walter F. Mondale (MN)

40th Ronald W. Reagan (1911-
Years in Office: 1981-1989
Party: Republican
State: CA
Vice Pres.: George H.W. Bush (TX)

41st George H. W. Bush (1924-
Years in Office: 1989-1993
Party: Republican
State: TX
Vice Pres.: J. Danforth Quayle (IN)

42nd William J. Clinton (1946-
Years in Office: 1993-
Party: Democratic
State: AR
Vice Pres.: Albert A. Gore (TN)

* *Home state at time of election*
1 *Died in Office*
2 *Until the 1970s there was no process for choosing a Vice-President to replace one who had become President because of death or resignation.*
3 *Resigned the office of President*

The Star-Spangled Banner

O! say can you see, by the dawn's early light,
What so proudly we hail'd at the twilight's last gleaming,
Whose broad stripes and bright stars, through the perilous fight,
O'er the ramparts we watched were so gallantly streaming?
And the rockets' red glare, the bombs bursting in air,
Gave proof through the night that our Flag was still there.
O! say, does that star-spangled banner yet wave
O'er the land of the free and the home of the brave?

On the shore, dimly seen through the mists of the deep,
Where the foe's haughty host in dread silence reposes,
What is that which the breeze o'er the towering steep,
As it fitfully blows, half conceals, half discloses?
Now it catches the gleam of the morning's first beam,
In full glory reflected, now shines on the stream.
'Tis the star-spangled banner; O! long may it wave
O'er the land of the free and the home of the brave!

And where is that band who so vauntingly swore
That the havoc of war and the battle's confusion,
A home and a country should leave us no more?
Their blood has washed out their foul footstep's pollution.
No refuge could save the hireling and slave,
From the terror of flight, or the gloom of the grave,
And the star-spangled banner in triumph doth wave
O'er the land of the free and the home of the brave.

O! thus be it ever when freeman shall stand,
Between their loved home and the war's desolation,
Blest with victory and peace, may the Heaven-rescued land
Praise the Power that hath made and preserved us a nation!
Then conquer we must, when our cause it is just,
And this be our motto, "In God is our trust."
And the star-spangled banner in triumph shall wave
O'er the land of the free and the home of the brave.

—*Francis Scott Key*

The Declaration of Independence

In Congress, July 4, 1776
The Unanimous Declaration of the Thirteen United States of America

When in the course of human events, it becomes necessary for one people to dissolve the political bands which have connected them with another, and to assume among the powers of the earth, the separate and equal station to which the laws of nature and of nature's God entitle them, a decent respect to the opinions of mankind requires that they should declare the causes which impel them to the separation.

We hold these truths to be self-evident, that all men are created equal, that they are endowed by their Creator with certain unalienable rights, that among these are life, liberty, and the pursuit of happiness. That to secure these rights, governments are instituted among men, deriving their just powers from the consent of the governed; that whenever any form of government becomes destructive of these ends, it is the right of the people to alter or to abolish it, and to institute new government, laying its foundation on such principles, and organizing its powers in such form, as to them shall seem most likely to effect their safety and happiness. Prudence, indeed, will dictate that governments long established should not be changed for light and transient causes; and accordingly all experience hath shown, that mankind are more disposed to suffer, while evils are sufferable, than to right themselves by abolishing the forms to which they are accustomed. But when a long train of abuses and usurpations, pursuing invariably the same object, evinces a design to reduce them under absolute despotism, it is their right, it is their duty, to throw off such government, and to provide new guards for their future security. Such has been the patient sufferance of these colonies; and such is now the necessity which constrains them to alter their former systems of government. The history of the present King of Great Britain is a history of repeated injuries and usurpations, all having in direct object the establishment of an absolute tyranny over these states. To prove this, let facts be submitted to a candid world.

He has refused his assent to laws, the most wholesome and necessary for the public good.

He has forbidden his governors to pass laws of immediate and pressing importance, unless suspended in their operation till his assent should be obtained; and when so suspended, he has utterly neglected to attend to them.

He has refused to pass other laws for the accommodation of large districts of people, unless those people would relinquish the right of representation in the legislature, a right inestimable to them and formidable to tyrants only.

He has called together legislative bodies at places unusual, uncomfortable, and distant from the depository of their public records, for the sole purpose of fatiguing them into compliance with his measures.

He has dissolved representative houses repeatedly, for opposing with manly firmness his invasions on the rights of the people.

He has refused for a long time, after such dissolutions, to cause others to be elected; whereby the legislative powers, incapable of annihilation, have returned to the people at large for their exercise; the state remaining in the meantime exposed to all the dangers of invasion from without and convulsions within.

He has endeavored to prevent the population of these states; for that purpose obstructing the laws for naturalization of foreigners, refusing to pass others to encourage their migrations hither, and raising the conditions of new appropriations of lands.

He has obstructed the administration of justice, by refusing his assent to laws for establishing judiciary powers.

He has made judges dependent on his will alone, for the tenure of their offices, and the amount and payment of their salaries.

He has erected a multitude of new offices, and sent hither swarms of officers to harass our people, and eat out their substance.

He has kept among us, in times of peace, standing armies without the consent of our legislatures.

He has affected to render the military independent of and superior to the civil power.

He has combined with others to subject us to a jurisdiction foreign to our constitution, and unacknowledged by our laws; giving his assent to their acts of pretended legislation:

For quartering large bodies of armed troops among us;

For protecting them, by a mock trial, from punishment for any murders which they should commit on the inhabitants of these states;

For cutting off our trade with all parts of the world;

For imposing taxes on us without our consent;

For depriving us, in many cases, of the benefits of trial by jury;

For transporting us beyond seas to be tried for pretended offenses;

For abolishing the free system of English laws in a neighboring province, establishing therein an arbitrary government, and enlarging its boundaries so as to render it at once an example and fit instrument for introducing the same absolute rule into these colonies;

For taking away our charters, abolishing our most valuable laws, and altering fundamentally the forms of our governments;

For suspending our own legislatures, and declaring themselves invested with power to legislate for us in all cases whatsoever.

He has abdicated government here, by declaring us out of his protection and waging war against us.

He has plundered our seas, ravaged our coasts, burned our towns, and destroyed the lives of our people.

He is at this time transporting large armies of foreign mercenaries to complete the works of death, desolation, and tyranny, already begun with circumstances of cruelty and perfidy scarcely paralleled in the most barbarous ages, and totally unworthy the head of a civilized nation.

He has constrained our fellow citizens taken captive on the high seas to bear arms against their country, to become the executioners of their friends and brethren, or to fall themselves by their hands.

He has excited domestic insurrections among us, and has endeavored to bring on the inhabitants of our frontiers, the merciless Indian savages, whose known rule of warfare is an undistinguished destruction of all ages, sexes, and conditions.

In every stage of these oppressions we have petitioned for redress in the most humble terms: our repeated petitions have been answered only by repeated injury. A prince, whose character is thus marked by every act which may define a tyrant, is unfit to be the ruler of a free people.

Nor have we been wanting in our attentions to our British brethren. We have warned them from time to time of attempts by their legislature to extend an unwarrantable jurisdiction over us. We have reminded them of the circumstances of our emigration and settlement here. We have appealed to their native justice and magnanimity, and we have conjured them by the ties of our common kindred to disavow these usurpations, which would inevitably interrupt our connections and correspondence. They too have been deaf to the voice of justice and consanguinity. We must, therefore, acquiesce in the necessity which denounces our separation, and hold them, as we hold the rest of mankind, enemies in war, in peace friends.

We, therefore, the representatives of the United States of America, in General Congress, assembled, appealing to the Supreme Judge of the world for the rectitude of our intentions, do, in the name and by authority of the good people of these colonies, solemnly publish and declare, that these united colonies are, and of right ought to be, free and independent states; that they are absolved from all allegiance to the British Crown, and that all political connection between them and the State of Great Britain is and ought to be totally dissolved; and that as free and independent states, they have full power to levy war, conclude peace, contract alliances, establish commerce, and to do all other acts and things which independent states may of right do. And for the support of this declaration, with a firm reliance on the protection of Divine Providence, we mutually pledge to each other our lives, our fortunes, and our sacred honor.

John Hancock, **President**

New Hampshire
Josiah Bartlett
William Whipple
Matthew Thornton

Massachusetts
Samuel Adams
John Adams
Robert Treat Paine
Elbridge Gerry

New York
William Floyd
Philip Livingston
Francis Lewis
Lewis Morris

New Jersey
Richard Stockton
John Witherspoon

Francis Hopkinson
John Hart
Abraham Clark
Pennsylvania
Robert Morris
Benjamin Rush
Benjamin Franklin
John Morton
George Clymer
James Smith
George Taylor
James Wilson
George Ross

Delaware
Caesar Rodney
George Read
Thomas M'Kean

Maryland
Samuel Chase
William Paca
Thomas Stone
Charles Carroll
of Carrollton
Rhode Island
Stephen Hopkins
William Ellery

Connecticut
Roger Sherman
Samuel Huntington
William Williams
Oliver Wolcott

Virginia
George Wythe
Richard Henry Lee
Thomas Jefferson

Benjamin Harrison
Thomas Nelson, Jr.
Francis Lightfoot Lee
Carter Braxton

North Carolina
William Hooper
Joseph Hewes
John Penn

South Carolina
Edward Rutledge
Thomas Heyward, Jr.
Thomas Lynch, Jr.
Arthur Middleton

Georgia
Button Gwinnett
Lyman Hall
George Walton

          For the People, By the People

Constitution of the United States & Bill of Rights

Preamble

We the People of the United States, in order to form a more perfect union, establish justice, insure domestic tranquillity, provide for the common defense, promote the general welfare, and secure the blessings of liberty to ourselves and our posterity, do ordain and establish this Constitution for the United States of America.

Article 1 Legislative Branch

Section 1 Congress

All legislative powers herein granted shall be vested in a Congress of the United States, which shall consist of a Senate and House of Representatives.

Section 2 House of Representatives

1. The House of Representatives shall be composed of members chosen every second year by the people of the several states, and the electors in each state shall have the qualifications requisite for electors of the most numerous branch of the state legislature.

2. No person shall be a representative who shall not have attained to the age of twenty-five years, and been seven years a citizen of the United States, and who shall not, when elected, be an inhabitant of that state in which he shall be chosen.

3. Representatives and direct taxes shall be apportioned among the several states which may be included within this Union, according to their respective numbers, which shall be determined by adding to the whole number of free persons, including those bound to service for a term of years, and excluding Indians not taxed, three fifths of all other persons. The actual enumeration shall be made within three years after the first meeting of the Congress of the United States, and within every subsequent term of ten years, in such manner as they shall by law direct. The number of representatives shall not exceed one for every thirty thousand, but each state shall have at least one representative; and until such enumeration shall be made, the State of New Hampshire shall be entitled to choose three; Massachusetts, eight; Rhode Island and Providence Plantations, one; Connecticut, five; New York, six; New Jersey, four; Pennsylvania, eight; Delaware, one; Maryland, six; Virginia, ten; North Carolina, five; South Carolina, five; and Georgia, three.

4. When vacancies happen in the representation from any state, the executive authority thereof shall issue writs of election to fill such vacancies.

5. The House of Representatives shall choose their Speaker and other officers; and shall have the sole power of impeachment.

Section 3 Senate

1. The Senate of the United States shall be composed of two senators from each state, chosen by the legislature thereof, for six years; and each senator shall have one vote.

2. Immediately after they shall be assembled in consequence of the first election, they shall be divided as equally as may be into three classes. The seats of the senators of the first class shall be vacated at the expiration of the second year, of the second class at the expiration of the fourth year, of the third class at the expiration of the sixth year, so that one third may be chosen every second year; and if vacancies happen by resignation, or otherwise, during the recess of the legislature of any state, the executive thereof may make temporary appointments until the next meeting of the legislature, which shall then fill such vacancies.

3. No person shall be a senator who shall not have attained to the age

of thirty years, and been nine years a citizen of the United States, and who shall not, when elected, be an inhabitant of that state for which he shall be chosen.

4. The Vice President of the United States shall be President of the Senate, but shall have no vote, unless they be equally divided.

5. The Senate shall choose their other officers, and also a President *PRO TEMPORE*, in the absence of the Vice President, or when he shall exercise the office of the President of the United States.

6. The Senate shall have the sole power to try all impeachments. When sitting for that purpose, they shall be on oath or affirmation. When the President of the United States is tried, the Chief Justice shall preside; and no person shall be convicted without the concurrence of two thirds of the members present.

7. Judgment in cases of impeachment shall not extend further than to removal from office, and disqualification to hold and enjoy any office of honor, trust, or profit under the United States; but the party convicted shall nevertheless be liable and subject to indictment, trial, judgment, and punishment, according to law.

Section 4 Congressional Elections and Meetings

1. The times, places, and manner of holding elections for senators and representatives shall be prescribed in each state by the legislature thereof; but the Congress may at any time by law make or alter such regulations, except as to the places of choosing senators.

2. The Congress shall assemble at least once in every year, and such meeting shall be on the first Monday in December, unless they shall by law appoint a different day.

Section 5 Congressional Powers and Duties

1. Each house shall be the judge of the elections, returns, and qualifications of its own members, and a majority of each shall constitute a quorum to do business; but a small number may adjourn from day to day, and may be authorized to compel the attendance of absent members, in such manner, and under such penalties, as each house may provide.

2. Each house may determine the rules of its proceedings, punish its members for disorderly behavior, and with the concurrence of two thirds, expel a member.

3. Each house shall keep a journal of its proceedings, and from time to time publish the same, excepting such parts as may in their judgment require secrecy; and the yeas and nays of the members of either house on any question shall, at the desire of one fifth of those present, be entered on the journal.

4. Neither house, during the session of Congress, shall, without the consent of the other, adjourn for more than three days, nor to any other place than that in which the two houses shall be sitting.

Section 6 Privileges and Restrictions of Members

1. The senators and representatives shall receive a compensation for their services, to be ascertained by law, and paid out of the Treasury of the United States. They shall in all cases except treason, felony, and breach of the peace, be privileged from arrest during their attendance at the session of their respective houses, and in going to and returning from the same; and for any speech or debate in either house, they shall not be questioned in any other place.

2. No senator or representative shall, during the time for which he was elected, be appointed to any civil office under the authority of the United States, which shall have been created, or the emoluments whereof shall have been increased, during such time; and no person holding any office under the United States shall be a member of either house during his continuance in office.

Section 7 The Legislative Process

1. All bills for raising revenue shall originate in the House of Representatives; but the Senate may propose or concur with amendments as on other bills.

2. Every bill which shall have passed the House of Representatives and the Senate shall, before it become a law, be presented to the President of the United States; if he approve he shall sign it, but if not he shall return it, with his objections, to that house in which it shall have originated, who shall enter the objections at large on their journal, and proceed to reconsider it. If after such reconsideration two thirds of that house shall agree to pass the bill, it shall be sent, together with the objections, to the other house, by which it shall likewise be reconsidered, and if approved by two thirds of that house, it shall become a law. But in all such cases the votes of both houses shall be determined by yeas and nays, and the names of the persons voting for and against the bill shall be entered on the journal of each house respectively. If any bill shall not be returned by the President within ten days (Sundays excepted) after it shall have been presented to him, the same shall be a law, in like manner as if he had signed it, unless the Congress by their adjournment prevent its return, in which case it shall not be law.

3. Every order, resolution, or vote to which the concurrence of the Senate and House of Representatives may be necessary (except on a question of adjournment) shall be presented to the President of the United States; and before the same shall take effect, shall be approved by him, or being disapproved by him, shall be repassed by two thirds of the Senate and House of Representatives, according to the rules and limitations prescribed in the case of a bill.

Section 8 Legislative Powers

The Congress shall have power:

1. To lay and collect taxes, duties, imposts, and excises, to pay the debts and provide for the common defense and general welfare of the United States; but all duties, imposts, and excises shall be uniform throughout the United States;

2. To borrow money on the credit of the United States;

3. To regulate commerce with foreign nations, and among the several states, and with the Indian tribes;

4. To establish a uniform rule of naturalization, and uniform laws on the subject of bankruptcies throughout the United States;

5. To coin money, regulate the value thereof, and of foreign coin, and fix the standard of weights and measures;

6. To provide for the punishment of counterfeiting the securities and current coin of the United States;

7. To establish post offices and post roads;

8. To promote the progress of science and useful arts, by securing for limited times to authors and inventors the exclusive right to their respective writings and discoveries;

9. To constitute tribunals inferior to the Supreme Court;

10. To define and punish piracies and felonies committed on the high seas, and offenses against the law of nations;

11. To declare war, grant letters of marque and reprisal, and make rules concerning captures on land and water;

12. To raise and support armies, but no appropriation of money to that use shall be for a longer term than two years;

13. To provide and maintain a navy;

14. To make rules for the government and regulation of the land and naval forces;

15. To provide for calling forth the militia to execute the laws of the Union, suppress insurrections, and repel invasions;

16. To provide for organizing, arming, and disciplining the militia, and for governing such part of them as may be employed in the service of the United States, reserving to the states respectively the appointment of the officers, and the authority of training the militia according to the discipline prescribed by Congress;

17. To exercise exclusive legislation in all cases whatsoever over such district (not exceeding ten miles square) as may, by cession of particular states, and the acceptance of Congress, become the seat of the government of the United States, and to exercise like authority over all places purchased by the consent of the legislature of the state in which the same shall be, for the erection of forts, magazines, arsenals, dock-yards, and other needful buildings; and

18. To make all laws which shall be necessary and proper for carrying into execution the foregoing powers, and all other powers vested by this Constitution in the government of the United States, or in any department of officer thereof.

Section 9 Powers Forbidden the United States

1. The migration or importation of such persons as any of the states now existing shall think proper to admit, shall not be prohibited by the Congress prior to the year one thousand eight hundred and eight, but a tax or duty may be imposed on such importation, not exceeding ten dollars for each person.

2. The privilege of the writ of habeas corpus shall not be suspended, unless when in cases of rebellion or invasion the public safety may require it.

3. No bill of attainder or ex post facto law shall be passed.

4. No capitation, or other direct, tax shall be laid, unless in proportion to the census of enumeration herein before directed to be taken.

5. No tax or duty shall be laid on articles exported from any state.

6. No preference shall be given by any regulation of commerce or revenue to the ports of one state over those of another; nor shall vessels bound to, or from, one state, be obliged to enter, clear, or pay duties in another.

7. No money shall be drawn from the treasury, but in consequence of appropriations made by law; and a regular statement and account of the receipts and expenditures of all public money shall be published from time to time.

8. No title of nobility shall be granted by the United States: And no person holding any office of profit or trust under them, shall, without the consent of the Congress, accept of any present, emolument, office, or title, of any kind whatever, from any king, prince, or foreign state.

Section 10 Powers Forbidden the States

1. No state shall enter into any treaty, alliance, or confederation; grant letters of marque and reprisal; coin money; emit bills of credit; make any thing but gold and silver coin a tender in payment of debts; pass any bill of attainder, ex post facto law, or law impairing the obligation of contracts, or grant any title of nobility.

2. No state shall, without the consent of the Congress, lay any imposts or duties on imports or exports, except what may be absolutely necessary for executing its inspection laws; and the net produce of all duties and imposts, laid by any state on imports or exports, shall be for the use of the treasury of the United States; and all such laws shall be subject to the revision and control of the Congress.

3. No state shall, without the consent of Congress, lay any duty of tonnage, keep troops, or ships of war in time of peace, enter into any agreement or compact with another state, or with a foreign power, or engage in war, unless actually invaded, or in such imminent danger as will not admit of delay.

Article 2 Executive Branch

Section 1 President and Vice President

1. The executive power shall be vested in a President of the United States of America. He shall hold his office during the term of four years, and, together with the Vice President, chosen for the same term, be elected, as follows:

2. Each state shall appoint, in such manner as the legislature thereof may direct, a number of electors, equal to the whole number of senators and representatives to which the state may be entitled in the Congress; but no senator or representative, or person holding an

For the People, By the People

office of trust or profit under the United States, shall be appointed an elector.

3. The electors shall meet in their respective states, and vote by ballot for two persons, of whom one at least shall not be an inhabitant of the same state with themselves. And they shall make a list of all the persons voted for, and of the number of votes for each; which list they shall sign and certify, and transmit sealed to the seat of the government of the United States, directed to the President of the Senate. The President of the Senate shall, in the presence of the Senate and House of Representatives, open all the certificates, and the votes shall then be counted. The person having the greatest number of votes shall be the President, if such number be a majority of the whole number of electors appointed; and if there be more than one who have such majority, and have an equal number of votes, then the House of Representatives shall immediately choose by ballot one of them for President; and if no person have a majority, then from the five highest on the list the said house shall in like manner choose the President. But in choosing the President, the votes shall be taken by states, the representation from each state having one vote; a quorum for this purpose shall consist of a member or members from two thirds of the states, and a majority of all the states shall be necessary to a choice. In every case, after the choice of the President, the person having the greatest number of votes of the electors shall be the Vice President. But if there should remain two or more who have equal votes, the Senate shall choose from them by ballot the Vice President.

4. The Congress may determine the time of choosing the electors, and the day on which they shall give their votes; which day shall be the same throughout the United States.

5. No person except a natural-born citizen, or a citizen of the United States, at the time of the adoption of this Constitution, shall be eligible to the office of President; neither shall any person be eligible to that office who shall not have attained to the age of thirty-five years, and been fourteen years a resident within the United States.

6. In case of the removal of the President from office, or of his death, resignation, or inability to discharge the powers and duties of the said office, the same shall devolve on the Vice President, and the Congress may by law provide for the case of removal, death, resignation, or inability, both of the President and Vice President, declaring what officer shall then act as President, and such officer shall act accordingly, until the disability be removed, or a President shall be elected.

7. The President shall, at stated times, receive for his services a compensation, which shall neither be increased nor diminished during the period for which he shall have been elected, and he shall not receive within that period any other emolument from the United States, or any of them.

8. Before he enter on the execution of his office, he shall take the following oath or affirmation:—"I do solemnly swear (or affirm) that I will faithfully execute the office of President of the United States, and will, to the best of my ability, preserve, protect, and defend the Constitution of the United States."

Section 2 Powers of the President

1. The President shall be commander in chief of the army and navy of the United States, and of the militia of the several states, when called into the actual service of the United States; he may require the opinion, in writing, of the principal officer in each of the executive departments, upon any subject relating to the duties of their respective offices, and he shall have power to grant reprieves and pardons for offenses against the United States, except in cases of impeachment.

2. He shall have power, by and with the advice and consent of the Senate, to make treaties, provided two thirds of the senators present concur; and he shall nominate, and by and with the advice and con-

sent of the Senate, shall appoint ambassadors, other public ministers and consuls, judges of the Supreme Court, and all other officers of the United States, whose appointments are not herein otherwise provided for, and which shall be established by law; but the Congress may by law vest the appointment of such inferior officers, as they think proper, in the President alone, in the courts of law, or in the heads of departments.

3. The President shall have power to fill up all vacancies that may happen during the recess of the Senate, by granting commissions which shall expire at the end of their next session.

Section 3 Duties of the President

He shall from time to time give to the Congress information of the state of the Union, and recommend to their consideration such measures as he shall judge necessary and expedient; he may, on extraordinary occasions, convene both houses, or either of them, and in case of disagreement between them with respect to the time of adjournment, he may adjourn them to such time as he shall think proper; he shall receive ambassadors and other public ministers; he shall take care that the laws be faithfully executed, and shall commission all the officers of the United States.

Section 4 Impeachment

The President, Vice President and all civil officers of the United States, shall be removed from office on impeachment for, and conviction of, treason, bribery, or other high crimes and misdemeanors.

Article 3 Judicial Branch

Section 1 United States Courts

The judicial power of the United States shall be vested in one Supreme Court, and in such inferior courts as the Congress may from time to time ordain and establish. The judges, both of the Supreme and inferior courts, shall hold their offices during good behavior, and shall, at stated times, receive for their services, a compensation, which shall not be diminished during their continuance in office.

Section 2 Jurisdiction

1. The judicial power shall extend to all cases, in law and equity, arising under this Constitution, the laws of the United States, and treaties made, or which shall be made, under their authority;—to all cases affecting ambassadors, other public ministers, and consuls; — to all cases of admiralty and maritime jurisdiction;—to controversies to which the United States shall be a party;—to controversies between two or more states—between a state and citizens of another state;—between citizens of different states;-between citizens of the same state claiming lands under grants of different states; and between a state, or the citizens thereof, and foreign states, citizens or subjects.

2. In all cases affecting ambassadors, other public ministers and consuls, and those in which a state shall be party, the Supreme Court shall have original jurisdiction. In all other cases before mentioned, the Supreme Court shall have appellate jurisdiction, both as to law and fact, with such exceptions, and under such regulations as the Congress shall make.

3. The trial of all crimes, except in cases of impeachment, shall be by jury; and such trial shall be held in the state where the said crimes shall have been committed; but when not committed within any state, the trail shall be at such place or places as the Congress may by law have directed.

Section 3 Treason

1. Treason against the United States shall consist only in levying war against them, or in adhering to their enemies, giving them aid and comfort. No person shall be convicted of treason unless on the testimony of two witnesses to the same overt act, or on confession in open court.

2. The Congress shall have power to declare the punishment of treason,

but no attainder of treason shall work corruption of blood, or forfeiture except during the life of the person attained.

Article 4 Relations Among the States
Section 1 Official Acts
Full faith and credit shall be given in each state to the public acts, records, and judicial proceedings of every other state. And the Congress may by general laws prescribe the manner in which such acts, records, and proceedings shall be proved, and the effect thereof.

Section 2 Privileges of Citizens
1. The citizens of each state shall be entitled to all privileges and immunities of citizens in the several states.
2. A person charged in any state with treason, felony, or other crime, who shall flee from justice, and be found in another state shall, on demand of the executive authority of the state from which he fled, be delivered up, to be removed to the state having jurisdiction of the crime.
3. No person held to service or labor in one state, under the laws thereof, escaping into another, shall, in consequence of any law or regulation therein, be discharged from such service or labor, but shall be delivered upon claim of the party to whom such service or labor may be due.

Section 3 New States and Territories
1. New states may be admitted by the Congress into this Union; but no new state shall be formed or erected within the jurisdiction of any other state; nor any state be formed by the junction of two or more states, or parts of states, without the consent of the legislatures of the states concerned as well as of the Congress.
2. The Congress shall have power to dispose of and make all needful rules and regulations respecting the territory or other property belonging to the United States; and nothing in this Constitution shall be so construed as to prejudice any claims of the United States, or of any particular state.

Section 4 Protection of the States
The United States shall guarantee to every state in this Union a republican form of government, and shall protect each of them against invasion; and on application of the legislature, or of the executive (when the legislature cannot be convened) against domestic violence.

Article 5 The Amendment Process
The Congress, whenever two thirds of both houses shall deem it necessary, shall propose amendments to this Constitution, or, on the application of the legislatures of two thirds of the several states, shall call a convention for proposing amendments, which in either case, shall be valid to all intents and purposes, as part of this Constitution, when ratified by the legislatures of three fourths of the several states, or by conventions in three fourths thereof, as the one or the other mode of ratification may be proposed by the Congress; provided that no amendment which may be made prior to the year one thousand eight hundred and eight shall in any manner affect the first and fourth clauses in the ninth section of the first article and that no state, without its consent, shall be deprived of its equal suffrage in the Senate.

Article 6 General Provisions
1. All debts contracted and engagements entered into, before the adoption of this Constitution, shall be as valid against the United States under this Constitution, as under the Confederation.
2. This Constitution, and the laws of the United States which shall be made in pursuance thereof; and all treaties made, or which shall be made, under the authority of the United States, shall be the supreme law of the land; and the judges in every state shall be bound thereby, anything in the Constitution or laws of any state to the contrary notwithstanding.

3. The senators and representatives before mentioned, and the members of the several state legislatures, and all executive and judicial officers, both of the United States and of the several states, shall be bound by oath of affirmation to support this Constitution; but no religious test shall ever be required as a qualification to any office or public trust under the United States.

Article 7 Ratification
The ratification of the conventions of nine states shall be sufficient for the establishment of this Constitution between the states so ratifying the same.

Done in convention by the unanimous consent of the states present the seventeenth day of September in the year of our Lord one thousand seven hundred and eighty-seven, and of the independence of the United States of America the twelfth. In witness whereof we have hereunto subscribed our names.

George Washington, President and Deputy from Virginia	Delaware George Read Gunning Bedford, Jr. John Dickinson Richard Bassett Jacob Broom
New Hampshire John Langdon Nicholas Gilman	
Massachusetts Nathaniel Gorham Rufus King	Maryland James M'Henry Daniel of St. Thomas Jenifer Daniel Carroll
Connecticut William Samuel Johnson Roger Sherman	Virginia John Blair James Madison, Jr.
New York Alexander Hamilton	North Carolina William Blount Richard Dobbs Spaight Hugh Williamson
New Jersey William Livingston David Brearley William Paterson Jonathan Dayton	South Carolina John Rutledge Charles C. Pinckney Charles Pinckney Pierce Butler
Pennsylvania Benjamin Franklin Thomas Mifflin Robert Morris George Clymer Thomas Fitzsimons Jared Ingersoll James Wilson Gouverneur Morris	Georgia William Few Abraham Baldwin Attest: William Jackson, Secretary

The Bill of Rights

Amendment 1 Freedoms of Expression
Congress shall make no law respecting an establishment of religion, or prohibiting the free exercise thereof; or abridging the freedom of speech, or of the press; or the right of the people peaceably to assemble, and to petition the government for a redress of grievances.

For the People, By the People

Amendment 2 Right to Keep Arms

A well-regulated militia being necessary to the security of a free state, the right of the people to keep and bear arms shall not be infringed.

Amendment 3 Quartering of Troops

No soldier shall, in time of peace, be quartered in any house, without the consent of the owner, nor in time of war, but in a manner to be prescribed by law.

Amendment 4 Searches and Seizures

The right of the people to be secure in their persons, houses, papers, and effects, against unreasonable searches and seizures, shall not be violated, and no warrants shall issue, but upon probable cause, supported by oath or affirmation, and particularly describing the place to be searched, and the persons or things to be seized.

Amendment 5 Rights of Accused

No person shall be held to answer for a capital, or otherwise infamous crime, unless on a presentment or indictment of a grand jury, except in cases arising in the land or naval forces, or in the militia, when in actual service in time of war or public danger; nor shall any person be subject for the same offense to be twice put in jeopardy of life or limb; nor shall be compelled in any criminal case to be a witness against himself, nor to be deprived of life, liberty, or property, without due process of law; nor shall private property be taken for public use, without just compensation.

Amendment 6 Criminal Proceedings

In all criminal prosecutions, the accused shall enjoy the right to a speedy and public trial, by an impartial jury of the state and district wherein the crime shall have been committed, which district shall have been previously ascertained by law, and to be informed of the nature and cause of the accusation; to be confronted with the witnesses against him; to have compulsory process for obtaining witnesses in his favor, and to have the assistance of counsel for his defense.

Amendment 7 Jury Trial

In suits at common law, where the value in controversy shall exceed twenty dollars, the right of trial by jury shall be preserved, and no fact tried by a jury shall be otherwise re-examined in any court of the United States than according to the rules of common law.

Amendment 8 Excessive Punishments

Excessive bail shall not be required, nor excessive fines imposed, nor cruel and unusual punishments inflicted.

Amendment 9 Rights of the People

The enumeration in the Constitution of certain rights shall not be construed to deny or disparage others retained by the people.

Amendment 10 Reserved Powers

The powers not delegated to the United States by the Constitution, nor prohibited by it to the states, are reserved to the states respectively, or to the people.

Amendment 11 Suits Against States

The judicial power of the United States shall not be construed to extend to any suit in law or equity, commenced or prosecuted against one of the United States by citizens of another state, or by citizens or subjects of any foreign state.

Amendment 12 Election of President and Vice President

The electors shall meet in their respective states and vote by ballot for President and Vice President, one of whom, at least, shall not be an inhabitant of the same state with themselves; they shall name in their ballots the person voted for as President, and in distinct ballots the person voted for as Vice President, and they shall make distinct lists of all persons voted for as President, and of all persons voted for as Vice President, and of the number of votes for each, which lists they shall sign and certify, and transmit sealed to the seat of the government of the United States, directed to the President of the Senate;—the President of the Senate shall, in the presence of the Senate and House of Representatives, open all the certificates and the votes shall then be counted;—the person having the greatest number of votes for President, shall be the President, if such number be a majority of the whole number of electors appointed; and if no person have such majority, then from the persons having the highest numbers not exceeding three on the list of those voted for as President, the House of Representatives shall choose immediately, by ballot, the President. But in choosing the President, the votes shall be taken by states, the representation from each state having one vote; a quorum for this purpose shall consist of a member or members from two thirds of the states, and a majority of all the states shall be necessary to a choice. And if the House of Representatives shall not choose a President whenever the right of choice shall devolve upon them, before the fourth day of March next following, then the Vice President shall act as President, as in the case of the death or other constitutional disability of the President—The person having the greatest number of votes as Vice President, shall be the Vice President, if such number be a majority of the whole number of electors appointed, and if no person have a majority, then from the two highest numbers on the list, the Senate shall choose the Vice President; a quorum for the purpose shall consist of two thirds of the whole number of senators, and a majority of the whole number shall be necessary to a choice. But no person constitutionally ineligible to the office of President shall be eligible to that of Vice President of the United States.

Amendment 13 Slavery

Section 1. Neither slavery nor involuntary servitude, except as a punishment for crime whereof the party shall have been duly convicted, shall exist within the United States, or any place subject to their jurisdiction.

Section 2. Congress shall have power to enforce this article by appropriate legislation.

Amendment 14 Rights of Citizens

Section 1. All persons born or naturalized in the United States, and subject to the jurisdiction thereof, are citizens of the United States and of the state wherein they reside. No state shall make or enforce any law which shall abridge the privileges or immunities of citizens of the United States; nor shall any state deprive any person of life, liberty, or property, without due process of law, nor deny to any person within its jurisdiction the equal protection of the laws.

Section 2. Representatives shall be apportioned among the several states according to their respective numbers, counting the whole number of persons in each state, excluding Indians not taxed. But when the right to vote at any election for the choice of electors for President and Vice President of the United States, representatives in Congress, the executive or judicial officers of a state, or the members of the legislature thereof, is denied to any of the male inhabitants of such state, being twenty-one years of age, and citizens of the United States, or in any way abridged, except for participation in rebellion, or other crime, the basis of representation therein shall be reduced in the proportion which the number of such male citizens shall bear to the whole number of male citizens twenty-one years of age in such state.

Section 3. No person shall be a senator or representative in Congress, or elector of President or Vice President, or hold any office, civil or military, under the United States, or under any state, who, having previously taken an oath, as a member of Congress, or as an officer of the United States, or as a member of any state legislature, or as an executive or judicial officer of any state, to support the Constitution of the

United States, shall have engaged in insurrection or rebellion against the same, or given aid or comfort to the enemies thereof. But Congress may by a vote of two thirds of each house, remove such disability.

Section 4. The validity of the public debt of the United States, authorized by law, including debts incurred for payment of pensions and bounties for services in suppressing insurrection or rebellion, shall not be questioned. But neither the United States nor any state shall assume or pay any debt or obligation incurred in aid of insurrection or rebellion against the United States, or any claim for the loss or emancipation of any slave; but all such debts, obligations and claims shall be held illegal and void.

Section 5. The Congress shall have power to enforce, by appropriate legislation, the provisions of this article.

Amendment 15 Black Suffrage
Section 1. The right of citizens of the United States to vote shall not be denied or abridged by the United States or by any state on account of race, color, or previous conditions of servitude.

Section 2. The Congress shall have power to enforce this article by appropriate legislation.

Amendment 16 Income Tax
The Congress shall have power to lay and collect taxes on incomes, from whatever source derived, without apportionment among the several states, and without regard to any census or enumeration.

Amendment 17 Election of Senators
Section 1. The Senate of the United States shall be composed of two senators from each state, elected by the people thereof, for six years; and each senator shall have one vote. The electors in each state shall have the qualifications requisite for electors of the most numerous branch of the state legislatures.

Section 2. When vacancies happen in the representation of any state in the Senate, the executive authority of such state shall issue writs of election to fill such vacancies: Provided, that the legislature of any state may empower the executive thereof to make temporary appointments until the people fill the vacancies by election as the legislature may direct.

Section 3. This amendment shall not be so construed as to affect the election or term of any senator chosen before it becomes valid as part of the Constitution.

Amendment 18 National Prohibition
Section 1. After one year from the ratification of this article the manufacture, sale, or transportation of intoxicating liquors within, the importation thereof into, or the exportation thereof from the United States and all territory subject to the jurisdiction thereof for beverage purposes is hereby prohibited.

Section 2. The Congress and the several states shall have concurrent power to enforce this article by appropriate legislation.

Section 3. This article shall be inoperative unless it shall have been ratified as an amendment to the Constitution by the legislatures of the several states, as provided in the Constitution, within seven years from the date of the submission hereof to the states by the Congress.

Amendment 19 Woman Suffrage
Section 1. The right of citizens of the United States to vote shall not be denied or abridged by the United States or by any state on account of sex.

Section 2. Congress shall have power to enforce this article by appropriate legislation.

Amendment 20 Change of Terms, Sessions, and Inauguration
Section 1. The terms of the President and Vice President shall end at noon on the 20th day of January, and the terms of senators and representatives at noon on the 3rd day of January, of the years in which such terms would have ended if this article had not been ratified; and the terms of their successors shall then begin.

Section 2. The Congress shall assemble at least once in every year, and such meeting shall begin at noon on the 3rd day of January, unless they shall by law appoint a different day.

Section 3. If, at the time fixed for the beginning of the term of the President, the President-elect shall have died, the Vice President-elect shall become President. If a President shall not have been chosen before the time fixed for the beginning of his term, or if the President-elect shall have failed to qualify, then the Vice President-elect shall act as President until a President shall have qualified; and the congress may by law provide for the case wherein neither a President-elect nor a Vice President-elect shall have qualified, declaring who shall then act as President, or the manner in which one who is to act shall be selected, and such person shall act accordingly until a President or Vice President shall have qualified.

Section 4. The Congress may by law provide for the case of the death of any of the persons from whom the House of Representatives may choose a President whenever the right of choice shall have devolved upon them, and for the case of the death of any of the persons from whom the Senate may choose a Vice President whenever the right of choice shall have devolved upon them.

Section 5. Sections 1 and 2 shall take effect on the 15th day of October following the ratification of this article.

Section 6. This article shall be inoperative unless it shall have been ratified as an amendment to the Constitution by the legislature of three fourths of the several states within seven years from the date of its submission.

Amendment 21 Repeal of National Prohibition
Section 1. The eighteenth article of amendment to the Constitution of the United States is hereby repealed.

Section 2. The transportation or importation into any state, territory, or possession of the United States for delivery or use therein of intoxicating liquors, in violation of the laws thereof, is hereby prohibited.

Section 3. This article shall be inoperative unless it shall have been ratified as an amendment to the Constitution by conventions in the several states, as provided in the Constitution, within seven years from the date of the submission hereof to the states by the Congress.

Amendment 22 Presidential Tenure
Section 1. No person shall be elected to the office of the President more than twice, and no person who has held the office of President, or acted as President, for more than two years of a term to which some other person was elected President shall be elected to the office of the President more than once. But this article shall not apply to any person holding the office of President when this article was proposed by the Congress, and shall not prevent any person who may be holding the office of President, or acting as President, during the term within which this article becomes operative from holding the office of President or acting as President during the remainder of such term.
Section 2. This article shall be inoperative unless it shall have been

For the People, By the People

ratified as an amendment to the Constitution by the legislatures of three fourths of the several states within seven years from the date of its submission to the states by the Congress.

Amendment 23 Presidential Electors for D.C.
Section 1. The District constituting the seat of government of the United States shall appoint in such manner as the Congress may direct:

A number of electors of President and Vice President equal to the whole number of senators and representatives in Congress to which the District would be entitled if it were a state, but in no event more than the least populous state; they shall be in addition to those appointed by the states, but they shall be considered, for the purposes of the election of President and Vice President, to be electors appointed by a state; and they shall meet in the district and perform such duties as provided by the twelfth article of amendment.

Section 2. The Congress shall have power to enforce this article by appropriate legislation.

Amendment 24 Prohibition of Poll Tax
Section 1. The right of citizens of the United States to vote in any primary or other election for President or Vice President, for electors for President or Vice President, or for senator or representative in Congress, shall not be denied or abridged by the United States or any state by reason of failure to pay any poll tax or other tax.

Section 2. The Congress shall have power to enforce this article by appropriate legislation.

Amendment 25 Presidential Succession and Disability
Section 1. In case of the removal of the President from office or his death or resignation, the Vice President shall become President.
Section 2. Whenever there is a vacancy in the office of the Vice President, the President shall nominate a Vice President who shall take the office upon confirmation by a majority vote of both houses of Congress.

Section 3. Whenever the President transmits to the President pro tempore of the Senate and the Speaker of the House of Representatives his written declaration that he is unable to discharge the powers and duties of his office, and until he transmits to them a written declaration to the contrary, such powers and duties shall be discharged by the Vice President as Acting President.

Section 4. Whenever the Vice President and a majority of either the principal officers of the executive departments, or of such other body as Congress may by law provide, transmit to the President pro tempore of the Senate and the Speaker of the House of Representatives their written declaration that the President is unable to discharge the powers and duties of his office, the Vice President shall immediately assume the powers and duties of the office of Acting President.

Thereafter, when the President transmits to the President pro tempore of the Senate and the Speaker of the House of Representatives his written declaration that no inability exists, he shall resume the powers and duties of his office unless the Vice President and a majority of either the principal officers of the executive departments, or of such other body as Congress may by law provide, transmit within four days to the President pro tempore of the Senate and the Speaker of the House of Representatives their written declaration that the President is unable to discharge the powers and duties of his office. Thereupon Congress shall decide the issue, assembling within 48 hours for that purpose if not in session. If the Congress, within 21 days after receipt of the latter written declaration, or, if Congress is not in session, within 21 days after Congress is required to assemble, determines by two thirds vote of both houses that the President is unable to discharge the powers and duties of his office, the Vice President shall continue to discharge the same as Acting President; otherwise, the President shall resume the powers and duties of his office.

Amendment 26 Eighteen-Year-Old Vote
Section 1. The right of citizens of the United States, who are eighteen years of age or older, to vote shall not be denied or abridged by the United States or by any state on account of age.

Section 2. The Congress shall have power to enforce this article by appropriate legislation.

Amendment 27 Congressional Pay Raises
Section 1. Congress can vote to give itself a pay raise, but the increased salary does not take effect until after the next Congressional elections.

Section 2. This amendment means that no Congress can give itself a quick pay raise.

The Constitution Made Easier

THE ORIGINAL SEVEN ARTICLES

THE PREAMBLE

We, the people of the United States, want to form a more perfect union between the states.
We also want to:
— establish justice
— ensure peace at home, between people and between states
— provide for our defense in case of war with other nations
— promote the welfare of all the people
— and protect the blessings of liberty for ourselves and our children.
Therefore we establish this constitution for the United States of America.

ARTICLE 1
The Legislative (Law-Making) Branch
Section 1. Congress
The power to make laws will be given to a legislature which we will call the Congress of the United States. Congress will be divided into two houses: the Senate and the House of Representatives.

Section 2. House of Representatives
1. The members of the House of Representatives will be elected every two years by the people of each state. The voters in each state must meet the requirements they would have to meet to vote for their state lawmakers.
2. In order to be a representative, a person:
   a. must be at least 25 years old,
   b. must have been a U.S. citizen for at least seven years, and
   c. must be a legal resident of the state he or she is elected to represent.
3. The number of representatives a state has and the taxes it pays depend on the number of people it has. (Each slave was to be counted as three-fifths of a person. That instruction is no longer in effect because of Amendments 13 and 14.)
   The people will be counted within three years of the first meeting of Congress. They will be counted every 10 years after that. (This *census* is still done.)
   Each state gets at least one representative no matter how small it is. (In 1929, Congress set a limit of 435 house members. Each state gets its share of the 435 depending on its population. Each state gets at least one representative.)
4. When a representative dies or resigns, the governor of the state must call an election so voters can pick a new representative.
5. The Chairman of the House of Representatives is called the Speaker of the House. The House chooses the Speaker and any other officers it wants. The House alone has the power to impeach a government official. (*Impeach* means accuse a public official of an important crime.)

Section 3. Senate
1. Each state will have two senators. Each senator will serve for six years. Each senator will have one vote in the Senate.
   (The Constitution at first said state legislatures would elect senators. In 1913, Amendment 17 gave voters the right to elect senators directly.)

2. When the Senate meets for the first time, it will be divided into three groups. The first group of senators will serve for two years. The second group will serve for four years, and the third group will serve for six years. Then in the future, the terms will be staggered so that one-third of the senators will be elected every two years.
   (If a senator dies or resigns, at first the Constitution gave state lawmakers the power to choose a new senator. Amendment 17 changed that. Now the governor calls for an election, or state lawmakers may tell the governor to choose a senator until the next election.)
3. In order to be a senator, a person:
   a. must be at least 30 years old,
   b. must have been a U.S. citizen for at least nine years, and
   c. must be a legal resident of the state he or she is elected to represent.
4. The Vice President of the United States will also be the president of the Senate. (This is the only job the Constitution assigns to the U.S. Vice President.) The Vice President will have a vote only when there is a tie.
5. The senators may elect any other officers they need. They will have a president *pro tempore* (for the time being), who will serve as chairman if the U.S. Vice President is absent.
6. If the House of Representatives impeaches a public official, the Senate is the jury for the trial. Senators are under oath during the trial. If the President of the United States is impeached, the judge will be the Chief Justice of the Supreme Court. It takes a vote of two-thirds of the senators at the trial for a person to be convicted (found guilty).
7. Officials who are convicted by the Senate are removed from government office. They cannot hold any other office. They will not be punished in any other way, but they may have to stand trial in the regular courts.

Section 4. Election and Meeting of Congress
1. Each state may decide when, where, and how its senators and representatives are elected. Congress can make laws to ensure the honesty and fairness of national elections.
2. Congress must meet at least once a year. (The Constitution set the opening day as the first Monday in December. Amendment 20 changed it to January 3.)

Section 5. Organization and Rules of Each House
1. The House and the Senate may each decide if members are qualified and have been elected fairly. More than half of the members (a *quorum*) must be present for a vote. A smaller number of members may agree to adjourn (stop meeting) for the day. Each house should have a way of calling members to meetings and of punishing them if they do not come.
2. Each house may make its own rules for its meetings. Each house has the right to punish a member for not behaving properly. If at least two-thirds of the members approve, a house may throw out a member.
3. Each house must keep a record of its business. It must publish the record, unless members agree that some parts of the record must be kept secret. (The records of both houses are published as the *Congressional Record*.) If one-fifth of the members vote for it, each member's vote on an issue must also be published. (This is called a *roll-call vote*.)

4. Neither house can adjourn for more than three days unless the other house agrees. Both houses must meet in the same city.

Section 6. Congressional Rights and Restraints

1. Senators and representatives will be paid a salary. How much they are paid is decided by law. Their salaries are paid out of the U.S. Treasury. While senators and representatives are in a meeting of Congress, or going to or coming from one, they cannot be arrested except for a felony, treason, or disturbing the peace. They have complete freedom of speech while talking in Congress. They cannot be arrested for what they say there.
2. While in Congress, senators and representatives may not hold any other government office. After leaving Congress, they may not take any government job that was created or received a pay raise while they were in Congress.

Section 7. How Bills Become Law

1. Only the House of Representatives can start a tax bill. The Senate may suggest changes in it. It must approve the bill (by a majority vote).
2. When any bill is approved by both the House and the Senate, it is sent to the President. There are four ways the President can deal with the bill:
   a. If the President likes the bill, he signs it. It becomes law.
   b. If the President does not like the bill, he may veto it and send it back to Congress. (*Veto* is a Latin word which means "I forbid.") If the members of Congress still like the bill, they can vote on it again. If two-thirds of the members of both houses vote for the bill this time, it becomes law without the President's approval. (This is called *overriding the veto*.) When this happens, everyone's votes must be recorded.
   c. If, while Congress is meeting, the President keeps a bill for 10 days without signing it or vetoing it, the bill becomes law without his approval.
   d. If less than 10 days remain before Congress adjourns, the President may hold the bill without signing it until Congress adjourns. The bill does not become a law. (This is called a *pocket veto*.)

Section 8. Powers Granted to Congress

1. Congress has the power to make and collect taxes, to pay debts, and to use taxes to protect the people. All federal (national) taxes must be the same throughout the United States.
2. Congress has the right to borrow money for the United States.
3. Congress has the power to control trade with foreign nations, between the states, and with the Indians. (*Trade* covers goods, people, and information, and the things that move them. That gives Congress control over everything from trucks and trains to roads to telephone and television hookups.)
4. Congress can decide which people who were not born in the United States can become citizens. It can set the rules that say what a person must do to become a citizen. Congress can pass laws about bankruptcy throughout the United States.
5. Congress has the right to coin (make) money and say how much it is worth. Congress also decides standards for weights and measures. (This ensures that a dollar, an ounce, or a mile will be the same in every state.)
6. Congress decides how to punish counterfeiters (those who make or use fake money).
7. Congress can set up post offices and build roads.
8. Congress can give copyrights to authors and patents to inventors so that they will have income from their ideas.
9. Congress can create any federal courts we need below the level of the Supreme Court.

10. Congress decides what *piracy* is and how to punish it. It decides punishment for crimes on the high seas because those crimes don't happen in a particular state.
11. Congress has the right to declare war.
12. Congress has the right to organize and pay an army. Money spent on the armed services has to be voted on every two years. (This gives Congress the power to draft citizens. It gives Congress power to buy what the armed forces need. This way, Congress keeps control over the army.)
13. Congress can organize and pay a navy.
14. Congress makes the rules for the armed forces.
15. Congress can call out the National Guard to enforce laws, stop riots, or stop invasions. (The National Guard is made up of the militia, or citizen soldiers, of the states.)
16. Congress may organize the National Guard, buy arms for it, and make rules on how it should be run. But the officers are appointed by each state. Training is conducted by each state, also.
17. Congress passes the laws for the District of Columbia (Washington, D.C.) because it is the headquarters of the national government. Congress passes laws for federal property such as army forts or national parks.
18. Congress can make any laws which are necessary and proper to carry out the powers given to the government of the United States. (This is called the *elastic clause*. It lets Congress stretch its powers to meet the nation's changing needs.)

Section 9. Powers Denied to the U.S. Government

1. Congress may not interfere with the slave trade before 1808.
2. The government may not suspend the right of *habeas corpus* unless the country is under attack and public safety requires it. (A *writ of habeas corpus* is a legal order from a judge telling the police to bring a prisoner to court. There, they must either show evidence against him and charge him with a crime or let him go. In some countries, people can be put in prison without being charged with a crime. The right of *habeas corpus* prevents this. The words *habeas corpus* mean "you may have the body." They begin a Latin sentence that says the prisoner must be brought to court.)
3. Congress may not pass a bill of attainder. (This would be a law to punish a person without letting him have a trial.) Congress may not pass an *ex post facto* law. (*Ex post facto* means "after the fact." An ex post facto law is passed after an act is committed. It makes that act a crime and punishes people who committed the act before the law was passed. Under this clause, if a law is passed today, it may not be used to punish people for things they did earlier.)
4. Direct taxes have to be the same for each person taxed. People in one state cannot be taxed more than people in another state. (Congress has not ordered many direct taxes. One is the income tax. Amendment 16, added to the Constitution in 1913, has changed this clause somewhat.)
5. No taxes can be put on goods sent out of a state. (Congress cannot use taxes to help one state's trade or hurt another's trade.)
6. The government cannot use trade and tax laws to favor the ports of any state over the ports of another state. Also, ships going from one state to another cannot be taxed.
7. No one can spend money from the U.S. Treasury unless a law says that the expense is proper. Accounts of money taken in and paid out must be published from time to time.
8. The government cannot give anyone a noble title. No

government official can accept a job, a salary, or a title from another country unless Congress approves.

Section 10. Powers Denied to the States

1. No state can enter into a treaty or a union with another state or country. No state can print money. No state can use a substitute for U.S. money. No state can pass a bill of attainder law to punish a person without a trial. No state can pass an ex post facto law. No state can change private contracts. No state can give a person a noble title.

2. Unless Congress agrees, no state may tax goods entering or leaving the state, except what is needed to pay the costs of inspection. Any profits on such taxes go to the U.S. Treasury. All such tax laws may be controlled and changed by Congress.

3. No state can have its own army or navy unless Congress agrees. No state can enter into treaty with another state or another country, or fight a war, unless it has been attacked and cannot wait for help.

ARTICLE 2
The Executive Branch
Section 1. The President and Vice President

1. The executive power (power to carry out laws) is given to the President of the United States of America. He will hold office for a term of four years. A Vice President will be chosen for the same term. (Amendment 22, adopted in 1951, limited the number of terms and made other changes.)

2. The President and Vice President will be elected as follows. Each state legislature will decide on a way to choose electors. Each state can have as many electoral votes as it has senators and representatives in Congress. No government official can be an elector.
(The electors together are known as the *electoral college*. On the ballot, you are really voting for a set of electors, not for the candidates themselves. Each set of electors on the ballot has promised to vote for a certain candidate for President and for Vice President when the electoral college votes.)

3. The electors will meet in their own states and vote for two people. At least one of the two must come from another state. (The effect is that the President and Vice President must come from different states.) The electors will send a list of the people they voted for and how many votes each one got to the government. The president of the Senate will open the lists and count the votes in front of the members of Congress. The person who got the most votes will be President. The person with the second highest number of votes will be Vice President. (Amendment 12, adopted in 1804, changed this. Now electors vote separately for President and Vice President.)
If there is a tie, the House of Representatives will choose which one is President. If there is a tie for Vice President, the Senate will choose. In either case, each state gets one vote.

4. Congress may choose the time for picking electors and the day when all electors must vote. All electors throughout the United States will meet at the same time.

5. In order to be President, a person:
a. must be a natural-born citizen of the United States;
b. must be at least 35 years old;
c. must have lived in the United States for at least 14 years.

6. If a President dies, resigns, is removed from office, or becomes too sick to do the job, the Vice President carries out the duties of the President. Congress can pass laws about what should be done if both the President and Vice President are unable to do the job.
(Laws passed by Congress say that if there is no President, the

Speaker of the House will become President. If the Speaker cannot, then the president pro tempore of the Senate becomes President. Amendment 25, approved in 1967, also tells more about what happens when the office of the President or Vice President is empty.)

7. The President will be paid a salary. The salary cannot be changed during his term. He cannot take any other pay from the government.

8. When the President takes office, he must take the following oath: "I do solemnly swear (or affirm) that I will faithfully execute the office of President of the United States, and will to the best of my ability preserve, protect, and defend the Constitution of the United States."

Section 2. Powers of the President

1. The President is commander in chief of the army, the navy, and the National Guard. The President may ask for written opinions from the heads of the executive departments (the Cabinet). The President may grant reprieves or pardons for any federal offense except in cases of impeachment.

2. The President has the power to make treaties with other countries. The Senate must approve a treaty by a two-thirds vote.
The President may choose ambassadors, judges of the Supreme Court, and other important government officials, but the Senate must approve by a majority vote. Congress may allow less important officials to be chosen by the President alone, or by the courts, or by the heads of departments.

3. If any of these important jobs is unfilled when Congress is not meeting, the President has the power to choose a person for it. When Congress meets again, the Senate votes for or against the person that the President chose.

Section 3. Duties of the President

The President must report to Congress on the state of the union. (This "State of the Union" speech is now given once a year.) He may suggest laws to Congress. He may call a meeting of one or both houses of Congress for special occasions. If Congress cannot agree on a time to adjourn, the President may decide.
The President receives (formally accepts) ambassadors and officials of other countries. He carries out foreign policy.
The President sees that laws are carried out.
The President appoints all officials of the United States.

Section 4. Impeachment

The President, Vice President, and any other civilian official can be removed from office if they are impeached for and convicted of treason, bribery, or other high crimes and misdemeanors. (*High crimes and misdemeanors* are acts that are morally wrong or against the law. *Treason* is anything that helps this country's enemies. *Bribery* is offering or taking money in return for special favors from the government.)

ARTICLE 3
The Judicial Branch
Section 1. Federal Courts

The judicial power (power to judge whether a law has been broken) is given to the Supreme Court and to other federal courts that Congress sets up. The judges of these courts keep their jobs for life during good behavior. They are paid a salary, which cannot be lowered during their time in office.

Section 2. Judicial Power of Federal Courts

1. Federal courts try cases having to do with:

For the People, By the People

— the Constitution
— federal laws (laws of the United States)
— treaties
— laws involving the sea
— ambassadors or other embassy officials.
Federal courts also try cases that involve:
— the United States government itself
— two or more states
— citizens of different states
— a state or its citizens against a foreign country or citizens of a foreign country.
2. Cases which involve officials of other countries or cases which involve states will go at once to the Supreme Court. (This is called *original jurisdiction*.) All other cases will be tried first in lower courts and can be appealed to the Supreme Court. (This is called *appellate jurisdiction*.)
3. The trials of all crimes except impeachment will be jury trials. A trial will be held in the state where the crime was committed. If the crime was not committed in any state (on a ship at sea, for example), the trial will be held wherever Congress decides.

Section 3. Treason
1. Treason against the United States means making war against the United States or helping the enemies of the United States. Treason can be proved only by the word of two witnesses or by a confession in open court.
2. Congress can decide what the punishment for treason will be. But the convicted person's family cannot be punished. Their property cannot be taken away.

ARTICLE 4
Relations of States to Each Other
Section 1. Official Acts
Official acts, records, or judgments of one state will be honored in every other state. Congress may pass laws saying what kinds of proof must be offered. (This means, for example, that a marriage or a will or a court decision that is legal in one state will be recognized by every state.)

Section 2. Duties of States
1 Citizens of a state will be protected by the laws of any state they happen to be in. (This does not include rights for which a person must live in the state, such as the right to vote.)
2. If a person commits a crime in one state and runs away to another state, the two states may agree to return the suspect to the first state to be tried. (The second state *extradites* the suspect to the first state.)
3. Slaves and other servants who run away from their masters to another state can be returned to their masters. (In 1865, Amendment 13 was adopted and made this clause meaningless. Amendment 13 outlaws slavery.)

Section 3. New States and Territories
1. Congress has the right to admit new states to the union. But a new state cannot be made out of another state or states without permission from the states involved.
2. Congress has the power to make laws for property, such as territories, that belongs to the federal government.

Section 4. Federal Protection for States
The United States guarantees to every state:
— a republican form of government. (This is not defined. Most people agree it means that the people and their elected representatives run the government.)

— protection from invasion.
— protection from riots or other violence within the state.

ARTICLE 5
How to Amend the Constitution
1. There are two ways that an amendment (change or addition) to the Constitution can be started:
   a. Two-thirds of both houses of Congress vote for the amendment.
      Or:
   b. The state legislatures of two-thirds of the states call for a constitutional convention. That convention then suggests changes.
2. There are two ways an amendment can be accepted:
   a. Three-fourths of the state legislatures approve it. *Or:*
   b. Special conventions in three-fourths of the states approve it. Congress decides which of these two ways will be used to approve any amendment.
3. The Constitution cannot be amended to take away a state's equal vote in the Senate unless that state agrees.

ARTICLE 6
Some Federal Rules
1 All debts that the United States agreed to before this Constitution was adopted will be paid.
2. This Constitution and the laws made under it will be the supreme law of the land. State laws and state constitutions cannot overrule federal laws and the U.S. Constitution.
3. Senators, representatives, members of state legislatures, judges, and other state and federal officials must promise to support this Constitution. But no one can be required to belong to any religion in order to hold federal office.

ARTICLE 7
Ratification (Approval) of the Constitution
This Constitution will be accepted and will take effect when it has been approved by nine states.
Done in convention by the unanimous consent of the states present on September 17, 1787, in the twelfth year of our independence.

George Washington
President of the Convention
(This was followed by the signatures of 38 of the people at the convention. Not everyone who had worked on the Constitution signed it.)
The Constitution was approved by nine states on June 21, 1788. It went into effect as the supreme law of the land on March 4, 1789. George Washington took office as the first President in April 1789. By the summer of 1790, all 13 states had approved the Constitution.

THE BILL OF RIGHTS

Most citizens of the United States of America had lived before under a government that could do anything it wanted. They thought the Constitution still needed strong statements protecting the rights of the people.
So the first Congress suggested 12 amendments to the Constitution. Ten of the 12 were ratified by the states in 1791. These 10 amendments together are known as the Bill of Rights.

AMENDMENT 1
Freedom of Opinion
Congress must not pass any law which:
— sets up a religion for the nation or keeps people from practicing their religion.
— interferes with the freedom of speech.
— interferes with the freedom of the press.
— interferes with the right to hold a peaceful meeting for a lawful purpose. (This is called the right of assembly.)
— keeps people from asking the government to correct something they think is wrong. (This is called the right of petition.)
(In fact, there are limits to all these freedoms. In using these rights, you must not break a law or take away someone else's rights. For example, you are not free to tell lies about a person that damage his reputation. You are not free to urge others to commit violent crimes.)

AMENDMENT 2
Right to Bear Arms
Each state has the right to have a militia, an army of citizens. (These militia make up the National Guard.) The people have the right to keep and bear arms (in other words, to own weapons).

AMENDMENT 3
Housing of Soldiers
In peacetime, the government cannot make you keep soldiers in your house without your permission. In wartime, the government can put soldiers in your house. Congress has to pass special laws first, telling how this should be done.

AMENDMENT 4
Searches and Seizures
People and their homes, papers, and property may not be searched by the police without good reason. The police must have reason to believe a person has something they are looking for. The police have to go to a judge first and show proof that the search is needed. The judge can then give the police a search warrant. The search warrant must say exactly what the police are looking for and where they are going to look for it.

AMENDMENT 5
Rights in Criminal Cases
No person can be tried for a felony (serious crime) unless he has been indicted (charged) by a grand jury. The only exception is for members of the armed forces during wartime. An indicted person also has these rights:
— If he has been tried and found not guilty, he cannot be tried again for the same crime.
— He does not have to testify (give evidence) against himself.
— He cannot be punished without "due process of law". In other words, the police and courts have to follow the laws, and the laws must be fair.
The government cannot take away a person's property for public use unless the person is paid a fair price for it.

AMENDMENT 6
Rights to a Fair Trial
If a person is arrested and accused of a crime, the person has these rights:
— the right to a fair, public trial as soon as possible.
— the right to a trial by a jury in the state where the crime was committed.
— the right to know what he is accused of doing, so he can prepare a defense.

— the right to be present when witnesses against him testify (tell what they know).
— the right to call witnesses to defend him, by force if necessary.
(The "force" to be used is a subpoena. That is legal paper telling a witness to show up or be thrown in jail for contempt of court.)
— the right to have a lawyer defend him.

AMENDMENT 7
Rights in Civil Cases
(Civil lawsuits deal with disagreements about persons' rights and their duties toward each other.)
People involved in a civil lawsuit in federal courts have the right to a jury trial. They may agree to do without a jury. A jury is not needed if the value in question is $20 or less.
A jury's decision can be reviewed (checked) by a higher court. But the higher court can change the decision only if the law was not understood correctly in the lower court or if the jury did not hear all the facts.

AMENDMENT 8
Bail, Fines, and Punishments
A person who is arrested cannot be held for an unfair amount of bail. (Bail is money paid to the court to ensure an accused person will show up for trial.) A person who is convicted cannot be fined or punished more than is fair. The government cannot use cruel or unusual punishments, such as torture.

AMENDMENT 9
Rights Not Mentioned
Just because a right is not described in the Constitution, that does not mean the people do not have it. (It wasn't possible to list all the rights the people wanted to keep. This amendment says the government cannot take away a right just because it isn't named in the Constitution.)

AMENDMENT 10
Powers Not Delegated
Any power the Constitution does not give to the United States or does not forbid to the states belongs to the states or to the people. (This amendment says once more that the federal government has only the power the Constitution gives it. Certain other power belongs to the states. All other power belongs to the people.)

AMENDMENTS SINCE THE BILL OF RIGHTS
(The date given is when the amendment was adopted by the states.)

AMENDMENT 11
Lawsuits against States – 1798
A person from one state cannot sue another state in a federal court. (This amendment was added to make clear Article 3, Section 2, Clause 1. A citizen who wants to sue a state he doesn't live in must sue in that state's courts, not a federal court.)

AMENDMENT 12
Presidential Elections – 1804
The electors will meet in their own states. They will vote on separate ballots for a President and a Vice President. (Before this, electors voted for both offices together. The person with the most votes became President. The second-highest vote-getter became Vice President.) At least one of these two people the electors vote for must not be from their own state. (This is the same as before. The effect is that the President and Vice President must come

from different states.) The list of votes is sent to Congress. The president of the Senate opens the ballots and counts the votes in front of the members of Congress.

If no candidate for President gets a majority of votes, the House of Representatives chooses a President from the top three vote-getters. Each state gets one vote. If the House doesn't choose a President before the next March 4, the Vice President will fill the office.

If there is no majority for Vice President, the Senate will choose between the top two vote-getters. The Vice President must meet the same requirements for office as the President.

(Amendment 12 changes Article 2, Section 1, number 3. The amendment was needed after there was a tie vote for President in the 1800 election. It also says for the first time that a Vice President must meet the same requirements as a President.)

AMENDMENT 13
An End to Slavery – 1865
1. Slavery and involuntary (unwilling) service are not allowed in the United States or its territories. The only exception is people who have been convicted of a crime. They may be put in prison and made to work.
2. Congress has the power to enforce this amendment by making needed laws.
   (Amendment 13, 14, and 15 were added soon after the Civil War. They extended the rights of citizenship to former slaves. They also gave the federal government power to make the states obey.)

AMENDMENT 14
Civil Rights – 1868
1. Any person born in the United States, or naturalized, is a citizen of the United States and of the state where he lives. No state can make a law that takes away any rights of citizens. No state can take a citizen's life, liberty, or property without due process of law. A state cannot deny anyone equal protection under the law.
2. When the people are counted to see how many representatives a state gets, everyone must be counted except Indians who do not pay taxes. (This charges Article 1, Section 2, Clause 3. It had said a slave should be counted as three-fifths of a person. But now slavery is banned.) If a state keeps any male citizens who are 21 from voting, that state will not be allowed to count those people when its number of representatives is decided. (This was to keep states from forbidding former slaves to vote.)
3. No one can hold a state or federal office who took an oath to support the Constitution and then took part in a rebellion against the United States. (This was meant to disqualify leaders of the South in the Civil War from holding public office. Many had once been U.S. or state officials.)
4. The United States will pay its debts from the war between the states. It will not pay the debts of the southern states. It will not pay for losses caused by the war.
5. Congress can pass laws needed to enforce this amendment.

AMENDMENT 15
The Right of Blacks to Vote –1870
1. The right of a citizen of the United States to vote cannot be taken away because of race or color. It cannot be taken away because he was once a slave.
2. Congress can pass laws needed to enforce this amendment.
   (This amendment was intended to apply to black men. Women did not yet have the right to vote. This amendment is now used to protect other ethnic minorities as well.)

AMENDMENT 16
Income Tax – 1913
Congress can collect taxes on incomes. It doesn't have to worry about whether income taxes are spread evenly throughout the states. (Earlier in the Constitution, rules said that direct taxes taken from a state must depend on the number of people living in that state. That did not allow for an income tax.)

AMENDMENT 17
The People Elect Senators – 1913
1. Senators will be elected by the voters of the state they represent. (This changes Article 1, Section 3, Clause 1. Until 1913, senators were chosen by their state legislatures, not by voters.)
2. If a senator dies or resigns before his term is up, the governor of his state will call for an election to fill the office. Or the state lawmakers may tell the governor to appoint someone to serve until the next election.
3. This amendment does not apply to any senator now in office.

AMENDMENT 18
Prohibition of Liquor – 1919
(In 1933, Amendment 18 was repealed, that is, made ineffective, by Amendment 21.)
1. One year after this amendment is adopted, it will be illegal to make, sell, carry, import, or export alcoholic drinks in the United States and its territories.
2. Congress and the states have the power to make laws to enforce this amendment.
3. This amendment will not go into effect unless it is ratified (adopted) within seven years.

AMENDMENT 19
The Right of Women to Vote – 1920
1. The right of a citizen to vote cannot be refused or taken away because of sex. (Some states already let women vote. This amendment gave all women in the United States the right to vote.)
2. Congress has the power to pass laws to enforce this amendment.

AMENDMENT 20
Terms of the President and Congress – 1933
1. The terms of the President and Vice President end at noon on January 20. The terms of senators and representatives end at noon on January 3. The terms of new officials begin at these times.
   (This shortened the time before newly elected officials take over after an election. It is sometimes called the "lame duck amendment." Lame ducks are officials who have not been re-elected but are serving out the rest of their term. Before this, the President and Congress stayed in office too long after being voted out. They had time to pass or hold back laws against the will of the voters. This amendment gives lame ducks less chance to do that.)
2. Congress shall meet at least once a year. The meeting will start at noon on January 3 unless the date is changed by law.
3. If the person elected President dies between the election and the time he takes office, the person elected Vice President shall become President. If a President is not chosen by January 20, the person elected Vice President shall act as President until a President is chosen. Congress may pass a law saying what happens if neither the President nor the Vice President can take office.

4. Congress may decide what to do if a candidate for President dies between the time the electors vote and the President and Vice President are chosen.
   (Two more clauses in this amendment told how it should take effect.)

AMENDMENT 21
Repeal of Prohibition – 1933
1. Amendment 18 is repealed (taken back).
2. Any state that wants to keep prohibition (laws against selling liquor) may do so.
3. This amendment will not go into effect unless it is ratified (adopted) within seven years.

AMENDMENT 22
President Limited to Two Terms – 1951
1. No one can be elected President more than twice. No one who has served more than two years of someone else's term as President can be elected President more than once. This does not apply to the person who is President when this amendment is proposed. (The first 31 Presidents served two terms or less. Most people thought that was long enough. Then Franklin D. Roosevelt was elected President four times–in 1932, 1936, 1940, and 1944. He died in office in 1945. This amendment was proposed in 1947. It did not apply to Harry S. Truman, who was President at the time. But, after serving almost eight years, he did not run again.)
2. This amendment will not go into effect unless it is ratified (adopted) within seven years.

AMENDMENT 23
Voting in Washington, D.C. – 1961
1. Congress can pass laws giving the District of Columbia electoral votes. The number of electors will be the same as for the state with the fewest people. The electors will vote for President and Vice President in the same way that the electors from the states do. (Until this amendment, people living in Washington, D.C. could not vote for President and Vice President.)
2. Congress can pass laws to enforce this amendment.

AMENDMENT 24
An End to Poll Taxes – 1964
1. The right of a citizen to vote in a federal election cannot be taken away because of failure to pay a poll tax or other tax. (Some states used to use taxes to keep poor people or blacks from voting. This amendment makes that illegal.)
2. Congress can pass laws to enforce this amendment.

AMENDMENT 25
Presidential Disability and Succession – 1967
1. In case the President dies, resigns, or is removed from office, the Vice President becomes President.
2. If the office of Vice President is empty, the President will nominate (name) a Vice President. He must be approved by a majority of both houses of Congress.
3. If the President says in writing that he is unable to do his job, the Vice President will be acting President until the President says in writing that he is able to do the job again. The President must send these messages to the president pro tempore of the Senate and the Speaker of the House.
4. If the Vice President and a majority of Cabinet officers think the President is unable to do his job, they must say so in writing. They must send this message to the president pro tempore of the Senate and the Speaker of the House. The Vice President will then become acting President. If the President later says in writing that he can do his job, he takes over unless the Vice President and a majority of Cabinet officers disagree. If they disagree, the Congress will decide. It must decide within 21 days. The President will stay on the job unless two-thirds of the Senate and two-thirds of the House decide he is disabled.

(Before Amendment 25, if the Vice President's job became empty, it stayed unfilled until the next election. And there were no rules to tell what happened if the President was ill and could not carry out his duties.)

AMENDMENT 26
The Vote for 18-Year-Olds—1971
1. Any person who will be 18 years old by election day is allowed to vote in national, state, and local elections.
2. Congress can pass laws to enforce this amendment.

AMENDMENT 27
Congressional Pay Raises
1. Congress can vote to give itself a pay raise, but the increased salary does not take effect until after the next Congressional elections.
2. This amendment means that no Congress can give itself a quick pay raise.

The Emancipation Proclamation

Whereas, on the twenty-second day of September, in the year of our Lord one thousand eight hundred and sixty-two, a proclamation was issued by the President of the United States, containing, among other things, the following, to wit:

That on the first day of January, in the year of our Lord one thousand eight hundred and sixty-three, all persons held as slaves within any State, or designated part of a State, the people whereof shall then be in rebellion against the United States, shall be then, thenceforward, and forever free; and the Executive Government of the United States, including the military and naval authority thereof, will recognize and maintain the freedom of such persons, or any of them, in any efforts they may make for their actual freedom.

That the Executive will, on the first day of January aforesaid, by proclamation, designate the States and parts of States, if any, in which the people thereof respectively shall then be in rebellion against the United States; and the fact that any State, or the people thereof, shall on that day be in good faith represented in the Congress of the United States by members chosen thereto at elections wherein a majority of the qualified voters of such States shall have participated, shall in the absence of strong countervailing testimony be deemed conclusive evidence that such State and the people thereof are not then in rebellion against the United States.

Now, therefore, I, Abraham Lincoln, President of the United States, by virtue of the power in me vested as Commander-in-Chief of the Army and Navy of the United States, in time of actual armed rebellion against the authority and government of the United States, and as a fit and necessary war measure for suppressing said rebellion, do on this first day of January, in the year of our Lord one thousand eight hundred and sixty-three, and in accordance with my purpose so to do, publicly proclaimed for the full period of 100 days from the day first above mentioned, order and designate as the States and parts of States wherein the people thereof, respectively, are this day in rebellion against the United States, the following, to wit:

Arkansas, Texas, Louisiana (except the parishes of St. Bernard, Plaquemines, Jefferson, St. John, St. Charles, St. James, Ascension, Assumption, Terre Bonne, Lafourche, St. Mary, St. Martin, and Orleans, including the city of New Orleans), Mississippi, Alabama, Florida, Georgia, South Carolina, North Carolina, and Virginia (except the forty-eight counties designated as West Virginia, and also the counties of Berkeley, Accomac, Northhampton, Elizabeth City, York, Princess Anne, and Norfolk, including the cities of Norfolk and Portsmouth), and which excepted parts are for the present left precisely as if this proclamation were not issued.

And by virtue of the power and for the purpose aforesaid, I do order and declare that all persons held as slaves within said designated States and parts of States are, and henceforward shall be, free; and that the Executive Government of the United States, including the military and naval authorities thereof, shall recognise and maintain the freedom of said persons.

And I hereby enjoin upon the people so declared to be free to abstain from all violence, unless in necessary self-defense; and I recommend to them that, in all cases where allowed, they labor faithfully for reasonable wages.

And I further declare and make known that such persons of suitable condition will be received into the armed service of the United States to garrison forts, positions, stations, and other places, and to man vessels of all sorts in said service.

And upon this act, sincerely believed to be an act of justice, warranted by the Constitution upon military necessity, I invoke the considerate judgment of mankind and the gracious favor of Almighty God.

In witness whereof, I have hereunto set my hand and caused the seal of the United States to be affixed.

Done at the city of Washington, the first day of January, in the year of our Lord one thousand eight hundred and sixty-three, and of the independence of the United States of America the eighty-seventh.

By the President: Abraham Lincoln

1. Declaration of Sentiments

When, in the course of human events, it becomes necessary for one portion of the family of man to assume among the people of the earth a position different from that which they have hitherto occupied, but one to which the laws of nature and of nature's God entitle them, a decent respect to the opinions of mankind requires that they should declare the causes that impel them to such a course.

We hold these truths to be self-evident: that all men and women are created equal; that they are endowed by their Creator with certain inalienable rights; that among these are life, liberty, and the pursuit of happiness; that to secure these rights governments are instituted, deriving their just powers from the consent of the governed. Whenever any form of government becomes destructive of these ends, it is the right of those who suffer from it to refuse allegiance to it, and to insist upon the institution of a new government, laying its foundation on such principles, and organizing its powers in such form, as to them shall seem most likely to effect their safety and happiness. Prudence, indeed, will dictate that governments long established should not be changed for light and transient causes; and accordingly all experience hath shown that mankind are more disposed to suffer while evils are sufferable, than to right themselves by abolishing the forms to which they are accustomed. But when a long train of abuses and usurpations, pursuing invariably the same object, evinces a design to reduce them under absolute despotism, it is their duty to throw off such government, and to provide new guards for their future security. Such has been the patient sufferance of the women under this government, and such is now the necessity which constrains them to demand the equal station to which they are entitled.

The history of mankind is a history of repeated injuries and usurpations on the part of man toward woman, having in direct object the establishment of an absolute tyranny over her. To prove this, let facts be submitted to a candid world.

He has never permitted her to exercise her inalienable right to the elective franchise.

He has compelled her to submit to laws, in the formation of which she had no voice.

He has withheld from her rights which are given to the most ignorant and degraded men—both natives and foreigners.

Having deprived her of this first right of a citizen, the elective franchise, thereby leaving her without representation in the halls of legislation, he has oppressed her on all sides.

He has made her, if married, in the eye of the law, civilly dead.

He has taken from her all right in property, even to the wages she earns.

He has made her, morally, an irresponsible being, as she can commit many crimes with impunity, provided they be done in the presence of her husband. In the covenant of marriage, she is compelled to promise obedience to her husband, he becoming, to all intents and purposes, her master—the law giving him power to deprive her of her liberty, and to administer chastisement.

He has so framed the laws of divorce, as to what shall be the proper causes, and in case of separation, to whom the guardianship of the children shall be given, as to be wholly regardless of the happiness of women—the law, in all cases, going upon a false supposition of the supremacy of man, and giving all power into his hands.

After depriving her of all rights as a married woman, if single, and the owner of property, he has taxed her to support a government which recognizes her only when her property can be made profitable to it.

He has monopolized nearly all the profitable employments, and from those she is permitted to follow, she receives but a scanty remuneration. He closes against her all the avenues to wealth and distinction which he considers most honorable to himself. As a teacher of theology, medicine, or law, she is not known.

He has denied her the facilities for obtaining a thorough education, all colleges being closed against her.

He allows her in Church, as well as State, but a subordinate position, claiming Apostolic authority for her exclusion from the ministry, and, with some exceptions, from any public participation in the affairs of the Church.

He has created a false public sentiment by giving to the world a different code of morals for men and women, by which moral delinquencies which exclude women from society, are not only tolerated, but deemed of little account in man.

He has usurped the prerogative of Jehovah himself, claiming it as his right to assign for her a sphere of action, when that belongs to her conscience and to her God.

He has endeavored, in every way that he could, to destroy her confidence in her own powers, to lessen her self-respect and to make her willing to lead a dependent and abject life.

Now, in view of this entire disfranchisement of one-half the people of this country, their social and religious degradation—in view of the unjust laws above mentioned, and because women do feel themselves aggrieved, oppressed, and fraudulently deprived of their most sacred rights, we insist that they have immediate admission to all the rights and privileges which belong to them as citizens of the United States.

In entering upon the great work before us, we anticipate no small amount of misconception, misrepresentation, and ridicule; but we shall use every instrumentality within our power to effect our object. We shall employ agents, circulate tracts, petition the State and National legislatures, and endeavor to enlist the pulpit and the press in our behalf. We hope this Convention will be followed by a series of Conventions embracing every part of the country.

2. Resolutions

WHEREAS, The great precept of nature is conceded to be, that "man shall pursue his own true and substantial happiness." Blackstone in his Commentaries remarks, that this law of Nature being coeval with mankind, and dictated by God himself, is of course superior in obligation to any other. It is binding over all the globe, in all countries and at all times; no human laws are of any validity if contrary to this, and such of them as are valid, derive all their force, and all their validity, and all their authority, mediately and immediately, from this original; therefore,

Resolved, That all laws which prevent woman from occupying such a station in society as her conscience shall dictate, or which place her in a position inferior to that of a man, are contrary to the great percept of nature, and therefore of no force or authority.

Resolved, That woman is man's equal—was intended to be so by the Creator, and the highest good of the race demands that she should be recognized as such.

Resolved, That the women of this country ought to be enlightened in regard to the laws under which they live, that they may no longer publish their degradation by declaring themselves satisfied with their present position, nor their ignorance, by asserting that they have all the rights they want.

Resolved, That inasmuch as man, while claiming for himself intellectual superiority, does accord to woman moral superiority, it is pre-eminently his duty to encourage her to speak and teach, as she has an opportunity, in all religious assemblies.

Resolved, That the same amount of virtue, delicacy, and refinement of behavior that is required of woman in the social state, should also be required of man, and the same transgressions should be visited with equal severity on both man and woman.

Resolved, That the objection of indelicacy and impropriety, which is so often brought against woman when she addresses a public audience, comes with a very ill-grace from those who encourage, by their attendance, her appearance on the stage, in the concert, or in feats of the circus.

Resolved, That woman has too long rested satisfied in the circumscribed limits which corrupt customs and a perverted application of the Scriptures have marked out for her, and that it is time she should move in the enlarged sphere which her great Creator has assigned her.

Resolved, That it is the duty of the women of this country to secure to themselves their sacred right to the elective franchise.

Resolved, That the equality of human rights results necessarily from the fact of the identity of the race in capabilities and responsibilities.

Resolved, That the speedy success of our cause depends upon the zealous and untiring efforts of both men and women, for the overthrow of the monopoly of the pulpit, and for the securing to women an equal participation with men in the various trades, professions, and commerce.

Resolved, therefore, That, being invested by the creator with the same capabilities, and the same consciousness of responsibility for their exercise, it is demonstrably the right and duty of woman, equally with man, to promote every righteous cause by every righteous means; and especially in regard to the great subjects of morals and religion, it is self-evidently her right to participate with her brother in teaching them, both in private and in public, by writing and by speaking, by any instrumentalities proper to be used, and in any assemblies proper to be held; and this being a self-evident truth growing out of the divinely implanted principles of human nature, any custom or authority adverse to it, whether modern or wearing the hoary sanction of antiquity, is to be regarded as a self-evident falsehood, and at war with mankind.

—edited by Henry Steele Commager

TITLE I—VOTING RIGHTS

SEC. 101. (2). No person acting under color of law shall—

(A) in determining whether any individual is qualified under State law or laws to vote in any Federal election, apply any standard, practice, or procedure different from the standards, practices, or procedures applied under such law or laws to other individuals within the same county, parish, or similar political subdivision who have been found by State officials to be qualified to vote; . . .

(C) employ any literacy test as a qualification for voting in any Federal election unless (i) such test is administered to each individual wholly in writing; and (ii) a certified copy of the test and of the answers given by the individual is furnished to him within twenty-five days of the submission of his request made within the period of time during which records and papers are required to be retained and preserved pursuant to title 111 of the Civil Rights Act of 1960. . . .

TITLE II—INJUNCTIVE RELIEF AGAINST DISCRIMINATION IN PLACES OF PUBLIC ACCOMMODATION

SEC. 201. (a) All persons shall be entitled to the full and equal enjoyment of the goods, services, facilities, privileges, advantages, and accommodations of any place of public accommodation, as defined in this section, without discrimination or segregation on the ground of race, color, religion, or national origin.

(b) Each of the following establishments which serves the public is a place of public accommodation within the meaning of this title if its operations affect commerce, or if discrimination or segregation by it is supported by State action:

(1) any inn, motel, or other establishment which provides lodging to transient guests, other than an establishment located within a building which contains not more than five rooms for rent or hire and which is actually occupied by the proprietor of such establishment as his residence;

(2) any restaurant, cafeteria, lunch room, lunch counter, soda fountain, or other facility principally engaged in selling food for consumption on the premises. . . .

(3) any motion picture house, theater, concert hall, sports arena, stadium or other place of exhibition or entertainment. . . .

(d) Discrimination or segregation by an establishment is supported by State action within the meaning of this title if such discrimination or segregation (1) is carried on under color of any law, statute, ordinance, or regulation; or (2) is carried on under color of any custom or usage required or enforced by officials of the State or political subdivision thereof. . . .

SEC. 202. All persons shall be entitled to be free, at any establishment or place, from discrimination or segregation of any kind on the ground of race, color, religion, or national origin, if such discrimination or segregation is or purports to be required by any law, statute, ordinance, regulation, rule, or order of a State or any agency or political subdivision thereof. . . .

SEC. 206 (a) Whenever the Attorney General has reasonable cause to believe that any person or group of persons is engaged in a pattern or practice of resistance to the full enjoyment of any of the rights secured by this title, the Attorney General may bring a civil action in the appropriate district court of the United States by filing with it a complaint . . . requesting such preventive relief, including an application for a permanent or temporary injunction, restraining order or other order against the person or persons responsible for such pattern or practice, as he deems necessary to insure the full enjoyment of the rights herein described.

TITLE VI—NONDISCRIMINATION IN FEDERALLY ASSISTED PROGRAMS

SEC. 601. No person in the United States shall, on the ground of race, color, or national origin, be excluded from participation in, be denied the benefits of, or be subjected to discrimination under any program or activity receiving Federal financial assistance.

—Edited by Henry Steele Commager

Glossary

Each entry gives the chapter in which the word was a vocabulary word.

A

abolitionist (ab uh LISH uh nuhst) a person who works to end slavery (Ch. 35)

academy (uh KAD uh mee) a school where certain kinds of skills are taught (Ch. 33)

advanced (ad VANST) ahead of in development (Ch. 4)

adviser (uhd VEYE zuhr) a person who shares knowledge or facts in order to be of help (Ch. 7, 89)

alien (AY lee uhn) being part of another country (Ch. 44)

alliance (uh LEYE uhns) two or more people or groups working for a common goal (Ch. 12, 57, 63, 82)

ambassador (am BAS uhd uhr) a person who goes to another country in order to represent his or her own government (Ch. 61)

ambush (AM boosh) to attack by surprise (Ch. 13, 19)

amendment (uh MEND muhnt) a change (Ch. 21)

annual (AN yoo uhl) happening once a year (Ch. 46)

apartheid (uh PAR tayt) the South African word for segregation (Ch. 97)

appeal (uh PEEL) a review by a higher court of a case tried earlier in a lower court (Ch. 22)

appeasement (uh PEEZ muhnt) the act of giving up one's demands so that a bullying power will not attack (Ch. 74)

appoint (uh POYNT) to choose someone for a job or office (Ch. 37)

armada (ar MAHD uh) a large group of war ships (Ch. 6)

armistice (AR muh stuhs) a short-term agreement not to fight (Ch. 80)

assassination (uh sas uhn AY shuhn) the killing of a person for political reasons (Ch. 44, 63)

assembly (uh SEM blee) a group of people who meet together to make decisions (Ch. 12)

astronaut (AS truh naht) someone who travels into space (Ch. 87)

atom (AT uhm) the smallest part of each kind of element, all of which combine to form everything that exists (Ch. 77)

atrocity (uh TRAHS uht ee) an act that is considered to be terribly wicked or cruel (Ch. 64)

auction (AHK shuhn) a sale in which people bid against each other until a price is reached that only one person is willing to pay (Ch. 70)

authority (uh THOR uh tee) the power to tell a person or group what to do (Ch. 34)

autobiography (aht oh beye AHG ruh fee) the story of a person's life as told by that person (Ch. 36)

B

balance (BAL uhnts) 1. to keep each side on the same level (Ch. 29) 2. having something to please all sides (Ch. 37)

balance of trade (BAL uhnts • uhv • trayd) the difference between the value of goods sold to other countries and the value of the goods bought from them (Ch. 93)

ballot (BAL uht) the time when a vote is held (Ch. 23, 66)

base (bays) a place where the military sets up full-time operations (Ch. 59)

basin (BAYS uhn) a low area of land (Ch. 2)

betray (bi TRAY) to fail someone in time of need (Ch. 46)

blackout (BLAK owt) a time when all lights are turned off as a protection from attack by plane (Ch. 76)

blitzkrieg (BLITZ kreeg) a surprise attack by land and air forces which carefully work together (Ch. 74)

blockade (blah KAYD) 1. the act of using ships on a country's coast to keep other ships from bringing in goods (Ch. 24, 40, 41, 82) 2. to surround an area so its people are cut off from the outside world (Ch. 83)

bluff (bluhf) a try at making someone believe something that isn't true (Ch. 12)

boom (boohm) a time when business grows quickly throughout an area or country (Ch. 66)

boycott (BOY kaht) 1. to refuse any dealings with a person or group until certain terms are met (Ch. 15, 85, 95) 2. the act of refusing any dealings with a person or group until certain terms are met (Ch. 56)

budget (BUHJ uht) a plan for collecting money and spending it (Ch. 71)

bunker (BUNG kuhr) an underground shelter used to protect people during war (Ch. 78)

C

campaign (kam PAYN) to perform the acts necessary to reach a goal, such as winning an election (Ch. 35)

canal (kuh NAL) a ditch or channel dug to move water from one place to another (Ch. 2, 61)

candidate (KAN duh dayt) one who runs for an office (Ch. 29, 37, 100)

capital (KAP uh tuhl) the city in which government is centered (Ch. 22)

capitalism (KAP uht uhl izm) a system in which people and companies decide what to buy and what to sell (Ch. 72)

carpetbagger (KAHR puht bag uhr) a person from the North who came to the South to make money after the Civil War (Ch. 45)

cavalry (KAV uhl ree) a group of soldiers who fight while riding horses (Ch. 43)

censure (SEN chuhr) to place blame for doing something that is wrong or bad (Ch. 84)

ceremony (SAIR uh moh nee) a formal act or gathering to do something or remember something (Ch. 19)

chart (chart) to record the movements of something (Ch. 6)

charter (CHAR tuhr) an agreement that is spelled out in writing (Ch. 7)

circumnavigate (sur kuhm NAV uh gayt) to go all the way around (Ch. 6)

circumstance (SUHR kuhm stants) the way things are at a certain time and place (Ch. 28)

citizen (SIT uh zuhn) a member of a city, state, and/or country (Ch. 14)

Glossary

civilian (suh VIL yuhn) not being part of any armed forces (Ch. 83)

civilization (siv uh luh ZAY shuhn) a group that has reached a stage where people use writing and keep records (Ch. 1)

civil rights (SIV uhl • reyets) all the privileges held by the citizens of a city, state, or country (Ch. 85, 88)

collaborate (kuh LAB uh rayt) to cooperate, especially with enemy forces occupying one's own country (Ch. 79)

colony (KAHL uh nee) a community of people living in a new place but keeping close ties to their original government (Ch. 8)

combine (KAHM beyen) a machine that handles every step of harvesting grain (Ch. 52)

commentator (KAHM uhn tay tuhr) someone who talks or writes about the news (Ch. 80)

committee (kuh MIT ee) a group of people chosen to carry out special duties (Ch. 14)

communicate (kuh MYOOH nuh kayt) to speak and write in order to share ideas (Ch. 86)

communication (kuh myooh nuh KAY shuhn) a way of sending speech and writing over long distances (Ch. 32)

communism (KAHM yuh niz uhm) the idea that government should own everything, that a central group should make all decisions, and that the people should work for the good of the government (Ch. 82)

communist (KAHM yuh nuhst) a person or country following the idea that government should own everything, that a central group should make all decisions, and that the people work for the good of the government (Ch. 63)

compromise (KAHM pruh meyez) 1. an agreement reached when the different sides each give up part of their demands (Ch. 21, 22, 35, 65) 2. to settle differences by each side giving up something it wants (Ch. 21)

computer (kuhm PYOOHT uhr) a machine that can deal with facts by handling electric currents (Ch. 50)

concentration camp (kahn suhn TRAY shuhn • kamp) a camp where people are held prisoner (Ch. 75)

confederation (kuhn fed uh RAY shuhn) a united group (Ch. 20)

confiscate (KAHN fuh skayt) to take away a person's belongings for use by the government (Ch. 43)

conquistador (kon KEES tuh dor) someone who conquers or takes over (Ch. 6)

conservation (kahn suhr VAY shuhn) the act of controlling a resource in order to protect it, such as stopping people from cutting down forests (Ch. 62)

conservative (kuhn SUHR vuht iv) a person who wants to keep things as they are or have been (Ch. 72)

containment (kuhn TAYN muhnt) the act of preventing the growth or spread of something (Ch. 81)

continent (KAHNT uhn uhnt) one of the globe's great land masses (Ch. 3)

controversial (kahn truh VUHR shuhl) causing heated quarrels or disagreements (Ch. 66)

convenience (kuhn VEEN yuhns) something that makes life easier (Ch. 27)

convention (kuhn VEN chuhn) a meeting held to choose a party's candidates for office (Ch. 91)

convinced (kuhn VINST) to be sure that something is true (Ch. 5)

corporation (kor puh RAY shuhn) a business owned by two or more people and set up under the laws of a certain state (Ch. 51)

corrupt (kuh RUHPT) filled with people who break the law by such acts as stealing and taking bribes (Ch. 82)

county (KOWNT ee) an area of a state or colony that is given some power to rule itself (Ch. 10)

crime (kreyem) 1. an act that is against the law and that can lead to some kind of punishment (Ch. 36, 54) 2. all these acts that government must deal with (Ch. 54)

crisis (KREYE sis) a time of great danger or a turning point (Ch. 38)

criticize (KRIT uh seyez) to find fault with someone or something (Ch. 28)

crusade (kroo SAYD) a spirited plan to do something or change something (Ch. 24)

current (KUHR uhnt) the force put out by water as it flows (Ch. 32)

D

debate (di BAYT) a public talk about issues between two or more people in a political race (Ch. 38, 86)

debt (det) money owed to another (Ch. 10, 91, 96)

declare (di KLAIR) to tell, state, or announce (Ch. 17)

defeat (di FEET) to beat, as in battle (Ch. 41)

defense (di FENTS) the act of protecting or rescuing (Ch. 82)

deficit (DEF uh suht) the money government must borrow to pay those bills not covered by tax money (Ch. 96)

delegate (DEL i guht) a person who is chosen to act for another person or group of people (Ch. 16)

demand (di MAND) some decision or action that a person or group insists upon (Ch. 15)

demilitarized zone (dee MIL uh tuh reyezd • zohn) an area where armed forces are not allowed (Ch. 83)

democracy (duh MAHK ruh see) a kind of government in which people rule themselves (Ch. 9, 30, 98)

demonstration (dem uhn STRAY shuhn) an event staged to show people's beliefs and ideas (Ch. 90)

deport (di PORT) to force a person to return to his or her own country (Ch. 68)

deposit (di PAHZ uht) money put into a bank (Ch. 31)

depression (di PRESH uhn) a time when the economy slows and people are put out of work (Ch. 31, 69, 86)

deregulate (dee REG yuh layt) to remove rules and laws that control some group or activity (Ch. 96)

desert (DEZ uhrt) a place where there is so little water that hardly anything can grow (Ch. 47)

dictator (DIK tayt uhr) a person who has total rule over a country (Ch. 72, 94)

diplomacy (duh PLOH muh see) the act of handling affairs between countries (Ch. 62)

diplomat (DIP luh mat) a person who handles dealings between governments (Ch. 64, 95)

For the People, By the People

Glossary

discrimination (dis krim uh NAY shuhn) the act of treating a person or group badly because of the mistaken idea that the group is inferior (Ch. 64, 76)

disease (diz EEZ) a sickness, such as smallpox or yellow fever (Ch. 6)

distance (DIS tuhnz) the space between two points or places (Ch. 5)

draft (draft) the selection of people who will be forced to serve in the military (Ch. 42)

E

economy (i KAHN uh mee) the system through which the people and companies of a certain area make their livings (Ch. 30, 62, 71, 98)

education (ej uh KAY shuhn) knowledge gained from schooling (Ch. 35)

efficiently (i FISH uhnt lee) without mistakes or waste (Ch. 33)

elect (i LEKT) to choose by voting; especially when choosing a person to fill an office (Ch. 29)

elevated (EL uh vayt uhd) placed or built above the ground (Ch. 54)

embargo (im BAR goh) an order to stop a certain kind of trade (Ch. 93, 99)

embassy (EM buh see) the home of a person who lives in one country in order to represent his or her country's government (Ch. 68)

embroider (im BROY duhr) to decorate by sewing with threads (Ch. 4)

empire (EHM peyer) a nation that is made up of many areas and people; ruled by a king or queen known as an emperor or empress (Ch. 3, 26, 63)

enforce (en FORS) to carry out or put into action some law or ruling (Ch. 34)

enslaved (in SLAYVD) in a state of being owned by another person (Ch. 26)

environment (in VEYE ruhn muhnt) the weather, living things, and geography that make up a place and that depend upon each other (Ch. 60, 89)

envy (EN vee) to want what someone else has

equal (EE kwuhl) being treated exactly like others who belong to the same group (Ch. 29)

ethnic origin (ETH nik • OR uh juhn) the culture and traditions of the country or group from which a person or family comes (Ch. 84)

evidence (EV uhd uhnts) proof (Ch. 79)

exclusion (iks KLOO zhuhn) keeping someone or something out (Ch. 53)

execute (EKS uh kyoot) to put to death as punishment for a crime (Ch. 80)

Executive Branch (ig ZEK yuh tiv • branch) the branch of the government that includes the President (Ch. 20)

Executive Order (ig ZEK yuh tiv • OR duhr) a rule created by the President that has the same strength as a law (Ch. 76)

exile (EG zeyel) a punishment; being sent far away or out of the country (Ch. 81)

expansion (ek SPAN shuhn) the growth of a country by adding more land (Ch. 33)

experiment (ik SPAIR uh muhnt) to try new methods to see what happens (Ch. 8)

expert (EKS puhrt) someone who is excellent at some skill (Ch. 25)

expire (ik SPEYER) to end; to run out (Ch. 23)

explore (ik SPLOR) to search the unknown in order to find facts (Ch. 8, 87)

extinct (ik STINGKT) none left alive (Ch. 1)

F

faction (FAK shuhn) a group that shares ideas that are opposed by another group or groups (Ch. 29)

factory (FAK tuh ree) a building where items are manufactured (Ch. 27)

fanatic (fuh NAT ik) a person who so strongly believes in certain ideas that they become more important than anything else (Ch. 99)

fascist (FASH uhst) a person or group who follows a dictator and believes that each person is less important than the country and its main race of people (Ch. 73)

favor (FAY vuhr) an act or gift done in exchange for another act or gift (Ch. 55)

favorable (FAYV ruh buhl) in one's favor or to one's advantage (Ch. 43)

feminism (FEM uh niz uhm) the idea of complete equality between the sexes (Ch. 90)

fertile (FUHR tuhl) good for growing plants (Ch. 11)

finance (FEYE nans) to pay money to support something (Ch. 46)

fleet (fleet) a group of armed ships that operate together (Ch. 61)

foreign (FOR uhn) not belonging to one particular country; coming from outside that country (Ch. 59)

foreign aid (FOR uhn • ayd) money and goods given to help another country (Ch. 94)

foreigner (FOR uhn uhr) a person who comes from outside the country he or she lives in (Ch. 98)

former (FOR muhr) at one time in the past (Ch. 44)

free enterprise (free • ENT uhr preyez) the right to run a business in open competition with others and with only that government control needed to protect the public (Ch. 60)

frontier (fruhn TEER) land that is still wild and has few people living there (Ch. 18, 49)

fugitive (FYOOH juht iv) a person who is running away from something (Ch. 36)

G

general assembly (JEN uh ruhl • uh SEM blee) a group elected to set rules and laws for the people or countries who have elected them (Ch. 65)

generation (jen uh RAY shuhn) a group of people born about the same time and sharing the same experiences (Ch. 90)

Glossary

geography (jee AHG ruh fee) the features of a place: where it is, what the land is like, what the weather is like, etc. (Ch. 11)

ghetto (GET oh) a city section in which only Jewish people must live (Ch. 73)

glasnost (GLAS nohst) openness, or the grant of freedoms and rights to the Soviet people (Ch. 97)

govern (GUHV uhrn) to keep order and make laws for (Ch. 9)

government (GUHV uhrn muhnt) the person or people who rule a certain place such as a state, colony, or country (Ch. 10)

gridlock (GRID lahk) a situation in which arguments become so heated that nothing is achieved (Ch. 100)

guerrilla (guh RIL uh) a kind of fighting that depends on hiding and surprise attacks (Ch. 19)

H

health care (helth • kair) the system a country follows in treating its people's illnesses (Ch. 100)

homeless (HOHM luhs) having no place to live (Ch. 70)

homelessness (HOHM luhs nuhs) the state of having no place to live (Ch. 96)

homestead (HOHM sted) a piece of land given away by the government in exchange for living on the land and turning it into a farm (Ch. 47)

hostage (HAHS tij) a person who is held as a prisoner until certain demands are met (Ch. 95)

humanity (hyoo MAN uht ee) all people (Ch. 79)

I

immigrant (IM i gruhnt) a person who moves to another country in order to live there (Ch. 23, 32, 48, 50, 53)

immigration (im uh GRAY shuhn) the act of moving to another country in order to live there (Ch. 53)

immunity (im YOO nuht ee) an agreement to drop charges if a person will confess a crime, especially while working as a witness (Ch. 97)

impeach (im PEECH) to charge a public official with crimes in office (Ch. 45, 92)

impressment (im PRES muhnt) the act of taking sailors from other ships to work on your own ship (Ch. 24)

income tax (IN kuhm • tax) a part of a person's earnings taken for government use (Ch. 62)

independence (in duh PEN duhnts) the state of being free from something (Ch. 17)

indigo (IN di goh) a plant from the pea family used to make a blue dye (Ch. 11, 27)

industry (IN duhs tree) all the work done by a country's factories (Ch. 50)

inflation (in FLAY shuhn) a time when prices continue to go up (Ch. 76, 84, 90)

influenza (in floo EN zuh) a virus that attacks a person's lungs, making it hard to breathe (Ch. 65)

installation (in stuh LAY shuhn) a place where the military sets up full-time quarters, such as a fort or base (Ch. 40)

integration (int uh GRAY shuhn) the act of opening membership to all people (Ch. 85)

interest (IN truhst) 1. the fee paid by banks for money they keep as people's savings 2. the fee charged for lending money to someone (Ch. 69)

invade (in VAYD) to attack another country by crossing its borders (Ch. 24, 75)

invent (in VENT) to make up something that never existed before (Ch. 34)

invest (in VEST) to use money so that profits are earned (Ch. 22, 98)

investigation (in ves tuh GAY shuhn) a check or examination to find out facts (Ch. 92)

investment (in VEST muhnt) money paid for some project in hopes of making more money back in profit (Ch. 9)

irrigate (IR uh gayt) to bring water to dry land so that plants can be grown (Ch. 47)

isolationism (eye suh LAY shuh niz uhm) the idea of avoiding dealings with other countries (Ch. 79)

issue (ISH ooh) something that needs to be settled or decided (Ch. 31)

J

Judicial Branch (jooh DISH uhl • branch) the branch of the government that includes federal judges and other officers of the court (Ch. 20)

L

labor (LAY buhr) workers (Ch. 56)

landslide (LAND sleyed) a win in which one candidate takes far more votes than anyone else (Ch. 92)

lease (lees) to rent something (Ch. 61)

Legislative Branch (LEJ i slay tiv • branch) the branch of the government that includes Congress (Ch. 20)

legislature (LEJ i slay chuhr) a group that makes laws (Ch. 20)

liberty (LIB uhrt ee) the state of being free or able to do what one wants (Ch. 53)

limit (LIM uht) to set a point that cannot be passed (Ch. 10)

lobbyist (LAHB ee uhst) a person whose only job is trying to influence government into passing laws that are good for the people that he or she works for (Ch. 55)

loot (looht) to steal great quantities of goods, especially during a time of war or violence (Ch. 99)

loyalty (LOY uhl tee) being faithful to a person, group, or government (Ch. 44)

M

majority (muh JOR uht ee) any number that is greater than one half (Ch. 39, 100)

mandate (MAN dayt) the voters' approval of a candidate's ideas and plans (Ch. 72, 86)

Manifest Destiny (MAN uh fest • DEST uh nee) the idea that the United States needed to spread from the Atlantic Ocean to the Pacific (Ch. 33)

Glossary

market (MAR kuht) all the buying and selling that goes on in one certain country or area (Ch. 57)

mercantilism (MUHR kuhn teel iz uhm) trade controlled by one country to help itself (Ch. 11)

mercenary (MUHRS uhn air ee) someone who fights in wars for pay (Ch. 18)

merchant (MUHR chuhnt) 1. a person who buys goods and sells them for a higher price, or profit, in order to make a living (Ch. 3) 2. used in buying goods and selling them for a higher price, or profit, in order to make a living (Ch. 64)

military (MIL uh tair ee) anything involved with the army, navy, air force, or marines (Ch. 40, 83)

militia (muh LISH uh) a state or local army made up of regular citizens (Ch. 24, 58)

mine (meyen) a hole dug in order to remove metals buried in the soil (Ch. 47)

minority (muh NOR uht ee) a group that is a small part of a country's population (Ch. 73)

missile (MIS uhl) a rocket fired as a weapon (Ch. 86, 99)

moderate (MAHD ur ruht) a person who does not support extreme ideas (Ch. 39)

monopoly (muh NAHP uh lee) total control of all the parts of a certain kind of business, such as all parts of the oil business (Ch. 51, 58)

N

negotiate (nuh GOH shee ayt) to talk about or bargain for (Ch. 19)

neutral (NOO truhl) refusing to take sides in some sort of disagreement (Ch. 63, 74)

nomination (nahm uh NAY shuhn) the state of being chosen by a political party to run for an office (Ch. 94)

nonaggression agreement (nahn uh GRESH uhn • uh GREE muhnt) a promise made between two or more countries not to attack each other (Ch. 74)

normalcy (NOR muhl see) a time when things work in patterns that people believe are regular and acceptable (Ch. 65)

nullify (NUHL uh feye) to strike down or cancel (Ch. 23)

O

occupy (AHK yuh peye) to use troops to control a foreign country (Ch. 75, 78)

offensive (uh FENT siv) an attack against an enemy during war (Ch. 89)

officer (AHF uh suhr) a person who is chosen to carry out special duties (Ch. 14)

outbreak (OWT brayk) a sudden burst of fighting (Ch. 37)

P

pacifist (PAS uh fuhst) a person who believes that war should never be used to settle disagreements (Ch. 64)

pamphlet (PAM fluht) a small booklet with a paper cover (Ch. 17)

panic (PAN ik) a time when people suddenly fear that the economy is failing (Ch. 31)

pardon (PAR duhn) an official act that forgives some crime or activity (Ch. 45)

Pentagon (PENT uh gahn) 1. the people who lead the U.S. Armed Forces 2. the building that houses these offices (Ch. 76)

perestroika (per uh STROY kuh) a plan for changing the Soviet Union's Communist government (Ch. 97)

persecute (PUHR si kyooht) to bring about suffering for a person or group (Ch. 79)

persuade (per SWAYD) to talk someone into doing something (Ch. 33)

petition (puh TISH uhn) a paper written to ask that something be done (Ch. 16, 60)

Pilgrims (PIL gruhmz) English people who came to America to worship in their own way (Ch. 9)

plain (playn) a place that is fairly flat, covered with grass, and has few trees (Ch. 47)

plank (plangk) each idea of a party's plan for running government (Ch. 39)

plantation (plan TAY shuhn) a very large farm that grows only one or two cash crops (Ch. 11)

platform (PLAT form) all the ideas that make up a party's plan for running government (Ch. 39)

policy (PAHL uh see) a plan for how to deal with something (Ch. 34)

political (puh LIT i kuhl) trying to affect or control government decisions (Ch. 22, 55)

politician (pahl uh TISH uhn) a person who tries to affect or control government decisions (Ch. 55)

pollution (puh LOO shuhn) those things that make land, water, or air dirty and dangerous (Ch. 89)

popular sovereignty (PAHP yuh luhr • SAHV ruhn tee) the freedom to choose whether or not to allow slavery (Ch. 35)

population (pahp yuh LAY shuhn) all the people who live in a specific area (Ch. 1, 59, 84)

port (port) a body of water that is protected by land, such as a harbor or bay, where ships can dock safely and stand at rest (Ch. 59)

prejudice (PREJ uh duhs) senseless hatred of a person or group (Ch. 48)

premier (pri MEER) the leader of a country's government (Ch. 74)

primary (PREYE mer ee) an election held to choose the people that a state's political parties will send to the parties' national conventions (Ch. 94)

process (PRAHS es) the steps in which some activity is completed (Ch. 67)

proclaim (proh KLAYM) to declare the beginning of something (Ch. 80)

produce (PROH doos) fruits and vegetables (Ch. 27)

professional (pruh FESH nuhl) having training in special skills that can be used to earn a living (Ch. 16)

profit (PRAHF uht) the money left over after all costs have been paid (Ch. 51, 69)

Prohibition (proh uh BISH uhn) a law making it a crime to make, sell, or use alcoholic drinks (Ch. 68)

progress (pruh GRES) to grow or become better (Ch. 60)

property (PRAHP uhr tee) something that is owned (Ch. 38)

protectionism (pruh TEK shuhn izm) the idea that the government should take actions to protect businesses (Ch. 30)

protest (PROH test) 1. to disagree or oppose (Ch. 7, 28, 98) 2. an act or statement that shows disagreement or opposition (Ch. 88, 98)

purge (puhrj) the act of getting rid of people thought to be enemies (Ch. 81)

pyramid (PIR uh mid) a building or structure that slopes inward from bottom to top (Ch. 2)

R

radar (RAY dar) a machine that uses radio waves to track moving objects, such as planes and ships (Ch. 75)

radiation (rayd ee AY shuhn) the energy released when an atom is split; poisonous for most living things (Ch. 78)

radical (RAD i kuhl) 1. being in support of extreme measures or changes (Ch. 44, 70) 2. a person who supports extreme measures or changes (Ch. 95)

ratify (RAT uh feye) to approve (Ch. 21, 95)

reaction (ree AK shuhn) a feeling or statement caused by some event (Ch. 38)

rebellion (ri BEL yuhn) a fight against one's government (Ch. 15)

receipt (ri SEET) a piece of paper that proves something was done or paid for (Ch. 48)

recession (ri SESH uhn) a time when the economy slows and people are put out of work (Ch. 93)

recognize (REK uhg neyez) to accept a new nation and its right to exist (Ch. 28)

reform (ri FORM) the act of making changes to clean up or improve something (Ch. 46, 58, 100)

refugee (ref yoo JEE) a person who tries to escape a place where battles are happening (Ch. 65)

regulate (REG yuh layt) to use laws to control some kind of action or actions (Ch. 57, 71)

reinforcements (ree in FORS muhntz) troops that are sent to help other troops in a war (Ch. 18)

religion (ri LIJ uhn) the beliefs a person or group holds about God (Ch. 7, 10)

represent (rep ri ZENT) to act for someone or something (Ch. 16)

representative (rep ri ZENT uht iv) a person who acts in place of another person or for a group of people (Ch. 17)

reservation (rez uhr VAY shuhn) land set aside for a group of people to live on (Ch. 25, 49)

resistance (ri ZIS tuhnts) a group that fights in secret against foreign troops that have taken over their country (Ch. 75)

resource (REE sors) something that can be sold and/or used to make an item that can be sold (Ch. 3, 50, 73)

retreat (ri TREET) to back away from danger (Ch. 18)

revenge (ri VENJ) to take action against someone in return for something they have done (Ch. 25)

revolution (rev uh LOO shuhn) the act of tossing out one kind of government and replacing it with another (Ch. 17)

rocket (RAHK uht) a metal tube that is pushed into flight by burning gas (Ch. 77)

S

sacrifice (SAK ruh feyes) the act of giving up enjoyable things in order to do a job (Ch. 80)

satellite (SAT uh leyet) 1. a country that is controlled by another country (Ch. 81) 2. a machine sent into space so it can circle a planet or moon and help send radio and television signals (Ch. 87)

scalawag (SKAL i wag) a person in the South who helped the North's Reconstruction government for gain (Ch. 45)

scandal (SKAN duhl) disgrace caused by doing something that offends people or is against the law (Ch. 46, 55, 66)

secede (si SEED) to leave the Union (Ch. 41)

secession (suh SESH uhn) the act of leaving or breaking away from a group or country (Ch. 25, 39)

segregate (SEG ruh gayt) to keep one group separate or set apart from another (Ch. 48)

segregated (SEG ruh gay tuhd) keeping one group separate or set apart from another (Ch. 61)

segregation (seg ri GAY shuhn) the act of closing membership to some people or groups (Ch. 85)

settle (SET uhl) to found a home or town in a new place (Ch. 8)

sewer (SOO uhr) a set of drain pipes that carry off water and waste material (Ch. 54)

sharecropper (SHAIR krahp uhr) a person who farms land owned by someone else and earns a share in the money made (Ch. 45)

shipping (SHIP ing) the act of moving goods by boat or ship (Ch. 26)

skill (skil) something that a person has learned to do well (Ch. 56)

slaughterhouse (SLAH tuhr hows) place where animals are butchered for meat (Ch. 52)

slum (sluhm) a part of a city that is very crowded, poor, and dirty (Ch. 54, 90)

society (suh SEYE uht ee) 1. a group of people who form a state or country and follow similar traditions (Ch. 67) 2. all the people of a country, including their ideas, relationships, and problems (Ch. 72)

soldier (SOHL juhr) a person who serves in an armed force (Ch. 13)

solidarity (sahl uh DAIR uh tee) a feeling of oneness, of working together for the same goal (Ch. 81)

space (spays) the area between planets and other heavenly bodies; contains no gravity or air (Ch. 87)

spoils (spoylz) the jobs a winning candidate can give to loyal supporters (Ch. 30)

stagflation (stag FLAY shuhn) a time when both inflation and a recession or a depression are happening (Ch. 93)

status (STAYT uhs) place or rank in society (Ch. 48)

stock market (stahk • MAR kuht) a place where shares in a company are bought and sold (Ch. 69)

strait (strayt) a narrow stretch of water flowing between two larger areas of water (Ch. 1)

strategy (STRAT uh jee) careful planning to achieve some goal (Ch. 13)

strike (streyek) the act of walking off a job until certain terms are met (Ch. 56)

style (steyel) a specific way in which something is made, such as writing a book or creating clothing (Ch. 67)

suburb (SUHB uhrb) an area or town with neighborhoods of houses located outside a large city (Ch. 52)

subway (SUHB way) a train that runs through a set of tunnels that have been dug under a city (Ch. 54)

sue (soo) to go to court to get something by law (Ch. 19)

suffrage (SUHF rij) the right to vote (Ch. 58)

supply (suh PLEYE) something needed, such as food or water (Ch. 13)

surrender (suh REN duhr) to quit or give up (Ch. 12, 43, 77)

surround (suh ROWND) to place people all around (Ch. 12)

sympathetic (sim puh THET ik) feeling of support or approval (Ch. 28)

T

tariff (TAIR uhf) a tax that must be paid on goods bought from another country (Ch. 30)

tax (taks) money people must pay to their governments (Ch. 14)

telegraph (TEL uh graf) a system that sends messages by using electrical clicks to form a code for letters of the alphabet (Ch. 32)

temple (TEM puhl) a building where people perform religious activities (Ch. 2)

tenement (TEN uh muhnt) a building divided into small rooms for family dwellings (Ch. 52)

term (tuhrm) 1. the length of time a person is elected to hold an office 2. the details set up in order to reach an agreement or goal (Ch. 78, 91)

territory (TAIR uh tor ee) an area of land (Ch. 27)

terrorist (TAIR uhr uhst) a person who uses violence and fear to gain his or her demands (Ch. 97)

thatch (thach) a mat of plant material that is used as a roof (Ch. 4)

ticket (TIK uht) the two people chosen by a party to run for President and Vice President (Ch. 92)

tobacco (tuh BAK oh) a plant grown for its leaves, which are dried so they can be chewed or smoked (Ch. 8)

traditional (truh DISH nuhl) in a manner that follows a long accepted pattern; customary (Ch. 68)

traitor (TRAY tuhr) someone who helps the enemy or joins the enemy side (Ch. 18)

transcontinental (TRANS kahnt uhn ent uhl) across a continent (Ch. 36)

transportation (trans por TAY shun) the way in which something is moved from one place to another (Ch. 32, 84)

treason (TREEZ uhn) the crime of betraying one's country (Ch. 43)

treaty (TREE tee) 1. an agreement reached by the parties after a war (Ch. 13) 2. a written agreement reached by two or more countries (Ch. 26, 91)

trench (trench) a ditch dug into the ground in which soldiers hide and fire at the enemy (Ch. 42)

troops (troops) members of the armed forces (Ch. 49)

truce (troos) an agreement to stop fighting (Ch. 34)

trust (truhst) a group of corporations that have joined together so that they do not compete with one another (Ch. 51, 58)

U

unassigned (uhn uh SEYEND) not given out or claimed (Ch. 49)

unemployment (uhn im PLOY muhnt) the state of having no job (Ch. 70)

unify (YOO nuh feye) to join parts together as one (Ch. 15)

unconstitutional (uhn kahnt stuh TOOHSH nuhl) not following the ideas of the U.S. Constitution (Ch. 85)

union (YOON yuhn) a group of workers that is set up to work for the good of the members (Ch. 56)

unorganized (uhn OR guh neyezd) not yet established or arranged (Ch. 36)

urban (UHR buhn) having to do with cities (Ch. 52)

V

value (VAL yoo) a belief or action that is held to be good and worthwhile (Ch. 68)

veteran (VET uh ruhn) 1. older and well tested (Ch. 25) 2. a person who has served in the armed forces (Ch. 70)

violence (VEYE uh luhns) the use of force against people (Ch. 37, 88)

volunteer (vahl uhn TEER) a person who chooses to join the army, navy, air force, or marines (Ch. 40)

voyage (VOY uhj) a trip made on the ocean (Ch. 5)

W

weapon (WEP uhn) a gun, bomb, knife, etc. (Ch. 38)

worship (WUHR shuhp) to pray or take part in a church service (Ch. 9)

Gazetteer and Index

How to Use the Gazetteer and Index:

1. Each entry has two parts. One part is an **index.** It tells the pages on which the words from the text can be found. The other part is a **gazetteer.** It tells how to pronounce the words from the text.

2. As in a dictionary or the glossary, the words are listed in alphabetical order. Most of the words are names. Some names have two or more words. For the names of places, things, and ideas, look at the letters that begin the first word. To find **St. Louis,** look in the S list.

3. People's names are included in this gazetteer. Remember, people's last names are used in putting them in alphabetical order. To find **George Washington,** look in the W list. To find **Juan Ponce de León,** look in the D list.

4. If a person has no last name, look at the letters that begin the person's first name. To find **Eric the Red,** look in E. Do not look for people's titles. To find **Prince Henry,** look in the H list.

5. To find the name of an organization, look at the letters that begin the first word. To find **Electoral College,** look in the E list. If a name begins with a common word like "department," "treaty," or "office," look at the letters that begin the main word of the name. To find the **Department of the Navy,** look in the N list. If you cannot find the name, look under the letters for the other words that are capitalized. For example, to find the **Department of the Navy,** you could look in D and N.

6. The last part of each entry also tells the page numbers where information about each topic can be found. For example, information about **George Washington** can be found on pages 76, 92, 95, 98-100, 103, 111-113, 118, 119, 130, 133, 134-137, 139, 243, 370, 461, and 527.

A

Abilene [Texas] (AB uh leen) 288
abolition (ab uh LISH uhn) 216, 218, 219, 225, 231
abolitionists (ab uh LISH uh nuhsts) 213, 214, 218, 219, 225, 231
Acadie [Canada] (a KAY dee) 47
Adams, Abigail (AB uh gayl • AD uhmz) 412
Adams, John (jahn • AD uhmz) 92, 95, 98, 105, 106, 119, 130, 139-142, 176, 412
Adams, John Quincy (jahn • KWIN zee • AD uhmz) 176, 177, 180
Adams, Samuel (SAM yuhl • AD uhmz) 92, 94, 130
Addams, Jane (jayn • AD uhmz) 331
Afghanistan (af GAN uh stan) 613, 614, 616, 629, 630, 636
Africa (AF ri kuh) 16-19, 21, 27, 50, 361, 372, 375, 387, 389, 420
African Americans (AF ri kuhn • uh MAIR uh kuhnz) 68, 90, 120, 137, 166, 190, 194, 195, 201, 216, 219, 221, 229, 231, 252-256, 259, 262, 268, 270-274, 278, 291-293, 295, 299, 300, 307, 312, 338-340, 345, 367, 368, 401, 420, 421, 422, 429, 453, 459, 460, 463, 471, 489, 498, 520, 545-549, 565, 575, 576, 578, 579, 589, 615
African National Congress (AF ri kuhn • NASH uh nuhl • KAHNG gruhs) 632
Africans (AF ri kuhnz) 21, 22, 24, 69, 162, 218, 219, 370, 469
Age of Steel (ayj • uhv • steel) 315
Agnew, Spiro (SPEER oh • AG noo) 607
Air Force 1 (air • fors • hwuhn) 566
air ships (air • ships) 398, 399
airplanes (air • playnz) 399, 400
Alabama (al uh BAM uh) 205, 236, 295, 498, 545, 546, 582
Alamo (AL uh moh) 197
Alaska (uh LAS kuh) 5, 11, 359, 415, 507, 576, 603, 605
Albany [New York] (AHL buh nee) 60, 78
alcohol (AL kuh hahl) 279, 425, 426, 431
Alcohol, Tobacco, and Firearms, Bureau of [ATF] (BYUHR oh • uhv • AL kuh hahl • tuh BAK oh • uhnd • FEYER ahrmz) 655
Aldrin, Edwin (ED wuhn • AHL druhn) 561
Aleut (al ee OOT) 11
Algeria (al JEER ee uh) 617
Algonquian (al GAHN kwee uhn) 76
Alien and Sedition Acts (AY lee uhn • uhnd • si DISH uhn • akts) 139-142
Allegheny [river] (al uh GAYN ee) 76
Allen, Ethan (EETH uhn • AL uhn) 95
alliances (uh LEYE uhnts uhz) 387, 389, 527, 528, 571, 603, 608, 631
Allied conferences (AL eyed • KAHN fuh ruhnts uhz) 500
Allied Forces (AL eyed • FORS uhz) 389, 395-401, 406, 407, 409, 479, 480-505, 642-647
Allied Powers (AL eyed • POW uhrz) 389, 395, 397-400, 405, 409, 468, 474, 479, 480, 482, 492, 494-498, 500, 502, 507, 508, 527, 528, 533, 535, 643, 642-647
Al-Wafre oilfield [Kuwait] (al WAH fruh • OYL feeld) 643
American Federation of Labor (uh MAIR uh kuhn • fed uh RAY shuhn • uhv • LAY buhr) 340, 341
American Indian Movement (uh MAIR uh kuhn • IN dee uhn • MOOV muhnt) 579
American Party, also known as Know-Nothing Party (uh MAIR uh kuhn • PART ee) 226
American Party [of the 1960s] (uh MAIR uh kuhn • PARTee) 582, 584
Anaconda Plan (an uh KAHN duh • plan) 241
anarchists (AN uhr kuhsts) 364
Anasazi (an uh SAHZ ee) 14
Anderson, John (jahn • AN duhr suhn) 617
Anderson, Marian (MAIR ee uhn • AN duhr suhn) 463
Annapolis [Maryland] (uh NAP uh luhs) 124
Anthony, Susan B. (SOOZ uhn • bee • AN thuh nee) 216, 412
Anti-Federalist Party (AN teye • FED uh ruh luhst • PART ee) 130, 134

Anti-Masonic Party (AN teye • muh SAHN ik • PART ee) 183
anti-war movement (AN teye • wor • MOOV muhnt) 577, 582, 583
anti-war protests (AN teye • wor • PROHtests) 200, 201, 577, 583
Apache (uh PACH ee) 12
apartheid (uh PAR tayt) 632, 658
Apollo 11 (uh PAHL oh • ee LEV uhn) 561
Apollo Program (uh PAHL oh • PROH gram) 561
Apollo 7 (uh PAHL oh • SEV uhn) 561
Apollo 13 (uh PAHL oh • thuhr TEEN) 561
Appalachians [mountains] (ap uh LAY chee uhnz) 75, 86, 192
appeasement (uh PEEZ muhnt) 474, 475
Appomattox Courthouse [Virginia] (ap uh MAT uhx • KORT hows) 259-261, 265
Arabs (AIR uhbz) 24, 517, 520, 602, 603, 643, 655
Arapaho (uh RAP uh hoh) 299
Arctic (ARK tik) 10
Argentina (ar jen TEE nuh) 171, 511
Aristide, Jean Bertrand (zahn • buhr TRAN • air uhs TEED) 29
Arizona (air uh ZOH nuh) 12, 33, 289, 301, 397
Arkansas (AR kuhn sah) 205, 247, 254, 268, 291, 548, 649
Arlington (AR ling tuhn) 243
Arlington National Cemetery (AR ling tuhn • NASH uh nuhl • SEM uh tair ee) 243
Armada (ar MAHD uh) 34, 44
arms race (armz • rays) 629
Armstrong, Louis (LOO ee • ARM strawng) 421
Armstrong, Neil (neel • ARM strawng) 561
Army Air Corps (ARM ee • air • kor) 498
Arnez, Desi (DEZ ee • ar NEZ) 541, 543
Arnold, Benedict (BEN uh dikt • ARN uhld) 95, 99, 100, 115
Around the World in Eighty Days (uh ROWND • thuh • wuhrld • in • AYT tee • dayz) 353
art (art) 420
Arthur, Chester A. (CHES tuhr • ay • AR thuhr) 335
Articles of Confederation (ART i kuhlz • uhv • kuhn fed uh RAY shuhn) 122-124
Aryans (AR ee uhnz) 469, 471
Asia (AY zhuh) 5, 10, 15, 17-19, 26, 28, 31, 41, 293, 294, 324, 325, 359, 377, 387, 467, 474, 475, 483, 485, 507, 510, 527, 536
Asian Americans (AY zhuhn • uh MAIR uh kuhnz) 547
assassination (uh sas uhn AY shuhn) 265, 266, 335, 364, 388, 405, 565-568, 646
assembly lines (uh SEM blee • leyenz) 309, 310, 419, 420
astronaut (AS truh naht) 560, 561
Atlanta [Georgia] (uht LANT uh) 258-260, 292
Atlanta Compromise (uht LANT uh • KAHM pruh meyez) 295
Atlantic Ocean (uht LANT ik • OH shuhn) 26, 28, 83, 192, 198, 249, 259, 301, 372, 387, 482, 527, 528, 609
atomic bombs (uh TAHM ik • bomz) 494, 501, 503-505, 510, 519, 527, 537, 559, 587, 613, 629
atomic missiles (uh TAHM ik • MIS uhlz) 555, 556
Attorney General (uh TUHRN ee • JEN uh ruhl) 134, 414, 430, 598
Attucks, Crispus (KRIS puhs • AT uhks) 90
Augusta [Georgia] (ah GUS tuh) 256
Augusta, Alexander T. (al ig ZAN duhr • tee • ah GUS tuh) 256
Auschwitz [Poland] (OWSH vits) 486
Austin, Stephen F. (STEE vuhn • ef • AH stuhn) 197
Australia (ah STRAYL yuh) 387
Austria (AHS tree uh) 474
Austria-Hungary (AHS tree uh • HUHNG uh ree) 65, 387-389, 391, 395, 398-400, 403, 405, 474
Autobiography of Frederick Douglass, The (thuh • aht oh beye AHG ruh fee • uhv • FRED uh rik • DUHG luhs) 222
automobile (AHT uh moh beel) 413, 418-420, 437, 438
Axis Powers (AK suhs • POW uhrz) 479, 480-505

B

B-29s (bee • TWEN tee • neyenz) 498
baby boom (BAYbee • boom) 539
balanced budget (BAL uhnst • BUHJ uht) 625, 627, 653
balance of powers (BAL uhns • uhv • POW uhrz) 459
balance of trade (BAL uhns • uhv • trayd) 601
Bahamas (buh HAHM uhz) 28, 240
Balkan Peninsula (BAHL kuhn • puh NIN suh luh) 387
Ball, Lucille (looh SEEL • bahl) 541, 543
balloons (buh LOONZ) 399
Baltic Sea (BAHLT ik • see) 387, 497
Baltimore [Maryland] (BAHL tuh mor) 150, 253, 317, 322
Baltimore, Lord (lord • BAHL tuh mor) 60, 62, 234
banking (BANGK ing) 182, 187, 188, 307, 381, 382, 384, 437-440, 442, 445-447, 452, 453, 455, 469, 483, 624, 631, 635
Bank of the United States, Second (SEK uhnd • bangk • uhv • thuh • yoo NEYET uhd • stayts) 182, 187
Banneker, Benjamin (BENJ uh muhn • BAN uh kuhr) 137
Baptist Church (BAB tuhst • church) 546

Bartholdi, Frédéric Auguste (FREED uh rik • AH goost • bar TAHL dee) 325
Barton, Clara (KLAIR uh • BART uhn) 262, 264
baseball (BAYS bahl) 413
Basie, Count (kownt • BAY see) 421
Bastogne [Belgium] (ba STOHN) 497
Bataan [Philippines] (buh TAN) 485
Batista, Fulgencio (ful JEN see oh • buh TEES tuh) 554
Bay of Pigs [Cuba] (bay • uhv • pigz) 555
Beauregard, Pierre G. T. (pee AIR • gee • tee • BOHR uh gard) 248
Beckworth, James (jaymz • BEK wuhrth) 190
Beckworth Pass (BEK wuhrth • pas) 190
Begin, Menachem (muh NAHK uhm • BAY guhn) 608, 610
Beijing [China] (BAY zhing) 587, 637
Beirut [Lebanon] (bay ROOT) 630
Belgium (BEL juhm) 152, 389, 398, 479, 496, 497, 528
Bell, Alexander Graham (al ig ZAND uhr • GRAY uhm • bel) 316
Bell, John (jahn • bel) 234, 235
Bennington [Vermont] (BEN ing tuhn) 112
Bering Strait (BAIR ing • strayt) 5
Berkeley, John (jahn • BUHRK lee) 62
Berle, Milton (MIL tuhn • buhrl) 541
Berlin [Germany] (buhr LIN) 471, 501, 502, 527
Berlin Airlift (buhr LIN • AIR lift) 527
Berlin Blockade (buhr LIN • blah KAYD) 527
Berlin Wall (buhr LIN • wahl) 525, 636, 639
Bernadotte, Folke (fohk • ber nuh DOT) 520
Bernstein, Carl (karl • BUHRN steen) 597
Berry, Chuck (chuk • BAIR ee) 585
Bessemer, Henry (HEN ree • BES uh muhr) 314
Bethune, Mary McLeod (MAIR ee • muh KLOWD • buh THYOOHN) 460
Bible (BEYE buhl) 370, 427
Bicentennial (beye sen TEN ee uhl) 604
big stick policy (big • stik • PAHL uh see) 372
Birth of a Nation (buhrth • uhv • uh • NAY shuhn) 422
Bitzer, Billy (BIL ee • BIT zuhr) 421
Black Kettle (blak • KET uhl) 299
Blackfeet (BLAK feet) 297
Black Muslims (blak • MUHZ luhms) 576
Black Panthers (blak • PAN thuhrz) 578
black power (blak • POW uhr) 578
Blaine, James G. (jaymz • gee • blayn) 335
Blair House (blair • hows) 531
"Bleeding Kansas" (BLEED ing • KAN zuhs) 224-226, 231
blitzkrieg (BLITZ kreeg) 473, 479, 494
Bly, Nellie (NEL ee • bleye) 353
Bolivia (buh LIV ee uh) 360
Bolsheviks (BOHL shuh viks) 429
bombing raids (BAHM ing • raydz) 500, 501, 503, 505, 534, 536, 572, 585, 643, 646
bombings (BAHM ingz) 341, 398, 399, 430, 502, 655
Bonaparte, Napoleon (nuh POH lee uhn • BOH nuh part) 139, 145, 150, 151, 159, 160, 162
Bonus Army (BOH nuhs • AR mee) 449
"Booker T. and W.E.B." (BOOK uhr • tee • uhnd • DUHB uhl yoo • ee • bee) 295
bootleggers (BOOT leg uhrz) 426
Booth, John Wilkes (jahn • wilks • booth) 265, 266
Bork, Robert (RAHB uhrt • bork) 598, 599
Bosnia (BAHZ nee uh) 387, 388
Bosnia-Herzegovina (BAHZ nee uh • hert suh goh VEE nuh) 391
Boston [Massachusetts] (BAH stuhn) 57, 88-90, 93, 94, 98-100, 106, 255, 316, 321, 330, 413, 604
Boston Common (BAH stuhn • KAHM uhn) 255
Boston, David (DAYvuhd • BAH stuhn) 545
Boston Harbor (BAH stuhn • HARbuhr) 89, 100
Boston Massacre (BAH stuhn • MAS i kuhr) 88, 90
Bourke-White, Margaret (MAHR guh ruht • boork • hweyet) 418
Bowser, Elizabeth (i LIZ uh buhth • BOW zuhr) 262
boycott (BOI kaht) 93, 339, 546, 614
Boyd, Belle (bel • boid) 262
Braddock, Edward (ED wuhrd • BRAD uhk) 81
Bradley, Omar (OH mar • BRAD lee) 497, 534
Brazil (bruh ZIL) 28, 171
Breckinridge, John C. (jahn • see • BREK uhn rij) 234
Breedlove, Sarah (SAIR uh • BREED luhv) 312
Breed's Hill, Battle of (BAT uhl • uhv • breedz • hil) 98, 100
Brewster, William (WIL yuhm • BROO stuhr) 54
Brezhnev, Leonid (LEE uh nid • BREZH nef) 618
bribery (BREYEB uh ree) 366
Bright, William (WIL yuhm • breyet) 416
British Columbia [Canada] (BRIT uhsh • kuh LUHM bee uh) 84
British Royal Air Force (BRIT uhsh • ROY uhl • air • fors) 480
British Royal Army (BRIT uhsh • ROY uhl • ARM ee) 477, 478, 480
British Royal Navy (BRIT uhsh • ROY uhl • NAYV ee) 477, 479, 480, 495, 496, 500
Brooklyn [New York] (BROOK luhn) 409
Brooks, Preston (PRES tuhn • brooks) 227

Brown, John (jahn • brown) 225, 227, 231, 236
Brown, Oliver (AHL i vuhr • brown) 545
Brown vs. Board of Education of Topeka (brown • VUHR suhs • bord • uhv • ed yoo KAYshuhn • uhv • toh PEEK uh) 545, 549
Bryan, William Jennings (WIL yuhm • JEN ingz • BREYE uhn) 352, 380
Buchanan, James (jaymz • byoo KAN uhn) 226, 229, 236
Buena Vista, Battle of (BAT uhl • uhv • BWAYN uh • VIS tuh) 237
buffalo (BUHF uh loh) 13, 287, 297, 298, 300
Buffalo Soldiers (BUHF uh loh • SOHL juhrz) 300
Bulgaria (buhl GAIR ee uh) 389, 398, 405, 497, 523
Bull Moose Party (bul • moos • PART ee) 383
Bull Run [Virginia] (bool • ruhn) 248, 258
Bull Run, First Battle of (fuhrst • BAT uhl • uhv • bool • ruhn) 248, 258, 260
Bull Run, Second Battle of (SEK uhnd • BAT uhl • uhv • bool • ruhn) 260
Bunche, Ralph (ralf • buhnch) 520
Bunker Hill, Battle of (BATuhl • uhv • bung KUHR • hil) 98-100
Burgesses, House of (hows • uhv • buhr juh SEEZ) 50, 89
Burgoyne, John (jahn • buhr GOYN) 98, 112
Burn, Harry (HAR ee • buhrn) 416
Burr, Aaron (AIR uhn • buhr) 140, 141
Bush, Barbara (BAR buh ruh • boosh) 650
Bush, George (jorg • boosh) 183, 605, 633, 635, 638, 642-647, 649, 650
businesses (BIZ nuhs uhz) 276, 304-306, 309, 311, 316, 323, 324, 333, 338, 339, 344, 349, 351, 368, 369, 380-384, 401, 414, 415, 419, 420, 425, 437, 440, 441, 444, 446-448, 451-454, 457, 458, 461, 462, 467, 518, 539, 540, 542, 577, 601, 608, 616, 624, 626, 629, 631, 632, 635
business owners (BIZ nuhs • OHN uhrz) 304, 306, 309, 310, 323, 324, 333, 339, 344, 366, 368, 401, 437, 438
business, regulation of (BIZnuhs • reg yuh LAY shuhn • uhv • BIZnuhs) 344, 345, 383, 415, 452, 601, 608, 616, 624, 653
Butler, Andrew (an DROO • BUHT luhr) 227
Byrd, Harry F. (HAIR ee • ef • bird) 554
Byzantine Empire (BIZ uhn teen • EM peyer) 16, 17

C

CBS (see • bee • es) 543
Cabinet [of the President] (KAB nuht) 133, 134, 181, 189, 271, 334, 382, 414
cable TV (KAY buhl • TEE vee) 153
Cabot, John (jahn • KAB uht) 31, 41
Cahokia (kuh HOH kee UH) 12
Calhoun, John C. (jahn • see • kal HOON) 145, 181, 182, 215
California (kal uh FOR nyuh) 10, 11, 14, 190, 198-200, 213-215, 218, 226, 287, 377, 397, 419, 422, 488, 489, 542, 543, 545, 557, 578, 579, 605, 607, 611
California, University of, at Berkley (YOO nuh vuhrs uht ee • uhv • kal uh FOR nyuh • at • BUHRKlee •) 578
Cambodia (kam BOHD ee uh) 585
Camden [South Carolina] (KAM duhn) 117
Camp David (kamp • DAY vuhd) 610
Camp David Accords (kamp • DAY vuhd • uh KORDZ) 610
Canada (KAN uh duh) 5, 12, 26, 41, 75, 83, 84, 86, 89, 95, 99, 100, 103, 112, 119, 146, 147, 150, 162, 219, 274, 301, 387, 423, 619
canals (kuh nals) 192, 193
Canary Islands (kuh NAIR ee • EYE luhndz) 27
Cape of Good Hope (kayp • uhv • good • hohp) 23
capitalism (KAP uht uhl izm) 457
Capitol [United States] (KAP uht uhl) 150, 247, 279, 416, 449
Caribbean (kar uh BEE uhn) 34, 373, 482, 531
Carlisle Indian Industrial School (KAHR leyeuhl • IN dee uhn • in DUHS tree uhl • skool) 385
Carmichael, Stokley (STOHK lee • KAR meyek uhl) 578
Carnegie, Andrew (an DROO • KAR nuh gee) 309
Carolana (kair uh LAHN uh) 42
Carolinas (kair uh LEYE nuhz) 61, 62
Carson, Rachel (RAY chuhl • KAR suhn) 573
Carter, Jimmy (JIM ee • KART uhr) 531, 537, 607-611, 613-618
Carter, Rosalyn (ROZ uh lin • KART uhr) 611
Cartier, Jacques (zhak • kar TYAY) 41, 47
cartoons (KARtoonz) 541
Cass, Lewis (LOO uhs • kas) 213
Castro, Fidel (fee DEL • KAS troh) 554-556, 638
Cateret, George (jorj • KAT uh ret) 62
Catholic (KATH uh lik) 41, 59, 62, 75, 426
Catholic Church (KATH uh lik • church) 525, 552
cattle (KAT uhl) 288
Cemetery Ridge [Pennsylvania] (SEM uh tair ee • rij) 253
Census Bureau (SEN suhs • BYUHR oo) 301, 359
Central America (SEN truhl • uh MAIR uh kuh) 6, 7, 11, 13, 28, 372, 373, 630
Central Committee (SEN truhl • kuh MIT ee) 429, 430
Central High School [Little Rock, Arkansas] (SEN truhl • heye • shool) 548
Central Intelligence Agency (SEN truhl • in TEL uh juhnts • AY juhn see) 482, 555, 597
Central Pacific Railroad (SEN truhl • puh SIF ik • RAYL rohd) 287
Central Powers (SEN truhl • POW uhrz) 389, 395, 398, 405, 408, 409, 468
Century of Dishonor, A (uh • SENCH uh ree • uhv • DIS ahn uhr) 300
Chamberlain, Neville (NEV uhl • CHAYM buhr luhn) 475, 477
Champlain, Lake (layk • sham PLAYN) 82, 146, 147
Chancellorsville, Battle of (BAT uhl • uhv • CHAN suh luhrz vil) 264

Chaplin, Charlie (CHAR lee • CHAP luhn) 422

Charbonneau, Toussaint (TOO sahn • shar BON oh) 159

Charles I (charlz • thuh • fuhrst) 55, 60, 61

Charles II (charlz • thuh • SEK uhnd) 60, 61

Charles IV (charlz • thuh • forth) 41, 42

Charleston [South Carolina] (CHARL stuhn) 89, 117, 234, 239, 258

Chase, Salmon P. (SAM uhn • pee • chays) 264

Chavez, Cesar (SHAV ez • SAY zar) 576

checks and balances, system of (SIS tuhm • uhv • cheks • uhnd • BAL uhnts uhz) 125, 127-129, 133,134, 139, 140, 145, 146, 199, 202, 203, 215, 224-226, 229, 230, 239, 240, 362, 382-384, 390, 397, 402-408, 451-454, 457-459, 476, 518, 523, 524, 534, 535, 553, 649-654

Cherokee (CHAIR uh kee) 203-206, 268, 301

Chesapeake Bay (CHES uh peek • bay) 118, 150

Cheyenne (SHEYE an) 297, 299

Chiang Kai-shek (chan • keye SHEK) 528, 529, 534, 536

Chicago [Illinois] (shuh KAHG oh) 220, 234, 277, 288, 316, 331, 341, 351, 397, 430, 567

Chickahominy, Valley of the (VAL ee • uhv • thuh • chik uh HAHMuh nee) 231

Chickasaw (CHIK uh saw) 203, 205, 268

Chief Justice (cheef • JUHS tuhs) 264, 397, 430, 567

child labor (cheyeld • LAY buhr) 329, 330, 368

Children's Bureau (CHIL druhnz • BYUHR oo) 381

Chile (CHIL ay) 171, 360

China (CHEYE nuh) 28, 214, 287, 293, 294, 324, 359, 360, 364, 375, 376, 381, 467, 483, 501, 507, 510, 528, 529, 533, 534, 536, 586, 587, 637, 638

Chinese Exclusion Act of 1882 (CHEYEN eez • iks KLOO zhuhn • akt • uhv • AYT teen • AYT tee • too) 324

Chippewa (CHIP uh wah) 298

Chisholm, Shirley (SHUHR lee • CHIS uhlm) 589

Choctaw (CHOK taw) 203, 205, 207, 268

Christ, Jesus (JEEZ uhs • kreyest) 16

Christmas Day (KRIS muhs • day) 111, 497

Christian (KRIS chuhn) 16, 338

Churchill, Winston (WIN stuhn • CHUHR chil) 477, 480, 482, 495, 500, 502, 509, 523

Cíbola (SEE boh luh) 33

cities (SIT eez) 194, 287, 293, 315-317, 321, 322, 327-331, 340, 366, 367, 429, 503, 510

citizenship (SIT uh zuhn ship) 291-294, 301

city departments (SIT ee • di PART muhnts) 367

city governments (SIT ee • GUHVuhrn muhntz) 334

city managers (SIT ee • MAN uh juhrz) 366

city problems (SIT ee • PRAHB luhmz) 327-331, 334, 542

Civil Disobedience (SIV uhl • dis uh BEED ee uhnts) 201

civil rights (SIV uhl • reyets) 216, 219, 273, 291, 292, 363, 367, 368, 421, 429, 459, 494, 518, 545-548, 566, 571, 575, 576, 578, 579, 582, 589, 609, 611, 614, 629, 638

Civil Rights Act of 1875 (SIV uhl • reyets • akt • uhv • AYT teen • SEV uhn tee • feyev) 291, 292

Civil Rights Act of 1957 (SIV uhl • reyets • akt • uhv • NEYENteen • SIKS tee • SEV uhn) 546, 547

civil rights movement (SIV uhl • reyets • MOOV muhnt) 545-547, 565

Civil Service Commission (SIV uhl • SUHR vuhs • kuh MISH uhn) 335

Civil War (SIV uhl • wor) 120, 237, 239-268, 274, 288, 291, 299, 304, 305, 309, 314, 316, 327, 330, 336, 338, 351, 422, 442, 462, 546, 611

civil wars (SIV uhl • worz) 609, 615

Clark, George Rogers (jorj • RAHJ uhrz • klahrk) 114

Clark, William (WIL yuhm • klahrk) 159

Clay, Henry (HEN ree • klay) 145, 176, 177, 182, 183, 187, 215, 230

Cleveland, Grover (GROH vuhr • KLEEV luhnd) 335, 346, 361

Clinton, William J. (WIL yuhm • jay • KLIN tuhn) 183, 537, 586, 646, 649, 650, 652-654

Clinton, Henry (HEN ree • KLIN tuhn) 98

coal (kohl) 305, 463

Cobb, Ty (teye • kahb) 413

Cochran, Woody (WOODee • KAHKruhn) 302

Coercive Acts (KOH UHR siv • akts) 89, 93

Cold Harbor [Virginia] (kohld • HAR buhr) 259

Cold War (kohld • wor) 523-525, 527, 528, 536, 540, 556, 586, 629, 630, 636, 637

Colfax, Schuyler (SHY luhr • KOHL faks) 276, 333

Collazo, Oscar (AHS kuhr • kuh LAT zoh) 531

Collins, Michael (MEYE kuhl • KAHL uhnz) 561

Colombia [South Carolina] (koh LAHM bee uh) 171, 260, 374, 375

Colombia (koh LAHM bee uh) 374, 375

Colorado (KAL uh rad oh) 285, 299, 301, 407

Columbus, Christopher (KRIS tuh fuhr • kuh LUHM buhs) 26-29, 162

Comanche (kuh MAN chee) 297

Commerce, Department of (di PARTmuhnt • uhv • KAM uhrs) 653

Common Sense (KAHM uhn • sens) 103

communication (kuh myooh nuh KAYshuhn) 153, 192-194, 199

Communism (KAHM yuh niz uhm) 391, 399, 429, 430, 457, 470, 473, 474, 476, 480, 519, 522, 524, 525, 527-530, 533, 536, 537, 540, 541, 555, 556, 567, 571, 572, 577, 585-587, 608, 609, 630, 636-639

Communist Party (KAHM yuh nist • PART ee) 429, 522

Communist Party of America (KAHM yuh nist • PART ee • uhv • uh MAIR uh kuh) 519, 540

Communist satellite countries (KAHM yuh nist • SAT uh leyet • KUHN treez) 523, 525, 528, 636

companies (KUHMpuh neez) 285, 287, 291

Compromise of 1850 (KAHM pruh meyez • uhv • ayt TEEN fif TEE) 215, 218

computers (kuhm PYOOT uhrz) 307

Comstock Lode (KAM stahk • lohd) 215, 218

concentration camps (kahn suhn TRAY shuhn • kamps) 481, 485, 486, 507, 509, 511

Concord [Massachusetts] (KAHN kord) 93, 94, 96, 100

Confederate Army (kuhn FED uh ruht • ARM ee) 243, 255, 260, 261

Confederate Congress (kuhn FED uh ruht • KAHNG gruhs) 237

Confederate Navy (kuhn FED uh ruht • NAV ee) 241, 255

Confederate States of America (kuhn FED uh ruht • stayts • uhv • uh MAIR uh kuh) 236, 237, 239, 241, 242, 247-249, 252-54, 258, 259, 261, 262, 264, 265, 267, 268, 270, 271, 273, 422

Congo (KON goh) 22

Congress, United States (YOOneyet uhd • stayts • KAHNG gruhs) 122-125, 128, 129, 133, 139, 141, 145, 146, 159, 160, 171, 175, 176, 182, 183, 188, 197, 200, 213, 214, 220, 224, 229, 230, 237, 243, 265, 267, 270-274, 279, 285, 286, 291, 292, 298, 299, 300, 301, 321, 324, 333, 340, 341, 344, 346, 351, 352, 360, 361, 362, 382, 383, 390, 397, 400, 408, 411, 412, 414, 425, 430, 441, 448, 449, 451, 453, 454, 458, 459, 482, 485, 488-490, 507, 518, 519, 523, 528, 530, 531, 534, 535, 539, 541, 542, 546-548, 559, 561, 565, 566, 568, 570, 572, 595-598, 601, 603, 608, 611, 613, 623-627, 630, 633, 635, 649, 650, 652-654

Congressional Medal of Honor (kuhn GRESH nuhl • MED uhl • uhv • AHN uhr) 250, 262, 496, 497

Connally, John (jahn • KAHN uh lee) 564-566, 568

Connally, Mrs. John (MIS uhz • jahn • KAHN uh lee) 564-566

Connecticut (kuh NET uh kuht) 56, 59, 61, 62, 94, 105, 130, 152

conservation (KAHN suhr VAY shuhn) 369, 382, 414, 573

conservatives (kuhn SUHR vuht ivz) 457, 545, 595, 596, 599, 601, 603, 608, 623, 624

Conservative Party (kuhn SUHR vuht iv • PARTee) 477

Constantinople (KAHN stan tuhn OH puhl) 16, 17

Constitution, United States (YOO neyet uhd • stayts • kahn stuh TOO shuhn) 124-126, 129-131, 133, 135, 140-142, 159, 182, 188, 235, 270, 273, 276, 292, 293, 363, 381, 404, 458, 534, 540, 546, 553, 578, 596, 611, 623, 627, 633

amendments (in numerical order)

12th Amendment (twelfth • uh MEND muhnt) 140, 141

13th Amendment (THUHR teenth • uh MEND muhnt) 265, 291

17th Amendment (SEV uhn teenth • uh MEND muhnt) 131, 381

18th Amendment (AYT teenth • uh MEND muhnt) 425, 427, 431

19th Amendment (NEYENteenth • uh MEND muhnt) 178, 216, 412, 416

22nd Amendment (TWEN tee • SEK uhnd • uh MEND muhnt) 627

26th Amendment (TWEN tee • siksth • uh MEND muhnt) 578

Rights, Bill of (bil • uhv • reyets) 132, 133, 140, 314

development of (duh VEL uhp muhnt • uhv) 121-137

ratification of (rat uh fuh KAYshuhn • uhv) 130

text of (tekst • uhv) 671-684

Constitution [Cherokee] (kahn stuh TOO shuhn) 204

Constitution [Cuba] (kahn stuh TOO shuhn) 363

Constitutional Convention (kahn stuh TYOO shun uhl • kuhn VEN shuhn) 124-126, 128, 129

Constitutional Processes (kahn stuh TYOO shun uhl • PRAH ses uhz)

checks and balances, system of (SIS tuhm • uhv • cheks • uhnd • BAL uhnts uhz) 125, 127-129, 133, 134, 139, 140, 145, 199, 202, 203, 215, 224-226, 229, 230, 239, 240, 362, 382-384, 390, 397, 402-408, 451-454, 457-459, 476, 518, 523, 524, 534, 535, 553, 649-654

declaring war (duh KLAIR ing • wohr) 145, 146, 199, 239, 240, 362, 390, 397, 485, 642, 643

effect on Presidential elections (uh FEKT ahn • prez uh DEN shuhl • i LEK shuhnz) 140, 141, 177, 178, 183, 277, 278, 594-598, 607

exercise of constitutional powers by (EKS suhr seyez • uhv • kahn stuh TOO shuhn uhl • POW uhrz • beye)

Executive Branch (ig ZEK yuht iv • branch) 125, 128, 129, 134, 180, 181, 188, 199, 252, 271, 368, 369, 372, 381, 382, 397, 403-408, 425, 426, 430, 451, 454, 457-459, 482, 483, 485, 488, 489, 500, 501, 509, 517, 523, 524, 528, 529, 534, 535, 545, 547, 553, 565-568, 570-572, 579, 584-588, 594-598, 601, 603, 604, 608, 609, 613-620, 625, 626, 629, 630-633, 635, 642-646

Judicial Branch (joo DISH uhl • branch) 125, 128, 129, 133, 142, 202, 203, 226, 229, 230, 293, 344, 368, 369, 458, 459, 545, 547, 548, 594-598, 619, 620

Legislative Branch (LEDJ uhs lay tuhv • branch) 125, 127, 128, 133, 134, 145, 146, 197, 229, 230, 271, 301, 341, 344, 403-408, 457-459, 476, 482, 483, 485, 509, 523, 524, 528, 529, 534, 535, 541, 546, 547, 559, 568, 587, 588, 594-598, 603, 604, 608, 609, 613, 614, 616, 625, 626, 631, 632, 635

setting up treaties and agreements (SET ing • uhp • TREE teez • uhnd • uh GREE muhnts) 134, 135, 137, 151, 152, 159, 170, 171, 198-204, 360-363, 372-377, 396, 397, 483, 484, 504, 507, 509, 528, 529, 535, 536, 572, 584-587, 609, 614, 617

Constitutional Union Party (KAHN stuh TOO shuhnl • YOO yuhn • PAHRT ee) 234, 235

consumers (kuhn SOO muhrz) 369

containment (kuhn TAYN muhnt) 523, 524, 527, 536

Continental Army (KAHNT uhn ENT uhl • ARM ee) 95, 98, 100, 112, 115

Continental Association (KAHNT uhn ENT uhl • uh soh see AY shuhn) 93

Contract with America (KON trakt • with • uh MAIR uh kuh) 653

Contras (KAHN truhs) 630, 632, 633

Coolidge, Calvin (KAL vuhn • KOO luhdj) 412-415, 438

copper (KAHP uhr) 285

Cornwallis, Charles (charlz • KORN wahl uhs) 112, 117-119

Coronado, Francisco (fran SIS koh • kor ah NOD oh) 33

corporate owners (KOR puh raht • OHN uhrz) 309, 312

corporations (KOR puh ray shuhnz) 309-312, 316

Corporations, Bureau of (BYUHR oh • uhv • KOR puh ray shuhnz) 369

Cortés, Hernando (her NAN doh • kor TEZ) 31, 32, 40

cotton (KAHTuhn) 151, 166, 167, 188, 194, 204, 309, 310

cotton gin (KAHTuhn • jin) 166, 168, 309

Cowpens [South Carolina] (KOW penz) 118

Cox, Archibald (ARCH uh bahld • kahks) 598, 599

Cox, James M. (jaymz • em • kahks) 411
Cradle of Liberty, nickname for Massachu-setts (KRAYD uhl • uhv • LIB uhr tee) 107
Crawford, William H. (WIL yuhm • aych • KRAH fuhrd) 176, 177
Crazy Horse (KRAY zee • hors) 300
Crédit Mobilier (KRED uht • MOH bil yay) 335
Creek (kreek) 170, 203, 205, 268, 301
crime (kreyem) 214, 219, 328, 425, 428, 429, 444, 491, 539, 542, 596, 597
Croatia (kroh AY shuh) 391
Croatoan (KROH uh TOH uhn) 44
Cromwell, Oliver (AHL uh vuhr • KRAHM wel) 60, 61
Crusades (kroo SAYDZ) 16
Crusaders (kroo SAYD uhrz) 16, 19
Cuba (KYOO buh) 361-363, 372, 374, 378, 543, 554-556, 637, 638
Cumberland River (KUHM buhr luhnd • RIV uhr) 249
Custer, George (jorj • KUHS tuhr) 299, 300
Custis, Martha (MAR thuh • KUHS tuhs) 243
Custis, Mary (MAIR ee • KUHS tuhs) 243
Czechoslovakia (chek uh sloh VAHK ee uh) 475, 476, 481, 523, 525

D

D-Day (dee • day) 495, 496, 500
da Gama, Vasco (VAS koh • duh • GAH muh) 17-19, 24
Dakotas (duh KOH tuhs) 300, 301
Daley, Richard (RICH uhrd • DAY lee) 582
Dallas [Texas] (DAL uhs) 317, 566, 567
Danbury [Virginia] (DAN ber ee) 259
Dare, Virginia (vuhr JIN yuh • dair) 43-45
Darwin, Charles (charlz • DAR wuhn) 427
Daugherty, Harry M. (HAR ee • em • DAH uhr tee) 414
Daughters of the American Revolution (DAHT uhrz • uhv • thuh • uh MAIR i kuhn • rev uh LOOH shuhn) 463
da Verrazano, Giovanni (gee oh VAHN ee • duh • vair uh ZAHN oh) 31, 41
Davis, Benjamin O. (BENJ uh muhn • oh • DAY vuhs) 489, 498
Davis, Jefferson (JEF uhr suhn • DAY vuhs) 231, 236, 237, 247, 260-262, 267, 268
Dawes Act of 1887 (dahs • akt • uhv • AYT teen • AYT ee • SEV uhn) 300
Dawes, William (WIL yuhm • dahz) 94
Daytona [Florida] (day TOH nuh) 460
Dead Sea (ded • see) 602
Dean, John (jahn • deen) 597
debates, presidential (prez uh DEN shuhl • duh BAYTZ) 553, 554
Debs, Eugene V. (yoo JEEN • vee • debz) 383
debt (det) 61, 86, 122, 134, 147, 187, 188, 327, 347, 372, 377, 382, 405, 408-09, 414, 425, 438-440, 442, 445-447, 453, 468, 507, 510, 582, 601, 626, 631, 635, 636, 652
de Champlain, Samuel (SAM yuhl • duh • sham PLAYN) 47
Declaration of Independence (dek luh RAY shuhn • uhv • in duh PEN duhns) 412
Declaration of Sentiments (dek luh RAY shuhn • uhv • SENT uh muhnts) 216
Declaratory Act (di KLAIR uh tohr ee • akt) 28
Deere, John (jahn • deer) 314
deficit spending (DEF uh sit • SPEND ing) 453, 460, 461, 625, 626, 635, 652
Delaney, Martin R. (MAR tuhn • ar • duh LAYN ee) 256
Delaware (DEL uh wair) 62, 130, 247, 252
Delaware River (DEL uh wair • RIV uhr) 48, 49, 62, 111
De La Warr, Lord (lord • DEL uh WAHR) 49
de León, Juan Ponce (whon • pahnts • day • lay AHN) 31
demilitarized zone (dee MIL uh tuhr eyezd • zohn) 536
democracy (di MAHK ruh see) 54, 55, 180, 183, 363, 372, 403, 429, 473, 536, 555, 571, 586, 636-639
Democratic Convention (dem uh KRAT ik • kuhn VEN shuhn) 234, 582, 607
Democratic Party (dem uh KRAT ik • PART ee) 143, 180, 183, 187-189, 213, 225, 226, 230, 234, 235, 258, 277, 278, 335, 345, 346, 352, 366, 367, 380, 383, 397, 407, 411, 448, 451, 457, 459, 460, 519, 535, 553, 554, 570, 582, 584, 595, 597, 607, 609, 617, 623, 625, 635, 649, 652-654
Democratic-Republican Party (dem uh KRAT ik • ri PUHB li kuhn • PART ee) 135, 136, 139-141, 143, 176, 180, 187, 527
Democratic Republic of Germany (dem uh KRAT ik • ri PUHB lik • uhv • JUHR muh nee) 527
de Montcalm, Louis Joseph (LOO ee • jo SEF • duh • mahnt KAHM) 82, 83
Denmark (DEN mark) 26, 321, 374
de Santa Anna, Antonio López (an TOHN yoh • LOH pez • day • SANT uh • AN uh) 197
desert (DEZ uhrt) 286, 301, 400
Desilu (DEZ ee loo) 543
de Soto, Hernando (her NAN doh • day • SOH toh) 33
Detroit [Michigan] (di TROYT) 146, 426, 489
Devereux Station (dev uh ROH • STAY shuhn) 272
Devil's Den [Battle of Gettysburg] (DEV uhlz • den) 252
Dewey, Thomas E. (TAHM uhs • ee • DOOH wee) 518, 519
Dial [family] (DEYE uhl) 45
Dickinson, John (jahn • DIK uhn suhn) 98
dictatorships (dik TAYT uhr ships) 468-470
Diogo Cão (jee OH goh • kow) 22
direct primaries (duh REKT • PREYE mair eez) 367
discrimination (dis krim uh NAY shuhn) 324, 401, 459, 469-471, 489, 498, 547-549, 570, 571
Distinguished Flying Cross (dis TING gwisht • FLEYE ing • krahs) 498
Distinguished Service Cross (dis TING gwisht • SUHR vuhs • krahs) 492
District of Columbia (DIS trikt • uhv • kuh LUHM bee uh) 134, 137, 215, 218
Dix, Dorothea (dor uh THEE uh • diks) 262

Dodds, Baby (BAY bee • dahdz) 421
Dodds, Johnny (JAHN ee • dahdz) 421
Dodge City [Kansas] (dahj • SIT ee) 288
Dole, Robert (RAHB uht • dohl) 653, 654
dollar diplomacy (DAHL uhr • di PLOH muh see) 381, 382
Dominican Republic (duh MIN uh kuhn • ri PUHB lik) 29, 372, 374
Dorchester Heights [Boston] (DOR ches tuhr • heyets) 98, 100
Douglass, Frederick (FRED rik • DUHG luhs) 201, 222, 295
Douglas, Stephen A. (STEE vuhn • ay • DUHG luhs) 215, 220, 230-232, 234
draft (draft) 255, 400, 483, 489, 492, 577, 614
drought (drowt) 442
Draft Riots (draft • REYEuhts) 255
Dred Scott case (dred • skaht • kays) 226, 229, 234, 235
drugs (druhgz) 578, 580
Du Bois, W.E.B. (w • ee • bee • doo BOYZ) 401
Dukakis, Michael (MEYE kuhl • doo KAHK uhs) 635
Dunkirk (DUHN kuhrk) 471
Durant [Oklahoma] (duh RANT) 207
Dust Bowl (duhst • bohl) 442, 463
Dutry, Honore (AHN uh ray • DOO tree) 421

E

Eagle (EEG uhl) 561
Eagleton, Thomas (TAHM uhs • EEG uhl tuhn) 595
Earth (uhrth) 559, 561
East (eest) 122, 148, 164, 190, 192, 285, 288, 293, 299
East Coast (eest • kohst) 321
Easten Europe (EE stuhrn • YUHR uhp) 323
Eastern Front (EE stuhrn • fruhnt) 398, 399
Eastern Woodland (EE stuhrn • WOOD luhnd) 12, 13
East India Company (eest • IN dee uh • KUHM puh nee) 88
East Indies (eest • IN deez) 26, 28
East Jersey (eest • JUHRZ ee) 60, 62
Economic and Social Council (ek uh NAHM ik • uhnd • SOHSH uhl • KOWN suhl) 510
economy (i KAHN uh mee) 180, 182, 187-190, 192-195, 247, 264, 315, 316, 327-329, 338, 344, 349-352, 366, 368, 369, 383, 384, 395, 397, 399, 401, 411, 413, 415, 420, 425, 437-441, 444-447, 451-454, 457, 458, 460-462, 467-469, 491, 507, 510, 517, 518, 522, 524, 539, 575, 577, 601, 603, 608, 610, 616, 624-626, 631, 635, 636, 639, 641
Ederle, Gertrude (GER trood • ED uhr lee) 413, 414
Edison, Louis (TAHM uhs • ED uh suhn) 315
Edison, Thomas (TAHM uhs • ED uh suhn) 315
editorial cartoon (ed uh TOR ee uhl • kar TOON) 79, 335
education (ej uh KAY shuhn) 270, 274, 291, 300, 329, 331, 368, 370, 371, 460, 518, 545, 589, 623
Education, Department of (di PART ment • uhv • ej h KAY shuhn) 653
Egypt (EE juhpt) 378, 602, 603, 608-610
Egyptian-Israeli Peace Treaty (ee JIP shuhn • iz RAY lee • pees • TREE tee) 608
Eichmann, Adolph (AY dahlf • EYEKH muhn) 511
Einstein, Albert (AL buhrt • EYEN steyen) 494
Eisenhower, Dwight D. (dweyet • dee • EYEZ uhn how uhr) 449, 497, 502, 528, 535, 536, 539-542, 545, 548, 553, 623
El Caney, Battle of (BAT uhl • uhv • el • kuh NAY) 362
Electoral College (i LEK tuh ruhl • KAHL ij) 129, 133, 140, 141, 176-178, 182, 183, 235, 557
Electoral Commission (i LEK tuh ruhl • kuh MISH uhn) 278
electric power (i LEK truhk • POW uhr) 315, 330
elevated railways (EL uh vayt uhd • RAYL wayz) 329, 330
elevated trains (EL uh vayt uhd • traynz) 316
Elizabeth I (i LIZ uh buhth • thuh • fuhrst) 42, 44
Elizabeth II (i LIZ uh buhth • thuh • SEK uhnd) 19
Ellington, Duke (dook • EL ing tuhn) 421, 422
Ellis Island (EL uhs • EYE luhnd) 328
Emancipation Proclamation (ee mant suh PAY shuhn • prahk luh MAY shuhn) 252, 254, 265
embassies (EM buh seez) 426
embargoes (em BAR gohz) 602, 603, 641, 642, 645
Emerson, John (jahn • EM uhr suhn) 229
Emerson, Ralph Waldo (ralf • WAHL doh • EM uhr suhn) 96
Emperor [of Austria] (EM puhr uhr) 403
Endicott, Andrew (AN droo • EN duh kaht) 137
energy crisis (EN uhr jee • KREYE suhs) 604, 608
Energy, Department of (di PART muhnt • uhv • EN uhr jee) 653
England (ING luhnd) 19, 27, 31, 39-45, 47-51, 53, 55, 59-62, 66, 67, 75, 78, 86, 98, 115, 119, 165, 187, 193, 222, 226, 240, 314, 387, 395, 414, 422, 427, 480, 580
England, Church of (chuhrch • uhv • INGluhnd) 53, 55, 56, 57
English Channel (ING luhsh • CHAN uhl) 413, 414, 479
English Civil War (ING luhsh • SIV uhl • wor) 60
environment (in VEYE ruhn muhnt) 369, 382, 573, 605, 611
Eric the Red (AIR uhk • thuh • red) 26
Ericson, Leif (leef • AIR uhk suhn) 26, 29
Erie Canal (EER ee • kuh NAL) 192
Ervin, Sam (sam • UHRV uhn) 597
Eskimo (ES kuh moh) 10
Europe (YUHR uhp) 16, 19, 21, 26, 28, 29, 31, 40-45, 47, 51, 66, 68, 81, 83, 126, 135, 145, 146, 150, 151, 159, 160, 162, 167, 171-173, 190, 192, 193, 240, 287, 298, 314, 321, 322, 331, 359, 360, 372, 375, 376, 381, 387-391, 395, 400, 401, 405, 409, 420, 421, 425, 449, 463, 467, 473, 475, 476, 477, 479, 481, 482, 485, 490, 494, 497, 498, 502, 503, 507, 509, 510, 523,

524, 527, 530, 535, 577
Europe, Eastern (EEST uhrn • YUHR uhp) 523-525, 528
Europe, Western (WEST uhrn • YUHR uhp) 495, 497, 527, 528, 539
Evolution, Theory of (THEE uh ree • uhv • ev uh LOO shuhn) 427
Executive Branch (ig ZEK yuht iv • branch) 125, 128, 129, 134, 180, 181, 188, 199, 252, 271, 368, 369, 372, 381, 382, 397, 403-408, 425, 426, 430, 451-454, 457-459, 482, 483, 485, 488, 500, 501, 509, 517, 523, 524, 528, 529, 534, 535, 565-568, 570-572, 579, 584-588, 594-598, 601, 603, 604, 608, 609, 613-620, 625, 626, 629, 630-633, 635, 642-646
Executive Order (ig ZEK yuht iv • OR duhr) 488, 489, 565, 595
exploring (ik SPLOR ing) 31-34, 40-45
extermination camps (ik stuhr muh NAY shuhn • kamps) 481, 486, 511
Exxon Valdez (EKS sahn • val DEEZ) 605

F

factory (FAK tuh ree) 165, 167, 168, 188, 193, 194, 199, 401, 413, 438, 440, 458, 463, 470, 486, 489-491, 494, 503, 510, 537, 577, 608
Fairbanks, Douglas (DUHG luhs • FAIR bangks) 422
Fair Deal (fair • deel) 517-519
Fall, Albert M. (AL buhrt • em • fahl) 414, 415
farming (FARM ing) 6, 7, 11, 13, 22-24, 32, 56, 65-68, 75, 111, 164-167, 175, 193, 194, 203, 401, 420, 425, 437, 442, 446, 454, 459, 470, 522, 588, 614
Far North (fahr • north) 10
Fascist Party (FASH uhst • PART ee) 468, 495, 496
Fascists (FASH uhsts) 473, 474, 476
Faubus, Orval (OR vuhl • FAH buhs) 548
Federal Bureau of Investigation [FBI] (FED uh ruhl • BYOO roh • uhv • in vest uh GAY shuhn) 566, 597, 655
Federal Courts (FED uh ruhl • korts) 129, 133
Federalists (FED uh ruh luhsts) 130, 133, 134, 136, 139-142, 152
Federal Republic of Germany (FED uh ruhl • ri PUHB lik • uhv • JUHR muh nee) 527
Federal Reserve Act (FED uh ruhl • ri ZUHRV • akt) 384
feminism (FEM uh niz uhm) 575
Ferdinand (FUR duh nand) 27
54th Regiment, Massachusetts Volunteer Infantry (FIF tee forth • REJ uh muhnt • mass uh CHOO suhtz • vahl uhn TEER • IN fuhn tree) 254, 255
Fillmore, Millard (MIL uhrd • FIL mor) 215, 226
Finland (FIN luhnd) 387, 479
Finlay, Carlos Juan (KAR luhs • hwahn • fin LEYE) 378
First Bank of the United States (fuhrst • bank • uhv • thuh • yoo NEYET uhd • stayts) 182
First Continental Congress (fuhrst • kahnt uhn ENT uhl • KAHNG gruhs) 92, 93, 95
fishing (FISH ing) 10, 11, 13, 41, 66
Five Civilized Tribes (feyev • SIV uh leyezd • treyebz) 203-207
flag [U.S.] (flag) 151
Florida (FLOR uhd uh) 12, 31, 41, 42, 50, 61, 119, 123, 134, 161, 170, 171, 205, 438, 460, 611
Foch, Ferdinand (FUHRD uhn and • fohsh) 400
Food and Drug Administration (food • uhnd • druhg • uhd min uh STRAY shuhn) 369
Force Bill (fors • bil) 182
Ford, Gerald (JAIR uhld • ford) 598, 604, 607, 613
Ford, Henry (HEN ree • ford) 396, 420
Ford's Theater (fordz • THEE uht uhr) 265, 266
foreign aid (FOR uhn • ayd) 524, 609
Forestry Service (FOR uh stree • SUHR vuhs) 382
Formosa (for MOH suh) 529
Fort Caroline (fort • KAIR uh leyen) 42
Fort Christina (fort • kris TEEN uh) 48
Fort Donelson (fort • DAHN uhl suhn) 249
Fort Duquesne (fort • doo KAYN) 76, 81, 82
Fort Halifax (fort • HAHL uh faks) 77, 100
Fort Henry (fort • HEN ree) 249
Fort McHenry (fort • muh KEN ree) 150
Fort Nassau (fort • NAS ah) 47, 60
Fort Orange (fort • OR uhnj) 60
Fort Sumter (fort • SUHMP tuhr) 239-241
Fort Ticonderoga (fort • teye kahn duh ROH guh) 82, 95, 99, 100, 112
Founding Fathers (FOWND ing • FAHTH uhrz) 124, 534
France (frants) 27, 31, 41, 42, 47, 75, 76, 78, 81-84, 86, 113, 118, 119, 126, 134, 135, 139, 135, 146, 150, 159, 160, 162, 173, 175, 240, 249, 298, 325, 360, 373-375, 378, 387-389, 395, 398, 400, 403, 405, 407, 409, 414, 421, 473, 475, 479, 482, 492, 495-497, 501, 510, 528, 602
Francis I (FRANT suhs • thuh • fuhrst) 41
Franco, Francisco (fran SIS koh • FRANG koh) 473
Franklin, Benjamin (BEN juh muhn • FRANGK luhn) 78, 79, 103, 105, 119, 126, 130
Franklin, William (WIL yuhm • FRANGK luhn) 103, 104
Franz Ferdinand (franz • FUHRD uhn and) 388, 405
Franz Josef (franz • JOH.zuhf) 388, 403
Fredericksburg [Virginia] (FRED ruhks buhrg) 264
free enterprise (free • EN tuhr preyez) 368, 369, 383, 384
Free-Soil Party (free • soyl • PART ee) 213
Free Staters (free • STAYT uhrz) 224
Frémont, John C. (jahn • see • FREE mahnt) 226
French and Indian War (french • uhnd • IN dee uhn • wor) 76-84, 86, 95
French Revolution (french • rev uh LOO shuhn) 134, 135
Friedan, Betty (BET ee • free DAN) 575
Fugitive Slave Act (FYOO juht iv • slayv • akt) 218
Fundamental Orders (fuhn duh MENT uhl • ORD uhrz) 56

G

fur trade (fuhr • trayd) 66, 75, 190

G-2 [British Intelligence Service] (jee • too) 482
Gage, Thomas (TAHM uhs • gayj) 93, 94, 98
Galena [Illinois] (guh LEEN uh) 336
Galt, Edith Bolling (EE duhth • BOHL ing • gahlt) 408
Galveston [Texas] (GAL vuh stuhn) 367
gangs (gangz) 328, 426, 427
Garbo, Greta (GRET uh • GAR boh) 422
Garfield, James A. (jaymz • ay • GAR feeld) 335
Gates, Horatio (huh RAY shee oh • gaytz) 117
Gemini program (JEM uh neye • PROH gruhm) 560, 561
General Assembly (JEN uh ruhl • uh SEM blee) 510
General Foods Corporation (JEN uh ruhl • foodz • KOR puh RAY shuhn) 312
Genoa [Italy] (JEN oh uh) 26
Gentlemen's Agreement (JENT uhl muhnz • uh GREE muhnt) 377
George II (jorj • thuh • SEK uhnd) 81
George III (jorj • thuh • thuhrd) 86, 93, 99, 104, 105, 106
Georgia (JOR juh) 61, 62, 92, 95, 98, 99, 107, 117, 130, 135, 170, 176, 204-206, 236, 261, 502, 607, 611, 652
German Air Force (JUHRM uhn • air • fors) 473, 480
German Americans (JUHRM uhn • uh MAIR uh kuhns) 488
German Army (JUHRM uhn • AR mee) 474
Germany (JUHRM uh nee) 111, 114, 387, 389, 390, 395, 396-401, 403, 405, 408, 409, 468-471, 473-477, 479, 480, 482, 485, 486, 492, 494-498, 501, 502, 507-509, 511, 522, 525, 527, 528, 618, 639
Gestapo (guh STAHP oh) 509
Gettysburg [Pennsylvania] (GET eez buhrg) 252, 253
Gettysburg, Battle of (BAT uhl • uhv • GET eez buhrg) 253, 254
Ghent, Treaty of (TREE tee • uhv • gent) 151
ghettos (GET ohz) 470
Gilbert, Humphrey (HUHMP free • GIL buhrt) 42
Gingrich, Newt (noot • GING ruhch) 652
Gish, Lillian (LIL ee uhn • gish) 422
glasnost (GLAZ nohst) 629
Glenn, John (jahn • glen) 560
Glory (GLOR ee) 255
gold (gohld) 204, 213, 214, 285, 287, 298, 351
Goldwater, Barry (BAIR ee • GOLD wah tuhr) 570
Gompers, Samuel (SAM yuhl • GAHM puhrz) 340
Gone with the Wind (gahn • with • thuh • wind) 462
Gorbachev, Mikhail (mik HEYEL • GOR buh chahf) 525, 629, 636
Gorgas, William (WIL yuhm • GOR guhs) 378
Gorges, Ferdinando (FUHRD uhn AND oh • GOR juhz) 59, 60, 62
grain mills (grayn • milz) 203
Granada (gruh NAY duh) 173
Grand Banks (grand • bangks) 41
Grandfather Clause (GRAND fahth uhr • klahz) 292
Grange (graynj) 345
Grant, Ulysses S. (yoo LIS eez • es • grant) 173, 249, 254, 259, 260, 276, 333, 334, 336, 347, 360, 414
Great Basin (grayt • BAY suhn) 10, 11
Great Britain (grayt • BRIT uhn) 66, 75-77, 81-84, 86-89, 92, 93, 95, 98-100, 103, 104, 111-115, 117-120, 123, 124, 134, 135, 139, 141, 145-148, 150-153, 160, 170, 171, 187, 197, 198, 203, 240, 241, 243, 298, 360, 361, 363, 375
Great Compromise (grayt • KAHM pruh meyeze) 128
Great Debate (grayt • di BAYT) 195
Great Depression (grayt • di PRESH uhn) 440, 442, 444-449, 451-455, 457, 458, 460-462, 467-469, 510, 601, 616, 635
Great Lakes [area] (grayt • layks) 7, 12, 14, 75, 82
Great Lakes [people] (grayt • layks) 12
Great Plains [area] (grayt • playnz) 12, 13, 285-288, 297-299, 301, 316, 321, 322
Great Plains [people] (grayt • playnz) 12, 13
Great Society (grayt • suh SEYE uh tee) 570, 582
Great Spirit (grayt • SPIR uht) 148
Greece (grees) 172, 523
Green, Ernest (UHRN uhst • green) 548
Greene, Nathaniel (nuh THAN yuhl • green) 118
Greenhow, Rose O'Neal (rohz • oh NEEL • GREEN how) 262
Greenland (GREEN luhnd) 26
Green Mountain Boys (GREEN • MOWN tuhn • boyz) 95
Greensboro [North Carolina] (GREENS buhr oh) 546
Grenville, George (jorj • GREN vil) 86
gridlock (GRID lahk) 649, 653
Griffith, D. W. (dee • w • GRIF uhth) 421, 422
Guadalcanal (gwahd uhl kuh NAL) 500
Guadalupe Hidalgo, Treaty of (TREE tee • uhv • gwahd uh LOO pay • hi DAHL goh) 200
Guam (gwahm) 485
Guernica [Spain] (GUHR ni kuh) 473
Guilford Court House [North Carolina] (GIL fuhrd • kort • hows) 118
Guiteau, Charles J. (charlz • jay • GOO toh) 335
Gustav V (GOOS tahf • thuh • fifth) 385

Gypsies (JIP seez) 469, 481

H

Haiti (HAYT ee) 29, 162, 374
Halifax [Canada] (HAL uh FAKS) 100
Hamilton, Alexander (al ig ZAN duhr • HAM uhl tuhn) 130, 134, 135, 139, 141
Hancock, John (jahn • HAN kahk) 94, 106
handicapped people (HAN dee kapt • PEE puhl) 469, 481
Handy, W. C. (w • see • HAN dee) 421
Hardin, Lil (lil • HAR duhn) 421
Harding, Warren G. (WOR uhn • HARD ing) 411, 412, 414, 415, 426
Harlan, John (jahn • HAR luhn) 293
Harpers Ferry [Virginia] (HAR puhrs • FAIR ee) 231, 234, 235
Harrison, Benjamin (BEN juh muhn • HAIR uh suhn) 346
Harrison, William Henry (WIL yuhm • HEN ree • HAIR uh suhn) 188, 189
Hartford [Connecticut] (HART fuhrd) 152
Hartford Convention (HART fuhrd • kuhn VEN shuhn) 152
Haupt, Hermann (HER muhn • hahpt) 277
Havana Harbor [Cuba] (huh VAN uh • HAR buhr) 362
Hawaii (huh WEYE ee) 324, 361, 362, 484
Hay, John (jahn • hay) 360
Hayes, Ira H. (EYE ruh • aytch • hayz) 302
Haymarket Riot (HAY mar kuht • REYE uht) 340, 341
Haymarket Square (HAY mar kuht • skwair) 341
Hayes, Lucy Webb (LOO see • web • hayz) 279
Hayes, Rutherford B. (RUHTH uh fuhrd • bee • hayz) 277-279
health care (helth • kair) 571, 611, 650
Henrietta Maria (hen ree ET uh • muh REE uh) 60
Henry, Prince (prints • HEN ree) 21
Henry, John (jahn • HEN ree) 307
Henry, Patrick (PA trik • HEN ree) 92, 130
Henry IV (HEN ree • thuh • forth) 47
Henry VIII (HEN ree • thuh • aytth) 41
Hessian (HESH uhn) 111
Hickam Field [Hawaii] (HIK uhm • feeld) 485
Hiding Place, The (thuh • HEYED ing • plays) 486
Hirihito (hir oh HEE toh) 484, 503
Hiroshima [Japan] (hir uh SHEE muh) 501, 504, 505
Hispanic Americans (his PAN ik • uh MAIR uh kuhns) 489, 547, 576, 589
Hispaniola (his pan YOH luh) 28, 29, 162
Hiss, Alger (AL juhr • HIS) 519
Hitler, Adolf (AY dahlf • HIT luhr) 468-471, 473-477, 479-481, 496, 497, 502, 509
Holland [the Netherlands] (HAHL uhnd) 53
Hollywood [California] (HAHL ee wood) 422, 423, 461, 543
Holocaust (HOH luh kahst) 481, 517
Holy Land (HOH lee • land) 16
Homestead Act of 1862 (HOHM sted • akt • uhv • AYT teen • SIKS tee • too) 285, 286, 314, 321
homosexuals (hoh muh SEK shuh wuhls) 481
Hood, John B. (jahn • bee • hood) 259, 260
Hooker, Joseph (JOH zuhf • HOOK uhr) 253
Hoover, Herbert (HUHR buhrt • HOOH vuhr) 414, 437, 440, 444, 446-449, 451, 535
Hoovervilles (HOOH vuhr vilz) 448
Hope, Bob (bahb • hohp) 541
Hopi (HOH pee) 12
hostages (HAH stuh juhz) 614-619, 630, 632, 641
Hottentots (HAHT uhn tahts) 22
House of Representatives [U.S.] (hows • uhv • rep ri ZEN tuh tivs) 213, 237, 449, 535, 553, 568, 570, 589, 611, 625, 627, 652, 653
housing (HOW zing) 518, 571, 624, 635
Houston, Sam (sam • HYOO stuhn) 197
Howe, William (WIL yuhm • how) 98, 100, 111, 112, 113
Huckleberry Finn (HUHK uhl ber ee • fin) 347
Hudson Bay (HUHD suhn • bay) 47
Hudson, Henry (HEN ree • HUHD suhn) 47
Hudson River (HUHD suhn • RIV uhr) 47, 192
Hughes, Charles Evans (charlz • EV uhnz • hyooz) 397
Hull House (huhl • hows) 331
Humphrey, Hubert (HYOO buhrt • HUM free) 582, 584
Hungary (HUHNG guh ree) 387, 497, 523, 525
hunting (HUHNT ing) 5, 10, 22, 203, 287, 297
Huron-Algonquian (HYOOR ohn • al GAHN kwee uhn) 76
Hussein, Saddam (suh DAHM • hooh SAYN) 153, 641-643, 645, 646, 655
Hutchison, Anne Marbury (ann • MAR buhr ee • HUHCH uhn suhn) 57

I

I Love Lucy (eye • luhv • LOOH see) 541, 543
Ice Age (eyes • ayj) 5
Iceland (EYES luhnd) 26, 528
Idaho (EYED uh hoh) 197
Illinois (il uh NOY) 175, 178, 201, 229, 230, 265, 288, 336, 557
immigrants (IM i gruhnts) 139, 193, 194
immigration (im uh GRAY shuhn) 4-7, 26, 28, 29, 30-34, 41, 42, 46-48, 52-57, 58-62, 75, 76, 191-195, 293, 294, 316, 321-325, 377, 395, 405, 506, 424, 428, 430,539
    African (AF ri kuhn) 50, 64, 68, 107, 194

Austrian (AHS tree uhn) 392
British (BRIT uhsh) 42-45, 48-62, 75, 76, 192, 395
Catholic (KATH uh lik) 60, 62, 75,323,428
Chinese (CHEYEN eez) 293-294, 324
Communist (KAHM yuh nuhst) 430
Danish (DAYN uhsh) 321
Dutch (duhch) 46-48, 321
French (french) 41, 42 46, 47, 75, 395
German (JUHRM uhn) 191, 321, 395
Irish (EYE ruhsh) 191, 193, 316, 405, 406
Italian (i TAL yuhn) 293, 316, 406
Japanese (JAP uh neez) 294, 377
Jewish (JOO ish) 323, 428
Native American (NAYT uhv • uh MAIR uh kuhn) 4-7, 28
Norwegian (nor WEE juhn) 321
Polish (POH luhsh) 293
Protestant (PRAHT uh stuhnt) 53-57, 59-62, 75, 323
Russian (RUSHSH uhn) 293, 395
Spanish (SPAN ish) 28, 29, 30-34, 42,46
Swedish(SWEED ish) 46-48, 321
Viking (VEYE king) 26
impeachment (im PEECH muhnt) 271, 595, 596, 598
impressment (im PRES muhnt) 145, 152, 160
inauguration (i nahg yuh RAY shuhn) 188, 239, 566, 598, 618
Inca (ING kuh) 31, 32
Inchon [Korea] (IN chahn) 533
income tax (IN kuhm • taks) 250, 346, 381
indentured servants (in DEN chuhrd • SUHR vuhnts) 194
independence (in duh PEN duhnts) 103, 104, 105, 106, 119, 197, 240, 242, 243, 258, 363, 372, 376
Independence, Declaration of (dek luh RAY shuhn • uhv • in duh PEN duhnts) 105, 106, 126, 216
Independence Hall [Philadelphia] (in duh PEN duhnts • hahl) 125
India (IN dee uh) 23, 27
Indiana (in dee AN uh) 178
Indian Territory (IN dee uhn • TAIR uh tor ee) 204-206, 268, 288, 299, 300, 301
Indian Wars (IN dee uhn • worz) 299, 300
indigo (IN duh goh) 165
Indochina (in doh CHEYE nuh) 483, 484
industry (IN duhs tree) 66, 122, 164, 165, 167, 175, 304-306, 309, 310, 312, 315, 316, 401, 414, 438, 440, 441, 467, 470, 522, 543
inflation (in FLAY shuhn) 491, 539, 575, 601, 603, 608, 616, 625, 626
integration (in tuh GRAY shuhn) 545, 548, 576, 582
Interior, Secretary of the (SEK ruh tair ee • uhv • thuh • in TIR ee uhr) 414, 415
Internal Revenue, Bureau of (BYUHR oh • uhv • in TUHRN uhl • REV uh noo) 425, 426
International Court of Justice (int uhr NASH uhn uhl • kort • uhv • JUS tuhs) 510, 616
International League for Peace and Freedom (int uhr NASH uhn uhl • leeg • fohr • pees • uhnd • FREE duhm) 331
Interstate Commerce Commission (INT uhr stayt • KAHM uhrs • kuh MISH uhn) 369
Intolerable Acts (in TAHL uhr uh buhl • akts) 89, 92, 95, 99
inventions (in VEN shuhnz) 166, 168, 192-194, 250, 314-316, 398, 419-421, 437, 442, 480
Iran (i RAHN) 613, 615-618, 630-633, 641, 655
Iran-Contra Affair (i RAHN • KAHN truh • uh FAIR) 631-633
Iran, Shah of (shah • uhv • i RAHN) 614, 615, 641
Iraq (i RAHK) 153, 602, 617, 631, 641-646
Ireland (EYER luhnd) 193, 387
Ireland, Republic of (ri PUHB lik • uhv • EYER luhnd) 207, 406
iron (EYE uhrn) 285, 305, 306, 315
Iron Curtain (EYE uhrn • KUHR tuhn) 522, 523, 525, 639
Iroquois (EER uh kwoy) 76, 78
irrigation (eer uh GAY shuhn) 286
Isabella (is uh BEL uh) 27
Islam (IZ lahm) 614, 630, 641
Israel (IZ ray uhl) 511, 517, 520, 602, 603, 608-610, 630, 643, 655
Italian Americans (i TAL yuhn • uh MAIR uh kuhnz) 488
Italy (IT uh lee) 26, 28, 31, 41, 293, 316, 360, 375, 387-389, 406, 422, 468, 473, 474, 479, 485, 492, 495-498, 502, 528
Iwo Jima (EE woh • JEE muh) 302

J

Jackson, Andrew (AN droo • JAK suhn) 151, 170, 171, 176, 177, 180-183, 187, 188, 189, 203-205, 225, 370
Jackson, Helen Hunt (HEL uhn • hunt • JAK suhn) 300
Jamaica (juh MAY kuh) 49, 151
James River (jaymz • RIV uhr) 47, 49
Jamestown [Virginia] (JAYMZ town) 47, 48, 49, 50, 51, 62, 65, 67, 194
James, Duke of York and Albany (jaymz • dook • uhv • york • uhnd • AHL buh nee) 60
James I (jaymz • thuh • fuhrst) 47, 51, 53, 55, 59
Japan (juh PAN) 28, 294, 302, 359, 360, 364, 376, 377, 381, 389, 467, 474, 475, 479, 483-485, 492, 494, 500-505, 507-509, 528, 529, 533, 631
Japanese Americans (JAP uh neez • uh MAIR uh kuhnz) 488, 489, 492
Japanese Army (JAP uh neez • AR mee) 461, 492, 503, 508
Japanese Navy (JAP uh neez • NAY vee) 504, 508
jazz (jaz) 421, 422
Jefferson, Thomas (TAHM uhs • JEF uhr suhn) 92, 105, 106, 134, 135, 139-143, 159, 160, 195, 203, 370

Jerusalem (juh ROOS uh luhm) 602, 603
Jewish (JOO ish) 323
Jewish Documentation Center (JOO ish • dahk yuh muhn TAY shuhn • SEN tuhr) 511
"Jim Crow" laws (jim • kroh • lahz) 547
jobs (jahbz) 220, 277, 304, 307, 316, 322, 327-329, 331, 333-335, 338-341, 366-368, 378, 401, 413, 415, 438, 440, 441, 444-449, 451-454, 457-461, 490, 517, 539, 540, 547, 575, 576, 611, 623, 624, 631, 635
John Paul II, Pope (pohp • jahn • pahl • thuh • SEK uhnd) 525
Johnson, Andrew (AN droo • JAHN suhn) 173, 266, 267, 270, 271, 359
Johnson, Bill (bil • JAHN suhn) 421
Johnson, Lady Bird (LAY dee • buhrd • JAHN suhn) 566, 573
Johnson, Lyndon (LIN duhn • JAHN suhn) 518, 547, 549, 559, 566, 570, 572, 579, 582
Johnston, Joseph E. (JOH zuhf • ee • JAHN stuhn) 248, 260, 261
Joint Chiefs of Staff, Chairman of (chair muhn • uhv • thuh • joynt • cheefs • uhv • staf) 534, 647
Jones, Bobby (BAHB ee • johnz) 413
Jones, John Paul (jahn • pahl • johnz) 115
Joplin, Scott (skaht • JAHP luhn) 421
Jordan (JOR duhn) 602
Judiciary Act (joo DISH ee air ee • akt) 142
Judicial Branch (joo DISH uhl • branch) 125, 128, 129, 133, 142, 202, 203, 226, 229, 230, 293, 344, 368, 369, 458, 459, 545, 546, 547, 548, 594-598, 619, 620
Jungle, The (thuh • JUHNG guhl) 351
Justice, Department of (di PART muhnt • uhv • JUHS tuhs) 430, 547, 568, 598

K

Kaiser Wilhelm II (KEYE zuhr • WIL helm • thuh • SEK uhnd) 375
Kansas (KAN zuhs) 33, 221, 224, 225, 227, 288, 299, 409, 431, 545, 654
Kansas-Nebraska Act (KAN zuhs • nuh BRAS kuh • akt) 221, 224, 225
Keaton, Buster (BUHS tuhr • KEE tuhn) 422
Kelly, William (WIL yuhm • KEL ee) 314
Kennebec River (KEN e bek • RIV uhr) 77
Kennedy, Anthony (AN thun ee • KEN uh dee) 599
Kennedy, Jacqueline (JAK wuh lin • KEN uh dee) 553, 564-566
Kennedy, John F. (jahn • ef • KEN uh dee) 549, 553-555, 557, 561, 564-568, 570, 595
Kennedy, Joseph (JOH sef • KEN uh dee) 475
Kent State University (kent • stayt • yoo nuh VERS uh tee) 579
Kentucky (kuhn TUHK ee) 140, 145, 151, 176
Key, Francis Scott (FRANT suhs • skaht • kee) 151
Keynes, John Maynard (jahn • MAY nuhrd • kaynz) 451, 452
Khomeini, Ayatollah Ruhollah (eye uh TOHL uh • ruh HOHL uh • koh MAY nee) 614
Kim Il Sung (kim • il • SUNG) 537
Kim Jong Il (kim • ZHAHNG • il) 537
King, Martin Luther, Jr. (MAR tuhn • LOOH thuhr • king • JOOHN yuhr) 545-547, 575, 578, 579
King's Mountain [North and South Carolina] (kingz • MOWN tuhn) 118
Kiowa [Kansas] (KEYE oh wuh) 431
Kirby-Smith, Edmond (ED muhnd • KUHR bee • smith) 260, 261
Kissinger, Henry (HEN ree • KIS uhn juhr) 595
Kitchen Cabinet (KICH uhn • KAB nuht) 181
Klansman, The (thuh • KLANS muhn) 422
Knights of Labor (neyets • uhv • LAY buhr) 340, 342
Knox, Henry (HEN ree • nahx) 100, 134
Know-Nothing Party (noh • NUHTH ing • PAR tee) 226, 235
Kongo (KONG goh) 22
Korea (kuh REE uh) 501, 529, 571
Korea, North (north • kuh REE uh) 529, 530, 533-537, 586
Korea, South (sowth • kuh REE uh) 529, 530, 533-536
Korean Peninsula (kuh REE uhn • puh NIN suh luh) 529
Korean War (kuh REE uhn • wor) 529-537, 647
Khrushchev, Nikita (nuh KEE tuh • KROOS chawf) 555, 556
Krazy Kat (KRAYZ ee • kat) 541
Ku Klux Klan (koo • kluks • klan) 273, 277, 278, 422, 428, 429
Kurds (kurdz) 646
Kuwait (kooh WAYT) 641-645

L

labor (LAY buhr) 168, 193, 194
Labor and Commerce, Department of (di PART muhnt • uhv • LAY buhr • uhnd • KAHM uhrs) 369
labor unions (LAY buhr • YOON yuhns) 338-342
Laika (LEYE kuh) 559
Lake Champlain (layk • sham PLAYN) 82
Lake Erie (layk • EER ee) 147, 192
Lake Erie, Battle of (BAT uhl • uhv • layk • EER ee) 147
Lake Placid (layk • PLAS uhd) 618
Lake Superior (layk • suh PEER ee uhr) 315
Landon, Alf (alf • LAN duhn) 458
land run (land ruhn) 301
Laos (lows) 585
Lathrop, Julia C. (JOOL ee uh • see • LAY thruhp) 381
Latin America (LAT uhn • uh MAIR uh kuh) 171, 173, 372, 378, 381, 608, 630
Laurel, Stan (stan • LOR uhl) 422
Lawrence [Kansas] (LAR uhnts) 224
Lazarus, Emma (EM uh • LAZ uh ruhs) 325
League of Nations (leeg • uhv • NAY shuhns) 403, 405-408, 467, 474, 475, 500, 509

Lebanon (LEB uh nahn) 602, 630
Lee, "Lighthorse" Henry (LEYET hors • HEN ree • lee) 243
Lee, Richard Henry (RICH uhrd • HEN ree • lee) 92, 104, 106
Lee, Robert E. (RAHB uhrt • ee • lee) 242, 243, 249, 253, 254, 259, 260, 265, 267
Left Hand (left • hand) 299
Leiden [the Netherlands] (LEYE duhn) 53
Legislative Branch (LEDJ uhs lay tuhv • branch) 125, 127, 128, 133, 134, 145, 146, 197, 229, 230, 271, 301, 341, 344, 390, 403-408, 457-459, 476, 482, 483, 485, 509, 523, 524, 528, 529, 534, 535, 541, 546, 547, 559, 568, 587, 588, 594-598, 603, 604, 608, 609, 613, 614, 616, 625, 626, 631, 632, 635
L'Enfant, Pierre (pee AIR • LAHN fahnt) 137
Lenin, V. I. (vee • eye • LEN uhn) 399, 429, 430, 522
Lennon, John (jahn • LEN uhn) 580
Lexington [Massachusetts] (LEK sing tuhn) 93, 94, 96, 100
Lewis, Meriwether (MAIR ih weth uhr • LOO uhs) 159
Liaotung Peninsula (lee OW dung • puh NIN suh luh) 376
Libya (LIB ee uh) 630
Life of General Villa, The (thuh • leyef • uhv • JEN uh ruhl • VEE yuh) 423
Liliuokalani (li LEE woh kuh LAHN ee) 361
Lima [Peru] (LEE muh) 32
limited government [federal level] (LIM uh tuhd • GUHV uhrn muhnt) 141, 143, 159, 167, 175, 176, 180, 181, 182, 187, 188, 333, 340, 344, 415, 437, 441, 446, 454, 457, 518, 519, 539, 570, 616, 623, 626, 649, 650, 653, 654
Lincoln, Abraham (AY bruh ham • LING kuhn) 201, 230-232, 234-236, 239, 240, 243, 247, 249, 252, 253, 255, 258, 260, 262, 264-267, 271, 359, 408, 459
Lincoln, Mary Todd (MAIR ee • tahd • LING kuhn) 243, 265
Lincoln-Douglas Debates (LING kuhn • DUHG luhs • duh BAYTZ) 230-232
Lincoln Memorial (LING kuhn • muh MOR ee uhl) 465
List of Resolves (list • uhv • ri SAHLVZ) 92, 93
Little Rock [Arkansas] (LIT uhl • rahk) 548
Liverpool [England] (LIV uhr pool) 580
Livingston, Robert (RAHB uhrt • LIV ing stuhn) 105
loans (lohnz) 187, 188, 327, 381, 382, 384, 425, 438-442, 445-448, 453, 601
Lodge, Henry Cabot (HEN ree • KAB uht • lahj) 404, 405
London [England] (LUHN duhn) 51, 399
London Company (LUHN duhn • KUHMP uh nee) 47, 48, 53, 62, 494
Long, Huey (HYOO ee • lahng) 457, 458
Loop [Nebraska] (loop) 13
Los Alamos [New Mexico] (lahs • AL uh mohs) 503
Los Angeles [California] (lahs • AN juh luhs) 199, 221, 419, 422, 578, 652
Louisbourg [Canada] (LOO uhs buhrg) 82
Louisiana (loo ee zee AN uh) 75, 159, 160, 162, 236, 260, 261, 277, 291, 293, 312, 457, 631
Louisiana Purchase (loo ee zee AN uh • PUHR chuhs) 159, 160, 164, 175, 190
Louis XIV (LOO ee • thuh • for TEENTH) 75
Louis XV (LOO ee • thuh • fif TEENTH) 75
Louis XVI (LOO ee • thuh • siks TEENTH) 134, 135
Louis XVIII (LOO ee • thuh • ay TEENTH) 160
Lowell, Francis (FRANT suhs LOH uhl) 165
Loyalist (LOY uhl uhst) 100, 103, 117, 118
Ludwig, Mary (MAIR ee • LUHD wig) 101
Luftwaffe (LOOFT waf uh) 480
Lumbees (LUHM beez) 45
lumbering (LUHM ber ing) 66
Lusitania (loo suh TAY nee uh) 396
Luxembourg (LUHK suhm buhrg) 479, 496
lynchings (LINCH ingz) 429

M

MacArthur, Douglas (DUHG luhs • muh KAR thuhr) 449, 485, 533-535
Macchu Piccu [Peru] (MAHCH oo • PEEK choo) 33
MacDonough, Thomas (TAHM uhs • muhk DAHN uh) 147
Madison, James (jaymz • MAD uh suhn) 130, 139, 142, 150, 195
Magellan, Ferdinand (FER duh nand • muh JEL uhn) 31
Maginot Line (MAZH uh noh• leyen) 479
mail (mayl) 192
Maine (mayn) 59, 62, 77, 99, 175
malaria (muh LAIR ee uh) 378
Malindi [Africa] (mah LIN dee) 23
Manassas [Virginia] (muh NAS uhs) 247, 248
Manchuria (man CHUR ee uh) 467, 501
Mandela, Nelson (NEL suhn • man DEL uh) 632, 638
Manhattan Island (man HAT uhn • EYE luhnd) 47
Manifest Destiny (MAN uh fest • DES tuh nee) 198
Manikongo [Africa] (man ee KON goh) 22
Manila Bay [Philippines] (muh NIL uh • bay) 362
manufacturing (man yoo FAK chuhr ing) 164, 165, 167, 168, 175, 193, 241, 304-306, 309, 310, 312, 315, 316, 401, 438, 489-491, 494
Mao Tse-dong (mow • zuh DAHNG) 528, 529, 537
Marbury, William (WIL yuhm • MAR buhr ee) 142
Marshall, George C. (jorj • see • MAR shuhl) 524
Marshall, John (jahn • MAR shuhl) 205
Marshall Plan (MAR shuhl • plan) 524
Marshall, Thurgood (THUHR good • MAR shuhl) 547, 549

Maryland (MAIR uh luhnd) 60, 62, 95, 124, 130, 134, 222, 247, 252, 317, 449, 540, 607
Mason, John (jahn • MAY suhn) 59, 62
mass production (mas • pruh DUHK shuhn) 309, 310
Massachusetts (mas uh CHOO suhtz) 54-57, 59-62, 89, 93, 94, 98-101, 105, 107, 120, 123, 130, 227, 255, 370, 412, 413, 553
Massachusetts Bay Company (mass uh CHOO suhtz • bay • KUHMP uh nee) 55
Massasoit (mass uh SOYT) 55
Maya (MEYE yuh) 11
Mayans (MEYE yuhns) 8, 11
Mayflower (MAY flow uhr) 53, 54
Mayflower Compact (MAY flow uhr • KAHM pakt) 54, 56
McCarthy, Joseph (JOH suhf • muh KAR thee) 540, 541
McCartney, Paul (pahl • muh KART nee) 580
McClellan, George B. (jorj • bee • muh KLEL uhn) 249, 258
McCormick, Cyrus (SEYE ruhs • muh KOR muhk) 314
McCormick Harvester Company (muh KOR muhk • HAR vuhst uhr • KUHM puh nee) 341
McDowell, Irvin (IR vuhn • muhk DOWL) 248
McGovern, George (jorg • muh GUHV uhrn) 595
McHenry, John (jahn • muhk HEN ree) 218
McIntosh, Dan N. (dan • en • MAK uhn tosh) 268
McKinley, William (WIL yuhm • muh KIN lee) 352, 360, 361, 363, 364, 373
McLean [family] (muh KLAYN) 260, 261
Medicaid (MED uh kayd) 571
Medicare (MED uh kair) 571
Medicine Lodge [Kansas] (MED uh suhn • lahj) 431
Mediterranean Sea (med uh tuh RAY nee uhn • see) 373, 378
Mein Kampf (meyen • kahmf) 477, 480
Mellon, Andrew (AN droo • MEL uhn) 414
Memphis [Tennessee] (MEM fuhs) 579
mercenaries (MUHRS uhn air eez) 111
Mercury Program (MUHR kyuh ree • PROH gram) 560
Metcalf, Ralph (ralf • MET kaf) 471
Mexican-American War (MEK si kuhn • uh MAIR uh kuhn • wor) 173, 198-201
Mexican Army (MEK si kuhn • AR mee) 423
Mexico (MEK si koh) 6, 11, 13, 14, 31, 33, 40, 41, 171, 197-200, 213, 215, 218, 219
Mexico City (MEK si koh • SIT ee) 199
Mexico, Gulf of (guhlf • uhv • MEK si koh) 192
Miami [Florida] (meye AM ee) 584
Michigan (MISH i guhn) 315
Middle Colonies (MID uhl • KAHL uh neez) 66, 69
Middle East (MID uhl • eest) 16, 17
Midway Island (MID way • EYE luhnd) 359
Midwest (mid WEST) 12
Miles, Nelson A. (NEL suhn • ay • meyelz) 363
militia (muh LISH uh) 93, 94, 95, 100
mining (MEYEN ing) 204, 213, 214, 285, 293, 463
Minnesota (min uh SOHT uh) 321
minorities (mun NOR uh teez) 481, 489
Minuit, Peter (PEET uhr • MIN yuh whuht) 47
minutemen (MIN uht men) 93, 94
Mississippi [state] (mis uh SIP ee) 205, 207, 231, 236, 237, 274
Mississippi River (mis uh SIP ee • RIV uhr) 12, 33, 81, 83, 114, 119, 123, 134, 151, 159, 164, 192, 203, 221, 237, 241, 298
Missouri (muh ZUHR uh) 12, 175, 177, 224, 229, 247, 252, 523
Missouri Compromise (muh ZUHR ee • KAM pruh meyez) 175, 221, 236
Mitchell, Margaret (MAR guh ruht • MICH uhl) 462
Moctezuma (mok tuh ZOO muh) 31, 32
Model T (MAHD uhl • tee) 420
Molino del Rey, Battle of (BAT uhl • uhv • moh LEE noh • del • ray) 199
Mombasa [Africa] (mahm BAH sah) 23, 24
Mongolia (mahn GOHL yuh) 501
Monmouth [New Hampshire] (MAHN muhth) 101
Monongahela [river] (muh nahn guh HEE luh) 76
monopolies (muh NAHP uh leez) 310, 311, 344, 349, 368, 380, 383, 440, 441, 359, 360, 372, 381, 382
Monroe Doctrine (muhn ROH • DAHK truhn) 172, 173
Monroe, James (jaymz • muhn ROH) 150, 170, 171, 172, 359
Montana (mahn TAN uh) 197, 300, 301
Monterey [Mexico] (mahnt uh RAY) 199
Montgomery [Alabama] (muhnt GUHM uh ree) 236, 247
Montgomery, Richard (RICH uhrd • muhnt GUHM uh REE) 99, 100
Montreal (mahn tree AHL) 47
Moody, Helen Wills (HEL uhn • wilz • MOOD ee) 413
Morgan, Daniel (DAN yuhl • MOR guhn) 118
Morocco (muh RAHK oh) 390, 473
Morris, Esther (ES tuhr • MOR uhs) 416
Morris, Lewis (LOO uhs • MOR uhs) 106
Moscow [Russia] (MAHS kow) 556, 587, 614
Mott, Lucretia (lu KREE shuh • maht) 216
movies (MOOV eez) 421, 422, 461, 462, 540, 543
Mozambique [Africa] (moh zahm BEEK) 23, 24
muckrakers (MUK rayk uhrz) 351

Mugwumps (MUHG wuhmps) 334, 335
Muhammad (moh HAHM uhd) 16
Munich [Germany] (MYOOH nik) 475, 476
Murrah Federal Building (MUHR uh • FED uh ruhl • BILD ing) 655
Muslim (MUHZ luhm) 16, 17, 22, 23, 388, 614, 630, 641, 655
Mussolini, Benito (buh NEET oh • mooh suh LEE nee) 468-470, 473, 479, 495, 496, 502
Mutual Film Company (MYOOHCH uh wuhl • film • KUHM puh nee) 423

N

Nagasaki [Japan] (nahg uh SAHK ee) 501, 503-505
Napoleon III (nuh POH lee uhn • thuh • thuhrd) 173
Nashville [Tennessee] (NASH vil) 259
Nast, Thomas (TAHM uhs • nast) 335
Nation, Carry (KAIR ee • NAY shuhn) 431
National Aeronautics and Space Administration [NASA] (NASH uh nuhl • air uh NAHT iks • uhnd • spays • uhd min uh STRAY shuhn) (NA suh) 559-601
National Association for the Advancement of Colored People [NAACP] (NASH uh nuhl • uh sohsh ee AY shuhn • for • thuh • uhd VANS muhnt • uhv • KUHL uhrd • PEE puhl) 401, 429, 549
National Colored Farmers' Alliance (NASH uh nuhl • KUHL uhrd • FAR muhrz • uh LEYE uhns) 345
National Congress of American Indians (NASH uh nuhl • KAHNG gruhs • uhv • uh MAIR uh kuhn • IN dee uhnz) 576
National Football Hall of Fame (NASH uh nuhl • FOOT bahl • hahl • uhv • faym) 385
National Football League (NASH uh nuhl • FOOT bahl • leeg) 385
National Guard (NASH uh nuhl • gard) 483, 548, 578, 579
National Labor Union (NASH uh nuhl • LAY buhr • YOON yuhn) 339, 340
National Organization of Women (NASH uh nuhl • or guh nuh ZAY shuhn • uhv • WIM uhn) 575
National Republican Party (NASH uh nuhl • ri PUHB li kuhn • PART ee) 180-183
National Youth Administration (NASH uh nuhl • yoohth • uhd min uh STRAY shuhn) 460
Native Americans (NAYT iv • uh MAIR uh kuhnz) 6, 10-14, 28, 31-34, 40-49-51, 54-56, 61, 65, 68, 75, 76, 81-83, 86, 90, 111, 114, 122, 145, 148, 152, 159, 160, 170, 176, 190, 192, 198, 203, 205, 268, 277, 288, 297-302, 305, 325, 335, 363, 385, 460, 547, 576, 579
Navajo (NAV uh hoh) 7, 12
Navy, Assistant Secretary of the (uh SIS tuhnt • SEK ruh tair ee • uhv • thuh • NAY vee) 364
Navy, Department of the (di PART muhnt • uhv • thuh • NAY vee) 139
Nazi Party (NAHT see • PART ee) 468-470, 474, 480, 481, 486, 509, 511, 639
Nebraska (nuh BRAS kuh) 13, 221, 224, 287, 301, 321, 345
Nelson, Donald M. (DAHN uhld • em • NEL suhn) 490, 491
Netherlands (NETH uhr luhndz) 34, 47, 50, 53, 62, 387, 388, 479, 486, 528
neutrality (noo TRAL uh tee) 390, 395, 396, 476, 482
Nevada (nuh VAHD uh) 190, 200, 285
New Amsterdam (noo • AM stuhr dam) 60
New Deal (noo • deel) 451-454, 457-462, 518
New Echota (noo • ee CHOH tuh) 204
New England (noo • ING luhnd) 12, 55, 56, 65, 66, 95, 100, 103, 111, 145, 152, 176, 180
New Federalism (noo • FED uh ruh liz uhm) 623
New France (noo • frants) 47, 75, 82, 83
Newfoundland Island (NOO fuhn luhnd • EYE luhnd) 26, 41, 42, 84, 119
New Hampshire (noo • HAMP shuhr) 59, 60, 61, 62, 94, 130, 178
New Jersey (nyoo • JUHRZ ee) 62, 66, 104, 111, 112, 130, 178, 376
New Jersey Plan (noo • JUHRZ ee • plan) 124, 125
New Mexico (noo • MEK si koh) 33, 199, 200, 214, 289, 301, 397, 501, 503, 576
New Netherlands (noo • NETH uhr luhndz) 47, 59, 60, 62
New Orleans [Louisiana] (noo • OR lee uhnz) 151-153, 159, 260, 261, 421
New Orleans, Battle of (BAT uhl • uhv • noo • OR lee uhnz) 151-153
New Spain (noo • spayn) 32
New Sweden (noo • SWEED uhn) 48, 62
New World (noo • wuhrld) 28, 32, 33, 34
New York (noo • york) 60, 62, 66, 88, 89, 99, 103, 105, 106, 111, 119, 130, 192, 335, 451, 518, 576, 589, 619
New York City (noo • york • SIT ee) 60, 69, 78, 87, 192, 216, 218, 221, 231, 255, 316, 322, 328-330, 334-336, 350, 351, 353, 375, 427, 439, 453, 463, 494, 503, 543, 655
Nicaragua (nik uh RAHG wuh) 630
Nicholas II (NIK uh luhs • thuh • SEK uhnd) 399
Nickerson, H. G. (aytch • jee • NIK uhr suhn) 416
Nightmare Alley (NEYET mair • AL ee) 533
Nixon, Richard M. (RICH uhrd • em • NIK suhn) 553, 554, 557, 582, 584-587, 595-599, 601, 603, 607, 613, 625
Nobel Peace Prize (NOH bel • pees • preyez) 520, 610
normalcy (NOR muhl see) 405, 411, 412
Normandy (NOR muhnd ee) 496, 500
North (north) 120, 128, 133, 134, 165, 167, 175, 181, 188, 197, 218, 224-226, 229, 234, 235, 240-243, 248, 249, 252-255, 258, 261, 262, 271-274, 277, 278, 291, 304, 310, 322, 340, 345, 401, 611
North Africa (north • AF ri kuh) 473, 495, 496, 498
North America (north • uh MAIR uh kuh) 5, 10-12, 26, 28, 31, 33, 41, 42, 44, 47, 50, 51, 55, 57, 61, 67, 75, 81-83, 86, 194, 298, 359, 387
North Atlantic Treaty Organization [NATO] (north • uht LANT ik • TREE tee • org uh nuh ZAY shuhn) 527, 528, 535, 571, 616
North Bridge (north • bridj) 94, 96, 100
North Carolina (north • KAIR uh leyen uh) 43, 45, 62, 117, 118, 130, 133, 166, 175, 247, 259, 546
North, Oliver (AHL uh vuhr • north) 633
North Pole (north • pohl) 10
Northern Alliance (NOR thuhrn • uh LEYE uhns) 345
Northern Europe (NOR thuhrn • YUHR uhp) 321, 323
Northern Pacific Railroad (NOR thuhrn • puh SIF ik • RAYL rohd) 276

Northern Securities Company (NOR thuhrn • si KYUHR uht eez • KUHMP uh nee) 368
North, Lord (lord • north) 88
North Star (north • star) 221
Northwest Coast (north WEST •kohst) 10, 172
Northwest Passage (north WEST • PAS ij) 31, 41
Northwest Territory (north WEST • TAIR uh tor ee) 135, 160, 197
Norway (NOR way) 26, 321, 388, 409, 479
Nova Scotia [Canada] (NOH vuh • SKOH shuh) 119
nullification (nuhl uh fuh KAY shuhn) 140, 182
nullify (NUHL uh feye) 140
Nuremburg (NYOOR uhm buhrg) 508

O

Oberlin College [Ohio] (OH buhr lin • KAHL ij) 216
O'Connor, Sandra Day (SAN druh • day • oh KAHN uhr) 623
ODESSA (oh DES uh) 511
Office of Strategic Service [OSS] (AHF uhs • uhv • struh TEE jik • SUHR vuhs) 482
Oglethorpe, James (jaymz • OH guhl thorp) 61, 62, 107
Ohio (oh HEYE oh) 75, 82, 114, 216
Ohio River (oh HEYE oh • RIV uhr) 82, 86
oil (oyl) 414, 483, 602, 603, 605, 608, 611, 613, 631, 641, 642, 645
Okinawa [Japan] (oh kuh NAH wuh) 501, 502
Oklahoma (oh kluh HOH muh) 33, 205, 207, 268, 301, 302, 385, 631
Oklahoma City (oh kluh HOH muh • SIT ee) 655
Oklahoma Territory (oh kluh HOH muh • TAIR uh tor ee) 301
Old Ironsides (ohld • EYE uhrn seyedz) 147
Olds, Ranson Eli (RAN suhm • EE leye • ohldz) 419, 420
Olive Branch Petition (AHL iv • branch • puh TISH uhn) 98, 99
Oliver, King (king • AHL iv vuhr) 421
Olmec (AHL mek) 11
Olympic Games (uh LIM pik • gaymz) 385, 471, 614, 619
Omaha [Nebraska] (OH muh ha) 287, 345
101st Airborne Division (hwuhn • HUHN druhd • uhnd • fuhrst • AIR born • duh VIZH uhn) 497
104th U.S. Colored Troops (hwuhn HUN druhd • uhnd • forth • yoo • es • KUHL uhrd • troops) 256
105th U. S. Colored Troops (hwuhn HUN druhd • uhnd • fifth • yoo • es • KUHL uhrd • troops) 256
Ontario [Canada] (ahn TAIR ee oh) 84
OPEC (OH pek) 603, 608, 631
Open Door Policy (OH puhn • dor • PAHL uh see) 360, 375, 376
Operation Desert Shield (ahp uh RAY shuhn • DEZ uhrt • sheeld) 642
Operation Desert Storm (ahp uh RAY shuhn • DEZ uhrt • storm) 643-646
Orders in Council (ORD uhrz • in • KOWN suhl) 145, 146
Orange and Alexandria Railroad (OR inj • uhnd • al ikz AN dree uh • RAYL rohd) 272
Oregon (OR uh guhn) 197, 198, 221
O'Reilly, Leonora Barry (LEE oh nor uh • BAIR ee • oh REYE lee) 342
Osceola (ah see OH luh) 205, 206
Oswald, Lee Harvey (lee • HAR vee • AHS wahld) 566-568
Ottoman [people] (AHT oh muhn) 17
Ottoman Empire (AHT uh muhn • EHM peyer) 387, 389, 398-400, 403, 405
outlaws (OWT lahs) 170
Oval Office (OH vuhl • AHF uhs) 598
Owens, Jesse (JES ee • OH wuhnz) 471

P

Pacific Coast (puh SIF ik • kohst) 324
Pacific Ocean (puh SIF ik • OH shuhn) 10, 31, 160, 198, 236, 301, 359, 360, 364, 372, 373, 377, 389, 474, 483, 485, 490, 492, 494, 502, 523
Pacific Railroad Act of 1862 (puh SIF ik • RAYL rohd • akt • uhv • AYT teen • SIKS tee • too) 286, 287
Pacifist (PAS uh fuhst) 396, 401
Paine, Thomas (TAHM uhs • payn) 103
Palestine (PAL uh steyen) 517, 602, 609, 655
Palestinian Liberation Organization [PLO] (pal uh STIN ee uhn • lib uh RAY shuhn • org uh nuh ZAY shuhn) 630
Palmer, A. Mitchell (ay • MICH uhl • PAHM uhr) 430
Panama (PAN uh mah) 373-375
Panama Canal (PAN uh mah • kuh NAL) 173, 372-375, 378, 484, 609
Panic of 1837 (PAN ik • uhv • AYT teen • THUHR tee • SEV uhn) 187-190
Panic of 1873 (PAN ik • uhv • AYT teen • SEV uhn tee • three) 276, 277
Panmunjon [Korea] (pan moon JAWN) 536
Paramount Studios (PAIR uh mownt • STOO dee ohs) 543
paratrooper (PAIR uh troop uhr) 302
Paris [France] (PAIR uhs) 119
Paris, Peace of (pees • uhv • PAIR uhs) 83, 496, 497
Paris, Treaty of (TREE tee • uhv • PAIR uhs) 119, 123, 126
Parker, John (jahn • PAR kuhr) 94
Parks, Rosa (ROH zuh • parks) 545, 546
Parliament (PAR luh muhnt) 60, 84, 86-89, 92, 93, 95, 98, 99, 105, 146, 477
Patriot (PAY tree uht) 93-95, 98, 99, 101, 104, 106, 111-115, 117, 118
Patton, George S. (jorj • es • PAT uhn) 449, 497
Pawnee (paw NEE) 13
Pea Ridge, Battle of (BAT uhl • uhv • pee • rij) 268
Pearl Harbor [Hawaii] (perl • HAR buhr) 484, 485, 488, 494, 500, 507

Peking [also Beijing, China] (pee KING) 587
Pendleton Act of 1883 (PEN duhl tuhn • akt • uhv • AYT teen • AYT tee • three) 335
Pennsylvania (pent suhl VAY nee uh) 61, 62, 78, 89, 95, 98, 103, 105, 107, 130, 252, 253, 271, 353, 385, 568
Penn, William (WIL yuhm • pen) 61, 62
Pensacola [Florida] (pen suh KOH luh) 170
perestroika (pair uh STROY kuh) 629
Perot, H. Ross (aytch • rahs • puh ROH) 183, 649
Perry, Matthew (MATH yoo • PAIR ee) 359
Perry, Oliver Hazard (AHL uh ver • HAZ uhrd • PAIR ee) 147
Pershing, John J. (jahn • jay • PUHR shing) 400
Persian Gulf (PUHRZH uhn • guhlf) 615, 645
Persian Gulf War (PUHRZH uhn • guhlf • wor) 153
Peru (puh ROO) 32, 33, 360
Petersburg [Virginia] (PEET uhrz buhrg) 259
Petrograd [Soviet Union] (PET roh grad) 399
Philadelphia [Pennsylvania] (fil uh DEL fee uh) 89, 92, 111-113, 124, 126, 134, 253, 409
Philip II (FIL uhp • thuh • SEK uhnd) 34
Philippines (fil uh PEENZ) 33, 360, 363, 364, 377, 483-485, 500, 501
Pickett, George E. (jorj • ee • PIK uht) 253
Pickford, Mary (MAIR ee • PIK fuhrd) 422
Pickney, Thomas (PIK nee • TAHM uhs) 140
Pickney, Charles Coatsworth (chahrlz • KOHTS wuhrth • PIK nee) 140
Pierce, Franklin (FRANGK luhn • peers) 224, 225, 237
Pike, Albert (AL buhrt • peyek) 268
Pike's Peak [Colorado] (peyeks • peek) 285
Pilgrim (PIL gruhm) 53, 54, 55, 56
Pima (PEE muh) 302
Pitcher, Molly (MAHL ee • PICH uhr) 101
Pitt, William (WIL yuhm • pit) 81, 82, 93
Pittsburgh [Pennsylvania] (PITS buhrg) 76, 82, 353
Pizarro, Francisco (fran SIS koh • pee ZAR oh) 32
Plains (playnz) 7
plantation (plan TAY shuhn) 67, 120, 194
Plessy, Homer (HOH muhr • PLES ee) 293
Plessy vs. Ferguson (PLES ee • VUHR suhs • FER guh suhn) 293
Plymouth [Massachusetts] (PLIM uhth) 56, 62
Plymouth Company (PLIM uhth • KUHMP uh nee) 47, 62
Plymouth Harbor (PLIM uhth • HAHR buhr) 54
Pocahontas (poh kuh HAHNT uhs) 49, 51
Poland (POH luhnd) 387, 476, 481, 497, 501, 522, 523, 525, 636
political conventions (puh LIT uh kuhl • kuhn VEN shuhnz) 183
political machines (puh LIT uh kuhl • muh SHEENZ) 334, 335, 351
polio (POH lee oh) 463
Polk, James (jaymz • pohk) 173, 197-201, 213
Poll Tax (pohl • taks) 292
pollution (puh LOO shuhn) 573, 605
Pope (pohp) 553
Popular Election (PAHP yuh luhr • i LEK shuhn) 8, 133, 140, 141, 176-178, 182, 187, 188, 192, 192
popular sovereignty (PAHP yuh luhr • SAHV ruhn tee) 214
population (pahp yuh LAY shuhn) 5, 7, 11, 54, 55, 128, 161, 193, 194, 205, 206, 219, 238, 241, 247, 316, 320-323, 326-328, 359, 377, 409, 424, 428, 442, 444, 485, 488, 489, 506, 507, 539, 611
Populist Party (PAHP yuh luhst • PART ee) 345, 346, 352, 411
Popul Vuh (POH puhl • vyoo) 8
Port Royal (port • ROY uhl) 42, 47
Portsmouth [New Hampshire] (PORT smuhth) 376
Portugal (POR chuh guhl) 17, 21, 26, 27, 28, 41
Portuguese (POR tyoo geez) 17, 18, 21, 22, 23, 27
Post, C.W. (see • w • pohst) 312
Post, Marjorie Merriwether (MAR juh ree • MAIR ee weth uhr • pohst) 312
Postum Cereal Company (POHST uhm • SEER ee uhl • KUHM puh nee) 312
potato (puh TAY toh) 42, 193, 207
potato famine (puh TAY toh • FAM uhn) 193, 207
Potomac River (puh TOH muhk • RIV uhr) 150, 364
Potomac, Army of the (AHRM ee • uhv • thuh • puh TOH muhk) 249, 253
Powell, Colin (KOHL uhn • POW uhl) 647
Powell, Lewis F., Jr. (LOO uhs • ef • POW uhl • JOON yuhr) 599
power loom (POW uhr • loom) 165
powers, separation of (sep uh RAY shuhn • uhv • POW uhrz) 125
Powhatan (pow HAHT uhn) 48, 49, 51
President [United States] (PREZ uh dent) 79, 129, 133, 134, 183, 349, 384, 407, 414, 441, 448, 451, 457-459, 461, 463, 504, 534, 548, 595, 596
Presidential Citation (prez uh DEN chuhl • seye TAY shuhn) 492
Presidential Election (prez uh DEN chuhl • i LEK shuhn) 133, 140, 141, 176-178, 182, 187, 188, 192
    of 1788 (uhv • SEV uhn teen • AYT ee • ayt) 133
    of 1796 (uhv • SEV uhn teen • NEYEN tee • siks) 140
    of 1800 (uhv • AYT teen • HUHN druhd) 140, 141
    of 1824 (uhv • AYT teen • TWEN tee • for) 176-178
    of 1832 (uhv • AYT teen • TWEN tee • too) 182
    of 1836 (uhv • AYT teen • THURH tee • siks) 187

For the People, By the People

of 1840 (uhv • AYT teen • FOR tee) 188
of 1848 (uhv • AYT teen • FOR tee • ayt) 213
of 1856 (uhv • AYT teen • FIF tee • siks) 226
of 1860 (uhv • AYT teen • SIKS • tee) 234
of 1864 (uhv • AYT teen • SIKS • tee • for) 258, 260
of 1876 (uhv • AYT teen • SEV uhn tee • siks) 277, 278
of 1896 (uhv • AYT teen • NEYEN tee • siks) 345, 346, 351, 352
of 1908 (uhv • NEYEN teen • oh • ayt) 380
of 1912 (uhv • NEYEN teen • twelv) 382, 383
of 1916 (uhv • NEYEN • SIKS teen) 396, 397
of 1920 (uhv • NEYEN teen • TWEN tee) 411, 412
of 1928 (uhv • NEYEN teen • TWEN tee • ayt) 437, 438
of 1932 (uhv • NEYEN teen • THUHR tee • too) 451
of 1936 (uhv • NEYEN teen • THUHR tee • siks) 458
of 1940 (uhv • NEYEN teen • FOR tee) 461
of 1944 (uhv • NEYEN teen • FOR tee • for) 461
of 1948 (uhv • NEYEN teen • FOR tee • ayt) 518, 519
of 1952 (uhv • NEYEN teen • FIF tee • too) 535, 541
of 1960 (uhv • NEYEN teen • SIKS tee) 553, 557
of 1968 (uhv • NEYEN teen • SIKS tee • ayt) 582
of 1972 (uhv • NEYEN teen • SEV uhn tee • too) 595
of 1976 (uhv • NEYEN teen • SEV uhn tee • siks) 607
of 1980 (uhv • NEYEN teen • AYT ee) 616, 617
of 1988 (uhv • NEYEN teen • AYT ee • ayt) 635
of 1992 (uhv • NEYEN teen • NEYEN tee • too) 649, 652
of 1996 (uhv • NEYEN teen • NEYEN tee • siks) 647, 653, 654
President's Committee on Unemployment Relief (PREZ uhd uhnts • kuh MIT ee • ahn • uhn im PLOY muhnt • ree LEEF) 447
Presley, Elvis (EL vuhs • PREZ lee) 580
prices (PREYES uhs) 344-346, 351, 384, 401, 420, 425, 437-441, 444-449, 451-454, 457, 458, 460-462, 491, 518, 539, 575, 601, 603, 608, 611, 631, 635
Prime Minister [British] (PREYEM • MIN uhs tuhr) 86, 88
Princeton [New Jersey] (PRINZ tuhn) 112
Princeton University (PRINZ tuhn • yoo nuh VUHR suht ee) 383
Prince William Sound (prints • WIL yuhm • sownd) 605
prison camps (PRIZ uhn • kamps) 470, 488, 492
prisoners of war (PRIZ uh nuhrz • uhv • wor) 507, 535, 536, 586
Proclamation of 1763 (prahk luh MAY shuhn • uhv • SEV uhn teen • SIKS tee • three) 86
Progressive (pruh GRES iv) 366-370, 380, 382, 383
Progressive Party (pruh GRES iv • PART ee) 383, 411, 415, 463
Prohibition (proh uh BISH uhn) 425, 426, 431
Promontory Point [Utah] (PRAHM uhn tor ee • poynt) 287
protectionism (pruh TEK shuhn iz uhm) 180, 181
Protestant (PRAHT uh stuhnt) 41, 75, 323, 428
protests (PROH tests) 546, 565, 576, 577, 579, 580, 582, 583, 632, 638
Providence [Rhode Island] (PRAHV uhd uhnts) 62
Providence Plantations (PRAHV uhd uhnts • plan TAY shuhnz) 63
Public Works (PUHB lik • wuhrks) 276
Pueblo [Colorado] 407
Pueblos (pwuh EB lohz) 12
Puerto Rico (PORT uh • REE koh) 363, 374, 531, 576
Puritan (PYOOR uh tuhn) 55, 56, 57, 59, 60, 61, 62, 370
Purple Heart (PUHR puhl • hart) 302, 492

Q

Qaddafi, Muammar al- (MOOH uh mar • al • kuh DAHF ee) 655
Quakers (KWAYK uhrz) 61, 62, 107
Quartering Act (KWORT uh ring • akt) 87, 88
Quebec [Canada] (kwuh BEK) 47, 82, 83, 84, 99, 100
Queenston Heights [Canada] (KWEENZ tuhn • heyetz) 146

R

Rabin, Yitzhak (YIT sahk • ruh BEEN) 655
racism (RAYS iz uhm) 428, 469-471, 539, 582
radiation (ray dee AY shuhn) 505
Radical Republicans (RAD i kuhl • ri PUHB li kuhns) 267, 268, 270, 271, 273, 274
radicals (RAD i kuhlz) 518, 599, 615, 619, 655
radio (RAY dee oh) 302, 413, 418, 419, 437, 438, 461
ragtime (RAG teyem) 421
railroads (RAYL rohdz) 193, 194, 221, 241, 258, 270, 272, 287, 288, 293, 304, 305, 307, 311, 315, 316, 321, 330, 333, 335, 340, 344, 345, 353, 368, 369, 381, 407, 502, 527
Raleigh, Walter (WAHL tuhr • RAHL ee) 42, 43
Rainey, Joseph (JOH suhf • RAY nee) 274
ranching (RANCH ing) 288, 289, 442
Randall, Dudley (DUHD lee • RAN duhl) 295
Randolf, Edmund (ED muhnd • RAN dahlf) 134
Randolph, A. Philip (ay • FIL uhp • RAN dahlf) 547
ratification (rat uh fuh KAY shuhn) 130
Ray, James Earl (jaymz • uhrl • ray) 579
Reagan, Ronald (RAHN uhld • RAY guhn) 173, 289, 599, 607, 616-618, 623-627, 629-633, 635, 649
Reaganomics (ray guh NAHM iks) 624, 625
recession (ri SESH uhn) 601, 624, 635
Reconstruction (ree kuhn STRUHK shuhn) 270-272, 276-278, 291, 292
Reconstruction Acts (ree kuhn STRUHK shuhn • akts) 270

Reconstruction Finance Corporation (ree kuhn STRUHK shuhn • fuh NANTS • kor pur RAY shuhn) 447
recycling (re SEYE kling) 573
Red Sea (red • see) 373, 378
Reed, Walter (WAL tuhr • reed) 378
reform (ri FORM) 334, 335, 347, 350, 366, 415, 652-654
religion (ri LIJ uhn) 8, 11, 16, 17, 31, 32, 41, 53-57, 59-62, 75, 76, 300, 350, 427, 428, 553, 578, 602, 603, 609, 610, 614-616, 630, 641, 643
Removal Bill of 1830 (ri MOO vuhl • bil • uhv • ayt TEEN • thuhr TEE) 205
Representatives, United States House of (yoo NEYET uhd • stayts • hows • uhv • rep ri ZINT uh tivz) 128, 129, 133, 134, 141, 146, 177, 183
Republican Convention (ri PUHB luh kuhn • kuhn VEN shuhn) 383, 411, 412, 584, 607, 623
Republican Party (ri PUHB luh kuhn • PART ee) 225, 226, 229, 230, 234-236, 258, 266, 270, 271, 273, 274, 276-278, 291, 292, 335, 345, 346, 352, 366, 367, 380, 382, 383, 397, 404, 405, 406, 408, 411, 412, 437, 441, 448, 451, 457, 458, 459, 518, 519, 535, 540, 554, 570, 584, 595, 607, 617, 624, 625, 649, 652, 653
reservation (rez uhr VAY shuhn) 152
reservationists (rez uhr VAY shuhn ists) 407, 460
resources (REE sor suhs) 305, 369, 399, 411, 467
Revels, Hiram (HEYE ruhm • REV uhlz) 274
Revere, Paul (pahl • ri VEER) 94, 604
revolution (rev uh LOO shuhn) 91-120, 122, 126, 134, 135, 161, 162, 193, 361, 362, 375, 423, 430, 457, 470, 554, 580
Revolutionary War (rev uh LOO shuhn air ee • wor) 91-120, 122, 126, 161, 243, 298, 325, 366, 395, 604
Rhineland [Germany] (REYEN land) 474, 475
Rhode Island (rohd • EYE luhnd) 56, 59, 61-63, 94, 107, 130, 133
rice (reyes) 166
Richardson, Elliot (EL ee uht • RICH uhrd suhn) 598
Richmond [Virginia] (RICH muhnd) 247-249, 259, 260, 330
Ridge, Major (MAY juhr • ridj) 206
Ridgeway, Matthew (MATH yoo • RIJ way) 534
Rights, Bill of [U.S. Constitution] (bil • uhv • reyets) 132, 133, 140
Rights, Declaration of (dek luh RAY shuhn • uhv • reyets) 92
Rio Grande [river] (REE oh • grand) 198
riots (REYE uhts) 565, 566, 579, 580, 582, 614, 652
roads (rohdz) 192
rockets (ROK uhts) 494, 527, 559, 560
Roanoke [Virginia] (ROH uh NOHK • EYE luhnd) 43, 44, 45
Robinson, Mary (MAIR ee • RAHB uhn suhn) 207
Rockefeller, John D. (jahn • dee • RAHK i fel uhr) 311, 351, 381
Rocky Mountains (RAHK ee • MOWN tuhnz) 190
Rolfe, John (jahn • rahlf) 49, 51
Roman Catholic Church (ROH muhn • KATH uh lik • chuhrch) 75, 226
Roman Empire (ROH muhn • EM peyer) 16, 468
Romania (roh MAYN ee uh) 497, 523, 525
Rome [Italy] (rohm) 16, 41, 495-497, 553
Roosevelt, Eleanor (EL uh nor • ROH zuh vuhlt) 463, 498
Roosevelt, Franklin D. (FRANG kluhn • ROH zuh vuhlt) 411, 451-455, 457-461, 463, 482, 483, 489-491, 494, 498, 500, 502, 507, 509, 518, 522, 565, 601, 627
Roosevelt, Theodore (THEE uh dor • ROHZ uh vuhllt) 173, 364, 366-370, 372, 375-377, 380, 382, 383, 397, 463, 496
Rosenberg, Ethel (ETH uhl • ROHZ uhn berg) 519
Rosenberg, Julius (JOOHL yuhs • ROHZ uhn berg) 519
Ross, John (jahn • rahs) 204, 206, 268
Rough Riders (ruf • REYED uhrz) 364
Ruby, Jack (jak • ROO bee) 566, 567
Russia (RUHSH uh) 172, 293, 359, 360, 376, 377, 381, 387, 389, 395, 398, 399, 429, 430, 457, 497, 522, 637, 638, 642
Russian Empire (RUHSH uhn • EHM peyer) 387
Russo-Japanese War (ROO soh • JAP uh neez • wor) 376, 377
Ruth, Babe (bayb • rooth) 413

S

SS [Nazi Secret Police] (es • es) 509, 511
Sacajawea (sak uh juh WEE uh) 159, 160
Sac and Fox (sak • uhnd • fahks) 385
Sacramento [California] (SAK ruh MEN toh) 213
Sadat, Anwar (AN war • suh DAHT) 608-610
Sakhalin Island (SAK uh leen • EYE luhnd) 376
Salt II Treaty (sahlt • too • TREE tee) 613, 614
Salt Treaty (sahlt • TREE tee) 587, 588, 613
Samoa (suh MOH uh) 360, 361
Samoset (SAM oh set) 55
Sampson, Deborah (DEB uh ruh • SAMP suhn) 101
San Antonio [Texas] (san • an TOHN yoh) 197
San Diego [California] (san • dee AYG oh) 199, 221
Sand Creek [Colorado] (sand • kreek) 299
San Francisco [California] (san • fran SIS koh) 199, 213, 221, 287, 377, 509
San Juan Hill [Cuba] (san • hwan • hil) 362, 364
San Salvador (san • SAL vuh dor) 28
Santa Maria (SAN tuh • muh REE uh) 27
Santiago [Cuba] (sant ee AHG oh) 362, 363
Santiago Bay (sant ee AHG oh • bay) 362

Sarajevo [Yugoslavia] (sair uh YAY voh) 388
Saratoga, Battle of (BAT uhl • uhv • sair uh TOH guh) 112, 113, 115
Saratoga [New York] (sair uh TOH guh) 113
satellite countries (SAT uh leyet • KUHN treez) 639
Saudi Arabia (SAH dee • uh RAY bee uh) 602, 642, 643, 645
Savannah [Georgia] (suh VAN uh) 117, 259, 260
scandals (SKAN duhls) 276, 333, 334, 366, 414, 415, 596-598, 632, 633
Scandinavia (skan duh NAY vee uh) 26, 321
Schindler, Oskar (AHS kuhr • SHIND luhr) 486
Schindler's List (SHIND luhrs • list) 486
Schwarzkopf, Norman (NOR muhn • SHWORTZ kahf) 647
Scotland (SKAHT luhnd) 115, 387
Scott, Dred (dred • skaht) 229
Scott, Winfield (WIN feeld • skaht) 206
Seaman, Elizabeth Cochrane (i LIZ uh buth • KAHK ruhn • SEE muhn) 353
Southeast Asia Treaty Organization [SEATO] (SOWTH eest • AY suh • TREE tee • org uh nuh ZAY shuhn) 571
secession (suh SESH uhn) 152, 235-237, 239, 242, 247, 266, 267
Second Bank of the United States (SEK uhnd • bank • uhv • thuh • yoo NEYET uhd • stayts) 182, 187
Second Continental Congress (SEK uhnd • kahnt uhn ENT uhl • KAHNG gruhs) 95, 98, 99, 103, 104, 106, 119, 122, 243, 412
Secretariat [UN] (sek ruh TAIR ee uht) 510
Secretary-General [UN] (SEK ruh tair ee • GEN ruhl) 510
Secretary of State (SEK ruh tair ee • uhv • stayt) 524, 595
Secretary of the Interior (SEK ruh tair ee • uhv • thuh • in TEER ee uhr) 382
Secret Service (SEEK ruht • SUHR vuhs) 249
Security Council [UN] (si KYOOR uht ee • KOWN suhl) 510, 529
segregation (seg ruh GAY shuhn) 489, 545-547, 570, 576, 582, 623, 632
Seminole (SEM uh nohl) 170, 203, 205, 268, 301
Senate [United States] (SEN uht) 128, 129, 131, 133, 134, 146, 159, 175, 213, 215, 227, 230, 231, 236, 237, 271, 274, 359, 375, 381, 382, 384, 390, 404-408, 411, 449, 457, 458, 535, 540, 541, 553, 568, 570, 588, 597, 599, 609, 611, 613, 614, 624, 625, 627, 649, 653
Senate Investigation Committee (SEN uht • in vest uh GAY shuhn • kuh MIT ee) 540
Seneca Falls [New York] (SEN i kuh • falz) 216
Sentiments, Declaration of (dek luh RAY shuhn • uhv • SENT uh muhntz) 216
separation of church and state (sep uh RAY shuhn • uhv • chuhrch • uhnd • stayt) 553
Separatists (SEP uh ruh tists) 53
Sequoyah (suh KWOY uh) 204, 301
Serbia (SUHR bee uh) 387-389
Seven Years War (SEV un • yeerz • wor) 81
Seward, William (WIL yuhm • SOO uhrd) 266, 267, 359
Shah (shah) 614, 615
Shanghai (shang HEYE) 467
shantytowns (SHAN • tee• townz) 445, 448, 449
sharecropping (SHAIR • krahp • ing) 273
Sharon [Massachusetts] (SHAIR uhn) 101
Shaw, Robert Gould (RAHB uhrt • goold • shaw) 254, 255
Shawnee (shaw NEE) 148
Shays, Daniel (DAN yuhl • SHAYZ) 122
Shays' Rebellion (SHAYZ • ri BEL yuhn) 122, 123
Shenandoah Valley (shen uhn DOH uh • VAL ee) 258
Sheridan, Philip (FIL uhp • SHER uhd uhn) 258
Sherman Anti-Trust Act (SHUHR muhn • ant eye TRUHST • akt) 368
Sherman, Roger (RAHJ uhr • SHUHR muhn) 105
Sherman, William T. (WIL yuhm • tee • SHUHR muhn) 258-260, 264
Shiloh, Battle of (BAT uhl • uhv • SHEYE loh) 249
shipping (SHIP ing) 67, 139, 145, 152, 159, 192, 193, 194, 395, 396, 403, 484, 542, 631
Shoshone (shuh SHOHN ee) 159
Shriver, Sargent (SAR juhnt • SHREYE vuhr) 595
Sicily (SIS uh lee) 495, 496
Sierra Nevadas [mountains] (see AIR uh • nuh VAHD uhz) 190
Silent Spring (SEYE luhnt • spring) 573
Sinai Peninsula (SEYE neye • puh NINT suh luh) 602, 610
Sinclair, Upton (Up tuhn • SIN klair) 351
Sioux (soo) 298, 300
Sirica, John (jahn • suh RIK uh) 598
Sitting Bull (SIT ing • buhl) 300
Six-Day War (siks • day • wor) 602, 603
Slater, Samuel (SAM yoo uhl • SLAYT uhr) 165
slaughterhouses (SLAH tuhr hows uhz) 316, 351
slaves (slayvz) 21, 50, 68, 90, 137, 195
slavery (SLAYV uh ree) 28, 50, 68, 69, 106, 107, 120, 129, 162, 166, 167, 175, 176, 194, 195, 197, 213, 216, 214-216, 218-220, 224-226, 229-232, 234-236, 239, 243, 247, 252, 264, 268, 273, 274, 278, 279, 291, 295, 378, 420, 421, 453, 459, 467, 486, 508, 547
slums (slumz) 327, 350, 463, 576
Smith, Jesse (JES ee • smith) 414
Smith, John (jahn • smith) 48, 49, 51
smuggling (SMUHG ling) 87, 426
Socialist Party (SOHSH uhl uhst • PART ee) 383
social programs (SOHSH uhl • PROH gruhms) 459, 624, 626, 649, 650
Social Security (SOHSH uhl • suh KYOOR uh tee) 459, 518
Sofala [Africa] (soh FAH lah) 23

Solomon Islands (SAHL uh muhn • EYE luhndz) 500
Sophie, Archduchess (arch DUCH uhs • SOH fee) 405
Souls of Black Folk, The (thuh • sohl • uhv • blak • fohk) 295
South (sowth) 111, 117, 118, 120, 129, 133, 134, 145, 165, 166, 167, 175, 180, 181, 188, 194, 195, 213, 214, 218, 220, 214, 224-226, 230, 231, 234-236, 239-243, 247, 252, 264, 268, 273, 274, 278, 279, 291, 295, 378, 401, 459, 462, 519, 547, 582, 611
South Africa (sowth • AF ruh kuh) 632, 638
South America (sowth • uh MAIR uh kuh) 5, 28, 31, 41, 44, 194, 214, 359, 373, 387, 511, 602, 603
South Carolina (sowth • kair uh LEYEN uh) 61, 62, 89, 117, 118, 130, 145, 166, 182, 227, 234-236, 239, 256, 258-260, 277
South Dakota (sowth • duh KOH tuh) 300, 301
Southeast (sowth • EEST) 203, 205
Southern Alliance (SUHTH uhrn • uh LEYE uhns) 345
Southern Christian Leadership Confer-ence (SUHTH uhrn • KRIS chuhn • LEE duhr ship • KAHN fuhr uhnts) 546
Southern Colonies (SUHTH uhrn • KAHL uh neez) 67, 69, 95, 106
Southern Europe (SUHTH urhn • YUHR uhp) 323
Southern Front (SUHTH uhrn • fruhnt) 398
Southwest (sowth • WEST) 7, 11, 12, 14, 151, 286, 301, 611
Soviet Union (SOH vee uht • YOON yuhn) 153, 173, 391, 470, 473, 476, 479, 480, 494, 495, 497, 500-502, 504, 507, 510, 519, 522, 524, 525, 527-530, 533, 534, 536, 540, 555, 556, 559, 561, 567, 586-588, 602, 609, 613, 614, 629, 636-639, 644
space race (spays • rays) 559-562
Spain (spayn) 27, 28, 31-34, 40-42, 44, 50, 53, 61, 122, 134, 135, 159, 161, 170, 171, 172, 175, 197, 297, 361, 363, 374, 375, 387, 388, 473
Spanish-American War (SPAN ish • uh MAIR uh kuhn • wor) 362-364, 372, 373, 378
Spanish Civil War (SPAN ish • SIV uhl • wor) 473
speakeasies (SPEEK ee zeez) 425, 426
Specter, Arlen (AR luhn • SPEK tuhr) 568
Spice Islands (speyes • EYE luhndz) 19
Spielberg, Stephen (STEE vuhn • SPEEL buhrg) 486
spinning jenny (SPIN ing • JEN ee) 165, 168
Spingarn Medal (SPING arn • MED uhl) 549
spoils system (spoylz • SIS tuhm) 180
Springfield [Illinois] (SPRING feeld) 265
Sputnik II (SPUHT nik • too) 559
Squanto (SKWAHN toh) 54, 55
stagflation (stag FLAY shuhn) 601, 624
Stalin, Joseph (JO zuhf • STAHL uhn) 430, 470, 476, 479, 480, 500, 502, 503, 522-524, 527, 528, 536, 537, 555
Stamp Act (stamp • akt) 87
Standard Oil Company (STAN duhrd • oyl • KUHM puh nee) 380, 381
Stanton, Edwin M. (ED win • em • STANT uhn) 243, 271
Stanton, Elizabeth Cady (i LIZ uh buhth • KAY dee • STANT uhn) 216
Star of David (star • uhv • DAY vuhd) 469, 481
"Star-Spangled Banner, The" (thuh • star • SPANG guhld • BAN uhr) 151, 471
state legislatures (stayt • LEJ i slay chuhrs) 183, 195, 367, 381, 416
State, Secretary of (SEK ruh tair ee • uhv • stayt) 134, 141-143, 177, 266, 267, 359, 360
states' rights (stayts • reyets) 140, 141, 143, 167, 176, 181, 182, 237, 344
Statuary Hall (STACH uh wair ee • hahl) 237, 416
Statue of Liberty (STACH oo • uhv • LIB uhrt ee) 321, 325, 637
St. Augustine [Florida] (saynt • AH guhs teen) 42, 61
steamboats (STEEM bohts) 192
steam power (steem • POW uhr) 192, 305, 307, 330
steel (steel) 250, 306, 309, 314, 315, 483
Steffens, Lincoln (LIN kuhn • STEF uhnz) 351
Steinem, Gloria (GLOR ee uh • STEYE nuhm) 575
Stephens, Alexander (al ig ZAN duhr • STEEV uhns) 236, 261
Stevens, Thaddeus (THAD ee uhs • STEE vuhnz) 271
Stevenson, Adlai E. (AD lay • ee • STEE vuhn suhn) 429, 535
St. Lawrence [river] (saynt • LOR uhnts) 47, 82
St. Lawrence, Gulf of (guhlf • uhv • saynt • LOR uhnts) 82
St. Louis [Missouri] (saynt • LOO uhs) 12, 221
Stockholm [Sweden] (STAHK holm) 385
stock market (stahk • MARK uht) 276
St. Paul [Minnesota] (saynt • PAHL) 221
Strauss, Levi (LEE veye • strows) 285
strikes (streyeks) 339-341, 349, 413, 415, 525, 539
strong government [federal level] (strahng • GUHV uhrn muhnt) 140, 141, 143, 167, 175, 176, 180-182, 340, 346, 350, 369, 383, 441, 448, 451, 452, 454, 457-459, 518, 519, 548, 570, 616, 623, 626, 649, 650, 653, 654
Student Non-Violent Coordinating Com-mittee [SNCC] (STOO duhnt • nahn VEYE luhnt • koh OR duh nayt ing • kuh MIT ee) 578
Students for a Democratic Society [SDS] (STOO duhnts • for • uh • dem uh KRAT ik • suh SEYE i tee) 579
submarines (SUHB muh reenz) 395-397, 401
suburbs (SUHB uhrbz) 542
Sudetenland (soo DAYT uhn land) 475, 486
Suez Canal (SOO ez • kuh NAL) 373, 378, 602
suffrage (SUHF rij) 216, 412, 416
sugar (SHOOG uhr) 166, 361, 362
Sugar Act (SHOOG uhr • akt) 86
Sultan [of Ottoman Empire] (SUHLT uhn) 403

For the People, By the People

Sumatra (soo MAH truh) 485
Summer Olympics (SUHM uhr • uh LIM piks) 614
Sumner, Charles (charlz • SUM ner) 227
Supreme Court (suh PREEM • kort) 129, 133, 142, 204, 205, 226, 229, 230, 264, 279, 289, 292, 293, 344, 368, 397, 430, 458, 459, 488, 545, 546, 549, 567, 598, 599, 623, 624
Sutter's Mill [California] (SUHT uhrz • mil) 213
Sweden (SWEED duhn) 26, 47, 62, 321, 385, 388, 396, 422, 481, 520
Switzerland (SWIT suhr luhnd) 387, 388
Syracuse [New York] (SEER uh kyoos) 218
Syria (SEER ee uh) 602, 603

T
Taft, Nellie (NEL ee • taft) 364
Taft, William Howard (WIL yuhm • HOW uhrd • taft) 364, 380, 381, 383
Taiwan (teye WAHN) 529, 534, 587
Tammany Hall (TAM uh nee • hahl) 351
Tarbell, Ida M. (EYE duh • em • TAR bel) 351
Tariff of 1832 (TAIR uhf • uhv • AYT teen • THUHRT ee • too) 181, 182
Tariff of 1828 (TAIR uhf • uhv • AYT teen • TWEN tee • ayt) 180-182
tariffs (TAIR uhfs) 180-182, 225, 382, 414, 440, 441
taxes (TAKS uhz) 69, 86, 87, 88, 93, 122, 129, 133, 139, 167, 181, 182, 188, 276, 334, 346, 361, 363, 382, 414, 440, 441, 451-455, 458, 459, 547, 571, 608, 616, 624, 627, 652, 654
Taylor, Sarah (SAIR uh • TAY luhr) 237
Taylor, Zachary (ZAK uh ree • TAY luhr) 198, 213-215, 237
Tea Act of 1773 (tee • akt • uhv • SEV uhn teen • SEV uhn tee • three) 88
Teapot Dome (TEE paht • dohm) 414
Tears, Trail of (trayl • uhv • teerz) 206
Tecumseh (tuh KUM suh) 145, 148
Tehran [Iran] (tay RAHN) 616
telegraph (TEL uh graf) 192, 199
telephone (TEL uh fohn) 316
television (TEL uh vizh uhn) 541, 543, 548, 553, 556, 580, 582, 637, 638
Temple, Shirley (SHUHR lee • TEM puhl) 462
Ten Boom, Corrie (KOR ee • ten • boom) 486
Tennessee (ten uh SEE) 117, 151, 175, 176, 247, 258, 259, 266, 416, 579
Tennessee, Army of (AHRM ee • uhv • ten uh SEE) 259, 260
Tennessee River (ten uh SEE • RIV uhr) 249
Tenochtitlán (tay nahch tee TLAHN) 11, 32, 33
Tenure of Office Act (TEN yuhr • uhv • AHF uhs • akt) 271
Texas (TEK suhs) 197, 198, 200, 236, 254, 288, 291, 317, 345, 367, 397, 547, 566, 589, 611, 631, 655
Texas School Book Depository (TEK suhs • skool • book • di PAHZ uh tor ee) 566
Thames, Battle of the (BAT uhl • uhv • thuh • temz) 148
Thanksgiving (thangks GIV ing) 55
Tienanmen Square [Beijing] (tee EN uh muhn • skwair) 637
Thomas, Jesse (JES ee • TAHM uhs) 175
Thoreau, Henry David (HEN ree • DAY vuhd • thuh ROH) 201
Thorpe, Jim (jim • thorp) 385
369th Infantry (three HUN druhd • uhnd • siks tee NEYENTH • IN fuhn tree) 401
Ticonderoga, Battle of (BAT uhl • uhv • teye kahn duh ROH guh) 82
Tilden, Samuel (SAM yoo uhl • TIL duhn) 277
tobacco (tuh BAK oh) 49, 50, 166
Tojo (TOH joh) 484
Tokyo [Japan] (TOH kee oh) 503, 508
Tolan, Eddie (ED ee • TOHL uhn) 471
Topeka [Kansas] (tuh PEE kuh) 545
"Topeka Constitution" (tuh PEEK uh • kahn stuh TOO shuhn) 224
Torresola, Giselio (hi SAYL ee oh • tor uh SOH luh) 531
Townshend Acts (TOWN shuhnd • akts) 88, 93
trade (trayd) 7, 13, 14, 16, 18, 19, 21, 60, 66-69, 75, 86-89, 92, 93, 111, 122, 128, 129, 139, 145, 147, 152, 159, 164, 167, 181, 192-194, 240, 285, 287, 293, 304, 311, 314, 316, 344, 359, 360, 364, 369, 376, 381, 395, 397, 401, 403, 425, 440, 441, 483, 491, 524, 542, 556, 577, 587, 588, 601, 608, 614, 616, 625, 642, 645
Trail of Tears (trayl • uhv • teerz) 206
transportation (trans por TAY shun) 164, 167, 192, 193, 194, 330, 542
treason (TREEZ uhn) 261
Treasury, Department of the (di PART muhnt • uhv • thuh • TREZH uhr ee) 188
Treasury, Secretary of the (SEK ruh tair ee • uhv • thuh • TREZH uh ree) 134, 414
Trenton, Battle of (BAT uhl • uhv • TRENT uhn) 111, 112
Trenton [New Jersey] (TRENT uhn) 111, 112
Truman, Harry S (HAIR ee • es • TROOH muhn) 502-504, 517-520, 523, 524, 527-531, 533-535, 539, 540, 547
Truman Doctrine (TROOH muhn • DAHK truhn) 524
Trusteeship Council [UN} (truhs TEE ship • KOWN suhl) 510
trusts (truhsts) 310, 311, 344, 349, 368, 380, 383, 415, 440, 441
Tsar (zahr) 387
Tubman, Harriet (HAIR ee uht • TUHB muhn) 219
Turkey (TUHR kee) 523
Tuskegee Airmen (tuhs KEE gee • AIR muhn) 498
Tuskegee Institute (tuhs KEE gee • IN stuh toot) 498
Twain, Mark (mark • twayn) 336, 347
Tweed, Boss (bahs • tweed) 335
Tydings, Millard (MIL uhrd • TEYED ingz) 540

Tyler, John (jahn • TEYE luhr) 188, 189
U
Unassigned Lands (uhn uh SEYEND • lands) 301
Underground Railroad (UHN duhr grownd • RAYL rohd) 219, 221
unemployment (uhn em PLOY muhnt) 444-448, 453, 459, 518, 616, 623, 625, 626, 631
U.N. forces (yoo • en • FORS uhs) 529, 530, 533-536, 530, 642-647
Union (YOON yuhn) 197, 203, 226, 231, 235-237, 239, 241-243, 247-249, 252, 254, 255, 258, 259, 261, 262, 264, 267-270, 413, 454, 525, 539
Union Pacific Railroad (YOON yuhn • puh SIF ik • RAYL rohd) 276, 287, 333
United Farm Workers (yoo NEYET uhd • farm • wuhrk uhrz) 576
United Nations (yoo NEYET uhd • NAY shuhns) 29, 391, 501, 509, 510, 517, 520, 529, 530, 533-535, 537, 587, 602, 613, 616, 642, 643, 645
United Nations War Crimes Commission (yoo NEYET uhd • NAY shuhns • wor • kreyems • kuh MISH uhn) 507
United States (yoo NEYET uhd • stayts) 5, 29, 41, 42, 105, 107, 113, 119, 125, 126, 128, 129, 135, 145-147, 151, 152, 159-165, 167, 168, 170, 171, 173, 178, 187, 193, 197-200, 203, 206, 218, 219, 221, 229, 230, 236, 237, 240, 241, 258, 264, 268, 285, 287, 295, 298, 299, 301, 302, 304, 306, 309, 312, 315, 316, 321-325, 330, 344, 346, 347, 349, 359, 360, 361, 363, 364, 372-377, 381, 385, 390, 391, 395-397, 400, 401, 407-409, 412, 413, 422, 423, 425-427, 430, 447, 449, 467, 473, 475, 476, 482-485, 492, 494, 495, 500, 503, 510, 517, 519, 522, 524, 527-531, 533-536, 539, 540, 554-556, 559, 572, 580, 585-587, 602-604, 608-610, 613, 616, 619, 626, 629-631, 633, 638, 641, 643, 646, 649, 655
Unorganized Territory (uhn OR guh neyezd • TAIR uh tor ee) 221
Untouchables, The (thuh • uhn TUHCH uh buhlz) 543
U.S. Armed Forces (yoo • es • armd • FORS uhs) 146-153, 198-201, 204, 205, 239-268, 270, 278, 299, 300, 302, 341, 349, 359, 360, 362-364, 372-374, 378, 400, 401, 406, 407, 409, 413, 449, 461, 480-505, 526, 529, 530, 533-536, 542, 548, 571, 572, 578, 582, 584-586, 588, 609, 615, 616, 624, 630, 631, 642-647
U.S. Army (yoo • es • AR mee) 241, 248, 253-256, 258, 264, 299, 300, 349, 362-364, 366, 372, 374, 378, 382, 397, 400, 401, 413, 449, 541, 548, 609
U.S. Cavalry (yoo • es • KAV uhl ree) 259
U.S. Court of Appeals (yoo • es • cort • uhv • uh PEELZ) 549, 599
U.S. Marines (yoo • es • muh REENZ) 302, 361, 502, 615, 630
U.S. Mint (yoo • es • mint) 351
U.S. Navy (yoo • es • NAYV ee) 397, 400, 401, 414, 495, 496, 502, 556, 609, 615, 631, 642
U.S. Post Office (yoo • es • pohst • AHF uhs) 401
U.S.S. Augusta (yoo • es • es • ah GUHST uh) 502
U.S.S. Hornet (yoo • es • es • HORN uht) 504
U.S.S. Maine (yoo • es • es • mayn) 362
U.S.S. Nashville (yoo • es • es • NASH vil) 375
U.S. space program (yoo • es • spays • PROH gruhm) 559-562, 588
U.S.S. Shaw (yoo • es • es • shah) 485
U.S.S. St. Louis (yoo • es • es • saynt • LOO uhs) 248
U.S.S. Stark (yoo • es • es • stark) 631
Utah (YOO tah) 200, 287, 301

V
Valentino, Rudolph (ROO dahlf • val uhn TEE noh) 422
Valley Forge [Pennsylvania] (VAL ee • forj) 113, 114
Van Buren, Martin (MAHR tuhn • van • BYUHR uhn) 187, 213
Van Lew, Elizabeth (i LIZ uh buhth • van • loo) 262
Vanderbilt, Commodore (KAHM uh dor • VAN duhr bilt) 349
Venezuela (ven uhz WAY luh) 372
Veracruz [Mexico] (vair uh KROOZ) 199
Vermont (vuhr MAHNT) 107, 112, 120, 178
Verne, Jules (joolz • vuhrn) 461
Versailles, Palace of (PAL uhs • uhv • vuhr SEYE) 403
Versailles, Treaty of (TREE tee • uhv • vuhr SEYE) 403-408, 474
Vespucci, Amerigo (uhm uh REE goh • ve SPOO chee) 28
veto (VEE toh) 129, 529
Vice President [United States] (veyes • PREZ uh dent) 133, 181, 183, 187, 333, 335, 364, 408, 531
Vicksburg [Mississippi] (viks BUHRG) 254
Vienna [Austria] (vee EN uh) 511
Vietcong (vee et KAHNG) 571, 572, 585
Vietnam (vee et NAHM) 571, 586
Vietnamization (vee et nuh muh ZAY shuhn) 584, 585
Vietnam, North (north • vee et NAHM) 571, 572, 585, 586
Vietnam, South (sowth • vee et NAHM) 571, 572, 582, 584-586
Vietnam Veterans Memorial (vee et NAHM • VET uhr uhnz • muh MOR ee uhl) 588
Vietnam War (vee et NAHM • wor) 571, 572, 575, 577, 582-586, 588, 595, 596, 647
Viking (VEYE king) 26
Villa, Pancho (PAHN choh • VEE yuh) 423
Vincennes [Indiana] (vin SENZ) 114
Vinland (VIN luhnd) 26
Virginia (vuhr JIN yuh) 42, 44, 47-49, 51, 53, 60, 62, 76, 89, 92, 95, 104, 105, 114, 117, 118, 124, 130, 134, 140, 166, 195, 231, 247, 248, 258-260, 264, 330
Virginia Company (vuhr JIN yuh • KUHMP uh nee) 42, 44, 47, 48
Virginia City [Nevada] (vuhr JIN yuh • SIT ee) 285
Virginia Plan (vuhr JIN yuh • plan) 124, 125
Virgin Islands (VUHR juhn • EYE luhndz) 374
Virgin Mary (vuhr JIN • MAIR ee) 60
von Steuben, Frederick (FRED rik • von • STOO buhn) 113, 114
voting rights (VOHT ing • reyets) 216, 219, 270, 271, 273, 274, 278, 291, 292, 367, 381, 546, 571, 589

Voting Rights Act of 1965 (VOHT ing • reyets • akt • uhv • NEYEN teen • SIKS tee • feyev) 178, 183, 274, 412, 416

W

Waco [Texas] (WAY koh) 655
wages (WAY juhs) 327-329, 338, 340, 346, 349-351, 366, 368, 401, 413, 425, 440, 441, 444, 446-449, 451-453, 457-461, 490, 491, 518, 539, 575, 576, 601, 631
Wake Island (wayk • EYE luhnd) 485, 533
Wales (hwaylz) 387
Walesa, Lech (lek • vuh LES uh) 525
Walker, C.J. (see • jay • WAHK uhr) 312
Walker, Mary (MAIR ee • WAHK uhr) 262
Walker, Quock (kwohk • WAHK uhr) 107
Wall Street [New York City] (wahl • street) 69
Walpi [Arizona] (WAHL pee) 12
War Hawks (wor • hahks) 145
War of 1812 (wor • uhv • AYT teen • twelv) 146-153, 160, 203
War of the Pacific, The (thuh • wor • uhv • thuh • puh SIF ik) 360
War of the Worlds (wor • uhv • thuh • wuhrldz) 461
War on Poverty (wor • ahn • PAHV uhr tee) 570
War Powers Act (wor • POW uhrz • akt) 596
War Production Board (wor • pruh DUHK shuhn • bord) 490
Warren Commission (WOR uhn • kuh MISH uhn) 566-568
Warren, Earl (uhrl • WOR uhn) 545, 566, 567
War, Secretary of (SEK ruh tair ee • uhv • wor) 134, 150, 488
Washington [state] (WAHSH ing tuhn) 197
Washington, Booker T. (BOOK uhr • tee • WAHSH ing tuhn) 295, 367
Washington, D.C. (WAHSH ing tuhn • dee • see) 134, 137, 150, 192, 206, 242, 243, 248, 253, 261, 268, 277, 335, 364, 384, 404, 408, 428, 449, 451, 463, 484, 502, 519, 528, 566, 587, 589, 597, 610, 654
Washington, George (jorj • WOSH ing tuhn) 76, 92, 95, 98-100, 103, 111-113, 118, 119, 130, 133, 134-137, 139, 243, 370, 461, 527
Washington Post (WAHSH ing tuhn • pohst) 597
Watergate (WAHT uhr gayt) 597-599, 607
Watie, Stand (stand • WAY tee) 268
Watts [California] (wahtz) 578, 579
Weaver, James B. (jaymz • bee • WEEV uhr) 345, 346
welfare (WEL fair) 623
Welles, Orson (ORS uhn • welz) 461
West (west) 114, 122, 145, 159, 164, 167, 175, 176, 180, 181, 187, 190, 192, 193, 197, 205, 206, 213, 214, 235, 241, 285-287, 300, 314, 352, 415
West Africa (west • AF ri kuh) 21
West Bank [Israel] (west • bangk) 602
West Berlin [Germany] (west • buhr LIN) 527
West Coast (west • kohst) 293, 362, 442, 488
Western Front (WES tuhrn • fruhnt) 398, 399
Western Hemisphere (WES tuhrn • HEM uhs feer) 5, 29, 172, 173, 360
West Indies (west • IN deez) 173
West Jersey (west • JUHRZ ee) 61, 62
West Point [New York] (west • poynt) 115, 199, 237, 489
West Virginia (west • vuhr JIN yuh) 247
Whig Party (hwig • PART ee) 187, 188, 189, 199, 213, 225, 235
Whisky Ring (HWIS kee • ring) 276
White House (hweyet • hows) 150, 153, 180, 181, 231, 234, 258, 271, 276, 277, 279, 334, 336, 345, 364, 367, 370, 382, 383, 396, 397, 408, 411, 412, 414, 415, 426, 437, 449, 451, 460, 461, 519,

556, 596-598, 608, 610, 627, 632, 633, 649
White House Counsel (hweyet • hows • KOWN suhl) 597
White, John (jahn • hweyet) 43, 44, 45
Whitney, Eli (EE leye • HWIT nee) 166, 309, 310
Wichita (WICH uh tah) 13, 297
Wiesenthal, Simon (SEYE muhn • VEES uhn tal) 511
Wilhelm II (VIL helm • thuh • SEK uhnd) 389, 403
Wilkins, Roy (roy • WIL kuhnz) 547
Williams, Roger (RAHJ uhr • WIL yuhmz) 55, 56, 59, 62, 107
Wilmot Proviso (WIL muht • pruh VEYE zoh) 213
Wilson, Edith (EE duhth • WIL suhn) 408
Wilson, James (jaymz • WIL suhn) 92, 130
Wilson, Woodrow (WOOD roh • WIL suhn) 261, 368, 383, 384, 396, 397, 400, 403-405, 407-409, 411
Winthrop, John (jahn • WIN thruhp) 55, 57
Wisconsin (wis KAHN suhn) 321, 540
Wolfe, James (jaymz • wuhlf) 83
Women's Christian Temperance Union [WCTU] (WIM uhnz • KRISH chuhn • TEM puh ruhnz • YOON yuhn) 431
women's rights (WIM uhnz • reyetz) 350, 353, 367, 368, 381, 412, 416, 418, 575
Woodward, Bob (bahb • WOOD wuhrd) 597
workers (WUHRK uhrz) 287, 295, 304, 307, 309, 310, 316, 322, 323, 327-329, 331, 333, 335, 338-342, 349, 366-369, 384, 401, 413, 415, 438, 441, 444-448, 452, 453, 459, 462, 470, 481, 485, 486, 489, 491, 525, 539, 575, 576, 611
Workers' Compensation (WUHR kuhrz • kahm puhn SAY shuhn) 368
Workingman's Party of California (WUHR king manz • PAR tee • uhv • kal uh FOR nyuh) 294
World, The (thuh • wuhrld) 353
World Trade Center (wuhrld • trayd • SENT uhr) 655
World War I (wuhrld • wor • hwuhn) 264, 389-401, 406, 409, 411, 413, 425, 429, 449, 467, 474, 509, 510, 517
World War II (wuhrld • wor • too) 264, 302, 449, 461, 476, 478-505, 482, 490, 507, 509, 522, 528, 529, 533-536, 539, 541, 547, 614, 636, 639, 571
Wright, Allen (AL uhn • reyet) 268
Wright, Martha Coffin (MAR thuh • KAHF uhn • reyet) 216
Wyoming (weye OH ming) 197, 414, 416

X

X, Malcolm (eks • MAL kuhm) 576
XYZ Affair (eks • hweye • zee • uh FAIR) 139

Y

Yalta (YAHL tuh) 500
Yalu River (YAL oo • RIV uhr) 534
yellow fever (YEL oh • FEEV uhr) 162, 378
Yeltsin, Boris (bor uhs • YELT suhn) 636, 637
Yom Kippur War (yahm • ki PUHR • wor) 602, 603
York [now Toronto] (york) 150
Yorktown [Virginia] (YORK town) 118, 119
Yugoslavia (yoo goh SLAHV ee uh) 391, 525

Z

Zaire [river] (zeye EER) 22
Zimmerman, Arthur (AR thuhr • ZIM muhr muhn) 397
Zimmerman Note (ZIM muhr muhn • noht) 396, 397, 401
Zuni (ZOO nee) 12